Hans Gerlach

Alpine Cookbook

Hans Gerlach with
Susanna Bingemer

Alpine
Cookbook

Comfort Food from
the Mountains

Photography by Hans Gerlach and Silvio Knezevic

Contents

Foreword   7

Snacks & Light Meals   8

Soups   38

Small Dishes & Vegetarian Cuisine   60

Cheese Dishes   92

Fish   118

Meat   138

Pastries & Desserts   172

Index   216

Acknowledgments   223

Foreword

My first food memory is round and sweet: Grandmother's *Zwetschgenknödel* (plum dumplings). As a child, I tried my hand at homemade apple strudel and was even somewhat successful—that is, if you ignore the amount of cinnamon that fell into the filling. Later I became a chef and was interested in other culinary specialties at first, from the French classics to Vietnamese cuisine. And yet, somewhere along the way, I realized how the cuisine of my childhood relaxed me: I did not have to learn how to make strudel, knödel, *Hendl*, *Rösti*, or palatschinken—it came naturally. Since then, my wife and I have been collecting the finest recipes in the Alps, from the Slovenian mountains to the Provence Alps that fall into the sea by Nice.

In this book, you will find important Alpine classics—the best gâteau *au fromage* from Lausanne, the finest Austrian schnitzel, our favorite potato pancakes from raw potatoes, wonderful, juicy fried chicken, the quintessential *Suure Mocke* (a fine Swiss sauerbraten), and much more. Many recipes are vegetable dishes, just as one would expect in a traditional cuisine where meat was primarily for Sundays and holidays. In each case, we tried to find the best recipe and to revise and describe it so it works well in every kitchen.

These classic recipes are joined by other more modern versions of regional recipes. My versions of *Brotsuppe*, *Topfenpalatschinken*, and *Chrut Gipfeli* are lighter, fresher, and more aromatic than the originals because the hard-working mountain farmer's food was primarily for delivering lots of energy. The idea of using up leftovers in *Brotsuppe* is still valid today, but there is no reason it cannot be a bit more flavorful and exciting than in earlier times. As a traveling chef, I smuggled in some dishes that give new interpretations to already wonderful mountain recipes—try pulled venison or Alpine pickles and Alpine chutney, which can lead savory and cheese dishes in a new direction.

The mountain cuisine of the Alps cannot offer many fish dishes, but the few that do exist come with my highest recommendation. Freshwater fish are often fished in an environmentally friendly manner and may reach your plate without a long journey. One recipe I would especially like to recommend from the bottom of my heart is the fried carp fillet. Carp farming is the most sustainable way to catch fish, simply because carps are vegetarians. These fried fillets are a wonderful way to enjoy a traditionally overlooked fish.

Most of the desserts in the mountains are pastries. Grandmother's dumplings are, of course, included—as well as juicy *Dinkelbuchteln* (spelt sweet rolls) with apricot *Powidl* and preserved fruit to line the shelves of your pantry. For the first time, we made the *Powidl* dumplings with choux pastry, which we thought was a bit old-fashioned at first, but it tastes fantastic.

Enjoy your culinary adventures through the Alps!

Hans Gerlach

Snacks & Light Meals

Alpine Hot Dog:
Bosna with Onion Mustard

Serves 4 • Prep: 15 minutes

For the onion mustard:

2–3 white onions, peeled and
 finely diced

3 tablespoons canola oil

salt

1–2 tablespoons herb vinegar

$1/3$ cup spicy mustard

2 tablespoons German sweet
 mustard

For the hot dog:

1 bunch parsley, removed from
 stalks and chopped coarsely

2 baby gherkin pickles or
 cornichons, diced

1 tablespoon vegetable oil

4 bratwursts (5½ oz (150g) total
 weight)

4 hot dog buns

curry powder

crushed red pepper flakes (to taste)

1½ in piece of fresh horseradish

pickled chilies or Alpine pickles
 (p. 13) for serving

1 For the onion mustard: Heat the canola oil in a pan and add the onions and a bit of salt; allow to sweat, covered, for 5 minutes. Deglaze the pan with the herb vinegar, remove from heat, and allow to cool. Mix with the spicy and German sweet mustards.

2 Heat the oil in a grill pan and cook the bratwursts for 6–8 minutes (or use a grill). Slice the buns in half lengthwise and toast them under the broiler or on the grill; spread with onion mustard. Place the bratwurst on the lower half of the roll and sprinkle with the curry powder, red pepper flakes (to taste), parsley, and diced baby gherkins.

3 Peel the horseradish and grate it over the hot bratwurst. Cover with the other half of the bun. Wrap each Alpine hot dog halfway with a paper napkin and serve hot with pickled chili peppers or Alpine pickles.

Tip:

For the Bratwurst you can use any long or short beef or pork sausages (every butcher shop has its favorite); some people even prefer a *Käsekrainer,* cheese-filled sausage. You should look for sausages that are not too large and whose filling is not too coarse. At the very first *Bosna* stand, the Balkan-Grill in Salzburg, they simply mix parsley and onions together instead of serving with onion mustard. Curry powder is often used as a spice, but try my Bosna Spice Mix instead. To create, combine the following ingredients in a food processor, being careful to mix rather than puree: 3 tablespoons sweet paprika, 1 tablespoon curry powder, 1 teaspoon crushed red pepper flakes, 1 teaspoon cumin, 1 tablespoon sumac or to taste (sumac is a slightly tart spice found in Turkish supermarkets or online), 1 tablespoon salt, and 1 tablespoon oil.

Alpine Pickles

The selection of vegetables in this recipe is only a suggestion; the pickling brine works well with all firmer vegetables, such as peppers, artichoke hearts, broccoli, and mushrooms. You can even use it to preserve peeled garlic cloves (leave out the sliced garlic in that case). The amount of chili peppers called for makes relatively spicy pickles; for a milder result, simply use fewer.

Makes 4 jars (17fl oz each) • Shelf life: About a year
Prep: 30 minutes + 15 days pickling time

½ cup salt

1lb 2 oz (500g) red kuri
 squash (*hokkaido*)

1lb 2oz (500g) cauliflower

14oz (400g) root vegetables
 (such as turnips)

9oz (250g) onions

9oz (250g) celery

3½oz (100g) mild chili peppers

For the brine:

6 young garlic cloves

1¾oz (50g) fresh horseradish

1 tablespoon brown mustard seeds

½ teaspoon caraway seeds

⅔ cup sugar

1 teaspoon turmeric

3 cups white wine vinegar

½ bunch savory

4 bay leaves

1 In a large pot, bring 2 quarts (2 l) water and salt to a boil and let cool. In the meantime, cut the squash in half, scoop out the seeds, and cut into slices. Break the cauliflower into small florets. Peel the root vegetables and the onion (keep the root base); cut in half and slice into wedges. Slice the celery into ½in pieces. Cut the chili peppers lengthwise and remove the seeds. Add the vegetables to the salted water and let stand for 1 day.

2 Peel and slice the garlic cloves and horseradish for the brine. Toast the mustard and caraway seeds in a large dry skillet until they become aromatic. Add the garlic, horseradish, sugar, and turmeric. Stir once and deglaze with the white wine vinegar. Add 3 cups water, savory, and bay leaves.

3 Strain the vegetables and boil them until they are al dente, approximately 6 minutes. Using a slotted spoon, remove the vegetables from the brine and pack them tightly into sterilized canning jars (see tip p. 14). Bring the brine back up to a boil and fill the jars; cover immediately. Let stand for at least 14 days.

Tip:

If you enjoy pickled chili peppers, try making some yourself: Bring brine to a boil and pour over whole chili peppers in a pot. Using a smaller lid, and weights if needed, press down the peppers and allow to cool overnight. Put the chilies in a separate bowl and bring the brine back up to a boil. Pour over chilies and allow to cool once more. Fill sterilized jars (see tip p. 14) with chilies, bring the brine back up to a boil, and pour over the chilies. Close the jars immediately.

Sour Onions

For the pantry

Sour onions go very well with sautéed pork and poultry. They also complement vegetables and potatoes. Consider using sour onions instead of onion mustard for the Alpine hot dogs (p. 10).

Makes 2 jars (12 fl oz each) • Shelf life: About 1 year
Prep: 25 minutes + 1 hour resting time

2¼lb (1kg) red or white onions

3 celery ribs

2–4 mild chili peppers

3 tablespoons salt

3½oz (100g) fresh ginger

²/₃ cup apple cider vinegar

7oz (200g) baby gherkin pickles
 or cornichons

1 cup sugar

1 tablespoon mustard seeds

½ teaspoon fennel seeds

freshly ground salt and pepper

1 Peel the onions and slice into thin rings. Cut the celery in half lengthwise and then chop into small slices. Cut the chili peppers in half, remove the seeds, and dice finely. Add the onions, celery, and chili peppers in a bowl along with the salt. Mash like you would sauerkraut and let stand one hour.

2 In the meantime, peel the ginger and slice into thin pieces against the fibers. Using a food processor, puree it with the apple cider vinegar. Dice the baby gherkins finely.

3 Rinse the salted vegetables in a colander under cold water and squeeze out the moisture using a clean kitchen towel. Add the prepared ingredients as well as the mustard and fennel seeds to a small pot. Bring to a boil and simmer covered over low heat for 15 minutes. Add salt and pepper to taste. Fill the jars with the hot mixture and close immediately.

Tip:

You can sterilize the jars for about 10 minutes in a 250°F (120°C) oven. Boil the lids and rubber rings (if using) for 5 minutes and allow to drip-dry on a cooling rack.

Cabbage Flatbread with *Bündnerfleisch* and Endive Salad

Serves 4 • Prep: 40 minutes + 15 minutes baking time

For the dough:

2¾ cups all-purpose flour plus extra
 for rolling

1 cup rye flour

1 teaspoon salt

11 tablespoons clarified butter

For the toppings:

9oz (250g) pointed cabbage (or
 other white cabbage variety)

2 tablespoons clarified butter

½ teaspoon caraway seeds

3 cups sour cream

freshly ground salt and pepper

2–3 tablespoons hazelnuts,
 coarsely chopped

3½oz (100g) *Bündnerfleisch* (or
 other cured beef, such as bresaola)

For the salad:

4 tablespoons peanut or canola oil

1 tablespoon white wine vinegar

1 teaspoon quince jelly

1 teaspoon spicy mustard

pinch of sugar

½ head endive (or another winter
 salad variety)

freshly ground salt and pepper

1 To create the dough, add the flours and salt to a bowl. Bring ⅔ cup water and the clarified butter to a boil, pour over the flour mixture, and knead into a smooth dough. (Careful, the dough is hot! Try starting with a wooden spoon until the dough has cooled, then continue kneading with your hands.)

2 To prepare the toppings, remove any wilted leaves from the outside of the cabbage and slice the rest thinly. Melt the clarified butter in a frying pan and sauté the cabbage with the caraway seeds for about three minutes. Remove from heat and allow to cool slightly. Add the sour cream and season to taste with salt and pepper.

3 For the salad, whisk all ingredients except the endive with 1 tablespoon water to create a vinaigrette. Season to taste with salt and pepper. Wash and dry the endive.

4 Preheat the oven to 460°F (240°C) or 430°F (220°C) (convection oven) and line two baking sheets with parchment paper. Divide the dough into four balls and, on a lightly floured surface, roll out each one as thin as possible into an oval (about 9¾ x 6in (25 x 15cm)).

5 Place two flatbreads on each baking sheet and spread a quarter of the cabbage mixture on each. Place the sheets in the middle oven rack one at a time and bake for about 8 minutes, or until crispy and browned. Sprinkle a quarter of the hazelnuts on each flatbread with 2 minutes to go.

6 Allow the flatbreads to cool and cut into pieces (or slices). Add the *Bündnerfleisch* by lightly covering each flatbread directly before serving.

Variations:

For a vegetarian flatbread, simply leave out the *Bündnerfleisch*. For a Swiss bacon flatbread, prepare the dough with lard and mix the sour cream with a finely diced onion (leave out the cabbage). Cover the flatbreads with very thin slices of bacon before baking.

Musque de Provence Pumpkin with South Tyrolean Speck, Mâche Lettuce, and Toasted Pumpkin Seeds

South Tyrolean speck, aged at least 22 weeks, tastes best raw. If you prefer to use crispy fried bacon, substitute thinly sliced Italian pancetta (or bacon) by frying it in oil until crispy and placing on paper towels to absorb excess fat. If you are unable to find Musque de Provence pumpkin, butternut squash is a good substitute.

Serves 4 • Prep: 35 minutes

1lb 2oz (500g) Musque de Provence pumpkin or butternut squash

3 tablespoons apricot or apple cider vinegar

3 tablespoons pumpkin seeds

4 tablespoons canola oil

2 sprigs fresh thyme

3 tablespoons lingonberry preserves

1 tablespoon pumpkin seed oil

2¾oz (75g) mâche lettuce or purslane

3½oz (100g) South Tyrolean speck (or fried pancetta or bacon)

freshly ground salt and pepper

1 Cut the pumpkin in half, scoop out the seeds, and cut into thin slices with a mandolin (or large, very sharp knife). Add to a bowl and lightly salt. Drizzle with 2 tablespoons vinegar and allow to sit for at least 15 minutes (but preferably an hour or more).

2 In the meantime, toast the pumpkin seeds in a frying pan with ½ teaspoon oil until they begin to jump. Remove and lightly season with salt. Pick the thyme leaves from the stem and chop. Mix the remaining vinegar with 1 teaspoon lingonberry preserves; season with salt and pepper to taste. Add the pumpkin seeds, thyme, and rest of the canola oil to create a marinade; season to taste.

3 Lightly salt the mâche lettuce and mix with 2 tablespoons marinade. Generously divide the pumpkin among four plates; sprinkle with pepper and the rest of the marinade. Divide the mâche lettuce, toasted pumpkin seeds, and sliced speck evenly among the plates. Garnish with the remaining lingonberry preserves and serve.

Potato Cheese Spread with Bacon and Rye Bread

Sandwich spread

This potato sandwich spread is especially popular in rural kitchens in Lower Bavaria and Austria. The name can be a bit misleading, as there is not actually any cheese in this recipe.

Serves 4 • Prep: 25 minutes

14oz (400g) starchy potatoes
 (such as Russet)

2 white onions

1 bunch chives

1⅓ cups sour cream

4–6 tablespoons cream or milk

sweet paprika

ground caraway seeds

8 slices rye bread

4 prunes, thinly sliced

4½oz (125g) smoked South
 Tyrolean speck

freshly ground salt and pepper

1 Cook the potatoes in boiling salted water for 10–15 minutes. In the meantime, peel the onions, cut in half, and chop finely. Slice the chives into small rings.

2 Drain the potatoes; peel and mash into a lumpy puree using a fork or potato masher. Mix in the onions, chives, sour cream, and cream. Season generously with salt, pepper, paprika, and caraway seeds. Mix thoroughly until the mixture is spreadable.

3 Spread the mixture on the rye bread and add the prunes. Cut the speck into thin strips and serve on top of or next to the bread.

Variations:

For *Topfenkas* (quark cheese spread), use 9oz (250g) quark, only 7oz (200g) potatoes, and the rest of the ingredients. For *Kürbiskas* (pumpkin cheese spread), preheat the oven to 350°F (175°C) or 320°F (160°C) (convection oven). Cut a small red kuri pumpkin in half, scoop out the seeds, and cut into slices. Line a baking sheet with parchment paper and spread out the pumpkin evenly. Bake for about 40 minutes in the middle rack. Allow to cool, and mash. Mix with 1 bunch chives (sliced in rings), 7oz (200g) cream cheese, and ⅔ cup crème fraîche. Season generously with salt, pepper, and caraway seeds.

Green Bean Salad with Egg, Potatoes, Sour Cream, and Dill

Vegetarian

Green beans are called fisolen *in Austria. This salad also tastes good with Bavarian, or even Sicilian, beans. They can be big or small, thick or thin—the most important thing is that they are crispy, fresh, and green.*

Serves 4 • Prep: 25 minutes

5½oz (150g) scallions

14oz (400g) small red potatoes

1 teaspoon caraway seeds

4 eggs

1lb 2oz (500g) green beans

½ bunch dill

⅔ cup sour cream

2 tablespoons mayonnaise

1–2 teaspoons spicy mustard

freshly ground salt and pepper

1 Slice the scallions into thin rings; salt, crush slightly, and set aside. Cook the potatoes with the caraway seeds in boiling water for 15–20 minutes.

2 In the meantime, hard-boil the eggs in salted water for about 10 minutes and cook the green beans in boiling salted water until al dente (depending on the type and size of beans, 5–10 minutes). Rinse the eggs with cold water, peel, and finely dice. Drain the beans, rinse under cold water, and allow to drip-dry. Chop the dill.

3 Drain the potatoes, peel if desired, and cut into thick slices. Combine 1 tablespoon water with the diced eggs, sour cream, mayonnaise, and mustard; season with salt and pepper. Combine the onions, potatoes, and beans and carefully fold in the sour cream mixture. Transfer to plates, sprinkle with dill, and serve lukewarm or cold.

Variation:

For an especially fine red beet salad without the normal vinegar dressing, pack 2lb 3oz (1kg) beets tightly in a baking dish and cover with aluminum foil. If there are any delicate leaves attached to the beets, set aside (or purchase a handful of baby greens, which are often baby Swiss chard or beet greens). Preheat the oven to 390°F (200°C) or 360°F (180°C) (convection oven). Place the beets on the middle rack and bake for about an hour. Remove from the oven, allow to cool slightly, and peel. Slice thinly using a sharp knife or mandolin, and combine with the egg-cream mixture and onions (but no potatoes or green beans). Garnish with beet leaves and serve.

Beet Carpaccio with Watercress Sour Cream

Thinly sliced smoked duck or crispy fried chicken breast strips go exceptionally well with Randen—which is what beets are called in Switzerland—carpaccio. The carpaccio is especially beautiful with striped beets; you can sometimes find the striped Italian variety, Chioggia, at the farmers market or purchase the seeds to grow yourself. You could also simply mix red beets with white and yellow beets, carrots, and parsnips.

Serves 4 • Prep: 30 minutes + 30 minutes inactive time

14oz (400g) red beets (or any other variety)

2 small red onions

½ organic orange

½ organic lemon

3 tablespoons canola oil and extra for the pine nuts

1 tablespoon pine nuts or *Zirbelnüsse* (see tip)

⅔ cup *Schmand* or sour cream

1 bunch watercress or parsley

freshly ground salt and pepper

1 Peel the beets and slice thinly with a mandolin (cut large beets in half first). Peel and dice the onion. Wash the orange and lemon with hot water and dry; zest and juice each and place the lemon zest and juice aside. Season the orange juice generously with salt and pepper and whisk with the canola oil. Marinate the beets and onions in the sauce for at least 30 minutes.

2 In the meantime, toast the pine nuts in a frying pan with a few drops of oil until golden brown. Allow to cool slightly, then chop coarsely; mix with the lemon zest and lightly season with salt. Whisk the lemon juice and *Schmand* or sour cream; season with salt and pepper. Coarsely chop the watercress and fold into the mixture.

3 Divide the marinated beet slices evenly among four plates and add a scoop of the watercress-*Schmand* mixture; sprinkle with pine nuts and serve.

Tip:

The *Zirbelkiefer*, *Arve*, or Swiss pine is the Alpine relative to the Mediterranean umbrella pines, just without the umbrellas. In the regions the *Zirbelkiefer* grows, its seeds (*Zirbelnüsse*) are used exactly like pine nuts.

Endive with Caramelized Onions

This hearty winter salad goes well with smoked fish fillets, including the not-so-Alpine herring fillets, as well as chopped herbs like chervil or dill. (And, of course, who could have guessed it— the salad also goes well with fried bacon.)

Serves 4 • Prep: 20 minutes

1 head endive

1¾oz (50g) walnuts, coarsely chopped

1¾oz (50g) stale white bread

4½oz (125g) goose fat or lard (or 3½fl oz (100ml) canola oil)

1 apple

3–4 tablespoons apple cider vinegar

1 medium onion, peeled and diced

1 clove garlic

1 teaspoon caraway seeds

freshly ground salt and pepper

1 Wash the endive, slice thinly, and add to a bowl. With the stale bread, form coarse bread crumbs with your hands or a food processor; you should have about 1 cup of bread crumbs. Melt 1 tablespoon goose fat in a frying pan and toast the walnuts and bread crumbs in the fat until golden brown while stirring frequently. Lightly season with salt then spread on a plate and allow to cool. Peel and quarter the apple, remove the core, and slice into thin pieces. Sprinkle with several drops of apple cider vinegar.

2 Melt the remaining goose fat in a pot and sauté the onion on low to medium heat until almost soft and golden brown.

3 In the meantime, peel the garlic and mince with the caraway seeds. Add to the onions and cook briefly. Deglaze with the remaining apple cider vinegar and remove from the stove. Season with salt and pepper.

4 Add the endive and the apple slices to the onion mixture, cover with the nut–bread crumb mixture, and serve immediately.

Cabbage Salad with Smoked Salmon

Serves 4 • Prep: 40 minutes

For the salad:

1 small pointed cabbage or other
 white cabbage variety (about
 1lb 10oz (750g))
1 pinch ground caraway seeds
1 onion, peeled and diced
2 tablespoons canola oil
2 tablespoons white wine vinegar
7oz (200g) smoked salmon (or
 other smoked fish)
freshly ground salt and pepper

For the dressing:

3 tablespoons mustard (or Dijon
 mustard)
2 tablespoons honey
2 tablespoons white wine vinegar
½ cup canola oil
1 bunch dill, finely chopped
freshly ground salt and pepper

1 For the salad, quarter the cabbage, remove stalk, and chop into thin slices. Add to a bowl with salt, pepper, and ground caraway seeds; lightly mash. Heat canola oil in a frying pan and sweat the onions for three minutes, then deglaze with the white wine vinegar. Fold in the cabbage mixture and allow to rest for 30 minutes, covered.

2 In the meantime, make the dressing by combining the mustard, honey, white wine vinegar, salt, and pepper. Whisk in the canola oil as if you were making mayonnaise: Add it little by little until emulsified (preferably with an immersion blender). Fold the dill into the dressing. Season to taste.

3 Cut the smoked salmon into thick slices using a sharp knife. Combine the cabbage mixture and dressing, then transfer onto plates along with the smoked salmon. Serve.

Potato Casserole

Good for guests

The traditional potato casserole from Graubunden and Engadin used to be baked directly over hot coals in a large baking dish or on a sheet in the oven. This variation of the Swiss casserole adds apples and dill to the base recipe to give it fresh and tart accents.

Serves 4 • Prep: 15 minutes + 40 minutes baking time

For the casserole:

2 white onions, peeled and diced

3½oz (100g) cured or smoked meat (such as *Salsiz*, *Bündnerfleisch*, or smoked bacon), diced

1lb 5oz (600g) red potatoes

1 tablespoon polenta

5 tablespoons soft butter plus extra for the baking dish

freshly grated nutmeg

salt

For the apples:

½ bunch dill

2 apples

2 tablespoons butter

freshly ground pepper

1 Preheat the oven to 370°F (190°C) or 340°F (170°C) (convection oven). Peel the potatoes and grate into a bowl. Add the diced onions, *Salsiz*, polenta, and 5 tablespoons butter; combine thoroughly and season with salt and nutmeg. Butter 4 small ramekins or a muffin tray and fill with the potato mixture. Place on the middle rack and bake for about 40 minutes, or until golden brown.

2 In the meantime, chop the dill. Peel and core the apples; cut into slices. Melt the butter in a frying pan, then sauté the apples for 3–4 minutes until golden. Season with pepper and dill.

3 Remove the casseroles from the oven and allow to cool slightly in the ramekins. Transfer to plates and serve with the apple mixture.

Tip:

The following winter salad goes well with this dish: Quarter an apple, remove the seeds, and slice. Wash an organic lemon with hot water and dry; zest and juice. Pick the leaves off four parsley stems and chop. In a tall jar, combine lemon zest, lemon juice, 1 teaspoon spicy mustard, 2 teaspoons quince jelly, and the chopped parsley. Season with salt and pepper and puree, preferably using an immersion blender. Add 1–2 tablespoons water and ¼ cup oil little by little until you have a creamy sauce. Break up a head of endive; combine with the apple slices and the dressing in a bowl, then serve.

Baked Swiss Dumplings

These baked Swiss dumplings with a cabbage filling go well in a lunch box but are also fit for a party. They taste different—but just as good—without Salsiz or bacon. Try serving with a fresh salad for a great lunch.

Serves 4 (makes 12 dumplings) • Prep: 35 minutes + 1 hour inactive time + 25 minutes baking time

For the dough:

2½ cups all-purpose flour plus extra for rolling

Salt

7 tablespoons clarified butter

½ cup milk

caraway seeds and Fleur de Sel to sprinkle on top

For the filling:

1lb 2oz (500g) pointed cabbage (or other white cabbage variety)

3½oz (100g) *Salsiz*, pancetta, or smoked bacon

2 tablespoons butter

¼ cup beer

1 bunch parsley

3½oz (100g) Tomme Vaudoise (a soft Swiss cheese) or Camembert

2 tablespoons shredded Alpine cheese (such as Sbrinz, Gruyère, or Allgauer Bergkase)

freshly ground salt and pepper

1 For the dough, combine flour and one large pinch salt in a bowl. Bring clarified butter, milk, and ½ cup water to a boil and pour over the flour. Stir using a large kitchen spoon until you have smooth dough. Cover and cool for about one hour.

2 In the meantime, prepare the filling: Quarter the cabbage, remove stalk, and chop into thin slices. Peel and dice the *Salsiz*. Melt the butter in a pot; add the cabbage, *Salsiz*, salt, and pepper. Steam for 5 minutes with the lid on, deglaze with beer, and cook for an additional 5 minutes without the lid until the liquid has almost all boiled off. Season to taste and allow to cool. Pick the parsley leaves from the stem and chop; cut the Tomme Vausoise into small cubes, and add to the cabbage mixture along with the parsley and shredded Alpine cheese.

3 Preheat the oven to 390ºF (200ºC) or 360ºF (180ºC) (convection oven). Roll out the dough on a lightly floured surface to about 14 by 19in (36 x 48cm), or until about 1/16in (2mm) thick. Cut into 12 squares (4–4¾in (10–12 cm) edge length). Add a heaping tablespoon of filling to each square, brush the edges with water, and form into triangles. Seal the edges using a fork or trim using a serrated pastry wheel.

4 Transfer the triangles to a parchment-lined baking sheet. Brush with water and sprinkle with caraway seeds and Fleur de Sel. Place on the second rack from the bottom of the oven and bake for 22–25 minutes or until golden brown. Serve warm or cold.

Potato Salad with Wild Mushrooms

Serves 4 • Prep: 35 minutes

1lb 5oz (600g) red potatoes

1 teaspoon caraway seeds

1 kohlrabi

3 scallions

1¼ cups vegetable broth

1 tablespoon mustard

¼ cup white wine vinegar

¼ cup canola oil

7oz (200g) wild mushrooms
 (chanterelles in the summer)

1 bunch chives, sliced into
 thin rings

1 bunch dill, chopped

freshly ground salt and pepper

1 Boil the potatoes with a large pinch of salt and the caraway seeds for 20 minutes. In the meantime, peel the kohlrabi, quarter, and slice very thinly. Chop the scallions into fine rings, setting the dark green ones aside. Bring the vegetable broth to a boil and pour over the kohlrabi and lighter green scallion rings in a bowl.

2 Drain the potatoes; allow to cool slightly, peel, and cut into slices directly into the broth mixture. Combine mustard, white wine vinegar, and 2 tablespoons canola oil; gently stir in. Season generously with salt and pepper and allow to rest for at least 10 minutes.

3 Clean the mushrooms with a cloth (only wash them if absolutely necessary then dry well with a paper towel); quarter or slice large mushrooms. Heat the remaining canola oil in a frying pan over high heat and sauté the mushrooms for 5 minutes.

4 Season the mushrooms with salt and pepper, and while still warm, add to the potato mixture along with the herbs and dark green scallion rings. Season to taste and serve.

Tip:

If there are no wild mushrooms available, slice a bunch of radishes very thinly and mix with a handful baby spinach or arugula; gently stir into the potato mixture.

Beef Salad

Use up leftovers

Serves 4 • Prep: 25 minutes

1lb 2oz (500g) cooked beef (such as soup meat, leftover roast, or top round; see tip)

2 red onions

1 tablespoon white wine vinegar

1 cucumber

2–3 baby gherkin pickles or cornichons

3½oz (100g) mâche lettuce or other leafy greens

3 tablespoons pumpkin seeds

oil for roasting

salt

For the dressing:

2 tablespoons white wine vinegar

1 teaspoon spicy mustard

1 tablespoon mayonnaise (or to taste)

¼ cup beef broth (preferably lightly gelatinized; see tip)

2 tablespoons pumpkin seed oil

freshly ground salt and pepper

1 Thinly slice the beef and then cut into strips. Peel the onions and slice into thin rings; season with salt in a bowl and mix with the white wine vinegar. Peel the cucumber in quarters lengthwise, remove the seeds with a spoon, and chop into pieces. Dice the baby gherkin pickles. Except for the pumpkin seeds, combine all salad ingredients in a bowl.

2 For the dressing, combine all ingredients except the pumpkin seed oil; season generously with salt and pepper then whisk in the oil.

3 Toast the pumpkin seeds in a frying pan with a few drops of oil until they jump. Add to a small bowl and lightly salt. Carefully combine the salad ingredients with the dressing, transfer to four plates, sprinkle with toasted pumpkin seeds, and serve.

Tip:

Homemade beef broth is especially aromatic if you boil top round and calves' feet. For the broth, cut two onions in half. Line a frying pan with aluminum foil and heat on high; place the onions cut side down and cook for 5 minutes, until nearly black. Peel and dice 4 cloves garlic, 2 carrots, and 1 parsley root. Combine 1lb 12oz (800g) calves' feet (ask your butcher to saw into slices) and onions in a large pot. Cover with 2 cups water, bring to a boil, reduce heat, and simmer for 30 minutes, skimming the foam off the top from time to time. Add 1lb 12oz (800g) top round, and after 2 hours, add the vegetables. Season generously with salt and pepper and add the stems from one bunch parsley. Simmer for about an hour then remove from heat and let set for 30 minutes. Pour the broth into a bowl through a fine sieve. Serve the top round with a bit of broth, boiled potatoes, and grated horseradish or allow to cool and use for this salad, along with the parsley leaves. If desired, use the meat from the calves' feet for the salad as well. Freeze the remaining broth.

Soups

Clear Pumpkin Soup with Chestnuts

Vegetarian

Serves 4 • Prep: 20 minutes + 15 minutes cooking time

14oz (400g) red kuri (*hokkaido*) squash, butternut squash, or Musque de Provence pumpkin

7oz (200g) soup vegetables (such as 3½oz (100g) celery root or two celery ribs and ½ leek; no carrots)

1 white onion

1 apple

7oz (200g) precooked chestnuts

2 tablespoons butter

1 teaspoon curry powder

1 sprig thyme

3½fl oz (100ml) white wine

5¼ cups vegetable broth

¼ cup shredded medium aged Alpine cheese

freshly ground salt and pepper

1 Peel the squash (unnecessary for red kuri), cut in half, and scoop out the seeds. Using a sharp knife, cut into ¾in (2cm) cubes.

2 If necessary, peel the vegetables and chop into small pieces. Peel the onion, cut in half, and slice. Peel the apple, quarter, remove core, and slice. Chop the chestnuts coarsely.

3 Melt the butter in a large pot over medium heat; add the squash, vegetables, onion, and apple. Season with salt, pepper, and curry. Cook for 5 minutes, covered, over low heat. Add thyme and cook another 5 minutes, covered; add chestnuts and deglaze with white wine. Pour in the broth and bring to a boil. Cook for 15 minutes or until the vegetables are soft.

4 Season to taste and portion into soup plates; sprinkle with shredded Alpine cheese and serve.

Tip:

A butter curler works even better than a spoon to remove the seeds from the squash—it's also a great tool for carving Halloween pumpkins.

Variation:

For a clear wild mushroom soup, replace the squash with cubed potatoes and the chestnuts with 9oz (250g) wild mushrooms. Clean the mushrooms and quarter or slice larger ones. Heat 2 tablespoons canola oil over high heat and sauté the mushrooms for 3 minutes. Add the mushrooms to the finished soup, bring to a boil, and let sit for a few minutes before serving.

Baked Cheese Soup

This soup is similar to the French classic, but it tastes even better with vacherin cheese. The fennel creates a subtle extra aroma.

Serves 4 • Prep: 30 minutes + 10 minutes baking time

7oz (200g) stale rolls or bread, thinly sliced

¼ cup canola oil

3oz (85g) smoked bacon, sliced or diced

4 white onions or 2 fennel bulbs

1 small bunch parsley

4 stalks marjoram or oregano

9oz (250g) Vacherin Mont d'Or (a soft Swiss cheese) or Alpine cheese

1 quart (1 liter) vegetable or beef broth

1–2 teaspoons lemon juice

1 Heat 2 tablespoons canola oil in a frying pan and cook the bacon until crispy. Remove from the pan and place on paper towels to drain. Cook the sliced bread in the bacon fat on each side until golden brown, remove, and place with the bacon.

2 Peel the onions, cut in half, and slice thinly (or cut the fennel in half and slice thinly). Heat the remaining canola oil. Sweat the sliced onions (or fennel bulbs) for 6–8 minutes. Remove the parsley and other herb leaves from their stems, chop, and add to the onions. Season with salt and pepper. Add the crispy bacon, cover, and let rest a few minutes. Cut the rind from the vacherin cheese (or grate the Alpine cheese).

3 Preheat the oven to 460°F (240°C) or 430°F (220°C) (convection oven). Layer the bacon mixture, the sliced bread, and the cheese in oven safe soup tureens or deep ramekins. To do so, spoon the vacherin from its container and spread onto the other ingredients (or sprinkle on the Alpine cheese), leaving some cheese for later use. Bring the vegetable broth to a boil; season with a bit of lemon juice and pour into the soup tureens. Cover with remaining cheese.

4 Place the soup tureens on the middle oven rack and bake 10 minutes or until golden brown; serve hot.

Vegetarian

Split Pea Soup with Swiss Chard

You can also make this split pea soup with spinach or turnip greens instead of Swiss chard, which will give it a slightly different taste.

Serves 4 • Prep: 20 minutes + 1 hour cooking time + soaking time

2 white onions

3 cloves garlic

½ cup olive oil

7oz (200g) Russet potatoes

5½oz (150g) split peas,
 soaked overnight in water

5 cups vegetable broth

½ bunch parsley

14oz (400g) Swiss chard or
 leaf spinach

1¾oz (50g) medium aged
 Alpine cheese, Trentingrana,
 or parmesan (to taste)

freshly ground salt and pepper

1 Peel and finely dice the onion and 2 cloves garlic. Heat 2 tablespoons olive oil in a pot; sweat the onions and garlic for 5 minutes. In the meantime, peel the potatoes and chop into pieces. Drain the peas and add to the pot along with the potatoes. Pour in the broth and simmer about 1 hour, uncovered. Near the end, remove the parsley leaves from the stems and add to the soup.

2 In the meantime, wash and dry the Swiss chard; chop large leaves into wide slices. Peel the last garlic clove and crush. Heat 2 tablespoons olive oil in a frying pan and sweat the garlic briefly. Add the Swiss chard, sauté for 2–3 minutes, then season with salt and pepper.

3 Puree the soup in a blender or with an immersion blender, then season generously with salt and pepper. Grate the Alpine cheese. Serve the soup with the Swiss chard, drizzle with the remaining olive oil, and sprinkle with Alpine cheese, if desired. Serve hot. Goes well with toast.

Herb Soup

Wild herb recipe

Serves 4 • Prep: 35 minutes

1 white onion, peeled and diced

5½ oz (150g) red potatoes, peeled and diced

1 bunch soup vegetables (such as turnips, celery, carrots, leeks, and parsnips) about 10½ oz (300g)), diced

1 tablespoon canola oil

5 cups chicken or vegetable broth

4 eggs

1 bunch wild or spring herbs (such as wild garlic, stinging nettle, watercress, young strawberry leaves, daisies, ground elder, ground ivy, dandelion leaves, and sorrel; or borage, sorrel, garden cress, chervil, chives, parsley, and salad burnet)

1 tablespoon herb vinegar

1¾ oz (50g) hard cheese (such as Trentingrana, Sbrinz, or parmesan)

freshly ground salt and pepper

1 Heat the canola oil in a pot and sauté all of the diced vegetables for 2 minutes; generously season with salt and pepper. Pour in the chicken broth and boil for 15 minutes until the vegetables are soft.

2 In the meantime, boil the eggs for 5 minutes until soft-boiled, run under cold water, and carefully peel. Pick the herb leaves from the stems and add to the soup. Using a regular or immersion blender, puree the soup and season with herb vinegar. Dish into deep soup plates along with the soft-boiled eggs. Grate the hard cheese over the soup and serve. Goes well with *Vinschgerl* (South Tyrolean flatbreads) or rye bread with butter and salt.

Tip:

Here is a bonus recipe for traditional *Kärntner Kirchtagssuppe* (Carinthian Church Day Soup) for 8 servings: Cut two unpeeled onions in half and place cut side down in a large pot; cook over medium heat until black. Add 1 gallon water to the pot along with 1lb 2oz (500g) soup meat, 1lb 2oz (500g) soup bones, and 1lb 2oz (500g) smoked meat. Bring to a boil and allow to simmer for 1 hour, occasionally skimming off the foam from the top. Add a chicken, bring to a boil, and again skim the foam. Coarsely grind 4 whole cloves, 1 teaspoon allspice, and 1 teaspoon whole peppercorns using a mortar and pestle. Add to broth along with 1 tablespoon salt and ½ cinnamon stick. Simmer for 30 minutes. In the meantime, bring 4¼ fl oz (125 ml) white wine to a boil and pour in two small jars saffron and set aside to steep. Pick the leaves from ½ bunch tarragon; crush 5 unpeeled cloves garlic. Peel and slice a 1½in (4cm) piece of fresh ginger. Add the tarragon, garlic, and ginger, then simmer for an additional 30 minutes. Peel and dice 1lb 12oz (800g) root vegetables. Pour the broth into a clean pot through a fine sieve or cheesecloth. Remove the meat from the bones and chop. Add to the broth along with the root vegetables, the saffron wine, and 1lb 2oz (500g) crème fraîche. Cook for an additional 10–15 minutes, season with about 1–2 tablespoons vinegar, and serve.

Use up leftovers

Bread Soup with Fried Onions and Blood Sausage

Serves 4 • Prep: 20 minutes

1 bunch soup vegetables (such as turnips, celery, carrots, leeks, and parsnips) about 10½oz (300g))

5 cups beef or vegetable broth

7oz (200g) dried farmhouse bread, thinly sliced and cut into 12–16 1¼in (3cm) pieces

2 white onions, peeled and sliced

1 pear or apple, peeled, seeded, and sliced

2 tablespoons clarified butter or vegetable oil

2 sprigs thyme

caraway seeds

5½oz (150g) coarsely ground blood sausage or liverwurst

1 small handful parsley, chopped

freshly ground salt and pepper

1 If necessary, peel the soup vegetables. Dice finely. In a large pot, bring the diced vegetables to a boil with the beef broth, season with salt, and boil for 5 minutes. Remove from heat.

2 Toast the bread for 4 minutes on each side in a dry frying pan, or in a toaster, until crispy. Transfer to four soup bowls.

3 Melt the clarified butter in a frying pan and add the pear, onion, and thyme. Sauté 6–8 minutes until golden brown, while stirring constantly. Season with salt, pepper, and caraway seeds. Divide the mixture over the toast.

4 Slice the blood sausage into 8 pieces and cook briefly in the onion pan. Carefully flip and cook briefly on the other side. Remove carefully and place two slices on each plate. Bring the broth and vegetables to a boil again and pour over the plates. Sprinkle with parsley, let sit for a moment, and serve.

Tip:

If desired, sprinkle the soup with chopped chives to serve.

Horseradish Dumplings

Serves 4 • Prep: 15 minutes

3 tablespoons butter
1¾ oz (50g) fresh horseradish or
 jarred minced horseradish
2 eggs
²/₃ cup semolina flour
freshly grated nutmeg
salt

Melt the butter in a small pot, remove from heat, and allow to cool slightly. Peel and finely grate the horseradish. Mix the butter, eggs, horseradish, flour, and 1 tablespoon water in a bowl. Season with salt and nutmeg and beat with a large kitchen spoon until the dough comes together but is slightly sticky (like the cheesy noodles, p. 109). Form the noodles directly into boiling salt water using a spätzle maker or a large metal colander. As soon as the noodles float to the surface, remove with a slotted spoon, allow to drip-dry, and add to desired broth.

Mini Mushroom Dumplings

Serves 8 • Prep: 15 minutes + 30 minutes resting time

5½ oz (150g) farmer's bread,
 crusts removed
1 tablespoon dried porcini mushrooms
½ cup milk
2 shallots
3½ oz (100g) porcini or wild mushrooms
1 small handful parsley
1 tablespoon butter
1 egg
1 tablespoon all-purpose flour
freshly grated nutmeg
freshly ground salt and pepper

Slice the bread and then cut into strips. Add to a bowl with the dried porcini mushrooms. Pour in the milk, cover, and let sit for 30 minutes. In the meantime, peel and finely dice the shallots. Clean the fresh porcini or wild mushrooms and also dice finely. Pick the parsley leaves from the stems and mince. Melt the butter in a frying pan and sweat the shallots and mushrooms for 3–4 minutes. Mix in the parsley then knead in the bread mixture, flour, and egg. Season with salt, pepper, and nutmeg. Form small dumplings with moist hands and cook for 5 minutes in boiling water. Remove with a slotted spoon, allow to drip-dry, and add to desired broth.

Mini Cheese Dumplings

Serves 8 • Prep: 25 minutes

2 tablespoons butter
½ cup milk
1 cup all-purpose flour
3 eggs
small handful chives
1¾ oz (50g) Alpine cheese
salt

Bring butter, milk, and a pinch of salt to a boil in a small pot. Add all of the flour and stir until the dough no longer sticks to the pot. Let the pastry cool for 5 minutes in a bowl then mix in the eggs one by one until the dough comes together. Snip the chives into thin rings and grate the Alpine cheese; fold into the dough. To prepare for a soup, either boil or bake them in pea-size pieces: pipe pea-size drops onto a parchment-lined baking sheet. Preheat the oven to 390°F (200°C) or 360°F (180°C) (convection oven) and bake for 7–9 minutes or until golden brown.

Butcher's Soup

The places that still slaughter are always the ones with the finest delicacies. They are usually from the parts generally considered less than noble and less than suitable for grand roasts or hams. In Carinthia and Styria, the butcher's soup is called Klachlsuppe. You can vary the meats depending on what your butcher has on hand, but avoid lean back, fillet, or leg pieces because they will only dry out and do nothing for the soup.

Serves 4 • Prep: 30 minutes + 2½ hours cooking time

2lb 3oz (1kg) pork knuckle, pig's
  head, pig's tail pieces (with rinds)
2 white onions
1 bunch soup vegetables (such as
  turnips, celery, carrots, leeks, and
  parsnips) about 10½oz (300g)),
  diced finely
1 teaspoon whole peppercorns
1 teaspoon juniper berries
½ teaspoon caraway seeds
4 sprigs thyme
1 bay leaf
2 tablespoons butter
1 heaping tablespoon
  all-purpose flour
1lb 5oz (600g) potatoes
1–2 teaspoons white wine vinegar
⅔ cup sour cream or crème fraîche
freshly grated nutmeg
2 scallions, sliced in fine rings, or
  ½ bunch chives to garnish
freshly ground salt and pepper

1 Bring the pork, 6 cups water, and 1 teaspoon salt to a boil in a large pot. Reduce heat to medium-low and simmer for 1½ hours, skimming the foam off the top from time to time.

2 While the broth simmers, cut the unpeeled onion in half and add to the pot with the diced soup vegetables. Grind the peppercorns and juniper berries or crush with the bottom of a heavy frying pan. Add to the pot along with the caraway seeds, thyme sprigs, and bay leaf. Simmer for another hour or until meat is soft.

3 With 30 minutes remaining, melt the butter in a pot over low heat and whisk in the flour. Cook for about 3 minutes, stirring constantly. Remove from heat and allow to cool. Peel the potatoes and cut into large pieces, then cook for 10–15 minutes in boiling salted water.

4 Drain the potatoes and meat, keeping the broth and discarding the soup greens and onions. Place the pot with the cooled roux back on the heat and whisk in the broth. Bring to a boil while whisking constantly. Season generously with salt, pepper, and white wine vinegar. Simmer over very low heat for 10 minutes, stirring occasionally, so that the flour taste disappears.

5 In the meantime, remove the meat and rind from the bones and slice. Add to the broth along with the potatoes. Stir in the sour cream and season with nutmeg. Garnish with scallions or chives and serve.

Barley Soup with Dandelion

Easy to vary

Cookbooks often show a skewed version of everyday life; bacon is not in the barley soup everyday—of course it tastes fantastic, but it is not really completely necessary. You can replace it with a few sprigs of herbs, such as thyme, to make a vegetarian version.

Serves 4 • Prep: 50 minutes

2¾oz (75g) smoked bacon slices

2 tablespoons canola oil

4½oz (125g) barley

5 cups vegetable broth

9oz (250g) root vegetables, such as carrots, beets, and parsnips

7oz (200g) Yukon Gold potatoes

2–3 cloves garlic

1 handful young dandelion leaves (about 1¾oz (50g)) or arugula, escarole, or endive if dandelion is not available

1 teaspoon lemon juice

4 eggs

freshly ground salt and pepper

1 Cut the bacon slices into small pieces and render down the fat over low heat in a pot with 1 tablespoon canola oil. Remove the bacon and lightly cook the barley in the same pot. Pour in the vegetable broth, bring to a boil, reduce the heat, and simmer for about 40 minutes.

2 In the meantime, peel the root vegetables, potatoes, and garlic, then slice. After 25 minutes cooking time, add the vegetables to the broth. Slice the dandelion leaves in 1–1½in (3–4cm) pieces. Combine with lemon juice, salt, pepper, and the remaining canola oil. Put aside.

3 Crack an egg into each of the four soup bowls. Taste and season the hot soup, and carefully ladle it over each egg; allow to sit a few minutes. Sprinkle with dandelion leaves and bacon to serve.

Variations:

You can also prepare a vegetarian risotto (for 4–6 servings): Peel and dice 1 onion, 2 carrots, and 2 parsley roots. Slice a leek in half lengthwise, then chop into 1cm cubes. Melt 2 tablespoons butter in a pot and cook 7oz (200g) barley for 2 minutes. Pour in 4½ cups vegetable broth and simmer for 30 minutes at medium heat. After 15 minutes, add the vegetables and season with salt and pepper. Coarsely chop the leaves from 2 bunches parsley or wild garlic. Add in at the end along with ¼ cup grated parmesan cheese. Serve hot.

Sauerkraut Soup with Smoked Sausage

The soup is often made with Saucisson Vaudois or Neuenburger sausage, which is usually pre-cooked in water for about an hour at 170°F (75°C). It is then sliced and served with leeks, potato gratin, legumes, or lettuce. Both varieties are protected with a geographical indication (IGP—Indication géographique protégée) and produced in Switzerland. Because of high import taxes, they are hard to find outside of Switzerland. A good substitution is smoked sausage, such as Polish sausage, bratwurst, or Italian sausage.

Serves 4 • Prep: 15 minutes + 70 minutes resting time

14oz (400g) Polish sausage, bratwurst, or Italian sausage

2 tablespoons clarified butter or canola oil

9oz (250g) white cabbage

1 onion

1 apple (such as Granny Smith), cored

3½oz (100g) starchy potatoes

¾fl oz (20ml) gin

3½fl oz (100ml) white wine

1 bay leaf

4½ cups vegetable broth

1 bunch chive or to taste

freshly ground salt and pepper

1 Remove the sausage from its casing, slice, and break into pieces. Melt the clarified butter in a pot and cook the sausage for 3–4 minutes over low heat. Remove from pot and set aside.

2 While the sausage is cooking, core and coarsely chop the cabbage. Peel the onion, apple, and potatoes. Cut everything into rings or slices. Cook for 5 minutes in the sausage pan along with the cabbage. Deglaze with gin and white wine; add the bay leaf and the broth. Boil for about 1 hour or until the cabbage is soft.

3 With about 10 minutes to go, add the sausage back into the pot and allow to steep (do not boil). In the meantime, chop the chives into thin rings, if using. Season with salt and pepper, sprinkle with chives, and serve.

Potato Leek Soup with Oregano Cream

Vegetarian

The genus origanum *is large and includes Italian oregano and marjoram. Wild oregano from a mountain meadow tastes different than its relatives, but they can still be substituted for one another. If you double the amounts in the oregano cream, it is easier to puree into a fine cream.*

Serves 4 • Prep: 40 minutes

1 leek

7oz (200g) white cabbage or 1 kohlrabi

14oz (400g) Yukon Gold potatoes

2 tablespoons butter

½ bunch savory or parsley

1 bay leaf

freshly grated nutmeg

salt and pepper

For the oregano cream:

½ bunch oregano

5 tablespoons canola oil

3 tablespoons pine nuts

salt

1 Cut the leek in half lengthwise and chop in pieces. Cut the cabbage in half and remove the stalk; chop finely. Peel and slice the potatoes.

2 Melt butter in a large pot and cook the leek, cabbage, and potato for 5 minutes over low heat. Pick the savory leaves from the stems and add to the vegetables along with the bay leaf. Pour in 4½ cups water and season with salt and nutmeg. Boil for 20 minutes or until the vegetables are cooked through.

3 In the meantime, prepare the oregano cream. Pick the oregano from the stems and puree with 5–6 tablespoons soup broth, canola oil, and a pinch of salt using a food processor or immersion blender. Toast the pine nuts in a frying pan over low heat until they become aromatic and add to the cream; puree. Season with salt, transfer to a bowl, and set aside.

4 Puree the potato-leek soup using an immersion blender; season with salt and pepper. Serve in soup bowls with a dollop of oregano cream on top.

Tip:

Aromatic, rustic sausages also go well with the soup: Simply add 14oz (400g) Saucisson Vaudois or raw Polish sausage to the soup as soon as it starts to simmer. Continue cooking over low heat for an hour, but do not boil. The ideal temperature is 170°F (75°C). Remove the sausage from the pot, puree the soup, slice the sausage, and add it back to the soup.

Small Dishes & Vegetarian Cuisine

Valais Asparagus Tart

Vegetarian

Instead of asparagus, you can also make this tart with spring carrots, finger-sized kohlrabi sticks, and scallions; sprinkle with toasted hazelnuts.

Serves 4–6 • Prep: 1 hour + 30 minutes baking time

For the crust:

2 cups flour plus extra for rolling

½ teaspoon salt

10 tablespoons cold butter

1 egg

pie weights or dried beans for
  blind baking

For the filling:

2lb 10oz (1.2kg) green and
  white asparagus

7oz (200g) cream cheese

½ cup crème frâiche

freshly grated nutmeg

¼ cup grated cheese (such as
  Gruyère or Raclette)

1 bunch chervil

1 tablespoon pine nuts, roasted

freshly ground salt and pepper

1 For the dough, mix flour and salt in a bowl. Cut the butter in cubes and add to the flour along with 2 tablespoons cold water and the egg. Use your fingertips to knead the dough until crumbly. Quickly form the dough into a ball, wrap in plastic wrap, and refrigerate for 30 minutes.

2 Preheat the oven to 390°F (200°C) or 360°F (180°C) (convection oven). Butter a quiche or tart pan and roll the dough out to about ⅛in (3mm) on a lightly floured surface. Line the bottom and sides of the quiche pan with the dough and poke the bottom multiple times with a fork. Cover with parchment paper and the pie weights or beans. Place in the hot oven on the second rack from bottom. Bake for 15–20 minutes.

3 In the meantime, peel the asparagus and cut in half. Cook in salt water for 10–12 minutes or until al dente, drain, and allow to dry. Whisk together cream cheese and crème fraîche then season with salt, pepper, and nutmeg. Take the quiche pan out of the oven and remove the parchment paper and pie weights. Add the asparagus pieces to the pan and cover with the crème fraîche mixture. Sprinkle with the grated cheese and bake at 430°F (220°C) or 390°F (200°C) (convection oven) for 25–30 minutes or until golden brown.

4 Pick the chervil leaves from the stems and chop coarsely. Remove the asparagus tart from the oven and sprinkle with chervil and pine nuts. Serve warm or cold.

Tip:

Leftover dough will keep in the freezer for about 6 months.

Ricotta Gnocchi

Potato dumplings and gnocchi are actually really easy to prepare, yet they often fail because the potatoes are too moist—in which case you have to add a lot of flour, making the gnocchi either become too hard or fall apart. If you prepare the potatoes in the oven, they'll lose a lot of their moisture while baking and the gnocchi will be perfect. This variation is from Trentino. The local Grana cheese resembles a high quality Parmesan and is perfect for this dish.

Serves 4 • Prep: 30 minutes + 90 minutes cooking and resting time

1lb 9oz (700g) large
  Russet potatoes
1lb 2oz (500g) ricotta
  or quark
3½oz (100g) grated hard
  cheese (such as Trentingrana
  or Parmesan)
1 cup semolina flour
3 tablespoons butter
2 eggs
¾ cup heavy cream
freshly ground nutmeg
2 scallions
salt

1 Preheat the oven to 370°F (190°C) or 340°F (170°C) (convection oven). Bake the potatoes on a baking sheet on the middle oven rack for 1 hour. Remove, cut in half, and scoop out the soft potato. Weigh 1lb 2oz (500g) of cooked potatoes—this will be a little more than 2 cups—and press through a potato ricer. Squeeze the excess liquid out of the ricotta using a clean dish towel and knead with the potatoes, 2½oz (70g) grated cheese, flour, 1 tablespoon butter, and a pinch of salt. Cool for 30 minutes.

2 Form the dough into finger-sized rolls and cut diagonally into ¾in (2cm) wide pieces. Add to a large pot of boiling salted water and reduce the heat so that the water is barely boiling. As soon as the gnocchi float to the top, let cook five more minutes. In the meantime, mix the eggs, cream, and remaining grated cheese; season with salt and nutmeg. Slice the scallions into fine rings and melt the remaining butter in a pot.

3 Remove the gnocchi with a slotted spoon, allow to dry, and sauté in the butter. Remove from heat and mix in the cream mixture and scallions. Serve immediately.

Tip:

To test if the dough has the right consistency, cook a sample gnocchi. If the dough is too soft and the gnocchi falls apart, fold in some flour. If it is too hard, add a spoonful of ricotta.

Spinach Dumplings in Beef Broth

Whether bacon dumplings, beet dumplings, cheese dumplings, or, like these, spinach dumplings, all of the aromatic dumplings from South Tyrol are delicious. For light dumplings that do not fall apart, there are a few tricks: Chop the bread especially fine or even crumble it so the dumplings hold together, dry the spinach well, and use room temperature milk.

Serves 4 • Prep: 30 minutes + 15 minutes cook time

7oz (200g) stale bread rolls or large
  bread crumbs

1 cup milk, at room temperature

7oz (200g) cooked spinach or
  defrosted frozen spinach

1 bunch parsley

1 onion

2¾oz (75g) Alpine cheese

2 tablespoons butter

2 eggs

1 tablespoon flour

3 cups beef or vegetable broth

salt

1 Slice the stale bread rolls then chop into small cubes (or chop the large bread crumbs into smaller pieces). Add to a bowl with a pinch of salt then pour in the milk. Cover and set aside for 30 minutes.

2 In the meantime, squeeze the liquid out of the spinach with a clean dish towel. Pick the parsley leaves from the stems and finely chop with the spinach. Peel and mince the onion. Grate the Alpine cheese. Melt the butter in a pot; steam the spinach, parsley, and onions for three minutes. Knead this mixture together with the bread crumbs, eggs, flour, 1¾oz (50g) grated Alpine cheese, and salt.

3 Bring a large pot of salted water to a boil. Form Ping-Pong ball–sized dumplings using moist hands. To test that the dough has the right consistency, cook a sample dumpling. If the dough is too soft and the dumpling falls apart, knead in more bread crumbs. Boil the dumplings gently for 15 minutes.

4 With a few minutes to go, bring the beef broth to a boil in a pot. Remove the dumplings with a slotted spoon, allow to dry, and transfer to the broth. Ladle into soup plates, sprinkle with the remaining cheese, and serve.

Variations:

For *Speckknödel* (bacon dumplings), dice 2¾oz (80g) of South Tyrolean speck and fry with the onions in place of spinach. Prepare the dough without flour and cook the dumplings as stated in recipe; serve in the broth. For *Semmelknödel* (bread dumplings), use the same instructions as for bacon dumplings, but leave out the bacon.

Puffed Potatoes with Sauerkraut

Serves 4 • Prep: 35 minutes + 90 minutes cook time

For the sauerkraut:

2 onions, peeled, halved, and
  thinly sliced

1 apple (such as Granny Smith),
  quartered, cored, and sliced

3 tablespoons butter or goose fat

1¼ fl oz (40ml) gin

6¾ fl oz (200ml) apple juice,
  pear juice, or white wine

2lb 3oz (1kg) white cabbage,
  thinly sliced

1lb 2oz (500g) smoked spare
  ribs (if desired)

freshly ground salt and pepper

For the puffed potatoes:

1lb 2oz (500g) Russet potatoes

2 egg yolks

²/₃ cup semolina flour plus extra
  for rolling

freshly ground nutmeg

1 teaspoon salt

1lb 2oz (500g) clarified butter
  or goose fat

1 For the sauerkraut, melt the butter in a pot and sweat the onions and apples for 5 minutes over low heat. Deglaze with gin and wine. Add the cabbage, bay leaf, smoked spare ribs (if using), and 2 cups water. Season with salt and pepper then simmer for 60–90 minutes.

2 With about 45 minutes remaining, start preparing the puffed potatoes. Boil unpeeled potatoes for 20 minutes in salted water. Drain and let stand briefly in the hot pot. Peel, push through a potato ricer, then knead with the egg yolks, flour, a bit of nutmeg, and salt. Roll out on a lightly floured surface until ¼ in (5mm) thick. Using a knife of pastry wheel, cut 2¼ in (6cm) rhombuses. Do not allow to stand too long because the dough will become too soft.

3 Melt the clarified butter or goose fat in a deep frying pan or deep fryer. Fry the potato dough in batches for 3–4 minutes or until golden brown. Place on paper towels to remove the excess oil and keep warm. Plate with sauerkraut and serve.

Zillertal Dumplings with Sautéed Beet Salad

This beet salad also tastes good raw. In some regions, red beets used to be fermented like sauerkraut. It is rare to find these days; it is most likely to be found at the markets on the eastern edge of the Alps such as at the Gurken-Leo stand at Vienna's Naschmarkt. Zerggl are the Zillertaler version of the South Tyrolean Kaspressknödel.

Serves 4 • Prep: 35 minutes + 90 minutes cook time

For the noodles:

7oz (200g) stale bread or large bread crumbs

14oz (400g) cooked potatoes (from the day before)

7oz (200g) Tyrolean gray cheese or hard blue cheese

4½oz (125g) low-fat quark, or regular quark if unavailable

2 small bunches chives

2 eggs

⅓ cup flour

freshly ground nutmeg

2–3 tablespoons butter or clarified butter

freshly ground salt and pepper

For the beet salad:

7oz (200g) young red beets

7oz (200g) white root vegetables (such as turnips and parsnips)

2 tablespoons apple cider vinegar

5 tablespoons peanut or canola oil

freshly ground salt and pepper

1 For the dumplings, dice the bread into cubes and place in a bowl, then pour ½ cup lukewarm water over them. Let rest for 30 minutes in a warm location. In the meantime, press the potatoes through a potato ricer and coarsely grate or crumble the Tyrolean gray cheese. Squeeze the excess liquid from the quark using a clean dish towel. Snip the chives into thin rings.

2 For the beet salad, peel the beets and turnips; coarsely grate and add to a bowl along with the apple cider vinegar and peanut oil. Season with salt and pepper and set aside until the dumplings are formed.

3 Knead together the soaked bread, potato puree, quark, chives, eggs, and flour. Season to taste with salt, pepper, and nutmeg. Form small dumplings from the dough using moist hands, and flatten.

4 Melt the butter in a large frying pan and fry the dumplings (if necessary, in batches) over medium heat for about 8 minutes on each side or until golden brown. In the meantime, add the beet salad to a pot and steam for about 6 minutes over low heat. Plate the dumplings and salad; serve.

Homemade Noodles with Ham

Serves 3–4 • Prep: 35 minutes + 30 minutes resting time

For the dough:

1¼ cups semolina flour plus
  extra for rolling
2 room temperature eggs
  (medium size if using a pasta
  machine, large size if rolling
  by hand)
1 large pinch salt

For the filling:

9oz (250g) cooked ham
7oz (200g) cream or crème fraîche
½ bunch watercress or
  1 small bunch parsley
2 tablespoons butter
freshly ground salt and pepper

1 For the dough, knead the flour, egg, and salt for 5 minutes until a smooth dough has formed. Wrap in plastic wrap and refrigerate for at least 30 minutes.

2 In the meantime, prepare the sauce. Slice the cooked ham; mix the cream with salt and pepper. Coarsely chop the watercress (or pick the parsley leaves and chop).

3 Sprinkle the dough with flour and roll (with a pasta machine, use the second thinnest setting or as thin as possible with a rolling pin). Occasionally wait a moment so the dough can rest. Use a pastry roller to cut the dough into irregular squares. Boil in salted water for 3–4 minutes (5–6 if hand rolled) or until al dente. Remove with a slotted spoon and allow to drip-dry.

4 Melt the butter in a frying pan and heat the ham. Add the noodles and cream; cook for 2 minutes. Plate the noodles and sprinkle generously with watercress to serve.

Tip:

Set some of the pasta water aside and use to thin the sauce if it becomes too thick during heating.

Variations:

For *Krautfleckerl* cabbage noodles, replace the ham/cream mixture with 1lb 12oz white cabbage. Quarter the cabbage, remove the stalk, and cut in thick slices. Melt a bit of butter in a pan and sauté the cabbage. As soon as it is lightly browned, deglaze with 1⅔ cups beef broth. Steam, covered, for 10 minutes. Mix with the cooked pasta and serve.

Cauliflower with Béchamel Sauce

A classic

In German, this dish is called Karfiol mit Einbrennsauce. *You could simply use the German name for cauliflower,* Blumenkohl, *but* Karfiol *is one of the most poetic words in the Austrian kitchen language. Related to the Italian word* cavolfiore, Karfiol *means nothing more than "cabbage flower," but it sounds much nicer. Béchamel sauce has also survived in the Austrian kitchen; this delicate and light sauce goes perfectly with cauliflower and bread crumbs.*

Serves 4 • Prep: 20 minutes

For the béchamel sauce:

2 tablespoons butter

3 tablespoons all-purpose flour

2 cups milk or (½ cup milk and
  ½ cup vegetable broth)

freshly grated nutmeg

freshly ground salt and pepper

For the cauliflower:

2lb 3oz (1kg) cauliflower

3 tablespoons butter

2¾oz (80g) bread crumbs
  (from the bakery or homemade,
  see tip p. 140)

1 bunch chives, sliced into thin
  rings (or mixed herbs, picked off
  their stems and chopped)

salt

1 For the béchamel sauce, melt the butter in a small pot. Whisking constantly, add the flour and cook for three minutes over low heat. Add the milk while still whisking and bring to a boil. Generously season with salt, pepper, and nutmeg then simmer very gently over low heat for 10 minutes in order to remove the flour taste.

2 Bring a large pot of salted water to a boil. Remove the cauliflower stem. Break cauliflowe into large florets and slice a cross into the bottom of any thick stems. Cook for 10–12 minutes in the boiling salted water until the cauliflower is a bit more than al dente, but not too soft. Drain and allow to drip-dry.

3 Melt the butter in a frying pan and cook the bread crumbs until golden brown while stirring constantly. Add the chives (or mixed herbs) to the sauce; stir once. Plate the cauliflower with the béchamel sauce and bread crumbs to serve.

Variations:

For dill green beans with béchamel: Cook 1lb 12oz (800g) green beans in salted water. Prepare the béchamel sauce as instructed but substitute ⅔ cup crème fraîche and 1½ cups beef broth for the milk. Right before serving, season with 1–2 teaspoons white wine vinegar and 1 teaspoon spicy mustard as well as 1 bunch chopped dill.

Baked Black Salsify

If you cannot locate black salsify for this dish, asparagus makes a delicious substitute—the instructions are the same.

Serves 4 • Prep: 20 minutes + 1 hour cook time

14oz (400g) celery

1lb 2oz (500g) black salsify

¼ cup white vinegar

6 tablespoons peanut or canola oil

¼ cup walnuts

2 cloves garlic

12 cherry tomatoes

4 sprigs thyme

2 teaspoons capers (from a jar)

1 cup vegetable broth

4½oz (125g) Appenzeller cheese or young Raclette cheese, sliced

2 tablespoons Alpine or balsamic vinegar (see tip)

freshly ground salt and pepper

1 Preheat the oven to 320°F (160°C) or 280°F (140°C) (convection oven). Cut the celery in half lengthwise then chop into thirds. Peel the black salsify then cut in half lengthwise— or for thick pieces, cut into quarters— and chop into thirds. (It is a good idea to wear gloves while handling black salsify; this prevents its sticky juice from discoloring your hands.) Place the celery and black salsify in a bowl with the vinegar and 4½ cups water.

2 In a shallow roasting pan over medium heat, heat 1 teaspoon peanut oil; cook the walnuts for 2 minutes, remove, coarsely chop, and salt. Add another tablespoon of peanut oil to the pan and cook the prepared vegetables for 3–4 minutes, then season with salt and pepper. Lightly crush the unpeeled garlic cloves. Cut the cherry tomatoes in half. Add to the vegetables along with the thyme and capers. Pour in the vegetable broth and bring to a boil.

3 Braise the vegetables, covered, for 45 minutes on the second rack from the bottom of the oven. After 45 minutes, raise the temperature to 430°F (220°C) or 390°F (200°C) (convection oven) and cover the vegetables with the sliced cheese. Cook for 15 minutes more.

4 Remove the roasting pan from the oven and arrange the vegetables on plates or a large serving platter. Remove the garlic. Mix the remaining pan liquid with the Alpine or balsamic vinegar and the remaining peanut oil. Season to taste. Pour over the vegetables. Sprinkle with the toasted walnuts and serve.

Tip:

Italian Aceto Balsamico vinegar is wonderful, but there are also some first-class vinegar producers in the Alps. Their products harmonize extremely well with black salsify. Try some Swiss balsamic vinegar from Baerg Marti or the mountain herb vinegar from Alpenwelt in the Mölltal region.

Potato Ravioli with a Liverwurst Filling

Easy to vary

Serves 4 • Prep: 50 minutes

For the dough:

1lb 2oz (500g) Russet potatoes

2 egg yolks

1 tablespoon soft butter and
 2–3 tablespoons butter to coat
 the ravioli

1²/₃ cups flour plus extra for rolling

freshly grated nutmeg

salt

For the filling:

1 teaspoon butter

7oz (200g) white cabbage,
 finely chopped

1 clove garlic, peeled and minced

½ teaspoon caraway seeds

1 bunch chives, sliced into
 thin rings

7oz (200g) liverwurst

freshly ground salt and pepper

1 For the dough, boil the potatoes in salted water for 10–15 minutes; drain and let stand for 10 minutes. Then peel and push through a potato ricer. Weigh 14oz (400g), or about 2 cups, potatoes and mix with egg yolks and butter; allow to cool. Once the mixture is cool, knead in the flour and season with salt and nutmeg.

2 For the filling, melt the butter in a pot and steam the cabbage with the garlic and caraway seeds, covered, for 15 minutes over medium heat. If necessary, add some water to the pot—at the end of steaming all of the liquid should be evaporated, though. Season with salt and pepper then let cool. Gently stir half of the chives into the cabbage mixture along with the peeled liverwurst. Set the rest of the chives aside.

3 Sprinkle the potato dough with flour and then roll out to ⅛in (3mm) thick. Slice into rectangles with a knife. Scoop a teaspoon of filling onto one half of each rectangle and brush the edges with water. Fold the rectangles in half and press the edges together with your fingers.

4 Cook the potato ravioli for about 5 minutes in lightly boiling salted water. Melt 2–3 tablespoons butter in a large, heavy frying pan and allow to brown. Remove the ravioli with a slotted spoon and allow to thoroughly dry before coating in the browned butter. Arrange on plates and sprinkle with the remaining chives before serving.

Variation:

Trinser Birnenravioli (Pear Stuffed Ravioli) are from Graubünden: Use the dough from the homemade noodles with ham (p. 72). For the filling, soak 6 dried pears in water overnight. Remove the stem and core, then coarsely chop. Melt 1–2 tablespoons butter in a frying pan and cook the pears, 2 tablespoons bread crumbs, and 2 tablespoons sugar for 4–5 minutes. Deglaze with 1 tablespoon pear liquor and season with salt, pepper, and a pinch of cinnamon. Form the ravioli the same way as in the potato ravioli recipe and cook for 3–5 minutes in lightly salted boiling water. Serve with melted butter and grated Alpine cheese.

Buckwheat Ravioli with a Burrata–Wild Garlic Filling

Buckwheat grows in barren soil and is very tedious to harvest. It is no surprise that it does not have a priority spot in supermarkets. Such a shame, though, since there are wonderful regional specialties from the south side of the Alps with buckwheat flour, such as Slovenian buckwheat ravioli and black polenta in Ticino and in the Provence.

Serves 4 (makes about 24 ravioli) • Prep: 1 hour 15 minutes

For the dough:

2 cups buckwheat flour

2 cups all-purpose flour plus extra
  for rolling

1 teaspoon salt

2 eggs

For the filling:

1 white onion

1 clove garlic

10½oz (300g) red kuri (*hokkaido*)
  squash or eggplant

3 tablespoons olive oil

5½oz (150g) burrata (Italian
  fresh cheese)

12 wild garlic leaves

ground chili powder or red
  pepper flakes

freshly ground nutmeg

salt

2 cups vegetable broth

¼ cup shredded Alpine cheese

salt

1 For the dough, mix flours and salt in a bowl. Pour in ¾ cup boiling water and thoroughly mix. Allow to cool. Separate one egg and set the egg white aside. Knead the egg and egg yolk into the flour mixture until you have a smooth dough. Cover and let rest at least 30 minutes.

2 In the meantime, peel the onion and garlic; cut in half and slice thinly. Cut the squash in half, scoop out the seeds, and also slice thinly; alternatively, peel, quarter, and cut the eggplant into fine slices. Heat the olive oil in a frying pan and cook the onions, garlic, and squash, covered, until very soft. Remove from heat and mash with a fork or potato masher; let cool.

3 While the mashed vegetables cool, coarsely chop the burrata and wild garlic leaves; set some of the chopped wild garlic leaves aside. Gently mix the cooled squash mixture with the burrata and wild garlic. Season to taste with salt, ground chili powder, and nutmeg.

4 Roll out the dough on a lightly floured surface until ¹⁄₁₆in (2mm) thick and cut out circles about 4in (10cm) in diameter. Scoop 1 tablespoon of filling onto each circle and brush the edges with egg whites. Fold the circles into half moons and press the edges together with a fork.

5 Bring a large pot of salted water just to a boil. In another pot, boil the vegetable broth. Cook the ravioli in the lightly boiling salted water for 8–10 minutes; remove with a slotted spoon, allow to drip-dry, and transfer to soup bowls. Ladle broth over the ravioli and serve with chopped wild garlic and grated Alpine cheese.

Carinthian Cheese Noodles with a Fried Potato Filling

Serves 4–6 (about 32 pieces) • Prep: 50 minutes

For the dough:

4 cups all-purpose flour plus extra
 for rolling

1 large egg at room temperature

2 tablespoons oil

1 pinch salt

For the filling:

10½ oz (300g) potatoes

1 white onion

2 cloves garlic

7oz (200g) wild mushrooms

4 tablespoons butter

½ cup ricotta or quark

1¾ oz (50g) grated Alpine cheese

1¾ oz (50g) sour cream

1 pinch freshly grated nutmeg

freshly ground salt and pepper

1 cup beef broth

2 sprigs marjoram

1 For the dough, knead the flour, egg, oil, salt, and ¾ cup lukewarm water to form a soft dough. Wrap in plastic wrap. Let rest 30 minutes.

2 While the dough rests, prepare the filling. Boil the potatoes, unpeeled, for 10–15 minutes; drain, let cool, and cut into cubes. Peel and dice the onions and garlic. Depending on the size of the mushrooms, either slice or leave them whole. Melt 2 tablespoons butter each in two frying pans. Cook the potatoes in one pan and the mushrooms in the other, both until golden brown. Season lightly with salt then add the onions and garlic to the mushrooms; sweat for a few minutes over low heat.

3 Remove both pans from heat. Mash the potatoes with a fork and chop the mushrooms. Mix together the potatoes, mushrooms, ricotta, Alpine cheese, and sour cream; then season to taste with salt, pepper, and nutmeg.

4 Place the dough on your work surface and lightly sprinkle with flour. Roll out until thin, about ⅛ in (3mm), and cut circles 3¼ in (8cm) in diameter. Scoop 1 tablespoon of filling onto each circle and fold into half moons. Press the edges together— or, as the Carinthians would say, *krendeln* (see tip).

5 Bring a large pot of salted water just to a boil. In another pot, boil the beef broth. As the broth heats, pick the marjoram leaves from the stems. Boil the filled noodles for 8–10 minutes in the water, remove with a slotted spoon, let drip-dry, and transfer to soup plates. Ladle broth over the ravioli and serve with marjoram.

Tip:

To *krendeln*: Put the dough circle in your left hand and add 1 tablespoon filling. Fold the dough in half to form a half moon, making sure no air bubbles form. Press the edges together and form a ½ in wide border. And now you can crimp the edges: Hold the dumpling in your left hand, fold the lower corner of the edge toward the filling with the thumb, and lightly press together. This creates a new corner on the edge. Again, fold this corner toward the filling and press together, supporting from below with your index finger. Repeat to *krendel* the entire edge.

Potato Goulash

Quick

Of course Austria also has a potato goulash, and it is especially fine with aromatic Kipfler potatoes. These are similar to Bavarian Bamberg potatoes and French Ratte potatoes. You can essentially use any flavorful potatoes that hold together well. The soup becomes especially creamy if you stir in a bit of butter at the end, preferably even spiced butter (see tip).

Serves 4 • Prep: 25 minutes

3 white onions

1lb 5oz (600g) red potatoes

2 carrots

2 tomatoes

2 tablespoons butter or
 vegetable oil

1–2 teaspoons thyme leaves
 or dried thyme

2 tablespoons sweet
 paprika powder

½ teaspoon caraway seeds

2 cups vegetable or beef broth

leftover roast and gravy
 (if available)

goulash spices (to taste)

freshly ground salt and pepper

1 Peel the onions, garlic, potatoes, and carrots. Cut the onions in half and dice. Mince the garlic and cut the potatoes into cubes. Quarter the carrots lengthwise and chop into pieces. Cut the tomato into eighths.

2 Melt the butter in a pot and sauté the prepared vegetables along with the thyme leaves for 5 minutes. Add paprika and caraway seeds; stir once then add the vegetable broth. Bring to a boil, cover, and boil over medium heat for 10 minutes.

3 If available, cut the leftover roast into small pieces and add to the vegetables along with the gravy. Season to taste with salt, pepper, and goulash spices; serve.

Tip:

For spiced compound butter: Beat 1 stick (8 tablespoons) soft butter with 2 tablespoons sweet paprika powder, 1 teaspoon red pepper flakes, 1 peeled, minced clove garlic, 1 teaspoon ground caraway seeds, 1 teaspoon organic lemon zest, chopped marjoram from 5 sprigs, and a small handful of parsley. Season with salt and pepper then chill or freeze. Stir 1–2 tablespoons into the goulash or use it like herb compound butter on top of roasts or grilled vegetables.

Red Beets with Horseradish Cream

You have never had red beets that taste so good: tender, juicy, and full of aroma—the vegetables cook perfectly in the salt crust. They are known as Randen im Salzmantel and make a great vegetarian appetizer when you have company. Smoked fish such as trout, arctic char, or carp also go well.

Serves 4 • Prep: 1 hour 15 minutes

4 cloves garlic

½ bunch thyme, leaves picked
 from their stems

8 red beets (4½ oz (125g) each),
 thoroughly washed

2lb 12oz (1.25kg) coarse sea salt

1 soft pretzel, sliced (or 1 slice
 farmer's bread, cubed)

3 tablespoons olive oil

2 blood oranges or oranges

1 bunch watercress or 1 package
 watercress

For the horseradish cream:

1 tablespoon butter

3 tablespoons flour

1²/₃ cups milk

freshly grated nutmeg

3½oz (100g) fresh horseradish
 or 4 tablespoons jarred minced
 horseradish

²/₃ cup sour cream

freshly ground salt and pepper

1 Preheat the oven to 390°F (200°C) or 360°F (180°C) (convection oven). Crush the unpeeled garlic. Mix the sea salt with the thyme, garlic, and 1 cup water. Put ¹/₃ of the mixture in a baking dish and place the beets on top of it; cover with the remaining salt mixture. Bake for 50 minutes on the middle oven rack.

2 In the meantime, prepare the horseradish cream by melting butter in a small pot. Whisk in flour and cook over low heat while stirring constantly. Whisk in the milk and bring to a boil. Season generously with salt, pepper, and nutmeg then simmer for 10 minutes over low heat, stirring occasionally. While it simmers, peel and finely grate the horseradish.

3 Heat the olive oil in a frying pan and toast the pretzel slices on each side. Peel the blood orange with a sharp knife (including the white pith). Cut out the fruit segments and discard the skin. Remove the red beets from the oven and open the salt crust with the back of a heavy knife (or a hammer). Remove the beets, peel if desired, and slice into wedges.

4 Before serving, bring the sauce back to a boil. Remove from heat and allow to cool for 2 minutes. Stir in the grated horseradish and sour cream. Plate the red beet wedges with the orange segments, watercress, and horseradish cream. Sprinkle with toasted pretzels and serve.

Cheese Dishes

Cheese Potato Pancakes

Serves 4 (as a side) • Prep: 15 minutes + 20 minutes cooking time

2lb 3oz (1kg) small or medium
 new potatoes

freshly grated nutmeg

2 tablespoons oil

2 tablespoons butter

2 tablespoons heavy cream or milk

2¾oz (75g) Gruyère, Appenzeller,
 or other Alpine cheese, coarsely
 grated

freshly ground salt and pepper

1 Thoroughly wash the potatoes and grate or slice into about $\frac{1}{16}$in (1–2mm) thick pieces. Season with salt, pepper, and nutmeg.

2 In a large, heavy frying pan, heat the oil and 1 tablespoon butter. Add the potatoes and press down with a large kitchen spoon. Drizzle with cream. Cover, leaving a small vent.

3 Fry over low heat for about 20 minutes or until golden brown, flipping after about 10 minutes. When flipping, rest the pancake on the lid and melt the remaining butter before returning the pancake to the pan. Sprinkle with cheese, cover, and finish cooking for 10 minutes.

4 Slide the potato pancake onto a wooden tray, cut into pieces, and serve with a mixed salad.

Tip:

If served with *Rahmschwammerln* (creamed mushrooms), this becomes a vegetarian main dish. For 4 servings: You will need 1lb 2oz (500g) mushrooms (such as cremini, oyster, or wild). Depending on their size, either quarter or cut the mushrooms into thick slices. Peel and dice a small onion and lightly crush 2 cloves unpeeled garlic. Pick the leaves from 1 bunch parsley and chop. Melt two tablespoons clarified butter over high heat and sauté the garlic and mushrooms for 2 minutes, stirring only once or twice in the second minute. Add the onions and cook for 1 minute. Deglaze with 3 tablespoons white wine; boil down the wine completely. Add 3 tablespoons vegetable broth and 1 cup cream. Cook down over high heat until creamy, 2–3 minutes. Beat ½ cup cream until almost stiff and mix with the mushrooms and parsley. Remove the garlic. Season with salt and pepper and serve with potato pancakes.

Gommer Potato Pie

Vegetarian

This specialty is also called Choleri *or* Chollera *and is from the Goms district. Gommer cheese is produced in the nearby mountains and goes best with this rustic potato pie. Unfortunately, the Swiss do not export this cheese, so make sure to take some home on your next vacation!*

Serves 4 • Prep: 30 minutes + 1 hour resting time + 1 hour baking time

For the filling:

10½oz (300g) potatoes

2 cloves garlic

2 ripe pears

1 leek (10½oz (300g))

butter for the leek

freshly grated nutmeg

7oz (200g) Gommer or Raclette cheese, grated

2¾oz (75g) walnuts, coarsely chopped

freshly ground salt and pepper

For the dough:

12 tablespoons butter plus extra to grease the baking dish

2½ cups all-purpose flour plus extra for rolling

1 pinch sea salt

1 For the filling, peel the potatoes and cut into ¹⁄₁₆in (1–2mm) thin slices. Peel and quarter the pears, remove the core, and slice thinly. Cut the leek in half lengthwise and then chop into pieces. Melt some butter in a pot and sweat the leek for 3–4 minutes. Add to the potatoes, garlic, and pear in a bowl. Season with salt, pepper, and nutmeg and let stand at least 1 hour.

2 In the meantime, cut the cold butter into small pieces. Knead with flour, sea salt, and 6 tablespoons cold water with your fingers until crumbly. Quickly form into a dough and wrap in plastic wrap; refrigerate for 30 minutes.

3 Preheat the oven to 350°F (175°C) or 320°F (160°C) (convection oven). Grease a quiche or tart pan with butter. Roll out ²⁄₃ of the dough on a lightly floured surface until round. Line the bottom and sides of the pan with the dough. Roll out the rest of the dough to form a cover.

4 Mix the potato-pear mixture with the grated cheese and walnuts and pour into the dough. Lay the cover over the filling and seal the edges. If there is leftover dough, use it to decorate the pie. Bake the pie for about an hour on the lowest oven rack until golden brown. Serve warm with a mixed salad.

Gruyère Cheese Tarts

Vegetarian

I prefer to bake these Swiss Gâteau au fromage tarts in small dishes instead of one large one because they are so rich and satiating. Served with a mixed salad, these savory cheese tarts make an excellent appetizer for guests. And of course, you could also bake it all together on a baking sheet.

Serves 4 (as a side dish) • Prep: 30 minutes + 30 minutes resting time + 30 minutes baking time

4 frozen puff pastry sheets
  (7 x 5½in (18 x 14cm), about
  2¾oz (75g) each)
1 leek, halved lengthwise and
  chopped
1 tablespoon oil
¾ cup cream or 1 cup milk
2 eggs
9oz (250g) Gruyère, grated
freshly grated nutmeg
butter for the pans
flour for rolling
pie weights or dried beans
freshly ground salt and pepper

1 Cover the puff pastry with plastic wrap to prevent it from drying out and allow to thaw. Heat oil in a frying pan and briefly sweat the chopped leeks; season with salt and set aside. Whisk together the sour cream and eggs. Stir the grated cheese into the mixture. Season with salt, pepper, and nutmeg.

2 Preheat the oven to 430°F (220°C) or 390°F (200°C) (convection oven). Lightly grease 4 mini tart pans (5½–6¼in (14–16cm) diameter) or 8 mini-tart pans (4in (10cm) diameter) with butter. Place the puff pastry on a lightly floured surface and roll out so they are slightly larger; cut in half, if necessary. Line the bottom and sides of each mini-tart pan with the dough, stretching slightly to fit. Poke the bottoms multiple times with a fork then line with parchment paper and pour in the pie weights or beans. Prebake the mini tarts for 8 minutes on the lowest oven rack.

3 Remove the tart pans from the oven. Generously fill with the leeks, then pour in the cream-and-cheese mixture. Bake for about 20 minutes on the lowest oven rack until golden brown. Remove from the oven and place on a cooling rack. Serve lukewarm or cold.

Tip:

Using puff pastry is easy, but you could make a homemade shortcrust pastry instead. For this, mix 2 cups all-purpose flour with ½ teaspoon salt and 10 tablespoons cold butter. Knead with your fingertips until it is crumbly, then quickly knead in ⅛ cup cold water. Wrap in plastic wrap and refrigerate for 30 minutes. Roll out the dough, fill the mini-tart pans, then bake as instructed (it will take 10 minutes longer).

A classic redone

Swiss Cheese Fondue

Serves 4–6 • Prep: 40 minutes

1lb 10oz (750g) small red potatoes
salt
14oz (400g) vegetables (such as
  carrots, leeks, parsley root, red
  beets)
3½oz (100g) oyster mushrooms
1 clove garlic
2-3 tablespoons butter
3 sprigs thyme

For the dip:
2 tablespoons lemon juice
2 tablespoons lemon preserves
2 tablespoons grainy mustard
½ cup canola oil
freshly ground salt and pepper

For the fondue:
2lb 3oz (1kg) Alpine cheese (such
  as Appenzeller cheese)
1 tablespoon cornstarch
13½–17fl oz (400–500ml) white
  wine
Ground mace or freshly grated
  nutmeg
1¼fl oz (40ml) kirsch (or to taste)

1 Thoroughly scrub the potatoes and boil for 15–20 minutes in salted water. In the meantime, peel the vegetables, if necessary, and cut into bite-size pieces. Boil the vegetables one after another until al dente. Remove the cooked vegetables and save ½ cup cooking water. Chop the mushrooms into wide strips and crush the unpeeled garlic. Melt the butter in a frying pan and add the mushrooms, thyme, and garlic. Sauté for 4 minutes then season with salt and pepper. Drain the potatoes and let dry.

2 For the dip, mix the lemon juice, lemon preserves, mustard, and ½ cup cooking water then season with salt and pepper. Stir in the canola oil and season to taste. If the dip is too thick, add more cooking water until creamy.

3 For the fondue, remove the cheese rinds and cut the cheese into ¾in (2cm) cubes. Sprinkle with cornstarch. Melt the cheese with the wine over medium heat, stirring often to bind the fondue. Season with ground mace and kirsch (if using) and allow to simmer. If the fondue becomes too hard, add a bit more wine.

4 Pour the cheese fondue into a fondue pot (such as a caquelon, a stoneware fondue pot often used in Switzerland) and place over a fondue burner. Serve with potatoes, vegetables, mushrooms, and dip. Guests can either dip the sides into the fondue or drizzle some fondue over the sides on individual plates with a bit of dip on the side.

Tip:

You can also dip white bread, green salad, Alpine pickles (p. 13), or Alpine chutney with quinces (p. 104).

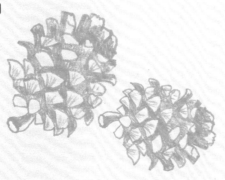

Raclette with Honey and Nuts

Something special

In Valaisan cabins, half cheese wheels are placed on a stone slab at the edge of a hot wood fire. The cut side melts in seconds and the edges brown. Right before the cheese starts to flow, it is transferred to a plate (with gloves!) and served immediately with sides. Not all of the guests can eat this Raclette at the same time because the cheese would get cold.

Serves 4 • Prep: 25 minutes + at least 30 minutes cooling time

1 organic lemon

1 organic orange

3 sprigs thyme

1 dried chili pepper

1 pinch salt

2 tablespoons sugar

4 pears or apples

1lb 5oz (600g) Raclette cheese

1 bunch scallions

3½oz (100g) hazelnuts or walnuts

¼ cup honey

1 Wash the citrus fruit in hot water and slice into rings. Add to a pot with 4 cups water, thyme, chili, salt, and sugar; bring to a boil and cook for 5 minutes. In the meantime, peel the pears, quarter, remove the cores, and slice into wedges. Add to the pot and cook for 2–3 minutes. Remove from heat and let sit for at least 30 minutes.

2 Slice the Raclette cheese. Cut the scallions diagonally into ¾in (2cm) thick pieces and coarsely chop the nuts. Remove the fruit from the liquid with a slotted spoon and let drip-dry. Dish into Raclette pans along with the scallions. Drizzle with honey and cover with sliced Raclette cheese. Sprinkle with chopped nuts. Bake the Raclette for 5 minutes (see tip) and serve immediately.

Tip:

There are two ways to prepare Raclette at home: The easiest way is to simply cook the cheese alone or with potatoes, fruit, and vegetables in the Raclette dishes in a preheated oven or in a Raclette grill. You can also find specialty grills that allow you to roast larger chunks of cheese until the top layer is melted and the edges start to brown. You then remove the cheese and scrape the melted layer directly onto a plate with a large knife and put the cheese back in the grill.

Alpine Chutney with Quinces

Makes 5 jars (8½ fl oz (250ml) each) • Shelf Life: about a year
Prep: 40 minutes + 1 hour resting time

9oz (250g) shallots

2lb 3oz (1kg) quinces

1lb 2oz (500g) ripe apricots

1–2 chili peppers

2 sprigs savory (lemon savory is
  especially delicious) or lemon balm

2 teaspoons juniper berries

2 teaspoons mustard seeds

½ cinnamon stick

1 cup freshly squeezed orange juice

2 teaspoons salt

1 cup sugar

½ cup apple cider vinegar

1 Peel the shallots, cut in half, and dice. Quarter the unpeeled quinces, remove the core, and dice finely. Cut the apricots in half, remove the stones, and slice. Cut the chili peppers into rings. Pick the savory from the stems and chop. Crush or coarsely chop the juniper berries.

2 Combine the prepared fruit, chilies, savory, juniper berries, mustard seeds, cinnamon stick, and shallots in a large pot along with the sugar and salt. Let sit for one hour, then cover and cook for 25 minutes over low heat.

3 Add the apple cider vinegar and cook for another 5 minutes. Remove the lid shortly before the end of the cooking time. If necessary, cook down like jam over medium to high heat. Fill sterilized canning jars (see tip p. 14).

Variations:

You can make aromatic vinegar fruit from apricots, Italian plums, or cherries. For this, cut 1lb 2oz (500g) apricots in half and remove the stones (or rub 1lb 2oz (500g) Italian plums with a clean dish towel and prick on all sides with a needle, or wash 1lb 2oz (500g) cherries but do not pit). Combine 6¾ fl oz (200ml) white wine for light fruit or red wine for dark fruit, ⅔ cup sugar, 4½ fl oz (125ml) wine vinegar, 4 whole cloves, 1 bay leaf, 1 teaspoon mustard seeds, and 2 sprigs thyme; bring to a boil. Pour over the fruit and let soak for at least a day. Pour the liquid into a pot through a sieve and reduce by one-third. Add the fruit back to a bowl and cover with the reduced liquid. Let soak for another day. Pour into a pot and bring to a boil over low heat. Remove the fruit with a slotted spoon and scoop into sterilized canning jars (see tip p. 14). Bring the liquid back up to a boil then pour over the fruit and close the jars immediately.

Pear Ketchup

For the pantry

Pampered fruits never develop any character; it is no different in the plant world than in the human world. That is why apricots from Valais, with their extreme temperature fluctuations, taste so good. It is also why some homemade mountain farmers' pear liquor is so aromatic. Two beautiful, ripe, and aromatic pears are vital for this recipe; then the ketchup will go perfectly with aromatic Alpine cheese and goat cheese as well as grilled items.

Makes about 17fl oz (500ml) • Shelf life: about a year • Prep: 10 minutes + 20 minutes cooking time

1 chili pepper
7oz (200g) mild chili peppers
2 ripe pears (7oz (200g) each)
$1/3$ cup white wine vinegar
¾ cup pear juice
1 teaspoon salt
$1/3$ cup brown sugar, packed

1 Remove the seeds from all of the chilies and chop coarsely. Peel the pears, quarter, remove the cores, and dice coarsely. Combine all ingredients in a pot, bring to a boil, and cook for 20 minutes or until soft.

2 Using an immersion blender, puree briefly, but not too fine. Bring back to a boil and transfer to sterilized canning jars (see tip p. 14).

Tip:

If you prefer a milder ketchup, feel free to substitute bell peppers for some of the chilies. If you prefer it hotter, make sure to use spicy chili peppers. You can substitute the pears with apricots, mirabelle plums, or any other local variety of plums. In any case, wash the fruit, cut in half, and remove the pits. You can even cook small plums with hard to remove pits without removing them; instead of pureeing, process with a food mill to remove the pits in the end.

Baked Cheesy Noodles

Serves 4 • Prep: 50 minutes

For the dough:

2 ½ cups semolina flour

7 eggs

½ cup seltzer water

1 large pinch freshly grated
 nutmeg

1 large pinch salt

For the filling:

1 fennel bulb

3 white onions

3–4 tablespoons butter

1 bunch parsley

5 ½ oz (150 g) Raclette or
 Limburger cheese

5 ½ oz (150 g) Alpine cheese

¼ cup bread crumbs (from the
 bakery or homemade, see tip
 p. 140)

3 tablespoons milk

freshly ground salt and pepper

1 For the dough, beat the flour, egg, seltzer water, nutmeg, and salt with a large kitchen spoon until it holds together but is slightly sticky and develops bubbles. Let set for 20 minutes.

2 Preheat the oven to 280°F (140°C). Cut the fennel in half and slice thinly; peel the onions, cut in half, and also slice thinly. Melt 2 tablespoons butter in a frying pan and cook both until golden brown. Steam, covered, with 4 tablespoons water for 10 minutes.

3 In the meantime, bring a large pot of salted water to a boil. Pick the parsley leaves from the stems and chop. Coarsely grate or crumble the Raclette and Alpine cheeses. Combine the parsley, bread crumbs, milk, and cheeses in a bowl. Season the fennel mixture with salt and pepper and set aside.

4 Using a spätzle maker, or a large collander, form the noodles directly into the salted water. As soon as they float to the top, remove with a slotted spoon, let drip-dry, and transfer to a casserole dish. Season with salt and sprinkle with some fennel mixture as well as the cheese mixture. Place in the oven to keep warm. Repeat until all of the dough is in the casserole dish. Sprinkle with remaining cheese and drop on the rest of the butter in small pieces. Heat the oven to 480°F (250°C) or turn on the broiler and bake for 6–8 minutes on the middle rack.

Variations:

The classic version is *Kasnockerl mit Zwiebeln*—cheese noodles with onions. To make, peel and slice 14oz (400g) white onions instead of the fennel. Melt 2 tablespoons butter in a frying pan and sauté the onions for 12–15 minutes until golden brown, stirring frequently; salt right at the beginning. Then follow the instructions from above for preparing and baking the casserole.

Stuffed Cabbage Rolls

Vegetarian

The vegetarian version of the chabisbünteli, *or stuffed cabbage rolls, has always been around, earlier because of frugality and today as an example of modern vegetarian fare. If you want, you can add an egg or some ground beef—the exact measurement does not really matter because the cabbage leaves will hold the filling together.*

Serves 4 • Prep 35 minutes + 1 hour cooking time

1 small pointed cabbage or white cabbage (about 2lb 3oz (1kg))
3½ oz (100g) stale bread rolls or white bread, crusts removed
2/3 cup hot vegetable broth or cooking water from cabbage
9oz (250g) turnip or 1 kohlrabi
2 cloves garlic
1 bunch parsley
3-4 sprigs lovage (or to taste)
3-4 tablespoons canola oil
½ teaspoon dried marjoram or oregano
2 white onions
2 tablespoons spicy mustard
freshly grated nutmeg
3½oz (100g) grated Gruyère
1 tablespoon flour
4½oz (125ml) white wine or beer
½ cup tomato sauce
freshly ground salt and pepper

1 Boil a large pot of salted water. Using a large fork or meat fork, dip the cabbage into the boiling water over and over to soften the outside leaves. Carefully remove the leaves one after another and repeat until you have 12 (as well as a few extra in case one or two tear later). Cut and discard the thick middle ribs out of the removed leaves; lay the leaves flat on a clean dish towel and pat dry. Cut the bread rolls into finger-size pieces. Pour vegetable broth over the bread and soak for 30 minutes.

2 Meanwhile, slice 7oz (200g) of the remaining cabbage in thin strips. Peel the turnips (or kohlrabi) and finely grate. Peel and finely dice the garlic or push through a garlic press. Pick the parsley and lovage leaves from the stems and chop finely. Heat 2 tablespoons canola oil in a small pot over low heat. Cook the cabbage, turnips, and garlic, covered, for 10 minutes. Stir in the marjoram, parsley, and lovage. Remove from heat and cool. Peel the onions, cut in half, and slice.

3 Squeeze most of the liquid from the bread, then mix the bread with the mustard and cooled vegetables. Season generously with salt, pepper, and a dash of nutmeg. Add cheese and knead together. Divide the filling among the 12 cabbage leaves. Fold the sides of the cabbage rolls into the middle then roll tightly. Keep closed with a toothpick.

4 Heat the remaining canola oil and sear the cabbage rolls on both sides, about 5 minutes. Add the onions and sprinkle everything with flour; cook for another 2 minutes. Deglaze the pan with a bit of white wine and add the tomato sauce. Cover and stew for 40–50 minutes, adding white wine from time to time to gradually form a creamy, glossy sauce. Once the wine is gone, you can add hot water. Serve the cabbage rolls with the sauce. Goes well with mashed potatoes.

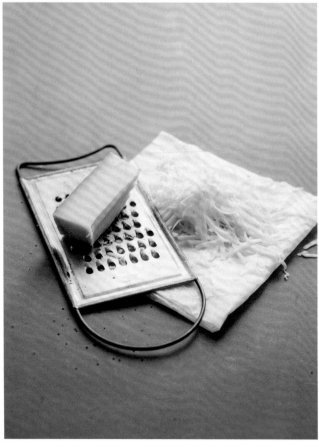

Spinach Casserole

Vegetarian

This luscious spinach or Swiss chard casserole is widespread in Graubünden. The beautiful name, Scarpatscha, stems from the Romansh language. Many of these melodious words have merged into the Bündner dialect through the kitchen. You can also use different vegetables in the recipe; steam heartier vegetables such as carrots first and then layer with the other ingredients.

Serves 4 • Prep: 35 minutes + 30 minutes baking time

7oz (200g) sliced dried farmer's bread, cut into thin strips

10½oz (300g) leaf spinach

5 scallions

2 celery ribs

2 carrots

1 bunch dill

2 tablespoons butter plus extra for the baking dish

¾ cup milk

3 eggs

freshly grated nutmeg

3½oz (100g) Gruyère cheese

freshly ground salt and pepper

1 Preheat the oven to 390°F (200°C) or 360°F (180°C) (convection oven). Soak the strips of farmer's bread in ½ cup warm water. Wash the spinach and chop the scallions into thin rings. Cut the celery into thin slices; peel the carrots, cut in quarters lengthwise, and slice thinly. Chop the dill.

2 Melt the butter in a frying pan and add the spinach, scallions, celery, carrots, and dill. Season with salt and pepper; cover and cook for 5 minutes. In the meantime, whisk the milk and egg in a bowl and season with salt, pepper, and nutmeg. Grate the Gruyère and grease a large baking dish (or 4 small ones) with butter.

3 Squeeze most of the liquid out of the bread. Layer the steamed vegetables, bread, and cheese one after another in the baking dish or dishes. Pour in the egg mixture and bake about 30 minutes on the middle rack until golden brown (in the smaller dishes, it will only take about 20 minutes).

Tip:

This recipe is enough for 6–8 servings as a side dish to braised meats. If you want to serve it as a main dish, serve with fresh salad or a light, fruity vinaigrette without oil. For this, cut 1 peach or 3 apricots in half, remove the pits, and dice finely. Peel and dice a shallot; mince a red chili pepper. Mix 2 tablespoons lemon juice, 1 teaspoon lemon preserves, 2 tablespoons almond butter, and 3 tablespoons vegetable broth or water. Add the fruit and chili to the sauce and season with salt. Pour over the casserole.

Cabbage Flan with Fondue

Vegetarian

Serves 4 (as a side) • Prep: 1 hour + 2 hours inactive time + 40 minutes baking time

10½oz (300g) Fontina cheese

½ cup milk

14oz (400g) savoy cabbage

9oz (250g) cooked chestnuts

4–5 shallots

3 tablespoons butter plus extra for the baking dishes

freshly grated nutmeg

1 cup heavy cream

4 eggs

bread crumbs for the baking dishes

freshly ground salt and pepper

1 Coarsely grate the Fontina cheese and mix with the milk; let stand at least 2 hours.

2 In the meantime, slice the cabbage, removing thick stems as you go. Chop the chestnuts into large pieces. Peel the shallots, cut in half, and slice. Melt half the butter in a large pot and sweat the shallots for 2–3 minutes over low heat. Add the cabbage and chestnuts; season with salt, pepper, and nutmeg. Pour in the cream, cover, and cook for 10 minutes over low heat until all the ingredients are cooked through.

3 Preheat the oven to 360°F (180°C) or 320°F (160°C) (convection oven). Using an immersion blender or vegetable chopper, puree the cabbage mixture, but not too fine. Separate 3 eggs and set the yolks aside. Mix the vegetables with 1 egg and the egg whites, then season to taste. Grease 4 timbale dishes or soufflé dishes (5fl oz (150ml) each) with butter. Sprinkle with bread crumbs and pour in the cabbage mixture. Place on the middle oven rack and bake for 35 minutes.

4 Shortly before the soufflés are done, melt the cheese-milk mixture with the remaining butter in a double boiler, stirring constantly with a wooden spoon. As soon as the mixture is relatively thick, add the egg yolks one by one. At first the mixture will be thinner, and then it will turn creamy. This usually takes about 5–10 minutes but sometimes longer. While cooking, the mixture should not get too hot, so make sure the water in the bottom is only just boiling. As soon as the fondue is creamy, remove from the stove immediately and pour into a new pot. Season, and if necessary, puree with an immersion blender until smooth.

5 Remove the cabbage flans from the oven and carefully turn out onto plates; serve with the fondue.

Polenta Dumplings with Gravy

Each year, 32 cheese makers in the cantons around Lucerne produce about 45,000 rounds of Sbrinz, each weighing 95lb (43kg). Sbrinz is similar to Parmigiano Reggiano in many ways, but there are two major differences that makes this hard-to-find cheese worth the search: Sbrinz cows are free to roam the entire year and many live half their lives in the high Alps. Different herbs grow there than at the Po Valley, which means the milk, and therefore the cheese, tastes different.

Serves 4 • Prep: 30 minutes

2 cups milk

2 cups vegetable broth

1 tablespoon butter

1 clove garlic, peeled and minced

1 pinch freshly grated nutmeg

2 cups instant polenta

¾ cup all-purpose flour

1 bunch chives

3½oz (100g) Sbrinz cheese or
 other Alpine cheese

6¾fl oz (200ml) gravy (or see tip)

freshly ground salt and pepper

1 Bring the milk, vegetable broth, and butter to a boil in a pot. Add the minced garlic to the pot. Season with salt, pepper, and nutmeg. Remove from heat and add in the polenta. Stirring constantly, follow the directions on the package.

2 Let the polenta cool slightly, knead with the flour, then form into walnut-sized dumplings with moist hands. Cook for 15 minutes in lightly boiling water that has been salted. In the meantime, slice the chives into thin rings, grate the cheese, and bring the gravy to a boil.

3 Remove the dumplings with a slotted spoon and let drip-dry. Serve with gravy; sprinkle with chives and grated cheese. You may also decide to skip the gravy and serve with braised meats, such as the veal roast (p. 150) or pulled venison (p. 159).

Tip:

The cooking time for polenta depends on the type you use. Instant polenta takes about 5-10 minutes whereas bramata (a coarser variety) takes about 30 minutes. For this, you would use 2½ cups each milk and vegetable broth to cook. The gravy for this dish should be homemade, but if you do not have any on hand, use creamed spinach, creamed mushrooms (see tip p. 94), or a tomato sauce. You could also prepare a simple vegetarian gravy: Peel and dice 1 onion, 2 cloves garlic, and 7oz (200g) root vegetables. Heat 2 tablespoons olive oil in a pot and sauté the vegetables with a pinch of salt for 3 minutes. Sprinkle with 1–2 teaspoons flour and sauté for an additional 2 minutes. Stir in 2 tablespoons tomato sauce and 1 tablespoon chopped herbs (such as sage, rosemary, or thyme) and deglaze with 2 tablespoons soy sauce. Add 1 cup vegetable broth or water and simmer for 10 minutes then season with salt and pepper.

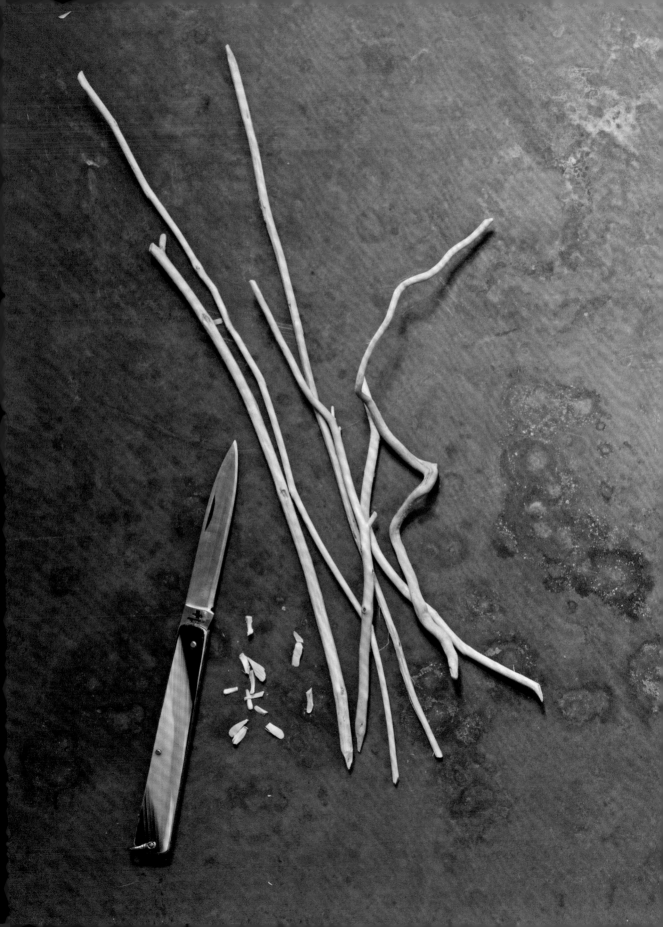

Fish

Skewered Fish in *Vinschgerl*

Serves 4 • Prep: 45 minutes + a few hours soaking time

For the marinade:

1 tablespoon spicy mustard

juice from ½ a lemon

1 tablespoon chili sauce or pear
  ketchup (p. 107)

1 teaspoon fennel seeds

1 teaspoon whole peppercorns

¼ cup olive oil

For the radish sauce:

1 bunch radishes (about 12)

½ cup sour cream

3 tablespoons mayonnaise

freshly ground salt and pepper

2 whole whitefish, arctic char,
  or trout

oil for the grill

4 *Vinschgerl* (South Tyrolean
  flatbreads) or rye bread rolls

1 piece fresh horseradish, about
  2in (5cm), or 3 tablespoons
  prepared horseradish from a jar

1 handful dandelion greens or
  arugula, cut into bite-size pieces

2 large wooden skewers, soaked in
  water for a few hours

1 For the marinade, mix the
mustard, lemon juice, and chili
sauce. Grind the fennel seeds and
peppercorns in a mortar and pestle
or spice grinder. Add to the marinade
along with the olive oil.

2 For the radish sauce, clean the
radishes, grate, and salt. Let stand
a few minutes then squeeze out
the excess liquid using a clean dish
towel. Mix the radishes in a bowl
with the sour cream and mayonnaise
then season with salt and pepper.

3 Preheat a charcoal grill, but not
too hot. Skewer the fish: Put the
skewer straight trough the tail, turn
it 90 degrees, and push it along the
spine and out through the mouth.

4 Rub the grill with an oiled paper
towel. Salt the fish, place them on
the grill, and cook for 12–15 minutes
total. Flip twice while cooking and
brush with marinade a few times.
Carefully lift the thickest part of the
fish with a knife—if the meat comes
off the bone easily, the fish is done.

Brush once more with marinade and
place on a cutting board or serving
platter. First remove the upper fillets
then carefully remove the backbone
along with the skewer. Finally free
the lower fillet from the remaining
bones and shred the meat.

5 Cut open the *Vinschgerl* and
toast lightly on the grill. Fill with the
radish cream, dandelion pieces, and
shredded fish. Generously grate
horseradish over the filling and
serve warm.

Tip:

You can also cut the skewers for this
dish from your garden or use metal
skewers, which do not need to be
soaked. If you are concerned the
fish might stick to the grill, use a fish
grilling basket instead of putting
the fish directly on the grill.

Fried Carp Fillet with Lemon Remoulade

Through the fusion of Asian and European kitchen tricks, you get wonderfully juicy and crispy carp without annoying fish bones. Careful—it can be addictive!

Serves 4 • Prep: 35 minutes + 18 hours resting time

1lb (450g) carp, whitefish, trout, or
  arctic char fillets, ready to use

2 tablespoons salt

5 tablespoons vinegar

2¼ cups clarified butter

1 lemon, in wedges, to garnish

For the batter:

⅔ cup all-purpose flour

1 egg

½ teaspoon sweet paprika or red
  pepper flakes

For the lemon remoulade:

1 organic lemon

6 young/fresh cloves garlic

2 tablespoons sugar

1 bunch parsley, chopped
  (about ½ cup)

2 teaspoons spicy mustard

½ cup sunflower oil

freshly ground salt and pepper

1 Place the fillets skin-side down on a cutting board. Score the back (the thickest part of the fillet) lengthwise every 1/8in (3mm). Place in a bowl and rub with 1 tablespoon salt. Cover with plastic wrap and refrigerate for 12 hours.

2 Remove the fish from the refrigerator, drizzle with about 2 tablespoons vinegar to remove the salt, then wash. Cut into 1¼in (3cm) wide strips. Drizzle the remaining vinegar over a paper towel and use to wrap the fish strips, then refrigerate for another 6 hours.

3 For the batter, nearly freeze ½ cup water or combine equal parts ice-cold water with crushed ice. Unwrap the fish strips and put in the freezer, along with the flour, egg, and paprika.

4 With the batter ingredients in the freezer, make the lemon remoulade. Wash the lemon under hot water, thinly peel, and juice. Peel the garlic and cut into thick slices. Add to a pot with ½ cup water and boil for 12 minutes. Drain, then gently boil down the garlic with sugar, lemon peel, and 2 tablespoons lemon juice.

Add the chopped parsley, lemon syrup, mustard, and 5 tablespoons water to a tall container and puree with an immersion blender. Season with salt and pepper then mix in the sunflower oil little by little until the remoulade is creamy.

5 Melt the clarified butter in a frying pan and heat to 350°F (175°C); this is when a drop of batter or a parsley leaf immediately begins to sizzle but not smoke when added. Remove the batter ingredients from the freezer and quickly combine with a fork, so there are clumps and ice cubes in the batter. Coat the cold fish strips in batter and fry in batches until crispy. Be careful, as the oil is likely to splatter. Remove with a slotted spoon and let drain on paper towels. Serve hot with the remoulade and lemon wedges. Goes well with salad.

Arctic Char with Sautéed Swiss Chard

Serves 4–6 • Prep: 30 minutes

3 tablespoons butter

2 shallots, peeled, sliced into rings

1lb 2oz–1lb 5oz (500–600g) arctic char fillets

3½ fl oz (100ml) white wine

3½ fl oz (100ml) dry vermouth (such as Noilly Prat)

¾ cup heavy cream

1 teaspoon spicy mustard

1 bunch dill, chopped

freshly ground salt and pepper

For the Swiss chard:

1lb 2oz (500g) Swiss chard or leaf spinach

2 cloves garlic

3 tablespoons olive oil

1 pinch freshly grated nutmeg

salt

1 Preheat the oven to 250°F (120°C). Melt 1 tablespoon butter in a large, oven-safe frying pan (the fillets should be able to fit next to each other) and sweat the shallots for 2 minutes. Season the fish with salt and pepper and place skin-side up in the frying pan. Dab 2 tablespoons butter on top of the fillets. Add white wine and vermouth then bring to a boil. Place on the middle oven rack and bake for 20 minutes.

2 For the Swiss chard, cut off the rough stem ends. Lightly crush the unpeeled garlic. Heat the olive oil in a large frying pan and sauté the Swiss chard and 1 clove garlic in 2 batches over high heat for 3 minutes. Season with salt and nutmeg and keep warm.

3 Turn off the oven and remove the fish from the oven. Place the fillets on a serving dish and place back in the oven to keep warm (keep the door open). Reduce the cooking liquid in the pan by two-thirds over high heat. Stir in the cream and cook until the sauce is creamy.

4 In the meantime, remove the skin from the fish fillets with a fork. Take the sauce off the heat, then stir in the mustard and chopped dill. Season to taste. Serve the fillets with the sautéed Swiss chard and sauce. Goes well with a side of potatoes or simple white bread.

Zander Pumpkin Patties

Serves 4 (12 pieces) • Prep: 1 hour 15 minutes

1lb 12oz (800g) red kuri pumpkin (*hokkaido*) or butternut squash

2 teaspoons lemon juice

6 tablespoons canola oil

14oz (400g) zander fillet or whitefish, ready for use

2 scallions

3 tablespoons pine nuts

1 teaspoon pumpkin seed oil

smoked salt, freshly ground salt and pepper

1 Preheat the oven to 390°F (200°C) or 360°F (180°C) (convection oven). Cut the pumpkin in half, scoop out the seeds, and cut into ¾in (2cm) wedges. Add to a bowl with lemon juice and 2 tablespoons canola oil then season with salt and pepper. Pour onto a parchment-lined baking sheet and bake on the middle oven rack for 15–20 minutes until firm to the bite.

2 Remove from the oven and finely dice one-third of the pumpkin. Set the rest aside. Finely chop the zander fillet with a large knife and add to a bowl. Season generously with smoked salt; mix well and cover with plastic wrap, then freeze for 30 minutes.

3 In the meantime, cut the scallions in half lengthwise and then into thin slices. Toast the pine nuts in a dry frying pan until golden brown then allow to cool. Heat 1 tablespoon canola oil with the pumpkin seed oil in a frying pan and sweat the scallions for 3 minutes. Add to a bowl along with the pine nuts and diced pumpkin. Season with smoked salt. Cover with plastic wrap and put in the freezer for 20 minutes, or until the fish is ready to come out of the freezer.

4 Remove the fish and pumpkin from the freezer and knead together thoroughly until a dough starts to form, similar to if you were making meatballs. Season to taste, then form 12 patties using moist hands. Heat 2 tablespoons canola oil in a large frying pan and fry the patties for 6–8 minutes (in batches, if necessary), flipping once. While they are cooking, sauté the remaining pumpkin in 1 tablespoon canola oil in another frying pan. Serve the patties with the sautéed pumpkin. Goes well with spicy mustard or tarragon-lemon mustard (p. 145).

Variations:

For classic *Fischpflanzerl* (fish patties), cube four slices (about 4½oz (125g)) stale white bread as small as possible. Pour ½ cup room temperature milk over the bread and let soak for 30 minutes. In the meantime, peel and dice 1 onion and mince 2 celery ribs. Chop 1 small bunch dill. Finely dice 14oz (400g) fish fillets (such as trout, arctic char, zander, or a mixture). Squeeze the milk from the bread, then mix the bread with 2 eggs, onions, celery, dill, and fish. Season with salt and form 12 patties with moist hands. Heat a bit of canola oil in a pan and fry the patties on both sides for 6–8 minutes total.

Smoked Trout Patties with Cucumber Salad

Serves 4 • Prep: 35 minutes

1 large zucchini (about 10½oz (300g))

½ cup milk

2 stale bread rolls (2¾–3½oz (80–100g)) or 4 slices white bread

1 white onion

2 cloves garlic

1 tablespoon butter

5½oz (150g) smoked trout fillet

1 egg

1 tablespoon mustard

freshly grated nutmeg

2 tablespoons canola oil

freshly ground salt and pepper

For the cucumber salad:

1 English cucumber

1 handful field herbs (such as watercress, dandelion, sorrel, and chickweed) or dill

⅔ cup yogurt or sour cream

1 tablespoon canola oil or pumpkin seed oil

freshly ground salt and pepper

1 Coarsely grate the zucchini; season with salt and lightly mash with your fist or a fork. Heat the milk until lukewarm. Cut the bread rolls in half then dice finely or crumble then soak in the warm milk. Peel the onions and garlic then dice finely. Melt the butter in a frying pan and sweat the onions and garlic for 2 minutes. Shred the smoked trout. Squeeze out the excess liquid from the grated zucchini using a clean dish towel and wring out the bread crumbs with your hands. Mix both with the smoked trout, egg, mustard, and onion mixture. Season with salt, pepper, and nutmeg; set aside.

2 For the salad, peel the cucumber, cut in half lengthwise, and scoop out the seeds with a spoon. Cut the cucumber diagonally in long, thin slices then season with salt and pepper. Coarsely chop the field herbs. Whisk the yogurt until smooth and lightly season with salt and pepper.

3 Form the fish mixture into small patties using moist hands. Warm the canola oil in a frying pan and fry the patties on both sides over medium heat for 6–8 minutes total (in batches, if necessary). Serve the cucumbers with yogurt and herbs and drizzle with canola oil. Serve with the smoked trout patties.

Tip:

If the fish mixture seems too soft before frying, knead in 1 tablespoon bread crumbs. If it seems too firm, mix in a tablespoon of milk or water—but don't worry, the patties should hold together.

Zander Stacks with Asparagus

Serves 4 • Prep: 30 minutes

1lb 9oz (700g) zander fillets with
  skin (from 2 zander fish, 1lb
  12oz–2lb (800–900g) each),
  ready for use
1 teaspoon lemon juice
2¾oz (75g) *Bündnerfleisch*
  (or other cured beef, such as
  bresaola), about 16–20 slices
1 clove garlic
1 tomato
1 sprig thyme
5fl oz (150ml) white wine
1²/₃ cups fish stock, packaged or
  homemade (see tip)
2lb 3oz (1kg) white or green
  asparagus
¼ cup olive oil
1 bunch chives
1 tablespoon cold butter
freshly ground salt and pepper

1 Cut the zander fillets into
16 pieces, season lightly with salt,
and drizzle with lemon juice. Lay
half of the fillets skin-side down on
a cutting board and place a slice of
Bündnerfleisch on each one. Cover
with another fillet, skin-side up, and
lightly press together; try to match
the pieces so that each stack is
close to the same height in the end.
Cool in the refrigerator.

2 Crush the unpeeled garlic clove
and coarsely chop the tomatoes.
Combine with the remaining
Bündnerfleisch, thyme, white wine,
and fish stock; reduce to ¾ cup
over high heat, then pour into a
measuring cup through a fine sieve.

3 Peel the asparagus (only
the lower end of green). Heat
2 tablespoons olive oil in a large
frying pan and cook the asparagus,
covered, for 10 minutes over medium
heat. Season with salt and pepper.
Deglaze with the tomato/wine sauce
and then reduce by a third over high
heat, uncovered. Season to taste.
Cut the butter into cubes and add it
to the asparagus; swirl the pan
around to combine the sauce.

4 Heat the remaining olive oil in
two pans and sauté the zander
stacks over medium heat for
6–8 minutes, flipping once. Bring
the asparagus sauce back to a boil
and serve with the zander stacks.

Tips:

If zander is not available, you may
substitute whitefish.

For homemade fish stock, have your
fish monger pack up the fish bones
and head (without the gills). Place in
a small pot and cover with water.
Peel and dice some vegetables (such
as tomatoes, leeks, celery root, and
fennel bulbs) and add them to the
pot. If desired, add 1 clove garlic,
1 sprig thyme, crushed whole
peppercorns, and a splash of
pernod (anise liquor). Bring to a
boil and simmer over low heat for
25 minutes. Scrape off the foam
from time to time and season lightly
with salt after 10 minutes. Pour the
finished stock through a fine sieve
or cheesecloth; use immediately
or freeze.

Baked Whitefish

In German, this dish is called Gebackene Renke. Renke *can also be called* Reinanke *or* Felchen. *If the whitefish rips open during cooking, it is not pretty, but it is a sign of absolutely fresh fish. They are still fresh a day or two after being caught, but they no longer rip open. You can fry them on the day of the catch as well as a day or two afterward.*

Serves 4 • Prep: 30 minutes

1lb 12oz–2lb 3oz (800g–1kg) potatoes

4 whole whitefish or trout (about 14oz (400g) each), ready for use

about ¾ cup semolina flour

5 tablespoons butter

3 tablespoons oil

1 small bunch parsley

2 lemons

freshly ground salt and pepper

1 Peel the potatoes, chop into large pieces, and boil for 15–20 minutes. In the meantime, wash the white fish under running water, let drip-dry, then pat fully dry with paper towels. Season the inside and outside of the fish with salt and pepper. Pour the flour in a deep plate and dredge the fish in it on both sides; shake off any excess flour.

2 About 10 minutes before the potatoes are done, heat a large frying pan over medium to high heat. Melt 4 tablespoons butter with the oil over medium heat until frothy. Lower the heat. Fry the fish for 5 minutes over low heat; gently shake the pan a few times to spread the butter. In the meantime, pick the parsley from the stems and coarsely chop. Juice 1 lemon and cut the other one in wedges.

3 Insert a fork right behind each fish head and carefully flip one at a time. Fry for another 5 minutes, basting often with butter. Drain the potatoes and let drip-dry. Carefully remove the fish using a spatula. Melt the remaining butter in the pan along with the lemon juice and parsley. Drizzle the sauce over the fish and serve immediately with potatoes and lemon wedges.

Tip:

To carve a fried whitefish or other round fish, prick the skin behind the head with the prong of a fork. Open the skin by moving the fork along the center of the fillet toward the tail. Now you can see a small line between back fillet and belly fillet. Hold the fish in place with the fork and separate the back fillet from the fish bones using a knife or fish knife. Then carefully separate the belly fillet from the bones. Remove and discard the head together with the center bone, so the lower two fillets stay on the plate. Finally, take out any remaining fish bones—pay special attention to the belly fillet, which usually has some bones.

Trout *Gröstl* with Potato Chips and Crispy Sage

Gröstl recipes are usually a way to use up leftovers. They are often simple and filling. The trout Gröstl is the exact opposite: refined, crispy, and juicy. It is best served as an appetizer with a glass of first-class South Tyrolean white wine on a relaxed Sunday afternoon. It is not advisable to increase the recipe size because potatoes only crisp up in small batches, and even the trout tastes best prepared like this.

Serves 4 • Prep: 35 minutes

For the *Gröstl*:

1lb 2oz (500g) trout or zander fillets, ready for use (if desired, without skin)

1lb 2oz (500g) small, red potatoes

1 handful sage

1 cup olive oil

freshly ground salt and pepper

For the spice mixture:

1 organic lemon

3 young garlic cloves

½ teaspoon fennel seeds

1 Cut the trout fillets into finger-sized pieces and lightly season with salt.

2 Scrub the unpeeled potatoes, finely slice, and soak in lukewarm water for 10 minutes. In the meantime, pick the sage leaves from the stems. Heat ²/₃ cup olive oil in a small pan and fry the sage leaves until crispy. Remove with a slotted spoon and let drain on paper towels; season lightly with salt. Drain the potatoes and pat dry with paper towels, then fry in the sage oil in batches until golden brown and crispy. Remove with a slotted spoon and let drain on paper towels; season lightly with salt.

3 For the spice mixture, wash the lemon in hot water, dry, and slice in half. Cut one half in wedges; zest and juice the other half. Peel and dice the garlic. Chop the fennel seeds. Mix the lemon juice, zest, garlic, and fennel seeds.

4 Heat the remaining olive oil in a new frying pan. Lay the trout in the oil skin-side down. Fry for 3–4 minutes over high heat, flipping once. Sprinkle with the spice mixture then flip again, carefully remove from the pan, and place on plates. Serve with potato chips, crispy sage, and lemon wedges.

Steamed Perch with *Bündnerfleisch*

Quick

Perch is the favorite fish of many Swiss chefs. The small predatory fish tastes delicious and is especially juicy. Outside of Switzerland, you should use perch or white fish—or whatever freshwater fish is available in your region because the freshest fish is always the best. In many areas, this often means fish from a lake or river.

Serves 4 • Prep: 35 minutes

2 tablespoons butter

2 tablespoons coarsely
 chopped walnuts

½ bunch arugula

1 white onion

1lb 2oz–1lb 5oz (500–600g)
 perch or white fish fillets

2½fl oz (75ml) white wine

Possibly ⅓ cup vegetable broth

¾ cup crème fraîche

1 tablespoon walnut or olive oil

2¾oz (75g) *Bündnerfleisch*
 (or other cured beef, such as
 bresaola), about 16–20 slices

salt

1 Melt 1 teaspoon butter in a frying pan and cook the chopped walnuts until they are aromatic and lightly browned. Remove from the pan and lightly salt. Remove any thick stems from the arugula and chop into pieces.

2 Grease a large ovenproof frying pan with butter. Peel, quarter, and slice the onion. Salt the perch and place in the pan. Add white wine and ⅓ cup water or vegetable broth and dot the remaining butter onto the fish. Cover with a lid or sheet of aluminum foil. Bring to a boil and steam over low heat for 6–8 minutes. Remove the cover, and using the lid or a spatula, pour off the liquid into another pot.

3 Mix the steaming liquid with the crème fraîche and cook for 2–3 minutes until creamy. In the meantime, mix the arugula with the walnut oil and lightly season with salt. Season the sauce with salt, as well, and froth the sauce using an immersion blender. Plate the perch fillets with the sauce. Divide the *Bündnerfleisch* among the perch fillets and sprinkle with the arugula and roasted walnuts. Goes well with polenta, mashed potatoes, or boiled potatoes.

Meat

Herb Fried Chicken

Serves 4 • Prep: 45 minutes

1 whole chicken (2lb 10oz–3lb 5oz
 (1.2-1.5kg)) or 2lb 3oz (1kg)
 chicken pieces

2–3 eggs

½ bunch oregano

1–2 tablespoons grainy mustard

½ cup all-purpose flour

7oz (200g) bread crumbs (from the
 bakery or homemade, see tip)

about 4 cups sunflower oil or 2lb
 3oz (1kg) clarified butter

1 lemon, in wedges, to garnish

freshly ground salt and pepper

1 Cut the chicken into eight pieces. Begin with two deep cuts, one on each side of the breastbone, to remove the chicken breasts.

2 Crack the eggs in a shallow bowl and beat with a fork. Pick the oregano leaves from the stems and chop; mix into the eggs along with the mustard. Pour the flour into one deep plate and the bread crumbs into another. Sprinkle the chicken with salt and pepper, dredge the chicken in the flour on both sides, and shake off the excess. Repeat in the egg mixture and then in the bread crumbs. Do not press down the breading to ensure that the chicken stays light and crispy when fried.

3 Heat the oil in a deep frying pan to 280°F (140°C) (a bread crumb will sizzle in the oil immediately but will not turn black right away). Fry the chicken for 15–20 minutes until golden brown, turning once or twice.

4 Carefully remove the fried chicken with a slotted spoon and let drip dry on paper towels. Serve with lemon wedges. Goes well with potato salad (p. 34) and pear ketchup (p. 107).

Tip:

It is very easy to make bread crumbs yourself and it often makes the difference between good and perfect fried chicken, schnitzel, or fried fish. Simply break apart some stale bread and add it to a food processor. The breading is especially good if the bread crumbs are not ground too finely. You can also use a vegetable chopper; however, they are much smaller. Store the bread crumbs in an airtight container.

Corn-fed Chicken Cordon Bleu with Wild Garlic

Serves 4 • Prep: 30 minutes

12 wild garlic leaves

4 corn-fed chicken breasts (with or
   without the skin and wings) or
   chicken breasts

3½ oz (100g) young Appenzeller or
   another mild Alpine cheese, sliced

5½ oz (150g) stale white bread or
   bread crumbs

2 eggs

½ cup all-purpose flour

2¼ cups clarified butter

freshly ground salt and pepper

To serve:

4½ oz (125g) lingonberry or
   cranberry sauce (preserved or
   homemade, see tip)

1 lime, in wedges

wild garlic leaves

1 Pick the wild garlic leaves from the stems. Slice the chicken three-fourths of the way through on the long side so that you can fill it; season with salt and pepper. Stuff with wild garlic and sliced cheese then seal with a toothpick.

2 Coarsely chop the bread crumbs then finely grind in a food processor or with an immersion blender. Pour into a deep plate. Crack the eggs into a shallow bowl and lightly beat with a fork. Pour the flour into a third deep plate. Dredge the stuffed chicken in the flour first, then the eggs, and finally the bread crumbs. Do not press down the breading to ensure that the chicken stays light and crispy when fried.

3 Melt the clarified butter in a large frying pan. Fry the chicken over low to medium heat on both sides for 12–15 minutes. Place on paper towels to absorb the excess oil. Serve with lingonberry sauce and lime wedges. Garnish with wild garlic leaves, if desired.

Tip:

Lingonberry sauce is easy to make yourself: Add 12½ oz (350g) fresh or frozen lingonberries (or cranberries), 8½ fl oz (250ml) applesauce, 1 cup packed brown sugar, 1 cinnamon stick, and the zest and juice from one orange to a small pot; boil for about 20 minutes until the berries start to pop. If you like it spicier, you can serve the cordon bleu with sour onions (p. 14).

Tri Tip with Tarragon-Lemon-Mustard

Serves 4 • Prep: 30 minutes + 3.5 hours cooking time

2 white onions

2lb 3oz (1kg) beef soup bones, including a few marrow bones

3lb 5oz (1.5kg) tri tip or top round

14oz (400g) root vegetables (such as 1 carrot, 1 parsley root, 3½oz (100g) celery root, ½ leek)

1 head white or savoy cabbage

1 sprig lovage or 1 sprig thyme

½ bunch parsley

2 bay leaves

4-6 cloves garlic

1 teaspoon whole peppercorns

salt

For the mustard:

1 piece fresh horseradish (1½in (4cm))

1 bunch tarragon

2 teaspoons coriander seeds

2 tablespoons lemon juice

3½oz (100g) grainy mustard

1 Cut the unpeeled onions in half and place cut side down in a large pot; roast for 10 minutes until dark brown. Remove and set aside. Add the soup bones to the same pot with 3 quarts water and bring to a boil, skimming the foam off the top from time to time. After 30 minutes, add the tri tip; season lightly with salt and simmer uncovered over low heat for an hour.

2 In the meantime, thoroughly wash the root vegetables, cabbage leaves, lovage, and parsley. Pick the parsley leaves from the stem and set aside. Bind the washed vegetables and bay leaves with kitchen twine. Cut the unpeeled garlic in half and crush the peppercorns. Add the vegetable herb bundle to the broth along with the onions, garlic, and peppercorns. Season the broth with salt and simmer over low heat for 1 hour. Turn off the heat but keep the pot on the stove for another hour.

3 In the meantime, prepare the mustard: peel the horseradish and finely grate most of it. Pick the tarragon leaves from the stems and puree in a vegetable chopper with the remaining ingredients.

4 Remove the meat from the broth. Pour the broth through a fine sieve into a clean pot. Season to taste and bring back to a boil. Slice the meat against the grain and arrange on deep plates; pour some broth over the meat. Grate the rest of the horseradish onto the meat then serve with tarragon-lemon-mustard. Goes well with fried potatoes.

Tip:

You can use the leftover broth to prepare soup, risotto, potato salad, or gravy. If the layer of fat that develops while cooling is very thick, discard some of it (but not all of it because there is lots of flavor in it). You can store the broth for at least 4 days in the fridge and up to 6 months in the freezer.

Swiss Sauerbraten

The quality of a pot roast depends on the grade of the meat. The most tender pieces are fine grain shoulder cuts from slowly grown free range or organic cows as well as cows raised by their mothers. Suure Mocke, the Swiss version of Sauerbraten, is classically served with mashed potatoes, polenta, or cheese noodles (p. 109), but it also goes well with a simple risotto.

Serves 4 • Prep: 4 hours 30 minutes + 3–5 days marinating time

7oz (200g) parsnips

7oz (200g) carrots

7oz (200g) celery root

2 small white onions

2 cloves garlic

2 bay leaves

4 whole cloves

1 teaspoon peppercorns

1 teaspoon juniper berries

½ bunch thyme

25½fl oz (750ml) red wine

½ cup red wine vinegar

2lb 10oz (1.2kg) beef shoulder

3 tablespoons sunflower oil

2¾oz (80g) Basler Leckerli (or another gingerbread with no glaze)

sea salt

1 Peel and roughly dice the parsnips, carrots, celery root, and onions; peel and crush the garlic. Add the spices to a spice bag or tea filter and bind with kitchen twine or a metal clip. Add to a flat baking dish along with the thyme, red wine, red wine vinegar, and the chopped vegetables. Add the beef shoulder and let marinate in the fridge for 3–5 days.

2 Remove the meat from the marinade, let drip dry and blot with a paper towel. Pour the marinade into a pot through a fine sieve. Let the vegetables, herbs, and spice bag drip dry and set aside; catch any liquid that drips off and add to the pot. Bring the marinade to a boil, skimming off any foam that forms on top. Lightly salt the marinated meat. Heat 2 tablespoons sunflower oil in a heavy Dutch oven or roasting pan and sear the meat on each side, about 10 minutes total. Ladle some hot marinade over the meat to deglaze the pan. Let the liquid cook down completely and repeat twice. Finally pour the remaining marinade over the meat, cover the pan, and stew for 3 hours, flipping occasionally.

3 Heat the remaining sunflower oil in a frying pan and sauté the chopped vegetables for 10 minutes. Crumble the gingerbread and add to the meat along with the vegetables, herbs, and spice bag. Stew for another hour.

4 Remove the roast from the pan and let rest on a cutting board. In the meantime, remove the herbs and spices from the sauce. Season the sauce with salt and cook down, if desired. Carve the roast into thin slices and serve with the stewed vegetables and sauce. Goes well with risotto.

Gremolata Pork Roast

Serves 4–6 • Prep: 30 minutes + 2 days marinating time + 2 hours cooking time

For the gremolata:

1 organic lemon

1 organic orange

1 young/fresh clove garlic

1 teaspoon cumin seeds

¼ cup pork lard

freshly ground salt and pepper

2lb 10oz (1.2kg) pork neck (without rind)

2 carrots

2 white onions

1 parsley root

2 fennel bulbs

3 tomatoes

2 tablespoons olive oil

1 bunch parsley

freshly ground salt and pepper

1 For the gremolata, wash the lemon and orange in hot water then dry. Peel thinly and juice. Peel the garlic and finely chop the cumin seeds. Mix the lard with garlic, cumin, and 1 teaspoon salt then season with pepper. Chill the lemon and orange juice.

2 Rub the pork neck with the gremolata and add to a bowl along with the citrus peels; cool, covered, for 2 days.

3 With a roasting pan inside, preheat the oven to 360°F (180°C) or 320°F (160°C) (convection oven). Peel the carrots, onions, and parsley root and chop into walnut-sized pieces. Slice the fennel greens from the fennel bulb and set aside; cut the bulb in half and slice. Quarter the tomato.

4 Remove the hot roasting pan from the oven and pour in the olive oil. Sear the meat on all sides for about 15 minutes total. Add the chopped vegetables and roast until light brown, about 6–8 minutes, then add the tomatoes. Deglaze the pan with the lemon and orange juice, cover, and braise for about 2 hours in the oven. In the meantime, bring 3 cups water to a boil and pour it into the roast little by little as it cooks.

5 Remove the pork roast from the oven and arrange on a serving dish. Pick the parsley from the stems and chop with the fennel greens. Add the herbs to the roasting pan and stir with the vegetables. Season the vegetables and sauce with salt and pepper and serve with the pork roast. Goes well with polenta.

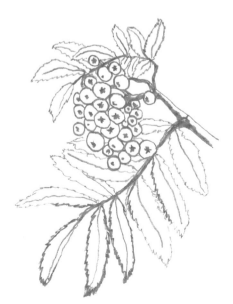

For guests

Veal Roast with Polenta and Juniper Berry Crumbs

Serves 4 • Prep: 30 minutes + 1 hour cooking time

For the roast:

2lb 3oz (1kg) veal leg without bones

1 tablespoon olive oil

1 tablespoon butter

2 red onions

3 cloves garlic

1 bay leaf

3 sprigs thyme

freshly ground salt and pepper

For the polenta:

5 cups vegetable broth or 2½ cups
  vegetable broth and 2½ cups milk

freshly grated nutmeg

2 cups instant polenta

7oz (200g) Vacherin Mont d'Or
  cheese (a soft Swiss cheese) or
  Raclette cheese

salt

For the juniper berry crumbs:

about 1oz (30g) stale white bread

3 sprigs thyme

12 juniper berries

1 tablespoon dried porcini
  mushrooms

2 tablespoons olive oil

For the sauce:

3½ fl oz (100ml) red wine

2–3 tablespoons currant jelly

1²/₃ cups wild game stock

1 tablespoon gingerbread crumbs
  (with no glaze)

freshly ground salt and pepper

1 Preheat the oven to 340°F (170°C) or 300°F (150°C) (convection oven). Season the veal leg with salt and pepper. Heat the butter and olive oil in an oven-safe frying pan or roasting pan and sear the meat evenly on all sides, for 8 minutes total. In the meantime, peel and quarter the onion; crush the unpeeled garlic. Add to the meat along with the bay leaf and thyme. Bake for 40 minutes uncovered on the lowest oven rack. Remove from the oven and place on a serving tray. Cover and place back in the turned off oven to rest; leave the door open. Set the pan aside.

2 For the polenta, bring the vegetable broth to a boil then season with salt and nutmeg. Whisk in the polenta then cover and let steep over low heat, stirring once or twice. Turn off the stove after 5 minutes. Cut the top rind off of the Vacherin Mont d'Or cheese then scoop out the soft cheese and let it melt into the finished polenta.

3 For the bread crumbs, puree the stale white bread in a mini food processor, but not too finely (or crumble in your hands); set aside. Pick the thyme leaves from the stems and chop with the juniper berries and mushrooms in a food processor. Heat olive oil in a small frying pan and roast the bread crumbs while stirring constantly until aromatic. Add the thyme mixture and stir a few times before removing from the stove.

4 For the sauce, heat the roast pan drippings in a frying pan or the roasting pan on the stove with red wine. Cook almost all the way down, then add the currant jelly, wild game stock, and the gingerbread crumbs. Reduce by half. Pour through a fine sieve and season to taste. Sprinkle the roast with the bread crumbs, slice then serve with sauce and polenta. Goes well with green beans.

Goulash with Elderberries

The classic Viennese Saftgulasch uses a similar recipe, just without the elderberries. The best meat to use is either beef shoulder or shank.

Serves 4 • Prep: 25 minutes + 2–2.5 hours cooking time

2lb 3oz (1kg) shoulder or leg from wild boar or domestic pig

4 sprigs marjoram or 1 teaspoon dried marjoram

1lb 12oz (800g) white onions

2 cloves garlic

1 teaspoon caraway seeds

¼ cup lard or clarified butter

2 tablespoons red wine vinegar

4 tablespoons sweet paprika powder

3½oz (100g) elderberry röster (store-bought or homemade, see tip), elderberry compote, or cranberry or lingonberry compote

freshly ground salt and pepper

1 Cut the meat in long 1¼–1½in (3–4cm) wide slices with the grain then against the grain in ½in (1cm) thick strips. Pick the marjoram leaves from the stems. Peel the onions and garlic; cut the onions in half and slice. Dice the garlic with the marjoram and caraway seeds.

2 Melt the lard in a heavy pot and roast the onions over high heat for 5 minutes until golden brown, stirring constantly. Mix the red wine vinegar with 1 cup water. Sprinkle the onions with the paprika powder and immediately deglaze with a bit of the vinegar and water mixture. Add the meat and season with salt and pepper. Braise for about 2–2.5 hours over low heat, almost all the way covered. Let the cooking liquid reduce all the way down again and again, pouring more water-vinegar mixture in each time it does.

3 Toward the end of the cooking time, bring a pot full of water to a boil. Mix the goulash with the elderberry röster and the garlic then barely cover with the hot water and boil for another 10 minutes, uncovered. Season to taste and serve with boiled potatoes or dumplings.

Tip:

You can order elderberry röster online or make it yourself. To make about 27fl oz (800ml) röster, wash and dry 2lb 3oz (1kg) elderberries then remove from the stems. Zest and juice one organic orange. Cut a vanilla bean in half and scrape out the seeds. Bring 4¼fl oz (125ml) red wine, 1 cup packed brown sugar, and the orange juice to a boil. Add the berries along with the orange zest, vanilla bean, and seeds. Boil for 8–10 minutes over low heat until the berries start to break up. Stir in 2fl oz (60ml) apricot liquor and pour into sterilized canning jars (see tip p. 14) and store like jam.

Venison Packets

Parchment paper is great for making small packets to cook meat, fish, and vegetables with short cooking times in their own juices. A few spoonfuls of stock accumulates in the packets and the meat stays nice and tender. Al-cartoccio recipes can also be made with aluminum foil, for example, for use on a covered grill. Parchment paper is better for baking in an oven, plus it looks nicer on a plate.

Serves 4 • Prep: 30 minutes + 20 minutes cooking time

1 clove garlic

1 teaspoon juniper berries

¼ cup soft butter

12 small venison medallions from leg or back (about 1lb 2oz (500g))

1lb 2oz (500g) chanterelles or other in-season wild mushrooms

2 shallots

2 celery ribs

6 tablespoons white wine

4 sprigs thyme

4 bay leaves

white bread for serving

freshly ground salt and pepper

1 Peel the garlic and chop with the juniper berries. Melt 2 tablespoons butter in a large frying pan and sear the venison medallions over high heat for 1 minute on each side. Season with salt and pepper; mix with the garlic and juniper berries, then transfer to a large plate.

2 Preheat the oven to 390°F (200°C) or 360°F (180°C) (convection oven). Clean the chanterelles, but only wash if necessary and dry thoroughly with a dish towel (thickly slice other varieties or leave small ones whole). Peel the shallots and slice into rings; cut the celery in pieces.

3 Grease the middle of 4 parchment paper sheets with the remaining butter (each about the size of a baking sheet). Add the venison, mushrooms, and vegetables to the buttered section and drizzle with a bit of white wine. Lightly season with salt and pepper. Add 1 sprig thyme and 1 bay leaf to each packet.

Place the left and right sides of the parchment paper over the filling and fold the edges three times, about ½in (1cm) wide. Now fold the small edges the same way. If necessary, use paper clips, staples, or a piece of string to hold the packet together. Transfer the packets to a baking sheet and bake for 8 minutes on the second oven rack from bottom.

4 Remove from the oven and transfer to plates. Do not open the packets until at the table; serve with white bread.

Venison Chestnut Meatballs

Serves 4 • Prep: 30 minutes + 30 minutes resting time

5½oz (150g) pre-cooked chestnuts

2 young/fresh cloves garlic

1 dried chile

¼ cup olive oil

1 tablespoon caraway seeds

1 tablespoon whole allspice

1 bunch cilantro

2 teaspoons organic lemon zest

¼ cup white wine

1lb 5oz (600g) venison or chamois
 shoulder, neck, or leg

3½oz (100g) raw pork belly

3½oz (100g) smoked bacon

1 tablespoon salt

1 Roughly chop the chestnuts; peel and mince the garlic. Crush the dried chile. Heat 2 tablespoons olive oil in a frying pan and sauté the chestnuts, garlic, and chile for 3 minutes. In the meantime, grind the caraway seeds and the allspice in a mortar and pestle. Chop the cilantro.

2 Add the spices and lemon zest to the pan then deglaze with white wine. Reduce until the liquid is gone then remove from the heat and let cool (best is if you put it in the freezer for a few minutes). Mix in the cilantro.

3 Slice the venison, pork belly, and bacon into ½in (1cm) strips then chop into small cubes. Next mince the cubes or put through the coarse setting of a meat grinder. Season with salt then freeze for at least 30 minutes. Knead the cold ground meat in a stand mixer for 10 minutes then mix in the cold chestnut mixture.

4 Form 3¼–4in (8–10cm) long finger-sized sausages (*Köfte*) with moist hands. Chill until ready to use, but definitely use them the same day or freeze them raw.

5 Heat the remaining olive oil in a large frying pan and sauté the sausages over medium heat for 8–10 minutes, turning occasionally.

Tip:

The *Köfte* go well with a lentil salad: Boil 4 cups salt water with ¾ cup brown lentils then cook according to package instructions. In the meantime, prepare the dressing by first zesting and juicing 1 organic lemon. Peel 1 clove garlic and mince with a red chile pepper. Mix everything together, season generously with salt, and mix with ½ cup olive oil. Dry roast ¼ cup hulled sesame seeds in a frying pan until lightly golden, aromatic, and they begin to jump. Drain the lentils and let drip dry, then mix with the roasted sesame seeds and dressing. Serve cold or warm and season once more before serving.

Pulled Venison in a Piandina

Take it to go

Pulled pork is not only a hit in New York—the meat is braised until so tender that it falls apart when you pull it. The Alpine street food version is game meat filled in a piadina, a thin Italian flatbread. You can substitute a store-bought tortilla instead.

Serves 4 • Prep: 50 minutes + 3 hours cooking time

7oz (200g) white onions

1 carrot

3½oz (100g) celery root

3 cloves garlic

1 teaspoon juniper berries

1–2 dried chiles

2lb 3oz (1kg) venison or wild boar
 leg or shoulder

3 tablespoons canola oil

5 sprigs thyme

½ cinnamon stick

¾ cup tomato sauce

2 tablespoons quince jelly

1 tablespoon all-purpose flour

13½fl oz (400ml) red wine

freshly ground salt and pepper

For the flatbread:

4 cups all-purpose flour

2 teaspoons salt

½ cup lard or clarified butter, at
 room temperature

1 For the pulled venison, peel and dice the onions, carrots, and celery root. Peel the garlic and chop with the juniper berries and chiles. Crush to a paste with a mortar and pestle along with 1 heaping teaspoon salt.

2 Cube the venison meat into 1½–2in (4–5cm) pieces. Heat the canola oil in a large, heavy pot or roasting pan over high heat and sear the meat. Add the diced vegetables and sauté for 3 minutes then lightly salt. Add the thyme, cinnamon stick, spice paste, tomato sauce, and quince jelly. Sprinkle with flour and stir. Deglaze with a bit of red wine and reduce until all of the liquid has cooked off. Repeat twice then pour in the remaining red wine and 4 cups water. Braise for 3 hours, covered, over low heat until the meat starts to fall apart when stirred. If the sauce is too thick, add a bit more hot water. .

3 In the meantime, mix the flour and salt in a bowl then knead with the lard and ¾ cup warm water until smooth. Form the dough into a ball then wrap in plastic wrap. Cool for 2–3 hours.

4 Divide the dough into 8 small balls and roll each out on a lightly floured surface until ¹/₁₆in (2mm). thick. Heat two frying pans and roast the piadine one at a time without oil for 2–3 minutes, turning once. Remove the thyme and cinnamon sticks from the pot and discard. Shred the meat with 2 forks and season with salt and pepper.

5 Fill the warm piadine with pulled venison, roll together, and enjoy warm.

Tip:

Line the piadine with lettuce and marinated grated pumpkin.

Smoked Meat with Pointed Cabbage

Serves 4 • Prep: 45 minutes + 2.5 hours cooking time

2 white onions

2lb 10oz (1.2kg) cured pork meat
(such as neck or knuckle; order in
advance from your butcher, if
necessary)

1 tablespoon whole peppercorns

1 bunch soup greens

3 bay leaves

4 sprigs thyme

salt

For the cabbage:

2 white onions

1 apple

1lb 12oz (800g) pointed cabbage

3 tablespoons lard or clarified
butter

4¼fl oz (125ml) white wine

¾fl oz (20ml) gin or 1 teaspoon
juniper berries

1 star anis

1 bay leaf

1 small potato

freshly ground salt and pepper

1 Cut the unpeeled onions in half and place cut side down in a large pot; roast for 10 minutes, until dark brown. Pour in 2½ quarts water along with cured meat. Bring to a boil, skimming off any foam that forms. Crush the peppercorns with a mortar and pestle then add to the pot along with the soup greens, bay leaves, and thyme. Lightly salt and cook for 2–2.5 hours over low to medium heat just under boiling.

2 With about an hour to go, prepare the cabbage. Peel the onions, cut in half, and slice thinly. Quarter the unpeeled apples, remove the core, and slice. Quarter the pointed cabbage, remove the stalk, and chop into ½in (1cm) thick pieces, removing any thick stems as you find them. Melt the lard in a pot and sauté the onions, apples, and cabbage over low heat for 5 minutes.

3 Deglaze the cabbage with white wine and gin. Add the star anise, bay leaf, and 2½ cups water. Season with salt and pepper, cover, and simmer over low to medium heat for 1 hour. In the meantime, peel and finely grate the potatoes. Add to the pot after 30 minutes. If it is cooking too intensely, add some water from time to time so that nothing burns.

4 Remove the cured pork from the pot and slice thinly. Season the cabbage to taste and serve with the meat. Goes well with mashed or boiled potatoes.

Braised Beef Cheeks

Serves 4 • Prep: 30 minutes + 4 hours cooking time

2 white onions

4 cloves garlic

1 tablespoon fennel seeds

2 sprigs sage

3lb 5oz (1.5kg) beef cheeks
 (preorder from your butcher shop)

¼ cup olive oil

3 tomatoes

17fl oz (500ml) white wine

freshly ground salt and pepper

1 Peel the onion and garlic. Cut the onion into ½–¾ in (1–2cm) cubes and coarsely chop the garlic with the fennel seeds. Pick the sage from the stems. Pat the beef cheeks dry using paper towels and trim some of the thicker pieces of fat. Season with salt and pepper.

2 Preheat the oven to 340°F (170°C) or 300°F (150°C) (convection oven). Melt the olive oil in a roasting pan and sear the beef cheeks over medium heat for about 5 minutes on each side. Add the onions, garlic fennel mixture, and sage. Dice the tomatoes and stir in. Wait a few moments, then deglaze with some of the white wine and cook down completely. Repeat until the white wine is all used up. Pour in 2 cups water, cover, and braise for 4 hours on the middle oven rack. Add a ladle of hot water from time to time so that the sauce slowly comes together.

3 Remove the beef cheeks, slice, and transfer to a serving tray. Season the sauce to taste and serve with the meat (if desired, pour through a fine sieve first).

Tip:

Goes well with boiled potatoes and spinach, barley, or quinoa. For this, add 1½ cups white or colorful quinoa, 2¾ cups water, and a pinch of salt to a pan. Cook for 15–17 minutes, covered. In the meantime, pick the parsley leaves from the stems and coarsely chop. Mix into the cooked quinoa along with 1 teaspoon organic lemon zest and 1 tablespoon roasted pistachios. Season with salt and ground cumin; serve.

Slow Braised Mountain Lamb Shoulder

Slow Cooking

The adage "good things are worth waiting for" also holds true in the kitchen. There are many recipes whose secret to success is giving them time, but you'll be rewarded with a new taste experience in the end. There are many well-known sheep breeds that are primarily raised in the Alps: various Sisteron lamb from the Provence Alps, Jezersko–Solčava sheep in Carinthia, or the Alpines Steinschaf in the northern Alps. And of course, the recipe tastes good with any grass-fed lamb.

Serves 4 • Prep: 45 minutes + 3 hours cooking time

2 sprigs rosemary

5 sprigs thyme

10 whole peppercorns

10 juniper berries

1 teaspoon fennel seeds

3 tablespoons hazelnuts

2lb 3oz (1kg) lamb shoulder or leg of lamb without bones

12 young cloves garlic

3 tomatoes

3 tablespoons olive oil

1lb 10oz (750g) small potatoes

1lb 2oz (500g) celery

1–2 tablespoons small olives with pit (such as from the Alpine regions in Nizza or Taggiasca olives from Liguria)

juice from ½ lemon

freshly ground salt and pepper

1 Preheat the oven to 280°F (140°C). Pick rosemary and parsley leaves from the stem and chop coarsely. Grind in a food chopper with the peppercorns, juniper berries, and fennel seeds. Add the hazelnuts and coarsely crush. Pat the lamb dry using paper towels and trim down large pieces of fat. Butterfly the lamb, then sprinkle with the spice mixture and salt. Roll the lamb together and bind with kitchen twine. Peel the garlic and coarsely chop the tomatoes.

2 Heat olive oil in a roasting dish or oven-safe frying pan and sear the lamb until golden brown on each side. Add the garlic and tomatoes and place the covered lamb on the second oven rack from bottom and braise for about 3 hours.

3 In the meantime, scrub or peel the potatoes and chop the celery into 1¼–1½in (3–4cm) long pieces. After an hour, add them to the meat and season with salt and pepper. Occasionally check if there is enough liquid in the roasting dish and add a bit of hot water, if necessary. After 2 hours baking, add the olives to the meat and then braise for about one more hour.

4 Remove from oven and cut away the kitchen twine. Let the lamb rest for 10 minutes, then slice. Season the sauce with lemon juice, salt, and pepper. Serve the lamb with the potatoes, braised vegetables, and sauce.

For the grill

Lamb Steaks with Mountain Herb Butter and Mashed Beans

Serves 4 • Prep: 1 hour

2 cloves garlic

1lb 5oz (600g) lamb steaks from the back or leg (¾in (2cm) thick)

2 tablespoons olive oil

2 organic limes or 2 small organic lemons

salt

For the herb butter:

1 cup soft butter

1 bunch mountain herbs (such as watercress, mountain mint, oregano, wild thyme, sorrel) or young shoots from spruce or mountain pine

1 handful edible flowers (such as stinging nettle, elder, deadnettle, or any of the above herbs

3 shallots

1 tablespoon lemon marmalade

ground cumin

salt

For the mashed beans:

14oz (400g) cooked beans (from a can, such as great northern beans)

1 white onion

2–3 tablespoons olive oil

ground cumin

4 sprigs oregano

freshly ground salt and pepper

1 Lightly crush the garlic; mix with the lamb steaks and olive oil in a bowl and marinate for at least 30 minutes.

2 In the meantime, prepare the herb butter: beat the butter until creamy (see tip). Pick the herb leaves from the stems and chop along with the flowers. Peel and dice the shallot. Melt 1 tablespoon creamy butter in a pan and sweat the shallots for 5 minutes with a pinch of salt over low heat, covered. Remove from heat and let cool. Puree together with the herbs, flowers, and lemon preserves in a mini food processor. Stir into the creamy butter and season with cumin and salt. Chill.

3 For the mashed beans, pour the beans into a sieve and rinse under cold water, then let drip dry. Peel and dice the onion. Heat the olive oil in a pan and sweat the onion. Add the beans and briefly sauté. Pour in ½ cup water and season with salt, pepper, and cumin then boil for 5 minutes. Pick the oregano from the stems and mash the beans in the pot with a fork. Transfer to a serving bowl and garnish with oregano; keep warm.

4 Wash the lime with hot water, cut in half, and slice into wedges. Skewer the lamb steaks and lime wedges; season with salt and place on a hot charcoal grill or in a grill pan. Cook on both sides for a total of 3–5 minutes. Serve with herb butter and mashed beans.

Tip:

The best way to cream the butter is with a stand mixer because you can just let it run for 10 minutes. If you use wooden skewers for the lamb, soak them in water first so they do not burn on the grill.

Veal Rolled Roast with a Dried Pear Filling

Easy to prepare in advance

Serves 4 • Prep: 1 hour + 2.5 hours cooking time + 12 hours soaking time

For the filling:

6–8 Kletzn (dried pears)

4 shallots

2 cloves garlic

2 tablespoons olive oil

1 bunch lemon thyme

freshly ground salt and pepper

For the roast:

2 tablespoons olive oil

2lb 3oz (1kg) chopped veal bones (preferably ribs)

4 shallots

1 fennel bulb

2 tablespoons quince jelly

about 8½fl oz (250ml) white wine

3lb 5oz (1.5kg) veal breast

freshly ground salt and pepper

1 For the filling, soak the dried pears over night in water then coarsely chop. Peel and mince the shallots and garlic. Heat the olive oil in a frying pan and sweat the shallots and garlic for 4 minutes. Pick the lemon thyme from the stems and chop. Mix with the pears, shallots, and garlic; season with salt and pepper, then set aside.

2 Prepare the roast: Preheat the oven to 460°F (240°C) or 430°F (220°C) (convection oven). Put the olive oil and veal bones in a roasting pan on the bottom oven rack. Roast the bones uncovered for 30 minutes until brown, flipping occasionally. In the meantime, peel the shallots and coarsely chop with the fennel. Add them to the veal bones with 5 minutes to go. Stir in the quince jelly and deglaze with a bit of white wine.

3 Season the veal breast with salt and pepper, then spread the filling on the inside. Tightly roll the meat, then bind with kitchen twine every 1½in (4cm). Turn the oven down to 320°F (160°C) or 280°F (140°C) (convection oven) then place the roast on top of the bones and roast for 1.5 hours, turning occasionally. Baste with a bit of white wine from time to time and later with the pan drippings, then with a bit of hot water, so that the bones are not quite covered.

4 Take the roast out of the oven and let rest for 5 minutes then cut away the kitchen twine. Remove the veal bones with a fork and discard. Skim off some of the fat then season the sauce to taste. Slice the roast and serve with the sauce. Goes well with gnocchi or mashed potatoes.

Tip:

You could also use prunes for the filling instead of dried pears.

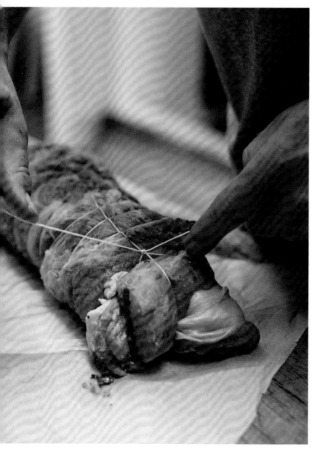

K.u.k. Schnitzel with Mashed Potatoes

A classic

You often find recipes for saftbraten or saftfleisch in old Austrian cookbooks. These classic roasts from the imperial and royal kitchen are characterized by their wonderful sauces, though sometimes the meat dries out easily. The variation described here comes together quickly and offers both tender, juicy meat as well as a delicate sauce.

Serves 4 • Prep: 30 minutes

For the schnitzel:

4 veal cutlets (6½oz (180g) each)

4 white onions

5½oz (150g) carrots

2 cloves garlic

2 tomatoes

2 tablespoons spicy mustard

½ cup all-purpose flour for the schnitzel

2–3 tablespoons oil

1 teaspoon organic lemon zest

1 teaspoon sweet paprika

½ teaspoon dried marjoram

1²/₃ cups beef broth or veal stock

freshly ground salt and pepper

For the mashed potatoes:

2lb 3oz (1kg) Russet potatoes

1 cup heavy cream or milk

freshly grated nutmeg

1–2 tablespoons butter

salt

1 For the schnitzel, allow the meat to come up to room temperature. Peel the onions and either cut into rings or quarter and slice. Peel the carrots, quarter lengthwise, then cube. Peel and dice the garlic. Quarter the tomatoes and remove the seeds.

2 For the mashed potatoes, peel and coarsely chop the potatoes. Cook for 10–15 minutes in boiling salt water.

3 In the meantime, lightly pound the veal, then season with salt and pepper. Brush lightly with mustard on each side. Pour flour in a deep plate then dip the veal in and coat both sides; shake off excess flour. Heat the oil in a frying pan and fry over high heat for 2 minutes. Then flip and fry for another minute. Remove from the pan and set aside. Add the onions and carrots to the pan and sauté for 5–6 minutes until lightly golden. Add the garlic, tomatoes, lemon zest, and spices.

Stir once then pour in the beef broth and reduce over high heat for 3–4 minutes. Transfer the schnitzel back into the pan and cook for 5 minutes, covered, over low heat.

4 In the meantime, drain the potatoes and let drip-dry. Bring the cream to a boil then season with salt and nutmeg and remove from the stove. Roughly mash the potatoes with a potato masher or a fork. Stir in the cream and add the butter in small pieces. Season with salt and nutmeg. Arrange the schnitzel onto plates with the vegetables and sauce; serve with mashed potatoes.

Tip:

The amount of liquid the potatoes need depends on the variety of potato and the time of year— sometimes you might need a bit more cream.

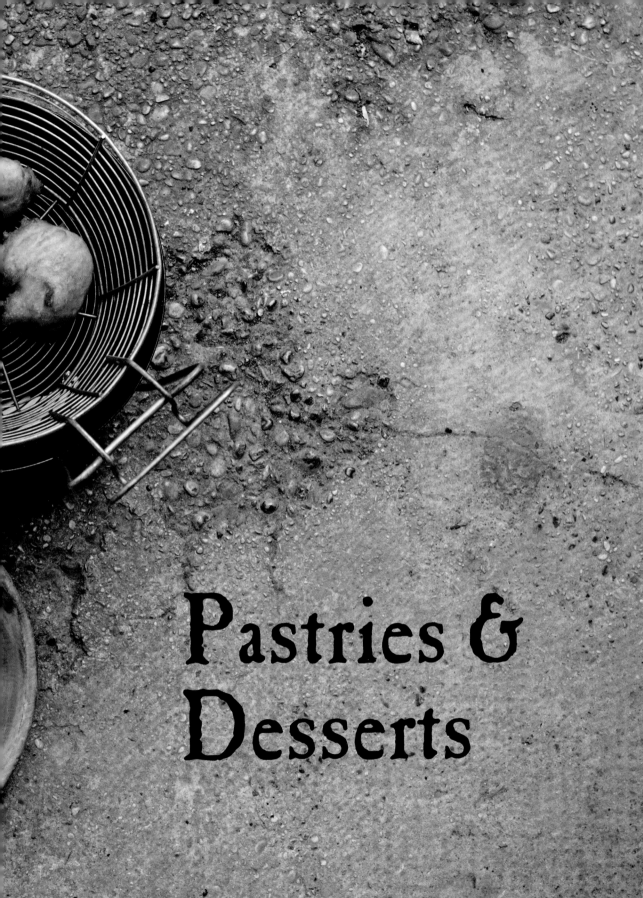

Pastries & Desserts

Engadin Nut Tartlets

Advanced

Makes 24 mini muffins • Prep: 1 hour 45 minutes

For the crust:

10 tablespoons butter, softened, plus extra for the muffin tins

⅓ cup sugar

2 eggs

3 tablespoons warm milk

3⅔ cups all-purpose flour plus extra for rolling

½ teaspoon baking powder

1 pinch salt

1 pinch organic lemon zest

confectioners' sugar for dusting (if desired)

For the filling:

4½ oz (125g) walnuts

¾ cup sugar

½ cup heavy cream

2 tablespoons honey

1 For the dough, cream the butter and sugar for 5–10 minutes with an electric mixer. Beat in the eggs one at a time, then add the milk. Mix the flour, baking powder, salt, and lemon zest, then knead into the butter mixture. Cool in the refrigerator for 1 hour.

2 Prepare the filling: Chop the walnuts and toast in a frying pan until aromatic. Transfer to a plate and let cool. Caramelize the sugar in a small pot over medium-low heat with ¼ cup water until it is golden brown, stirring as little as possible. At the same time, bring the cream and honey to a boil in another pot. Stir into the sugar mixture and boil over low heat until the caramel has fully dissolved. Set 4–5 tablespoons of the caramel cream aside and mix the rest with the toasted walnuts, then pour onto a piece of parchment paper. Cool. As soon as the nut caramel has cooled to the touch, place another piece of parchment paper over it and roll out until ½ in (1.5cm) thick.

3 Preheat the oven to 390°F (200°C). Grease a mini muffin tin with butter. Roll the cooled dough out on a lightly floured surface to ⅛ in (3mm) thick. Cut out 24 circles (2in (5cm) diameter) and carefully press them into the mini muffin tin. Remove the upper sheet of parchment paper from the nut caramel and cut out 24 circles to fit the muffin cups. Place 1 caramel circle in each muffin cup. Knead the leftover dough together again and roll out a little thinner. Cut out 24 circles (1½ in (4cm) in diameter) and put on top of the tarts. Carefully seal the edges then press with the prongs of a fork.

4 Bake the tartlets on the second oven rack from the bottom for about 30 minutes. Take out of the oven, slightly cool, then remove from the muffin pan. Warm up the remaining caramel and drizzle over the tarts. Dust with confectioners' sugar, if desired, and serve.

Spelt Reindling

Makes 1 cake • Prep: 45 minutes + 2½ hours resting and baking time

For the filling:

4½ oz (125g) raisins

2 fl oz (6ml) rum for soaking (if desired)

3½ oz (100g) coarsely chopped walnuts

1 teaspoon ground cinnamon

⅓ cup sugar

For the dough:

2 cups warm milk

¼ cup sugar

2 teaspoons organic lemon zest

1¼ fl oz (40ml) rum

1 cube fresh yeast (1½ oz (42g))

4¾ cups spelt flour plus extra for rolling

1¼ cups spelt semolina flour or spelt flour

10 tablespoons melted butter plus extra for the baking dish

2 eggs

3 tablespoons apricot jam

1 For the filling, soak the raisins in rum or lukewarm water. As they soak, mix the milk, sugar, lemon zest, and rum in a bowl and stir with a kitchen spoon. Crumble in the yeast. Add the spelt flour and spelt semolina flour little by little as you continue stirring. As soon as the dough becomes too stiff to stir, knead it with your hands or a stand mixer. Add 6 tablespoons melted butter and eggs and thoroughly knead. Cover with a dish towel and let rise for 45 minutes–1 hour in a warm location until it has doubled in volume. Briefly knead the dough then let rise for 45 minutes more.

2 Preheat the oven to 390°F (200°C). Roll the dough out on a lightly floured dish towel to about ¼ in (5 mm) thick and brush with a bit of melted butter. Sprinkle evenly with raisins, chopped hazelnuts, cinnamon, and sugar, then roll the dough together tightly (the Reindling is not very sweet. If you want, you can sprinkle with a few more tablespoons sugar). Grease a deep baking sheet (8 x 12in (20 x 30cm)) with butter and lay in the dough in a spiral form. Brush with the remaining butter, let rise 10 minutes, and bake on the lowest oven rack for 45–50 minutes until golden brown.

3 In the meantime, mix the apricot jam with 2 tablespoons water and push through a fine sieve. Remove the spelt reindling from the oven, brush with the glaze, and serve warm or cold.

Variations:

For an especially festive filling, coarsely chop 3½ oz (100g) dried fruit (such as cranberries, apricots, raisins) and soak overnight in 3 tablespoons rum. Bring ½ cup cream to a boil and stir in 3 tablespoons sugar, 6¼ oz (175g) ground poppy seeds, and 2¾ oz (75g) ground walnuts. Stir for 2 minutes over heat then remove from the stove. Add the soaked fruit, 1 teaspoon organic lemon zest, and ½ teaspoon ground cinnamon. Allow to cool then spread evenly onto the dough.

Mini Cheese-filled Pancakes with Raspberries

For the classic pancakes with apricot jam, double the batter recipe, make 12 pancakes, and brush with apricot Powidl (p. 194) or jam (see tip).

Serves 6 • Prep: 1 hour + 30 minutes baking time

For the pancakes:

about 4 tablespoons butter plus
  extra for the pans

$2/3$ cup all-purpose flour

2 eggs

¾ cup milk

1 pinch salt

For the filling:

1 organic lemon

2 tablespoons butter

3 tablespoons sugar

1 pinch salt

2 eggs

3½oz (100g) low-fat quark,
  or ricotta cheese if not available

¼ cup sour cream

1 tablespoon all-purpose flour

To garnish:

confectioners' sugar

5½oz (150g) raspberries

1 For the pancakes, melt a heaping tablespoon butter in a small frying pan (7–8in (18–20cm) diameter) and let brown. Mix the flour, eggs, and milk with an immersion blender, then add the browned butter and salt. Let stand for at least 30 minutes.

2 In the meantime, wash the lemon with hot water, then dry and zest until you have 1 teaspoon. Beat the butter, 1 tablespoon sugar, salt, and lemon zest with an electric mixer. Separate the eggs and beat in the egg yolks one at a time. Wring out the quark or ricotta in a dish towel, then fold in. Add the sour cream and flour. Beat the egg whites with the remaining sugar until stiff, then fold into the batter.

3 Preheat the oven to 360°F (180°C) or 320°F (160°C) (convection oven). Melt a pat of butter in a small frying pan and make 6 pancakes, one at a time. Grease 6 mini baking dishes (2¾in (7cm) diameter) with butter and add the pancakes. Pour in the filling, then bake for 25 minutes on the second rack from the bottom.

4 Remove from the oven and let cool for a few minutes. Carefully remove the filled pancakes from the baking dishes and transfer to plates. Serve with confectioners' sugar and garnish with raspberries to serve.

Tip:

For the perfect apricot jam: Cut 2lb 3oz (1kg) apricots in half, remove the pits, and mix in a large pot with 4 cups sugar. Zest and juice 2 organic lemons; add to the pot, cover, and let steep for 12 hours. Bring to a boil, cool, and let steep for another 12 hours. Pour the fruit into a sieve over another pot. Bring the juice to a boil and cook down until it starts to thicken, about 10 minutes. Add the fruit and cook for another 10 minutes. To test if it is set, dip a spoon into the mixture and let drip off. If the last drop hardens, the jam is set. Remove the pot from the stove and pour into sterilized canning jars (see tip p. 14).

Caramelized
Kaiserschmarren

Serves 4 • Prep: 20 minutes + soaking time + 30 minutes inactive time

2 tablespoons raisins

3 tablespoons rum

²/₃ cup all-purpose flour

ᵉ/₃ cup milk or heavy cream

1 pinch salt

1 tablespoon vanilla sugar

3 eggs

5 tablespoons butter

¹/₃ cup sugar

confectioners' sugar for dusting
 (if desired)

1 Mix the raisins with the rum and let soak (preferably for a few days).

2 Mix the flour with the milk, salt, and vanilla sugar until smooth (do not whisk). Cover and let rest for 30 minutes, then carefully stir in the eggs.

3 Preheat the oven to 360°F (180°C) or 320°F (160°C) (convection oven). Melt half the butter in an oven-safe frying pan over medium heat until frothy. Pour the batter into the frying pan and cook for 3 minutes (the underside is slightly browned and the top is still liquid). Sprinkle on the raisins and bake on the middle oven rack for 10 minutes. Remove and tear into 1¼–1½ in (3–4cm) pieces with 2 forks.

4 Add the remaining butter in small pieces to the *Kaiserschmarren*. Sprinkle with sugar, flip in the pan, and caramelize on the stove for 3 minutes. Transfer to plates, sprinkle with confectioners' sugar, if desired, and serve. Goes well with caramelized cherries (see tip), applesauce, or a fruity *Röster* (such as cherry *Röster*, p. 190).

Tip:

For caramelized cherries, cut 1lb 2oz (500g) cherries in half and remove the pits. Boil 3 tablespoons sugar and 3 tablespoons water in a pot until light brown. Add a dash of cherry juice or red wine—be careful, the hot sugar might splatter. Stir until the sugar is completely dissolved. Add the cherries, bring to a boil, and transfer to a plate or serving dish. Let cool.

Croissant *Koch*

Serves 4 • Prep: 40 minutes + 45 minutes baking time

5½oz (150g) stale croissants, rolls, or baguettes
10 dried apricot halves
3 eggs
1½ cups heavy cream or milk
2 apples (such as Granny Smith)
cinnamon sugar (3 tablespoons sugar with ½ teaspoon ground cinnamon)
2 tablespoons of butter in pieces, plus extra for the pan
confectioners' sugar for dusting (if desired)

1 Slice the croissants (or cut the rolls or baguettes) in half, then slice into strips. Slice or chop the apricot halves and add to a bowl with the croissant pieces. Separate 1 egg and set the yolk aside. Whisk together 1 cup of the cream or milk with 2 eggs and the egg white. Pour over the croissants. Cover, and let steep for 20 minutes.

2 As the croissants steep, peel, quarter, core, and slice the apples.

3 Preheat the oven to 360°F (180°C) or 320°F (160°C) (convection oven). Grease a loaf pan with butter. Pour one-third of the croissant mixture into the dish, then cover with a layer of apple slices and sprinkle with cinnamon sugar. Repeat, then cover with the rest of the croissant mixture. Whisk the remaining ½ cup cream or milk with the egg yolk and pour over the baking dish. Sprinkle on the remaining cinnamon sugar and pieces of butter. Bake on the second oven rack from bottom for about 45 minutes, until golden brown and crispy.

4 Remove the croissant *Koch* from the oven, dust with confectioners' sugar, if desired, and serve hot with *Röster*, compote, or fresh fruit.

Variations:

You could also prepare the croissant mixture in a frying pan to make a croissant *Schmarren*. For this, prepare the croissant mixture as in step 1. In a large frying pan, melt 2 tablespoons butter until frothy; pour in the mixture and leave to cook for 2–3 minutes over medium heat. Tear the croissant *Schmarren* into large pieces with 2 forks. Cook for 3–4 minutes until golden brown, then flip. Add a tablespoon of butter, then cook for another 3–4 minutes. Sprinkle with 2 tablespoons sugar and a pinch cinnamon, then stir. Serve as soon as the sugar is caramelized.

A classic

Salzburger Sweet Dumplings

Salzburger nockerl (sweet dumplings) are very sensitive soufflés, which means you have to be very exact during preparation. The timing plays a large role. You have to wait for the nockerl and not the other way around: When the nockerl are ready, they should be enjoyed right away.

Serves 4 • Prep: 20 minutes

5 egg whites

2 teaspoons sugar

3 egg yolks

1 packet (about 2 teaspoons) vanilla sugar, or 1 teaspoon vanilla extract if unavailable

3 tablespoons all-purpose flour

1 teaspoon organic lemon zest

1 tablespoon butter and 2 teaspoons sugar for the pans

confectioners' sugar for dusting

1 Preheat the oven to 360°F (180°C). Beat the egg whites and sugar until stiff. Just barely fold in the egg yolks, vanilla sugar or vanilla extract, flour, and lemon zest; there will still be yolk visible in the batter.

2 Grease 4 soufflé dishes or ramekins with butter and sprinkle with sugar. Using 2 tablespoons, form 2 dumplings and place next to each other in each soufflé dish, so that peaks form.

3 Place on the second oven rack from bottom and bake for 6–8 minutes until lightly golden but creamy on the inside. They collapse as soon as they cool, so immediately dust with confectioners' sugar and serve.

Tip:

Raspberry sauce goes well with the nockerl: Puree 9oz (250g) raspberries with 1–2 tablespoons confectioners' sugar for 10 minutes; this binds the sauce. Push through a fine sieve to remove the seeds, then chill in the refrigerator.

Yogurt *Koch* with Blueberries

Koch is the Austrian word for a small dessert somewhere between a pudding and a soufflé—lighter than a pudding but much more stable than a soufflé. It works best in baking dishes with straight sides.

Serves 6 • Prep: 40 minutes + 35–45 minutes cooking time

4½oz (125g) blueberries

½ cup soft butter plus extra for the baking dishes

1 tablespoon vanilla sugar

6 tablespoons confectioners' sugar plus extra for dusting

5 eggs

²/₃ cup Greek yogurt or sour cream

¹/₃ cup all-purpose flour plus extra for dusting

3 tablespoons ground walnuts or hazelnuts for the baking dishes

1 Wash and thoroughly dry the blueberries. Using an electric mixer, cream the butter, vanilla sugar, and half the confectioners' sugar for 5 minutes. Separate the eggs and beat the egg yolks one by one into the butter-sugar mixture. Stir in the yogurt. Beat the egg whites with the remaining confectioners' sugar until nearly stiff, then fold into the other mixture. Sift the flour over the batter and fold in.

2 Preheat the oven to 340°F (170°C) along with a deep baking sheet. Grease 6 oven-safe glasses (4¾–5fl oz (140–150ml) capacity, such as small canning jars) with butter and line with ground nuts. Bring 2 quarts water to a boil. Sprinkle the blueberries with flour and stir. Scoop the batter tablespoon by tablespoon into the jars, adding 1 teaspoon blueberries between each layer.

3 Place the jars onto the hot baking sheet and carefully pour the boiling water into the baking sheet until the jars are submerged just about ¾in (2cm). Cook the jars for 10 minutes, then reduce the heat to 300°F (150°C) and bake for 25–30 more minutes. Remove from the oven and sprinkle with confectioners' sugar before serving.

For guests

Walnut *Koch*

Serves 6 • Prep: 45 minutes + 30 minutes baking time

3½ oz (100g) couverture chocolate
  or other good quality chocolate

2 tablespoons sugar

2¾ oz (80g) walnuts

1 tablespoon butter for the
  caramelizing and extra for the
  baking dish

3 tablespoons all-purpose flour

3 tablespoons ground walnuts (or
  other nuts) to line the baking dish

½ cup butter

¾ cup confectioners' sugar plus
  extra for dusting

5 eggs

¾ cup heavy cream

1 Chop the chocolate and melt in a double boiler. Caramelize the sugar with 1 tablespoon water in a small frying pan over medium-low heat until golden brown. Add the walnuts and butter; stir until the nuts are covered in caramel. Remove from the pan and spread on a parchment-lined tray. Allow to cool, then chop coarsely. Sprinkle the chopped walnut brittle with flour and stir.

2 Place a deep baking sheet in the oven and preheat the oven to 360°F (180°C). Grease 6 small ramekins or small canning jars (4¾–5fl oz (140–150ml) capacity) with butter and sprinkle with ground walnuts. Separately, bring 2 quarts water to a boil.

3 Using an electric mixer, cream the butter and confectioners' sugar for 5–10 minutes. Separate the eggs and beat the egg yolks one by one into the butter-sugar mixture. Stir in the melted chocolate and the chopped walnut brittle. In a separate bowl, beat the egg whites until stiff. Fold into the other mixture. Divide among the prepared jars. Place the jars onto the hot baking sheet and carefully pour the boiling water into the baking sheet until the jars are submerged about ¾ in (2cm). Bake for 30 minutes.

4 Shortly before the end of baking, beat the heavy cream until nearly stiff. Remove the dishes from the oven and turn out onto plates. Sprinkle with confectioners' sugar and serve with whipped cream. Goes well with strawberries.

Tip:

You can also make one large *Walnusskoch* (walnut *Koch*) in a large, covered pudding mold. Preheat a deep baking sheet on the lowest oven rack with a little more water than called for in the recipe. Place the filled, covered pudding mold in the water and make sure it is at least half submerged. Bake for about 1 hour. Turn out onto a serving tray and serve.

Simple and easy

Port Wine *Kletzn*

**Serves 6 or 12 • Prep: 10 minutes + 40 minutes cooking time
+ 2 hours cooling time + 12 hours soaking time**

6 or 12 *Kletzn* (dried pears)
25½ fl oz (0.75l) port wine
½ cinnamon stick
1 teaspoon whole allspice
5½ oz (150g) honey
¾ cup heavy cream

1 Soak the dried pears overnight in cold water.

2 Add the port wine, cinnamon stick, and whole allspice to a small pot; bring to a boil. Drain the pears, saving ²/₃ cup soaking water. Add the pears and soaking water to the port wine mixture. Simmer for about 40 minutes, then let cool.

3 Remove the pears from the wine mixture and dish onto 6 or 12 plates. Add the honey to the wine mixture and boil down until syrupy. In the meantime, beat the cream until stiff. Pour the port wine syrup over the pears and serve with whipped cream.

Cherry *Röster*

Makes 27 fl oz (800ml) • Prep: 40 minutes

2lb 3oz (1kg) cherries
1 organic orange
¼ cup sugar (more to taste)
1¼ fl oz (40ml) orange liquor or
    apricot liquor (or to taste)
1 pinch ground mace

1 Wash the cherries and remove the pits. Wash the orange with hot water and dry, then slice an extremely thin, long piece of peel and juice the orange. Add the cherries, sugar, orange peel, and juice to a small pot and bring to a boil. Steam, covered, for 15 minutes over low heat, until the cherries are soft. If using, add the orange liquor. Season with the ground mace and possibly a bit more sugar.

2 Fill sterilized canning jars with the boiling hot mixture (see tip p. 14). Has a shelf life of about 2–3 months, if stored in the fridge.

Tips:

The *Kletzn* has a shelf life of at least a year if prepared like a *Powidl* (p. 194). Cherry *Röster* goes well with many desserts and pastries (like Mini Cheese-filled Pancakes, p. 178, or quark dumplings, p. 203). Apricots, Italian plums, and wild plums can also be used to make a *Röster*. The major difference from a compote is that the fruit is steamed with little liquid (you could almost say roasted). This creates a juicier result when compared to similar compotes, which are prepared with lots of water or wine.

Blueberry Compote

Serves 4 • Prep: 10 minutes + 12 hours marinating time

2lb 3oz (1kg) blueberries

½ cup packed brown sugar
 (preferably muscovado sugar,
 more to taste)

3 tablespoons freshly squeezed
 lemon juice

1 cinnamon stick

1¼ fl oz (40ml) apricot liquor (or to
 taste)

1 teaspoon vanilla sugar, or
 ½ teaspoon vanilla extract

sugar-free gelling agent, for a
 fruit:sugar ratio of 3:1

1 Mix the blueberries with sugar, lemon juice, a cinnamon stick, and apricot liquor, then lightly mash with a fork. Cover and let stand for at least 12 hours.

2 Pour the blueberry mixture into a pot and mix in the gelling agent. Bring to a boil over medium heat and boil for 2 minutes. Remove the cinnamon stick and pour into sterilized canning jars (see tip p. 14). Close immediately.

Tip:

Because the gelling agent is not prepared according to package directions, the compote remains fluid. You can also leave it out, although it does give the compote a pleasant texture.

Rhubarb Compote and Rhubarb Strawberry Sauce

The rhubarb compote tastes great with pastries, panna cotta, and creamy ice cream. Or try adding 1 teaspoon of the liquid to a glass of champagne. If you fill sterilized canning jars (see tip p. 14) with the hot compote, it will keep for up to a year.

Serves 4 • Prep: 10 minutes + 12 hours marinating time

14oz (400g) rhubarb

7oz (200g) pomegranate syrup
 (grenadine)

1lb 2oz (500g) ripe strawberries for
 the sauce

1 Slice the rhubarb into ½in (1cm) chunks. In a pot, mix with ¾ cup water and the pomegranate syrup. Boil for 6–8 minutes or until almost soft.

2 For the sauce, add the strawberries to the hot rhubarb and puree. The sauce will keep for up to 2 weeks if stored in an airtight container.

Apricot *Powidl*

This is one of the original methods to preserve fruit: no added sugar and often cooked in a cooling bread oven. The classic variety uses Italian plums mixed with a few prunes, but you should take advantage of ripe summer apricots and make a large batch. It also tastes delicious with granola and on top of fresh bread.

Makes: 4–5 jars (200ml each) • Shelf life: about one year • Prep: 15 minutes + 3 hours cooking and baking time

5lb 8oz (2.5kg) apricots

1 vanilla bean

7oz (200g) dried apricots

8½ fl oz (250ml) dessert wine or
  fruity white wine

1 Wash the apricots; cut in half and remove the pits. Slice the vanilla bean in half lengthwise and scrape out the seeds. Combine the vanilla bean and seeds with the rest of the ingredients in a pot. Boil for 30 minutes, stirring occasionally. Drain the mixture over another pot using a fine sieve; remove the vanilla bean. Boil down the juice for about 15 minutes until syrupy.

2 Preheat the oven to 300°F (150°C). Pass the apricots through a food mill, puree with an immersion blender, or push through a fine sieve. Mix the puree with the reduced juice and pour into a baking dish. Bake on the middle oven rack for 2¼ hours. Stir occasionally at first but more frequently during the last half hour. Pour into 5 sterilized canning jars (see tip p. 14) and close the jars. The apricot *Powidl* will keep for many months if stored in the fridge.

Tip:

If you want to store the apricot *Powidl* at room temperature, you should boil the jars. To do this, find a pot that fits the canning jars perfectly and line the bottom with a folded dish towel. Place the warm jars in the pot in one or more layers. Pour in hot water until the glasses are mostly covered but not swimming (it is ok if the lids are not fully covered—the steam from boiling is hot enough). Bring the water to a boil, and as soon as bubbles rise in the glasses, boil for another 15 minutes. Remove from the pot and place on a cooling rack.

Spelt Sweet Rolls

From the oven

Instead of a metal baking sheet, you can also use a ceramic baking dish (this would require a bit longer in the oven). The sweet rolls also taste good with other fillings, such as vanilla pudding or a poppy seed filling (see tip p. 177).

Makes 30 sweet rolls • Prep: 20 minutes + about 2 hours resting and baking time

1¼ cups milk

5 cups spelt flour plus extra for rolling

1 package (7g) dry yeast

3 tablespoons sugar

2 eggs

½ cup soft butter and ½ cup melted butter to grease the baking dish

1 pinch salt

10½oz (300g) apricot *Powidl* (p. 194) or Italian plum *Powidl*

confectioners' sugar for dusting

1 Heat the milk until lukewarm and pour into a bowl or a stand mixer, along with the spelt flour, dry yeast, sugar, eggs, ½ cup butter, and salt. Knead for 5 minutes, until you form a soft dough. Cover with a dish towel and let the dough rise in a warm spot until it has doubled in size (about an hour).

2 Preheat the oven to 340°F (170°C) or 300°F (150°C) (convection oven). Brush some of the melted butter onto a baking sheet. Roll out the dough on a lightly floured surface to about a finger thickness and cut into 30 squares. Add a heaping teaspoon apricot *Powidl* to the middle of each square, fold together, and press the edges together, so that the sweet roll is sealed.

3 Place the seam side down on the baking sheet, brush with butter, and let rise for 15 minutes. Bake for about 20 minutes on the second rack from the bottom, then brush on the rest of the butter. Bake for another 5 minutes. Remove from the oven and allow to cool slightly.

4 Dust with confectioners' sugar and serve lukewarm or cold. Goes well with a vanilla sauce or ice cream.

Tip:

If you have enough time, chill the dough for 12 hours then remove from the bowl and lightly knead. Put back in the bowl and let rise another hour, until it has doubled in size. This develops more aromas in the dough and the sweet rolls stay juicy even longer.

Milk-Cream Strudel

Makes 12 pieces • Prep: 1 hour 15 minutes + 50 minutes baking time

For the dough:

1²/₃ cups all-purpose flour plus
 extra for rolling

1 pinch salt

2 tablespoons oil plus extra for
 drizzling

1 room temperature egg yolk

about 4 tablespoons melted butter
 to grease the pan and for the
 parchment paper

For the filling:

1 organic lemon

4 tablespoons soft butter

1 pinch salt

¹/₃ cup sugar

2 eggs and 2 egg yolks

7oz (200g) low-fat quark or
 ricotta cheese

²/₃ cup sour cream

¼ cup all-purpose flour

3 tablespoons ground hazelnuts

For the icing:

3 tablespoons sugar

2 eggs

½ cup milk

½ cup heavy cream

confectioners' sugar for dusting

1 For the dough, mix the flour, salt, oil, egg yolk, and ¹/₃ cup lukewarm water in a bowl. Firmly knead the dough for at least 5 minutes, then form into a ball. With interlocked fingers, *schleifen* the dough: With even, circular motions, lightly knead the dough until it has a velvety and smooth surface. Brush with a bit of oil, place in a bowl, cover with plastic wrap, and allow to rest for 30 minutes.

2 In the meantime, prepare the filling: Wash a lemon with hot water, dry, and zest until you have 1 teaspoon. Beat the butter, lemon zest, salt, and 1 tablespoon sugar with an electric mixer until soft and creamy. Separate the eggs and set the egg whites aside. Beat in the egg yolks one at a time. Squeeze the excess moisture from the quark or ricotta using a dish towel, then also stir into the mixture together with the sour cream and flour. Beat the egg whites with the remaining sugar until stiff and fold into the filling.

3 Preheat the oven to 320°F (160°C) or 280°F (140°C) (convection oven). Line a baking sheet (or small roasting pan) with parchment paper greased with butter. Spread a large dish towel on a table and sprinkle with flour. Lightly roll out the dough on the towel then cut in half. Successively pull each half in all directions until thin. For this, insert your floured hands one at a time under the dough with the backs of

your hands facing up. Carefully pull toward the edge of the table. Repeat this motion in all directions until the dough is very thin (you can cut off any thick edges). Brush on some of the melted butter and sprinkle with half the ground hazelnuts. Pour half the filling along the short edge of the dough, leaving a 1¼in (3cm) wide border. Use the dish towel to help roll the strudel, then transfer to the baking sheet. Fill the second strudel using the same method and place next to the first. Bake on the middle oven rack for 45–50 minutes.

4 In the meantime, mix the sugar and eggs together. Bring the milk and cream to a boil and pour into the egg-sugar mixture, while stirring. Evenly pour the glaze over the strudels after 25 minutes in the oven and coat the strudels twice with the remaining melted butter— first after 40 minutes and again once removed from the oven. Dust with confectioners' sugar and serve hot, though it also tastes good cold.

Mini Puff Pastry Pear Strudels

Makes 6 mini strudels • Prep: 30 minutes + at least 3 hours soaking time + 30 minutes baking time

1lb 5oz (600g) pears

17fl oz (500ml) white wine

¼ cup sugar

1 star anise

1 cinnamon stick

6 sheets frozen puff pastry
 (7in x 5½in (18 x 14cm))

2 tablespoons butter

flour for rolling

¼ cup sour cream

3–4 tablespoons ground almonds

4 tablespoons raisins

1 tablespoon cinnamon sugar

confectioners' sugar for dusting

For the pear cream:

¾ cup heavy cream

1–2 tablespoons pear liquor

1 Peel the pear, cut into eighths, and remove the core. Bring to a boil in a small pot with white wine, sugar, and spices. Remove from the heat and let soak for at least 3 hours; overnight would be even better.

2 Preheat the oven to 340°F (170°C) or 300°F (150°C) (convection oven). Line a baking sheet with parchment paper. Wrap the puff pastry with plastic wrap and allow to thaw. In the meantime, remove the pears from the pot with a slotted spoon and either let drip-dry or blot with a dish towel. Reduce the liquid until syrupy and set aside. Melt the butter. Sprinkle the puff pastry sheets with flour and roll out until 1½–2 times larger, then brush with butter. Spread the sour cream and ground almonds over the puff pastry sheets. Add the pears then sprinkle with the raisins and cinnamon sugar.

3 Roll each sheet into a small strudel. Press the edges together and place the strudels seam-side down on the baking sheet. Brush with a bit of melted butter and bake on the middle oven rack for about 30 minutes until golden brown. While they bake, brush with the remaining melted butter once or twice.

4 Right before the strudels are done, prepare the pear cream. Beat the cream until stiff, then stir in 3 tablespoons pear syrup and the pear liquor. Remove the strudels from the oven and let cool slightly. Arrange on plates and sprinkle with confectioners' sugar; serve with the pear cream.

Tip:

Reduce the remaining pear syrup by half and allow to cool. Add 1 teaspoon syrup to a glass of white wine to make a refreshing drink for mild summer evenings.

Italian Plum Cheese Dumplings

Serves 4 • Prep: 30 minutes + 2 hours resting time

1lb 2oz (500g) low-fat or normal
 quark or ricotta cheese

10 tablespoons soft butter

1 cup confectioners' sugar

10½oz (300g) bread crumbs (from
 the bakery or homemade, see
 p. 140)

2 egg yolks

2 eggs

1 teaspoon organic lemon or orange
 zest

1 pinch salt

16 Italian plums or small apricots,
 pitted

16 cubes sugar

2–3 tablespoons cinnamon sugar

1 Squeeze out the excess liquid from the quark or ricotta using a dish towel. Beat the butter and confectioners' sugar with a hand mixer until creamy. Beat in 7oz (200g) bread crumbs, the egg yolks, eggs, lemon zest, and salt. Stir in the quark or ricotta, cover, and cool in the fridge for 2 hours.

2 Bring a large pot of water to a boil. Form ping-pong ball sized dumplings from the cheese mixture with moist hands; press flat between the palms of your hands. Lay an Italian plum on each dumpling then wrap the edges around it, making sure to seal thoroughly. Roll into balls and place in the boiling water. Bring back up to a boil and place the lid on halfway; cook for 10 minutes.

3 In the meantime, melt the butter in a frying pan. Cook the remaining bread crumbs until golden brown, while stirring constantly. Mix with the cinnamon sugar.

4 Remove the dumplings with a slotted spoon and let drip-dry. Arrange on plates and sprinkle with the cooked bread crumbs. Goes well with vanilla sauce.

Tip:

To make sure the dumplings do not fall apart while cooking, make a sample dumpling out of the cheese mixture. Add it to the boiling water and cook as described. If it falls apart, knead 1 egg yolk and some more bread crumbs into the mixture. The dumplings turn out especially light if the bread crumbs are coarse and uneven in size.

Poppy Seed Dumplings with Glazed Quinces

Something special

Although quince jelly or jam is very easy to make, the hard fruit has to be cut up first and then cooked. Softer varieties (such as Limon Avasi or Esme) can be found at many Turkish markets.

Serves 4–6 • Prep: 35 minutes + 2 hours inactive time

1lb 5oz (600g) Russet potatoes

2 egg yolks

¾ cup all-purpose flour

2 tablespoons cornstarch

1 egg white

sugar for the boiling water

4 tablespoons butter

¼ cup ground poppy seeds

2–3 tablespoons sugar

salt

For the quinces:

2 soft quinces (such as Esme)

1 tablespoon lemon juice

2 tablespoons butter

3 tablespoons ground hazelnuts

2 tablespoons sugar

¾ fl oz (20ml) apricot liquor

1 For the dumplings, boil the unpeeled potatoes for 20 minutes in salted water. Peel while hot and push through a fine sieve. Allow to cool completely. Stir in the egg yolks, flour, and cornstarch, one after the other. Beat the egg white until stiff and fold into the mixture. Cover and chill in the refrigerator for one hour.

2 In the meantime, wash, quarter, and core the quinces then cut into wedges. Drizzle with lemon juice. Melt the butter in a frying pan and cook for 10 minutes, covered, over low heat (see tip). Add the hazelnuts and sugar and caramelize for 2 minutes. Deglaze with the apricot liquor and set aside.

3 Bring a large pot of water with a pinch of salt and sugar to a boil. Form walnut-sized dumplings from the potato mixture using moist hands. Cook in the boiling water for 10 minutes. While they cook, melt the butter in a frying pan and cook the ground poppy seeds until aromatic, while stirring constantly. Add the sugar and remove from the stove.

4 Remove the dumplings with a slotted spoon and let drip-dry, then add to the poppy seed mixture and coat. Lightly heat the glazed quinces and serve with the dumplings.

Tip:

The quinces should be almost soft after 10 minutes cooking, depending on the variety. If not, simply add a few spoonfuls water and cook a bit longer.

Powidl Dumplings

Advanced

Serves 4–6 • Prep: 40 minutes

For the dough:

1 cup milk

2 tablespoons butter

2 cups all-purpose flour plus extra
 for rolling

2 eggs

1 egg, beaten, for brushing

salt

For the filling:

3½ oz (100g) *Powidl* (see p. 194)

1–2 tablespoons rum

1–2 teaspoons sugar

1 pinch salt

For the bread crumb butter:

10 tablespoons butter

1¾ oz (50g) bread crumbs (from
 the bakery or homemade, see tip
 p. 140)

cinnamon sugar for dusting (if
 desired)

1 For the dough, bring the milk, a pinch of salt, and ½ cup water to a boil. Remove from the stove and stir in the flour. Put back on the stove and stir until the ingredients have combined thoroughly and there is a white layer on the bottom of the pot. Remove from the heat and let cool for 5 minutes. Beat in the eggs one at a time with an electric mixer.

2 Bring a large pot of salted water to a boil. Transfer the dough to a work surface and sprinkle with a little flour. Roll out until ⅛ in (3mm) thick. Cut out palm-sized circles. Alternatively, lightly flour small portions of dough and press into circles.

3 For the filling, season the *Powidl* with rum, sugar, and cinnamon. Add 1 teaspoon filling to the middle of each circle and brush the edges with beaten egg. Fold the dough circles into half moons and press the edges together. Add to the lightly boiling salted water and cook for 5 minutes until they rise to the surface.

4 In the meantime, melt the butter in a frying pan and cook the bread crumbs until golden brown while stirring constantly. Remove from the stove and set aside.

5 Carefully remove the dumplings with a slotted spoon and briefly rinse in cold water then let drip-dry. Serve with the cooked bread crumbs and dust with cinnamon sugar, if desired.

Tip:

You can also prepare these dumplings with a potato dough. For that, boil 1lb 5oz (600g) unpeeled potatoes for 20 minutes in salted water, peel, and press through a potato ricer. Let cool to room temperature, then knead with 1 egg and 1¼ cups semolina or all-purpose flour, along with a pinch of salt and nutmeg. Then continue as described in the recipe.

Mini Linzer Tortes with Quince Jelly

Strictly speaking, Linz is not in the Alps. On the other hand, Linzer tortes are a good example of a cuisine that magically uses up leftovers to create something delicious. Professional bakers especially love this cake because it is made with the crumbs that fall when they cut cakes. Ask your baker for some cake crumbs.

Makes 8 tortes • Prep: 30 minutes + 35 minutes baking time

¾ cup soft butter plus extra for the baking dishes

¾ cup confectioners' sugar

1 teaspoon ground cinnamon

1 pinch ground cloves

1 packet (about 2 teaspoons) vanilla sugar, or 1 teaspoon vanilla extract if unavailable

1 teaspoon organic lemon zest

1 pinch salt

2 eggs

4½oz (125g) ground almonds plus sliced almonds for the baking dishes

6oz (175g) dried cake crumbs or crushed ladyfingers

⅔ cup all-purpose flour

2 ripe pears

4½oz (125g) quince jelly

confectioners' sugar for dusting

1 Preheat the oven to 320°F (160°C) or 280°F (140°C) (convection oven). Cream together the butter and confectioners' sugar. Mix in the spices together with 1 egg, then stir in the other egg. Combine the ground almonds, cake crumbs (or crushed ladyfingers), and flour, then fold into the butter mixture.

2 Grease 8 tartlet pans (4in (10cm) in diameter, or 1 muffin tin) with butter and line with sliced almonds. Transfer the batter to a pastry bag and use about two-thirds of it to fill the tart pans in a spiral pattern. Spread the batter to the edges with a spoon.

3 Peel, quarter, core, and dice the pear. Mix with the quince jelly and scoop a teaspoon onto each tart, leaving a border.

4 Pipe borders or crosses onto the tarts with the remaining batter. Place on the second rack from bottom and bake about 35 minutes or until golden brown. Let cool in the pans, dust with confectioners' sugar, and serve.

Blueberry Pancakes with Sour Cream

There are as many Schwarzbeeren (blueberry pancakes) recipes as there are locations to find the berries. Some recipes call for more berries and little batter; some are made without egg. These small, thick ones are especially delicate: fluffy and juicy, but not too moist.

Serves 4 • Prep: 15 minutes

3 eggs

½ cup sour cream

¾ cup all-purpose flour plus extra for dusting

1 teaspoon organic lemon zest

1 pinch salt

3 tablespoons sugar

9oz (250g) blueberries

butter for the pan

confectioners' sugar for dusting

1 Separate the eggs. Mix the egg yolks, sour cream, flour, lemon zest, and salt. Beat the egg whites and sugar until stiff. Carefully fold the egg whites into the batter.

2 Wash the blueberries and dry them well. Sprinkle with 1 teaspoon flour and carefully fold them into the batter. Melt the butter in a frying pan and scoop 1 tablespoon of batter at a time into the pan to form 12 small pancakes. Fry on both sides until golden.

3 Dust with confectioners' sugar and serve.

Fried Dough with Strawberries and Cream

Deep fried pastries, such as Krapfenblätter, Tirteln, or Schmalznudeln, are especially popular in the winter. There are many sweet and savory varieties; some are filled with dried fruit, poppy seeds, or cabbage—whatever is available in the cold time of year. Here, the contrast between the crumbly Krapfenblättern and the fresh tangy strawberries is terrific.

Serves 6 • Prep: 50 minutes + 1 hour inactive time

1¼ cups flour

1¼ cups rye flour

3 tablespoons butter

2 eggs

1 pinch salt

1lb 2oz (500g) strawberries

1¼ cups heavy cream

2¼ cups clarified butter or sunflower oil

confectioners' sugar for dusting

7oz (200g) rhubarb-strawberry sauce (p. 193) or pureed strawberries with a bit of confectioners' sugar

1 Mix the flours in a bowl; melt butter and add. Knead together with eggs and salt for about 30 minutes; cover and let rest for 1 hour. In the meantime, wash the strawberries, cut into thick slices, and set aside. Whip the cream until stiff; keep cool in the refrigerator.

2 Roll the dough out on a lightly floured surface to ⅛in (2–3mm) thick and cut out 18 circles (3¼in (8cm) diameter). Heat clarified butter in a flat pan until it bubbles immediately when you insert the handle of a wooden spoon. Fry the dough in batches until golden, remove with a slotted spoon, and place on paper towels to drain. Immediately dust the fried dough with confectioners' sugar so it can lightly caramelize.

3 Layer 3 fried dough circles with cream and strawberries on each plate and drizzle with rhubarb strawberry sauce. Dust again with confectioners' sugar and serve immediately.

Cheese Doughnuts with Rhubarb Raspberry Compote

**Serves 6–8 (about 24 doughnuts) • Prep: 35 minutes
+ 75 minutes resting and cooking time**

For the doughnuts:

2 cups all-purpose flour

1 tablespoon sugar

1 pinch salt

½ cup milk

Fresh yeast (about ¾oz (20g))

9oz (250g) quark or ricotta cheese

3 tablespoons soft butter

2 eggs

1 quart oil for frying

cinnamon sugar for rolling

For the compote:

2lb 3oz (1kg) rhubarb

13½fl oz (400ml) elderberry syrup

3½oz (100g) raspberries

1 For the doughnuts, add the flour, sugar, and salt in a bowl and make a well in the middle. Add the milk and yeast to the well and stir. Cover and set in a warm place to rise for 15 minutes. Knead in the quark or ricotta, butter, and eggs until a soft dough forms. Cover and set in a warm place to rise for 1 hour.

2 In the meantime, preheat the oven to 390°F (200°C) or 360°F (180°C) (convection oven). For the compote, slice the rhubarb into 1½in (4cm) long pieces. Bring the elderberry syrup to a boil. Transfer the rhubarb and raspberries to a baking dish and pour in the elderberry syrup; cover with a sheet of parchment paper (fold under the edges of the dish) and bake for about 35 minutes on the middle oven rack.

3 Heat the oil in a deep frying pan (or large pot). Stir the doughnut dough and scoop out pieces of dough with a teaspoon and let them slide into the hot oil. Fry for about 1–2 minutes on each side until golden brown. Remove from the oil with a slotted spoon and place on paper towels to absorb any excess fat. Immediately roll in cinnamon sugar and serve with the warm or cold rhubarb raspberry compote.

Tip:

Like jam, you can fill sterilized canning jars (see tip p. 14) with the hot rhubarb compote directly after cooking and store for about a year.

Index

A

Alpine chutney and quinces, 104
Alpine hot dog: *Bosna* with onion
　　mustard, 10
Alpine pickles, 13
apricots
　　apricot jam, 178
　　apricot *Powidl,* 194
　　croissant *Koch* or *Schmarren,* 183
　　pancakes with apricot jam, 178
　　Powidl dumplings, 207
　　Powidl dumplings with potato
　　　　dough, 207
　　spelt sweet rolls, 197
Arctic char with sautéed Swiss
　　chard, 124
asparagus
　　Glarus macaroni, 87
　　Valais asparagus tart, 62
　　zander stacks with asparagus, 130

B

bacon. *See* speck (bacon)
baked black salsify, 77
baked cheese soup, 43
baked cheesy noodles, 109
baked whitefish, 133
baking. *See* desserts and pastries
balsamic vinegar, 77
barley
　　barley soup with dandelion, 55
　　vegetarian risotto, 55
beans
　　dill green bean with béchamel
　　　　sauce, 74

green bean salad with egg,
　　potatoes, sour cream, and dill,
　　23
lamb steaks with mountain herb
　　butter and mashed beans, 167
béchamel sauce, 74
beef
　　beef salad, 37
　　braised beef cheeks, 163
　　cabbage flatbread with
　　　　Bündnerfleisch and endive
　　　　salad, 17
　　Carinthian Church Day Soup, 47
　　goulash with elderberries, 153
　　steamed perch with
　　　　Bündnerfleisch, 137
　　Swiss sauerbraten, 146
　　tri tip with tarragon-lemon
　　　　mustard, 145
beef broth
　　homemade beef broth, 37
　　spinach dumplings in beef broth,
　　　　67
beets
　　beet carpaccio with watercress
　　　　sour cream, 24
　　fermented red beets, 71
　　red beet salad with egg, potatoes,
　　　　sour cream, and dill, 23
　　red beets with horseradish
　　　　cream, 91
　　Zillertal dumplings with sautéed
　　　　beet salad, 71
black salsify, baked, 77
blood sausage, bread soup with fried
　　onions and, 48
blueberries
　　blueberry compote, 193
　　blueberry pancakes with sour
　　　　cream, 210
　　yogurt *Koch* with blueberries, 187
Bosna spice, 10
bread
　　cabbage flatbread with

Bündnerfleisch and endive
　　salad, 17
piadina flatbread, 159
potato cheese with bacon and rye
　　bread, 20
Swiss bacon flatbread, 17
vegetarian flatbread, 17
Vinschgerl (South Tyrolean
　　flatbread), 120
bread crumbs, homemade, 140
bread dumplings, 67
bread soup with fried onions and
　　blood sausage, 48
broths. *See* soups; stocks and
　　broths
buckwheat ravioli with burrata–wild
　　garlic filling, 81
Bündnerfleisch
　　cabbage flatbread with
　　　　Bündnerfleisch and endive
　　　　salad, 17
　　steamed perch with
　　　　Bündnerfleisch, 137
burrata cheese, 81
butcher's soup, 52
butter
　　mountain herb butter, 167
　　spiced compound butter, 84

C

cabbage
　　baked Swiss dumplings, 33
　　cabbage flan with fondue, 114
　　cabbage flatbread with
　　　　Bündnerfleisch and endive
　　　　salad, 17
　　cabbage noodles, 72
　　cabbage salad with smoked
　　　　salmon, 29

puffed potatoes with sauerkraut, 68

sauerkraut soup with smoked sausage, 57

smoked meat with pointed cabbage, 160

stuffed cabbage rolls, 110

cakes. *See* desserts and pastries

caramelized cherries, 180

caramelized *Kaiserschmarren,* 180

Carinthian cheese noodles with fried potato filling, 82

Carinthian Church Day Soup, 47

carp, fried fillet with lemon remoulade, 123

casseroles

baked cheesy noodles, 109

cheese noodles with onions, 109

potato casserole, 30

spinach casserole, 113

cauliflower

Alpine pickles, 13

cauliflower with béchamel sauce, 74

cheese dishes

baked cheese soup, 43

baked cheesy noodles, 109

baked Swiss dumplings, 33

buckwheat ravioli with burrata–wild garlic filling, 81

cabbage flan with fondue, 114

Carinthian cheese noodles with fried potato filling, 82

cheese noodles with onions, 109

cheese potato pancakes, 94

Gommer potato pie, 97

Gruyère cheese tarts, 98

mini cheese dumplings, 51

Raclette with honey and nuts, 103

ricotta gnocchi, 65

Swiss cheese fondue, 100

Swiss mac 'n' cheese (*Älplermagronen*), 87

cherries

caramelized cherries, 180

cherry *Röster,* 190

chestnuts

cabbage flan with fondue, 114

clear pumpkin soup with

chestnuts, 40

venison chestnut sausages, 156

chicken

chicken cordon bleu with wild garlic, 143

herb fried chicken, 140

chile peppers, pickled, 13

Choleri/Chollera, 97

chutneys and jams

Alpine chutney and quinces, 104

apricot jam, 178

elderberries, 153

lingonberry sauce, 143

pear ketchup, 107

vinegar fruit, 104

compotes

blueberry compote, 193

rhubarb compote, 193

rhubarb raspberry compote, 215

storing, tips on, 215

condiments. *See* chutneys and jams; pantry items; sauces and creams

creams. *See* sauces and creams

croissant *Koch,* 183

croissant *Schmarren,* 183

cucumber salad, smoked trout meatballs with, 128

D

dandelion, barley soup with, 55

desserts and pastries

apricot jam for, 178

apricot *Powidl,* 194

blueberry compote, 193

blueberry pancakes with sour cream, 210

croissant *Koch,* 183

croissant *Schmarren,* 183

Engadin nut tartlets, 174

fried dough with strawberries and cream, 212

Italian plum quark dumplings, 203

Kaiserschmarren, caramelized, 180

milk-cream strudel, 198

mini cheese-filled pancakes with raspberries, 178

mini Linzer tortes with quince jelly, 209

mini puff pastry pear strudels, 200

pancakes with apricot jam, 178

poppy seed dumplings with glazed quinces, 204

port wine *Kletzn,* 190

potato dough for, 207

Powidl dumplings, 207

quark doughnuts with rhubarb raspberry compote, 215

rhubarb compote and rhubarb strawberry sauce, 193

rhubarb raspberry compote, 215

Röster, 190

Salzburger sweet dumplings, 184

shortcrust pastry for, 98

spelt Reindling, 177

spelt sweet rolls, 197

walnut *Koch,* 189

yogurt *Koch* with blueberries, 187

dill

dill green bean with béchamel sauce, 74

green bean salad with egg, potatoes, sour cream, and dill, 23

red beet salad with egg, potatoes, sour cream, and dill, 23

dumplings, savory

baked Swiss dumplings, 33

bread dumplings, 67

cheese dumplings, mini, 51

for soup add-ins, 51

horseradish dumplings, 51

mushroom dumplings, mini, 51

polenta dumplings with gravy, 117

speck (bacon) dumplings, 67

spinach dumplings in beef broth, 67

Zillertal dumplings with sautéed beet salad, 71

dumplings, sweet

Italian plum quark dumplings, 203

poppy seed dumplings with
    glazed quinces, 204
potato dough for, 207
Powidl dumplings, 207
Salzburger sweet dumplings, 184

E

elderberries, 153
endive
    cabbage flatbread with
        Bündnerfleisch and endive
        salad, 17
    endive with caramelized onions, 27
    endive winter salad, 30
Engadin nut tartlets, 174

F

fish
    Arctic char with sautéed Swiss
        chard, 124
    baked whitefish, 133
    cabbage salad with smoked
        salmon, 29
    carving roundfish, tips on, 133
    fried carp fillet with lemon
        remoulade, 123
    skewered fish in *Vinschgerl*, 120
    trout *Gröstl* with potato chips and
        crispy sage, 134
    zander stacks with asparagus, 130
    zander pumpkin patties, 127
fish patties (*Fischpflanzerl*), 127
fish stock, 130
fondue
    cabbage flan with fondue, 114
    Swiss cheese fondue, 100
fried dough with strawberries and
    cream, 212

G

garlic
    buckwheat ravioli with burrata–
        wild garlic filling, 81
    chicken cordon bleu with wild
        garlic, 143
    slow braised mountain lamb
        shoulder, 164
Glarus macaroni, 87
gnocchi, ricotta, 65
Gommer potato pie, 97
goulash
    goulash with elderberries, 153
    potato goulash, 84
gravy, 117
green beans. *See* beans
gremolata pork roast, 149
grilled dishes
    Alpine hot dog: *Bosna* with onion
        mustard, 10
    lamb steaks with mountain herb
        butter and mashed beans, 167
    skewered fish in *Vinschgerl,* 120
Gröstl, 134
Gruyère cheese tarts, 98

H

ham, homemade noodles with, 72
herbed dishes
    barley soup with dandelion, 55
    herb fried chicken, 140
    herb soup, 47
    lamb steaks with mountain herb
        butter and mashed beans, 167
    potato leek soup with oregano
        cream, 58
    spiced compound butter, 84
    tri tip with tarragon-lemon
        mustard, 145
horseradish

horseradish dumplings, 51
red beets with horseradish
    cream, 91

I

Italian plum quark dumplings, 203

J

jams. *See* chutneys and jams
jars, sterilizing, 14

K

K.u.k. schnitzel with mashed
    potatoes, 171
Kaiserschmarren, caramelized, 180
ketchup, pear, 107
Kletzn, 190
Koch desserts, 183, 187, 189
krendeln, 82

L

lamb
    lamb steaks with mountain herb
        butter and mashed beans, 167
    slow braised mountain lamb
        shoulder, 164
leeks
    potato leek soup with oregano
        cream, 58

leftovers, using, 37, 48
lemon remoulade, fried carp with, 123
lentil salad, 156
lingonberry sauce, 143
Linzer tortes with quince jelly, 209
liverwurst filling, potato ravioli with, 78

M

meats
   braised beef cheeks, 163
   chicken cordon bleu with wild garlic, 143
   gremolata pork roast, 149
   herb fried chicken, 140
   K.u.k. schnitzel with mashed potatoes, 171
   lamb steaks with mountain herb butter and mashed beans, 167
   pulled venison in a piadina, 159
   slow braised mountain lamb shoulder, 164
   smoked meat with pointed cabbage, 160
   Swiss Sauerbraten, 146
   tri tip with tarragon-lemon mustard, 145
   veal roast with polenta and juniper berry crumbs, 150
   veal rolled roast with a dried pear filling, 168
   venison chestnut sausages, 156
   venison packets, 154
   See also sausages
milk-cream strudel, 198
mushrooms
   clear wild mushroom soup, 40
   creamed mushrooms, 94
   mini mushroom dumplings, 51
   potato salad with wild mushrooms, 34
Musquee De Provence pumpkin with South Tyrolean speck, mâche lettuce, and roasted pumpkin

seeds, 18
mustards
   Alpine hot dog: *Bosna* with onion mustard, 10
   tri tip with tarragon-lemon mustard, 145

N

nockerl (sweet dumplings), 184
noodles. *See* pastas and noodles
nuts
   cabbage flan with fondue, 114
   Engadin nut tartlets, 174
   Raclette with honey and nuts, 103
   spelt reindling, 177
   Swiss pine nuts, 24
   walnut *Koch,* 189
   See also chestnuts

O

onions
   Alpine hot dog: *Bosna* with onion mustard, 10
   bread soup with fried onions and blood sausage, 48
   cheese noodles with onions, 109
   endive with caramelized onions, 27
   sour onions, 14
oregano cream, potato leek soup with, 58

P

pancakes
   blueberry pancakes with sour

cream, 210
   cheese potato pancakes, 94
   mini cheese-filled pancakes with raspberries, 178
   pancakes with apricot jam, 178
pantry items
   Alpine chutney and quinces, 104
   Alpine pickles, 13
   apricot jam, 178
   balsamic vinegar, 77
   pear ketchup, 107
   pickled chile peppers, 13
   sour onions, 14
   vinegar fruit, 104
parchment paper, 154
parsnip puree, 88
pastas and noodles
   baked cheesy noodles, 109
   buckwheat ravioli with burrata–wild garlic filling, 81
   cabbage noodles, 72
   Carinthian cheese noodles with fried potato filling, 82
   cheese noodles with onions, 109
   Glarus macaroni, 87
   homemade noodles with ham, 72
   pear stuffed ravioli, 78
   potato ravioli with liverwurst filling, 78
   ricotta gnocchi, 65
   Swiss mac 'n' cheese (*Älplermagronen*), 87
pastries. *See* desserts and pastries
pastry dough, shortcrust, 98
pears
   Gommer potato pie, 97
   mini puff pastry pear strudels, 200
   pear ketchup, 107
   pear stuffed ravioli, 78
   port wine *Kletzn,* 190
   veal rolled roast with a dried pear filling, 168
peas
   split pea soup with Swiss chard, 44
perch, steamed with *Bündnerfleisch,* 137
piadina flatbread, 159
pickles and pickled dishes

Alpine pickles, 13
pickled chile peppers, 13
sauerkraut, 57, 68
sour onions, 14
sterilizing jars for, 14
pickling brine, 13
pies. *See* desserts and pastries;
  tarts and pies
plums
  Italian plum cheese dumplings, 203
  Powidl dumplings, 207
  spelt sweet rolls, 197
polenta
  polenta dumplings with gravy, 117
  veal roast with polenta and juniper
    berry crumbs, 150
poppy seed dumplings with glazed
  quinces, 204
pork
  butcher's soup, 52
  gremolata pork roast, 149
  homemade noodles with ham, 72
  potato ravioli with liverwurst
    filling, 78
  smoked meat with pointed
    cabbage, 160
port wine *Kletzn,* 190
potato chips, 134
potato dough, 207
potatoes
  Carinthian cheese noodles with
    fried potato filling, 82
  cheese potato pancakes, 94
  Gommer potato pie, 97
  green bean salad with egg,
    potatoes, sour cream, and dill,
    23
  mashed potatoes, K.u.k. schnitzel
    with, 171
  parsnip puree, 88
  potato casserole, 30
  potato cheese with bacon and rye
    bread, 20
  potato goulash, 84
  potato leek soup with oregano
    cream, 58
  potato ravioli with liverwurst
    filling, 78
  potato salad with wild

mushrooms, 34
puffed potatoes with sauerkraut,
  68
red beet salad with egg, potatoes,
  sour cream, and dill, 23
ricotta gnocchi, 65
Swiss mac 'n' cheese
  (Älplermagronen), 87
trout *Gröstl* with potato chips and
  crispy sage, 134
Powidl
  apricot *Powidl,* 194
  Powidl dumplings, 207
  Powidl dumplings with potato
    dough, 207
puffed potatoes with sauerkraut, 68
pumpkin seeds, 18, 37
pumpkins
  Alpine pickles, 13
  buckwheat ravioli with burrata–
    wild garlic filling, 81
  clear pumpkin soup with
    chestnuts, 40
  Musquee De Provence pumpkin
    with South Tyrolean speck,
    mâche lettuce, and roasted
    pumpkin seeds, 18
  pumpkin cheese, 20
  zander pumpkin patties, 127

quark
  cheese doughnuts with rhubarb
    raspberry compote, 215
  Italian plum cheese dumplings, 203
  milk-cream strudel, 198
  mini cheese-filled pancakes with
    raspberries, 178
  quark cheese, 20
quinces
  Alpine chutney and quinces, 104
  mini Linzer tortes with quince
    jelly, 209
  poppy seed dumplings with

glazed quinces, 204
quinoa, 163

Raclette with honey and nuts, 103
raspberries
  cheese doughnuts with rhubarb
    raspberry compote, 215
  mini cheese-filled pancakes with
    raspberries, 178
  raspberry sauce, 184
ravioli
  buckwheat ravioli with burrata–
    wild garlic filling, 81
  pear stuffed ravioli, 78
  potato ravioli with liverwurst
    filling, 78
reindlings, 177
rhubarb
  quark donuts with rhubarb
    raspberry compote, 215
  rhubarb compote and rhubarb
    strawberry sauce, 193
ricotta gnocchi, 65
risotto, vegetarian, 55
roasts
  gremolata pork roast, 149
  slow braised mountain lamb
    shoulder, 164
  Swiss Sauerbraten, 146
  veal roast with polenta and juniper
    berry crumbs, 150
  veal rolled roast with a dried pear
    filling, 168
Röster, 190

salad dressings
  balsamic vinegar, 77

fruity vinaigrette, 113
salads
    beef salad, 37
    beet carpaccio with watercress
        sour cream, 24
    cabbage flatbread with
        Bündnerfleisch and endive
        salad, 17
    cabbage salad with smoked
        salmon, 29
    endive with caramelized onions, 27
    endive winter salad, 30
    green bean salad with egg,
        potatoes, sour cream, and dill, 23
    lentil salad, 156
    potato salad with wild
        mushrooms, 34
    red beet salad with egg, potatoes,
        sour cream, and dill, 23
    smoked trout meatballs with
        cucumber salad, 128
    Zillertal dumplings with sautéed
        beet salad, 71
salmon, smoked with cabbage
    salad, 29
Salzburger sweet dumplings, 184
sandwich spreads
    potato cheese with bacon and rye
        bread, 20
    pumpkin cheese, 20
    quark cheese, 20
sauces and creams
    béchamel sauce, 74
    creamed mushrooms, 94
    elderberries, 153
    gravy, 117
    horseradish cream, red beets
        with, 91
    lemon remoulade, fried carp fillet
        with, 123
    lingonberry sauce, 143
    oregano cream, potato leek soup
        with, 58
    raspberry sauce, 184
    rhubarb strawberry sauce, 193
    tarragon-lemon mustard, tri tip
        with, 145
    watercress sour cream, beet
        carpaccio with, 24

sauerkraut
    puffed potatoes with sauerkraut,
        68
    sauerkraut soup with smoked
        sausage, 57
sausages
    Alpine hot dog: *Bosna* with onion
        mustard, 10
    bread soup with fried onions and
        blood sausage, 48
    choosing types of, tips on, 10
    potato leek soup with oregano
        cream, 58
    sauerkraut soup with smoked
        sausage, 57
    venison chestnut sausages, 156
Savoy cabbage flan with fondue,
    114
Sbrinz cheese, 87, 117
schnitzel with mashed potatoes,
    K.u.k., 171
skewered fish in *Vinschgerl,* 120
smoked trout meatballs with
    cucumber salad, 128
soups
    baked cheese soup, 43
    barley soup with dandelion, 55
    bread soup with fried onions and
        blood sausage, 48
    butcher's soup, 52
    Carinthian Church Day Soup, 47
    clear pumpkin soup with
        chestnuts, 40
    clear wild mushroom soup, 40
    dumplings for, 51
    herb soup, 47
    potato leek soup with oregano
        cream, 58
    sauerkraut soup with smoked
        sausage, 57
    split pea soup with Swiss chard, 44
sour onions, 14
spätzle. See pastas and noodles
speck (bacon)
    baked cheese soup, 43
    barley soup with dandelion, 55
    Musquee De Provence Pumpkin
        with South Tyrolean speck,
        mâche lettuce, and roasted

pumpkin seeds, 18
    potato cheese with bacon and rye
        bread, 20
    speck dumplings, 67
    Swiss bacon flatbread, 17
    turnip puree, 88
spelt reindling, 177
spelt sweet rolls, 197
spiced compound butter, 84
spinach
    spinach casserole, 113
    spinach dumplings in beef broth,
        67
steamed perch with *Bündnerfleisch,*
    137
stews. *See* goulash; soups
stocks and broths
    beef broth, 37, 67
    fish stock, 130
strawberries
    fried dough with strawberries and
        cream, 212
    rhubarb strawberry sauce, 193
strudels
    milk-cream strudel, 198
    mini puff pastry pear strudels, 200
stuffed cabbage rolls, 110
Swiss bacon flatbread, 17
Swiss chard
    Arctic char with sautéed Swiss
        chard, 124
    split pea soup with Swiss chard, 44
Swiss cheese fondue, 100
Swiss dumplings, baked, 33
Swiss mac 'n' cheese
    (Älplermagronen), 87
Swiss pine nuts *(Zirbelnüsse),* 24
Swiss sauerbraten, 146

T

tarts and pies
    cabbage flan with fondue, 114
    Engadin nut tartlets, 174
    Gommer potato pie, 97

Gruyère cheese tarts, 98
Valais asparagus tart, 62
trout
   smoked trout meatballs with
      cucumber salad, 128
   trout *Gröstl* with potato chips and
      crispy sage, 134
turnip puree, 88

V

Valais asparagus tart, 62
veal
   K.u.k. schnitzel with mashed
      potatoes, 171
   veal roast with polenta and juniper
      berry crumbs, 150
   veal rolled roast with a dried pear
      filling, 168
vegan potato salad with wild
   mushrooms, 34
vegetarian dishes, 109
   Alpine chutney and quinces, 104
   Alpine pickles, 13
   baked black salsify, 77
   barley soup with dandelion, 55
   beet carpaccio with watercress
      sour cream, 24
   buckwheat ravioli with burrata–
      wild garlic filling, 81
   cabbage flan with fondue, 114
   cabbage flatbread with endive
      salad, 17
   cauliflower with béchamel sauce,
      74
   cheese dumplings, mini, 51
   cheese potato pancakes, 94
   clear pumpkin soup with
      chestnuts, 40

dill green bean with béchamel
   sauce, 74
Glarus macaroni, 87
Gommer potato pie, 97
green bean salad with egg,
   potatoes, sour cream, and dill, 23
Gruyère cheese tarts, 98
herb soup, 47
horseradish dumplings, 51
lentil salad, 156
mushroom dumplings, mini, 51
parsnip puree, 88
pear ketchup, 107
pear stuffed ravioli, 78
polenta dumplings with gravy, 117
potato leek soup with oregano
   cream, 58
potato salad with wild
   mushrooms, 34
puffed potatoes with sauerkraut,
   68
Raclette with honey and nuts, 103
red beet salad with egg, potatoes,
   sour cream, and dill, 23
red beets with horseradish cream,
   91
ricotta gnocchi, 65
risotto, 55
sour onions, 14
spinach casserole, 113
split pea soup with Swiss chard, 44
stuffed cabbage rolls, 110
Swiss cheese fondue, 100
Valais asparagus tart, 62
See also desserts and pastries
venison
   pulled venison in a piadina, 159
   venison chestnut sausages, 156
   venison packets, 154
vinegar fruit, 104
vinegar, balsamic, 77
Vinschgerl (South Tyrolean
   flatbread), 120

W

walnuts
   Engadin nut tartlets, 174
   spelt reindling, 177
   walnut *Koch,* 189
whitefish, baked, 133

Y

yogurt *Koch* with blueberries, 187

Z

zander stacks with asparagus, 130
zander pumpkin patties, 127
Zillertal dumplings with sautéed
   beet salad, 71

Acknowledgments

For *Alpine Cookbook*, I looked for the sources of our culinary culture, for recipes that our grandmothers cooked and that have sometimes been preserved in some of the more remote mountain regions. First and foremost, I want to thank my wife, the author Susanna Bingemer, with whom I have researched and written many articles and a large cook and travel book about the Alps. For Alpine Cookbook, we captured the perfect versions of the classics together, adding our fresh takes and lightness to the recipes—always with lots of flavor.

Additionally I would like to thank my stylist, Barbara Dodt, who finds the perfect props for every dish—and if not, builds or restores them herself. From casual textile printing to fine carpentry, no techniques are foreign to her. The photo production was especially fun, and for that, I would like to thank chefs and food stylists Marcel Sumpf and Sven Christ, who cooked wonderfully. My thanks also goes to Silvio Knezevic, my partner during photo production: We not only both photographed and assisted each other, as chefs we also gladly spent time together in the kitchen.

Monika Schlitzer, editorial director of DK Verlag, had the brilliant idea for this book. Dr. Gabriele Kalmback and Sarah Fischer lovingly looked after it at the publishing house. My editors Lara Tunnat and Katharina Lisson have worked with me extensively on the recipe wording over the past months—now everything is right, everything fits together well.

About the Author

Hans Gerlach worked for many years as a trained cook and chef in award-winning European restaurants; then he got a degree in architecture. For a while, he worked as a food stylist in Munich and today is an author, food photographer, and "kitchen coach." He is well known to a wide audience from his column in the *Süddeutsche Zeitung* magazine.

Recipes Hans Gerlach, Susanna Bingemer
Photography Hans Gerlach, Silvio Knezevic, p. 6 top left PRCreativeTeam, Fotolia.com;
top right jm, Fotolia.com; bottom Thomas Neumahr, Fotolia.com
Food styling Marcel Sumpf, Sven Christ
Props Barbara Dodt
Design, typography, and illustration Silke Klemt

DK US
Translation Allyson Upton
Editors Allison Singer, Rebecca Warren
Senior designer Jessica Lee
Editorial director Nancy Ellwood

DK Germany
Publishing director Monika Schlitzer
Project editors Gabriele Kalmbach, Sarah Fischer
Production director Dorothee Whittaker
Producer Christine Rühmer
Production coordinator Madlen Richter

First American Edition, 2015
Published in the United States by DK Publishing
345 Hudson Street, New York, New York 10014

A catalog record for this book is available from the Library of Congress.
ISBN 978-1-4654-3795-2

DK books are available at special discounts when purchased in bulk for sales promotions, premiums,
fund-raising, or educational use. For details, contact: DK Publishing Special Markets, 345 Hudson Street,
New York, New York 10014 SpecialSales@dk.com.

Printed and bound in China
All images © Dorling Kindersley Limited
For further information see: www.dkimages.com

A WORLD OF IDEAS:
SEE ALL THERE IS TO KNOW

www.dk.com

TUPOLEV
THE MAN AND HIS AIRCRAFT

PAUL DUFFY

ANDREI KANDALOV

SAE
INTERNATIONAL®

To SLK and Lidia

Copyright © 1996 Paul Duffy and Andrei Kandalov

First Published in the UK in 1996 by Airlife Publishing Ltd

This edition published 1996 by SAE International

Library of Congress Cataloguing in Publication Number
  96-70235

ISBN 1 56091-899-3
SAE Order No. R-173

Printed in Hong Kong

Society of Automotive Engineers, Inc.

400 Commonwealth Drive, Warrendale, PA 15096-0001, USA

Dear Readers,

I am pleased to introduce a book about the history of our Tupolev Joint Stock Company in the name of academician A. N. Tupolev, well-known in the countries of former Soviet Union and its allies. Its history is not so well-known in the West. This book is one of the first publications in the West about our Design Bureau and aviation industry, especially all-metal aircraft, one of the most influential founders of which was Andrei Nikolaevich Tupolev.

This, I hope, will help make our work better known and understood by more people. Our country and our industry are going through a very difficult period of time. We need to develop our contacts with the aviation industry and airlines in other countries and we hope that this book will help us to do so.

General Director
of the Tupolev Joint Stock Co.

Valentin T. Klimov
Moscow, 1996

Preface and Acknowledgements

The aviation industry in the Soviet Union was organised very differently to that of the West. With the government essentially the producer and consumer, different ministries controlled almost every aspect of the industry. The Ministry of Aviation Industry was responsible for everything to do with the design and production of aircraft, aero engines and components, and the Ministry of Defence plus the Ministry of Civil Aviation were responsible for the operation of these aircraft, and for aerodromes and maintenance facilities. Thus, while the ministries maintained contact as necessary between each other, at lower levels this was not usual, sometimes even within the same ministries.

The Aviation Industry was divided into several specialist categories. Highest amongst these were the design bureaux, from where the ideas were developed into reality. Each bureau had its own specialist workshop where it produced one, or sometimes two, prototypes. The prototypes were test-flown by the bureau and by a specialist government research and test facility. If all went well, then the bureau would pass over production drawings to a production factory and send a team to the factory to ensure that any problems were solved; while it kept an eye on the programme, there were no commercial links with the factory or the operator.

So preparing a book about Tupolev was very different to writing about a Western producer, where the design and production facilities maintain close contact. I was fortunate to be working with Andrei Kandalov. Andrei has worked with Tupolev the man and the bureau for fifty-four years. His approach to much of the work matched mine, although there were times when he told me that he couldn't understand why I wanted particular data; nevertheless, he went searching for it. And, even though he was first deputy to the general designer until 1991, much of the data was difficult and occasionally impossible even for him to obtain.

With the consent of Tupolev, we asked permission to visit many of the production factories and repair factories. Few replied, and all except one said no. Fortunately, in my six years working in Russia and the Soviet Union I had made many of my own contacts, and thus was able to visit Ulyanovsk, where the

Tu-204 is in production. My thanks to my friends at Aviastar for that, particularly Viktor Mikhailov, director general, and Nikolai Katchalov, commercial director, for their courtesy. And Kharkov, where the Tu-124 and 134, along with some missiles, were built. Anatoli Myalitsa, the deputy director for foreign economic matters, assisted me there. Repair factory N407 in Minsk, now called the Minsk Aircraft Repair Works, was also very helpful; I would like to thank general director Arkadi Yamov and chief technologist Anatoli Igumnov for their friendliness and helpfulness. They gave me an excellent insight into the Soviet system and the reasons behind the system.

The former Aeroflot division which is now Vnukovo Airlines was one of the operators which helped me understand Soviet aircraft and operations. I would like to thank Yuri Kashitsin, the general director, Mikhail Bulanov, and his unrelated colleague, Nikolai Bulanov, both deputy directors general. I must also make mention of Igor Pikalov, their ever helpful chief of protocol, and pilots, navigators and flight engineers – Mikhail Lila, Anatoli Dymnov, Mikhail Pkhedo, Yurgi Parfentiev and Viktor Borzenin; and Yuri Sitnik, who flew the Vnukovo 204 exactly as I had requested for the cover of this book, and for company promotion.

The Domodedovo division, now the Civil Aviation United Enterprise, was also very helpful. My thanks to general director Leonid Sergeev of Domodedovo and Olga Tokareva for their help, and to Tu-114 pilots and engineers Trifon Bashilov, Mikhail Shidlovski, Veniamin Malishev and Vladislav Konopko; and to Ivan Levandovski and Vladimir Kuznetsov, then of Krasnoyarskavia, for their help at the beginning of the project.

In Tupolev itself, my thanks are due to Valentin Klimov, the current director general, and Yuli Kashtanov, his first deputy for putting up with my questions over the last few years. Lev Lanovski and Yuri Vorobiev, chief designer of the Tu-204 programme and the -204C respectively, and Igor Kalygin, chief designer of the Tu-334, were always friendly and willing to help, as was Vladimir Rigmant, director of the excellent A. N. Tupolev museum, who gave considerable help in preparing the chart of the design programmes undertaken by the bureau. It was

Paul Duffy (left) and Andrei Kandalov
Lidia Kandalova

disappointing, however, to receive virtually no photographs from the bureau; those that are credited to Tupolev in the book came from Andrei Kandalov's personal files. However, I was very fortunate to receive an impressive range from Maksimillian Saukke, an engineer working in the design bureau and author of several books in Russian on A. N. Tupolev; although he is not a photographer, he has collected photographs of relevance to the Tupolev story for many years. He also provided the three-view drawings.

Konstantin Udalov, the general director of Avico Press, has been a Soviet aviation author and historian for over twenty years now. He opened his files freely to augment the photographs in this book. Valentin Vetlitski, Avico's artist, who had previously worked as a technical artist with MiG, provided the line drawings, and Vasili Karpi, the editor-in-chief of the Russian aviation newspaper *Vozdushni Transport* also provided some photos and a lot of background material. Thierry Montigneaux, executive officer of the Fédération Aéronautique International, came up with the current list of Tupolev records.

I would also like to thank my long-term friend John W. R. Taylor for his help, advice and assistance in preparing this book.

A special word of thanks must go to Svetlana Kirillova for the assistance she has given in the translation of the huge volume of documents involved in the preparation of the book. My Russian is very limited, and without her work the book would have had to wait another ten years. And to Lidia Kandalova, Andrei's wife, who provided enthusiasm and support for the project, not to mention excellent catering, as Andrei and I argued the text.

In closing, I would like to remind readers that although Russian people are very like their Western counterparts, sometimes their traditions are a lot different; for instance, a Russian would usually address a colleague by the colleague's name and patronym, so I should call my co-author 'Andrei Inokentievich'. I didn't, and he didn't expect me to. Similarly, in this book, I have adopted the Western practice in most places of just giving the first name (when known).

In the three years of research for this book I have become painfully aware of how much is missing from it. I am conscious that there are several chapters and details not covered as well as I would like. The Soviet system is changing, but it will take some time to bring it to the standards of information normally available to the West. Production details is a principal example: Andrei and I have done what we can, but it is far from complete, and virtually all of Tupolev's pre-war records were destroyed as the Nazis advanced on Moscow in 1941. So there are still gaps. If anyone has any information which adds to the contents, please let me know.

And whatever about people, Russia's Cyrillic alphabet is very different to the Roman alphabet used in the English speaking world. Thus it might just happen that I have spelt a word or name slightly differently in various chapters of the book. If you find it, it follows that I didn't at the proof reading stage. I apologise.

Paul Duffy
Shannon, Ireland
June 1995

Contents

Author's note on A. N. Tupolev	8	ANT-21/MI-3	64
A. N. Tupolev	9	ANT-22/MK-1	65
Aleksei Andreevich Tupolev	19	ANT-23/I-12	67
Valentin Tikhonovich Klimov	20	ANT-25	68
The Design Bureau Story	21	ANT-26/TB-6	73
Aerosleighs	28	ANT-27/MDR-4, MTB-1	73
Airships	29	ANT-28	74
Torpedo Boats and Cutters	29	ANT-29/DIP	74
ANT-1	31	ANT-31/I-14	75
ANT-2	32	ANT-32	76
ANT-3 [R-3]	34	ANT-34	76
ANT-4/TB-1	36	ANT-35/PS-35	76
ANT-5	40	ANT-36/DB-1	77
ANT-6/TB-3	42	ANT-37/DB-2	78
ANT-7/R-6	47	ANT-38	79
ANT-8/MDR-2	50	ANT-39	79
ANT-9	51	ANT-40	80
ANT-10/R-7	55	ANT-41/T-1	84
ANT-11	55	ANT-42/TB-7	84
ANT-12/I-5	55	ANT-43	86
ANT-13/I-8	56	ANT-44/MTB-2A	86
ANT-14	57	ANT-45	87
ANT-15	59	ANT-46/DI-8	87
ANT-16/TB-4	59	ANT-47	88
ANT-17	60	ANT-48	88
ANT-18	60	ANT-49	88
ANT-19	60	ANT-50	88
ANT-20	61	ANT-51	88
[*Maksim Gorki*]	61	The PE-2	89

ANT-End	89
ANT-58 to -62; -65 to -67; Samolet 103 – The Tu-2	89
ANT-63P/Tu-1	94
The ANT-64 and the Tu-4	94
ANT-63/Tu-6	99
ANT-68/Tu-10	99
ANT-69/Tu-10	99
Tu-70	99
Tu-72/Tu-73/Tu-74 and Tu-78/Tu-79	102
Tu-75	103
Project 77/ The Tu-12	103
Tu-80	104
Tu-81/Tu-14	105
Tu-82 – The First Tu-22	105
Tu-85	106
Tu-88 – The Tu-16	108
Tu-89	112
Tu-91	112
Tu-92/Tu-16P	113
Tu-95 'Bear'	113
Tu-96	116
Tu-98	116
Tu-104	117
Project 105 – The Tu-22	123
Tu-110	126
Tu-114	126
Tu-116	131
Tu-119	132
Missiles	132
Tu-124	134
Tu-126	136
Tu-128	138
Tu-134	141
Tu-134 Modifications	150
Tu-142	151
Tu-144	153
Project 145	158
Tu-154	161
Tu-154 Modifications	167
Tu-155	168
Tu-160	169
Tu-204	173
Tu-234	179
Tu-334	179
Future Designs	182
Tu-134 Production List – Aircraft in Service in 1995	184
Tu-154 Production List	188
Tu-204 Production List	194
Glossary of Terms	195
Bibliography	197
Designs of A. N. Tupolev OKB 1923–1993	199
Corporate Structure of A. N. Tupolev ANTK	206
Specifications of ANT Aerosleighs	207
Specifications of Aircraft	207
World Records	211
Specifications of Torpedo Boats	218
Production Figures	219
Index	228

Author's Note on
A. N. Tupolev

Andrei Nikolaevich Tupolev did not make friends easily. He took his time getting to know people and to trust them. But if he did place his trust in anyone, he stood by them, relied on them, and if they should make a mistake or let him down, he looked at it not as their fault, but as his.

A strong leader, and a fighter for projects and causes in which he believed, his strength and loyalty won him strong support from his staff and friends. But this contrasted with the family man at home, who according to some of his colleagues was a 'pussycat'. He drew much of his strength from his wife, Julia Nikolaevna, whom he met while working in his student days as a medical 'brother' in a Moscow hospital. They remained together throughout their lives.

There were many legends about him. He was reported to be able to look at an aircraft, or even at drawings, and correctly state its ability to fly or not; or to pinpoint problems and suggest answers. Here, for example, he is said to have looked at Petliakov's Pe-2 (fighter turned bomber) and commented that larger vertical tailplanes would be needed for stability, and they were. Before the first flight of a new Tupolev aircraft type, he would often walk down the runway and stop at the point he expected it to lift off, and he is reported as always being right. He could look at an engineering project and pinpoint the weak points in design, even if it had little relationship to aviation. These qualities resulted from a combination of his talent, his skill, his experience and his 'nose' for his profession.

He was also a skilled manager and organiser of people and projects. His staff he regarded as an extension of his family – he would help them through their problems, sometimes helping them find a new home, or the appropriate medical assistance, or even to sort out arguments.

When he decided to do something, he put his heart into it, and didn't give up until it was completed. This combination of professionalism, judgement and management plus thoroughness made his capability respected not only in the Soviet Union, but throughout the aviation world.

One of Tupolev's early gliders in flight
Maksimillian B. Saukke Collection

A. N. Tupolev

Andrei Nikolaevich Tupolev was born in his family's home in the village of Pustomazovo, near the town of Kimry, in north-west Russia on 29 October 1888 (the date accords with the Julian calendar; in February 1918, Russia switched to the Gregorian calendar and the date became 10 November). He was the sixth child of a family of seven; he had two brothers and three sisters older, and one sister younger.

His father, Nikolai Ivanovich Tupolev, came from the town of Surgut in Siberia from a Cossack family. He had graduated from Tobolsk gymnasium (the equivalent of the British secondary school) and had become a teacher; his subjects were arithmetic and geometry. After some years he decided to further his education and entered university in Moscow. There, he became involved in student unrest, and was watched by police and eventually sent down from the university. After that, he went to the Tver (later Kalinin) region, where he became a notary serving a regional court in the town of Korchev. Then he changed career and direction again, bought a small plot of land in Pustomazovo and became a farmer. Tupolev's mother, Anna Vasilievna Lisitsyna, was born in 1850 in Torzhok, a small town near Tver. The daughter of a court investigator, she graduated from Tver gymnasium. She spoke French and German, and played the piano.

From his early childhood, Andrei Nikolaevich was adept at building models and making furniture for himself and his family. With his parents' support and approval, he developed these skills. At the age of thirteen, he entered Tver gymnasium, his mother's old school. Here, his teachers did not notice any special qualities about him except that he developed an interest in astronomy. By the time of his graduation in summer 1908, he had decided that he should 'proceed in the technical sphere'. He applied for courses in two third level institutes (the Russian equivalent of universities or colleges). He was awarded a place in two of them, following admittance examinations: the Moscow Imperial Technical High School (IMTU) and the Institute for Railroad Engineers. He chose the IMTU, and did not regret his choice. At the end of his first year, he told friends that he had 'done more than I had planned or expected'.

Then, in autumn 1909, a new course began at IMTU. Given by Nikolai Yegorovich Zhukovski, the subject was aerodynamics. A few months later, enthusiastic students formed a new branch in the subject with Zhukovski as chairman. The students organised their first aeronautical exhibition, which was held in the IMTU, in April 1910. Among the exhibits were a scale model of the Antoinette biplane (built in France) and an early example of a wind tunnel which was designed and built by Tupolev; it was described as a 'flat aerodynamic tube' and was intended to study the effects of new developments prior to actually flying them. Later he developed a rounded tube, and this led to the formation of an aerodynamic laboratory at the IMTU, where Tupolev's 'aerodynamic tubes' served until 1923.

After the exhibition, Tupolev and his fellow students began to build a 'balance glider'. Using Lillenthal's theories, this involved the pilot's weight serving to change pitch and direction, and is a system still used on hang gliders today. The first flights were made in Moscow's Lefortovo Park. The first ever photograph to be published of Tupolev was as pilot of one of these gliders in flight at the park; it appeared in the first issue of the *Bulletin of the Moscow Aeronautics Society*, in 1910.

His studies and his work in the IMTU aerodynamic laboratory were interrupted in the spring of 1911. He was accused of allowing his home address to be used for correspondence of the 'city coalitional committee of higher educational institutions of Moscow and St Petersburg'. Because of the political climate prevailing in Russia at that time, on 14 March he was arrested, and despite the strenuous efforts of his mentor, Zhukovksi, he was released only to attend his father's funeral on 21 April; later he was released on condition that he was confined to Pustomazovo village. (Tupolev had no involvement in the forthcoming 1917 revolution, but was of course aware of it. As did most of his countrymen, he had to accept the results.) He applied to be readmitted to the IMTU at the end of 1912, and was accepted, but he could not resume his attendance there until February 1914 because of his confinement to the village, and also because of the need to support his mother and younger sister.

In 1916, an aviation test and calculations bureau was established with Zhukovski as its head. Tupolev was appointed deputy head, with responsibility for the supervision of the laboratory installations and equip-

A. N. Tupolev in his office with a portrait of N. E. Zhukovski behind him
Maksimillian B. Saukke Collection

ment. The bureau did considerable work in calculating aerodynamic loads and in experimental developments in aircraft construction.

On 11 June 1918, at the end of his (initial) studies, Tupolev received his degree of engineer-mechanic when he presented his thesis for diploma on 'Hydroplane design, based on tests in hydro tubes.' (Hydroplane is the Russian equivalent of the seaplane, an aircraft capable of landing and taking off from water; as the Cyrillic alphabet has no direct equivalent of the letter 'h', it is usually referred to as 'Gidroplan'.) Later that year, at the second All-Russia Aviation Congress, Zhukovski (then and still regarded as the father of Russian aviation) praised his student's work by saying, 'The paper on hydroplane research presented by A. N. Tupolev is an outstanding piece

of research which used experimental results from English research as well as his own. This has made clear to all that aircraft can in fact both take off from and land on water. If this research is published, it will greatly enhance the fame of Russian aviation.' (This citation has been paraphrased into English terminology.)

By 1920, the IMTU had been renamed the Moscow Higher Technical School (MVTU) and Tupolev was giving a course of lectures on 'the basics of aerodynamic calculations'.

TsAGI – The Birth of an Industry

Two years earlier, in 1918, Zhukovski and Tupolev had submitted proposals to the new Soviet government for the establishment of an aerodynamics research centre under the title of 'Provisions for TsAGI'. TsAGI is the Russian initials for the 'Central Aero/Hydrodynamics Institute'. The government gave its approval, and on 1 December 1918, the TsAGI was established with offices and laboratories at Radio Street (then called Voznesenskaya Street) on the banks of the River Yauza, some five kilometres from the Kremlin, Moscow's centre. Tupolev was responsible for the establishment of the Institute's research and test facilities, appropriately called the experimental base.

By mid-1919, there were thirty-three people working at the TsAGI, including Zhukovski and Tupolev; the largest section was the aviation division, which had six staff working on a variety of projects. But Tupolev was beginning to suffer from health problems. He developed a lung illness, a form of pleurisy, which doctors suspected might develop into tuberculosis; at that time, this was incurable. His doctors recommended that he should move to the better climate of the Crimea, so in autumn 1919 he moved there, and for the next year worked as a medical orderly in a sanatorium. He stayed there until late 1920, spending some of his time resolving resort matters.

Shortly after his return to Moscow, he married a girl he had met six years earlier when, as a student, he had worked as a 'nursing brother' in a Moscow hospital. Julia Nikolaevna Zheltiakova was there at the same time working as a nursing sister. She turned out to be a strong woman and gave him much of the strength he needed for the years ahead. He and Julia lived in house no. 29 in Ulitsa Kaliaeva, Moscow from their wedding until 1952.

On 5 April 1921, Tupolev was elected by a staff vote to be Zhukovski's deputy. At that time, this earned him the title of 'comrade to the director' (a Russian term for deputy). Now he began work on the introduction of light metals for aircraft construction which would be vital for the future development of the industry. He ran into considerable opposition from the advocates of wooden aircraft and the wood industry, but he persisted. First of all, he had to determine the specifications needed for the metals, including grades and quality, although from the start it was clear that duraluminium would be the principal material. To do this, he needed to determine accurately the strengths and qualities of each metal, then to establish production.

Once he had selected a metal, he began to test it. One of his ways of testing was to design and build aerosleighs and speedboats, and to study the effects of their use. By the summer of 1922, the first bars of aviation grade aluminium were rolling off the production lines at the Kolchuginsk metallurgical factory.

By October 1922, Tupolev had succeeded in setting up a 'commission for the construction of all-metal aircraft', a new division of TsAGI. Although it was not to bear his name officially until after his death, this was regarded by Tupolev in later years as being the birth of the Tupolev Design Bureau. The commission was established on 22 October. Tupolev, as the TsAGI's director deputy responsible for AGOS (the division covering aviation, hydroplanes and test aircraft), also took on aviation metals.

Tupolev and his team had built several aerosleighs which proved to be tough and reliable, even in the polar regions where they were used. With the new metals, it now became possible to construct sleighs entirely from metal. The first one was completed in February 1923, and after trials they were put into production in two factories, the Marti metallurgical plant in Leningrad (now St Petersburg) and, appropriately, Kolchuginsk, under the designation ANT-I and continuing to the ANT-IV, which was displayed at the 1928 Berlin exhibition.

October 1921 saw construction begin on the first of Tupolev's speedboats, the ANT-1, a designation used less than a year later for his first aircraft. This boat was made mainly from wood. It led to the establishment of a test base in the Crimea for the trials and development of both speedboats and hydroplanes. This base was also used to test the effects of salt water corrosion on the new metals. The experience gained in the development and service of the aerosleighs and speedboats added to his knowledge and prepared the path for Tupolev and his team for the construction and manufacture of all-metal aircraft.

Six months later, in April 1922, he began working on the design of his first aircraft. It was a single-seat cantilever sports monoplane of mixed metal and wood

construction with a 7.2 metre wingspan, and was capable of aerobatics. Eighteen months later it was completed, and its first flight was made on 21 October 1923, flown by Yevgeni Pogosski.

Meanwhile, in May 1923, Tupolev had started to design the ANT-2, the first Soviet all-metal aircraft, a high-wing cantilever monoplane with the pilot sitting in an open cockpit and an enclosed passenger cabin for two people facing each other. It was powered by an air-cooled Bristol Jupiter engine of 100 hp. Nikolai Petrov was the pilot when the ANT-2 made its first flight on 26 May 1927. A small number of ANT-2s were built at the Kolchuginsk factory. The first aircraft is still preserved at the Monino museum of the Soviet/Russian Air Force. Some five were built there, and they served the Moscow–Gorki route. Gorki is now Nizhni Novgorod.

By the early 1920s, Tupolev had a team which included thirteen engineers, and much of his time and energy was spent on the development and testing of aluminium alloys suitable for aircraft manufacture. His first visit to a foreign country was in January 1925, when he led a team to Germany and France to study how the aviation industries in those, and other, countries were dealing with corrosion and other problems. Although he was impressed enough with the work being done in these countries, nonetheless he decided that the anodising method used in the British industry would best suit Russia's requirements, and soon anodisation was the norm in Russia.

In July 1924, the TsAGI was requested by the Air Force to design a two-seat reconnaissance aircraft. Naturally, the task fell to the AGOS division headed by Tupolev, and the result was the ANT-3, his first biplane – actually a sesquiplane, as the lower wing was much shorter than the top one. The choice of a biplane format was dictated by the availability of engines at the time. The shorter wingspan needed on a biplane also added manoeuvrability to the performance, which was (and still is) a necessity for fighter and reconnaissance aircraft. The ANT-3's first flight was in August 1925, and the aircraft was immediately put into serial production at GAZ5 – Gosudarstvenni Avia Zavod (State Aero Works) 5 (in 1927, it was renamed Red October, to commemorate the tenth anniversary of the 1917 October revolution).

When designing the ANT-3, Tupolev used a corrugated surface to add strength to the wing and fuselage duraluminium plates. Corrugation had been an original patent of Junkers, the German aircraft manufacturer. In 1923, the Soviet Narodny (National) Commissariat of Production had reached agreement with Junkers to help the Soviet Union set up an aluminium production factory and to train Russian engineers in the manufacturing process. In the event, this did not happen and the agreement was cancelled, Tupolev and his team designed corrugated aluminium with what was called a TsAGI wave (instead of the Junkers' wave), which he calculated to be twenty-five per cent stronger and five per cent more durable. It proved to be more complicated to manufacture, and more difficult to rivet, and led to strong resistance from the industry; but Tupolev had his way, and the new corrugation was introduced. Junkers then brought the Soviet Ministry (or Narodny Commissariat) of Production before the international court in The Hague, Holland on the basis that it held international patents for corrugated aluminium, but the case was dismissed.

Tupolev now turned his thoughts to the difficulties of manufacturing aircraft without having test aircraft built first in order to try out new concepts and sort out difficulties. He concluded that test aircraft were needed, and set about establishing an experimental base as part of his AGOS division. TsAGI had been formed as a scientific study and research body, and many senior people did not agree with adding on an experimental division, but again Tupolev fought his way through the difficulties and the new section was set up on 14 November 1924 as part of the AGOS in TsAGI.

Work began on new offices and a factory to house the new AGOS on a site near that of the TsAGI on the corner of Voznesenskaya Street and Nemetskaya Street (today called Radio Street and Bauman Street). It was tasked with the development of test technologies for serial production, and it included a factory for the construction of test aircraft. Shortly after its opening, 183 out of TsAGI's total staff of 305 worked there. These buildings are still part of today's Tupolev Aviation Complex, and helped Tupolev to undertake design and development of a growing range of aircraft. Over the next few years, they included the ANT-4/TB-1; ANT-5 fighter (1927); ANT-7/R-6 (1929); ANT-9 passenger airliner (1929); ANT-6/TB-3 four-engined bomber (1930); and the ANT-14 (1931). Even in these busy times, Tupolev sought to increase his knowledge and contacts and undertook a number of foreign journeys, to Austria and Italy in 1927; Germany (1928); Germany, France, Austria and England (1929); and to the United States (1930). In 1930, Tupolev was appointed chief designer and head of the AGOS; he began preparations for the Zavod Opytnikh Konstruktsii (ZOK), the factory of experimental productions, and to enlarge the design offices.

In 1931, the government decided to reorganise the growing aviation industry, and appointed Sergei Ilyushin to TsAGI's experimental aviation depart-ment, with Tupolev as his deputy. Indeed, all Soviet industry was being transferred from one ministry to another. About four months later, another rethink saw Tupolev reappointed head of the department.

He was adamant on the need for test aircraft, and rejected the idea that all test aircraft should go into production. For example, when asked whether Grigorovich's MT-1 (a naval torpedo carrier) design should be produced, he said, 'We should reject the idea that [all] test aircraft should go into serial production. The idea of a test is to test. Nobody has yet been able to step over the evolution of technology.' He was also not in favour of buying and copying foreign aircraft unless there was a real advantage in so doing because, 'They offer us aircraft that have already shown good results – in other words, yesterday's designs, and not today's, not the designs of the future, the ones still only in designer's briefcases. It would take at least two years for us to put foreign aircraft into production in our factories and we would end up with obsolete aircraft instead of modern ones.' But when there was an advantage, he was prepared to back it. As chief engineer of the aviation department of the National Commissariat of Heavy Industry, he authorised and insisted on purchasing a licence to build the Douglas DC-3 in Russia and to obtain its 'Loft Mould' construction process. Under the name of its Soviet adapter, this led to 6,157 Lishunov Li-2s being produced for service in the Soviet Union and its allied countries.

In 1929, he also encouraged the government to purchase licences for the manufacture of the Wright Cyclone engine range; these formed the basis for the ASh range of air-cooled engines still produced in the 1990s and updated by Arkadi Shvetsov. Another licence was bought from Hispano Suiza for liquid-cooled engines produced by the French company.

In 1933, he was elected to the Soviet Academy of Sciences as Correspondent Member for Science and Technology. This was, and is, regarded as one of the highest qualifications in the Soviet Union for any technical grade, with only Academician ranking higher.

In the 1930s, Tupolev and his team designed, tested and developed the ANT-20 (Maksim Gorki), ANT-25, ANT-9, ANT-6/TB-3, ANT-40/SB, ANT-35 and ANT-42/Pe-8. Prototypes of each of these, and some other, aircraft were built at the new factory. These significant designs contributed to the Soviet Union's growing reputation in world aviation as a leader in the industry.

1936 was a significant year for Tupolev. On 5 January he was appointed chief engineer of the Main Department of the Aviation Industry (GUAP) of the

People's Commissariat (Ministry) of Heavy Industry (NKTP), a position which gave him a leading influence over Russia's aviation industry. Furthermore, on 1 July, his 'factory of experimental constructions N156' was officially separated from the TsAGI to become an independent body. By then also, the bureau's premises had been substantially extended and included the buildings on the embankment of the Yauza river. It would be almost another 40 years, until just after his death, before the factory would be named after its founder.

But the good days were coming to an end. With Josef Stalin tightening control over the Soviet Union, there came a paranoia about state security, a paranoia to the point where even an unconfirmed suggestion of betrayal was enough to end a career or even a life. Senior figures in political, military, industrial and cultural circles were not exempt, and many were imprisoned, sent to concentration camps or executed. It was a dark period in Russia's turbulent history, and people lived in fear.

On 21 October 1937, a knock on the door of Tupolev's office late in the evening was followed by his arrest. He was brought to the Lubianka prison, interrogated and then transferred to cell number 58 in Moscow's Butyrskaya prison, which he shared with forty other prisoners, in a cell built for four. He was accused of sabotage and espionage, contrary to article 58 of the criminal code. Who his accusers were was never made clear, but at that time prisoners were usually subjected to severe torture, and many would accuse others to ease their own torment. It is possible that Levanevski's tirade to Stalin after his failed flight on the ANT-25 to America may have been one of the factors: he accused Tupolev of being an enemy of the people, saying that he had deliberately sabotaged the flight, even though this had subsequently been accomplished by Chkalov and Gromov. Under torture, Tupolev pleaded guilty to even the most outlandish and unproven charges.

With public disquiet over Tupolev's arrest, stories about his alleged crimes soon began to spread among the back street gossips of Moscow. He was said to have stored bomber drawings in the longerons of the ANT-25 before its flight to America, had them removed there and sold to Messerschmitt in Germany, and that they had been recovered by the American Secret Service. Rumours of this kind persisted until the 1960s, despite the following facts: drawings weighing 500 to 800 kilograms would have made the ANT-25 unable to reach America – at that time, Gromov had even removed safety equipment to make his flight; drawings by Soviet designers had to be converted with special equipment with the right tools even for Soviet

production factories; and by 1937 nobody needed 1932 vintage drawings to improve their technology. A short while after Tupolev's arrest, his wife Julia was also arrested and brought to Butyrskaya prison where she was held for twenty-eight months before her release in spring 1940. During their imprisonment, their son and daughter, Aleksei and Julia, were looked after by friends of the family.

It did not take Stalin and the head of his secret service, Beria, very long to realise that development in the aviation industry had virtually stopped, as it had in several other industries, so they began to organise design bureaux and research facilities in different prisons and concentration camps by transferring specialists from relevant industries, including shipbuilding, chemical and aviation, military tracked vehicles, artillery and others, to the one prison. Thus was born the Central Design Bureau N29 (TsKB N29) of the NKVD, the State Security Police for Interior Affairs. Established for aviation projects, it included over 150 leading industry specialists.

It is difficult for those who did not live in the Soviet Union at that time to understand how people imprisoned, usually unjustly, by the state could agree to work for the state in such conditions. But factors involved in their decision could have included patriotism with a looming war, fear of punishment against family and friends, and the conditions facing prisoners in the concentration camps. Tupolev agreed to work at TsKB N29, and was transferred to Bolshevo prison in the Moscow region to join the other aviation specialists. He did this on the conditions that he could receive a letter from his wife, and that his children would be allowed to live with their Niania (family nurse) at the family home in Ulitsa Kaliaeva (now renamed Dolgomilovskaya Ulitsa). These conditions were accepted, and late in autumn 1938 he was transferred from Butyrskaya prison to Bolshevo, where he headed the group working on 'Project 103', a dive bomber soon designated the ANT-58, and which later was redesignated Tu-2. Other aviation groups in Bolshevo at that time included Project 101 headed by Myasishchev, Project 102 headed by Petliakov, and Project 110 headed by Tomashevski. Other well known aviation industry prisoners included Korolev, Rumer, Scillard and Nekrasov, as well as directors of major aircraft factories. One of the specialists working on Project 103 was Georgi Frenkel, stepfather of this book's co-author, Andrei Kandalov. Tupolev spent his fiftieth birthday, 10 November 1938, in Bolshevo prison.

At first, Beria insisted on Tupolev designing a long-range, four-engined dive bomber, Project N6Y. Tupolev considered this an almost impossible task, and, with considerable difficulty, set about convincing Beria to allow him to design and build a twin-engined aircraft, something which Tupolev felt was possible with the engines and technology of the time. To proceed with his design work, Tupolev drew up a list of the names of specialists he needed, and the NKVD went to seek them out in the prisons and camps. Soon the group was at work, but without the workshops and test facilities necessary for their task. With great difficulty, a full scale mock-up of Project 103 was constructed of timber in a nearby forest. Here it was seen from the air by pilots from an air base in the region, who reported a crashed aircraft to their commanding officer. The local NKVD quickly ordered it to be dismantled, and Tupolev experienced considerable trouble in persuading the 'technically illiterate' officers of the need for a mock-up. Eventually, the problem was solved by covering the wooden structure with a camouflage net. But the difficulty of designing, building and testing aircraft was evident, and so the aviation prison group was transferred back to Moscow, to relocate, still as prisoners, in Plant 156. Ironically, this building today carries a memorial plaque, mounted in 1973, which reads: 'The Tupolev Embankment was named in 1973 in honour of academician Andrei Nikolaevich Tupolev (1888–1972), the outstanding aviation designer, three times hero of Socialist Labour.'

But in 1940, it was Tupolev's prison; admittedly a more acceptable prison than the Lubianka or Bolshevo because at least the needs of his craft were at hand. His bedroom was on the sixth floor, while the design offices were on the third and the fourth. A covered passageway connected the design offices with the test factory, so it was not even necessary to put on a coat to visit the workshops, and problems could be quickly and easily solved.

One problem for designers was that, as prisoners, they had no right to a name, and were not permitted to sign their drawings – a normal procedure at that time in the industry to show that the designer had completed his section of his work and approved the result. So each designer was given a rubber stamp with his number on it to approve his drawings. Tupolev's was number 011, and all the designers working on his project had numbers the sum of which would equal 11 – 065, 074, 083, 092 etc. 029 was the number of Georgi Frenkel.

In the design offices and factories, many 'civilians' – that is, non-prisoners – worked alongside the prisoners daily. For the most part, they treated their prisoner comrades not as 'enemies of the people' but as friends in trouble, and many risked their own freedom by helping them in different ways. The

designer prisoners were always followed around the workshops by guards, which was not always conducive to working efficiently. The prisoner specialists were not allowed to receive information, even relating to their own skills and the needs of their profession. This obviously limited their work, and eventually it was decided to apply to the NKVD for permission to visit some factories. The need was obvious, and the NKVD organised a visit – but on one occasion only.

At the factory, the prisoners were greeted with great warmth by the staff. This resulted in the NKVD bringing subsequent information to the designers rather than allowing another visit. But the non-technical NKVD staff very often mixed up the data, and the results were usually useless. Very often, the NKVD staff relaying the information had little or no general education, even apart from technical know-how.

Despite all this, Tupolev eventually told the NKVD that he wanted to meet an Air Force commission to present Project 103. The commission approved the design, and the prototype ANT-58 (Tu-2) was built at Plant 156, then brought to Chkalovsk aerodrome (then called Shelkovski) near Monino, from where it made its first flight on 22 December 1940, flown by Mikhail Nukhtikov. It was tested by the Air Force from December 1940 until June 1941, and was regarded by the military authorities as being 'superior to the Pe-2 in speed and bomb load, defensive armaments and manoeuvrability'.

For the Soviet Union, World War Two – the Great Patriotic War – started on 22 June 1941. A month later, Tupolev was released, despite a Supreme Court decision taken at a closed session, and without a case being presented, on 28 May 1940 that he be sentenced to fifteen years of 'reformatory works'. At that time, the sentence was stated to be final and not subject to appeal. On 9 July 1941, Tupolev and twenty of his prisoner colleagues were 'granted mercy' and had their convictions set aside by a special decision of the Praesidium of the Supreme Court of the USSR allowing them to be officially rehabilitated.

Tupolev had to wait until the XXIInd Congress of the Communist Party of the Soviet Union in 1956 to be officially rehabilitated and restored to all his rights. There, Stalin's successor Nikita Khrushchev accused his predecessor of many crimes during his two periods of terror, 1935 to 1941 and 1945 to 1953, and that the tests carried out on the Project 103 and 103U aircraft by the Air Force Research Institute (NII-VVS) showed that these aircraft powered by an AM37 exceeded the performance of any other aircraft in their category (at that time) and fully met the requirements of the Red Army Air Force for combat dive bombers.

The War Years

With his release, Tupolev found himself immediately involved in relocating his facilities to Omsk, in western Siberia, because the German invasion of Russia had left Moscow under threat. The actual evacuation of Plant 156 began on 19 July, three days before his release. In Omsk, the factory section moved into an uncompleted motor (car) assembly works, while the design staff took over the offices of the Irtysh river steamship line.

The Omsk factory was given the number 166, and was soon producing the ANT-58, now renumbered the Tu-2, but production of the Tu-2 was stopped at the end of 1942 in favour of Yak-9 fighters which the military authorities decided were more urgently required. Tu-2 production resumed in 1944. Its 635kph/395mph speed at 8,000 metres/26,248 feet altitude made it virtually invincible as a bomber. But a decision to stop production of the AM37 water-cooled engine forced Tupolev to select instead the ASh-82 air-cooled engine, which dropped performance to 540kph/336mph at 5,000 metres/16,405 feet. This allowed increased production of the ASh-82, which was also needed for the Il-2 then being produced in huge numbers.

Meanwhile, in autumn 1943 Moscow was deemed safe from the German threat and Tupolev and the design staff returned to their own offices and factory. On their return, the design bureau concentrated on improving the Tu-2; a prototype was built with substantially reduced weights: electric wiring weight was halved; the hydrosystem was simplified; hydraulic lines were shortened from a total length in the aircraft of 447 metres/1,466 feet to 112 metres/367 feet; and the fuel system was simplified, as was the navigation and cockpit equipment. All in all, some 400kg/882lb was trimmed off the aircraft's weight.

Tupolev's next major task came in 1945. Russia was not at war with Japan, but after a 1944 raid on Japanese cities, four US Army Air Force Boeing B-29 Superfortresses, which had been damaged by Japanese anti-aircraft fire and could not have made it back to their bases, landed near Vladivostok, on the Soviet Pacific coast. Stalin decided that an exact copy should be produced, and three B-29s were flown to Moscow. One was given to factory N30 where it was completely stripped down. Two others went to the LII Flight Research Institute in order to measure its performance capability and handling characteristics, and the fourth was kept as a comparison. Early in 1945, Tupolev was given the task of reproducing the B-29, and in doing this, to bring the Soviet aviation industry back on a par with that of the United States, where it had

A. N. Tupolev, in uniform, reading a note
Konstantin Udalov/Avico Press Collection

advanced with major progress during the war years.

To carry out this job, Tupolev was made responsible for all technical decisions, and his decisions were given the status of 'obligatory'. They were required to be acted upon by any ministry, and thus by any industry or research body that Tupolev considered necessary. That in itself eliminated many of the delays inherent in the aviation industry, whether in the Soviet Union or elsewhere, and allowed the programme to advance very quickly. Thus the first flight of the Soviet B-29, the Tu-4, took place in May 1947, some twenty months after the project was launched.

This project tested Tupolev to the maximum, for it literally involved the modernisation of the Soviet aviation industry as well as the construction of a large, very complex aircraft. One of the methods he used to speed up the programme was to set aside a large area in a mock-up workshop as an exhibition centre which displayed all the components for the Tu-4 as they came in from the manufacturing factories. This allowed Tupolev and his team to judge the quality of each unit and producer, and to decide which needed extra effort and resources in order to keep the programme on schedule.

Even at his early stage, production of the Tu-4 was beginning at Moscow factory N23 (GAZ5, called Red October) and at factory N22 in Kazan. To speed up development, twenty pre-production aircraft were completed to take part in the flight tests which were carried out by the LII Flight Test Institute at Zhukovski, the airfield for developmental flying, near

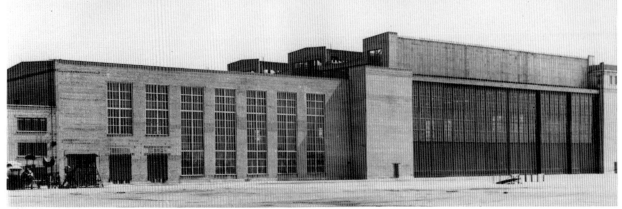

One of Tupolev's flight test hangars at Zhukovski
Maksimillian B. Saukke Collection

the town of Ramenskoe in the Moscow region. A combination of a fear of Stalin and Tupolev's determination to minimise problems and programme time led to some unusual decisions; one of these was that reproduction of the electrical system was to Western specifications (400 kiloHertz and 115 volts for the aircraft, and 500 kiloHertz for onboard missiles), as well as using imperial thicknesses for wiring and airframe skins.

Tupolev was never a man to waste opportunities, and the development of the Tu-4 went side by side with a passenger aircraft, the Tu-70. Originally intended as a twenty-eight-seater, it soon developed into a less luxurious but still comfortable seventy-two-seater. Using parts of the Boeing aircraft including the wings, tailplane, undercarriage, engines and some instruments and equipment, the Tu-70 actually flew before the Tu-4, lifting off in November 1946. With a seventy per cent commonality with the Tu-4, it would have been a simple production task, but Aeroflot did not yet need an aircraft of that size. A cargo version, the Tu-75, was designed and built. Capable of carrying 100 parachutists/paratroopers, it featured a tail ramp. The last in the series with piston engines, the Tu-85, was built in the early 1950s; with sixteen crew and a take-off weight of seventy-five tonnes, it had a range of 12,000km/7,450 miles at 10,000m/32,810 feet and a speed of 665kph/413mph with a payload of five tonnes – impressive figures for the time. But turbines were just about to enter service, and the jet and turboprop engines left no demand for new piston-engined aircraft.

Concurrently with the Tu-4 programme, Tupolev had begun work on Project 77, which was an aircraft intended to serve as an introduction of jet engines on to large aircraft. Project 77 started just at the end of the war, using a production Tu-2 (which was redesignated Tu-12). It involved fitting two Rolls-Royce Nene jet engines, which gave a thrust of 2,270kgp/5,004lb, in place of the two piston engines. These effectively maintained the aircraft's balance/CG (centre of gravity) position.

Modifying a standard Tu-2 allowed the actual construction of the Tu-12 to be completed in two and a half months, although the design work necessary had taken almost two years. As jet engines operate most effectively at higher altitudes – 11,000 metres/36,091 feet was deemed suitable for the Tu-12 – it was necessary to pressurise the cockpit. A new wing and horizontal tailplane were also needed. First flight was in July 1947, and some problems were soon evident: the thinner kerosene fuel (compared to petrol) leaked easily, and it was found necessary to pressurise the fuel system; new materials had to be found to improve the installation.

To meet these needs, the project was renumbered 73; flight tests showed that the 77 was underpowered, so it was decided by Tupolev to mount a third engine, this time a Rolls-Royce Derwent, in the tail – unheard of in 1947, although later many jets would feature tail-mounted engines. First flight on 29 December 1947 was followed by a successful test programme and led to Project 81, which became the Tu-14 and was the first Soviet jet bomber to enter production and service; it was powered by two VK-1 engines designed by Vladimir Klimov.

With the Tu-4 and -14 programmes working well, Tupolev began the design of a long-range strategic bomber. By now, new design techniques were evolving from the mass of experience built up over the war period. The mathematics of design had improved and a combination of these factors helped designers select the optimum shapes for new projects. This led him to decide on a swept wing layout. With a family relationship to the Tu-14, the Tu-82 made its first flight in March 1949 as an experimental/research prototype. With the flight test results, Tupolev then updated it as Project 88, to take advantage of the new Mikulin AM-3 engines which offered 9,000kgp/19,841lb of thrust. In Project 88, Tupolev refined a procedure known as the 'tadpole rule' which the bureau had begun to use on the Tu-2. Internationally, this became known as the 'area rule' when formulated by R. T. Whitcomb in the United States in 1953. It is a technique used to determine the best fuselage shape and wing geometry formula to meet transonic Mach requirements; with the power and drag characteristics available in the later 1940s and early 1950s, this resulted in a requirement for fuselages to be narrower in the centre and rear, giving Tupolev's tadpole effect.

Project 88 made its first flight in April 1952, and attained a speed of 1,012kph/629mph, but the production aircraft was overweight, and could not meet its range requirements. Tupolev decided to eliminate most of the fuselage joints and create a more monocoque/monolithic fuselage, and to limit the aircraft's speed at altitudes below 6,000m/19,686 feet, saving almost six tonnes in weight. This done, the aircraft went into production at Kazan, and later at Voronezh as the Tu-16, and it was also built under licence in China. Most Tu-16s were withdrawn from the Soviet Air Force in the late 1980s, although a few were still in service in 1992.

By the early 1950s, the Soviet government was concerned over progress being made in the West on very long-range, large strategic bombers, and Tupolev was ordered by the government on behalf of the Air Force to develop a large, high-speed aircraft capable of exceeding 10,000km/6,214 miles range to a high specification. A close study of engine availability led him to the conclusion that it would not be possible to meet this requirement with the jet engines then available. But Tupolev didn't give up. He issued a request to the industry for turboprop/turboshaft engines which could offer 10,000 shaft horsepower and for high efficiency propellers. The Kuznetsov Design Bureau in Molotov near Perm took on the engines, and the Zhdanov Design Bureau based in Stupino, near Moscow, the propellers.

Taking the piston-engined Tu-85 as a basis, Tupolev began work early in 1951. Eighteen months later, the remarkable Tu-95 made its first flight, although as Kuznetsov's new engines were not yet ready, an interim choice of fitting TV-2F engines was made. These were in fact TV-2 engines with increased power and modified to take a gearbox which drove contra-rotating propellers. Indeed Zhdanov's propellers were the real key to the aircraft's subsequent success. But success did not come easily.

On 11 May 1953, an engine caught fire during a test flight. The crew were unable to put out the fire, and the prototype Tu-95 crashed, killing pilot Aleksei Pereliot and other crew members. Tupolev himself took the deaths very badly and regarded them as his own fault. In the event, quite a few construction improvements were made before the second Tu-95, now powered with Kuznetsov's NK-12 engines, made its first flight in February 1955.

While most of his work since the late 1930s had been on military aircraft, Tupolev had not forgotten the needs of civil aviation. The Tu-70 had proved to be too big and too early for Aeroflot. By the end of the war Great Britain had established the Brabazon Committee to determine the future needs for its commercial aviation. This had led to the choice of turbine engines, both jets and turboprops, to power a new generation of airliners. The de Havilland Comet had been one of the results of this, and in May 1952 it operated the first ever commercial jet service (from London to Johannesburg). Tupolev began to plan a Soviet jetliner in the middle of 1952. His plans met with considerable opposition, but Tupolev had never been afraid of a battle. Some of the opposition came from those who felt that military jet experience needed to be built up; more came from those who were not ready for the substantial infrastructural costs of developing airports and ATC equipment. But Tupolev won, and drew up concept plans which he submitted to the government with a proposal to develop a jetliner. Early in 1954, the project was approved.

Tupolev had already decided to build on the experience gained on the Tu-16 in Project 88. He used the cockpit layout and many of the systems. The new jetliner retained the wing shape and angle of sweep and similar engine mounts in the wing root, although it was to have more span and greater chord. This simplified much of the work, and shortened the time needed. It also allowed a high degree of commonality to be shared in the aircrew training programmes for both types.

The major difference between the two programmes was the jetliner's need to have a large pressurised cabin in order to give passengers a reasonably normal atmosphere. By now, the Comet accidents had happened, and major investigations were in place to determine their cause. Tupolev had no more insight than anyone else, but right from the start he thought that pressurisation could be part of the problem, and he worked on the design of the new fuselage with that in mind. So he arranged for the TsAGI to design and build a watertank to simulate flight cycles.

The Tu-104 emerged from the programme to make its first flight in June 1955; unknown in the West, it caused a major sensation when it turned up at Heathrow, London's main airport, in June 1956 bringing in a high-level delegation. The aircraft entered service in September 1956, flying mainly to military airports as most of the airports in the Soviet Union were not yet ready to handle jets. But the introduction of the Tu-104 acted as a catalyst for the modernisation of many airports.

With the Tu-104 programme established, Tupolev

set about preparing a large aircraft to meet the growing passenger and cargo traffic volumes, and combined with these, the Soviet Union's needs for long-range aircraft. The targets set were for 8,000km/4,971 miles and 180 to 220 passengers. Now well established in Air Force service, the Tu-95 offered an excellent basis for the new airliner. With only minor changes, its wings, tailplane, engines and undercarriage, along with primary systems, were all selected. The main change was, again, in the fuselage, which called for a capacity virtually three times that of the Tu-104. The resulting Tu-114 made its first flight in November 1957. Two visits were made to the USA in 1959, with the second carrying the CPSU General Secretary and Soviet President, Nikita Khrushchev. This flight was met at cruising level several hundred miles off the US coast by a USAF jet escort.

Later that day, Tupolev, who had travelled with Khrushchev, met a USAF General and asked him if they had checked the aircraft's speed (the USAF had expressed doubts about the ability of a turboprop airliner to fly at 800kph/500mph). He replied, 'What? Oh yeah – we sure did. Incredible!' The Tu-114 won Tupolev a gold medal for design from the Fédération Aéronautique International (FAI). It also received the Grand Prix award at the 1958 Brussels International Exhibition.

Before the visit to the United States, the KGB expressed concern over the number of dignitaries flying over long stretches of ocean in one aircraft. Tupolev was taking his full family, for example. So they insisted that everyone must be trained in the aircraft's safety equipment. The design bureau was instructed to build a special mock-up of the Tu-114 for emergency evacuation training. This was brought to the swimming pool of a governmental dacha (rest house) in Moscow's Lenin Hills. As a concession to the rank of the travellers, the mock-up was connected by bridge to a balcony which had changing rooms. Each cabin had the name of its user on a door plaque – Khrushchev, his wife Khrushcheva, (deputy premier) Kozlov, (designer) Mikoyan, Tupolev, Tupoleva etc. The mock-up had seats installed, with life vests and inflatable rafts. During the rehearsals, Khrushchev, his wife and Tupolev were excused from actually jumping into the water, but everyone else was thoroughly trained, and all the other VIPs had to jump in.

On arrival at Edwards Air Force Base near Washington, it turned out that there were no steps at the base high enough to reach the aircraft's door. So the Soviet leaders, their wives and the delegation had to travel the final few steps to the United States down a stepladder!

In 1962, Tupolev's wife, Julia Nikolaevna, died of cancer after a long and difficult illness. She was buried in the cemetery at Moscow's famous New Maiden's Convent. She had given her husband much of the strength he had needed in the difficult times he had faced over the last forty-five years, and he took her death with a heavy sense of loss. They had been very close, and he, sometimes impatient with the restrictions imposed by indifferent health, had relied on her. After her death, his daughter Julia, a doctor, took on the task of looking after him. She travelled with him on all his business trips at home and abroad.

In the 1960s, although he was now well into his seventies, he worked on a range of military and commercial aircraft, including the Tu-128 fighter/interceptor, the Tu-22 and the similarly designated Tu-22M 2 and 3 strategic bombers. Commercial programmes included the Tu-124 and 134; the Tu-154; and the Tu-144 supersonic airliner, in which his son, Aleksei Andreevich, played a major role.

In December 1972, Andrei Nikolaevich Tupolev fell ill; he was brought to hospital, and, after a short illness, he fell asleep in the evening of 22 December and died peacefully. He is buried in the cemetery of the New Maiden's Convent in Moscow, close to those who died in the ANT-20 *Maksim Gorki* accident, and to the crew of the Tu-144 which was lost at the 1973 Paris Air Salon, and alongside many of his co-workers.

Советский авиаконструктор, трижды Герой Социалистического Труда, академик А. Н. Туполев. 1888–1972

A commemorative cover issued after Tupolev's death
Maksimillian B. Saukke Collection

Aleksei Andreevich Tupolev

The only son of the founder of the design bureau, Aleksei Tupolev was born in Moscow on 20 May 1925. He began his career in aviation working at factory 166 in Omsk in 1942 as a designer, part of the team maintaining contact between the bureau and the production factory.

In 1943, he returned to Moscow with the bureau as the Nazis began their retreat from the Soviet Union. He worked for another year in the same role at factory 156 beside the design offices, working on the construction of prototype aircraft and equipment. In 1944, he enlisted at the Moscow Aviation Institute, the third level college in the Soviet capital for students intending to work in the aviation industry. He graduated in 1949, and later submitted his first thesis in 1953.

By then, factory 156 had been renamed the Moscow engineering Plant 'Opyt'. He rejoined initially as an aerodynamics engineer, then becoming a deputy chief designer and chief designer. In 1958, the bureau opened a new department to develop missiles, and A. A. Tupolev was appointed to head it. Under his design leadership, six missile programmes were completed, three of which went into production. He was also appointed chief designer for the Tu-144, the Soviet supersonic jetliner which was the first in the world to fly. In the late 1960s, he was appointed deputy general designer of the bureau, which also ranked him as the deputy chief executive.

After his father's death in 1972, he was appointed general designer, a post he took up in April 1973. He led the bureau through the difficult years of the 1970s and 1980s, when the Soviet Union reduced its expenditure on aircraft programmes. During these years, the bureau worked on aircraft in current service, including the Tu-134 and -154 airliners, and military programmes such as the Tu-16, Tu-20, Tu-22, Tu-28 and Tu-22M. New programmes were scarce, but the Tu-160 'Blackjack' supersonic strategic bomber and new generation Tu-204 airliner were developed under his leadership, as was the Tu-155, an adaptation of the Tu-154 passenger jet for new cryogenic fuels.

In 1992, a staff meeting voted him out of office as general director of the bureau, although he retained the position of general designer. He is a Doctor of Technical Sciences (1963); a Correspondent Member of the USSR Academy of Sciences (1982); and an

Aleksei Tupolev
General designer of ANTK named after A. N. Tupolev

Acting Member of the USSR Academy of Sciences (1984). He has received a number of awards and distinctions from the Soviet government; these include the Znak Pocheta (Sign of Honour), 1957; the Order of the Labour Red Banner, 1966; the 'Hammer and Sickle' Gold Medal of a Hero of the Socialist Labour, 1972; and the Order of the Bulgarian People's Republic (1st Degree), 1986. For the Tu-123 missile, he was awarded a 'Laureat of the State Premium' in 1967, and for the Tu-154B, he received a Laureat of the Lenin Premium in 1980.

Valentin Tikhonovich
Klimov

Valentin Klimov
General Director of ANTK

Born in Moscow on 15 August 1939, Valentin Klimov graduated from the Moscow Aviation Technical Institute, a third level college for aeronautical engineers, in 1961. He submitted his first thesis in 1972, and was awarded the qualification of Doctor of Technical Sciences in 1982. He is an Academician of the Russian Federation Academy of Quality Problems.

In September 1961, he joined what would become the Tupolev Design Bureau twelve years later, as an engineer. Later, he became an engineer-designer, rising through the third category to the first and attaining the level of leading engineer by 1982. In April of that year he was appointed head of the Tupolev flight test and development base at Zhukovski, where he worked on programmes including the Tu-160 'Blackjack', the Tu-22M, the Tu-154M and Tu-155, and the Tu-204.

In December 1990, he became general director of Aviaexport, the Soviet government's sole sale agents for the aviation industry in international markets. However, when he was elected to the position of general director of the ANTK, named after A. N. Tupolev in May 1992, he returned to his first employer.

Valentin Klimov has taken on a difficult job at a time when the aviation industry and Russia are having to face enormous problems in learning to deal with a new order. The first noticeable effect of his leadership was the Presidential decree issued on 6 June 1995 regarding the formation of the Russian Aviation Consortium – a union of business, operational and financial interests to promote Tupolev airline development and marketing.

The Design Bureau Story

What was to become the Tupolev Design Bureau and the Tupolev Aviation Complex was never actually founded; rather, it evolved. And its evolution is a story in itself.

Fifty years later, Andrei Nikolaevich Tupolev ascribed its foundation to the establishment by the TsAGI (the Central Aero and Hydrodynamics Institute, where he was deputy to N. E. Zhukovski, the director) of a 'commission on the construction of metal aircraft'. The commission was set up on 22 September 1922. Tupolev was its chairman, and the other members were I. I. Sidorin, G. A. Ozerov and I. I. Pogosski. The commission took responsibility for two new TsAGI divisions, one for testing aviation materials and construction methods, the О И АМ и К, or OIAM and K in English, and the second, the division of aviation, hydroaviation (seaplane) and experimental test construction, the А Г ОС or AGOS, which were fully established by 1924/25. In the first months of the commission, Tupolev had four assistants – I. I. Pogosski (a commission member), V. M. Petliakov, A. I. Putilov and N. S. Nekrasov – and five engineers and pilots – B. M. Kondorski, N. I. Podkluchnikov, E. I. Pogosski, T. P. Saprykin and N. I. Petrov, the pilot. There were also three designers: D. N. Osipov, A. P. Golubkov, and I. F. Nezval. This nucleus stood at 11,200 by the beginning of the 1990s, having peaked at 16,423 in 1979.

The first workshops of the commission were not elaborate – the first aircraft built by the team, the ANT-1, was constructed on the second floor of a merchant's mansion in Radio Street, which later became the scientific memorial museum dedicated to N. E. Zhukovski. The second aircraft, the ANT-2, which had a ten-metre (almost thirty-three-foot) wing span, just could not be fitted in, so it was built piece by piece in an empty storage area on the second floor of a barn then being used as a fire shed, and was assembled in the yard under a cover.

All this was somewhat impractical, and Tupolev sought better accommodation. This he found at No. 16 Radio Street, a three-storey building still in existence seventy years later. Machine tools and equipment were set up on the ground floor; on the second floor was V. M. Petliakov's design team and an area for the assembly of large parts (such as wings). The ANT-4's twelve-metre/39.4-foot wings were assembled there. They were brought out by knocking down a wall, carrying them out by hand, and lowering them to the ground on a purpose-built pandus/hoist. Then the wall was fitted with gates for a while before it was eventually rebuilt. Even in 1994, the patchwork was still visible on the wall. In 1927, the ANT-3 boat was built there, and was brought out in the same way.

The first buildings purpose-built for the commission were completed by the beginning of October 1925; they comprised laboratories for aerodynamics, engine development and experimental materials. Meanwhile, at the corner of Nemetskaya and Voznesenskaya streets the new building for the AGOS was well under way, and late in 1926 it was occupied. The ANT-6/TB-3 was built there, but by the early 1930s it was obvious that more space was needed as aircraft were growing in size and complexity. So design work began for a new building for the KOSOS (the design division for test construction) and for the ZOK (the factory of experimental constructions).

The design bureau offices on the Yauza Embankment at the corner of Radio Street
Maksimillian B. Saukke Collection

Aleksander Nekrasov
Academician, author of a number of works on mechanics

Evgeny Stoman
Head of Test Flight service

Timofei Saprykin
Head of the Undercarriage Development Department

Aleksei Cheremukhin
Deputy Chief Designer on durability

Konstantin Polishuk
Head of Design on heated glass and meters for measurement of fuel capacity

Georgy Ozerov
Deputy Chief Designer

In 1931, the People's Commissariat of Heavy Industry decided to reorganise the TsAGI. In August, it was joined with factory N39 under the design bureau led by Sergei Ilyushin, and Tupolev was appointed his assistant with responsibility for TsAGI and the Central Design Bureau (TsKB). In a further reorganisation in May 1932, the TsKB was restructured into the SOS (section for experimental aircraft construction) with S. V. Ilyushin as its deputy director, and responsible for the TsAGI. There were a number of divisions in the SOS, including Tupolev's design division.

But in January 1933, the TsAGI regained its former independence and the ZOK factory had begun to work. The first aircraft to be built here was the ANT-16/TB-4, a large six-engined aircraft. By 1934, the ZOK included three aircraft-building workshops situated in a large assembly hall, with five OKB brigades (design teams) supporting them. By then the design brigades had been reorganised into specialist categories. Up until then, for example, the brigade led by V. M. Petliakov was responsible for the design of the wings for all ANT aircraft. Now the teams were assigned to different categories. These were:

		LED BY
N1	Heavy Aircraft	V. M. Petliakov
N2	Hydroplanes	I. I. Pogosski (after he died in April 1934, he was succeeded by A. P. Golubkov)
N3	Fighters and Experimental Aircraft	P. O. Sukhoi
N5	High-Speed Military Aircraft including Passenger Modifications	A. A. Arkhangelski
N6	Experimental Aircraft	V. M. Myasishchev
N10	Torpedo Boats	N. S. Nekrasov

Additionally there were brigades set up for particular tasks, including:

		LED BY
N7	Propellers/Airscrews	V. L. Aleksandrov
N8	Power Installation	E. I. Pogosski
N9	Undercarriages	M. N. Petrov

This system simplified Tupolev's responsibility for technical leadership, and added authority and responsibility for the brigade leaders as well as increasing their independence. It substantially sped up the design work.

Aleksander Arkhangelski
First Deputy; Chief Designer, ANT-9, SB (ANT-40)

In July 1936, KOSOS and ZOK were made into factory N156 of NKTP – the People's Commissariat of Heavy Industry. Also that year, Arkhangelski's brigade was separated, and became an independent OKB. It moved to new premises at serial production factory N22. Staff numbers had reached 4,391 by 1936. These structures lasted until October 1937. However, on the evening of the twenty-first Tupolev was arrested, as were many other leaders of industry at that time. The TsAGI's OKB was effectively split up, and for almost two years virtually no design work was done.

With the advent of World War Two, Josef Stalin and his security chief Lavrenti Beria set up a special design bureau of prisoners under Beria's secret police, TsKB (Central Design Bureau) – N29 of the NKVD. Although by that time Tupolev had spent over a year in prison, when he was called to work in TsKB-29 he agreed. He was tasked with designing a combat dive bomber, and first of all selected his team from prisoners in the NKVD gulag system. Early in 1940, the 150 or so prisoner experts were moved to Moscow, back to Tupolev's facilities in the KOSOS building. Effectively, their selection by Tupolev and their agreeing to work with TsKB-29 saved their lives, for few survived the desperate conditions of the gulag camps in the war years. His new team was literally most of Soviet aviation's technical élite. There were some specialists from other industries with skills which were useful to the team's work, including automobile/car factories, metalworks, electronics, physics, materials (including plastics), as well as senior specialist members of the Academy of Sciences and Research bodies.

The invasion of the Soviet Union by German forces on 22 June 1941 resulted in the prisoners increasing their determination and their effort. Apart from their standard twelve-hour working day, one of their first extra tasks was to build a bomb shelter; Tupolev himself worked on it using a spade and an axe. The shelter was completed by 20 July, two days before the first German bombs fell on Moscow. The next day, 21 July, Tupolev did not turn up for work, something unheard of in prison terms. It turned out that he, and some twenty others, had been granted clemency (but not pardoned) by the Supreme Soviet twelve days earlier. The other prisoners were informed of this and of their own reprieve on 8 August while they were being transferred from Moscow to Omsk as part of the major industrial evacuation of the city caused by the German advance.

In Omsk, still under the designation TsKB-29 of the NKVD, the bureau was put to work in a partially completed factory intended to assemble cars and trucks. They continued to work on the dive bomber, which by now was designated the Tu-2/ANT-58/103, and the vehicle factory was developed into an aircraft production facility. That autumn, TsKB-29 was 'released' from its NKVD connections and redesignated factory N156. A year later, in autumn 1943, the design bureau was returned to Moscow, leaving the production factory at work in Omsk. It is still at work there today producing the An-72/74, with little connection to Tupolev. The bureau was re-established in its former facilities, the KOSOS and ZOK buildings on the Yauza river embankment. At the end of the war, there were 3,397 staff working in the design bureau. Two years later, this figure had grown to 5,226.

With the Tu-4 programme and the development of jet aircraft, the years following the great patriotic war were busy indeed for the design bureau. The Zhukovski Flight Test and Development Base, the ZLiDB, was established between 1949 and 1951, and some 4,000 staff worked there at the beginning of the 1990s. The premises on the Yauza embankment were expanded between 1952 and 1954 with a new factory building (N8) and design offices (N14) being constructed.

The first branch office was created in 1945 at Kazan at factory N22. It has worked since then on the serial production questions for the Tu-4, Tu-16, Tu-22, Tu-145 (Tu-22M) and Tu-160. It includes both a design office and an experimental production facility. A second branch design office was established in the town of Tomilino, some thirty kilometres from Moscow, in 1954. It had its own separate design and test production facilities. The first projects on which it worked included Tu-4, Tu-104 and Tu-16 modifications, and the development of pilotless (drone) aircraft. The next branch was set up in March 1956 at Kuibyshev in aircraft factory N18. Today, Kuibyshev has been renamed Samara. There is a design office and a small test production division there, and it has worked mainly on the Tu-95/-142 programme and on the Tu-154, including modifications, assembly parts and spares for both types. The Voronezh branch office was set up in 1961 at factory N64, where the Tu-16, Tu-128 and Tu-144 were produced. Although today more associated with Ilyushin production, it still retains Tupolev design offices.

Ulyanovsk also had a branch office formed in 1988 with Tupolev representation for the Tu-204 programme. In 1993 it was re-formed as a separate legal body still retaining its ANTK branch office status. Representation offices are situated in Taganrog at the Dimitrov production factory where the Tu-142 was produced, and at the Kiev production factory where the new Tu-334 will be built. Another branch office had been established in Moscow as far back as 1945 at the timber processing facility of factory N301. This built wooden test models as well as furniture for the workshops and design offices; in 1949 it began to produce metal components, including flaps, slats, tailplanes and large-scale wind tunnel models.

The 1950s and up to the mid-1960s was a golden period for Soviet aviation. Tupolev's design bureau developed the first Soviet jet bombers just after the war, and went on to design the Tu-95, a strategic bomber which led on to the Tu-114, the world's largest aircraft which served from the late 1950s until the early 1970s on long-range commercial routes. The bureau also developed what could reasonably be described as the world's first successful jet airliner, the Tu-104; using the Tu-16 *Badger* as a basis, the -104 entered passenger service in 1956 and stayed in service until 1975. It led to a range of other jetliners – the Tu-110, -124, -134 and -154 – and the first supersonic airliner to fly, the Tu-144.

Staff numbers grew as the programmes grew: from 5,205 in 1949, the bureau's employment had reached 11,255 ten years later, passing through 10,000 in 1958. In 1972, at the time of Tupolev's death, 15,240

A. N. Tupolev at his desk in 1970
Maksimillian B. Saukke Collection

worked in the bureau.

Tupolev remained general designer (and effectively chief executive) of the bureau until his death. Almost uniquely in Soviet industry, he was succeeded by his son Aleksei, whom Tupolev had appointed a chief designer of pilotless aircraft in the 1950s and of the Tu-144 supersonic airliner programme in the 1960s.

In 1973, the design bureau was at last named after its founder and father. To mark his huge contribution to Soviet aviation, a government decree changed the name to MMZ 'Opyt' ANTK imeni A. N. Tupolev – the Moscow Engineering Factory 'Opyt' (experience) Aviation Scientific and Technical Complex named after A. N. Tupolev. It was normal for industries to be posthumously named after their founder. This title lasted until 1989, when the MMZ 'Opyt' section was dropped.

Tupolev had always stood by his workers: with the low pay rates normal in the Soviet Union, he had arranged that most of his staff would live in apartment houses built for the bureau. That, too, was normal in the USSR, but Tupolev staff lived either close to the bureau or at least on a direct metro/underground line which meant that most took no longer than twenty to thirty minutes to reach work, and he arranged better health care than was available to most Soviet citizens. He also organised rest resorts for his staff near Moscow and on the Black Sea coast. Termed 'health resorts', these were in fact holiday resorts.

For the next nineteen years the bureau felt the slow-down in economic activity that affected the whole of

Soviet industry. Some work continued on unmanned vehicles and missiles, and programmes which were in production had to be maintained, but the number of new programmes dropped considerably. Only two new aircraft made their first flights under the leadership of Aleksei Tupolev – the world's largest production bomber, the supersonic Tu-160, in 1981, and a new 214-seat airliner, the Tu-204, in 1989. He also led the Tu-155 programme in a search for aviation fuels of the future.

After the April 1992 bureau staff vote, the new task of negotiating with the new Russian government for funds to pay salaries and to develop new and existing programmes fell to Valentin Klimov. With money shortages and rampant inflation in the country, and with the old structures giving no part of the sales income to the designers, he had, and has, a very difficult job. The money problems contributed to delays of three years and more to the Tu-204 programme, vitally needed both by the bureau and by the region's airlines; also held back was the new 100-seater Tu-334.

The collapse of the Soviet Union had another effect – industrial privatisation. Before, the people (with the government as their representative) owned everything. Now the time had come to transfer ownership from the people collectively to the people individually. As a first step, the government issued every citizen of Russia with a privatisation voucher which entitled them to get a share (in the Western sense of 'stocks and shares') in a body of their choice. Many chose to invest in their employer. In some cases, including that of the Tupolev Aviation Complex, the government retained a strategic interest usually for a finite specified period, and the balance of the equity was to be sold for what-

A

B

C

A Leonid Kerber
Deputy Chief Designer on equipment

B Aleksei Mesheriakov
Chief Engineer of the experimental factory

C Aleksander Nadashkevich
Deputy Chief Designer for armaments

D Aleksander Bonin
Deputy Chief Designer for hydraulic systems

E Abram Fainshtein
Head of the works for installation of plastics

D

E

Left: **Yuri Voroblev** *Chief Designer Tu-204C*
Centre: **Aleksander Pukhov** *Chief Designer of Tu-144 laboratory*
Back right: **Oleg Alasheev** *Deputy Chief Designer 204 programme*
Front right: **Yuli Kashtanov** *Deputy Director-General, Interpre*

Tupolev Management at Mosaeroshaw Conference 1995
Left: **Aleksei Tupolev** *General Designer*
Right: **Valentin Klimov** *General Director*

The current headquarters of the Tupolev Aviation Complex on the Yauza Embankment
Maksimillian B. Saukke Collection

ever cash could be raised in order to give the organisation much needed money. So, in December 1992 the Tupolev Aviation Complex was registered as a 'shareholders' society of the open type' with a 'constitutional capital' of 462.5 million roubles (at 1992 prices). The new company began by negotiating new agreements with the factories building Tupolev designs; for the first time, these were commercial agreements defining the responsibilities and benefits for each side.

The first major result of all this work was announced on 6 June 1995. Russia's president, Boris Yeltsin, issued a decree which announced the formation of the Russian Aviation Consortium, a grouping of Tupolev, the Aviastar production factory at Ulyanovsk, Aviadvigatel – the Perm-based designers of the Tu-204's PS-90A engine and the engine's manufacturer, Aeroflot – Russian International Airlines, the state-owned (at the time) airline likely to be a major -204 and -334 customer, and the Universal Scientific Production Centre. The consortium was given worthwhile fiscal concessions and promises of government support to solve the problems delaying the badly needed new generation of aircraft.

At the time of writing, Russia and the former Soviet Union has ten major design bureaux and some thirty-four aircraft production factories. It seems unlikely that all will survive unless the country returns to communism. Valentin Klimov and his team have a complex job ahead of them.

Back:
Boris Levanovich *Deputy Chief Designer of Tu-160*
Leonid Kulokov *Chief Designer of missiles*
Vladimir Andreev *Chief Designer of Tu-155*

Front:
Interpreter *(Irina)*
Lev Lanovski *Chief Designer – Tu-204 programme*
Igor Kalygin *Chief Designer – Tu-334*

Aerosleighs

Although Tupolev had decided under Zhukovski's tutelage that his future lay in aviation, and that metal aircraft would become the norm, he still needed to develop and test his theories.

In August 1919, the Council for Labour and Defence decided to build sleighs for the use of the Red Army. A commission was set up to build these powered sleighs, called aerosleighs, and Tupolev was appointed deputy chairman of the commission. This gave him the opportunity to use metals, and to observe the results. Six sleighs were constructed; Tupolev described their evolvement as: 'Gradual, step by step from detailed research of the shapes, the tubes and pipes, the riveting and corrugation, the designs were developed into logical possibilities.' This was to be his way of working for the whole of his life. Step by step. Experience gained in each stage led on to the next move forward. No giant steps – just one at a time, thoroughly.

He designed his first aerosleigh with a body similar in many respects to that of an aircraft. Tests proved that his understanding of the qualities of the materials was accurate. Completed in 1921, the ANT-I was 5.13m/16.8 foot long including skis, and was powered by a 38hp Bristol Anzani engine; it was made of wood and metal. A second ANT-I was built in 1925. Both were two-seaters. The ANT-II was bigger, with five seats. Powered by a Clerget 115hp engine, its empty weight was 680kg/1,500lb, and it could carry a 480kg/1,057lb load. It was also made of wood and metal.

The ANT-III was the first all-metal aerosleigh and was completed in February 1923. A three-seater, it was powered by an 80hp Gnôme-Rhône engine. The ANT-IV and -V were completed together in January 1924. The first was a five-seater and the second carried three. They were powered by 100hp engines – the Mikulin M-11 for the IV and the Bristol Lucifer for the V. After state tests, they were put into production in 1926 at Kolchuginsk, where duraluminium was manufactured. In 1933 they were also put into production in Leningrad (now St Petersburg). The ANT-IV was shown at an international exhibition in Berlin in 1928.

Tupolev's aerosleighs were widely used by the Red Army. They served in expeditions in the Arctic and in the Far East, and in the Finnish war in 1939–40, and in the Great Patriotic War (1941–1945).

The ANT-VI followed in 1926, and ANT-VII in 1934. Then, in 1961, G. Makhotkin was the chief designer of a new range of amphibious aerosleighs called the AZ which, with no modification, could be used in any climatic conditions. The AZ was demonstrated widely in Europe, the Americas, Canada, and Asia, where its abilities led to 150 examples being built at Moscow factory N81, and, later, another 650 at Mukhachev in the western Ukraine. They served until the late 1980s.

The ANT-IV aerosleigh
Maksimillian B. Saukke Collection

Airships

In the 1910s, Tupolev had designed and built a few gliders to test out some of his theories on aerodynamics. Control of these was exercised by the pilot leaning his weight in the direction he wished to go, much like the hang gliders of the 1980s.

In September 1924, he designed and built some experimental models for airship sections, and went on to build a nacelle, or cabin, and the empennage for an airship named *Chemist – Resinshik to Ilych*. The airship was a non-rigid and the cabin held four people. It made its first flight on 7 June 1926, with R. N.

Nizhevski in command. Later, in 1931 and 1932, the TsAGI, under Tupolev's leadership, designed and manufactured metal (duraluminium) nacelles, the empennages, equipment and engine mounts for two Soviet airships, the USSR-V-1/D3 and the USSR-V-2/D4. Both airships made their first flights in April 1932. The V-1 had a volume of 2,200 cubic metres, and was powered by two 55hp motors and had a payload of 780kg/1,720lb; the V-2 was larger, with a volume of 5,000 cubic metres and two 169hp engines. Its payload was 1,842kg/4,061lb.

Torpedo Boats and Cutters

Two Tupolev-designed G-5/ANT-5s, at sea
Konstantin Udalov/Avico Press Collection

With the research he had done in the IMTU, working under Zhukovski, and on the thesis for his degree (which was on hydroplane design), it was natural that Tupolev would wish to expand his knowledge of the relationship between water and vessels. So, in preparation for his first hydroplane, he began to design boats. In October 1920, work started on a speedboat,

the ANT-1. It was completed in autumn 1922, and Tupolev himself tested it on the Moskva River in November that year; with a 160hp engine, the boat gave good results, achieving a speed of 40.4 knots/75kph. Meanwhile, a base was being established in the Black Sea port of Sevastopol (then in Russia, but later given by Stalin to the Ukraine), which would serve as a test centre for ships and boats.

The first all-metal boat, the ANT-2, was begun in

June 1923, and five months later Tupolev again was testing it, this time on the Yauza River beside the TsAGI's base; with a 30hp engine it could travel at 21.5 knots/40kph. Later the engine was replaced with a 75hp, and it served between Cheboksari and Vasilsursk.

That year, 1923, Tupolev was asked to design a twin-engined torpedo boat, with a provision that it had to be faster than cutters captured from England's Royal Navy. He started by designing shapes which he had made up at Kolchuginsk, and by testing them in tanks. The result was the GANT (Hydro, or Gidro ANT-) -3 which he named *Pervenets* (first born). It was completed in March 1927 and was sent to Sevastopol for testing. With a nine-tonne displacement, it was the first duraluminium speedboat designed to serve in the open sea. It carried a 450mm/ 17.7 inch torpedo, and two 7.62mm machine-guns. With two 600hp engines, its maximum speed was fifty knots, and cruise was thirty knots. It carried radios for receiving and transmitting, and had a crew of four. In trials, it turned out that the propeller pitch needed adjustment which Tupolev himself did on site with a hammer.

Tupolev, with the head of the Technical Department of the Navy, got an English cutter to ride parallel with his new GANT-3; he had the throttle set at 1,400rpm (instead of the maximum 2,400rpm) and allowed the rival vessel to draw a little ahead. The other crew were delighted. Then they turned around to head back. Now, he ordered full power, and the engineer on the other boat had to check his engine to see why it had stopped. It hadn't! Corrosion was soon evident, and led Tupolev to anodise his metals for naval use.

Next came the ANT-4, called the Sh-4. Fifty-nine were built in Leningrad between 1927 and 1931, and it served in the Caspian Sea, the Baltic, the Black Sea and the Far East. It entered service on 8 April 1929, under the decreed name *Tupolev*. Later came the G-5/ANT-5, which carried two 533mm/21-inch torpedoes. Some 329 were built in Leningrad between 1933 and 1943, and they served in the war. Single copies of the G-6 and G-8 were built, in 1933 and 1936, although another G-8 was factory-built in 1939.

The ANT-1 in the yard at Radio Street
Konstantin Udalov/Avico Press Collection

A. N. Tupolev (with his hand on the cockpit) and his workers beside the ANT-1
Tupolev

The ANT-1

Tupolev's First Aircraft

Tupolev's first aircraft followed his initial work on aerosleighs and boats. It was never intended to be any more than a method of checking out his theories and to advance Soviet understanding of the use of metals in the construction of aircraft. It was a simple, single-seat, single-engine, low-wing cantilever monoplane, described as an aerobatic sports plane, made from a combination of wood and metal with linen fabric coverings. Aluminium was used in the wing partitions and ribs, on the vertical and horizontal tailplanes, and in some other smaller areas. All other load bearing structures were made of wood, and linen was used to cover the wings and fuselage. Power was provided by a thirty-five horsepower Bristol Anzani engine, a six-cylinder radial.

Design of the ANT-1 was not officially started until early 1922 – it had evolved in Tupolev's thinking in the course of the previous year. Construction began in the backyard of the Raek Tavern, close to TsAGI's design offices, in June 1922, and continued for sixteen months. It was completed in October 1923, brought to Ekaterininskaya Square, now Krasnokazarmenaya

Street, from where it made its first flight on the twenty-first of that month. Yevgeni Pogosski was the pilot; he earned his place in Tupolev's history as the first person to fly a Tupolev-designed aircraft. With a maximum take-off weight of 360kg/794lb and an empty weight of 230kg/507lb, the ANT-1 could only carry 130kg/287lb, including the weight of the pilot and fuel. This resulted in a maximum range of 540 kilometres/335 miles.

The ANT-1 was flown regularly over the next two years to help evaluate Tupolev's theories. Later, it was stored in the KOSOS assembly workshop in factory N156. In the late 1930s/early 1940s, it was suspended from the ceiling at an altitude of about eight metres/twenty-six feet. However, with the disruptions to the bureau caused by imprisonment and the war, it had disappeared by the time the war ended. Its subsequent fate is not known, although it is likely to have been destroyed along with all the early Tupolev records at the time of the German advance on Moscow in the summer of 1941. Only one example was built.

ANT-2

The first Soviet all-metal aircraft

The first ANT-2 in the yard at Radio Street
Konstantin Udalov/Avico Press Collection

By late 1922, Tupolev was convinced that metal offered many advantages for the fledgling Soviet aviation industry. The greater durability of light metal alloys compared to wood, combined with their construction potential and their advantages in the severe Russian winters, led him to the view that wood held few prospects of meeting the needs of the industry's future.

Thus, a special commission was established at TsAGI to promote the construction of metal aircraft. Its formation, on 21 October 1922, was later regarded by Tupolev as the birth of the bureau which would, after his death, bear his name. It was headed by Andrei Nikolaevich and its first task was to establish facilities for the production of duraluminium alloys which could be used for aircraft manufacture. A factory had already been selected in the town of Kolchuginsk in the Vladimir region, some 120 kilometres/75 miles from Moscow. A high-grade alloy was developed there, which was named Kolchugaluminium; the first ingots of the new metal were produced in September 1922, and this in turn led to the establishment of the commission with a mandate to begin work on constructing an all-metal aircraft, and to develop ways of testing the strengths of components. Tupolev set up a design bureau within TsAGI, with fifteen engineers, technicians and draughtsmen, and the first components produced were used to train craftsmen in

the new materials.

Tupolev regarded the birth of duraluminium as the birth of the aviation industry of the Soviet Union. Combined with the development of the crafts skills needed were the problems of developing alloy production skills; Tupolev and TsAGI, along with the Kolchuginsk factory, had to find answers to all the questions. Alloy production methods were developed which proved to be very different to those of Junkers, the German leaders in the field, but just as effective – some would say even better. All this led to Tupolev taking the then courageous decision to produce an all-metal aircraft. Tupolev was later to gain great respect for his ability to make progress without taking major risks, so his first venture into this new area was made cautiously. Many of the trials on the new materials were made on his aerosleighs and boats, and on gliders before he was satisfied that it was safe to move on.

Work began on the first Soviet all-metal aircraft, the ANT-2, in 1923. It was built in the AGOS division of TsAGI, on the first and third floors of 16 Radio Street. It emerged as a high-wing monoplane with an unusual triangular fuselage cross-section – an arrangement which proved useful both because of the extra strength and rigidity which it offered, which avoided most of the need for fuselage struts to maintain shape, and because of the aerodynamic benefit which avoided vortex drag under the rear fuselage. The fuselage was in three sections: the first allowed easy access to the engine for inspection; the second was an enclosed compartment which could hold two passengers, facing each other; and the third section, left vacant, was the tail elements. Entrance to the second section was through a door on the left side of the fuselage. The passenger compartment was located behind and below the cockpit, where the pilot sat with an open canopy.

The wing had two spars (a double spar) which supported ribs, and was attached to the fuselage by four bolts. The forward spar featured a cutaway section to allow cockpit space. The tail was a cantilever section; in early flight trials, this was the only element of the design which needed any change, and the fin and rudder were both increased slightly in size on the

funds to purchase a squadron of reconnaissance aircraft, consisting of nineteen Dux R-1 aircraft, a Soviet-built 'combination' of the de Havilland DH-4 and DH-9. When all nineteen R-1s were lined up for the presentation, the new ANT-2 was added to the right of the line as the twentieth aircraft.

The ANT-2 had a take-off weight of 837.5kg/1,846lb and an empty weight of 523kg/1,153lb, giving it a payload of 314.5kg/693lb, which, according to the flight test report published in mid-1924, allowed it to carry 'a pilot – 80kg; two passengers – 160.7kg; fuel 54.9kg and oil 4.8kg; other items – 11.6kg'. This gave the aircraft a range of 750km and a ceiling of 3,300m, with a maximum speed of 169kph/105mph. The second aircraft, the ANT-2bis, joined in the extended test programme to prove the theories of Tupolev. It

One of the production ANT-2s shown on skis
Maksimillian B. Saukke Collection

second aircraft – two only were built by TsAGI. Power was provided by a single Bristol Lucifer three-cylinder radial engine which generated 100hp.

The first aircraft was completed in May 1924, and Nikolai Petrov was its pilot on the first flight, which took place on the twenty-sixth of that month, an important date in Soviet aviation history. Handling qualities on the ANT-2 were good, particularly when the tail had been enlarged; for the first flight, two sacks filled with sand represented passengers in weight terms.

A few days later, on 1 June, there was an 'air parade' held at the Central Moscow Aerodrome, Khodinka. The Society of Friends of the Air Fleet had gathered

was also built at the AGOS. The ANT-2 could be fitted with either a wheel or ski undercarriage.

While the small cabin of the ANT-2 allowed two passengers to be carried, its size and economics made it unsuitable for most airline services. But it paved the way for later airliners, and was an important factor in their development. Some sources report that up to twenty ANT-2s were produced, but Tupolev are confident that five is the correct production figure. These were used for a short while on a route linking Moscow and Nizhni Novgorod (then called Gorki). Unfortunately, no documents can be found to support this. The first ANT-2 is preserved at the Monino air force museum near Moscow.

ANT-3 (Military Designation R-3)

Tupolev's First Production Aircraft

The experience gained on his first two aircraft was put to good effect on Tupolev's next design, the ANT-3. With the Air Force commanders now convinced of the practicalities and capabilities of metal in aircraft construction, the AGOS-TsAGI team led by Tupolev set about designing the first all-metal aircraft for the Soviet military.

Design work started on 1 August 1924, and July 1925 saw the prototype ANT-3, a two-seat 'sesquiplane' (a biplane where the lower wing was noticeably shorter than the upper wing), being rolled out from the AGOS factory. The first flight was made on 6 August, flown by V. N. Filippov, who conducted TsAGI's tests of the aircraft which continued until October. Air Force and State tests continued until May 1926 in a programme headed by M. M. Gromov, and produced very favourable reports which led to orders from the Air Force.

The ANT-3 was designed as a reconnaissance aircraft, hence its later Air Force designation R-3 (R = Razvedchik = Reconnaissance). It was a two-seater permitting the pilot to be supported by a gunner/observer who stood in a second cockpit immediately behind the first. The sesquiplane arrangement was supported by a single strut on each wing with cross bracing wires in a very conventional arrangement for the time. Again, Tupolev used a triangular fuselage section and the fuselage skin was of

corrugated duraluminium.

The prototype was powered by a single 400hp Liberty engine, and the second aircraft, also built at AGOS, by a 450hp Napier Lion. But Tupolev had intended from the start that a range of different engines could be used on the aircraft, and production aircraft were fitted initially with the 450hp Lorraine-Dietrich (seventy-nine aircraft), one with a BMW-V1 engine which gave 500hp, and twenty-one more with the 450hp Mikulin M-5. Production continued at Gos Avia Zavod (GAZ) 5 from 1926 until 1929. Later this factory was to be called 'Krasnyi Oktiabr' (Red October), and later again, Factory No. 22.

The Soviet government and the Air Force were well pleased with the ANT-3, as much for its capabilities and service as the image it portrayed to the world of the modern and efficient capabilities of Soviet industry. But more would have been built if industry had been able to build them: metal supply was not as plentiful as the government or industry would have liked. Still, the government decided to avail itself of the propaganda opportunities offered by the aircraft, and a commission was established to prepare foreign itineraries for the ANT-3.

In summer 1926, a French pilot, Michel Arroshar, visited Moscow, flying in from Paris. The commission decided to respond to this by sending Mikhail Gromov to the major European capitals in an ANT-3, registered RR-SOV. On the journey, he was accompanied by a mechanic, Yevgeny Radzevich. He set out at 3.00

ANT-3 RR-SOV *Proletarii* **at Khodinka in 1926**
Maksimillian B. Saukke Collection

A line of Red Air Force R-3s
Konstantin Udalov/Avico Press Collection

a.m. on 30 August, and headed west at about 300 metres/975ft altitude. But 120 kilometres/75 miles later, an expansion tank holding water for the Napier Lion engine suffered three fatigue cracks, and water started spraying into the cockpit. Gromov, who lived till he was eighty-five, exercised prudence and returned home. (Newspapers reported his return as being due to poor weather conditions. Heavy rain in the cockpit!) Tupolev advised that the tank should be given a convex base, and the following morning the *Proletarii*, as the aircraft was named, headed out again.

By the time it landed at Koningsberg (now Kaliningrad), the radiator was leaking. Gromov decided to head for Berlin, where the local mechanics were not able to solve the problem. So he headed on to Paris. There, a French mechanic discovered that some putty sealant had fallen off. He took a radiator from another aircraft, made some small changes, and fitted it to the ANT-3. Then Gromov was off again, this time heading for Rome. On the rollout from the hangar, a black cat crossed in front of the aircraft. For Russians, this means bad luck; but it did not deter Gromov – he decided to take the English version, which regards it as lucky. Weather on take-off from Paris was poor, but by Lyons, it had cleared up allowing Gromov to fly over the Alps and head for Turin, then to Genoa and finally to Rome. It took longer than expected to refuel the aircraft, and darkness was not very far away when they took off again, heading north for Vienna. The sun was setting as they crossed the Swiss Alps, and twilight came when they were 120km/75 miles from Vienna; 20km/12 miles away, it was pitch dark, but the competent Gromov saw campfires around the city's airport, and landed safely. On the following morning, the flight was due to have been seen off by VIP delegates, including the Soviet ambassador to Austria, but the delegates arrived late, and Gromov, anxious to make his deadline for Moscow, had gone.

Bad weather prevented their landing at Prague, but the time of their overflight was noted, and they continued to Warsaw, where Soviet Embassy staff gave them flowers which they asked should be dropped from the aircraft over Soviet territory. This was done, even though it was also considered to be unlucky to do so. In less than three days, Gromov had covered 7,150km/4,443 miles in thirty-four hours and fifteen minutes' flight time.

In 1927, the British minister at the Foreign Office, Austin Chamberlain, a brother of the later Prime Minister, Neville, broke off diplomatic relations with the Soviet Union. So the next foreign venture by an ANT-3, from Moscow to Tokyo and back, which was made between 20 August and 1 September 1927, was made by an aircraft named *Our Reply* (to Chamberlain). The voyage was named 'The Great Eastern Overflight', and the pilot for the journey was Semion Shestakov; it covered some 22,000 kilometres/13,671 miles in 153 flying hours. The route was Moscow–Sarapul–Omsk–Novosibirsk–Krasnoyarsk–Irkutsk–Chita–Blagoveshensk–Nanian–Yokohama–Tokyo, and back, not perhaps the most direct of routes, but valuable for propaganda purposes. Today, the return trip takes eighteen flying hours. For this flight, the ANT-3 was a version powered by the Mikulin M-5.

Tupolev proposed an upgraded ANT-3, the R-4, to the Air Force with a 500hp Mikulin engine, but production difficulties prevented its being built. One aircraft, with a Lorraine–Dietrich engine, was delivered to Aeroflot's Yakutsk division. Under the designation PS-3 it served as a mail plane until about 1930.

The ANT-3 was Tupolev's first practical aircraft. Adequately powered, its range (950km/590 miles) and payload (790kg/1,742lb) gave it a cruising speed of 194kph/121mph and a service ceiling of 5,000 metres/16,400 feet – very acceptable for its day and its role.

ANT-4/TB-1

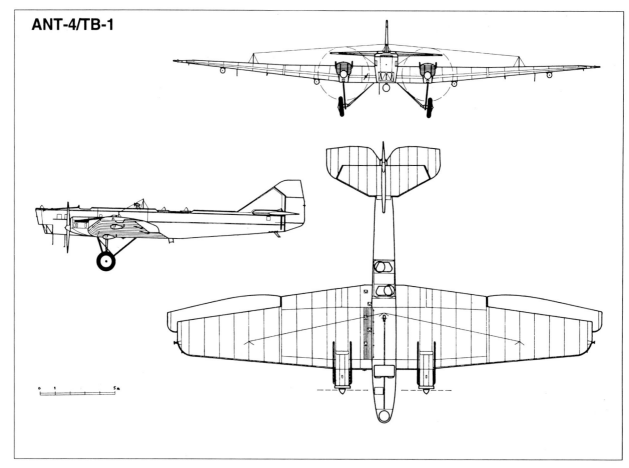

ANT-4/TB-1

Tupolev's First Multi-Engined Design

By the beginning of the 1920s, the Soviet Army had begun to examine the possibilities of heavy bombers. Before the 1917 revolution, Igor Sikorski had designed and built several four-engined aircraft, including the Ilya Muromets, five of which formed the nucleus of a bomber unit until they were retired in 1921. Sikorski, however, had emigrated to America where he was to find fame and fortune with his helicopter designs, so leaving a void in the ranks of Soviet designers; thus, with the industry not yet established, the Army and Air Force decided to order the design work of the aircraft from England. But the company approached, thought to be Bristol, asked for $2 million and two years, which the Soviet government decided was too much and too long.

Tupolev and TsAGI were just beginning to establish their names, and Tupolev offered to design and build the prototype within nine months. His offer was

accepted, and work began on the ANT-4 on 11 November 1924. The engines were to be two 450hp Napier Lions, and duraluminium was to be a major construction material. Design and construction work were carried out on the second floor of the AGOS–TsAGI workshop in Radio Street, a three-storey building. The design was to the principles by now established in Tupolev's work: it featured an all-metal corrugated skin of duraluminium, with steel used for the ribs and frame, the undercarriage, engine mounts and in the control systems. The wings consisted of a centre plane of 13.5m/44.29ft with detachable outer planes of 7.6m/24.9ft on each wing which were fixed in place by casing bolts. In order to take the wing section, when completed, out of the workshops, one of the building's walls had to be knocked down. For a while, the wall was patched up with wooden gates, which allowed the other sections of the aircraft to be taken out as they were completed; later, it was rebuilt with bricks. Seventy years later, the patchwork is still noticeable.

The prototype aircraft was completed by 11 August

1925. Tupolev had kept his word. This ANT-4 was the world's first all-metal heavy bomber and served as a prototype not only for later production ANT-4s, but also for succeeding generations of large all-metal aircraft. The aircraft was brought piece by piece to Moscow's central airfield at Khodinka, later the home of the constructors' bureau headed by S. V. Ilyushin. After reassembly, on 26 November 1925 it took off for the first time piloted by Apolinari Tomashevski, and few problems were encountered even though the ANT-4 was Russia's largest aircraft built up to that time, and few other larger aircraft had been built in other countries. The first aircraft did not carry any armaments, and was equipped with single controls for one pilot only. The test programme continued until 2 July 1926, with twenty-five flights being made in the final three weeks. It was decided that further development was required. Initially, it was decided to change the engines for more powerful Lorraine–Dietrich examples, but in April 1927, this was changed to the BMW-V1, which could give 500 to 600hp. Eventually, when the Soviet licence-built version, the Mikulin M-17 engines, became available, these would be used.

Meanwhile, the second ANT-4 was being built, again at the AGOS–TsAGI works. Powered by BMW-V1Z engines, which could give up to 730hp, it was fitted with three turrets – in the nose, mid-fuselage and tail, each of which held a Lewis machine-gun. It also had new radios and camera equipment installed. It was completed in the summer of 1928, and made its first flight on 15 August. The flight test programme

continued until 26 March 1929, and the test report was satisfactory.

The five years since design work had begun had been difficult for the Soviet aviation industry due to the problems of obtaining suitable metals. But bauxite had been found in the northern mountains and ways of producing high-grade alloys had been developed, so the nation's dependence on imported alloys was coming to an end. Thus, the ANT-4 was put into serial production at Moscow Aircraft Factory N22, with Vladimir Petliakov heading the project. The first production aircraft, fitted with BMW-VI engines of 500 to 680 hp, was completed in July 1929. Its acceptance tests were carried out between 1 August and 19 October. In the next three years, 216 ANT-4s were built there.

The ANT-4 was given the Air Force designation TB-1 (TB = Tyazheli Bombardirovshik = heavy bomber) – it was the first heavy bomber for the Soviet Air Force. In military service, it carried six crew, including three gunners each of whom operated a double set of Diagtirev machine-guns. It also carried up to a one-tonne bomb load. The TB-1 had an empty weight of 4,520kg/9,965lb and a standard take-off weight initially of 6,500kg/14,330lb, later increased to 6,810kg/15,013lb. But it was permitted, when extra fuel tanks were fitted, to increase its take-off weight to a maximum of 8,790kg/19,378lb, which greatly augmented its capabilities.

The availability of an aircraft with the range and capacity of the ANT-4 opened possibilities for the

Vakhmistrov's Zveno trials; an ANT-5/I-4 mounted on the wing of an ANT-4/TB-1
Konstantin Udalov/Avico Press Collection

Soviet leadership. The first of these was for long-range flights. To start the programme, a relatively short flight was carried out – Moscow to Voronezh and back without a stop (1,600km/994 miles). It went well. Then Stalin agreed that an intercontinental flight should be accomplished. The target selected was New York. Although crossing the Atlantic would have been the shorter route, the long, over-water stage would have been difficult, and the propaganda value of visiting important cities in Russia would have been lost, so the flight was planned for an easterly journey of more than twice the distance. Two aircraft were prepared for the journey and stripped of their armaments.

On 8 August 1929, Semion Shestakov and co-pilot Bolotov took off from Moscow in an ANT-4 named *Strana Sovetov* (Country of the Soviets). But an emergency landing in the Omsk region of Siberia damaged the aircraft, and the crew returned to Moscow. Fifteen days later in the second ANT-4 with the same name, they were off again. This time all went well. Their route brought them to Omsk, Novosibirsk, Krasnoyarsk, Chita and Khabarovsk. Here, the aircraft's wheeled undercarriage was replaced by floats, which were used for the next 7,950km/4,940 miles as Shestakov and Bolotov flew to the Aleutian Islands of Stewart and Sitka; here another engine problem resulted in an emergency landing and an engine change. Fortunately, the planning had been thorough, and a spare engine was soon on its way. Then they were airborne again, bound for Seattle. In Seattle, wheels replaced the floats, and they headed on to San Francisco, Chicago, Detroit and New York, which they reached on 3 November. They had flown 21,242km in 137 flying hours. It was the first time a Tupolev design had been seen in America, but it certainly was not to be the last. The aircraft, painted white to represent peace, returned to the Soviet Union by ship.

Meanwhile, Soviet industry was beginning to develop, and Aleksander Mikulin's aero-engine design bureau had produced a Soviet-built version of the BMW-V1 which was called the M-17. Its performance was not as high as that of its German equivalent: with BMW engines, the ANT-4 could fly some 12kph/7.5mph faster and its service ceiling was 100m/328 feet higher. But the availability of domestically produced engines was a worthwhile achievement from both the national economic and national technological points of view.

ANT-4s were quite widely used as early industry flight test beds. Apart from a single aircraft fitted with extra fuel tanks for long range, another had 'power boosters' fitted under and over each wing – three pairs on each side. These early equivalents of JATO bottles

shortened take-off from around twenty-seven seconds to a mere five. They were also used on the first of the remarkable 'links' developed by V. S. Vakhmistrov, an engineer at the VVS's Scientific and Research Institute. He proposed that long-range bombers should have fighters (which he termed 'destroyers') mounted on its wings; the 'link', as he called it, would take off with all engines running, then the fighters could throttle back, until they were needed. This would greatly increase their range for escort duty and would allow the bomber to bring its own defenders far into enemy territory. When the fighters had finished their work, they could link back on to the mother aircraft for a ride home. The idea had been tried before in other countries, but with airships, not aircraft.

Vakhmistrov's idea was well received, and he was authorised to go ahead. He developed a three-linkage system to hold each fighter, with a snap lock at the tail to catch it on retrieval to the mother ship. He called the combination 'Zveno' (aircraft group). His first mother ship was an ANT-4/TB-1; later he was provided with ANT-6/TB-3 aircraft. For the first experiment, Zveno 1, he fitted pivot pyramids and struts on the wing of the ANT-4, and wooden ramps were used to 'load' the 'destroyers' – two ANT-5/1-4 fighters. Vakhmistrov's biggest difficulty for the project was to be allowed to fly on the first mission. Originally, he had planned to go as co-pilot to release the 1-4s, but the airfield commander decided that only a suitably rated pilot should fly. After some arguing, Vakhmistrov and his assistant were allowed to go, travelling in one of the turrets. The ANT-4 was flown by A. I. Zalevski, and the fighters by V. P. Chkalov, by now the most famous Soviet aviator, and A. F. Anisimov. The take-off went well, but the co-pilot by mistake released Chkalov's aircraft too early, and only Chkalov's remarkable skill prevented an accident. Anisimov was released a few seconds later, proving that the aircraft mounted on the wings need not be released simultaneously. All three pilots and Vakhmistrov were awarded the Order of the Red Star for their work. Vakhmistrov continued his work until 1940, but the Stalin purges in the late 1930s resulted in the arrest of many of his high-level supporters. This, combined with the developing range of fighter aircraft, eventually brought an end to his projects.

Between 1933 and 1935, the ANT-4/TB-1 was used for in-flight refuelling experiments similar to the work being carried out in England where Handley Page Harrows, converted from bombers into tankers, were used to increase the range of the long-distance aircraft for Atlantic crossings. The first experiments involved a Polikarpov R-5 feeding fuel into the ANT-4; next an

A single ANT-4 survives; SSSR-N317 of Avia Arktika was preserved at the Ulyanovsk Civil Aviation Museum and shown there in 1992
Paul Duffy

ANT-4 was used as a tanker to fuel Polikarpov 1-15 and 1-16 fighters; and finally, an ANT-4 tanker was used to fuel standard ANT-4s. The ANT-4s involved in the programme were fitted with little refuelling equipment – the line had to be caught by hand on the receiving aircraft, a job which was usually left to the unfortunate gunner. ANT-4s were also used by the Air Force in parachute trials of heavy drop methods; among the loads dropped were cars, artillery cannon and even small tanks.

Some fifty-five TB-1s were modified to TB-1-P standard. This involved replacing the standard undercarriage with floats (Poplavok, which gave the 'P' suffix). These were used in coastal areas, mainly the Far East, for coastal patrols. Other TB-1s were fitted with skis for use in northern regions.

One of the highlights of the TB-1's career came in 1934. The previous summer, the steamship *Cheluskin* had left Leningrad on a voyage intended to bring it along the north coast of the Soviet Union to the Pacific. Unfortunately, almost within sight of the Bering Strait in November, the ice became impassable and the ship stuck hard. The ship was tough, and it, along with the 104 people on board, settled down for the winter. But on 12 February 1934, the ice won, and the ship was crushed. The crew, and some family members, settled down on the ice and prepared a landing strip. The first aircraft to arrive was an ANT-4 flown by Anatoli Lyapidevski, a military pilot

now working with Avia Arktika in the Far East. It reached the survivors on 5 March. Over the next week, all 104 people from the *Cheluskin* were rescued by air, in the largest aerial rescue mission mounted in the world up to that time.

The ANT-4/TB-1 served the VVS well until its retirement in 1941, at the beginning of the Great Patriotic War. From about 1933, a number of TB-1s fitted with Mikulin M-17s were withdrawn from Air Force service and transferred to Aeroflot and Avia Arktika to help in the development of civil air services under the designation G-1. The last G-1 served with Avia Arktika on reconnaissance work and carrying cargo to polar ice stations until 1948.

ANT-5/I-4

Tupolev's First Fighter

In building up his team, Tupolev had selected some outstanding and talented people. One of these was Pavel Sukhoi, later to lead his own design bureau specialising in fighter aircraft. Sukhoi was given the responsibility in autumn 1925 of developing the first fighter to be designed by the TsAGI, working within Tupolev's section. Up to then, all of Tupolev's programmes had been orientated towards developing and producing materials and systems for larger aircraft. Sukhoi's design was the first of several exceptions to this general policy.

As usual with TsAGI/Tupolev aircraft, it was constructed entirely of metal, the first Soviet fighter aircraft so developed. It was another sesquiplane, and many of the design features of the ANT-2 and ANT-3 were retained on the ANT-5. The prototype was completed in July 1927 and was fitted with a nine-cylinder Gnôme-Rhône Jupiter VI engine which developed 420hp; it underwent a factory test programme from 10 August until 25 September 1927. It was then transferred to the NII-VVS, the Scientific Research Institute of the Air Force, where Mikhail Gromov, A. Anisimov, Andrei Yumashev and A. Kozlov carried out an extensive test programme to determine its suitability for military needs. By December, before the programme was completed, the decision was taken to put the ANT-5 into production under the designation I-4 (Istrebitel = Fighter).

Soviet fighter production had got off to a slow start. In 1922, the government decided to buy abroad, and for the next five years or so, British Martinsyde F4 Buzzards, Italian Ansaldo A-1s and Dutch Fokker DXIs provided most of the numbers of Soviet fighters. But from 1925, local aircraft began to join the VVS; first came Grigorovich's I-2; then came the I-4, followed by Polikarpov's I-3. A second prototype joined the programme in July 1928, and underwent NII-VVS tests between December 1928 and April 1929. It was fitted with a Gnôme-Rhône Jupiter 9 Asb, which increased available power to 480hp.

Meanwhile, the I-4 had gone into production at factory N22 in Moscow and the first production aircraft was completed on 18 October 1928. It turned out to be heavier than the prototypes, and this reduced its performance. But the Soviet government and the Air Force had adopted a decree to replace foreign aircraft as quickly as possible in military service, and the I-4's performance was well up to international standards, so the programme continued.

The production I-4 was fitted with a Mikulin M-22 radial engine which gave 480hp. This was in fact a licence-built version of the Jupiter engine. Armament was two 7.62mm fuselage-mounted machine-guns, synchronised to fire through the propellers. Sukhoi considered the production I-4 to be 'not one of the best'. He felt that the corrugated skin, the wing ribs and stringers, the absence of strut fairings and under-carriage fairings all increased the aircraft's drag, and on a relatively small aircraft these led to substantial performance penalties. This led him to develop the I-4bis in 1931, with major external differences

The prototype ANT-5 with lower wings in place
Tupolev

Mechanic working on cylinder head of Mikulin M-22 of ANT-5/I-4
Konstantin Udalov/Avico Press Collection

including the removal of the lower wing, an increase in the length of leading edge slats, and the fitting of a new engine cowling which incorporated the engine's cylinder heads. Although this version was tested by the NII-VVS, by now the I-4 was nearing the end of its front-line service, and the version was dropped.

Altogether, production of the I-4 amounted to 369 plus the two prototypes. In common with most of its contemporaries, it stayed in front-line service for only a relatively short four and a half years before its withdrawal, in late 1933, to training duties. At its peak, the I-4 equipped some eighteen squadrons and played a valuable role in the development of Soviet fighters.

A number of I-4s were modified for test and experimental programmes. These included three aircraft prepared for Vakhmistrov's Samolet Zveno programme, where an ANT-4/TB-1 mother ship was used to launch two or more fighters. For this, the I-4s were fitted with much smaller lower wings, with connector clips to hold them in place, and with release controls. Others were tried out with different armaments. One was fitted with machine-guns on the top wing, another with two 76.2mm DEP cannons mounted under the lower wing – this was tested only against ground targets – and another had 'dynamo

reactive' (jet) cannons, designed by Kurchevski, fitted to test their effectiveness. One aircraft was fitted with 'jet boosters' (JATO bottles); three were fitted under each wing, each generating a thrust of 450kg which lasted for 2.5 seconds, by which time the aircraft was airborne. This compared to a usual twenty seconds or so. One aircraft was fitted with floats; while this was useful for water landings and take-offs, the drag reduced performance considerably.

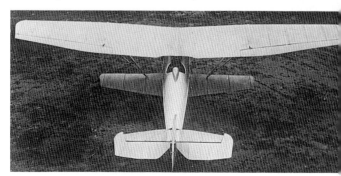

ANT-5, photographed from above and behind, clearly showing the sesquiplane layout
Konstantin Udalov/Avico Press Collection

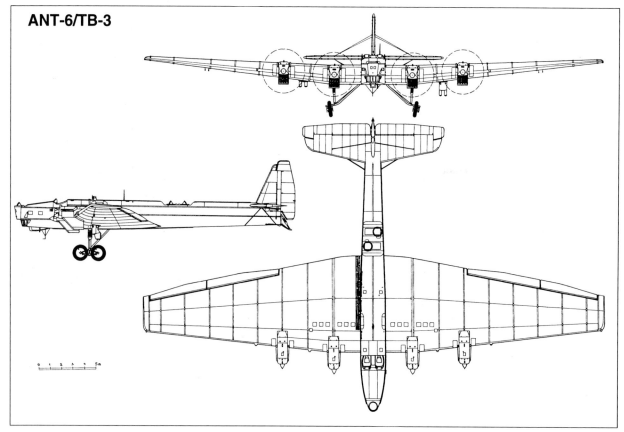

ANT-6/TB-3

ANT-6/TB-3

Aeroflot Designation – G-2

With the first flight of the ANT-4, later the TB-1, in November 1925 having proved that the Soviet Union could successfully build and operate a heavy bomber, TsAGI and Tupolev were soon being urged to develop bigger and better models. The Soviet Air Force was anxious to develop a family of bombers with similar construction and characteristics, differing only in size and capacity.

Thus, early in 1926, Vladimir Petliakov and his team were given another project – the world's first four-engined monoplane with engines mounted on the leading edge of the wing. It was an ambitious programme for the time; even more so because the customer, the VVS, took until 1929 to develop fully its requirements.

Under Tupolev's guidance, Petliakov developed a trapezoid fuselage (parallel upper and lower surfaces with sloping sides) but with the upper surface slightly convex. The fuselage was in three sections: the first contained the nose section and cockpit. Here, a nose

gunner and bomb aimer were positioned and also the pilot and co-pilot. The next section held two more gunners, one on each side of the fuselage. Last came the tail section. Two more gun positions were carried in turrets which retracted into each wing outboard of the engines. Fuel tanks, each holding 1,950 litres/429 gallons, were riveted into the wings. The prototype was fitted with Curtiss V1760 Conqueror engines which gave 600hp. With a wingspan of 39.5 metres/129.6 feet, the ANT-6, designated TB-3 by the Air Force, was one of the biggest aircraft of the time.

The first flight took place on 22 December 1930 from Monino, with Mikhail Gromov at the controls. It was fortunate that a man of his experience was in command. On take-off, he pushed the four engine throttles fully open, and then moved both hands to the control column because of the force levels needed. As the aircraft lifted off, spectators heard the engines beginning to lose power. Gromov quickly realised that vibration was causing the throttles to slip backwards. He shoved them forward immediately, and ordered a mechanic to hold them there. After an otherwise successful flight, the throttles were fitted with a tighter support which solved the problem. State tests began at

A Red Air Force Mikulin AM-34R-powered TB-3 photographed air to air
Maksimillian B. Saukke Collection

the NII-VVS in February 1930. During the tests, the engines were replaced with BMW-VIs, and later again by Mikulin M-17Fs which gave 500 to 730hp.

The aircraft was put into immediate production, starting with factory N22 in Moscow. Here, 763 TB-3s were built between 1932 and 1938. Another fifty were built at factory N31 in Taganrog between 1932 and 1934, and a further six at Voronezh between 1934 and 1937, giving a production of 819 aircraft plus one prototype.

Petliakov and the TsAGI were kept busy for the next few years seeking ways to solve problems and to improve the TB-3. The VVS wanted the aircraft quickly. When the state tests were concluded on the first production aircraft, it was found to weigh more than a tonne heavier than the prototype, and its performance suffered because of this. The causes were established as being due to adding extra joints and more equipment, to using thicker metals for the skin, increased thickness on ribs and tubes, and heavier materials being substituted in production – all of these added 1,127kg/2,485lb to the weight. So Petliakov's first job was to sort out the production engineering and to source the right materials needed. This brought the production weight back down to 10,230kg/22,553lb, some 150kg/330lb heavier than the prototype, and 977kg/2,154lb lighter than the initial production version.

The first production aircraft was flown on 4 January 1932 by A. B. Yumashev. It was fitted with rotating turrets, and could carry a bomb load of up to two tonnes mounted, despite the large fuselage, externally on racks. A turret was also mounted in the nose which was fitted with a single plus a double machine-gun. The rudder and elevators were enlarged to reduce input forces on the controls; after some years, the small tandem-mounted twin wheels on each main undercarriage leg were replaced with much larger single wheels which improved ground control capabilities.

Meanwhile, despite its extra power, the M-17-powered production aircraft was unable to meet the

The nose of a TB-3
Konstantin Udalov/Avico Press Collection

service ceiling of the V1760-powered prototype. So they were changed for M-34s with a power output of 675 to 830hp. Now the top speed fell by 8kph from the 215 achieved with M-17s, although as the aircraft climbed higher it improved. So, in 1933, geared M-34s were fitted, with notable improvements in all performance aspects despite an increase in empty weight to 12,230kg/26,962lb. In 1936, the M-34RN blower-fed supercharger version of the engine gave the TB-3 its best capabilities – a maximum speed of 288kph/179mph at 4,200m/13,780 feet and a service ceiling of 7,740m/25,395 feet. Final engine choices were the AM-34FRN and AM-34FRNV supercharged which gave 900hp power. By now, Petliakov had covered the corrugated wing surface with fabric and streamlined the connections of the wing to the fuselage. Development of the TB-3 continued until 1936, some ten years after design work began.

With its state acceptance tests behind it, the TB-3 was quickly assimilated into VVS service. Indeed, for some time in 1932, production at two factories resulted in one and a half aircraft being completed per day. On May Day (1 May – the day of workers' international solidarity, a Soviet holiday) 1932, only five months after the first flight of a production TB-3, no fewer than nine flew in formation over Red Square in Moscow with the annual parade.

The TB-3 was also used in Vakhmistrov's Zveno (Link) experiment. Beginning in August 1934, his group Zveno-2 used a TB-3 as the mother ship. First experiments were with the Polikarpov/I-5 fighters, one mounted over the fuselage and two over the wings. Later, he used the TB-3 with two Grigorovich I-Z fighter monoplanes, one mounted under each wing. All separations trials went according to plan, but Vakhmistrov realised that recovering the fighters to the mother ship was not going to be easy.

On 23 March 1935 the first attempt to join up in the air went successfully. The TB-3, with P. M. Stefanovski in command, took off from Monino and was followed a few minutes later by Vasily Stepanchenok in an I-Z. At an altitude of 2,000 metres/6,562 feet they rendezvoused as arranged. Stefanovski lowered a horizontal pole with a trapeze attached, and Stepanchenok positioned his I-Z carefully under the TB-3, matched speeds, and attached the fighter securely to the trapeze. All went well.

Vakhmistrov's experiments climaxed in November 1935 when his Aviamatka (mother aircraft) formation took off – a TB-3 with three I-5s mounted above the wings and two Polikarpov I-16s mounted below – and climbed to 2,000 metres/6,562 feet, where Stepanchenok once again attached his I-Z under the central fuselage. Then all six aircraft separated from the mother ship and landed separately.

Although his works continued until 1941, even seeing limited action at the beginning of the Great Patriotic War (as World War Two was called in the Soviet Union), his invention was overtaken by improved fighter design and changing politics. An example of its war service was the destruction of a railway bridge at Chernovodsk in August 1941; after a number of unsuccessful raids by fighters, two Zveno Z-6SPBs (or an ANT-6/TB-3 with two Polikarpov I-16s attached = one Z-6SPB) based at Yevpatoria in the Crimea were dispatched to destroy the bridge. Each I-16 carried a single 250kg/551lb bomb. The raid was successful, but only a few such operations were carried out, for by then the TB-3 was outdated, and only its heavy armament and armour allowed it to survive. It had seen action in 1938 when the Soviet Union and Japan had skirmishes. The TB-3 had been a formidable opponent for the Japanese; a year later, in further clashes, new Japanese fighters had won most of the battles. By the Finnish War of 1939, the TB-3 was relegated to a mainly transport role.

Zveno 2 at state tests in August 1933 with three Polikarpov 1-5s mounted on top of an ANT-6/TB-3
Maksimillian B. Saukke Collection

Vasily Stepanchenok's Grigorovich I-2 after hooking on underneath the TB-3 in March 1935 as part of the Zveno experiments
Konstantin Udalov/Avico Press Collection

The VVS also used the TB-3 in early paradrop exercises. In a major military exercise near Kiev in 1937, some 700 paratroops were dropped while designer P. I. Grokhovski came up with para equipment to carry and drop everything from a T-27 light armoured car or truck right up to a four-tonne T-37 truck (which had to be dropped into water). Here the pilot was expected to maintain a level of only one metre above the surface till the load was released.

Earlier in its career, the size and shape of the TB-3 had earned it recognition throughout the world. Thus, a number of international goodwill flights were served with the aircraft. Over the winter of 1933–1934, nine aircraft were withdrawn from the VVS. Their armaments were removed and they were painted white to represent peace. In flights of three aircraft the following summer the following journeys were made: Moscow–Warsaw–Moscow (29 July–1 August); Moscow–Kiev–Vienna–Paris–Lyons–Strasbourg–Prague–Moscow (5 to 17 August; both these journeys were flown by Baidukov, Yefimov and Leonov); Moscow–Kiev–Kharkov–Rome–Vienna–Moscow (5 to 16 August; pilots were Sokolov, Golovachev and Riabchenko). The visit to Rome was in response to a visit by Italian Savoia Marchetti SM-55 flying boats to Odessa.

A number of international records were set by the TB-3. In September 1936 A. Yumashev flew a TB-3 carrying a five-tonne load to an altitude of 8,116m/26,629 feet. A month later, he lifted another five tonnes to 8,980m/29,463 feet. The following year,

in September, he carried ten tonnes to 6,605 metres/21,664 feet, and twelve tonnes to 2,700m/5,952 feet, each time flying a TB-3 fitted with the supercharged AM-34FRN or FRNV engine.

By the mid-1930s, a number of TB-3s were beginning to be transferred to civil aviation. The new Aeroflot directorate of Turkmenistan was equipped with several under the designation G-2 which were used to carry twenty passengers or for cargo. Also, Aeroflot's department of Polar Aviation, better known as Avia Arktika, received four new ANT-6/G-2s in 1936. These were fitted out from the start for Arctic service; during the winter, they were fitted with skis, and they changed to wheels normally in early June for the short summer season. They also had supercharged engines, the AM-34RNs, heated cabins, and brake parachutes installed to allow short landings as well as extra emergency and rescue equipment. With them, Avia Arktika planned the first aerial mission to the North Pole.

Preparations began in March 1936 when a two-aircraft survey party left Moscow to find a suitable base for the main expedition. Rudolf Island, the most northerly landpoint of the Soviet Union, was selected as 'not perfect, but not impossible'. Later that summer, a small village was built on the island – two eight-roomed houses plus a kitchen, office, radio beacon, garage, bath house and stores, as well as an aerodrome equipped with fuel storage and a 'movable house'. And they set up 'Severny Polus-1' (North Pole 1), an ice-mounted station, which drifted with the polar icecap.

All this was planned by Dr Otto Schmidt, known as the Ice Kommisar. He picked Mikhail Vodopianov to head the aviation detachment. On 22 March 1937, five aircraft left Moscow with forty-three people plus supplies on board. First to go was Pavel Golovin in an ANT-7 which was to be the expedition's survey aircraft. Four ANT-6s followed, flown by Vodopianov, Vassili Molonov, Anatoli Alekseev and Ilya Mazuruk. Two intermediate stops were made, at Arkhangelsk and Naryan Mar. They reached Rudolf Island on 18 April because of the weather delays at the closing stages of Russia's severe winters. There they stayed for another month, although Golovin managed a few survey flights including one which brought him over the Pole. But eventually the weather improved, and on 21 May at 5 a.m., Vodopianov took off for the Pole, which he reached at 11.35. He overflew it and landed some twenty kilometres past it when he found a suitable landing strip. He radioed the conditions to Rudolf Island from his aircraft (SSSR-N170). Four days later, Alekseev arrived and landed nearby, as did Molonov on the fifth day. Mazuruk did not arrive until 5 June, landing some 50km from the Pole. One month later, all four ANT-6s headed back to Rudolf Island, leaving four research scientists on Severny Polus 1, then situated at 88°54", 20°W. When they were picked up by two icebreaker ships the following February, they had drifted to 70°54"N and 19°50"W – just off the Greenland coast! Ivan Papanin led the team of research scientists.

One of these four aircraft, SSSR-N169, also flew on the last pre-war polar expedition in 1941. A number of other ex-military TB-3s were converted for Avia Arktika service, with the last being withdrawn in 1947. Conversion included covering over the cockpit, diverting exhaust gases to heat the interior, and fitting skis in place of wheels.

The ANT-6 started its life well ahead of any Western rival in terms of size and ability. That ten years later it was still a formidable rival is a tribute to its creators. By the time of its entry to service, Soviet aviation had come of age, and had been able to set its own standards. Unfortunately, no TB-3s or ANT-6s are preserved – all were scrapped by the mid-1950s.

ANT-6; one little known trial carried out on an ANT-6 was this kamikaze flying torpedo. It was intended that the volunteer pilot should fly it straight at the enemy, and that he would die in the attack
Konstantin Udalov/Avico Press Collection

ANT-7/R-6

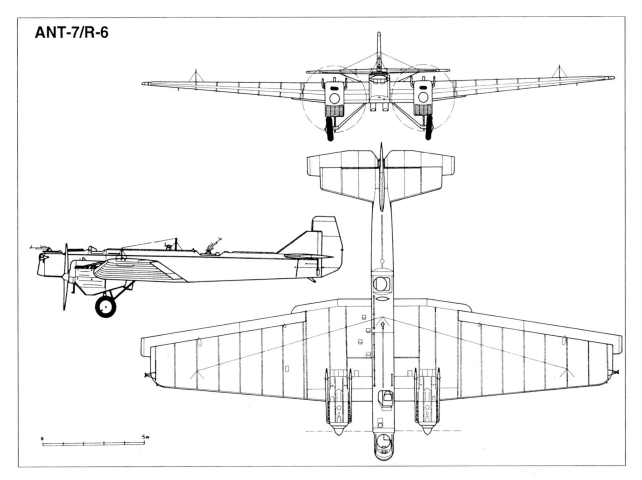

ANT-7/R-6

Early in 1928, the Soviet Air Force outlined a requirement for a multi-role aircraft. It was needed for long-range support, for defensive patrols, reconnaissance (hence its military designation R-6, where R = Razvedchik = Reconnaissance), light bombing and torpedo roles.

Never ones to waste a good idea, the TsAGI team, under Tupolev's guidance and led by Ivan Pogosski, took the design of the ANT-4 and scaled it down by approximately one third. The new design was intended to carry either two Hispano Suiza engines of 520 to 610hp or two Bristol Jupiter VIs of 420hp. Instead, the prototype was powered by BMW-VIs which gave 500 to 710hp. The open cockpit layout of the ANT-4 was retained. When Pogosski died in the crash of the prototype ANT-27 in 1934, Vladimir Petliakov, leader of the ANT-4 programme, also took on the ANT-7 work.

The first flight of the scaled-down aircraft took place on 11 September 1929, almost four years after

that of its big brother. This time Mikhail Gromov was the pilot. TsAGI let the winter go by before it began flight trials in March 1930. State tests, carried out by the NII-VVS, were conducted in the summer, with Mikhail Gromov taking charge. The tests quickly discovered a heavy buffeting in the tailplane – this was solved by increasing the size of the elevators by the simple expedient of riveting duraluminium strips to the trailing edges. On the next flight, an engine radiator was damaged and the engine failed. Gromov, with considerable difficulty, made an emergency landing. Despite two setbacks in quick succession, the tests continued and the ANT-7 passed through the test programme successfully.

The first production ANT-7, fitted with Mikulin M-17F engines, rolled off the assembly line of Moscow factory N22 in November 1931, one year after production began. Over the next three years, 410 aircraft were built in three production factories: 385 were completed at N22 and a further five were constructed at factory N31 in Taganrog – these were KR-6P floatplanes; the final twenty were built at factory N12 in Komsomolskna-Amure. One of those built at N22 in 1932 was a 'passenger limo'. With a covered-in cockpit, a passenger door and a cabin with glass windows and a luggage compartment, it could seat seven passengers in a luxury not usually associated with the ANT-7. A year after its rollout, on 5 September 1933, it was lost in an accident attributed to a technician's oversight.

training aircraft.

With the original design of the R-6 dating back to 1924, it comes as no major surprise to find that by 1935 the VVS found the R-6 to be outdated, and their withdrawal from service began. But this did not mean retirement for many of them – they were handed over to Aeroflot and Avia Arktika as the PS-7-2M17 (the

Golovin's ANT-7/PS-7-2M17 at the North Pole in March 1937
Boris Vdodenko via Konstantin Udalov/Avico Press Collection

The R-6, as the ANT-7 was designated by the VVS, was produced in four versions; the standard aircraft was the R-6 for reconnaissance duties. As such, it carried a crew of three: a pilot, an observer, and a gunner who controlled two DA-2 twin machine-guns. It could also carry up to a 500kg bomb load and had a range of 1,000km. A small number of floatplanes served with the Soviet Navy, either as patrol KR-6Ps or as torpedo carrier MR-2Ps. The KR-6 (the K represented Kreiser = Cruiser) was equipped with two PV-2 machine-guns, with the second crew member acting as a gunner. Some of these were later used as

last indicating two M-17 engines) for passenger and cargo services, or as the MP-6-2M17 if fitted with floats.

As has already been mentioned, in 1937 an ANT-7 piloted by Pavel Golovin led Vodopianov's five-aircraft flight to the North Pole, becoming the first aircraft to overfly the pole on 5 May 1937. In the open cockpit of SSSR-N166, Golovin must have been very cold indeed.

With Aeroflot, the PS-7 saw widespread service in Siberia until the start of the Great Patriotic War.

An ANT-7/R-6 at Khodinka in 1929
Tupolev

The only ANT-7 with an enclosed cockpit was this 'Passenger Limo', URSS-J5, which served for just one year before being lost in an accident
Maksimillian B. Saukke Collection

SSSR-N29 over a ship in the Arctic Ocean (from a painting)
Konstantin Udalov/Avico Press Collection

ANT-8/MDR-2

Although Tupolev and the TsAGI had been requested to construct a flying boat in 1925, higher priority had been given to his long-range bomber projects and little work was done. But in 1930, with Ivan Pogosski as head, work began in earnest on the ANT-8, which was given the military designation of MDR-2 (MDR = Morskoi Dalnii Razvedchik = Naval Long-Range Reconnaissance).

The designation ANT-8 indicated how long the TsAGI had held back this project, for shortly after its first flight, the ANT-14 flew. The flying boat's wings and tailplane were derived from the ANT-9, and again an all-metal construction was chosen. The fuselage was given a lot of attention by the design team, and the opportunity was taken to make the floats part of the load bearing structure as well as surface balancing devices. Power was provided by two BMW-VI pusher engines mounted on struts over the wings. It was piloted by S. Riballschuk on its first flight which took place on 30 January 1931. Armament was two DA-2 machine-guns, and it could carry an underwing bomb load of 900kg.

Tupolev regarded the ANT-8 as a proof of concept machine for further development, particularly of hulls. In fact, it turned out to be a worthwhile design in its own right, although the Soviet Navy decided not to proceed with it as it considered the design already dated and unlikely to meet its developing needs. It would have to wait another five years for Beriev's MBR-2. Only the prototype ANT-8 was built; although several modifications were made to its hull, it remained essentially a one-off experimental aircraft.

The ANT-8 beginning its take-off at Sevastopol
Tupolev

The ANT-8 anchored at Sevastopol
Konstantin Udalov/Avico Press Collection

ANT-9

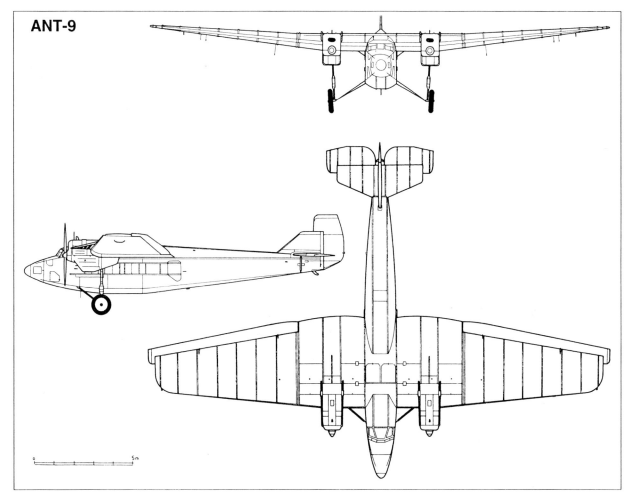

ANT-9

In autumn 1927, Tupolev put a proposal for a three-engined airliner to the Soviet governmental for international air services. The proposal was well received; although several Soviet airliners were in service, none were deemed good enough to meet international standards. So in October that year TsAGI's design office, AGOS, was given instructions to design and build the nine-passenger airliner prototype.

Working under Tupolev, the design was headed by Ivan Pogosski, who adopted much of the wing and tailplane of the ANT-7 in creating his high-wing design. Initial powerplants were three 250hp Gnôme-Rhône Titans. The aircraft was included for development and production in the first five-year economic plan (for 1928–1932). The prototype was displayed in Moscow's Red Square for the 1929 May Day parade. Its first flight took place in mid-May, piloted by Mikhail Gromov. State tests were started

immediately, again headed by Mikhail Gromov.

Tupolev was impressed with the ANT-9. After three or four flights had been successfully completed, he brought his wife and two children on a flight, with Gromov piloting. His confidence in the aircraft left a strong impression throughout Russia.

As a part of the state tests, which were completed late in June 1929, a flight from Moscow to Odessa, Sevastopol, Odessa, Kiev and back to Moscow was undertaken between 6 and 12 June. Pilots for the series were Gromov, Mikheev and Spirin. After the state tests, the ANT-9 was handed over to the NII-VVS for further tests. Here some of the pilots complained of its lack of lateral stability. Gromov checked the aircraft and found that some control cables were too tight. After resetting them, the problem was solved, but the vibrations caused by the cables had a consequence on the next flight when liquid leaked from the magnetic compass, and the instrument itself fell from the control panel.

An early flight to European capitals was planned. In preparation for this, to test the aircraft in an operational environment, a Moscow–Kiev–Odessa––Kiev–Moscow flight was organised. With Gromov in command, the ANT-9 left Moscow on a very wet July morning. Poor visibility and a low cloud base kept the aircraft down to fifty metres/164ft. By Serpukhov, the weather improved and Gromov climbed to 300m/984ft. He decided to head straight for Odessa, where Tupolev was waiting to join the flight. After refuelling, they set off for Kiev, but quickly ran into heavy rain, and had to descend again to 100m/328ft. As they approached the Dnepr River, a strange noise was heard, and although the engine power was maintained, speed began to drop. Gromov increased the power, but they continued to lose speed and a forced landing became inevitable as the speed fell to 118kph/73mph. They found an acceptable field, and Gromov made a successful landing.

It turned out that the aircraft's three-bladed propellers, which had wooden frames with fabric covering, had begun to lose the fabric which had been shredded by the heavy rain, and this had formed pockets which increased the drag substantially and resulted in the speed loss. Tupolev examined the blade, asked for a penknife, then Pogosski sat on Gromov's shoulders (because Gromov was tall) and cut away the linen. Some of the passengers were disembarked and some fuel detanked, and the ANT-9 was off again to Kiev, and later to Moscow.

A few days later, on 10 July, the ANT-9, now named *Krylia Sovetov* (Wings of the Soviets) began its tour of European capitals. Berlin was the first stop. The only problem en route was that passengers kept going to the toilet at the back of the cabin, and this resulted in Gromov, the pilot, and Rusakov, the co-pilot and mechanic, having to constantly retrim the aircraft. Ten flying hours brought them to Berlin, where they were

The prototype ANT-9 in Red Square for the May Day Parade in 1929
Maksimillian B. Saukke Collection

Aeroflot ANT-9 SSSR-L113 mounted on skis
Konstantin Udalov/Avico Press Collection

given a tour of the city. Then they flew on to Paris and to Rome, where they met Benito Mussolini, the Italian dictator and leader, and on to Marseille, where they re-fuelled before heading off for London. Over the middle of France they ran into bad weather, and Gromov had to descend below the solid cloud base to maintain visibility.

Unexpectedly, the aircraft began to descend rapidly. Gromov pulled back the control column to climb just as Rusakov pulled back the throttles; Gromov shouted at him and full power was applied, with Gromov looking for a suitable landing ground. A few minutes later, they were on the ground in a large meadow. There the only problem Gromov could find was an open hatch over the centre wing. They closed it, and they took off again, but with Gromov on the alert, he soon noticed buffeting. He landed again in the same field, and they found the same hatch open, but Gromov wasn't satisfied, so they checked further

and found a burst relay tube in one of the engines. A garage was located in a nearby village, and by the next morning the tube was welded and the hatch was dead-locked. They crossed the French coast below cloud at only 20m/65ft, but made it successfully to Croydon. From London, they headed back to Moscow via Paris, Berlin and Warsaw, reaching home on 8 August. They had covered 9,037km/5,616 miles in fifty-three flying hours, at an average speed of 170.5kph/106mph.

The ANT-9 was put into production in factory N22 in Moscow, which built sixty-one aircraft between 1930 and 1932. A further five were built in Taganrog in factory N31. Six aircraft were fitted with two Mikulin M-26 engines, but production defects in the M-26 caused them to be changed for the more reliable, but larger, M-17 which involved strengthening the wing to hold the extra weight. Several of the M-26-powered aircraft had their engines replaced by Wright J-4 Whirlwinds which gave 365hp each; this increased

A late production ANT-9, URSS-S186, with two Mikulin M-17F engines
Konstantin Udalov/Avico Press Collection

the speed by 20kph to 205kph but reduced the range from 900km to 700km. Two Whirlwind-powered ANT-9s were delivered in 1932 to Deutsch-Russisch Luftverkehrs, better known as Deruluft, a joint German–Russian airline which operated international services from 1922 to 1937, when it was closed down. In the next few years, four more aircraft were transferred from Dobrolet to Deruluft. They stayed in service with the joint venture airline until its closure on 31 March 1937. Deruluft covered the corrugated wings with fabric which improved the performance.

As the PS-9 (PS = Passazhirski Samolet = Passenger Aircraft) the ANT-9 entered service with Dobrolet, Aeroflot's predecessor, early in 1931. This was the first Soviet passenger aircraft good enough to face foreign competition; indeed contemporary reports indicate that it may well have been Europe's best in the early 1930s. It served on international services from Moscow and other western Soviet cities mainly to Europe until the impending world war forced these services to be dropped. It continued serving domestic routes until its withdrawal from service in 1945. All in all, sixty-two PS-9s served with Dobrolet and Aeroflot, including four seconded to Deruluft for some years. One aircraft, registration number SSSR-L183, built up 5,205 flight hours in its eight years of service from 1934 to 1942, an impressive enough figure for those times.

Two PS-9s were assigned to the Maksim Gorki propaganda squadron in 1933, when the 'Agiteskadrilia Maksima Gorkogo' (the Maksim Gorki Agitation Squadron) was formed with the object of spreading propaganda or beneficial information about Soviet progress throughout the Soviet Union. The squadron flew from city to city, organising film shows, leaflet drops and flights for workers who had given exceptional service. It was normal to name each aircraft after a Soviet newspaper or magazine, and the PS-9s were named after the satirical magazine *Krokodil* (crocodile). To live up to their name, Vadim Shavrov redesigned the forward fuselage of the aircraft to give them the appearance of a crocodile's mouth, and a matching paint scheme, one smiling with teeth visible and one with a closed mouth, made these two of the best known aircraft in the Soviet Union of the 1930s.

ANT-9; the smiling crocodile taking off
Konstantin Udalov/Avico Press Collection

ANT-10/R-7

Under the military designation R-7, a single ANT-10 was built as a possible alternative to Polikarpov's R-5, which first flew in 1928 and went on to have a production run of 4,995 in the 1930s.

The sole ANT-10 at Khodinka in 1930
Konstantin Udalov/Avico Press Collection

Tupolev's project was an all-metal sesquiplane. The shortage of metal was one of the factors which worked in favour of the simple wooden airframe chosen by Polikarpov. For both aircraft the BMW-VI engine was specified, due to its planned Soviet production as the Mikulin M-17.

TsAGI began design work on the R-7 in 1928, when the R-5 was already flying. Its first flight was made on 30 January 1930, flown by Mikhail Gromov. As it was not appreciably better than the R-5, the programme was discontinued six months later.

ANT-11

Programme cancelled. It would have been a multi-role seaplane.

ANT-12/I-5

With the development of the Soviet Union's first five-year economic plan came a national desire to be self-sufficient in as many spheres as possible. The Soviet Union's fighter aircraft were mostly imported, and the VVS was anxious to replace them with nationally made aircraft as quickly as possible.

So, in 1928, Tupolev was instructed to design a new fighter, which was designated the I-5 by the Air Force, and the ANT-12 by the TsAGI. The engine was specified as the Gnôme-Rhône Jupiter VI or the Soviet licence-built derivative, the Mikulin M-36. Some work was done by the TsAGI, but pressure of bomber projects led the VVS, which was in a hurry, to seek another designer for the project; thus the TsKB, the Central Design Bureau, was given the project instead, with Nikolai Polikarpov leading the team. His I-5 went on to serve with the Soviet Air Force until at least 1941, and some 800 were built. This also expanded Polikarpov's experience and reputation, and he went on to design several more outstanding biplane fighters.

ANT-13/I-8

Tupolev's second visit to Germany, in 1928, gave him the chance to visit Krupp's huge metal works in Essen. Here he was given samples of several new alloys, among them stainless steel, which he had thoroughly tested on his return to Russia. He was a believer in trying out new materials, and his opportunity to test stainless steel came two years later with the ANT-13, a non-braced (no struts) biplane fighter which was given the military designation I-8. The full spars of the aircraft's upper and lower wings were made of the new alloy.

The project was organised by Vladimir Rodionov, and the construction of the prototype, and the only example to be built, was done with each designer and engineer giving seventy hours of his time on a 'social basis' (i.e. unpaid). It was completed by the end of October 1930. Its engine was a 625 to 700hp water-cooled Curtiss Conqueror V1570. The aircraft was, unusually, given the name *Zhokei* (Jockey) because of its diminutive size.

Mikhail Gromov was the pilot for its first flight, which was made on 12 December 1930, and was impressed with it from the beginning. In its trials, it became the first Soviet aircraft to exceed 300kph when, in January 1931, it reached 303kph. But although it achieved its design targets, the VVS had by now committed itself to the I-5, and another factor against it was its foreign engine, so its development was stopped.

The sole ANT-13 *Zhokei* at Khodinka in 1931
Maksimillian B. Saukke Collection

ANT-14

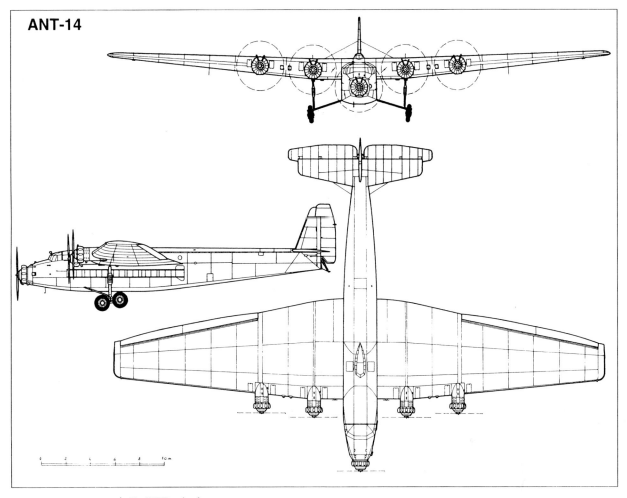

ANT-14

The next aircraft in the series was the ANT-14. Essentially conceived as a much larger version of the ANT-9, Tupolev developed it as a thirty-six-seat passenger airliner with a crew of five. To speed up the programme, the wings and undercarriage of the ANT-6/TB-3 were used, with the only major change being lengthened undercarriage legs because of the ANT-14's high wings. Power came from five 480hp Gnôme-Rhône Jupiter VI engines, with two mounted on each wing and the fifth in the aircraft's nose. It was one of the biggest aircraft of its time – which was to be its undoing, because its size was beyond the then needs of Soviet air transport.

The programme was headed by Vladimir Petliakov, in a programme which worked particularly well, for when Mikhail Gromov flew it for the first time on 14 August 1931, less than a year after the start of design work, very little adjustment was needed to anything.

Its test programme was completed by spring 1932. But a short evaluation by Dobrolet/Aeroflot, then flying the eight-passenger Kalinin K-5 and just beginning to receive the nine-passenger ANT-9, revealed no worthwhile routes for a thirty-six-seat airliner, so the AGOS/TsAGI-built prototype remained the sole example of the ANT-14.

Its life was not over; shortly after its test flying was completed, the idea of forming an agitation, or propaganda, squadron was approved by Stalin and it was established on 17 March 1933. It was named after Maksim Gorki, the famous Russian writer who had begun his writing career forty years earlier in 1891. Gorki was Stalin's favourite writer, which added to the support for the idea. The available ANT-14 was the first lead aircraft of the squadron, which named each aircraft after a newspaper or magazine of the time. As leader, the ANT-14 was given the name *Pravda* (truth) after the nation's leading daily newspaper.

For the next ten years, the ANT-14 served the

The sole ANT-14 shows its size with a line up of parachutists underneath
Konstantin Udalov/Avico Press Collection

squadron well. It made well over 1,000 flights, and carried over 40,000 passengers. These included officials and workers being rewarded for their services as well as fare-paying passengers on tourist flights over Moscow. It operated mainly within Russia and, to a lesser extent, the wider Soviet Union. It flew two tourist flights from Moscow to Kharkov in the Ukraine, and one to St Petersburg, then called Leningrad. Its only journey outside the USSR was in

October 1935 when it visited Bucharest, the Romanian capital, to mark a festival being held there at the time.

During its service no major technical snags were experienced, a remarkable tribute for the time. With the outbreak of the Great Patriotic War in 1941, the squadron's days drew to a close. In 1942, after its withdrawal from service, the fuselage of the aircraft was parked in a children's playground, where it continued its propaganda work for a short while.

The ANT-14 arriving at Bucharest on 27 October 1935 on its only journey outside the USSR
Maksimillian B. Saukke Collection

The ANT-14 URSS-N1001 before the Soviet Union adopted SSSR as its nationality marks
Konstantin Udalov/Avico Press Collection

ANT-15

Project not proceeded with.

ANT-16/TB-4

The success of the TB-1 and TB-3 led the VVS to want bigger and better bombers with more capacity to carry bigger bomb loads. Earlier in the development story, in 1929, TsAGI experts had calculated that, theoretically at least, there should be no insurmountable problems in designing and building bombers with the then available technology up to a maximum take-off weight of seventy tonnes, including a twenty-tonne bomb load. The ANT-6's MTOW of some seventeen tonnes had been less than a quarter of that. A leap from seventeen tonnes to seventy was considered too ambitious, so an interim point was the development of the TB-4, the ANT-16, with a MTOW of 32,380kg.

But this was not a project to be rushed. Even with Vladimir Petliakov, whose experience on the TB-1 and

TB-3 was second to none, it took over three years to build the prototype. Design work was started in March 1930. The general concepts of the TB-3 were retained but expanded. Now the wingspan grew from the 39.5m/129.6ft of the older aircraft to 52m/170.6 feet; and the four Curtiss Conqueror engines of 600hp each on the prototype TB-3 were changed for six Mikulin M-34 engines which offered 500 to 680hp each. Still Tupolev and TsAGI looked on the TB-4 as being a half scale model of the full size seventy tonner.

The wing thickness was increased to a scale where a mechanic could crawl through a tunnel to reach any of the four engines mounted in the leading edge of the wing, even when in flight, to make any adjustments or repairs deemed necessary. The fifth and sixth engines were mounted on pylons over the centre fuselage, with one being a puller and the other a pusher. On the ground, the engine nacelles opened downwards and formed a step ladder to simplify pre- and post-flight inspection, and to allow maintenance work to be carried out. The fuselage held two large bomb compartments, one forward of the main strut's intersection with the fuselage, the other behind it. Each was

The sole ANT-16/TB-4 at Khodinka
Maksimillian B. Saukke Collection

5m/16.4ft long and width and height was 1.8m/5.9 feet. Normal bomb load was four tonnes, but the maximum take-off weight could be exceeded allowing the TB-4 to carry a ten-tonne load. Armament included ten machine-guns and two variable angle 20mm cannons. Normal crew was eight, but with a full complement of gunners, this grew to twelve. The prototype TB-4 was built at the AGOS-TsAGI factory at Radio Street, then disassembled and brought by road to Khodinka, where it was reassembled.

On 3 July 1933, Mikhail Gromov started the engines of the world's largest aircraft of the time; after warming them up, he taxied to the runway. A few minutes later, the giant was airborne. Unlike most of its predecessors, the ANT-16 was not a joy to fly. Gromov quickly found that a very high pressure was needed to be kept on the controls – almost at an impossible level. He got the aircraft down safely, however; there the design team decided to enlarge the rudder and elevators. A few weeks later, Gromov was airborne again in the new bomber. But now there was much too little pressure: during a minor turn to the right, unless both feet maintained sufficient force on the left pedal, the right pedal would go forward by itself and the rate of roll could quickly develop into a spin. It took quite a while to sort everything out. Eventually, the flight characteristics were worked out.

But the TB-4 did not live up to its expectations. Five-tonne bomb loads could only be carried 775km/481 miles; four tonnes, 1,000km/621 miles; the TB-3 load of two tonnes it could only carry 2,200km/1,366 miles, 120km/69 miles less than could the older aircraft, which had a service ceiling of 7,740m/25,395ft. The TB-4 with a four-tonne load could only get to 2,750m/9,023ft. It was not an improvement on the TB-3. The project was discontinued late in 1933.

ANT-17

In 1933, TsAGI were instructed to design a heavily armoured ground attack fighter; it was given the project number ANT-17, and the military designation TShB (Tiazheli Shturmovik Bronirovannii = heavy armoured ground attack). Its purpose was to attack enemy ground forces behind the lines, and its heavy armour was needed to defend it against ground arms.

Tupolev conceived it as a flying armoured car and it was designed to carry one tonne of armour, with over one third being built into the airframe as load supporting. Powerplants were two Mikulin M-34s, and armament was six machine-guns, including a moveable twin unit mounted and four forward shooting in fixed positions; a 1,500kg/3,307lb bomb load was also to be mounted under the wings.

But the VVS reconsidered its ground attack requirements, and the ANT-17 was discontinued before the prototype was completed.

ANT-18

A redesign of the ANT-7/R-6 for the TShB role – see ANT-17; the project was cancelled before any construction work began.

ANT-19

Not proceeded with.

ANT-20

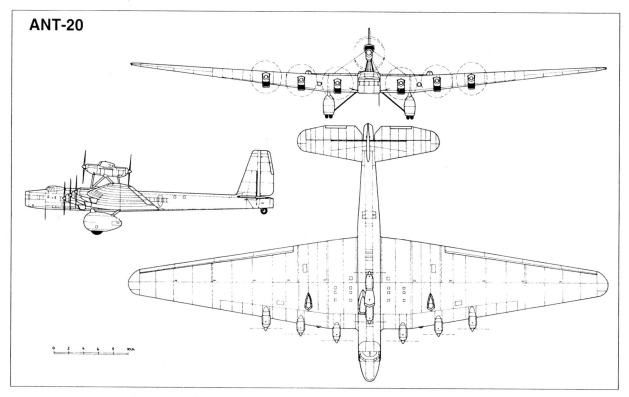

ANT-20

The *Maksim Gorki*

In October 1932, Mikhail Koltsov, a Russian jour-
nalist, promoted the idea of building a 'giant
aeroplane' to commemorate the fortieth anniversary
of Maksim Gorki's first publications. As Josef Stalin,
the Soviet leader, regarded Gorki as his favourite
writer, the idea quickly gained support, and a public
collection of money for the project was organised. It
raised almost eight million roubles, and the TsAGI,
under Tupolev, was commissioned to carry out the
work which was given the project number ANT-20.
(Incidentally, five years later, in 1937, Koltsov was
arrested and executed without a trial.)

The design work went ahead quickly, and construction of what was to be the world's largest aircraft (until
the Hughes Hercules, some thirteen years later – a
flying boat which flew just once, attaining an altitude
of twelve feet/approximately four metres; and a land-
plane, the Bristol Brabazon, which first flew in 1949)
began on 4 July 1933 and was completed nine months
later, on 3 April 1934. Because of the great size of the
aircraft, by the world standards of the 1930s – its
length was 32.5 metres/106.6 feet and its span 63
metres/206.7 feet – the design was kept essentially

simple. The ANT-16/TB-4 was used as the basis for
design. Tupolev retained the proven all-metal corrugated system for the aircraft's skin, wings and
empennage. The fuselage was made in five sections,
bolted together with high tensile bolts.

The first section included the cabin and the navigator's seat. In the second section was the cockpit for
the pilots and radio operator, and some passenger
accommodation. In the centre section, between the
wing spars, were a telephone station, the toilets and
a working compartment. The fourth section held a
buffet, cinema equipment, a photo laboratory and
a radio station – the essentials of a propaganda
machine. The last section, the tail section, was left
empty and was for structural purposes only. Entrance
to the aircraft was from underneath: a section of the
cabin floor could be lowered to form a stairs and
banisters allowing crew and passengers to board
and disembark. The four fuselage sections which
comprised the working area of the aircraft had a floor
area of 100 square metres/1,077 square feet; maximum
capacity was seventy-two passengers and eight crew.

The ANT-20 was powered by eight Mikulin
M-34FRN engines, each generating 900 horsepower.
Three engines were mounted on each wing, while the
seventh and eighth were mounted in tandem above
the fuselage centre section, one a pusher. Six engines,

each giving 900hp, were deemed insufficient to power the mighty aircraft, which was given the name of its 'sponsor', Maksim Gorki. The enormous wing thickness needed to generate lift on a relatively slow aircraft of its size and weight gave the advantage of allowing engineers standing access in flight to the six wing-mounted engines. The engines each drove a large two-bladed propeller of four metres/13.12 feet in diameter. The ANT-20 was fitted with an autopilot, the first of Tupolev's designs to do so. It was one of the first aircraft in the world to use this new control, which could control the directional, altitudinal and pitch/yaw controls of the aircraft.

The ANT-20 took off for the first time on 17 June 1934, from Khodinka with Mikhail Gromov as pilot. Unlike the TB-4, it proved to be stable and easily controlled, and its flight test programme was completed by August, and resulted in no changes in the design.

It entered service with the Maksim Gorki propaganda squadron on 18 August 1934, beginning a career that took it to many of the cities and towns of the Soviet Union where it was used to laud the aims and achievements of communism and Josef Stalin by flying over the region and transmitting music and information from its loudspeakers. (These were called 'Golos s Neba', or 'the voice from the sky'.) Local dignitaries were often invited to the aircraft's cinema, which was a big screen with people sitting on benches outside the aircraft to watch the films/movies, and leaflets could be printed on board and dropped to the people below. A photo laboratory could process films and quickly print the results, sometimes for inclusion in the propaganda leaflets; a pneumatic mail system could transfer mail or messages from one section of the aircraft to another, and the aircraft had its own sixteen-number

telephone exchange. To power all this equipment, an electricity generator was driven by an auxiliary engine.

With all this equipment and its huge size, the take-off weight of the aircraft came to forty-two tonnes/92,568lb, a huge figure for the time, and considerably above the thirty-two-tonne standard maximum take-off weight of the ANT-16. The *Maksim Gorki* drew considerable attention wherever it went, greatly helping the propaganda squadron to achieve its purpose.

But fate intervened on 18 May 1935. While flying a formation detail from Khodinka, Moscow's central airport, the *Maksim Gorki* was struck by a Polikarpov I-5 fighter flown by N. P. Blagin, a TsAGI test pilot; the formation had already made two circuits of Moscow, and had just begun its third when Blagin began to do aerobatics around the giant ANT-20, pretending, apparently, to loop around it. Certainly, from film footage taken from another aircraft in the formation, he carried out two rolls, then seemed to lose speed and hit the ANT-20 in the rear of the fuselage. The reports published later said that he had struck the wing – they were not correct.

The ANT-20 continued flying for a short while, but then a wing broke off, and the aircraft began to disintegrate; finally the fuselage broke up. The aircraft and the forty-five people on board – two inspector pilots, ten crew members and thirty-three passengers, mostly TsAGI technical staff, but including six children – fell to the ground near the then small town of Sokol, now a region of Moscow city. There were no survivors. Blagin also died. All were buried with impressive ceremony in the cemetery in the grounds of Moscow's New Maiden Convent.

There was considerable controversy about the crash. Blagin was alleged to have written a letter on the

The *Maksim Gorki* at Khodinka
Maksimillian B. Saukke Collection

SSSR-L760, the ANT-20bis with six Mikulin M-34FRNV engines, served with Aeroflot; shown here at Kazan
Konstantin Udalov/Avico Press Collection

day before it happened saying that he intended to ram the *Maksim Gorki* to protest against the communist regime in the Soviet Union. Certainly the letter was published in the Polish newspaper *Mech* (Sword) and was reprinted in *Vozrozhdenie* (Revival), the Russian emigrant newspaper which was published in Paris. But Blagin's co-workers in TsAGI cast doubts on these reports, saying that he was a professional, a leading test pilot for Tupolev and TsAGI. Nonetheless, Blagin did commit a serious violation of air practice by performing aerobatics close to a passenger aircraft. There was also speculation that he had been ordered to impress Moscovites by flying around the ANT-20. But whoever, if anyone, gave such an order is unlikely to be traced now.

As the New Maiden Cemetery was reserved for distinguished people and heroes, these matters were reported to have been brought to Stalin's attention by the head of the commission set up to investigate the collision, Nikita Khrushchev, later Soviet leader, who asked where to bury Blagin. Stalin is said to have taken some time before stating that he should be buried with the others.

But the *Maksim Gorki* had proved its worth, so it was decided to build a second example. This time, the work was headed by V. M. Petliakov, and the aircraft was constructed at factory N22 in Kazan. By now, Mikulin had developed the 1,200hp AM-35, and it was decided to use six of these, mounted in the wing, instead of the eight AM-34s. This allowed the two engines mounted in tandem above the wing to be omitted. It was not equipped for the propaganda role

of its predecessor, but was instead delivered to Aeroflot at Khodinka, Moscow's central airport, under the designation PS-124 and was registered SSSR-L760. It was used for the busy Moscow–Mineralnie Vody (a health resort) route from 1937 to 1941 in a sixty-four-passenger configuration. Shortly after the Soviet Union entered World War Two, it was transferred to the Uzbekistan Department of the Civil Air Fleet, or Aeroflot section, where it served on the Tashkent–Chardzhou–Urgench and the Tashkent–Kuibyshev (now Samara) routes.

Its career ended on 14 December 1942. Late that morning, it took off from Chardzhou with twenty-six passengers and ten crew on board and headed for Tashkent. Two hours ten minutes later, some fifty kilometres from its destination, it was seen to lose height – it was flying at 500m above the ground. Despite all its engines remaining in operation, the aircraft entered a steep dive, hitting the ground at an angle of 80°. It was totally destroyed, and all on board died. During the investigation it was discovered that the pilot was not at the controls when the aircraft crashed. It seems that he gave the controls to a passenger who disconnected the autopilot and lost control. Thus ended the story of the remarkable ANT-20, a story more strange because of the unusual circumstances resulting in the losses of the only two examples of the world's biggest aeroplane of its day.

It had been planned to build eighteen PS-124s at Kazan for Aeroflot, but the disruption to the industry following Stalin's purge in the late 1930s meant that there were no longer the specialists available for the work.

ANT-21/MI-3

The first prototype ANT-21 at Khodinka on 26 August 1933; note the double tailfin and rudder
Maksimillian B. Saukke Collection

Aleksander Arkhangelski's first assignment as chief designer came in 1932; working under Tupolev's guidance as part of the TsAGI team, he was tasked with the design and construction of a twin-engined high-speed fighter/cruiser in a programme intended to increase substantially the speeds of combat aircraft.

He broke away from the angular family of aircraft associated with Tupolev and TsAGI up to that time by designing a rounded fuselage for a cantilever low-wing monoplane. Another first was a retractable undercarriage. He retained the strengthening corrugated wing, but it was fabric-covered to reduce drag and improve lift. It had a twin tail, with fin and rudder mounted at the outer end of each of the horizontal tailplanes. Two Mikulin M-17 engines provided the power, each generating 500 to 680hp. Armament was

two sets of twin machine-guns of 7.62mm calibre, one mounted in the nose and one in a dorsal turret in the rear fuselage. These were operated and aimed by gunners – the ANT-21 had a crew of three, which led to its military designation of MI-3 (MI standing for Mnogomestnii Istrebitel = many, or multi-, seat fighter).

The prototype was constructed at AGOS–TsAGI in Radio Street; when completed, it was brought by road to Khodinka from where the first flight was made on 23 May 1933, with Ivan Kozlov in command. Few problems arose in the test programme until, in September, an attempt was made to increase maximum speed beyond the already achieved 350kph/217mph. As it neared 400kph/248mph, a severe flutter began on the flying controls and this had a serious effect on the aircraft's controllability. So Arkhangelski set about constructing a second aircraft, the ANT-21bis, again at AGOS–TsAGI. This time, he replaced the twin tail with a more conventional single but larger fin and rudder after the TsAGI had investigated the causes of the controls flutter. On the first aircraft, the tailplane had retained the corrugated surfaces of earlier aircraft; on the second, a smooth skin was achieved, with the horizontal tailplane mounted halfway up the fin. This time, two of the improved and more powerful Mikulin AM-34RN supercharged engines were installed. The second aircraft was designated MI-3D.

This time, tests went much better; the handling qualities proved satisfactory. But the Air Force had developed its requirements beyond the MI-3, and the programme was cancelled.

The ANT-21bis/MI-3 with a single fin and rudder at Khodinka on 19 May 1934
Maksimillian B. Saukke Collection

ANT-22/MK-1

The second TsAGI/Tupolev flying boat, the ANT-22, was conceived in a programme headed by Ivan Pogosski in response to a naval specification for a 'flying cruiser', a large amphibious seaplane with long range and endurance to seek out and destroy enemy warships.

Early work for this project was carried out under the programme number ANT-11, but the pressure of work on other projects caused it to be put aside with only the programme outlines being submitted in late 1929. Other design bureaux proceeded with submitting more detailed proposals, but in 1932 the naval authorities came back to TsAGI and requested the project be completed. The designation MK-1 (Morskoi Kreiser = sea cruiser) was applied.

For this, the largest seaplane to be built in the Soviet Union until at least the 1960s, Pogosski chose a twin-hull arrangement, with two identical boats. In a design more to be expected from Italy's Savoia Marchetti, it seems likely that the spectacular long-range flights of Pinedo and the formation flights of Balbo in the S-55

had not gone unnoticed in the Soviet Union. At the rear of each boat was a tail turret with twin DA-2 machine guns of 7.62mm calibre, each pair operated by a gunner. Two similarly equipped turrets were mounted forward, one in each nose. The wing had a 51m/167.3ft span and was mounted on top of the twin hulls; mounted on pylons on the wing were three pairs of Mikulin M-34Rs, with one pusher and one puller in each nacelle. Each engine generated 750 to 830hp. The tail featured a biplane arrangement, supported by a centre strut, with the elevators on the upper surface. The cockpit was mounted on the leading edge of the wing at the centre; here, the two pilots had good forward visibility, but the twin hulls must have seriously impeded most other angles. Once again, the aircraft was constructed of duraluminium, with corrugated surfaces. In addition to the machine-guns listed above, two Oerlikon cannons were mounted in ring turrets behind the wing, one in each hull.

The aircraft was constructed at TsAGI/ZOK. Completed in late 1933, it was disassembled and brought by train to Sevastopol, on the Black Sea coast, where, after reassembly, it made its first flight from Omega Bakt (Bay) on 8 August. It was flown by

The ANT-22 shown air to air, with the twin hulls visible
Maksimillian B. Saukke Collection

Four workers relaxing in front of the ANT-22
Maksimillian B. Saukke Collection

Timofei Riabenko. Without armaments, in factory tests it achieved a maximum speed of 233kph/145mph, but a disappointing service ceiling of only 3,500m/11,484 feet. For state tests the following summer with a full military load, including a six-tonne bomb load, the speed fell to 205kph/127mph and the ceiling to 2,250m/7,382 feet. The poor performance would have left the MK-1 very open to attack. So the Navy did not progress the programme.

But the ANT-22 flew well and performed well on water. So Tupolev and TsAGI built up more knowledge with it, and it proved its load-carrying capabilities by setting a world record. In December 1936, Riabenko and Ilynski carried 10,040kg to 1,942m/6,371 feet. Later, they lifted a 13,000kg payload for the first time, but no record was sought. But the programme had ended.

The ANT-22 at anchor in Sevastopol
Tupolev

ANT-23; the unusual shape of the I-12 is shown in this view from above
Maksimillian B. Saukke Collection

ANT-23/I-12

The next TsAGI aircraft was unusual in several different respects. Firstly, it was a single-seat fighter/interceptor. Although Tupolev's team had begun work on several such projects, none had actually been completed or flown since the ANT-5/I-4 made its first flight in 1927. This was to be the second single-seat fighter to fly with Tupolev's initials.

But more unusual was the fact that the idea for the I-12, to give it its military designation, came from a group of young designers and engineers working in TsAGI under Pavel Sukhoi, led by Vladimir Chernyshov. His idea was to mount two of the new 76mm APK-100 recoilless cannons then being developed by Leonid Kurchevski, not only as armament for the aircraft but also as part of the load bearing structure, using the exhaust areas of the cannon, fitted with long pipes much akin to a car exhaust, as the twin fuselage booms needed to hold the tailplane because of the unusual (particularly for the early 1930s) push-pull engine arrangement.

To attain the targeted design performance, Chernyshov's design team calculated they needed an engine which could give 800 to 900hp power output, something that would take a few more years to arrive, for work on the ANT-23 began in December 1929. So the decision was taken to use two Bristol Jupiter VI engines of 420 to 525hp mounted back to back in a short fuselage with a single-seat cockpit and a fuel tank between the cockpit and the rear engine.

Design and construction work continued throughout 1930, being carried out mainly by young designers and engineers. In the second quarter of 1931, it was given the name *Baumanski Komsomolets* (Young Communist of Bauman). Bauman was an early socialist; at the end of the Czar's era, he had lived and worked in the district around Radio St, the TsAGI headquarters. Later the district was named after him. He was killed during civil unrest in 1905, close to what would become the design bureau's base.

The aircraft was constructed, as usual for TsAGI design, of duraluminium, and although the tail featured the usual corrugated pattern, the wing had extension panels fitted into the corrugation valleys, leaving many fewer 'ribs' on the surface. The twin booms, acting as cannon exhausts, were made of steel piping with a 170mm diameter. Made in three sections, they screwed together with a thread cut into the ends. Because the tailwheeled fixed undercarriage needed to be high to cater for the ground clearance of the rear engine with its 2.9m/9.5 feet propeller, Chernyshov designed a long pyramid-shaped undercarriage leg.

The enthusiasm of the youthful design team overlooked one or two problems. The major one was noticed immediately by test pilot Ivan Kozlov, who pointed out that a pilot attempting to bale out of the I-12 would run a severe risk of being hit by the rear propeller. Despite this, he agreed to fly the aircraft. The first flight took place on 29 August 1931. Although the aircraft flew well enough, its performance was disappointing. The rear engine and its propeller did not give the anticipated power level; the drag from the fixed undercarriage and corrugated tail also slowed the aircraft down. On one flight, during firing trials, a cannon exploded and its exhaust pipe, which was one of the two supports for the tail, broke. Kozlov, with great difficulty, managed to land the aircraft as he could not evacuate. For this, he was awarded the Red Star, a decoration for bravery. The test proved worthwhile; the cannon was returned to the designers, who established the cause and eliminated the chance of it happening again.

That finished the short career of the I-12; work on the second aircraft was stopped and the project was cancelled.

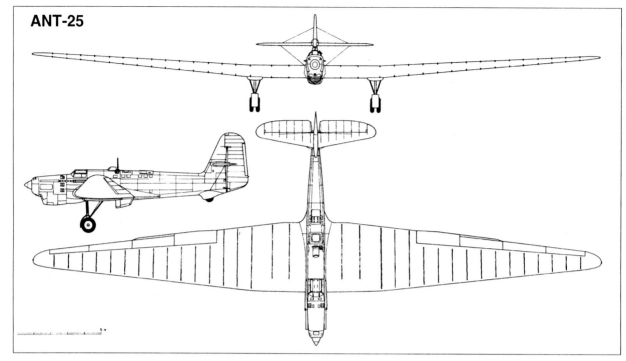

ANT-25

The ANT-25

Setting Long-Range Records

In 1931, the Soviet Military Revolutionary Council decided that a long-range bomber was needed for the Air Force, and in August that year it set up a commission to establish the design requirements. It was decided that none of the TB class aircraft was suitable, so the commission proposed a more streamlined, single-engined design with a slow-running engine in order to reduce drag and to save fuel. Tupolev was instructed to prepare proposals.

The proposals were approved in December, and Tupolev set up a team headed by Pavel Sukhoi to design the aircraft around a Mikulin M-34 engine. The designers set out to achieve a still-air range of 13,000km/8,078 miles, while Tupolev guaranteed that a minimum of 10,000km/6,214 miles would be possible. It was given the designation ANT-25RD (Rekord Dalnosti, or long-range record), and the military designation DB-1 (Dalnii Bombardirovshik = long-range bomber). The design was finalised as a single-engined, low-wing monoplane with a very high aspect ratio of more than 13:1 – span was 34m and chord was 2.62m. The spar was in two sections, with the flanges manufactured from steel chromatised tubes. A third spar was mounted to the rear of the (wing) chord. Duraluminium braces were fixed

between the spars and were part of the load-carrying structure, as were the riveted fuel tanks, seven metres long, which were mounted in each wing. The wing surfaces consisted of corrugated metal.

The fuselage was made of two sections: forward, the front was monolithic and integral with the wing, while the rear was a monocoque of oval sections. The tailplane was also corrugated. The undercarriage retracted by folding backwards into the wing; the wheels were solid discs rather than the usual spoked versions; and the suspension featured oleo-pneumatic shock absorbers. The tailwheel was covered by a spat to minimise drag. The large, three-blade propeller could have its pitch adjusted, but only on the ground. It measured 3.9m/12.8 feet, from tip to tip.

Exhaust gases were used to heat the cockpit. The pilot sat on a canvas-covered seat directly behind the engine. Behind him, on the wings' centre spar (and over the integral fuel tanks), was a bed for crew rest. Then came the navigator who was provided with a sextant and observation hatch to allow him to fix position by star/astral readings. He also doubled as radio operator, so the aircraft's radio equipment was mounted alongside the navigation area. Last came the second pilot, with a simplified instrument panel and full controls. With no forward visibility, he could only fly on instruments and served only as a back up, and short-term relief, for the first pilot.

The ANT-25 was equipped with the latest developments in blind flying instruments for its time, including an artificial horizon and a turn and bank indicator. It also featured an early gyromagnetic compass, a solar course indicator, and a radio transceiver with a range of up to 5,000km/3,107 miles. To improve the possibilities of evacuation time in the event of ditching, inflatable rubberised bags were fitted which would increase buoyancy.

Work began on the first aircraft at the TsAGI/ZOK on 7 December 1931. Completed in June 1932, it was then disassembled and brought by road to Monino where it was reassembled and readied for flight, fitted with a 750hp Mikulin M-34. On 22 June 1933, the ANT-25 made its first flight, piloted by Mikhail Gromov, which lasted for just over an hour. In September, the original Mikulin engine was replaced by an uprated version which gave 874hp.

The test results proved to be disappointing. The second aircraft, which was constructed in August/September at Monino, made its first flight on 10 September, again flown by Gromov. This was fitted with the uprated M-34R engine, which gave 900hp. It showed that the ANT-25's range in still air would not exceed 11,000km/6,835 miles. So Sukhoi and his team looked again at the design, and decided that the corrugated surfaces on the wings and tailplane might be increasing the aircraft's drag coefficient. They decided to cover these surfaces with linen, using a special needle which was fed into machined holes on the riser surfaces. The corrugated 'valleys' were filled with lightweight balsa wood, and the new wing surfaces were varnished as was the engine cowling. The propeller was then highly polished, all with the aim of reducing drag.

It worked. Test flying began again in summer 1934, and noticeable improvements in performance were evident right from the start. Tupolev and Sukhoi were quickly convinced that 13,000km/8,078 miles could be achieved. In August a thorough pre-flight preparation began, which included the crew spending long periods flying in cloud, flying the proposed route in a Polikarpov U-2 training aircraft, and locating possible emergency landing strips en route, and trying them out. The next training session was a triangular Moscow–Ryazan–Tula circuit, a distance of 520km/323 miles, which was to be flown as many times as the aircraft's endurance would allow.

The ANT-25 at the XVth Paris Air Salon at Glahd Palace in November 1936
Konstantin Udalov/Avico Press Collection

Gromov's Route, 10 to 13 September 1934

	DISTANCE IN KM	NUMBER OF CIRCUITS	TOTAL
Monino–Shelkovo–Moscow	34	1	34
Moscow–Tula–Ryazan–Moscow	520	9	4,680
Moscow–Liubertsy–Shelkovo–Moscow	92	39	3,588
Moscow–Tula–Moscow	358	1	358
Moscow–Liubertsy–Moscow	56	1	56
Moscow–Shelkovo–Moscow	64	1	64
Moscow–Tula	179	1	179
Tula–Ryazan	148	1	148
Ryazan–Podlesnaya–Ryazan	110	1	110
Ryazan–Tula	148	1	148
Tula–Tsaritsyno	158	1	158
Tsaritsyno–Kharkov	630	1	630
Kharkov–Dnepropetrovsk–Kharkov	393	1	393
Kharkov–Balaklaya–Kharkov	155	3	465
Kharkov–Rogan–Kharkov	40	1	40
Kharkov–Chuguev–Kharkov	80	16	1,280
Kharkov–Emiev–Kharkov	80	1	80
Kilometre Total			12,411

Time 75 Hours 2 minutes

Early in September, Mikhail Gromov took off from Monino, near Moscow, accompanied by crew members Aleksander Filin and Ivan Spirin. Because it was necessary to chart strictly the aircraft's track, it was decided to fly at minimum speed and at low altitude; 200m/656 feet was chosen for the sector to Ryazan. About an hour into the journey, they encountered fog and the engine began to lose power. Gromov decided to jettison fuel and to seek a landing spot. To jettison he had to switch off the engine or face a possible explosion. Fuel jettisoned well from the right tank, but only a thin trickle came from the left. But he landed the aircraft on a wet field and despite the wheels digging in up to the axles, the aircraft did not nose in.

The carburettor jets were replaced, and they returned to Monino on the next day. Two days later, they tried again. Thirty-four hours into the flight, they were some 120km/75 miles beyond Ryazan, flying at 3,500m/12,000ft, when a fire started in the starboard engine block, and they began to lose power. Gromov turned back to Ryazan, and began to descend. Thirty-five minutes later they landed beside a river and had to jump out to hold the aircraft so it wouldn't fall into the water. It turned out that a carburettor float had failed when Gromov switched tanks. It was repaired and they returned to Monino. On 10 September they were off again. By the third night of the journey, they had flown the Moscow–Ryazan–Tula circuit nine times plus a wide range of other sectors in order to avoid boredom (see chart above), but because of bad weather, they were advised by radio to fly westwards, towards Kharkov in the Ukraine. There they flew another complex sector pattern. They were flying near Kharkov at 4,200m (almost 13,000 feet) when they ran into more bad weather. They realised that fuel for a return to Moscow was doubtful, so they continued to Kharkov, where they landed. There was only thirty kilograms of fuel remaining, perhaps ten gallons! They had covered 12,411km/7,712 miles in seventy-five hours and two minutes. While this exceeded the existing record of 9,104km/5,657 miles set by French pilots Maurise Rossi and Paul Codos in August 1933 when they flew a Blériot 110 from New York to Rayak in Syria, Gromov's flight was not recognised by the Fédération Aéronautique Internationale, as the Soviet Union was not then a member of the FAI.

Now that Gromov and his crew had proved that the ANT-25 could beat the record, the government gave instructions to prepare for a long-distance record-breaking flight. It was decided to fly non-stop from Moscow to the United States over the polar icecap and the North Pole.

The winter months were used in preparation for the flight, and the following May the second ANT-25 took off from Monino, this time commanded by Sigismund Levanevski. They headed due north, aiming for the Pole. Some twenty hours later, over the frozen Barents Sea, oil began to leak from an engine pipe, and Levanevski decided to return to Moscow rather than face the prospect of a forced landing on the icecap. On his return, Levanevski berated Tupolev and accused him of attempting to sabotage the flight. He also stated that he would never again fly a Tupolev aircraft. He never did, for tragedy followed.

Levanevski also suggested that it was madness to attempt to fly such a long distance in a single-engined aeroplane. Ironically, shortly after Chkalov and Gromov had successfully flown ANT-25s over the Pole to America, Levanevski and a crew of five set out in a four-engined DB-A designed by M. M. Shishmarev in Zhukovski's Military Aviation Academy, heading for America in an attempt to break the long-distance record. They reported passing the North Polc, and that they were heading for Fairbanks in Alaska. Then they reported the loss of an engine. Two garbled messages followed, but they were never seen again.

Levanevski's return did nothing to inspire confidence in the ANT-25, and for six months it looked as if no further flights would be allowed. But Georgi Baidukov, Levanevski's co-pilot, did not share his lack of trust, and he persuaded Valeri Chkalov, perhaps the best known Soviet pilot and well known to Josef Stalin, to support the programme. Previously, he had flown only fighters, and he was reluctant to fly the ANT-25. But after one flight, he was enthusiastic. Chkalov's intercession resulted in Stalin giving approval for him to undertake a long-range flight within the Soviet Union. A route plan was drawn up: starting from Moscow, the flight would proceed north to Spitsbergen, then fly east along the north coast to Franz Josef Land, on over the Northern Lands to Tiksi, then south-east to Petropavlovsk-Kamchatski and Nikolaev-Petropavlovsk-Kamchatski-na-Amure (Nikolaev on the Amur river).

All of this had delayed the programme by a year, but on 20 July 1936, at 5.45 a.m. Moscow time, Chkalov, with co-pilot Georgi Baidukov and navigator Aleksander Belyakov, lifted off from Monino and headed north. Fifty-six hours and twenty minutes later, bad weather forced them to land on Udd Island at the mouth of the Amur river. They had established a record, which was recognised by the FAI, of 9,347km/5,825 miles. Udd Island was renamed Chkalov Island by Stalin in commemoration of the event.

With confidence in the ANT-25 re-established, Stalin gave approval to proceed with the transpolar flight to the United States. At first, the plan was for both aircraft to fly with a separation of thirty minutes. The Soviet government set about preparing for the flight by establishing 'Severny Polus 1' (North Pole 1), a meteorological centre floating on the polar ice which would broadcast weather reports for the flight from the top of the world.

In the winter months while preparing for the attempt, Baidukov flew the ANT-25 via Cologne to Le Bourget, from where the aircraft was brought by road to the XVth Paris Air Salon at Glahd Palace (November 1936). It returned to Moscow in December, routing through Berlin.

The plan to fly both aircraft to America on the same day did not work out, because Chkalov's engine needed some maintenance. So the engine was removed from both aircraft, and that of the second was fitted on Chkalov's ANT-25. On 18 June 1937, at 4.04 a.m. Moscow time, Chkalov, again with Baidukov and Belyakov, took off from Monino and headed due north along the 38°E line of longitude. Five hours into the flight, Chkalov noticed an oil spillage, just like Levanevski's, but he decided to continue. After a while, the spillage reduced. At nine o'clock, Baidukov took over for a four-hour duty, and was soon flying in icy conditions in cloud at 2,600m/ 8,530 feet. When Chkalov resumed control, he climbed first to 3,000m (9,843ft) then eventually to 4,250m (13,944ft) to avoid

Chkalov's ANT-25 taking off from Shelkovo in 1937
Maksimillian B. Saukke Collection

ice. At this level, oxygen was needed, and there was only enough for nine hours on board. By 11 p.m., Chkalov calculated that fuel burn was higher than planned by about 300 litres/66 Imperial gallons – two flight hours. At 4.15 a.m. on 19 June, the aircraft was heard passing the North Pole by the crew of Severny Polus 1; Chkalov then flew south along the 133°W meridian. By late morning they were into cloud and icy conditions again. Chkalov climbed to 4,850m (15,913ft), then 5,500m (18,046ft). Oxygen was now running short. They had to descend to 3,000m (9,843ft).

They crossed the Canadian coast at 4.15 p.m. and flew on towards Bear Lake. Four hours later, as they crossed the Mackenzie River, they saw the Rocky Mountains and had to climb again. As they flew by Portland, Chkalov discovered that, of the 500 litres/110 gallons of fuel remaining, only about 120/26 could be fed to the engine and this would not be enough to reach San Francisco, their target. So they landed at Vancouver, Washington. There they were met by General Marshall, and, a few hours later, by Soviet Ambassador Troianovski. They had covered a straight line distance of 8,504km (5,284 miles) and a track distance of 9,130km (5,673 miles) in sixty-three hours and twenty-five minutes. It was the first non-stop flight from Moscow to the United States.

They were hailed as heroes both in the United States, where President Roosevelt spent one hour and forty minutes with them instead of the planned fifteen minutes, and where they received a New York ticker-tape parade, and in Russia, where Chkalov's home town of Vasilevo was renamed after him. The ANT-25 was disassembled in the United States and shipped back to Russia, and is preserved in Chkalovsk. Chkalov died in an air accident in 1938 in circumstances still regarded as controversial.

Three weeks later it was Gromov's turn. He added an extra 500kg fuel by leaving off survival gear, including an inflatable boat, a rifle, food supplies, and oil and grease, saving some 250kg/551lb weight. His crew were Andrei Yumashev and Sergei Danilin. After a normal take-off from Monino, things went well for

them, although they also had some icing problems. They dropped several markers en route to confirm their track. They passed the Pole some fourteen minutes early and calculated that they had used less fuel than expected. They overflew Prince Patrick Island exactly on their plotted course but ran into bad weather shortly after reaching Canada. In icy conditions, many of their instruments ceased to work, but luck was on their side and they passed through the ice layer. They passed Chkalov's landing point and flew on by San Francisco, right down to the Mexican border. As they had no permission to overfly Mexico, even though they had enough fuel to reach Panama, they turned back and landed in a meadow near San Jacinto, but only after several low passes were made at about 10m/33 feet to persuade two calves to move, which they did. They had covered 10,148 kilometres/6,306 miles in sixty-two hours and seventeen minutes, a record which would last only one year. In November 1938, two modified Vickers Wellesley bombers of the Royal Air Force's long-range development flight, led by Squadron Leader Kellett, increased the record distance to 11,526km/7,162 miles by flying from Ismailia in Egypt to Port Darwin, Australia.

After their landing, crowds quickly arrived, many looking for autographs. The landowner, obviously a resourceful businessman, was soon charging admission fees; when Gromov allowed him to take the remaining fuel, he poured it into small glass phials and quickly sold it all. They visited Hollywood, where their guide was six-year-old Shirley Temple; then San Francisco, then Washington where they met President Roosevelt. Then back to Le Havre on the *Normandie* liner, then to Paris where the FAI awarded them the Henri de Lavo medal. And from there back to a heroes' welcome in Moscow.

Tupolev, the designers, built two ANT-25s. In 1934, the Voronezh production factory received orders from the government to build fifty for the Soviet Air Force. These were improved versions and were redesignated ANT-36, and their story is outlined under that project number. In 1989, staff of the Tupolev Design Bureau built another ANT-25, this time a replica for preservation at the State Aviation Museum, fittingly located at Monino where it holds pride of place.

Some US sources doubt that these flights took place, pointing out that Gromov's aircraft was unpainted when it arrived in California, and that photos published in Soviet newspapers of the time show it with titles on the side. It must be remembered that Soviet photographs were frequently 'improved' by artists before release. Indeed, this practice has posed a difficulty in selecting photos for this book.

Tupolev (left) with Belyakov, Chkalov and Baidukov after their return to Moscow
Maksimillian B. Saukke Collection

ANT-26/TB-6

The disappointing results of the ANT-16/TB-4 led to the cancellation of the full-scale seventy-tonne maximum take-off weight ANT-26/TB-6. Tupolev and Petliakov had undertaken a considerable amount of work on the design of the giant bomber which was to have had a 95m/311.7-foot wingspan and twelve Mikulin M-34FRN supercharged engines, six mounted on the wing's leading edge, two mounted on the trailing edge near each wingtip, and four mounted in two pusher/puller pairs set on pylons above the wings. Crew was to have been twenty, including four gunners to operate fuselage-mounted machine-guns, plus four more to operate cannons, one in a turret above the fuselage, one in a tail turret, and two others in wing turrets mounted in the nacelles of the pusher engines.

With the cancellation of the TB-6 went the largest possible aircraft of its time. No Soviet aircraft was ever to have a wingspan to match the 95m of this giant. The Antonov An-22, which first flew in 1965 and measured 64.4m/211.3ft from tip to tip, was the largest to enter service, and the massive An-225, which first flew in 1988 and had a MTOW of 600 tonnes, measured just 88.4m/290 feet from tip to tip.

ANT-27/MDR-4, MTB-1

The next aircraft to bear Tupolev's initials had an unusual start. The TsKB, Central Design Bureau, began work on a long-range reconnaissance flying boat in 1931 with a project led by Igor Chetvertikov. Powered by four BMW-VI engines, the result, the TsKB-11/MDR-3, flew for the first time in January 1932. Results, however, were disappointing, and late in 1932 TsAGI were asked to take over the programme.

Tupolev gave the project to Ivan Pogosski, who was already working on the ANT-22/MK-1 programme. A new designation was applied, that of ANT-27, while the military designation became the MDR-4 (MDR = Morskoi Dalnii Razvedchik = naval long-range reconnaissance). So Pogosski and his team had two major projects running concurrently.

Unusually, and because of the design's origination, little use was made of duraluminium. Pogosski and Tupolev were satisfied with the hull of the MDR-3; in state tests, the hydrodynamic results were good, so Chetvertikov's fuselage was taken with very little modification. But the wing was another matter. A new wing was designed with a 39.15m/128.5ft wingspan, up from the MDR-3's 32.2m/105.6ft, and a wing area of

177.7 square metres/1,913 square feet – the MDR-3's area was 153 sq.m/1,647 sq.ft. A new tailplane was constructed with a single fin and rudder instead of the twin-boom arrangement on the MDR-3, and the powerplants were replaced by three Mikulin M-34R engines with 750 to 830hp each. These had an unusual arrangement: mounted on overwing pylons directly above the floats, the two outer engines were conventional pullers, while the centre engine, mounted over the fuselage, was a pusher. This was done to give a smoother airflow, so Pogosski produced two very different flying boats, both of which were to make their first flights in 1934, with the ANT-27 preceding the ANT-22.

Construction of the prototype ANT-27 was completed early in 1934 at TsAGI's ZOK; it was brought by road to Taganrog. Its first flight took place in March 1934, with Timofei Riabenko in command. Flight tests went according to plan for the next week, but on 15 April the aircraft was lost in a take-off accident, in which its designer, Ivan Pogosski, died.

Tupolev was present in a small motorboat to watch the take-off. At that time, many of the Soviet flying boat pilots had learned their craft on the Dornier Wal, a fine aircraft with just one bad habit: it was difficult to lift off from the water. So they had developed a technique of rocking the wings from float to float to separate the aircraft from the water. But on that day there was a subsurface roll coming in from the sea which was not visible from the sheltered bay where the flying boat began its take-off run. Tupolev noticed the roll when its effect was felt in his boat, and tried to warn the crew by waving his arms; in those days, no short-range radios were available. They did not notice. The aircraft emerged from the bay at high speed, lifted on the first wave and hit the sea just in front of the next wave. The pylon struts of the centre engine broke off, and the engine fell into the cockpit killing all on board. A commission was appointed to investigate the accident. It found no fault with the design or construction of the aircraft. By that time, the Soviet Navy badly needed a large flying boat.

Pogosski was replaced by Aleksander Golubkov and the work went on. A second ANT-27, the -27 bis (or 'duplicate') was completed in Taganrog by October, and it was tested throughout the winter. It was given a new designation for a new role – MTB-1 (for Morskoi Torpedonosets Bombardirovshik = naval torpedo bomber). Its performance was not remarkable, it was moderate at best. Maximum speed without armaments was 232kph/144mph, and service ceiling was only 5,000m/16,405ft. But the flying boats were badly needed, so it was ordered into production.

The ANT-27bis at Sevastopol on state tests in January 1935
Tupolev

The ANT-27bis was lost in another accident in September 1935, when a tear in the fabric covering the wing resulted in a large strip of the material ripping off the surface and a consequent loss of lift. This did not change the Navy's go-ahead decision. Fifteen ANT-27s were completed as MTB-1s; the production aircraft had a maximum take-off weight of 16,250kg/35,831lb, up from the prototype's 14,660kg/32,325lb. Its weapons load was two tonnes of bombs/torpedoes. Five were delivered in 1936, and ten in 1937. Not an ideal choice for Soviet needs, but the only one available at the time. Later, one of the naval aircraft was also lost following a tear in the fabric covering.

ANT-28

Designed in conjunction with the ANT-26, the ANT-28 was intended as a transport aircraft capable of carrying a field company including combat vehicles or field guns. Span was to be 60 metres/196.9ft, and power would have come from twelve Mikulin M-17s. With the cancellation of the ANT-26 came the same fate for the ANT-28.

ANT-29/DIP

The Soviet Air Force's interest in cannon fighters resulted in Aleksander Arkhangelski's design group at TsAGI beginning work on a twin-engined fighter in 1932, but pressure of other work delayed completion of the prototype until February 1935.

Much more conventional than the ANT-23/I-12, the Arkhangelski design was a smooth-skinned, twin-engined aircraft with a retractable undercarriage. It was powered by two Hispano Suiza 12Ybrs engines which gave 860hp each. The more unusual aspect of the design was the location of the two APK-100 cannons. They were mounted in a relatively deep fuse-

The sole ANT-29 with TsAGI titles on the tail at Khodinka in early 1935
Maksimillian B. Saukke Collection

lage thus acting as the floor on which the pilot and the gunner, located behind him, had their seats mounted. It had the advantage of the gunner being able to reach and load/reload the weapon, something not possible on other cannon fighters. The cannon exhausts then merged into a single tube which came out under the tail. It was given the military designation DIP (Dvukhmestnii Istrebitel Pushechnii = two-seat fighter with cannons).

Its first fight took place on 14 February 1935 with Sergei Korzinshikov in control. Unfortunately, its control surfaces proved to be too small, and a degree of longitudinal instability resulted. The days when this type of problem could be easily solved by clipping on extra surface area were gone with the more modern design of the DIP, and this, combined with the invention of recoilless weapons, meant that the aircraft did not go into production.

Flight trials showed that the DIP could reach 352kph/219mph at 4,000m/13,124ft, which was quite creditable. But, as usual with Tupolev designs, some aspects of the DIP were to prove valuable in later models.

ANT-31/I-14

The Air Force's need for faster fighters led in 1932 to a competition between three design teams for a low-wing monoplane fighter with a retractable undercarriage. Two of the teams were from the TsKB, the Central Design Bureau, and the third was Pavel Sukhoi's team at TsAGI, working under Tupolev's direction.

Initial armament was intended to be one or two synchronised PV-1 machine-guns plus two cannons, either the recoilless APK-37 or the ShVAK automatic,

and Sukhoi designed the I-14 as a cantilever monoplane with a monocoque fuselage made of stressed metal to avoid the need for corrugation, although the wings retained their corrugation. The undercarriage retracted backwards into the wing. The prototype was constructed at TsAGI's ZOK, and it was completed in May 1933. Its first flight was made that month from Monino and it was flown by Konstantin Popov. In tests, the I-14, with the somewhat underpowered Bristol Mercury engine, achieved 384kph/240mph at 5,000m/16,400ft, which, while not bad, was not considered good enough. At lower levels, the supercharged Mercury gave slower speeds. So Sukhoi built a second I-14, the I-14bis, sometimes called the I-142, with a 640hp Wright Cyclone. With this engine, speed increased to 414kph/257mph.

Some control problems were experienced with the I-142, particularly in high-speed tight turns, and this led to a redesign of the rear fuselage in 1936, which solved the problem. The delay had the benefit of allowing the development of the ShVAK cannon to be completed. The Air Force then ordered fifty-five I-14s. Production was set up at factory N23 in Moscow and the first aircraft were completed in 1935, and delivered to the Air Force. However, by the time the eighteenth aircraft had been completed, one of its rivals, the Central Design Bureau's I-16 from Nikolai Polikarpov's team, which had experienced its own teething problems, had been developed into an impressive and formidable rival, and the Air Force chose it instead of Sukhoi's I-14. So the remaining thirty-seven I-14s were cancelled while the rival I-16 went on to a production run of just over 7,000 aircraft. Because the Air Force concentrated its resources on the I-16, Sukhoi's eighteen I-14s did not remain long in uniform.

The prototype ANT-31 shown on skis after its state test programme
by Tupolev via Konstantin Udalov/Avico Press Collection

ANT-32

The ANT-32 was a project for a single-seat fighter which was cancelled at an early stage.

ANT-34

Prepared in response to an Air Force requirement for a twin-engined 'fighter-cruiser', the ANT-34 was to have been powered by two Wright Cyclone engines, but the proposal was cancelled.

ANT-35/PS-35

Although this book has been prepared in chronological order by numbers, not all the design projects were to run so smoothly. The ANT-35 is evidence of this, because its design team, led by Aleksander Arkhangelski, developed it from the SB-2, otherwise known as the ANT-40.

The SB-2 was a twin-engined high-speed medium-range bomber, and the design work needed to produce a ten-passenger airliner from it was not very great. First flight of the SB-2/ANT-40 took place in April 1934; work on the ANT-35 began in July 1935, with Arkhangelski in charge of both projects. The SB-2's wing was adopted with only minor changes, although the engines for the prototype ANT-35 were Mikulin M-85s, a licence-built version of the Gnôme-Rhône 14K, which gave 800hp. The fuselage was replaced with a new design featuring a ten-seat cabin, with a large passenger door on the port side. Undercarriage and tailplane stayed essentially the same.

The prototype was constructed at TsAGI's ZOK

and it was completed by August 1936. On the twentieth of that month, Mikhail Gromov flew it on its first flight. Tests went well, and included a Moscow–Leningrad–Moscow return flight of 1,266km/787 miles, which he completed in three hours and thirty-eight minutes. This resulted in Stalin's approval that the ANT-35 should be shown at the XVth Paris Air Salon. So early in November, Gromov, accompanied by co-pilot Sergei Korzinshikov, navigator Sergei Danilin and a mechanic, Anikeev, took off from Monino for Paris, routing via Koningsberg (now Kaliningrad), Berlin and Cologne. Just before they landed at Cologne, Gromov noticed the right engine was beginning to lose power, but after checking it on the ground, they continued their journey the next day. As they landed at Le Bourget, the engine failed completely, and a spare had to be brought from Moscow for their return. The aircraft was brought by road to the Air Salon's presentation at Glahd Palace, where it was shown close to the ANT-25.

Meanwhile, in 1934, the aviation branch of the Scientific and Technical Research Organisation of the whole Union, Aviavnito, had published details of a competition to modernise Soviet air transport aircraft. The ANT-35 was assessed by Aviavnito, which had received quite a number of not very promising proposals, and was judged to be the best of the twin-engined aircraft.

The ANT-35 was put into production in 1936 at factory N22 in Moscow; the production aircraft was fitted with Mikulin M-621Rs which offered increased power of 1,000hp, thus raising the maximum speed to 432kph/268mph. They proved to be efficient and reliable, and, for their day, the aircraft were well

ANT-35; Mikhail Gromov in front of PS-35 URSS-No. 35 at Shelkovo Aerodrome before his flight to Paris for the XVth Air Salon in November 1936
Maksimillian B. Saukke Collection

equipped. Aeroflot used them initially on international services including Moscow–Stockholm via Riga, and Moscow–Prague, with services beginning in 1937. But industry criticism that the cabin size could not be enlarged, and that the aircraft were not particularly economical, meant that Aeroflot restricted the number it took to eleven. In airline service, it was called the PS-35 (Passazhirski Samolet = passenger aircraft). From 1939 on it served some domestic routes, including Moscow–Lvov and Moscow–Odessa, both linking the Soviet capital with cities in the Ukraine. The eleven PS-35s served with Aeroflot until June 1941, when the German invasion of Russia began the Great Patriotic War for the Soviet Union.

Arkhangelski began work on another passenger aircraft, which would have been the ANT-50, in 1937, using the Mikulin M-34, in response to a more detailed Aeroflot specification, but despite the urgent needs of the airline industry in the Soviet Union of the late 1930s, the project was dropped.

ANT-36/DB-1

and slow, and its limited armaments, low service ceiling and large wing meant it was very vulnerable to fighters, so the planned production of fifty was cut to twenty which were never to see service in the role for which they were intended.

By spring 1936, these twenty had been delivered to the Air Force base at Ismailova, near Moscow. Two of these were fitted with diesel engines, and flight tests indicated that this version could achieve a range of 25,000km (15,535 miles). It was planned to circumnavigate the world on the 57°N line of latitude, but the build-up to the Second World War caused the plans to be put aside. The remaining thirty aircraft were not built.

The aircraft was not a military success. Labelled the DB-1, the Air Force soon realised that the almost five years it took to develop had left the aircraft too slow, and that against contemporary fighters it was outclassed and virtually defenceless. But the twenty military aircraft went on to further flight trials; two were fitted with Junkers Jumo diesel engines, as has already been mentioned. Most of the others were used by the TsAGI's BOK, a department headed by

The different engine, two-blade propeller and the squared tip of the tail tells an ANT-36/DB-1 from its predecessor ANT-25

Konstantin Udalov/Avico Press Collection

The ANT-36 was a redesigned ANT-25, and the twenty aircraft built for the Soviet Air Force under the military designation DB-1 were actually ANT-36s. This has caused some confusion as the sometimes reported production figures of the ANT-25 are quoted as two (the correct figure) and twenty-two, the total which includes both the -25 and the -36.

The major differences between the two Sukhoi-led programmes was armaments: on two aircraft, the Mikulin M-34R of the ANT-25 was changed for a Junkers Jumo 4 diesel and, later, the Soviet-built AN-1 diesel. But these engines left the DB-1 underpowered

Vladimir Chizhevski which was developing pressurised cabins for high-altitude test flights. In 1936, Chizhevski had worked in Kharkov developing pressurised cabins for high-altitude balloons. He lightened the airframe and shortened the span for his first version, the BOK-1. The engine chosen was the M-34RN with a turbocharger fitted to permit a ceiling of 10,000m/32,810ft to be attained. In early trials Piotr Stefanovski reached 10,700m/35,107ft; later, after further lightening of the aircraft, he brought it up to 14,100m/46,262ft. In June 1937, the engine was replaced by the new M-34RNV, fitted with two turbochargers. With some lightening, the aircraft reached heights of over 12,000m/39,372ft.

In 1938, Chizhevski modified another ANT-36 to BOK-7 standard. He substantially modified the cabin, so now the two crew sat with their heads in small doubleglazed domes which rose above the line of the fuselage. It was powered by a M-34FRN which developed 860mph, and had two superchargers. With this, the Soviet Air Force set its plans for a non-stop round the world flight approximately on the 53° North line of latitude. The programme was headed by Aleksander Filin, one of Chkalov's crew, and targeted for 1939 or 1940. But Filin was arrested in Stalin's purge, and executed in 1940. This and the war ended the project.

ANT-37/DB-2

Construction of the DB-2 was commenced early in 1934 at the TsAGI's ZOK works in Radio Street. It was completed by the end of April 1934, disassembled and brought by road to Moscow's central airport, Khodinka; there it was reassembled, and it made its first flight on 15 June, with Konstantin Popov in command. But its performance was disappointing: as speed went above 250kph/155mph, a major tail flutter was encountered, and on 20 July Mikhail Gromov was fortunate to survive a crash-landing which destroyed the aircraft after the rear fuselage and tailplane began to disintegrate in flight at a speed of almost 340kph/211mph. This incident gave the TsAGI another impetus to solve the flutter problem. Eventually, it was traced to inadequate production

The prototype ANT-37/DB-2. The markings on the tail indicate it belongs to the Ministry of the Aviation industry (И) and is experimental (Е)
Konstantin Udalov/Avico Press Collection

Late in 1933, Pavel Sukhoi was instructed to begin work on another long-range bomber. This time, however, a twin-engined aircraft was required capable of carrying a one-tonne bomb load some 3,500km/2,175 miles. Speed was specified as 350kph/217mph at 3,500m/11,483 feet.

His experience on the ANT-25/-36 programmes was put to good use on the ANT-37, or DB-2, its military designation. He used a slightly shorter version of the ANT-25's wing, at 31m/101.7 feet. Like the ANT-25, the wing was made of corrugated aluminium with the valleys filled in with balsa wood and a linen cover 'sewn' into the raisers. With two engines, the undercarriage had room to retract into the rear of the nacelles. The engines were 800hp Gnôme-Rhône 14Ks in the Soviet-built Mikulin M-85 version. The prototype was fitted with a rotatable turret with a single machine-gun, and a second turret, with twin machineguns, was located behind the pilot, giving a crew of three – one pilot and two gunners.

techniques in the horizontal tailplane, which led to a major redesign of that section of the ANT-37. A second aircraft was built by TsAGI, with a reinforced rear fuselage and toughened ribs in the horizontal stabiliser. Its first flight took place on 25 February 1936, with Mikhail Alekseev in command.

The DB-2bis began its flight test programme in the spring of 1936. Its speed was disappointing: cruising speed was only 213kph/132mph, but its range was substantially better. In August 1936, it flew Moscow–Omsk–Moscow non-stop, a distance of 4,995km/3,104 miles. Although the Air Force concluded that it did not want the DB-2, it was decided to modify it for long-distance record attempts, so it was taken back to the TsAGI/ZOK works, where the armaments were removed; it was fitted with the uprated Mikulin M-86 development of the original M-85 engines. These offered 950hp, and with new variable pitch propellers and increased capacity fuel tanks, the aircraft was expected to have a range of between 7 and 8,000km (4,350 to 4,971 miles).

The *Rodina* crew, left to right, Marina Raskova, Valentina Grizodubova and Polina Osipenko
Maksimillian B. Saukke Collection

The aircraft was named *Rodina* (motherland) to represent Russia, and on 24 September 1938, it took off from Monino and pointed eastwards. Three women made up the crew: Valentina Grizodubova was pilot; Polina Osipenko, co-pilot; and Marina Raskova, navigator. Osipenko had already set a number of international records in the MP-1, a Beriev-designed seaplane, between May and July of that year, including altitude and distance records for seaplanes.

minutes later, and 5,908km/3,761 miles to the east, they made a wheels-up landing near the remote village settlement of Kerbi, on the banks of the Amur river. The aircraft was still there in the early 1990s, locked in by the difficult terrain, but little damaged by the landing.

Although not a success in the role for which it was designed, the DB-2 proved its value by adding to the growing list of internationally recognised records set by the Soviet aviation industry.

The *Rodina* after its wheels-up landing near the village of Kerbi on 25 September 1938. Polina Osipenko is shown on the left wing
Maksimillian B. Saukke Collection

Now, as co-pilot, she was part of a team which would set a new women's long-range record by flying non-stop from Moscow to the far eastern region of Khabarovsk, where twenty-six hours and twenty-nine

ANT-38

A proposal for a high-speed bomber similar to the ANT-40 was not proceeded with.

ANT-39

Another project which was cancelled.

ANT-40

Late in 1933, TsAGI received an Air Force requirement for a light high-speed bomber. With Sukhoi already working on the long-range DB-2/ANT-37, Tupolev assigned the task to Aleksander Arkhangelski's team, and design work began immediately.

As the TsAGI considered the Air Force's specifications, which called for a speed of 330kph/205mph, service ceiling of 8,000m/26,248ft, and a range of 800km/497 miles with a bomb load of 500kg/1,102lb, to be inadequate to meet the needs of the next five to ten years, Tupolev instructed Arkhangelski to build two different versions of the SB (Skorostnoi Bombardirovshik = high-speed bomber), as the military designated the project. TsAGI gave it the ANT-40 designation.

The Air Force had selected radial engines for the SB – two air-cooled Wright Cyclone F-5s, a nine-cylinder engine giving 730hp each for the prototypes, with the intention of fitting production aircraft with Mikulin M-87 radials of 900hp. But for his own ideas, Tupolev selected the in-line Hispano Suiza 12Ybrs. Arkhangelski concentrated on reducing drag and on keeping the aircraft's weight down. The TsAGI's wind tunnels were used extensively as each new idea was made into a model, and the wind speed effects tested on it. Flush riveting techniques were developed for the duraluminium fuselage and wing surfaces, and new alloys were developed – super duraluminium and new high tensile steels.

On the wing, ailerons were equipped with weight and axis balancers, and a trimmer was fitted internally to each aileron; landing flaps were used to slow the low drag design to a reasonable approach speed. The undercarriage retracted into the rear of the engine nacelles, although the lower wheel remained uncovered – semi-retracted would better describe it. The undercarriage was raised and lowered by an electro-hydraulic system with a mechanical backup. A crew of three was carried: a pilot, a navigator who also acted as both bombardier and gunner, and a radio operator who also was a gunner. Five retractable machine-guns were carried: two in the nose turret, two in the rear fuselage turret, and one mounted on a hatch in the lower fuselage which could swing down. Tankage of 940 litres/207 gallons was carried on the prototype fitted into the 19m/64.4ft span.

Arkhangelski's design was approved in March 1934, and construction began immediately at TsAGI-ZOK. It was flown for the first time on 7 October 1934. The test pilot was Konstantin Popov. The flight tests were not very promising, and when the aircraft was badly damaged in a landing accident on 31 October, the opportunity was taken to make some changes to the wing design. The rebuilt aircraft was completed by February 1935, by which time the second aircraft, the ANT-40-1, was flying.

Fitted with water-cooled Hispano Suiza 12Ybrs in-line engines, the ANT-40-1 made its first flight on 30 December 1934 when it was flown by K. Zhurov. Both aircraft were tested extensively until July 1935, and the lessons learnt in these tests were taken into account for the next aircraft, dubbed the ANT-40-2, which was the outcome of Tupolev's discussion with Arkhangelski almost two years earlier. While the SB and the SB-1 (the second aircraft) were somewhat disappointing, the need for an aircraft of this category was strong enough for the Air Force to issue instructions for production to be put in progress, and the preparatory work for serial production was initiated.

State tests on the second aircraft, the SB-1, had found some wing turbulence, particularly in tight turns, but problems like this were resolved in the ANT-40-2, which was soon given the designation SB-2. From its entry into state testing in September 1935, the improvements were noted almost immediately. Top speed of 325kph/207mph grew to 404kph/251mph; service ceiling improved from 6,800 metres/22,311ft to 9,400m/30,841ft; and the extra tankage for fuel in the SB-2 allowed range to grow to 1,250km/777 miles from 700km/435 miles. The SB-2 was a winner. By now, the Soviet Union had secured production rights to the Hispano Suiza 12Ybrs engine, which was given the Soviet designation Mikulin M-100. The first production SB-2s were powered by 750hp M-100s which gave a maximum speed of just 395kph/245mph, but within six months Mikulin had improved the engine to French levels, and the new variant produced 860hp, which allowed bomb payload to be raised to 600kg/1,323lb and increased maximum speed to 423kph/263mph.

The first aircraft began to come off the production line at Moscow's Factory N22 early in 1936, and by the end of March their factory and state flight acceptance tests had been completed, and deliveries to the Air Force were under way. Production was also established in Factory N125 at Irkutsk in central Siberia. By the time production was discontinued in 1941, no less than 6,831 aircraft had been built, 5,695 in Moscow and 1,136 in Irkutsk. Another 161 were built in Czechoslovakia. The number of ANT-40/SBs built has usually been given as 6,656 – indeed even the Tupolev Design Bureau have given out this figure. But during the research for this book some omissions from production records were noted, and those built in Czechoslovakia were omitted from earlier counts and

ANT-40; coded '9', this SB is shown from above on a taxiway
Maksimillian B. Saukke Collection

are now added. So the total numbers built, including the three prototypes constructed at the TsAGI–ZOK, amounted to 6,995. Up to the ANT-40, total production of Tupolev aircraft had only reached 2,084 (ANT-1 to ANT-37). No other Tupolev aircraft had come close to this.

The SB-2's first active service was in Spain during the civil war in that country. Altogether, some 210 SB-2s were delivered by sea to Franco's forces, with the first arriving in October 1936. They made a decisive difference: faster than most of the government's fighters, their manoeuvrability and toughness made them difficult opponents. Some of them had the Mikulin engines replaced by French-built HS 12Ybrs after the civil war had ended, and served in front-line and, later, training squadrons until the mid-1940s.

By the beginning of the Great Patriotic War in June 1941, some ninety-four per cent of the Soviet Air Force's serviceable bomber strength were SB-2s. With the German invasion, they were soon in action against Russia's former allies; before the end of June, SB-2s were used to attack an airfield captured by the Luftwaffe near the town of Demidov. On 1 July, thirty-nine aircraft – SB-2s, Pe-2s and I-153s with an escort of MiG-3s – destroyed a bridge near Skulen. Later that month, eighteen SB-2s were attacked by about thirty Messerschmitt Bf 109 fighters. In a battle lasting half an hour, three Bf 109s were shot down along with one SB-2; on the same day, three SB-2s were attacked by twelve German fighters, and both sides lost two aircraft. In an eight-day operation in August 1941, SB-2s were flying three to four missions each night against the 2nd Panzer Gruppe of the German Army as it laid siege to Leningrad (St

Petersburg). SB-2s of the 10th Guard Short-Range Bomber Regiment saw extensive action in the battle for Stalingrad (now Volgograd), attacking enemy aerodromes, infantry and tank/panzer units.

The role of the SB-2 was not just confined to bombing missions: they also saw service as transport and liaison vehicles linking Red Army HQ with the front, as glider tugs bringing troops and supplies behind enemy lines, as reconnaissance aircraft, and, when needed, as airborne searchlight carriers which would light up enemy aircraft attacking Moscow, thus making them easier targets for ground defenders.

Several cases are reported of pilots aiming their badly damaged SB-2s at the enemy. On 22 June 1941, Captain A. S. Portasov, the officer in command of the 16th High-Speed Airbombing Regiment, after being badly damaged by cannon fire from a Luftwaffe bomber, deliberately rammed and destroyed his opponent. A few weeks later, on 4 July, Captain L. V. Mikhailov, squadron commander of the 10th Bombing Regiment/41st Bombing Division, after receiving major damage from ground fire, crashed his aircraft on to a column of tanks and destroyed several of them. Both pilots died in the crashes.

Extraordinarily, some SB-2s served with the Luftwaffe. They entered German service because the Soviet government had granted production rights to the Czechoslovakian manufacturer Avia, and between 1937 and 1939, the Skoda subsidiary company had produced 161 aircraft, including 101 in a bombing version and sixty as long-range reconnaissance aircraft. With the German invasion of Czechoslovakia in 1938, many of the SB-2s were captured; these, and those under construction, entered

ANT-40/SB, arriving back from a night bombing mission in 1941 – note the skis
Konstantin Udalov/Avico Press Collection

Luftwaffe service as trainers and for target towing for gunnery practice. Some Avia- and Aero-built aircraft were also delivered to the Bulgarian Air Force. Other SB-2s were exported to China, some of the earliest Soviet exports to this major Far Eastern country. These saw service, sometimes with Soviet crews, against Japanese forces in 1941–43.

Some other pre-war developments are worthy of inclusion. One SB-2 was built with a non-retractable tricycle undercarriage in order to test the advantages of the newly developed undercarriage system. While it had little effect on the war effort, by the end of hostilities most new aircraft designs included tricycle landing gear. It was the first Soviet aircraft to have a nosewheel undercarriage.

As the Soviet aero engine industry developed the M-100 engine, the newer versions began to become available for the SB production, and this allowed Arkhangelski to improve the aircraft. When the 860 to 960hp M-103 was introduced in 1936, variable pitch propellers were installed for the first time and the SB-2bis, as this version was called, with water-cooling

radiators fitted under the engine, could attain speeds of up to 450kph/280mph. On 2 September 1937, Mikhail Alekseev set a world record in an ANT-40/SB-2bis by carrying a one-tonne payload to 12,246.5 metres/40,180 feet. Actually, some time earlier, he had carried one tonne to 12,695m/41,652 feet, but the Soviet Union had not yet joined the Fédération Aéronautique Internationale (FAI), so the record was not recorded.

The M-103A, introduced in 1937, gave 950 to 1,000hp, and resulted in the SB-3, which featured an enlarged turret under the rear fuselage, and a slightly higher maximum speed of 455kph/283mph. A trainer version of the SB-3 was produced, the USB (Uchebnii Skorostnoi Bombardirovshik), with a stretched forward fuselage which included an open cockpit for the instructor located forward of the cockpit in which the trainees sat.

A proposed SB-3bis, with design improvements, was not built, but a prototype ANT-40MMN was, with two 1,050hp M-105 engines. This had an enlarged cabin which was constructed as an extension of the nose turret used by the bombardier. The MMN was used by Aeroflot, which called it *Shuka* (Pike), flying

The first Soviet aircraft with a nosewheel undercarriage was this modified ANT-40/SB which was converted at TsAGI by Igor Tolstikh, Chief Engineer of the institute
Konstantin Udalov/Avico Press Collection

mail and cargo at high altitude for the first time. The MMN had an empty weight of 4,183kg and a take-off weight of 5,706kg, so payload, freight and crew could come to 1,568kg/3,456lb.

Experience in the Spanish Civil War led Arkhangelski to design a dive bomber version called the SB-RK (the 'RK' stood for Razreznoe Krylo = Slotted Wing) which was intended to have a complex system of variable slotted flaps. But these would have taken too long to develop, so instead he strengthened the wing, reduced its surface area and installed suppressor grids in the leading edges. He fitted 1,100hp M-105Rs into streamlined nacelles and cooled the engines by installing air intakes into the wing leading edges which forced air over the radiators. With a two-

stage supercharger for each engine, the SB-RK could climb to 10,500m/34,450 feet; it could carry a one-tonne bomb load 1,000km/621 miles, and could fly at 480kph/298mph at 4,700m/15,420 feet. Although the RK was put into production in 1940, only 200 were completed by the time the German invaders forced the evacuation of Kazan. They served in the VVS under the designation Ar-2 (for Arkhangelski, as Tupolev was by that time a prisoner).

Stalin's post-war clean-up in the early 1950s saw any ANT-40s still around being scrapped. But one aircraft had force-landed in a snowstorm in 1939 near the Yuzhne Muiski mountain range on the banks of the Ukshum river in the Baikal region. Over the next thirty years its broken fuselage had been noted many times, and in the late 1970s *Vozdushni Transport*, the

ANT-40, SSSR-L2440, with Aeroflot titles; although not yet converted, it served as a mailplane
Konstantin Udalov/Avico Press Collection

Soviet aviation newspaper, sent an expedition led by Evgeny Konoplev to survey the aircraft. Konoplev found the results encouraging: the aircraft was in fairly good condition, so a group of VVS pilots arranged an expedition to recover it from its remote site, brought it to a military aerodrome and loaded it on to an Antonov An-22 which carried it to Moscow. It was transferred by road to Tupolev's facility on the Yauza embankment, and a group of young Tupolev employees volunteered to restore it. In April 1982, it was unveiled fully restored at the VVS museum at Monino, some sixty kilometres from Moscow, the only survivor of the almost 7,000 ANT-40s built.

ANT-41/T-1

Vladimir Myasishchev led a project to develop a torpedo bomber on the basis of the ANT-40/SB-2. TsAGI gave it the ANT-41 designation, while the VVS designated it T-1 (Torpedonosets = torpedo carrier). It was fitted with two Mikulin M-34FRN engines of 890hp. It was a low-winged monoplane with three crew.

It was completed early in 1936; on its first flight on 2 June the pilot, Aleksander Chernavski, encountered the same heavy tail flutter as had been experienced on early ANT-40 flights. Later, on its fourteenth flight, the aircraft broke up, and Chernavski and his two crew were lucky to be able to successfully evacuate the aircraft. The programme was discontinued.

ANT-42/TB-7

The Soviet Union's need for a large, modern, four-engined bomber was known to all the industry's designers, and in July 1934 Vladimir Petliakov's design team at TsAGI, under the overall leadership of Tupolev, began to research the problem of developing a suitable aircraft. He determined that speed and high-altitude cruising levels were essential requirements, and that this meant a low drag profile and super-charged engines offering as much power as possible. There were no suitable powerplants available in the Soviet Union at that time.

Petliakov began by designing a smooth-skinned, semi-monocoque fuselage of oval section with large bomb doors under the central fuselage. This was more easily conceived than done, as the metal industry was still producing duraluminium in corrugated sheets, and Tupolev had to use his considerable skills in arguing that it was time for the producers to adapt to new needs.

All this took time, so the prototype ANT-42, by now designated TB-7 by the Air Force, was not completed until December 1936. Its engines were four M-34FRNs of 930hp, but without the benefit of superchargers. Petliakov and Tupolev had given a lot of thought to the problem and had come up with an answer – to install a fifth engine in the rear fuselage which would act as a compressor/supercharger for the other four engines and which could provide pressurisation. But this was not fitted on the first ANT-42.

Petliakov located the nineteen fuel tanks in the wings. They were welded tanks, covered by a thin layer of rubber to reduce leakages. Five were mounted in the centre section, five in each of the outer wing panels between the double spars, and two in each wing's leading edge.

First flight took place from Khodinka on 27 December 1936 with Mikhail Gromov in command and Nikolai Rybko as co-pilot. Although the aircraft handled well, the lack of superchargers meant that its maximum service altitude was only 4,500m/14,765ft. As the flight test programme of the prototype progressed, Petliakov introduced changes to improve performance. By June 1937, work had been completed on the development of the fifth engine, an ATsN-2, derived from the M-100 – the licence-built Hispano Suiza 12Ybrs – and it was installed in the rear fuselage to power a supercharger. Although the aircraft's empty weight increased by some two tonnes because of the installation, performance was much better. Maximum speed at 403kph/251mph was as good as most fighters in foreign service, and the service ceiling was now 10,800m/35,435ft.

Meanwhile, work on the construction of the second TB-7 had begun in April 1936, and the lessons learned with the first aircraft resulted in several changes on the second. The engines were replaced by four AM-34FRNVs which gave 1,000hp each, and the supercharger was driven by a M-100A which produced 860hp, and it joined the test programme as it drew to a close in July 1938. While the tests were in the main satisfactory, the extra weight of the fifth engine substantially reduced the bomb load, and the M-34 engines were by now being outclassed by new designs, so Petliakov had to find a suitable replacement. This took until 1939, by which time he and many others had become prisoners in the purges sweeping the Soviet Union. But he was permitted to install the new Mikulin AM-35A, a 1,200hp supercharged engine, on the TB-7. This allowed the maximum take-off weight to increase to 27,000kg/59,535lb, and speed to rise to 427kph/265mph. Range also improved: now the TB-7 could carry two-tonne bomb loads 4,700km/2,921 miles, but the service ceiling reduced to 9,300m/30,513ft.

The first two aircraft had been built in factory N156, as the TsAGI-ZOK works were now known, and serial production was set up in factory N22 in Kazan. Production aircraft not only had new engines, they also featured a slimmer nose and new armaments. The nose turret now housed twin machine-guns, while cannons were mounted on pivots, one above the fuselage and one in the tail. The inner engine nacelles featured not only the radiators for both engines on that wing, but also a rear-facing turret with a pivoted machine-gun. Heavy armour was fitted, with 9mm plates to protect the pilots and thinner sheets for the navigator and the gunners, including those in the turrets mounted behind the engines. Thus the crew numbered ten – pilot and co-pilot, navigator, flight engineer, bombardier, and five gunners.

Later some TB-7s were fitted with M-40 diesel engines – a 1,000hp twelve-cylinder in-line engine – and the range with a two-tonne bomb load increased greatly to 7,820km/4,860 miles; speed and service ceiling both suffered, so the experiment was cancelled. Owing to a shortage of AM-35s, some aircraft were fitted with ASh-82 radials, but again performance suffered, so most of the ninety-three TB-7s built stayed with the AM-35A. The numbers were limited by the shortage of engines, as priority for high-performance piston engines was being given for fighter aircraft such as the MiG-3.

While plans were drawn up for a passenger version of the TB-7, intended to carry seventy, they were not put into production. But two of the last TB-7s were built as passenger aircraft. The ninetieth and ninety-first aircraft were fitted with a special cabin for twelve passengers which was mounted in the aircraft's rear fuselage, aft of the bomb bays. As Petliakov had died in an air accident in 1942, this work was headed by Iosef Nezval, who succeeded him as chief designer of the aircraft, which had been redesignated Pe-8 as a belated and posthumous honour to its designer.

The passenger compartment had cabin walls featuring a layer of noise and heat insulation material; a buffet was installed, as was a toilet. A luggage compartment was fitted into one of the bomb bays, and was capable of carrying 1,200kg/2,646lb of baggage. The bomb doors were replaced by a conventional fuselage skin. Aft of the cockpit there was sleeping accommodation for three people. While the upper fuselage machine-gun fitting was omitted from these two aircraft, other defensive weapons were retained.

These aircraft were completed in 1944. They were followed by two more standard TB-7 bombers, then production was closed.

In military service, the TB-7/Pe-8 was assigned to the 45th Air Army, where it equipped squadrons in two divisions. Its war career began on 8 August 1941, some seven weeks after the German invasion, when aircraft from two squadrons of the N412 long-range bomber regiment of the 81st Division bombed Berlin. Two nights later, they were airborne again; this time each Pe-8 carried six 500kg/1,102lb high-explosive avia bombs (FAB 500). The return flight from Pushkino aerodrome near Leningrad to Berlin took almost thirteen hours. While the damage the small numbers of the Pe-8s did to the German capital was relatively small, its effect on both German and Russian morale was considerable.

In September 1941, Pe-8s bombed Nazi-occupied Bucharest, and in 1942 they provided support to the Soviet army under siege in the battle for Stalingrad (Volgograd) by bombing positions near the enemy's front line. April 1943 saw the Pe-8 in action against the

The four-engined ANT-42/TB-7
Konstantin Udalov/Avico Press Collection

then German city of Koningsberg – today it is Russia's Kaliningrad. On 5 April, in a night operation against the city, a Pe-8 dropped a five-tonne bomb for the first time. In June, more five-tonne bombs were dropped in the major battle for the city of Kursk, when enemy tanks and armour were the targets. Other cities to be targeted by the largest Soviet bomber of the time included Danzig, Stettin and Budapest.

TB-7/Pe-8s, with their long range and high speed, were used for several VIP flights during the war. On 28 April 1942, the Soviet deputy people's commissar for foreign affairs (deputy foreign minister) flew to England as head of a delegation preparing for a visit by Viacheslav Molotov, the commissar. They landed at Tilling, where deputy commissar Pavlov remained while his pilot Aziamov and three members of the delegation left for London on a de Havilland DH95 Flamingo. Unfortunately, the DH95 caught fire en route and exploded, killing all on board. The following day, 1 May, the remainder of the Soviet delegation flew back to Moscow, with Aziamov's co-pilot, Endel Pusep, now in command.

Nevertheless, on 19 May Pusep returned to Tilling with Molotov and a delegation of nine. Josef Stalin, the Soviet leader, had instructed Molotov to conduct talks with Winston Churchill and Franklin Delano Roosevelt on the opening of a second front against the Germans. For the mission, the Pe-8 was fitted with oxygen equipment. The flight to England, some 2,700km/1,678 miles, took fifteen hours and was flown at altitudes of 3,000 to 6,000m/9,843 to 19,686 feet. Pusep noted that the outside air temperatures fell to -45°C/-49°F en route.

On 24 May they were off again, this time en route to Washington, which they reached via Prestwick, Reykjavik and Goose Bay, landing in the US capital on 30 May. In the landing, several of the aircraft's tyres burst; fortunately for Molotov and his team, the American tyre manufacturer B. F. Goodrich measured the wheel size and made up a new set in just two days.

Roosevelt took the trouble of meeting the aircrew and welcoming them to America. On 4 June they headed east, routing through Gander, Reykjavik and Prestwick, and from there direct to Moscow's Kratovo Aerodrome which they reached on the thirteenth. Most of the ocean crossing was flown at 8,000m/26,248 feet, and they had successfully flown through German-occupied airspace without hindrance. They had covered some 17,800km/11,061 miles.

Despite the huge advances in aircraft design, the TB-7/Pe-8 continued in VVS service until the mid-1950s. Unfortunately, all surviving examples were scrapped in the latter part of the decade.

ANT-43

Tupolev proposed a six-passenger single-engined low-wing monoplane in 1936. However, instead of using conventional drawings, the plans were prepared on stencils which were to be applied to sheet metal for cutting. Because of this, approval for construction was refused, and the project was scrapped.

ANT-44/MTB-2A

In December 1934, Tupolev was asked to design a naval heavy bomber (Morksoi Torpedonosets Bombardirovshik = naval torpedo bomber = MTB). With his seaplane specialist Ivan Pogosski dead, he gave the project to Aleksander Golubkov who came up with a more conventional design than the earlier ANT 'hydroplanes' – a single hull with a high-wing profile, made entirely from duraluminium. It was an amphibian with a retractable wheeled undercarriage, and the floats, mounted near the wingtips on struts, were load-carrying. Powerplants were four Gnôme-Rhône 14Krsds, which gave 810hp each, and were conventionally mounted in the wing leading edges. The wings' shape resulted in the ANT-44, as the project was designated, being called the *Chaika* (Seagull).

Construction of the prototype began on 4 October 1935, and the aircraft was manufactured with smooth sheets of duraluminium, which were now becoming available in place of the former corrugated ones. The work was carried out in the TsAGI–ZOK factory N156. It was completed in March 1937, and brought by road to Khodinka, from where it made its first flight on a fixed wheeled undercarriage (because the retractable mechanisation was not yet ready) on 19 April 1937. Its pilot was Timofei Riabenko. State tests were conducted with the undercarriage fixed down; maximum speed was measured at 355kph/221mph, maximum take-off weight at 18,500kg/40,792lb, and range with a bomb or torpedo load of 2,500kg/5,512lb was 2,500km/1,554 miles. The state tests were completed in July.

A second aircraft was completed in June 1938; by now, the first had its undercarriage modified to retract, while the second aircraft had a retractable one from the start. It had 840hp Mikulin M-87As fitted and was dubbed the ANT-44bis or -44D.

By September, both aircraft were taken on service with the Soviet Navy, as the MTB-2A. No production was ordered, and they served some operations in the Great Patriotic War from bases in the Black Sea. Led by Ivan Sukhomlin, the MTB-2As were used to bomb

The ANT-44bis, with four-blade propellers at Khodinka
Konstantin Udalov/Avico Press Collection

oil refineries in Bulgaria and Romania, both then under Nazi occupation. But before the Soviet Union was invaded by Germany, Ivan Sukhomlin had earned four world records, with the ANT-44bis. In June 1940, he set several records lifting different loads to record altitudes for amphibians, and on 7 October he achieved a record for amphibians by carrying a two-tonne load over a 1,000km/621 mile closed circuit at an average speed of 241.999kph/150.378mph. Although this record was not acknowledged by the FAI until after the war, it stood unbeaten until 1957.

ANT-45

In 1935, the TsAGI began work on the design of a low-wing, two-seat fighter, but the project was cancelled the following year.

ANT-46/DI-8

Arkhangelski's ANT-40 was the basis of a two-seat, low-wing fighter monoplane on which design work began early in 1935. The ANT-46 was later given the

VVS designation DI-8 (Dvukhmestnii Istrebitel = double-seat fighter). It was designed as a mount for two APK-100 cannons, which were mounted on the wings outboard of the engines. Again, the project was headed by Aleksander Arkhangelski, working under the general leadership of Tupolev.

The aircraft was a mid-wing twin-engined fighter with a close resemblance to its larger brother, the ANT-40/SB-2. Two Gnôme-Rhône 14Krsd 800hp engines were fitted, and it was also equipped with four ShKAS 7.62mm machine-guns which were mounted in fixed positions in the aircraft's nose.

The sole example, the prototype, was manufactured in the KOSOS–TsAGI works, and its first flight took place on 1 August 1935 when its pilot was Mikhail Alekseev. In tests, the ANT-46 achieved a speed of 400kph/249mph; but because of pressure of work for the ANT-40/SB project, Arkhangelski did not offer the ANT-46 for state tests and the programme was dropped.

ANT-46/DI-8 at factory tests in 1935
Maksimillian B. Saukke Collection

ANT-47

A proposed single-seat fighter which was not developed.

ANT-48

A proposed development of ANT-40/SB which was not progressed.

ANT-49

A proposed long-range reconnaissance development of the ANT-40/SB with aerial cameras installed in the bomb bay, and with larger fuel tanks. The project was cancelled before a prototype was built.

ANT-50

Passenger aircraft. Project not started.

ANT-51

In 1936, the VVS announced a competition for a light reconnaissance bomber under the codename 'Ivanov'. The results of the competition were a foregone conclusion, because the specifications were drawn around an aircraft which had already flown, the Kharkov-built KhAI-5; still, it attracted quite a number of designs which were useful comparisons for the VVS. Four aircraft were selected for the development to prototype stage, but the timescale allowed was short and only the KhAI-5 was ready in time.

However, development of the winner proceeded perhaps a little too quickly, and as the production aircraft entered service, problems were soon evident. By now, the three other contenders were flying. One of these was the ANT-51, the TsAGI project headed by Pavel Sukhoi under the leadership of Tupolev. It was a single-engined low-wing monoplane with a large cockpit powered by a nine-cylinder Mikulin M-62 of 830hp, and carried a crew of two. It carried four ShKAS machine guns fitted into the leading edge of the wings, and two more in a turret at the rear of the cockpit. The first example was constructed at KOSOS–TsAGI.

Mikhail Gromov flew the prototype on its first flight from Khodinka on 25 August 1937. As the retraction equipment was not available, it was fitted with a fixed undercarriage but with spats to reduce drag. It achieved a speed of 403kph/251mph at 4,700m/15,420 feet, a very creditable performance with fixed undercarriage, and even at low levels attained 360kph/223mph. It looked an obvious choice for the Air Force, but Russia was in the midst of Stalin's purges, and in November 1937 Tupolev was arrested and imprisoned. However, in 1938 Sukhoi was appointed the general designer of a new bureau. With the war looming, aluminium was in short supply, so he redesigned the fuselage to be constructed in the more plentiful material wood, and installed the new 950hp Mikulin M-87. Two examples of the BB-1 (Blizhnii Bombardirovshik = short-range bomber), as the redesign was designated by the VVS, were ready by late 1939. A third, fitted with an M-88, was completed early in 1940, and this was the model selected for production. As they began to roll off production lines, the industry designation was changed from ANT-51 to Su-2.

By the start of the Great Patriotic War in June 1941, just over 100 Su-2/BB-1s had entered service with the VVS, but the enforced move of most of the industry from Moscow with the German advance saw the end of production for the last of the pure ANT series and the first Su. Its military pilots and engineers used to say of the BB-1, 'Ni Tu, Ni Su' (not a Tu, not a Su).

ANT-51, a retouched photo, with the undercarriage painted out, to represent the ANT-51; the sole ANT-51 only flew with a fixed undercarriage
Konstantin Udalov/Avico Press Collection

The PE-2

An Almost ANT

Vladimir Petliakov was another victim of Stalin's purges. From his cell, he proposed a design which he initially called the VI-100 (Vysotnii Istrebitel = high-altitude fighter). It was a low-winged, high-speed fighter fitted with two supercharged Mikulin M-105R engines. Along with the pilot was a gunner who operated a turret fitted with a machine-gun. Just before the prototype was completed, the VVS changed its mind and instructed him to continue development as a bomber.

The prototype was completed as a mix between the two roles, and made its first flight in December 1939. By now, the VVS had amended its bomber requirements from high altitude to high speed level and dive bombing for close co-operation with ground forces, but despite these problems Petliakov managed to develop an outstanding aircraft. The prototypes of the bomber had a better performance than any Soviet production fighters – 540kph/336mph at 5,000m/16,405ft. Some 462 Pe-2s, as the aircraft was best known, were delivered by the start of the war on 22 June 1941, and soon proved their worth even though few crews had been trained by then. By the end of the war, more than 11,400 Pe-2s had been delivered to the VVS, and they had played a vital role in the Soviet Union's victory.

But Vladimir Petliakov had died, in an air crash, in 1942. He had been released from prison in 1940, and with Tupolev still a prisoner had been permitted to head his own design bureau. In 1942, he was travelling in a Pe-2 from the factory at Kazan to Moscow when the aircraft crashed in bad weather conditions. After this, all chief designers were required to receive permission in advance before being permitted to travel by air.

ANT-End

With the arrest and imprisonment of Tupolev came an effective end to the early years of what is today named the Tupolev Aviation Complex. While ANT designations would continue to be applied until the late 1940s, the projects were better known by their Tu designations, so they are listed as such in this section; sometimes, for reasons usually of secrecy, other designations were used, such as Samolet (aircraft) N, Yu, 103. These will be outlined and explained in the appropriate places.

ANT-58 to -62; -65 to -67; Samolet 103 – The Tu-2

(NATO Codename 'Bat')

After his arrest and imprisonment, Tupolev had only the daily routines of prison to keep him occupied. But his profession was not forgotten and his mind kept developing new ideas.

As signs of an impending war drew closer, Lavrenti Beria, the people's commissar (minister) for internal affairs, began to realise that much of the capability of Soviet industry had been damaged by the imprisonment of so many industrial leaders and specialists, and he put the idea to Stalin that prisoners should be put to work, in prisons, using their talents and capabilities to organise and develop new product designs. When Tupolev was offered the chance to lead a design team, he agreed on the terms outlined earlier in the chapter on his life story. His two years of no activity had left him eager for work. At least he had the opportunity to select his new team from a huge number of specialists in the prison camps and to form Central Design Bureau N29 of the NKVD (security police of the Department of the Interior).

Once he had gathered a team of prisoners who were expert in the skills needed to produce combat aircraft, Beria instructed Tupolev to begin work on a four-engined dive bomber. Tupolev quickly realised the impracticability of such a design, but it took some time, working from prison, to convince Beria to have second thoughts, and then to issue instructions to Tupolev and his team to design instead a twin-engined combat dive bomber which could also be used in a medium- to high-altitude role. Eventually, as a matter of practical sense, Beria authorised that TsKB N29 of the NKVD should be transferred to the TsAGI's offices in Radio Street, and that this building should become a prison. This at least allowed the design team facilities for their work and the building of a prototype. The mock-up was built in prison, with considerable difficulties for both the prisoners and the guards.

Once the need had been redefined, the team got down to work. This time, Tupolev was the chief designer with just one project to control; in the past, he was usually in charge of five or more projects, each of which he assigned to a particular team. Work on the Samolet 103 – the project's codename – began on 1 March 1940. Tupolev chose an all-metal construction once again; the aircraft's frame, wings and skin were manufactured from smooth duraluminium, with the engine mounts and undercarriage made from steel.

The design featured a conventional twin-engined

ANT-58

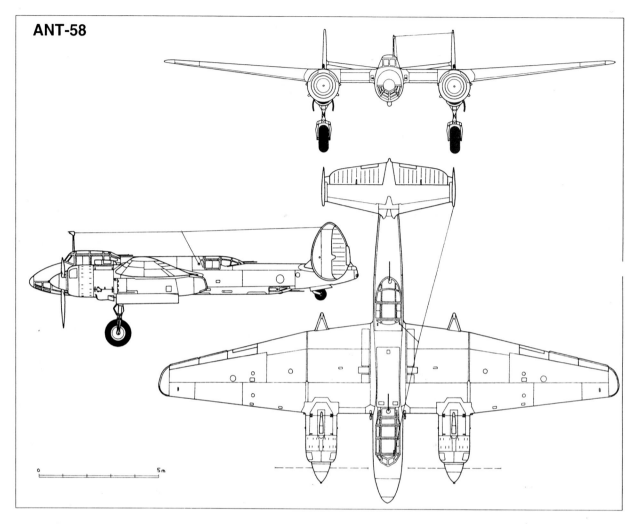

layout, but with a twin fin and rudder tailplane. The tailwheel undercarriage had the main wheels retracting backwards into the rear of the engine nacelles. The wings were mounted to the mid-fuselage, and the initial crew numbers were three. A large bomb compartment began just behind the cockpit and took up most of the fuselage. The gunner sat in a mid-fuselage turret over the bomb bay. Engines for the first aircraft were Mikulin AM-37s, which gave 1,400hp each. Variable pitch three-blade propellers were fitted. Hydraulic systems were used to control the flaps, wheel brakes and undercarriage for retraction and lowering. The cockpit had single controls, although provision was made for the installation of dual controls. The aircraft carried two cannons which were fired forward from the fuselage sides, and from three to five machine-guns which were aimed to the rear. Bomb load was up to 4.5 tonnes depending on the category and target requirements.

Considering the difficulties of the prison regime, the aircraft was completed in remarkably quick time at factory N156. It was first rolled out six months after the programme began, on 3 October 1940. It was transferred by road to Chkalovskaya AFB, where it was reassembled, and began tests on 1 December with the State red banner NII-VVS.

The first tests were ground runs of the engine and ground testing of the systems. The first flight was made on 29 January 1941, piloted by Mikhail Nukhtikov. During the tests, which continued until June, the aircraft was found to have an outstanding performance: at an altitude of 8,000m/26,248 feet, maximum speed was 635 to 640kph/395 to 398mph, and service ceiling was 10,800m/35,435 feet. Its range was 2,500km/1,554 miles. It was better than the VVS requirements in every respect. The only problem was that the engines, as well as the aircraft, were at an early stage of development. Tupolev had secured them from the designers before they were put into production, and production quality would be a problem for Soviet industry for quite some time yet. At that time, Mikulin and his team were more concerned with problems relating to more urgently needed engines for fighters.

The second aircraft was given the coded designation of Samolet 103U by the VVS and ANT-59 by Tupolev and his team. Tupolev incorporated a number of changes in it following the early tests with the Samolet 103/ANT-58, including a larger cockpit, with a higher roof. A second gunner was carried in a new tail turret to protect a weak area evident on the first aircraft. Although its early flights, which began on 18 May 1941, flown by Nukhtikov again, were made with AM-37 engines, these were soon changed for the ASh-82 radial; although top speed fell from 610kph/379mph to 530kph/329mph, at least the engine was available and reliable. The 103U also carried extra armament in the form of ten rockets mounted on pylons under the wing.

By that time, production of Samolet 103 had begun at a former car factory at Omsk. Based on the ANT-58 the first production aircraft, the 103V, had taken from

A Tu-2S coded '8' in flight over Moscow, near Gorki Park

Konstantin Udalov/Avico Press Collection

1 August to 13 November 1941 to complete. It was fitted with the air-cooled ASh-82 radial, a development of the Mikulin M-82, which gave 1,330hp. With this, service ceiling fell to 9,000m/29,529 feet and range to 2,000km/1,243 miles. But demands on production capacity were great, and after only nineteen had been produced the government ordered the Omsk factory to switch production to the more needed Yak-1 fighter. The design team designated the 103V as the ANT-60.

In 1942, Tupolev constructed the first ANT-61s, or Samolet 103S. Based on the 103V, it differed only in details which would allow it to become a production aircraft. This was the first aircraft to be designated Tu-2 by the VVS, and three early production examples were tested from 13 September until 28 October 1942 and then delivered to an Air Force front-line bomber unit near Kalinin (now Tver) where they were enthusiastically received by commanders and aircrew. So the government ordered the Tu-2 back into production at Omsk.

The shortage of materials and components forced Tupolev to make modifications yet again. But at least the more powerful ASh-82FN, rated between 1,460 and 1,850hp, was now available. Now called the Tu-2S, this version made its first flight on 26 August 1943 and the first examples began arriving with squadrons in spring 1944. Some 1,111 examples were delivered by the end of the war, although the VVS could happily have used many more. The fuel-injected engines of the Tu-2S gave it a speed of 530kph/329mph and its range was 2,100km/1,304 miles. Its standard bomb load was one tonne.

Other Tu-2 versions included:

ANT-62, or Tu-2D: With the D standing for Dalnii (long range), this version had ASh-83 engines of 1,900hp; its wingspan was increased by 3.34m/10.96 feet which allowed fuel tankage to be increased. The crew numbered five, and up to four-tonne bomb loads could be carried. Range with a one-tonne load was 2,790km/1,734 miles. Duplicate controls allowed a second pilot to be carried to relieve the first on long sectors. It went into production after the war to meet a need for long-endurance patrol aircraft.

ANT-62T, or Tu-2T: A torpedo carrier version with two ASh-82FN engines and extra fuel tanks installed in the bomb bay. Its first flight took place on 2 August 1946 with Fiodor Opadchi in command. After its trials, it was handed over to the Navy and a small production run followed. Tu-2Ts replaced the Ilyushin Il-4T in naval service and were assigned to squadrons based on the Black Sea and Baltic Sea. It remained in service until the mid-1950s.

A version of the Tu-2D with AM-44TK engines
Konstantin Udalov/Avico Press Collection

Tu-2SDV, or ANT 63: Only two examples of this high-speed day bomber were built; the first flew on 21 May 1944 on its maiden flight, piloted by Aleksei Pereliot. It was fitted with in-line AM-39s which offered 1,500 to 1,870hp, and reached 645kph/401mph. The second, fitted with AM-39F engines, had a crew of three, one more than the earlier example; it reached a speed of 640kph/398mph. It first flew on 14 October 1944 piloted by Mikhail Nukhtikov.

ANT-65, or Tu-2DB: A long-range version equipped with Mikulin supercharged AM-44 engines. Its first flight was made on 1 July 1946, the pilot being Fiodor Opadchi. Because of problems with the engine, the programme was stopped.

ANT 67, or Tu-2ACh-39VF: A diesel-engined version – the ACh-39VF referred to the engines which were designed by Aleksei Charomski; though they were of 1,900hp, speed dropped to 509kph/316mph, but the range grew to 4,100km/2,548 miles. However, with a take-off weight of 17,170kg/37,860lb, this version was substantially heavier than the other Tu-2s. Difficulties with the engine resulted in the programme being discontinued.

Tu-2S4: A two-seat version equipped with two 45mm cannons and two of 37mm installed in the nose. Some aircraft had a movable cannon for defence aimed to the rear. Another had a 75mm cannon for use against trains and another was a testbed for forty-eight machine-guns aimed vertically downwards to attack ground targets.

Tu-2R/Tu-2P/Tu-6: A long-range photo-reconnaissance version with cameras mounted in the bomb bay.

Tu-2 Paravan: A version designed to cut the cables holding barrage balloons in place. The Paravan had a 6m/19.7ft 'Pinocchio' type nose which had cables made of 13.5mm wire running to the wingtips where a cutter was fitted. Two Paravans were built. Paravan is the Russian equivalent of 'minesweeper'.

Other aircraft based on the Tu-2 included the Tu-8/ANT-69, the Tu-10/ANT-68 and the Tu-12. Tu-2 production figures include the numbers for the Tu-6, Tu-8 and Tu-10.

Although it took some time before the Tu-2 began to appear in reasonable numbers, they were used in many battles. Their first actions were operated from Kalinin, as already mentioned. Later, in the battle for Kursk in June 1944, eighteen Tu-2s of division N285 were used to bomb enemy forces and to attack positions behind the lines. In the battle for Vyborg, which began on 9 June 1944, over 600 Tu-2s led by Colonel I. Piskok of Division N334 took part. They were used to bomb enemy positions in nearby posts as well, including those in the Kiviniemi, Valkiarvi and Kivennopa regions of the pre-Baltic. On 7 April 1945, a force of 516 Tu-2s and Pe-8s attacked defences in Koningsberg (now Kaliningrad) prior to the city being taken by Soviet forces. They also took part in the battle for Berlin. On the first day of the battle, Tu-2s dropped ninety-seven tonnes of bombs on the city.

By the end of the war, the VVS had begun to realise the value of the Tu-2, and thus development of the aircraft continued until 1948 when production was terminated. But several versions of the versatile design remained in operation with Soviet forces until the mid-1950s. With the cessation of hostilities, many Tu-2s were transferred to training roles. But it was still a front-line aircraft, and what was needed was an aircraft to train crews for the Tu-2, so Pavel Sukhoi's bureau was asked to develop an aircraft to do just that. He substantially lightened the design and produced the Sukhoi UTB (Uchebno Trenirovochnii

Tu-2 Paravan, one of only two Paravans built for the role of cutting cables of barrage balloons
Konstantin Udalov/Avico Press Collection

Bombardirovshik = Learning Training Bomber) which served the VVS until the late 1950s.

Tu-2s also saw service with other air forces, including that of China. Several, but unquantified, dozens of aircraft were delivered to the Chinese Air Force, and the Tu-2 was produced in unknown numbers in China. Many Tu-2s were still in China in 1996, some with museums and some still on air force bases, although out of service. Tu-2s were also used as flying laboratories and engine test beds. Several jet engines were tried out for the first time suspended under a Tu-2, including the RD500, a 1,600kp engine used for the Lavochkin La-15 fighter and the RD-45 used on the MiG-15bis. It was also used in

experiments to carry a GAZ-6TB cross-country jeep-type vehicle in the bomb bay, half retracted into the body of the aircraft. From there it could be paradropped to the ground. It was also the test vehicle for Soviet radar bomb sighting equipment.

Production of the Tu-2 series started and ended in 1941, and was restarted in 1943 and continued in Omsk until 1948. Dates or numbers for Chinese-built Tu-2s are not known, but Russian production totalled 2,527. Several Tu-2 versions are preserved in China. Some of these had been fitted with Chinese HS8 engines in a programme begun in 1963. More than 50 aircraft had been fitted with these engines in the mid 1960s.

A rare Tu-2 survivor, this Chinese Air Force example is preserved at the Beijing Datang Shan Museum, shown here in November 1995. It was re-engined in the 1960s.
G. M. Nason

ANT-63P/Tu-1

A slimmed-down version of the Tu-2, the ANT-63P/Tu-1 served as a fighter
Konstantin Udalov/Avico Press Collection

Although the Tu-2 was NKVD N29's first programme, the VVS gave the designation Tu-1 to a Tu-2 development which converted the high-speed medium bomber into a two-seat long-range fighter intended to escort and defend bomber forces and convoys.

Tupolev scaled down the Tu-2 slightly and reduced its weight. The crew was reduced from four to two. Design work began late in 1943, and the prototype was completed in early 1945. Only the size and the cockpit were substantially different to the Tu-2, except for the engines. On the prototype were two AM-39UVs, designed by Mikulin, which generated 1,640hp each. It was constructed at factory N156, and made its first flight from Zhukovski on 21 May 1945. Performance was impressive: it reached 680kph/423mph and its range was 2,500km/1,554 miles. Ceiling was 10,000m/32,810ft.

Although the war was ending, it was put into production at factory N166 in Omsk. Production aircraft were fitted with AM-43Bs with a power output of 1,900hp each. Production aircraft were armed with four fixed trajectory NS-23 cannons and a ShVAK cannon operated by the gunner from the rear cockpit.

The ANT-64 and the Tu-4

(NATO Codename 'Bull')

One of the most remarkable stories of aviation engineering in the 1940s is undoubtedly that of the Tu-4.

In 1944, Tupolev had begun work on a large, long-range bomber with four turbocharged engines under the designation ANT-64, but the programme did not go ahead. While the industry of the Soviet Union had made considerable advances in the previous twenty years, the country's leaders were well aware that Western industry, and particularly that of the United States, was still well ahead in terms of technology. A large number of Western aircraft had been supplied to the Soviet Union under the Lend–Lease programme, but few of these were of the latest technology, and Stalin and his ministers/commissars were particularly anxious to see the Soviet Union close the gap.

In the summer of 1944, fate took a hand. On 7 July, a US Air Force B-29-5BW, serial 42-6526 of 771st Squadron, 462nd Bomb Group, made a forced landing in eastern Siberia. It had been on a bombing mission to Japan and had suffered damage, so the crew elected to land in Russia rather than be lost in the Pacific. They were well received and were returned to the United States shortly afterwards. However, as the Soviet Union was not at the time at war with Japan, the B-29 was impounded. Several more B-29 crews took the same option. On 8 August, 42-93829 crashed in an east Siberian mountain range. The surviving crew were returned home. Although the aircraft was badly damaged, some parts could be salvaged. And in November, two aircraft landed safely, serial 42-6365 on the eleventh, and 42-6358 on the twenty-first, both from the 794th Squadron, 468th Bomb Group.

With three virtually complete examples of one of the United States' more advanced aircraft at his disposal, the Soviet leader, Josef Stalin, decided that this could be a key to modernising the Soviet aviation industry. He selected Tupolev, still not quite in favour but no longer a prisoner, and Vladimir Myasishchev to work on ways to do this. Tupolev had forced modernisation in the industry over twenty years earlier. Now he was instructed to build a duplicate B-29 and to give the Soviet Union a strategic bomber. He was also given Stalin's authority to carry out whatever he deemed necessary, including a full industry modernisation, for the task.

The Georgian leader of the Soviet Union had moulded a network of authority throughout the entire nation, and Tupolev set about using the network to achieve his target. He appointed Dmitri Markov as chief designer and he remained project leader. The work was not given a project number; with an already existing finished product, it was not considered appropriate.

It might seem a straightforward task to copy

another aircraft, but it is not. Eddie Allen, leader of the design team of the B-29, had been far-seeing and had stretched the capabilities of the industry; now Tupolev had to close the existing gap and take the same step forward with Soviet industry, materials, components and engines. Tupolev started with a thorough examination of the three surviving B-29s which had been flown to the new research airport now called Zhukovski. Situated some forty kilometres/twenty-five miles east of Moscow, this airfield would be known to the West only as Ramenskoe, the name of a small nearby town, until the late 1980s. Although the design was, by early 1945, already three years old at a time of rapid industrial development, Tupolev was very impressed with it. He told Stalin it would take a minimum of three years to produce a duplicate. Stalin told him that the first examples were to participate in the air parade held to mark the aviation industry – the day of the Air Fleet, in August 1947, just over two years away.

Tu-4

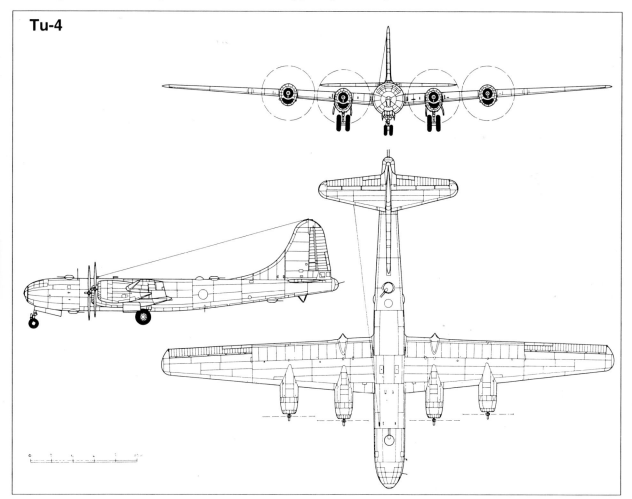

Tupolev started by reorganising the bureau. With Markov heading the team, he assigned each of his department heads a range of responsibilities in line with his skills. Then it was decided to completely strip down one of the B-29s and to use the components to make detailed technical drawings. A second aircraft was used for flight testing in order to determine its performance and capabilities, and the third was held in reserve and to act as a comparison later.

One of Tupolev's outstanding strengths was his organisational capability. He needed it over the next few years. As components were stripped from the B-29 they were examined, weighed and a technical description was written, then they were broken down for technical drawing, and the drawings were sent out to Soviet industry for a high-priority duplicate to be made. He bore the responsibility of determining what was acceptable and what was not. This was done to everything – pipes, tubes, cables, fuselage skin, frames and spars. He convened regular meetings of his team to compare items. On one side was the American original, on the other the samples built by different Soviet factories or design bureaux. Test reports would be compared, weights checked, then opinions would be garnished before a decision was made. And very often the decision was, 'You have to do better, and quickly'.

One of the major questions was that of measure-ments. The Soviet Union used the metric system, the US industry measured in feet and inches. So when it came to measuring the thickness of wires or cables, for example for electrical circuits, which to use? By choosing the nearest metric size, the weight would be greater or lesser, but the conductive capability would also vary. And on the aircraft's skin, minor thickness differences could make big differences in weight and strength, although it was easier to predict the effects. Without the luxury of time, Tupolev decided to stay with the American system. In several cases the Soviet industry had to adjust to imperial measurements. For more than twenty years Soviet craftsmen continued to use imperial measurements in many different industries.

Instruments were also a major difficulty. Some were possible to duplicate, but with others, in particular the American IFF system (Identity: Friend or Foe), there was no choice but to substitute a Soviet replacement. With radio equipment there were also some difficul-ties. The short-wave system on the B-29, although better than that on Soviet aircraft, was of old design. There were better examples on the B-25 Mitchells received under the Lend–Lease programme. Although the radio industry agreed to duplicate the newer system, VVS consent was needed. Mindful of Stalin's instructions, the VVS agreed that while the aircraft

A line of nine Tu-4s at LII in Zhukovski being operated by the VVS for the National Kommissariat of the Aviation Industry in 1947–1948
Maksimillian B. Saukke Collection

A Tu-4LL at LII in Zhukovski with an NK-12 engine mounted for testing. The NK-12 was the Tu-95's powerplant
Konstantin Udalov/Avico Press Collection

should have the better equipment, it could not give its consent. But it agreed that it would accept an undertaking from the design bureau that the new system would meet all requirements. In addition, rubbers, plastics and synthetics were very different to those used in Russia, so these industries had to change too. As only one of the three flyable B-29s was equipped with a de-icing system (Goodrich was the manufacturer), this was a difficult problem which had to be solved. All these problems were solved by summer 1946; by then, a representation from the design bureau had been set up in factory N22 at Kazan; later it would become the first branch office of the OKB.

With three prototypes already in existence, and little time in which to meet Stalin's order, the first Tu-4, as the Soviet B-29 was designated, made its first flight from Kazan on 19 May 1947 piloted by Nikolai

Rybko. State tests were passed without serious problems, and the Akt (a Soviet certificate of airworthiness) was for the first and only time personally signed by Josef Stalin. On 3 August 1947, the first three production Tu-4s, along with the Tu-70, a passenger version, took part in the National Air Parade at Tushino aerodrome near Moscow. The Tu-4s were the first of twenty test aircraft, and were flown by Nikolai Rybko, Mark Gallai and Aleksander Vasilchenko. Tupolev had met Stalin's deadline.

The Tu-4 was an all-metal design, although the ailerons, rudders and elevators had linen skins to reduce weight. The fuselage was semi-monocoque of 2.9m/9.51 feet diameter and comprised five sections, which were bolted together. The cabin was pressurised to give an equivalent altitude of 2,500m/8,202 feet when flown at 7,000m/22,967 feet. All control cables

This Tu-4 is preserved at the VVS Museum in Monino, shown here in the winter of 1990
Paul Duffy

were duplicated, thus a break in any control line did not mean a loss of control. The wheel brakes were operated hydraulically.

The aircraft was well armed: it carried ten 20mm cannons mounted in five turrets, one in the nose, one above the centre fuselage and one in the tail, with another immediately behind the cockpit and the fifth fitted under the rear fuselage, an arrangement allowed by the nosewheel tricycle undercarriage. In an unusual arrangement for the time, all guns could be aimed and fired from any gunnery position by means of a remote control. The Boeing's Wright R-335D Turbo Cyclone 18-cylinder, turbocharged two-row radial engines were also duplicated, this time by Arkadi Shvetsov's engine design bureau, so the Tu-4 was powered by four ASh-73TKs which were fitted with large four-blade propellers of 5.056 metre/16 feet 7 inches diameter. These gave a power output, comparable to their American equivalent, of 2,000hp at 2,400rpm (maximum cruise) or 2,400hp at take-off power of 2,600rpm.

Bomb load was normally six tonnes, with a maximum of eight tonnes. Like the B-29, the Tu-4 could also carry nuclear bombs. It was, in fact, the first Soviet aircraft to drop an atom bomb. Some 47.5 tonnes was the normal take-off weight, but the Tu-4 could have this raised to sixty-six tonnes when necessary, with bomb load and fuel representing the extra weight. Maximum landing weight was forty-eight tonnes. This compared to 54 tonnes normal on the B-29, and 63.5 tonnes maximum on early versions.

Production began in Kazan in 1946, and the first twenty aircraft were used for a speedy test programme which experienced few difficulties – as already said,

Rybko made the first flight in May 1947, and Mark Gallai flew the second in June. The VVS began to receive the aircraft early in 1949, and set about training the eleven-man crews for the bomber. Much of its equipment was new to the VVS, including the radar which allowed bombs to be accurately dropped from 12,000 metres/39,372 feet at night and in all weather conditions. Performance of the Tu-4 was good, although not quite as good as its American counterpart (figures in brackets). Maximum speed was 570kph/354mph (576kph/358mph). Range without refuelling with five-tonne bomb load at 47.5 tonnes take-off weight was 4,900km/3,045 miles (5,000km/3,107 miles).

Although its primary role was as a strategic bomber, the Tu-4s also served as in-flight refuelling tankers and as long range reconnaissance aircraft. One Tu-4T was built as a paratroop transporter which could carry twenty-eight fully equipped soldiers. During the Hungarian uprising against Soviet authority in 1965, Tu-4s were on standby to drop 250kg bombs on Budapest. Fortunately they were not needed.

A second production line was opened at Moscow factory N23. By the time production ceased, 847 had been manufactured. Stalin had originally ordered that 1,000 be built, but later developments reduced the number.

Three Tu-4s were used as aerial test platforms for the NK-12 turboprop, which was mounted in place of the inner starboard engine. With substantially larger propellers, they were easy to identify.

After the VVS began to withdraw the Tu-4 in 1956 several were transferred to Avia Arktika, where they

The Chinese Air Force fitted turboprop engines on several Tu-4s; two of these are preserved at the Datang Shan museum near Beijing; This aerial laboratory example . . .
Paul Howard

. . . and this AWACS version, one of two modified to monitor US nuclear tests in the Pacific in the 1950s and 1960s.

Malcolm Nason

served as supply transports and search aircraft until Avia Arktika was absorbed into Aeroflot in January 1960. Military service continued into the 1960s; after withdrawal from the front-line units, they served with the reserve forces for some years.

The Soviet Union seemed reluctant to tell the Tu-4 story. Certainly, it showed that Soviet industry was not on a par with that of the United States, but it also told a remarkable story of adapting to meet the requirements when called on to do so by two strong leaders, Stalin and Tupolev.

Twenty Tu-4s were delivered to the Chinese Air Force in the early 1950s. Two were converted to an AWACS role in order to monitor US atomic tests in the Pacific; two others were converted in China for turboprop engines and remained operational in the early 1990s. Several of the piston Tu-4s remained operational in China at the beginning of the 1990s.

ANT-63/Tu-6

The Tu-6 was a photo-reconnaissance version of the Tu-2, and also bore the designation Tu-2R and Tu-2F. It was powered by two ASh-82FNs. It had a greater wingspan than most other Tu-2s, 22.2 metres/72.8 feet instead of 18.86m/61.9 feet, which allowed extra fuel tanks to be carried to increase range and patrol endurance. It carried aerial cameras fitted in the bomb bays; these could be either daylight or infra-red cameras for night operations.

A small production run of Tu-6s was completed; the numbers are included in the Tu-2 totals. They remained in service until the mid-1950s.

ANT-68/Tu-10

Another Tu-2 variant was the Tu-10. This was a four-crew aircraft fitted with in-line Mikulin AM-39FNVs of 1,850hp. Its first flight took place on 19 May 1945, and it proved to have perhaps the best performance of any Tu-2. At 8,600m/28,217 feet, it attained a speed of 641kph/398mph. Ceiling was 10,450m/34,286 feet but range fell to 1,740km/1,081 miles. A small batch was produced in Omsk between 1945 and 1947.

ANT-69/Tu-8

Another Tu-2 derivative, a single Tu-8 was completed by the end of 1946. It was basically a Tu-2D but with a greater wing area (61.26 square metres/659.4 square feet) compared to that of the Tu-2S and -2D (48.4 square metres/525.3 square feet). Again its engines were Shvetsov's ASh-82FNs. Its role was intended to be a long-range bomber. It was fitted with four-blade propellers, and its armament was improved by fitting 23mm NS-23 cannons in the wing and replacing the machine-guns in the rear cockpit with 20mm cannons.

Tu-70

The B-29 and Tu-4 were to lead, under Tupolev's guidance, to a range of other aircraft which would keep the design bureau and production factories busy until the 1990s.

The first development was a large passenger airliner, the Tu-70. Not only was much of the B-29 design

The fastest version of the Tu-2, the Tu-10 was the last to go into production with piston engines
Maksimillian B. Saukke Collection

Tu-70

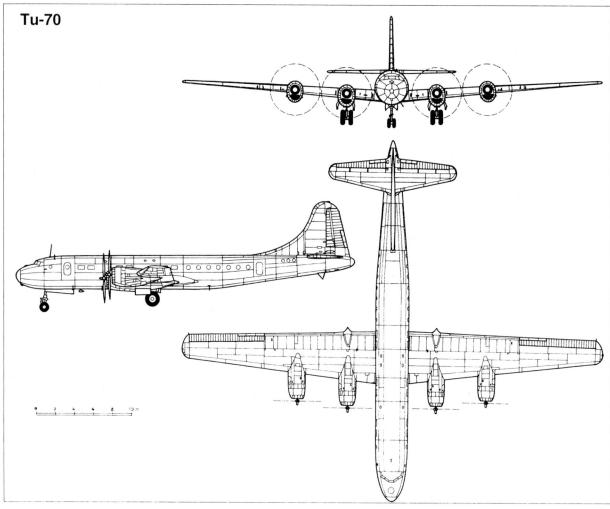

joined to a new passenger fuselage designed by Dmitri Markov and his team, but the engines, wings except for the centre section, undercarriage and tailplane were all Boeing-built. They were removed from one of the three B-29s at Zhukovski and joined to the new fuselage and wing centre section which was needed because the Tu-70 featured a low-wing arrangement rather than the mid-wing of the B-29. Some of the instruments and systems from the American aircraft were also used.

While Boeing's commercial version of the B-29 was the double-decker Stratocruiser, Tupolev and Markov went for a more conventional cabin. The fuselage was a semi-monocoque pressurised cabin and cockpit. At first, the cabin was reminiscent of pre war luxury, for a forty-eight-seat passenger interior was installed with heating and ventilation, as well as an in-flight kitchen, refrigerator, wardrobes and toilets. But travel had begun to change, and soon the luxury cabin was replaced by a not so luxurious, but still comfortable, seventy-two-seater. The original version was intended for a crew of eight – two pilots, an engineer, a navigator and four cabin attendants; without the luxury, cabin attendants became two.

and the new Ilyushin Il-18 sixty-six-passenger piston-engined airliner, could have been useful additions for the airline which had only begun to operate the twenty-seven-passenger Il-12; its other main equipment was the Lisunov Li-2, a twenty-eight passenger Soviet licence-built DC-3. Although these were short-range aircraft, the lack of alternatives meant that they were serving both light-volume routes that would have justified larger aircraft, and long-range routes that should have needed them. Thus the 700km/435-mile flight from Moscow to Leningrad was in 1949 being flown by a twenty-eight-seater Li-2, which took three hours, and Il-12s were serving much longer distances carrying a maximum of eighteen passengers. The longest route served by the Il-12 in the late 1940s was Moscow to Vladivostock, a distance of 6,800km/4,226 miles. The flight required nine refuelling stops and took over thirty-two hours, at a cruising speed of 350kph/217mph. The Tu-70 could have covered it in under twenty hours with two en route stops allowing for fuel reserves.

One factor prevented Aeroflot ordering the Tu-70, or the Il-18 – the state of Soviet airports. Both aircraft

Tu-70 – a lot of the B-29 parts were used to build the passenger Tu-70
Tupolev

The civilianisation of the B-29 to the Tu-70 still left one distinctly military feature that would remain on later Tupolev passenger aircraft – a glazed nose, in which the navigator's position was placed to allow him to get visual references when conditions allowed.

The passenger aircraft was completed almost six months before the first of the military Tu-4s due to the availability of the B-29 sections. Fiodor Opadchi flew it on its first flight from Zhukovski on 27 November 1946. In state tests, few problems were encountered. The aircraft had a maximum speed of 563kph/350mph, a service ceiling of 5,000 to 6,000m/16,405 to 19,686 feet, and a range of 4,900km/3,045 miles.

By late 1947, when the state tests were completed, Aeroflot, the Soviet state airline, was beginning to experience a growth in passenger numbers. The Tu-70,

needed long concrete runways and not many airports in the Soviet Union of the late 1940s had hard runways or planned to have them in the foreseeable future. So the Tu-70 was ahead of its time. Even in the communist world, where economy was not given a high priority, the cost of updating a large number of airports was not even considered. It would take another Tupolev aircraft and at least six more years to make that happen.

But the Tu-70 was not discarded. It was transferred to the VVS as an executive transport, and was used when available by Stalin's son, Vasili, who was Marshal of the VVS at the time. After Josef Stalin's death in 1953, his son retired, and the Tu-70 had finished its short career.

Tu-72/Tu-73/Tu-74 and Tu-78/Tu-79

Continuing the ANT number sequence, Tupolev progressed jet bomber development, with Sergei Yeger as chief technical officer.

The Tu-72 was developed as a naval bomber in 1946/1947. It was to be a mid-winged, twin-engined aircraft without sweep, and the engines were due to be hung under the wings. Rolls-Royce Nenes were the chosen powerplants, but Air Force worries over the adequacy of two engines to power an aircraft of this size and weight led Tupolev to design a similar, but slightly larger aircraft, the Tu-73, with a third engine, this time a 1,600kp Rolls-Royce Derwent, fitted in the tail but with an air intake noticeable at the front of the fin in what would become a classic feature of trijets twenty years later. While design work of both aircraft continued in parallel, it was the three-engined Tu-73 that was actually built, again at factory N156.

Its first flight was made on 29 December 1947, with Fiodor Opadchi in command. It went well. During state tests, its performance was measured as top speed 870kph/541mph, range 2,800km/1,740 miles, and service ceiling 11,500m/37,738 feet.

The Tu-74 (or Tu-73R) was a proposed photo-reconnaissance version which was not developed.

The Tu-78 and Tu-79 were essentially the Tu-73 but with Soviet licence-built Rolls-Royce engines. The two Nenes were now called the RD-45, and the Derwent, the RD-500. The prototype was built at factory N156 with Sergei Yeger in charge. It made its first flight on 17 April 1948 and its state tests were completed by December. It was approved for serial production under the VVS designation Tu-20, but this was not actually carried out because of the shortage of produc-

Sergei Yeger
Chief Designer Tu-73, Tu-78, Tu-79, Tu-81, Tu-82 and first head of the division of technical projects

tion facilities. The Tu-20 designation would be used again later.

The Tu-79 was a long-range reconnaissance aircraft originally designated Tu-73R. By then, 1949, Klimov had developed the Nene/RD-45 to produce 2,700kp/5,952lb thrust, and the Tu-79 was to have been fitted with two of these VK-1 engines in place of the lower powered RD-45s. The VVS allocated the designation Tu-22 to planned production. Although this one was never actually built, the Tu-22 designation would also be used later.

The prototype Tu-73 shown at Zhukovski in 1948
Maksimillian B. Saukke Collection

Tu-75

The sole Tu-75 at Zhukovski
Konstantin Udalov/Avico Press Collection

Next in the extended B-29/Tu-4 family was a military transport, basically a version of the Tu-70. Its design was very similar to its civilian counterpart. Again Dmitri Markov had gone for a low-wing, four-engined transport, with the wings, undercarriage and tailplane virtually identical to those of the B-29/Tu-4; only the wing's centre section had any major differences in order to fit a low- rather than a mid-wing arrangement. The fuselage was also almost a direct copy of the Tu-70 in length, cockpit and cross-section, but its military purpose resulted in some differences. These included the interior: rather than a luxury passenger cabin, the Tu-75 had a pressurised cargo hold with an underbody loading ramp which swung downwards on hinges to allow ramp access for its planned military cargoes. These could include vehicles such as jeeps or small tracked armoured personnel carriers. General cargo could be loaded or unloaded using a hoist which was mounted in the aircraft beside the loading ramp. Ahead of its time, even aero engines could be carried in the hold. Alternatively, 100 fully equipped para-troops could be carried, and could exit the aircraft while in flight.

Like the Tu-70, powerplants were those of the B-29, but this time Shvetsov's copy, the ASh-73K, was used, with each engine giving 2,300hp. It was armed with three pairs of machine-guns, one on the upper fuse-lage, one below and one in the tail.

Work began on the Tu-75 in 1947, and the proto-type was built at factory N156. Its first flight was made on 22 January 1950 with Viacheslav Marunov in command. Marunov was one of the pilots who had ferried the B-29s from Vladivostok to Zhukovski. Although the aircraft was not put into production, it was another step on the road to the VVS building up its strategic transport and bomber capability.

Project 77/The Tu-12

The Tu-12 was the last derivative of the Tu-2, but this was not just another variant of a well-tried theme. It was also, better perhaps, known as the Tu-77, really as a follow-on of the ANT numbering sequence. The VVS gave it the designation Tu-12.

This Tu-12 (Tu-77) served as a testbed for Bondaruk's rocket engine of the Kh-10 missile
Konstantin Udalov/Avico Press Collection

The Tu-12 was the Soviet Union's first jet bomber. Tupolev intended it as an interim measure to develop later aircraft and to train crews in the handling of larger jet aircraft. Sergei Yeger, working under Tupolev's supervision, led the programme. He took the basic Tu-2 fuselage, wings and tailplane, and adapted them only for the higher speeds of a jet. It was one of very few jets of the 1940s to feature a twin tail. The undercarriage was changed from a tailwheeler to a tricycle, and under the wings were fitted Rolls-Royce Derwent engines; for several years after the war, the British government allowed engines, and some other aviation components, to be sold to the USSR. Although Soviet designers were hurriedly developing jet engines, by the time of the Tu-12 in 1947 even MiG-15s were using either Rolls-Royce engines or licence-built copies of them. Only Lyulka's jet engines were of Soviet design and manufacture, and these at that time had hardly half the power of the Nenes fitted on the Tu-12, which gave a static thrust of 2,270kp/5,004lb.

The Tu-12 (Tu-77) was the last design derived from the Tu-2; silhouetted against the snow, its Tu-2 ancestry is evident
Maksimillian B. Saukke Collection

The first Tu-12 was built at factory N156, the new title for the former KOSOS–TsAGI works attached to the design offices. It was completed in May 1947, and after transfer to Zhukovski and reassembly, Aleksei Pereliot flew it on its first flight on 27 June. There were no major difficulties found in the test programme. For an interim aircraft its performance was reasonable: maximum speed was 783kph/487mph, range was 2,200km/1,367 miles, and its service ceiling was 11,300m/37,075 feet.

The VVS accepted the prototype Tu-12, and production began at factory N23 in Moscow with an order for five. However, only three were completed.

These were completed by 1950, and were used by the Air Force in a training role for a short while. One was used as a flight test aircraft by the LII for experimental work with rocket engines, which were mounted on a pylon above the centre fuselage.

Tu-80

Under the project number 64 Tupolev, with Dmitri Markov as chief designer, had begun to work on a long-range strategic bomber in 1945. The arrival of the B-29s and the subsequent Tu-4 programme (which, because it started with a finished product, was never given a project number) put a stop to this project.

At the end of 1948, just as production Tu-4s were beginning to be delivered to the VVS, Tupolev and Markov began work on a replacement. In a sense, it was an improved B-29 design, with a major programme to trim weight and thus to improve performance. Once again, the wing was raised (after the Tu-70 and Tu-75) back to mid-fuselage position, but a new wing with better aerodynamic qualities and with a lighter but stronger spar was developed. The fuselage was also redesigned; it was lightened and the round Tu-4 nose of the same chord as the fuselage

The sole Tu-80 at Zhukovski
Konstantin Udalov/Avico Press Collection

was replaced with a more usual one in which the cockpit was raised above the nose for improved visibility. A new, more angular tail was also built, with a distinctive dorsal fin. Its engines were four of Shvetsov's ASh-73TKFNs, a Soviet-built turbocharged version of the original B-29 engines.

All these changes resulted in the Tu-80 being substantially lighter than the Tu-4, and this allowed it to carry more fuel. Its first flight was made by Aleksei Pereliot on 1 December 1949 from Zhukovski. In state tests, its maximum speed was established as

640kph/398mph. But the Tu-80 was just another step on the way to the Soviet Union achieving a long-range strategic bomber. With the coming of age of turbines, it was not developed beyond its test programme.

Tu-81/Tu-14

(Nato Codename 'Bosun')

The work done on the Tu-72, -73, -74, -78 and -79 projects were all stages in the development of Soviet jet bombers. Next step was the Tu-81, which would later enter service with the VMS (Voenno Morskie Sili = Navy) as the Tu-14.

Sergei Yeger was again programme leader, but the Tu-81 went back to the twin-engined Tu-72 rather than stay with the three-engined designs of the Tu-73, -74, -78 and -79. This came about because of Klimov's improved Nene/RD-45, the VK-1, which offered an increase in power from the 2,270kp/5,004lb static thrust of the Rolls-Royce Nene and the RD-45 to 2,740kp/6,040lb, which, combined with a lower empty weight, allowed the third engine to be omitted.

Work on the design and construction began in July 1944. Tupolev and Yeger aimed to keep the aircraft as light as possible, so an uncomplicated result was achieved. Still showing some considerable resemblances to the Tu-72, the Tu-81 was a mid-winged twin-jet bomber still without wing sweep. It was completed in factory N156 in 1948, and its first flight was made on 13 October 1949. State tests were completed by autumn 1950, and the aircraft was approved for production under the military designation Tu-14T for a VMS role as a torpedo carrier.

Test results showed the Tu-14T as having a performance of 860kph/534mph, a range of 3,000km/1,864 miles, and a service ceiling of 11,200m/36,747 feet. Some eighty-seven aircraft were built in Irkutsk between 1950 and 1952, and the first examples entered service in 1951. They were armed with two fixed-fire NK23 cannons and two machine-guns mounted on a tail turret. It served in a patrol role, with the ability to bomb naval targets.

Tu-82 – The First Tu-22

Continuing his development of jet bombers, the next Tupolev aircraft was the light twin-engined Tu-82, which was the first Soviet bomber to feature swept wings.

Sergei Yeger continued as project leader, and he incorporated a wing with a sweep of 35°; while the Tu-14 range had already featured a swept-back horizontal tailplane, the Tu-82 also had the fin swept at an angle of 40°. Engines were two Nene derivative VK-1s of 2,740kp.

The Tu-82 was provisionally given the designation Tu-22 by the VVS. This was not used for long, although there are photographs available to show that it was painted on the aircraft for a while; later the Tu-22 designation would be used again (and again). Conceived as a test and development aircraft for the purpose of determining the flight qualities of large swept-wing aircraft, only the single example constructed at the design works was built. Construction began at the end of 1947, and the aircraft was completed at the beginning of 1949. It made its first flight from Zhukovski on 24 March with Aleksei Pereliot at the controls.

Its performance was good. Maximum speed was established to be 934kph/580mph, service ceiling was an excellent 14,000m/45,934 feet, and range 2,750km/1,709 miles. A relatively small aircraft, the Tu-82 had an empty weight of just 9,526kg/21,005lb, compared to the more than fourteen tonnes of the three-engine jets of the family. Its normal take-off weight was thirteen tonnes (13,000kg/28,665lb), but it had little difficulty in performance when this was increased to eighteen tonnes. A production version of the Tu-82 was planned, the slightly bigger Tu-86, but the programme was cancelled.

Although planned for production, only the prototype Tu-82 was built
Tupolev

Tu-85

At the end of the 1940s, Vladimir Dobrynin's engine design bureau had developed a new air-cooled, twenty-four-cylinder in-line piston engine, the VD-4K, which offered a 4,300hp supercharged power output.

Dmitri Markov set about designing a very long-range strategic bomber with these engines. Starting from the Tu-80 he began by designing a high-aspect wing with increased span – now it was 55.94m/183.5 feet compared to the 43.83m/143.8 feet of the Tu-75 and -80, and wing area was 273.6 square metres/2,945 square feet, compared to 162.7/1,751. Wing aspect ratio was 11.4:1. This allowed the new aircraft to carry some forty-four tonnes of fuel which would give it a range of 12,000km/7,457 miles. He streamlined the fuselage, and provided accommodation for a second crew which would be needed with the aircraft's twenty-six-hour endurance capability. Normal crew was eight so the Tu-85 carried sixteen in a pressurised cabin. The Tu-85 was fitted with large four-blade propellers, and it was armed with five turrets each fitted with a pair of NR-23 cannons which could be remotely controlled by a gunner, who had a screen to show the arc of fire from each position – a development of the B-29/Tu-4 system.

The Tu-85 was constructed at factory N156 in 1949 and 1950. When completed, it was brought to Zhukovski aerodrome, reassembled and readied for flight. On 9 January 1951, Aleksei Pereliot was in command as it took off for the first time. In factory and state tests, it gave excellent results. Although its empty weight was 55.4 tonnes and its normal take-off weight seventy-five tonnes, it could take off at 107 tonnes when necessary, allowing it to carry the enormous fuel load needed to achieve its 12,300km/7,581 miles range with a five-tonne payload, or to increase its normal five-tonne bomb load to twenty tonnes. Cruising speed for maximum range was established at 450kph/280mph, but maximum speed was much higher. At low level, it was measured at 563kph/350mph, and at a level of 10,000m/32,810 feet it reached 665kph/413mph.

But by now, turbine engines were establishing themselves and offering higher speeds with lower fuel burns. The Tu-85 was the end of the line for Tupolev's piston-engined, and also for Soviet, aircraft. Although the United States would stay with pistons for another five years, for the Soviet Union, and for Europe, the time had come to move on.

Only one Tu-85, the prototype was built. It was the last large Tupolev aircraft without swept wings.

Tu-85

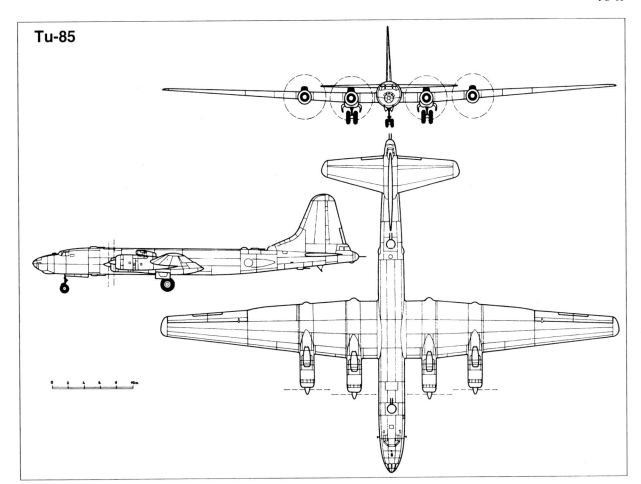

The last large piston-engined Tupolev design, the Tu-85 did not go into production because of turbine engine developments
Maksimillian B. Saukke Collection

Tu-88

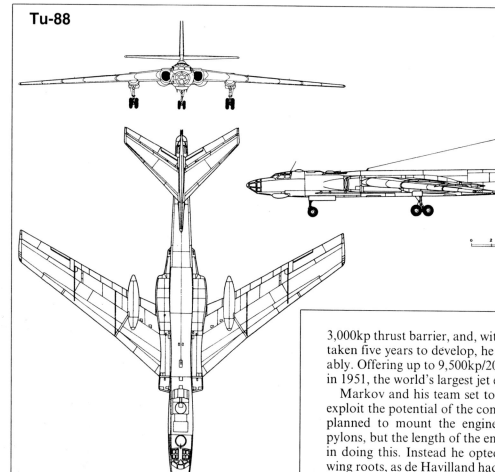

Tu-88 – The Tu-16

(NATO codename 'Badger')

With the experience gained on many programmes that had kept the design bureau busy in the years since the end of the war, a jet bomber ready for production had to become a reality.

The Tu-4 had grown into the Tu-70, -75, -80 and -85, while the Tu-2 had evolved into the Tu-72, -73, -74, -78, -79 and -81. The first of these families had built up experience with large, long-range aircraft and the second with smaller jet bombers. Now Tupolev and Dmitri Markov would bring the two developments together in Project 88, which was to become better known under its military designation, the Tu-16.

The catalyst was a huge increase in power offered by Aleksander Mikulin's new generation of turbojet engines. At last a way had been found to break the

3,000kp thrust barrier, and, with the AM-3 which had taken five years to develop, he had done this remarkably. Offering up to 9,500kp/20,944lb, the AM-3 was, in 1951, the world's largest jet engine.

Markov and his team set to work early in 1950 to exploit the potential of the coming engine. At first he planned to mount the engines under the wing on pylons, but the length of the engine meant a difficulty in doing this. Instead he opted to place them in the wing roots, as de Havilland had done with the Comet. To compensate for the effect of exhaust heat on the fuselage, he turned the engine axis a few degrees outwards. The prototype's AM-3s were rated at 8,750kp/19,290lb static thrust.

Before the AM-3 was fitted to the Tu-88, it had been tested on a Tu-4LL (flying laboratory), with the jet installed in place of the inner right engine. Markov evaluated a range of swept wings at the TsAGI wind tunnels at Zhukovski, before deciding on a 35° sweep with a 40.5° angle at the wing roots. Span was 34.5m/113.3 feet. The circular section fuselage had a family resemblance to that of the Tu-85, and its pressurised cabin was occupied by a crew of seven. A pilot and radio operator sat in the cockpit, while the navigator and bombardier used the glazed nose for visibility; two gunners were in the rear fuselage and a third in the tail turret.

The prototype was completed in factory N156 by the end of 1951. It was disassembled and brought by road to Zhukovski, from where, after reassembly and ground tests, it made its first flight on 27 April 1952, with Nikolai Rybko in command. Shortly afterwards, in August 1952, a rival design, the Ilyushin Il-46, made its first flight. The Tu-88 and the Il-46 were close to each other in most performance aspects: maximum speed was 945kph/587mph for the Tupolev and 930kph/578mph for the Ilyushin, service ceiling 12,000m/39,372 feet against 12,300m/40,356 feet, and bomb load/range was six tonnes/4,800km/2,983 miles for the Tu-88 and three tonnes/5,000km/3,107 miles for the Il-46. But with a three-tonne load, the Tupolev had a range of 6,400km/3,977 miles. That was the deciding factor. The VVS chose the Tu-16, and in December 1952 it was ordered into serial production.

As usual in Soviet industry, Tupolev prepared production drawings and made allowances for the differences between prototype production and serial production. It was soon evident that the serial aircraft would be overweight and that it would not meet its range requirements, so a major programme was begun to bring the production aircraft's weight down from 41.5 tonnes to a target of 37.2 tonnes. In a novel scheme for the Soviet Union, each design leader was promised a cash bonus for whatever weight he

trimmed off production assemblies.

Everything was checked – the engines, fuselage and wing skin, ribs, spars, even the wiring and hydraulic systems. Effectively, only the shape was retained in a major redesign which delayed production by a year, but the resulting aircraft was 5.5 tonnes lighter, and now it could exceed its planned range. Weight was down to thirty-six tonnes. The programme resulted in some operational restrictions, including speed limitations at altitudes below 6,600m/21,655 feet. Pilots were advised to avoid combat while climbing to this level, but on descent there were no such limits. Among the changes were reductions in the number of connection points, rivets and fasteners. The alloy for the fuselage and wing skins, D16, was changed to a pre-stressed one, V95. Anything which could trim a kilogram was done.

Production was set up in factory N22 at Kazan, and first deliveries to the VVS were made in early 1954; the first nine service Tu-16s flew in formation over Moscow in the May Military Parades that year. Soon it was given the NATO codename 'Badger'.

The Tu-16 'Badger'; the first Soviet nuclear bomber saw widespread service from the mid-1950s until the early 1990s. A line of nine, of different marks, is shown here
Konstantin Udalov/Avico Press Collection

A line of 13 Chinese Air Force Tu-16s/H-6
Chinese Social Science Press

Soon Kuibyshev (now Samara) factory N18 and Voronezh factory N64 were producing the Tu-16. By the time production ended in 1961, 1,507 examples had been built in Russia. Approximately 120 more were licence-built in China under the designation H-6.

Tu-16s were delivered to the air forces of Egypt, India, Indonesia and Iraq. In VVS service, the Tu-16 served with the long-range Air Force squadrons, and was based in the North, the Far East, the Ukraine and the Crimea. It was the first Soviet bomber to drop a hydrogen bomb, and it saw extensive service in the Afghan conflict. One of its tasks was to bomb open areas in enemy regions at night. In the Arab–Israeli war in 1967, the Iraqi forces used it in raids against Israel and found it to be reliable and needing little attention. The Indonesians used it in the 1960s during their conflict with Malaya/Malaysia to launch 'short, sharp attacks' on defence positions over the border, and to use the Tu-16's high speed to escape the defending RAF Gloster Javelins.

The production Tu-16, with its lower weight, was equipped with the later AM-3M engine, which offered 9,500kp/20,950lb thrust. These, combined with its trimmed-down weight, gave the service aircraft a top speed of 992kph/610mph. Even with two KSR-11 (NATO code 'Celt' or AS-56) missiles mounted below the wing, its speed was 786kph/488mph. Armament consisted of six pairs of AM-23 cannons, which could be operated by remote control, plus one cannon in a fixed position in the nose. Their rate of fire was up to 900 rounds per minute. Two KSR missiles of varying marks could also be carried, either on pylons under the wings or in the bomb bay.

The Tu-16 served in many different roles, and so almost fifty versions of the aircraft were developed. The principal ones include (first flight year in brackets):

Tu-88 – the prototype (1952)
Tu-16 – production aircraft (1954)
Tu-16R (Tu-92) – reconnaissance (1956)
Tu-16K-10 – missile carrier for K-10 (NATO code 'Kipper' AS-2) (1961)
Tu-16K-11 – missile carrier for KSR (NATO code 'Celt' AS-5A) (1962)
Tu-16REB – radio electronic jammer (1962)
Tu-16K-26 – missile carrier for KSR-5 (NATO code 'Kingfish' AS-6)
Tu-16Z – refuelling tanker (1976)
Tu-16LL – flying laboratory (1980)

By the early 1990s, relatively few Tu-16s remained in VVS service, although a number continued mainly in the flying laboratory roles. Several Tu-16s were used to train Aeroflot pilots on the Tu-104; they were called the Tu-104G.

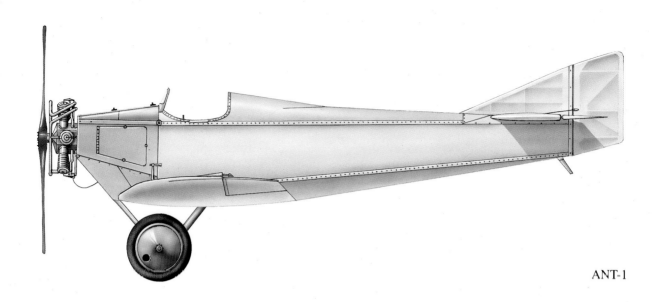

ANT-1

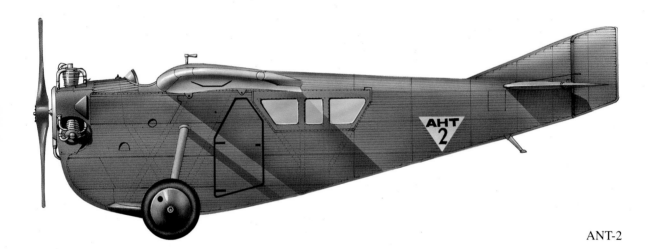

ANT-2

ANT-3

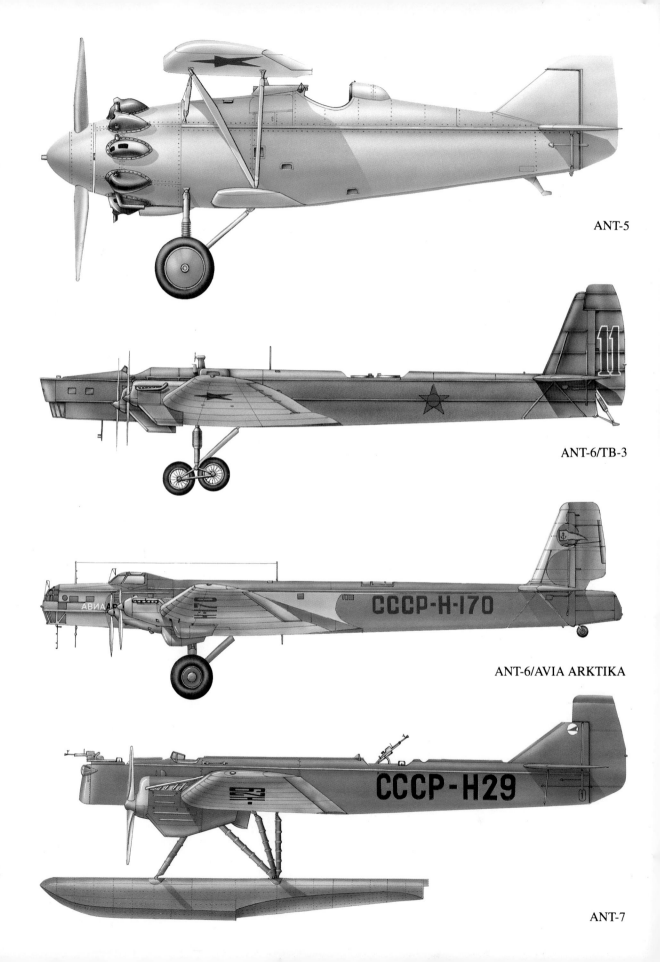

ANT-5

ANT-6/TB-3

ANT-6/AVIA ARKTIKA

ANT-7

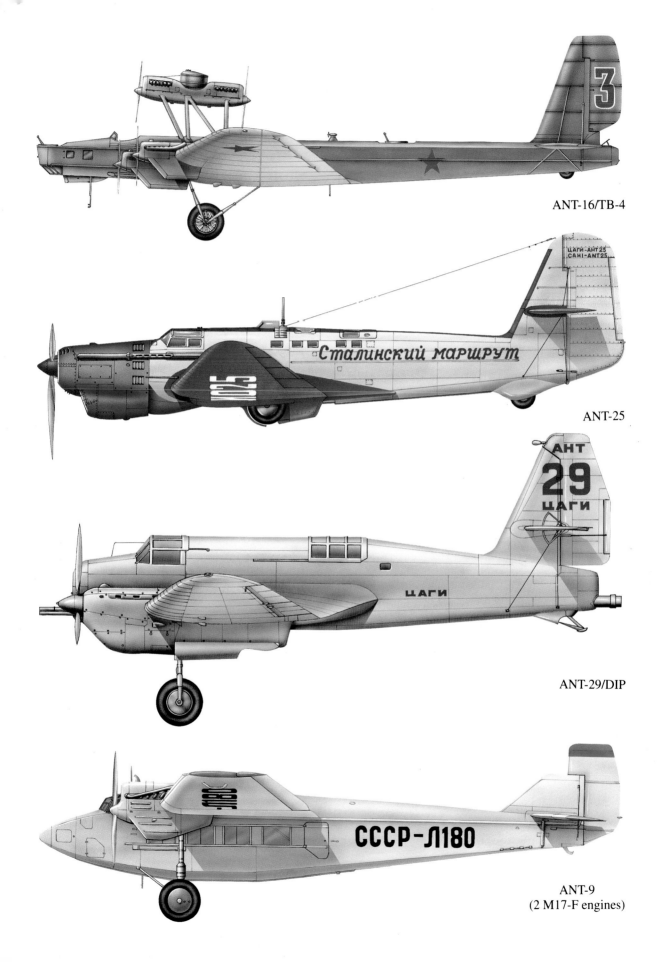

ANT-16/TB-4

ANT-25

Сталинский маршрут

ANT-29/DIP

АНТ
29
ЦАГИ

ЦАГИ

СССР-Л180

ANT-9
(2 M17-F engines)

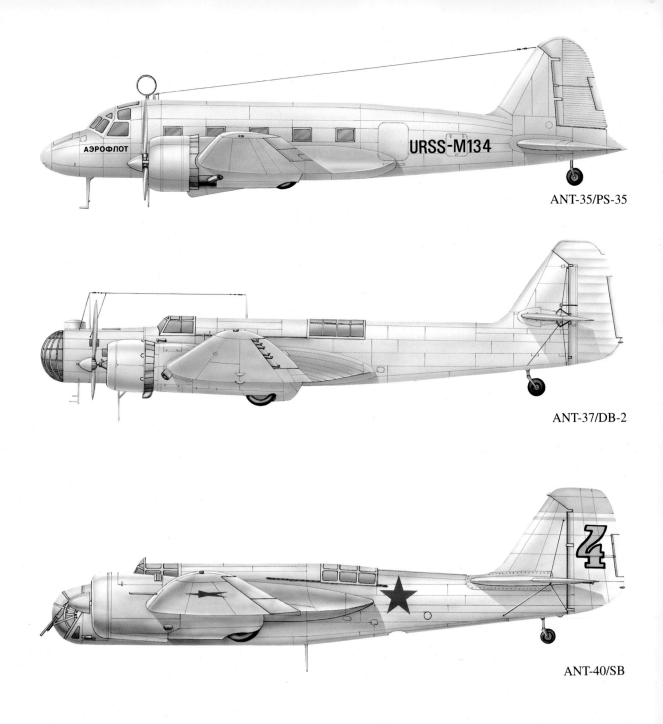

ANT-35/PS-35

ANT-37/DB-2

ANT-40/SB

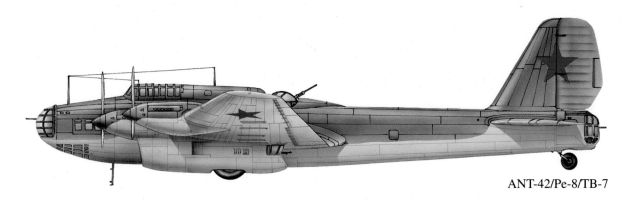

ANT-42/Pe-8/TB-7

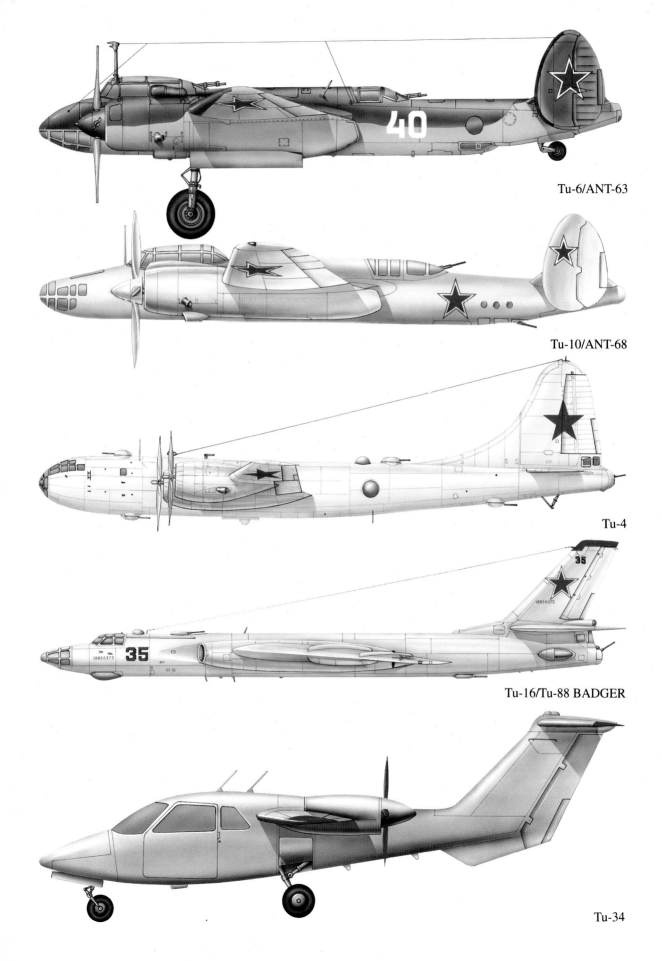

Tu-6/ANT-63

Tu-10/ANT-68

Tu-4

Tu-16/Tu-88 BADGER

Tu-34

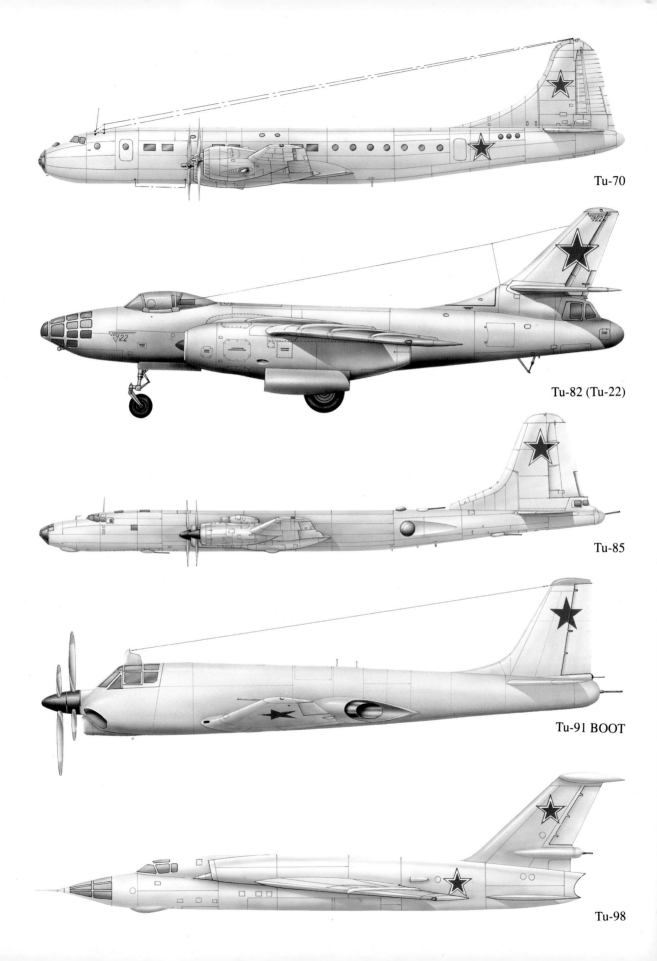

Tu-70

Tu-82 (Tu-22)

Tu-85

Tu-91 BOOT

Tu-98

Tu-104

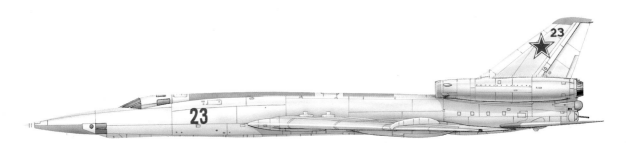

Tu-22/Tu-105 BLINDER

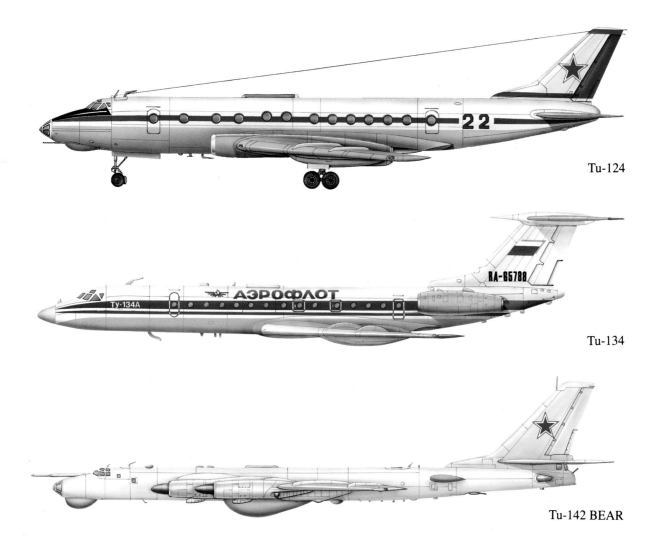

Tu-124

Tu-134

Tu-142 BEAR

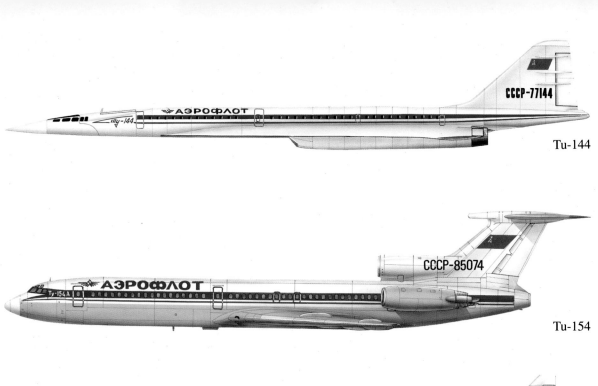

Tu-144

Tu-154

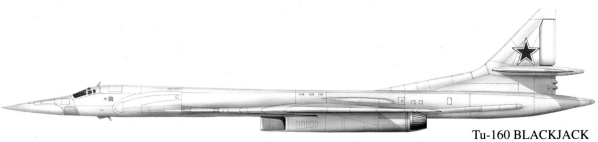

Tu-160 BLACKJACK

Tu-204

Tu-334

A Tu-16LL, coded 41, serving as a flight test bed for a Soloviev PS-90A engine. For take-off and landing, the engine could be semi-retracted into the bomb bay
Maksimillian B. Saukke Collection

In 1957, the Soviet government granted China a licence for the local production of the Tu-16. China began to set up production at the Harbin Aircraft and Engine factory under the designation H-6. Harbin was also preparing the H-5 programme – the local version of the Il-28, and the resulting strain on its capacity was resolved by transferring the programme to Xilan. At Harbin, several Tu-16s were assembled from Soviet-made components, and the first of these was flown 3 days prior to National Day (October 1st) 1959.

Although Tupolev would claim that full technical drawings were provided, China's industry states that they were incomplete and local specialists had to undertake substantial design work, resulting in the preparation of some 15,400 technical drawings. Design changes included fuselage, vertical tailplane, nose undercarriage and fuel system in the most complex work undertaken up to that time by the industry.

The first Chinese atomic bomb was dropped from a H-6 on 14 May 1965. Several were converted for an electronic counter-surveillance role.

Delayed by the transfer of production, the first Chinese manufactured H-6A made its first flight on 24 December 1968, flown by Li Yuanyi.

Later Chinese variants included the H-6D, an air-to-surface missile carrier for the Chinese Naval Air Force which entered service in 1986; and several flight testbeds on which aero-engines, drones, and 'defence counter-measure' equipment were evaluated.

A Tu-16Z refuelling a standard 'Badger' over a winter landscape
Konstantin Udalov/Avico Press Collection

Tu-89

One Tu-89 was built as a development aircraft for a reconnaissance version of the Tu-81/Tu-14. It made its first flight in February 1951, and was a long-range version, but the -88 programme offered better prospects, and so development was stopped in mid-1951. For a short while, it was given the VVS designation Tu-16.

Tu-91

The Ugly Duckling (NATO Codename 'Boot')

At the end of the 1940s, the Soviet government took a decision to expand the Voenno Morskoi Flot (VMF, the Navy). It was decided to include an aircraft carrier fleet, and development of aircraft suitable for carriers was a part of the programme. Tupolev was given the task of designing a strike aircraft for the new fleet.

Tupolev asked two of his teams to prepare design proposals. One of these, Project '509' (1950 – ninth project) was a Tu-14 version, essentially taking a Tu-14T and equipping it with folding wings (for below deck storage), an arrestor hook and boosters, like JATO bottles, to accelerate its take-off from a carrier deck. But there was little prospect of a Tu-14T version having any range capability, so this development was stopped. Pavel Sukhoi, then head of Tu-14 production, was an adviser on Project 509 – his own design bureau had been closed, although it would later re-open. The second team was that led by Boris Kondorski, the head of the future aircraft conception unit. His design, Project 507, was based on the new Kuznetsov-designed TV-2 turboprop which was then being tested on a Tu-4LL flying laboratory. By then, the British Royal Navy had begun to operate the Westland Wyvern, and the Fairey Gannet was under development. Also, in the United States, the Navy had selected the Douglas Skyshark. The ability of a turboprop to offer higher speeds than piston engines and a lower fuel burn than jets made it worth looking at.

Vladimir Chizhevski was appointed chief designer – up until then, he had designed nacelles for airships and worked on high-altitude aircraft. His team developed a two-seat low-wing monoplane, with a straight wing and with the engine located in the centre fuselage driving a long propeller shaft, which ran through the middle of the cockpit, and drove, through gears, two contra-rotating three-blade propellers. When it was completed in factory N156 (the old TsAGI–ZOK and KOSOS works) at the end of 1953, it was brought by road to Zhukovski for reassembly in the Tupolev

hangar. As it was being rolled out from there, one of the workers gave it the nickname 'Bychek' after the goby fish, because it appeared to have eyes on the top of its head. The name stuck. Today, in 1995, few aviation workers remember the Tu-91, but many remember the 'Bychek'.

Josef Stalin died in March 1953, and the new leaders cut back the VMF expansion plans and thus the requirements for carrier-borne aircraft was cancelled. The naval chiefs, however, still saw a need for a strike aircraft, and Tupolev was asked instead to prepare a land-based aircraft for the role. This time Chizhevski was requested to design a dive bomber for attacking naval surface and submarine vessels; instead of carriers, it had to be capable of operating from runways of limited length.

The Tu-91 required only relatively minor changes to meet the revised needs. The folding wings were now unnecessary and, with the arrestor hook, were removed and were replaced with conventional wings. One unusual feature about the pre-flight tests of the Tu-91 was that, while the engine was being tested, it was mounted on a Tu-4LL complete with cockpit section and the full length propeller shaft. This experience allowed Chizhevski to develop less complicated engine maintenance procedures and shortened the ground test programme.

As was usual for Tupolev, and for other design bureaux, specific personnel from the flight and engineering test staff had been appointed to follow the aircraft's development from the early days of the programme. The flight crew selected had been Dmitri Ziuzin, pilot, and Konstantin Malkhasian, navigator. Taxying trials began in autumn 1954 – unfortunately, no exact dates were recorded – and went well. On the third last taxying run, Ziuzin lifted the Bychek off the runway and held it at 1.5 to two metres (four to six feet) off the ground before landing back. The first official flight took place a few days later.

The test programme went well. Both the factory tests and the state tests, flown by Lt-Col Alekseev and Major Sizov, which were carried out by the State Commission at the Scientific and Research Institute of the Air Force (NII VVS), gave good results, and the aircraft was approved for production. Only the politicians remained to give their approval, which was usually just a formality.

Every so often, new programmes and equipment were shown to party leaders. In the summer of 1956, the latest examples of military aviation were unveiled to a group of high level officials, including the new General Secretary of the Communist Party, Nikita Khrushchev, then in effect the Prime Minister. Among

The sole Tu-91 'Bychek' shown at Zhukovski
Konstantin Udalov/Avico Press Collection

all the gleaming examples of power and speed was the straight-winged Tu-91, one of very few propeller aircraft present and looking awkward in comparison with its neighbours. 'What's that?' Khrushchev asked a naval officer attending the Bychek. Confused momentarily by being addressed by Khrushchev, the officer, instead of replying that the aircraft could deliver firepower equal or greater than that of a heavy cruiser, answered that it could do the job of a cruiser. The jovial Khrushchev then asked: 'So why do we need cruisers?'

The career of the Tu-91 was over. Although Tupolev used all his connections and experience it was impossible to gain support from those under the leader. A few years later, when inspecting the latest range of gleaming new aircraft at Zhukovski, Khrushchev saw the Tu-91 again in the background. Just back from some short field tests on unpaved runways, it was looking dirty and grimy. 'Is that still here?' he asked. A few days later, it wasn't.

As the war in south-east Asia would show, the Soviet Union could have made use of a Bychek. But there were none around.

Tu-92/Tu-16P

The Tu-92 was the reconnaissance version of the Tu-88/Tu-16; with the VVS designation Tu-16R, it was produced at Kuibyshev, and is included in the Tu-88 story.

Tu-95 'Bear'

The Tu-4 Grows Up

By the end of the 1940s, the development of turbine engines had marked the closing of the piston era. Initially, the new turbojets were small, and were not of any use for long-range bombers, but by the early 1950s they had started to develop. So had turboprops.

In the West, the turboprop was confined mainly to commercial aircraft – the Bristol Britannia, Vickers Viscount and Lockheed Electra helped to bridge a gap between the piston and jet ages. Some military transports would use turboprops. Particularly well-known is the Lockheed Hercules, and a few mainly carrier-borne strike aircraft such as the Fairey Gannet. But little thought was given to the possibility of using turboprops to power strategic bombers by anyone except Tupolev and his team.

In 1949, he set up a team headed by Nikolai Bazenkov to develop the Tu-85 and make use of the new developments in Soviet turboprops, specifically Nikolai Kuznetsov's new NK-12, due to be available in 1953, which offered a power of up to 15,000 shaft horsepower (shp). Pending their availability, development work began using TV-2 and TV-12 engines of 12,000shp each.

Two prototypes were constructed in factory N156 beside the design offices, using, as usual, the design bureau's specialist engineers working alongside Bazenkov and his team, with Tupolev visiting the works almost every day as was the norm. Although substantially based on the Tu-85, a considerable

Nikolai Bazenkov
Deputy Chief Designer, chief designer of Tu-95, Tu-114

amount of work was needed to adapt the design for the much higher speeds targeted for the Tu-95. Most important was the wing; the Tu-85 had a maximum speed of 563kph/350mph, but the -95 was expected to achieve 900 to 950kph/559 to 590mph, almost sixty to seventy per cent faster. In an effort to achieve this, Bazenkov developed a wing which measured 51m/167.33 feet from tip to tip, despite a 35° angle of sweep. The 6m/19.7-foot-long engines were installed in large nacelles on the wings, with the inner ones having a pod which extended eight metres to the rear into which the four-wheeled undercarriage legs retracted rearwards.

The cabin was pressurised, which improved crew conditions on long-distance flights – cruising at 750kph/466mph, patrols could last up to twenty hours. One thing missing was ejection seats. Although normal equipment in most high-performance military aircraft since the late 1940s, the Tu-95 did not have them. The crew in the forward section had to evacuate by using an emergency lift which would bring them from the cockpit and drop them through a hatch near the nose-wheel door while those in the aircraft's tail exited through escape hatches.

The prototype Tu-95 (called Tu-95/1) was completed by September 1952, and was brought by road to Zhukovski. After reassembly, it began its ground trials early in November; on 12 November, with Aleksei Pereliot in command, the first flight took

place. As mentioned earlier, its engines were the 12,000shp TV-2FS. In state tests, they exceeded 900kph/559mph, something considered impossible by many aerodynamic specialists for propeller aircraft. Tupolev gave particular credit for the excellent performance to the design and production of Konstantin Zhdanov's propeller and gearbox developed at Stupino, near Moscow.

Work proceeded on the second prototype relatively slowly, but late in 1953 the first aircraft crashed due to an engine fire which resulted in the engine falling off. Three people died: Pereliot, a flight engineer and a research scientist; nine escaped by evacuating the aircraft by parachute. The second was completed only in July 1954. Delays in engine production meant that it did not receive its TV-12s until the end of the year. Early in 1955, the Tu-95/2 was rolled out at Zhukovski for its pre-flight trials, including engine runs and taxying tests. It made its first flight on 16 February, flown by Mikhail Nukhtikov.

Meanwhile, serial production of the Tu-20, as the VVS designated it, had been set up at Kuibyshev factory N18 under General Director Mitrofan Yevshin. Work started in January 1955 and the first two production aircraft were completed in October and began state tests. They were powered by the first production examples of Kuznetsov's NK-12, which gave 12,000shp. As was usual in the Soviet system, production examples were not built to the same standards as the virtually hand-made prototypes, and Soviet designers made allowances for this. The production Tu-95, with lower powered engines and higher weight, was measured to have a performance of 882kph/548mph in speed, a range with a five-tonne payload of 15,040km/9,346 miles, and a service ceiling of 11,300m/37,075 feet – not quite up to VVS requirements. The second production aircraft was fitted with the NK-12M, a higher powered version which gave 15,000sph and a lower fuel consumption. With these, performance improved to a maximum speed of 905kph/562mph, range to 16,750km/10,408 miles, and ceiling to 12,150m/39,864 feet. These figures met the requirements.

The Tu-95 was first shown to the public at the 1955 Aviation Day air show at Tushino, in Moscow's north-west, in August, when the second prototype made a flypast. The VVS accepted delivery of its first Tu-95s in August 1957, and it went into service as a long-range strategic bomber. It was armed with six pairs of AM-23 cannons, providing almost complete coverage: one pair was in the nose, two above the fuselage, just behind the cockpit and forward of the tail, one was in a tail turret and the others under the fuselage. Some of these could be remotely operated by a

A VVS Tu-95K 'Bear C' shown air to air
Konstantin Udalov/Avico Press Collection

gunner who sat between two glazed blisters in the rear fuselage. The bomb load varied from a maximum range version with five tonnes to fifteen tonnes with a fall off in range; it was possible to carry two nuclear bombs, or conventional warheads.

An accident in March 1957, when the failure of one engine plus a problem in propeller feathering caused the loss of the aircraft and the death of the crew, resulted in the installation of NK-12MVs, modified versions of the engine with automatic and manual systems of feathering.

Production of the Tu-95 continued until 1959, in several different versions listed below. Production totalled 173 aircraft plus the two prototypes. All these were strategic aircraft. While most of them continued in service until the late 1980s/early 1990s, the effects of the Strategic Arms Limitations Talks (SALT) caused many of them to be cut up in the 1990s. Some of the Tu-95s – or, to give them their worthy NATO codename, Bear – were modified after their withdrawal from front-line bomber units to carry missiles or for reconnaissance roles. Two Tu-95s were removed from the production line in 1958 and were completed as Tu-116s. By the mid-1990s all Tu-95s were grounded or scrapped.

Later, the Tu-95 would appear again as the non-strategic Tu-142. Although differing mainly in equipment from the Tu-95, the -142 was not a bomber, and so did not come under the auspices of the SALT treaty. Its story is related later.

A Tu-95 was modified as a Tu-95LAL (=Letavshaia Atomnaia Laboratoriya = Flying Atomic laboratory). Although no engine power was generated from atomic sources, the aircraft carried a VVR-100 reactor, and made 42 flights to test ecological problems; after these tests, the decision was taken not to proceed with the Tu-119 which remained a paper project.

Production and Modifications

Tu-95	Bear A	(1955) Strategic Bomber
Tu-95A		Strategic Bomber with Nose Radar
Tu-95M		Modified
Tu-95K	Bear B	(1959) Strategic Bomber – Missile Kh-20
Tu-95KM		(1959) Strategic Bomber (modified) – Missile Kh-20
Tu-95MR		(Modified) Reconnaissance
Tu-95RTs	Bear E	(1960) Long-Range Reconnaissance
Tu-95K-22		(1964) Strategic Bomber Missile – Kh-22
Tu-95MS		(1981) Strategic Bomber Missile – Kh-55

Note: Tu-95K represents the missile carrier version; any suffix after the K refers to the type of missile.

Tu-96

A single Tu-96 was built. It was a standard Tu-95 airframe but it was intended to be fitted with Kuznetsov's NK-16 engine, of 16,000shp, for use as a high-altitude strategic bomber. As the NK-16 was not developed in time, the aircraft was given NK-12s which proved inadequate. Its first flight was in 1956, but the VVS decided it was not needed, so development stopped.

Tu-98

(NATO Codename 'Backfin')

back into the fuselage, with two large air intakes located just behind and on either side of the cockpit. The engines selected were Arkhip Lyulka's AL-7Fs, which developed 10,000kg/22,046lb static thrust, and were fitted with afterburners. With a maximum take-off weight of 39,000kg/85,980lb, the Tu-98 was close in size to the Tu-16, but the extra power, and particularly the afterburners, gave it the extra energy to go through the sound barrier.

The first aircraft was completed by early 1956 at factory N156, and, as usual, after road transfer, it was reassembled at Zhukovski and made ready for flight. Unfortunately details of its first flight are not available except that it was made in spring 1956 by Valentin Kovaliov. A second aircraft joined the first in the state

The first Tu-98

Maksimillian B. Saukke Collection

trials. Performance was measured at a maximum speed of 1,238kph/769mph (with afterburners on) at 12,000m/39,372 feet.

The Tu-98 received quite wide Western press coverage as it was one of the Soviet aircraft shown to a high-level US Air Force delegation invited by the flamboyant Soviet leader, Nikita Khrushchev, to see the latest Soviet aircraft in 1956. The delegation, led by General Nathan Twining, was brought to the single runway transport base of Kubinka, some 40km/25 miles west of Moscow, where a range of mainly development aircraft was lined up. Following the visit, the Tu-98, which was not identified by name or number to the party, was given the NATO codename 'Backfin'.

Tupolev's progress in the development of aircraft design rarely came about by huge technical leaps; rather it was a progressive, but time-consuming, step by step advancement. Thus when work began on the Tu-98 at the beginning of 1954, it was not intended for production; instead it was a bridge to evaluate the problems of supersonic flight, and a stepping stone to the Tu-105 and the Tu-128 programmes which would follow later.

Chief designer on the project was Dmitri Markov; he based the wing design on that of the earlier Tu-88/Tu-16, but cleaned it up and moved the engines

The Tu-96 at Zhukovski
Konstantin Udalov/Avico Press Collection

Tu-104

On 22 March 1956, a large number of people gathered at London's Heathrow airport. For several days rumours were rife that the high-level Soviet delegation due to visit the British government would arrive in a new jet airliner. But the Soviets didn't have a jet airliner.

Britain had introduced the world's first jetliner into service just four years earlier. In May 1952, the de Havilland DH106 Comet had begun passenger services. But a year later, one of BOAC's Comets had broken up in the air, and two others followed. Now, in 1956, Britain was nearing the end of a major two-year investigation of the accidents whose cause was

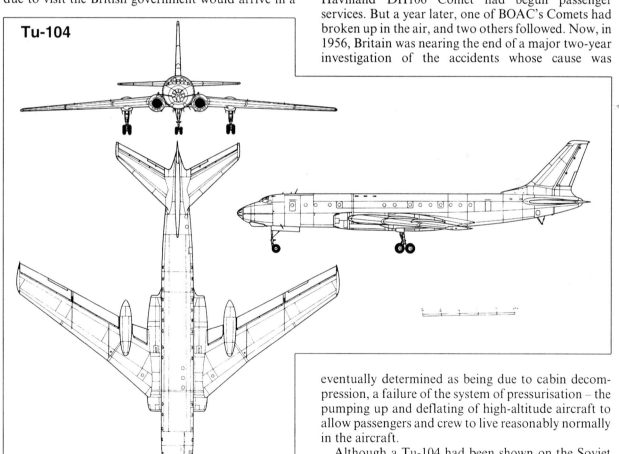

Tu-104

eventually determined as being due to cabin decompression, a failure of the system of pressurisation – the pumping up and deflating of high-altitude aircraft to allow passengers and crew to live reasonably normally in the aircraft.

Although a Tu-104 had been shown on the Soviet Aviation Day flypast at Tushino in August 1955, Western attenders had apparently assumed it to be just a Tu-16 bomber – the idea of it being an airliner had not even been considered.

The sixth Soviet five-year (economic) plan, for the years from 1956 to 1960, was being drawn up in the early 1950s; the fifth plan had achieved targets of 9.8 million passengers carried by Aeroflot and 2.4 million tonne kilometres (mtk) of freight. At that time, most of Aeroflot's passengers were being carried on the Lisunov Li-2 (the Soviet version of the Douglas DC-3), or on the Ilyushin Il-12 and -14, with thirty-two being the maximum number any of these slow piston aircraft could carry. Now, for the sixth plan, passenger numbers were to increase by a factor of 4.5 to 44.8 million and cargo mtks by a factor of 2.6. To achieve such a rapid growth, a major investment was needed for civil aviation: faster and larger aircraft were needed urgently, and airports would need modernisation to their runways, taxiways and terminals. Thus civil aviation received a high priority for the next fifteen years or so. In the years from 1955 to 1960, Antonov would fly the An-10, An-10A, An-12 (both civil and military), the An-14 and the An-24. Ilyushin would develop the turboprop Il-18 and begin work on the long-range Il-62, and Tupolev would see the Tu-104, Tu-110, Tu-114 and Tu-124 take to the air.

some of the problems of pressurisation, and he followed the widely reported investigation into the Comet accidents with interest. He and Markov had selected circular windows right from the start, but whether this was because of knowledge, prescience or luck is now just a matter of conjecture. The Comet's weak point turned out to be the corners of its rectangular windows in the passenger cabin. The -104 did not have these, so the problem did not arise.

Markov designed a semi-monocoque fuselage with a cross-section of 3.2m/10.5 feet; at first, seating was to be for fifty passengers. Later the seating was rearranged for seventy. The wing was attached to the fuselage in a lower relative position to that of the Tu-16, and its sweep remained the same 35°. For civilian use, the Mikulin AM-3s were derated to 8,700kg/19,180lb static thrust. In military service their resource (to use the Russian term for service life, or time between major overhauls) was short; by derating them, longer service lives could be achieved. Markov designed the -104 for a service life of 25,000 flight hours and 12,000 cycles. Because of the Comet's experience, a large pool was constructed at Zhukovski,

The prototype Tu-104, SSSR-L5400, at Zhukovski
Konstantin Udalov/Avico Press Collection

Tupolev began work on the Tu-104 in 1953. Head of the programme was Dmitri Markov. Together, they selected their team, and to save time the Tu-16 was chosen as a good basis for the airliner. The bomber had made its first flight in April 1952, and already a lot of experience had been gained on the type. While an airliner would certainly need a new fuselage, the wings, undercarriage, tailplane and engines could be taken with little change from the bomber, as could many of the aircraft's systems – hydraulics, electrical, instruments and controls. And, unlike de Havilland, Tupolev had already built pressurisation into the Tu-70, Tu-75, Tu-85 and Tu-95. Thus he had learned

and in it a complete fuselage was pressurised and depressurised to represent flight cycles for the operational life of the aircraft.

Although no problems of any significance were found, it was nonetheless decided, in view of the Comet report, to reinforce the window frames. The -104 was pressurised to equal a 2,500m/8,202 feet atmosphere when the aircraft was at a height of 10,000m/32,810 feet, representing a pressure differential of 0.57 atmospheres. In the early design stages, Tupolev and Markov considered the biggest risk to come from the possibility of a broken cockpit window; thus, the cockpit crew were provided with oxygen masks, while in the first two prototypes a hermetically sealed wall was installed between the cockpit and the

An Aeroflot Tu-104B, SSSR-42477, taking off from Sheremetyevo
Konstantin Udalov/Avico Press Collection

cabin. As confidence was built up in both the test airframe and in flight trials, this was considered unnecessary in production aircraft. The -104 was also the first Soviet aircraft to be fitted with a 'Panoramic Radio Location Station', the Soviet term for omnidirectional radar.

In order to prepare for the -104, the Ministry of the Aviation Industry (MAP) arranged for five Tu-16s to be converted as crew trainers under the designation Tu-104G at Aviaremont (aircraft repair factory) N400 at Vnukovo near Moscow. Meanwhile, the Ministry of Civil Aviation set about developing the Aviaremonts to the system that would remain up to the end of the Soviet Union in 1991: each aircraft type would be allocated to one repair factory; only in the event of large fleets would two or more factories be used, such as the An-2 of which 14,000-plus were built. Minor maintenance, Forms 1 and 2 checks (approximately equal to Western A and B checks) would be carried out by the operator, but Forms 3 and 4 (C and D equivalent checks) would be carried out at the dedicated overhaul factory.

While all this was going on, Markov and his team had completed the first true Tu-104 by early 1955 at factory N156, beside the design offices. It was then disassembled, brought by road to Zhukovski and reassembled. Its engine runs, ground trials and taxying tests were completed early in June, and on the seventeenth of that month, Yuri Alasheev was in command for its first flight. It took part, as mentioned, in the August Aviation Day flypast, apparently unnoticed by Western observers.

Factory tests went smoothly, with few problems despite the complexity of the aircraft. State tests followed. One problem needed ironing out: at high level (of altitude) near thunderstorms and vertical airstreams it was important to avoid getting into high angles of attack (nose high); thus the designers tightened the CG (centre of gravity) limits by moving forward the rear limits. (This was just a way of ensuring that the aircraft's payload was better positioned – it did not involve any engineering changes). Markov also increased the angle of the horizontal stabiliser, and the maximum angle it was possible to turn the elevator.

The flight to London mentioned at the beginning of this section was a part of the test programme. Tupolev was one of the visiting delegation. He was very pleased at the sensation caused by the jet's arrival in London, and at the level of media attention it attracted. He later regarded it as 'putting an end to the myth that Soviet civil aviation continued to lag behind that of the West'.

Now production had begun in Kharkov factory N135 and Omsk factory N166; later Kazan factory N22 would also add to the production. In 1956, twelve Tu-104s were delivered to Aeroflot, followed by twenty-two more in 1957. Altogether, 201 production examples were built between 1956 and 1960. Five were delivered to the Czechoslovakian airline CSA between 1957 and 1959, with a sixth delivered, ex-Aeroflot. An undetermined number went to the VVS, including some after service with Aeroflot. At least four of these served in a cosmonaut training role, and two are reported still to exist, although out of service, at Chkalovsk Air Force aerodrome in 1995.

For Aeroflot and its pilots and engineers, the arrival of the Tu-104 meant a huge move forward from the technology of the 1930s as represented by the Li-2 and the Ilyushin piston aircraft. In only fifteen months after the first flight, the Ministry of Civil Aviation and Aeroflot had managed to upgrade many airports and to train controllers, flight crew and technical staff to operate, fly and maintain a totally new product – the jet airliner. The first Aeroflot unit to receive the -104 was at Vnukovo, Moscow's major domestic airport since the 1930s. Early in 1995, flight crew who had served on the -104 told of their experiences:

'The first scheduled service was from Vnukovo to Omsk and Irkutsk and it took place on 15 September 1956. Trial route proving flights had begun five months earlier, when a crew headed by K. P. Sapelkin had flown the same route, covering the 4,570km/2,840 miles in a flying time of just seven hours ten minutes, just over half the time that it was taking Il-14s to fly the route. As military pilots were familiar with the Tu-16, they became instructors at a special training centre set up in Novosibirsk to convert Aeroflot pilots from piston-engined aircraft on to the -104. Everyone working on the -104, which we called by its codename "Strela" (Arrow) was trained there, and had to become used to the new power, speed and altitude of the new aircraft. It was a huge change from the Li-2.'

While some systems on the -104 were standard, others were new – pressurisation and the air change system had not been on older airliners; these were worked off the engines, and the resulting hot air left a very dry cabin, so the air needed to be humidified. Many of the instruments were also new to the crews and much emphasis was paid to the need to control rate of climb and CG limits.

'As we got to know it, we built up confidence in it; soon we loved it for its power and reliability. As we came near our destination, for the first few years other aircraft were ordered to leave the zone to make the way clear for us. In those days, many of the runways were a bit short for the -104, so we had brake parachutes installed, which we used. But as our experience and confidence built up we gradually learned to slow the aircraft without a parachute. We sometimes had a problem with it; if we touched down too fast, the

parachute could break away – if, for example, it was deployed above 250kph/155mph. Each airport had a specialist parachute packing staff who would rarely take more than ten minutes to replace one, although how long it took to collect, clean and repack one from a wet runway, I don't know.'

By the end of 1956, the -104 was also flying to Tbilisi, Tashkent and Khabarovsk in the Far East. Later, holiday (health) resorts such as Mineralnie Vody and Simferopol were added as well as Alma Ata, Leningrad, and Sakhalin on the Pacific Coast. The flight from Leningrad to Sakhalin now took 8.5 hours' flying time plus two one-hour stopovers compared to the twenty-eight flying hours plus nine stops in the Li-2 or Il-14s previously used.

'On one flight from Sverdlovsk [now Yekaterinburg], the captain ordered the co-pilot to retract the undercarriage. Beside the lever was one to release the tail parachute, and he chose the wrong one. The navigator reported that speed was dropping just as the engineer announced that the 'chute was out. The captain ordered "release 'chute, retract gear, dump fuel for emergency return". He climbed to circuit altitude until the fuel had been dumped, then landed. They found two parachutes and the fuel plugs on the strip – all was OK.'

Shortly after this incident, the parachute release lever was relocated to the engineer's position.

Faults on the -104 were described as, 'not enough fuel, the range was too short, and it needed a long runway'. In the 1950s, on the transcontinental route from Moscow to Khabarovsk, there were only four airports long enough to take it – Irkutsk, Omsk, Novosibirsk and Sverdlovsk, although Chelabinsk was added later.

The -104 served with six Aeroflot squadrons (rather than invent new titles, military ones were often used): No. 200 at Vnukovo; 201 at Irkutsk; 202 at Khabarovsk; 203 at Leningrad; and 204 at Novosibirsk. The sixth was at Sheremetyevo, where the Moscow directorate based its international services. Later this became the TsUMVS – Central Department of International Air Services. Omitting the converted Tu-16s, designated Tu-104Gs, a total of 203 were built – two prototypes, including the structural tests airframe at factory N156, ninety-six at Kazan, forty-five at Kharkov and sixty at Omsk.

The original fifty-seat cabin was soon found to be too small, and even rearranging it to accommodate

One of the last Tu-104s built, SSSR-42507, is shown at Bourgas in Bulgaria, about to start in this night shot taken in 1971
Paul Duffy

seventy proved inadequate. The first new version, the Tu-104A, retained the same dimensions as the original -104, but operational experience allowed it to be converted with worthwhile weight savings, and with an improved version of the AM-3 engine, the RD-3M, which gave an increased power of 9,700kp/21,385lb, but with service life now at 1,500 hours, well up from the 200 to 300 of the older engine. CSA, the Czechoslovakian airline, introduced the -104A into service shortly after its first one was delivered to Prague on 2 November 1957. It was the only foreign customer for the -104, and it served routes to Europe, the Soviet Union and the Middle East until 1974; the three surviving -104s of the CSA fleet were preserved, one in the Czech Aviation Museum, and the other two as bars/restaurants.

In 1959, a new model, the Tu-104B, was introduced. This featured a 1.2m/3.94 feet stretch in the fuselage and a complete cabin redesign; by eliminating crew rest accommodation and changing galley layouts, passenger accommodation was increased to 100, although some had an all 'tourist class' arrangement which could carry 115. A final version offered to Aeroflot was the -104E, designed to carry 122. The -104A began to serve international routes in 1958, with Delhi, Cairo and London being the first destinations. The first -104B service was 15 April 1959 on the Moscow–Leningrad route. By 1960, one third of all Aeroflot's passengers were being carried on the -104 – in its first ten years in service, twenty-eight million passengers travelled on -104s.

As was usual with Soviet aircraft, the Tu-104 was used to establish new FAI recognised world records. Twenty-two were set including:

September 1957:	(SSSR-L5421) the first jetliner to cover a 2,000km/1,243-mile closed circuit – pilot Yuri Alasheev, who covered 2,002.6km/1,244.4 miles.
21 September 1957:	1,000km/621 miles with ten-tonne load flown at average speed of 970.821kph/603.268mph. Again Yuri Alasheev was the pilot.
1 August 1959:	100km/62.1 miles with fifteen-tonne load covered at 1,015.816kph/631.259mph. Pilot – Valentin Kovaliov in a Tu-104B.
14 August 1959:	altitude of 12,896 metres/42,311 feet with a twenty-five-tonne load. Yuri Alasheev in a Tu-104B.

The -104 continued in Aeroflot service until the 1970s. With the arrival of new aircraft, Vnukovo began their withdrawal in October 1973, and two years later the last one was withdrawn from Irkutsk, but service was not finished. A number had been delivered to the VVS, and others were transferred as they were withdrawn from Aeroflot. They served as VIP transports, flying laboratories and for cosmonaut training; on these missions, the Tu-104 would climb to high altitudes, then cut power, descend 1,000m, then climb again and repeat the procedure to simulate weightlessness. This of course put severe strain on the airframe and shortened the service life considerably. Military service ended after an accident on 7 February 1981, when a badly loaded and overweight Tu-104A (serial number 76600402) belonging to the VMF Pacific Fleet, crashed on take-off from Pushkino airport, near Leningrad, at the start of a return trip to Khabarovsk, killing all six crew and forty-five passengers. Although the accident was established as being due to the poor loading, the fact that among the dead passengers were the Deputy Commander of the Pacific Fleet, the Commander of Aviation for the Pacific Region, and the Chief of Staff of Naval Aviation of the Pacific Fleet, led to the grounding of the remaining aircraft. Reports that two Tu-104s continued in service at Chkalovsk until the late 1980s have been discounted by the VVS.

On 11 November 1986, the last (known) flight of a Tu-104 took place: SSSR-42322 was flown from Sheremetyevo to the Aeroflot museum at Ulyanovsk. Present at the departure was the Minister of Civil Aviation, Boris Bugaev, who, thirty years earlier, had been one of the first Tu-104 pilots. He said at the time that 'any experienced pilot could fly the -104'.

Studies on the -104, including stress tests, continued right through its career. Three withdrawn aircraft and wings from five others were tested to destruction. These proved that 35,000 flight hours or 15,000 cycles could have been safely achieved. One Tu-104G (a converted Tu-16) was equipped with a large quantity of research equipment and, operated by the GosNII GA (the State Scientific Research Institute for Civil Aviation), served as a weather laboratory for the Soviet Hydro Meteorological Service, investigating weather systems. It was used in Cuba to check thunderstorms and hurricanes, and was called *Tsiklon* (Cyclone).

SSSR-42400 achieved the highest flight cycles, over 18,000, without any major structural cracks. The first passenger flight was made on SSSR-L5412. After 8,000 cycles, when it was the high time aircraft, it was withdrawn and tested for signs of fatigue. Later, another -104 was painted with its number and preserved at Vnukovo, where it still stands (in mid-1995).

Andrei Tupolev made a point of meeting and knowing all the first Aeroflot pilots to operate the -104; at that time, there was a gap in communications between the two aviation ministries, and the pilots still remember him with pride.

One Tu-104A was completed in 1958 at Omsk as a development for a military transport. Called the Tu-107, it was not put into production.

This Tu-16/88 (or Tu-104G), SSSR-42355, became a weather research laboratory, called *Tsiklon*. It was operated by the GosNII GA in Aeroflot marks. It spent some time operating from Cuba
Konstantin Udalov/Avico Press Collection

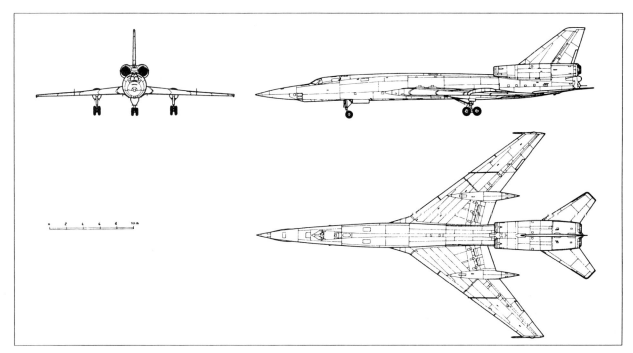

Project 105 – The Tu-22

(NATO codename 'Blinder')

The developments in aircraft and engine technology in the years after the Great Patriotic War/World War Two can be well demonstrated by a VVS decision to order development of a new long-range bomber intended to replace the Tu-16 'Badger' just as it entered service (by the mid-1950s, even Soviet industry often used the NATO codenames, particularly if they were liked). Once again, Dmitri Markov was appointed chief designer. His brief was to create a new twin-engined long-range bomber and missile carrier which could also serve in a reconnaissance role; it was required to be capable of exceeding the sound barrier for short periods. It was designated Tu-105 by the bureau.

Markov chose an almost low-wing layout – low-mid-wing might be a better description, with a 55° sweep. The horizontal tailplane and the fin were even more swept. The fuselage was all-metal, and was manufactured of V95 aluminium alloy, with added AK-8 steel aluminium and ML5-74 magnesium alloys for extra strength where needed. Frames and stringers were used to reinforce the skin. A pressurised cabin fitted with K-22 ejection seats which released downwards was set in the forward fuselage, and accommodated the crew of three – pilot, navigator and weapons operator. The rear fuselage held the bomb compartment, with the bomb load fitted into 'cassette holders'. Alternatively, on missile carriers, a Kh-22 'Kitchen'/AS-4 long-range air-to-surface missile was carried semi-sunk under the fuselage. On the reconnaissance version, the Tu-22R, cameras were carried instead, fixed into place in the fuselage over viewing holes through which photos were taken.

Fuel was carried in rubberised tanks; seven were mounted in the fuselage, and twelve in the wings, which consisted of a centre section with four outer, removable, boxes. The rear fuselage housed a container for the two parachutes used to slow the aircraft when landing. The aircraft's controls were operated by hydroboosters, with two back-up systems, one mechanical and the other electrical, which could be used in the event of a failure in the primary system. These systems were used for ailerons, stabilisers and rudders, and also for wing flaps. Visually, the aircraft's most unusual feature was the location of its engines, which were mounted over the rear fuselage on either side of the tail. The engines were single duct turbo-boosted RD-7s designed by Piotr Kolesov of the Dobrynin engine design bureau at Rybinsk. At first, the 16,000kg/35,275lb static thrust TRD-VD7M was used, but later these were replaced with the RD-7ND version, which increased output to 16,500kg/36,375lb. Normal bomb load was three tonnes, but it was possible to take up to thirteen tonnes with some range penalties.

The prototype Tu-22 'Blinder' at Zhukovski
Konstantin Udalov/Avico Press Collection

Design and construction of high-performance aircraft was becoming increasingly complex, and even with a high priority, it was almost four years before the engineers and technicians at factory N156 completed the prototype in February 1958. After transfer by road to Zhukovski, reassembly and ground trials, its first flight was made on 21 July with Yuri Alasheev making the last first flight of his career.

It proved to be a complex and difficult aircraft to fly in some regimes. At high subsonic speeds, the position of the engine caused severe air turbulence over the tailplane which was installed under the exhausts (later tail-engined jets would usually feature the horizontal tailplane at the top of the fin, four or five metres above the exhaust). Poor all-round visibility, particularly with a nose-high attitude on approach, and a high landing speed which resulted in a requirement for a 2,700 metre/8,860 foot runway length, were other difficulties for the crew.

Shortly before the Tu-105A, the second prototype, made its maiden flight on 7 September 1959, the first one was lost in an accident during flight trials, killing its three crew including Alasheev. He was later awarded the title of 'Hero of the Soviet Union', the highest military honour of the nation, for his

A Tu-22 'Blinder A' about to link up with its refuelling tanker
Konstantin Udalov/Avico Press Collection

outstanding work in the development and testing of aircraft.

In 1959, the VVS ordered the aircraft into production in Kazan factory N22 under the designation Tu-22. This was the third aircraft to bear the Tu-22 military designation – the Tu-79 of 1948, and the Tu-82 of 1949 were both earlier bearers of the number, but neither went into production. In Kazan, 311 aircraft were built between 1959 and 1969. Even so, another Tu-22 would appear later.

Ten Tu-22s took part in the Aviation Day flypast at Tushino in 1961, before service entry. Some later flypasts had formations of twenty-two aircraft in recognition of the type number. The Tu-22 was given the NATO codename 'Blinder'. Service entry began in 1962; although it was intended to replace the Tu-16 in service, a role was found for both aircraft, and they served side by side until the early 1990s.

Five main versions served with the VVS:

Tu-22 – Blinder A – long-range bomber
Tu-22K – Blinder B – missile carrier
Tu-22P – electronic jammer
Tu-22R – Blinder C – reconnaissance patroller, with both day and night equipment.
Tu-22U – Blinder D – trainer, with the instructor seated in an extra cockpit mounted above and behind the normal position.

The suffix 'D' was applied (e.g. Tu-22RD) when the Tu-22 was fitted with an inflight refuelling system. Fuel was downloaded usually from a Tu-16Z tanker using '3MS-2' male-female probes; as the SALT negotiations progressed throughout the 1980s, Tu-22s were removed from the strategic category simply by the dismantling of this equipment to shorten the aircraft's range. In service conditions, the Tu-22 could be re-equipped from a bomber to a reconnaissance role and vice versa at its base in a period of a few hours. Early in the 1980s, some aircraft were modified to Tu-22RDM standard by the fitting of new radio interference equipment.

The Tu-22 had a single defensive NR-33 cannon mounted in the tail, which was remotely controlled by the weapon's operator from the pressurised cabin. He also controlled the release of the missiles or bombs. With afterburners on, the Tu-22 had a top speed of 1,600kph/994mph or Mach 1.51 at 12,200m/40,028 feet when fitted with RD-7ND engines; it was 190kph/118mph slower with the less powerful VD-7M version. Service ceiling was 13,500m/44,294 feet with the RD-7NDs; range without refuelling was 5,650km/3,500 miles. Normal take-off weight was eighty-five tonnes, but ninety-two could be reached when necessary.

By the early 1990s, most Tu-22s had been withdrawn from service, with only a few remaining with the VVS and VMS on long-range patrol duties. Some Tu-22Rs and -22Us were exported: nine were delivered to Iraq in the mid-1960s, and seven went to Libya.

A Tu-22U 'Blinder D', coded '06', on its landing roll. Note the training instructor's cockpit above the normal cockpit
Konstantin Udalov/Avico Press Collection

Tu-110

5600, probably the prototype Tu-110 which bore the civilian number SSSR-L5600, in military marks at Kazan
Konstantin Udalov/Avico Press Collection

In order to meet Aeroflot's requirement for a 100-seat jetliner, Dmitri Markov installed four 5,000shp Lyulka AL-7P engines in place of the two larger AM-3s in a slightly stretched fuselage of a Tu-104 – the stretch, of 1.2m, gave the Tu-110, as the new version was numbered, a fuselage length of 40.06m/131.44 feet. The span was also increased by 2.96m/9.7 feet to give space for the extra two engines to be installed. The third change was to the interior, where the cabin was divided into two sections to provide for first and economy class passengers. Take-off weight of the four-engined aircraft, at 79,300kg/174,825lb, was 3,300kg/7,273lb higher than the original Tu-104. With a maximum speed of 1,000kph/621mph, a ceiling of 12,000m/39,372 feet, and a range of 3,300km/2,049 miles, there was little difference in performance.

One aircraft was built at factory N156 from parts manufactured at factory N22 in Kazan and brought to Moscow, and it made its first flight on 11 March 1957, with Dmitri Ziuzin in command. Although it flew well, it offered little advance on the -104, and no production orders followed, although two others were completed at Kazan. Instead, Aeroflot and Tupolev agreed that the slightly larger body should become standard on the -104B, which began service in 1959.

Tu-114

By the mid-1950s, the Soviet government was anxious to see Aeroflot expanding its services beyond national frontiers in order to broaden its communications and

influence with non-aligned countries, particularly in the less developed areas of the world. This gave impetus to a programme to produce long-range airliners.

There was also growing traffic volume within the USSR, so in 1955 work began on a new range of turbo-prop airliners to meet these needs. Antonov produced the eighty-four-passenger An-10 for domestic routes; Ilyushin's second Il-18, a four-engined turboprop for 100 passengers, was soon to be built in large numbers, and was to be Aeroflot's medium- and long-range standard bearer for more than a decade; but for high-density or very long-range services, Tupolev's Tu-114 was unbeatable. All made their first flights in 1957.

Starting with the Tu-95, Nikolai Bazenkov, working under the direction and supervision of Tupolev, set about building an airliner. The Tu-95 had first flown in 1952; it had experienced some early problems in perfecting the design of its engines, gearbox and propellers, but by 1955 the new Kuznetsov NK-12s were proving to be reliable and relatively economical. Tupolev was never a man to ignore a good design feature, and he and Bazenkov elected to speed up the airliner programme by adapting the wings, engines, tailplane and undercarriage of the 'Bear' and adding a new fuselage designed to accommodate passengers.

This cut the time needed to design and build the prototype to just eighteen months. A double-deck arrangement was selected with a fuselage diameter of 3.7m/12.14 feet. The Tu-114, which was given the NATO codename 'Cleat', was designed to carry up to 220 passengers, and from its inception until the

Tu-114

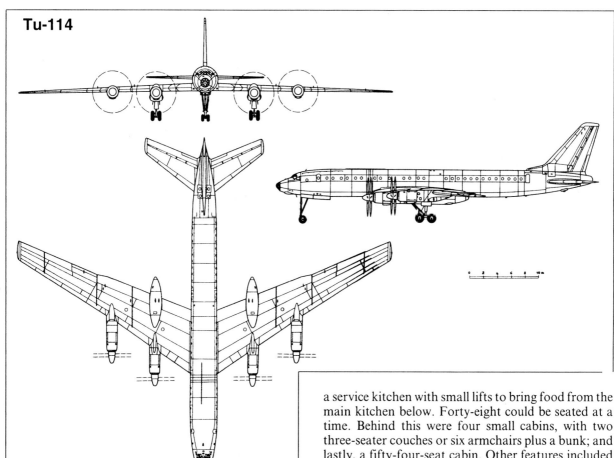

appearance of the first Boeing 747 more than a decade later, it was the world's largest passenger aircraft. Indeed, until the Antonov An-22, which first flew in 1965, it was the largest aircraft to enter service in the world, with only a prototype flying boat exceeding its size – the Hughes Hercules, which made just one flight in 1947.

The new fuselage was a semi-monocoque construction and was 47m/154.2 feet in length. The lower deck was for cargo and baggage, and was described as consisting of two compartments 'each as large as a (railway) freight carriage'. On the upper deck, and behind the cockpit, there was sleeping accommodation for passengers and crew and a staircase gave access to the flight kitchen. Normally two cooks were carried to cater for the numbers of people on board. Two seating arrangements were offered. On routes of up to 6,000 kilometres/3,728 miles, 220 passengers could be carried. In one version, behind the sleeping area was a forty-two-seat cabin, followed by a dining hall and

a service kitchen with small lifts to bring food from the main kitchen below. Forty-eight could be seated at a time. Behind this were four small cabins, with two three-seater couches or six armchairs plus a bunk; and lastly, a fifty-four-seat cabin. Other features included a cloakroom for hanging coats, which was in line with the propellers, then came toilets, washrooms and a powder room. Today, many of these features would be regarded as a waste of space, and be used instead to carry even more passengers. This came to a total of 168 passengers; alternatively a single cabin tourist arrangement could hold 220. On the very long-range version, called the Tu-114D (for Dalnii) by Aeroflot, the forward cabin held extra fuel tanks, and passenger numbers were restricted to just 120 – even that was more than any other propeller airliner, and matched the seating of early Western jetliners.

The fuselage was, of course, pressurised, to a maximum differential of 0.59kg/cm², representing an atmosphere of 2,500m/8,202 feet at an altitude of 10,000m/32,810 feet. The prototype was built at factory N156 and, when completed, was disassembled and brought to Zhukovski. After ground trials and engine tests – the first two aircraft were fitted with 12,000shp NK-12s; later aircraft had 14,000shp NK-12Ms or 14,795shp NK-12MVs – the maiden flight of the first Tu-114 took place on 15 November 1957 with Aleksei Yakimov in command. With the experience built up on the Tu-95, by now Kuznetsov's engines and Zhdanov's propellers and gearbox were working particularly well, and the flight trials went smoothly.

A need for a long-range airliner to fly the Soviet premier to a United Nations General Assembly meeting in September 1959, and doubt as to whether the -114 would be available by then, led to the hurried production of the two Tu-116s.

During its development programme and in the year following, a number of records were set by the Tu-114. On 24 March 1960, with Ivan Sukhomlin in command, a Tu-114 carried a payload of twenty-five tonnes over a 1,000km/621-mile closed circuit at an average speed of 871.38kph/541.45mph. It set eight world records with this flight, all recognised by the FAI – for speed with payloads of 0kg, 1,000kg, 2,000kg, 5,000kg, 10,000kg, 15,000kg, 20,000kg and 25,000kg. Later, on 1 April, he set another eight records over a 2,000km/1,228-mile course at 857.277kph/532.69mph. And, on 9 April, he took the same eight categories over a 5,000km/3,107-mile course at an average speed of 877.212kph/545.07mph. Two years later, on 21 April 1962, over a 10,000km/6,214-mile closed circuit, he set a speed record of 737.352kph/458.2mph for all categories up to ten tonnes payload. On 12 July 1961, with a payload of 35,035kg, he climbed a Tu-114 to 12,073m/39,610 feet and set altitude records for twenty-five-tonne and thirty-tonne payloads.

Meanwhile, Aeroflot had begun to prepare for the Tu-114 by setting up a ground school at Moscow's Vnukovo airport. Vnukovo was also the maintenance centre established for the -114 at repair factory N400. All those built were operated by the Moscow Region of Aeroflot, initially based at Vnukovo for domestic services and at Sheremetyevo when it began international flights. Later, in 1967, when Domodedovo airport was opened, the domestic -114s were transferred there to the new Domodedovo directorate. These two were the only Aeroflot units to operate the giant airliner.

As the prototype began flight tests, Tu-114 production was set up at Kuibyshev factory N18, under the leadership of general director Mitrofan Yevshin. Between 1957 and 1968, thirty-two aircraft were built. In a tribute to their design and construction, and in view of the service they would give, it is remarkable that only one accident occurred to a Tu-114, and that was due to a pilot fault. On 2 December 1966, SSSR-76457 was lost in a take-off accident at Sheremetyevo when a wingtip struck a large mound of snow as it began a flight to South Africa.

Before it entered service, the -114 was used for two VIP flights to the United States. On 28 July 1959, the prototype -114, SSSR-L5611, flew deputy premier Kozlov to New York on a diplomatic mission combined with a route-proving flight as a preparation for Premier Khrushchev's forthcoming visit to the United Nations, which followed on 15 September. As these were the longest non-stop and overwater flights ever made by top-level Soviet delegates, before each

The prototype Tu-114, SSSR-L5611, at Vnukovo in 1959
Konstantin Udalov/Avico Press Collection

Tu-114 SSSR-76470 of the TsUMVS Aeroflot division shown at Paris–Le Bourget in the late 1960s
J. Bigley

flight they were all given emergency evacuation training in a swimming pool near Moscow by the KGB, worried for their safety.

A number of route-proving flights were made prior to service entry to European destinations, and in June 1959 the -114, appropriately called *Rossiya* (Russia) since the 1957 fortieth anniversary of the Socialist Revolution, visited the Paris Air Salon. Earlier, it visited Brussels for EXPO–57, where it won for Tupolev the 'great gold Medal of distinction.'

The first scheduled passenger flight took place on 24 April 1961, flying from Moscow to Khabarovsk, near the Russian Pacific coast, non-stop. The scheduled time for the 6,810km/3,675-mile route was just eight hours fifteen minutes, shorter even than that of the Tu-104 which needed two refuelling stops en route.

In 1962, the long-range Tu-114D version with fewer passengers was introduced; operating with 120 passengers, it began services to Cuba on 7 January 1963. Because on a great circle route, Murmansk was closer to Havana, and because the difficult political situation of the time sometimes made overflights by Soviet aircraft diplomatically impossible, the -114 services were operated from Sheremetyevo through this northern city to the Caribbean island. In ten years of operation and with over 1,400 return flights completed, no significant technical problems arose. On one occasion, an eastbound TWA Boeing 707 reported a near miss with a -114 over the mid-Atlantic; in those days, political isolation and imperfect navigation and radio systems meant that there was no possible communication between Soviet and Western aircraft. In those ten years no -114 diversions to any Western airport were made. The flight took almost twenty hours, including the stopover.

Tu-114s served the Moscow to Delhi route from March 1963; Moscow to the West African cities of Conakry and Accra from August 1965; and Moscow to Tokyo in a code-sharing arrangement with Japan Airlines from August 1966 (although the joint service only began in April 1967 with a mix of Japanese and Soviet cabin crew); and Moscow to Montreal from November 1966. Other routes, including Moscow to Paris and London, used -114s when capacity required, with Paris being serviced once a week in summer months by the -114.

Pilots and engineers of the Domodedovo Civil Aviation United Enterprise, who had flown and worked with Tu-114s in the 1960s and 70s, outlined some of their experiences early in 1995. Some had previous experience on the Il-18 and some on the Il-12/-14. It was not a very big step from the turboprop Il-18, although the large size of the Tu-114 and a 50kph/31mph increase in approach speed meant that some extra attention was needed. But it was quite a jump from the piston-engined Il-14. Even captains of the Il-18 had to spend a year as co-pilot on the Tu-114, building up at least 450 hours' experience, before being given command.

'We attended a two-month ground training course at Vnukovo before each pilot was given eight hours of flight training. The Tu-114 was easy to fly; we had no simulators in those days. To begin, the first Aeroflot pilots were trained by Tupolev crews from Zhukovski, but later ones went to Kuibyshev where we were trained by factory pilots.

The Tu-114 fleet moved to Domodedovo from Vnukovo six months after the airport was opened in 1964. We flew it from here for twelve years, until 1976, to cities such as Khabarovsk, Novosibirsk, Tashkent, Alma Ata and Anadir. The shortest of these flights was about four hours, although Khabarovsk took seven to seven and a half to reach, and the return flight took about an hour longer. The aircraft would stay about three hours at the out airport, then return to Domodedovo, where it would take about four to six hours to get ready for the next trip. Very often, it would fly back to Khabarovsk the next day.

The engines were very powerful and gave few problems. At the start their time between overhauls was quite short, just 600 hours; later it grew to 2,000 hours which was good for the 1960s. Their total service life was 8,000 hours. The fuel burn was 7.2 tonnes for the first hour, including take-off and climb-out; in the cruise it was five to 5.5 tonnes, about the same as the Tu-154M today, but with up to 220 passengers instead of the -154's maximum of 180.

The propellers and gearboxes were very reliable, but they produced a lot of noise and vibration; while the cockpit was quiet, the fuselage area near the propellers was definitely noisy, although normal conversation was possible in the rear cabin. The propellers took three hours to change – they were developed for military aircraft, but in civilian service had to fly perhaps ten times as much, up to 2,000 hours per year.

On one occasion, with a full load of over 200 passengers, a -114 returning from Khabarovsk to Moscow met strong headwinds, then found Moscow airports closed and had to divert to Leningrad, which closed just as the flight drew near, so it diverted to Kiev, about one hour's flight away on the other side of Moscow. As it neared Kiev, it closed, but Moscow reopened. It made it back to Domodedovo with about forty minutes' fuel remaining – about half the journey time to either Leningrad or Kiev.'

As the Tu-114 was withdrawn from service, several went to museums. SSSR-76464 was fittingly displayed at Domodedovo in 1977. But one interesting footnote to history was the last flight of SSSR-76485 which was delivered to an (engineering) technical training college

The Tu-114's height is shown in this photo of the second Tu-114, SSSR-L5412, at Vnukovo
Konstantin Udalov/Avico Press Collection

Tu-114 SSSR-76478 in flight
Konstantin Udalov/Avico Press Collection

at Krivoi Rog in the Ukraine in September 1976. The problem was that the airstrip near the college had only a 2,100m/6,890-foot grass runway. It was flown there by captain Trifon Bashilov and co-pilot Nikolai Riabinin, with flight engineer Arkhalinin the third crew member. Touch down, evidenced by track marks, was eighty metres/262 feet from the beginning of the runway, and the ground run was just 1,300m/4,265 feet, one of the shortest made by the large turboprop. One other Tu-114 went to Novgorod, a second to Tyumen and a third to the Ulyanovsk Civil Aviation Museum.

As Il-62s began to be delivered to Aeroflot, the operation of Tu-114s was scaled back; although a few remained in service at Domodedovo until 1980, most were withdrawn in 1975 and 1976.

Tu-116

The Soviet government had planned for several years that the General Secretary of the Communist Party and Premier of the Soviet Union, Nikita Khrushchev, should address the United Nations General Assembly. As a matter of national prestige, he had to travel on a Soviet airliner.

When this matter first arose, in the mid-1950s, the Soviet Union had no medium- or long-range aircraft in commercial service. Although the Tu-104 was shortly to enter service, it was not considered suitable because of its relatively short range. The -114 was in

the early stages of design, but whether it would be operational before the end of the decade was difficult to determine. The Soviet Union had, of course, the remarkable Tu-95, but the nation's leader could not travel in a strategic bomber – or could he? Tupolev was called in.

Nikolai Bazenkov was diverted from other duties to prepare a passenger version of the Tu-95. Two aircraft were taken from the production line at Kuibyshev. No armaments were fitted, and all military equipment was removed. With the original airframe of the Tu-95, a passenger compartment was installed behind the wing spar; it consisted of a pressurised cabin with two sections, each of which could accommodate twenty passengers in VIP luxury. A kitchen, toilet and service room were also installed. A fitted stairs was installed so passengers could board and disembark without a need for special airport equipment.

Although the work began only in mid-1957, the Tu-116, which was sometimes called the Tu-114D, was airborne by spring 1958. Usually, the 'D' suffix in an aircraft designation represented 'Dalnii' (long distance), but this time it stood for 'Diplomaticheskii' (diplomatic).

In April 1958, the prototype Tu-116, Air Force Number 7801, a number probably derived from its manufacturer's block and line number, made a high-altitude, long-distance trial flight to demonstrate its ability for the task. Flying at levels between 10,000m/32,810 feet and 12,200m/40,028 feet, it flew non-stop from Moscow to Irkutsk and back to

The first Tu-116, SSSR-76462, is preserved at the Ulyanovsk Museum of Civil Aviation
Paul Duffy

Moscow, covering 8,500km/5,282 miles at an average speed of 800kph/497mph. After landing, it was calculated still to have fuel for another 1,500 to 2,000km/932 to 1,228 miles. The second aircraft was intended as a reserve in the event of a problem with the first, but neither were needed. Instead, Khrushchev flew to the New York headquarters of the United Nations Assembly in the prototype Tu-114.

Never intended for normal commercial service, the two Tu-116s were little used. Originally painted in military marks (7801 and 7802), one aircraft was later given the civilian registration SSSR-76462, and is now preserved in the Ulyanovsk Museum of Civil Aviation.

Tu-119

In the late 1950s, the Soviet government was intent on developing its nuclear industry. The idea of a nuclear-powered strategic bomber was put forward, and Tupolev was asked to study its feasibility.

Work began on the project, designated 119, by converting a Tu-95 flying laboratory, the Tu-95LAL.

The Kuznetsor engine design bureau developed an NK-12 to take nuclear power, and the flying Laboratory was fitted with a nuclear reactor installed in the fuselage; power was provided by two nuclear-fuelled NK-14s plus two normal NK-12MVs.

However, the programme was discontinued before the aircraft flew.

Missiles

Projects 121, 123, 130, 139, 141 and 143

Military thinking in the mid-1950s moved away from piloted aircraft and more towards unmanned aviation, or missiles. Meanwhile, Tupolev had begun to prepare his son, Aleksei, to succeed him. Aleksei had by now graduated from the Moscow Aviation Institute and was working in the aerodynamics department of the OKB. In 1958, Tupolev set up a new division to undertake work on 'pilotless aircraft'; Aleksei was appointed head of the department. His task was to design and construct missiles for reconnaissance, strike and space purposes.

His first missile, with project number 121, was built only as a prototype. It was a strategic strike missile, or ICBM. Under the designation 'S', it was launched in 1959. His next project, the 123, was a strategic reconnaissance missile which could be launched from a mobile platform for a pre-programmed course and height. The data gathered could be transmitted to a ground station, and the missile could be recovered, after a parachute landing, for reuse. Its range was 3,650km/2,268 miles, speed was 2,700kph/1,678mph, and its cruise altitude was 19,000m/62,338 feet at the beginning of its mission, rising to 21,000m/68,901 feet at the end. Launch weight was 36.8 tonnes. Its thrust came from a KR-15-300 turbojet engine and its output was ten tonnes. Fifty-two missiles were produced between 1964 and 1972 at Voronezh.

Next came an unmanned space missile, the 130,

which was only built as a prototype. It was launched in the early 1960s. Project 139 followed. Developed from the 123, it was given the military code DBR-2. It was a strategic reconnaissance missile equipped with an intelligence gathering system under the name Yastreb (Hawk). Only one was produced, which was launched for the first time in July 1968. It was recoverable.

Next came Project 143, a tactical reconnaissance missile with a range of just 190km/118 miles. It was equipped with a 'Reis' (Flight) intelligence gathering system, and flew at 850 to 950kph/528 to 590mph at altitudes of 50 to 3,000m/164 to 9,843 feet. It was powered by a TRZ 117 engine which gave 580kg/1,279lb thrust. It was produced at Kumertau between 1973 and 1989, and 950 were manufactured. It was sold to the air forces of Syria, Czechoslovakia and Romania.

The last missile was Project 141. Another tactical reconnaissance unit, it was equipped with a 'Strizh' (Swift [bird]) intelligence gathering system. Its range was 1,000km/621 miles and speed was 1,100kph/683mph. Its altitude could vary from 50m/164 feet to 6,000m/19,687 feet. Launch weight was 6,215kg/13,702lb and it was powered by a KR-17A motor which gave 2,000kg/4,409lb thrust. Between 1979 and 1989, 152 were built at Kharkov factory N135.

A Tu-123 reconnaissance missile with its mobile platform
Tupolev

Tu-124

The Little Tu

The targets for air traffic set in the sixth economic plan were being met in 1957 and 1958, and part of the progress was due to the introduction of the Tu-104 on trunk routes. Meanwhile, piston-engined airliners continued to carry virtually all the short- and medium-distance traffic of the Soviet Union. The Soviet planners were impressed with the results from the -104, and decided to include a smaller passenger jet into the seventh economic plan (1959 to 1965) for medium-length routes, and thus to speed up the development of inter-city transportation. For shorter routes, turbo-props would be developed.

Tupolev was the obvious choice to develop the new aircraft for the medium routes, and he delegated the

in the wing roots. Unlike the -104, the turbofan engines were a lot quieter than the pure jets of earlier aircraft, and the turbofan offered a longer service life (initially 1,100 flight hours) and a lower fuel burn per aircraft tonne/km, or passenger kilometre than earlier jets. Fuel tankage was 13,500 litres/2,970 gallons.

As usual for Soviet aircraft, Markov designed the -124 to be capable of using unpaved runways, so he fitted two-axle, four-wheeled bogeys on each of the main undercarriage legs. He also fitted double-slotted flaps, an under-fuselage airbrake and rapid retraction devices to assist the aircraft's soft field performance.

In 1962, Leonid Seliakov took over his position as programme chief for the -124, when he joined Tupolev from the Myasishchev design bureau. Markov was needed on other programmes, particularly the new Tu-22M.

Although it looked like a -104, most of the aircraft's

An Aeroflot Tu-124, SSSR-45013, air to air
B. Vdodenko via Konstantin Udalov/Avico Press Collection

task to Dmitri Markov. Working with the -104 as a basis, Markov designed a similar looking, but smaller version which was given the project number 124. Its cabin was designed to accommodate forty-four passengers in three sections of four abreast seating. Cabin width, at 2.70m/ 8.6 feet was narrower than the 3.2m/10.5 feet of the five abreast -104, and its length, at 20.7m/67.9 feet, but including galley and toilets, was slightly larger than that quoted for the -104, but without galley and toilets, of 20.1m/66.0 feet. All in all, the -124 is often quoted as being twenty-five per cent smaller than the -104, and was called 'Malenkii Tu' (Little Tu) by the travelling public.

It was the first Soviet airliner to use turbofans, and the first jetliner in the world to do so on short to medium routes. The engines were developed for the -124 by Pavel Soloviev's engine design bureau based in Perm, and were D-20Ps rated at 5,400kg/11,905lb static thrust. Like the -104, the engines were mounted

systems, as well as its cross-section (fuselage diameter) were new. Markov's work began in late 1958 at factory 156; the completed aircraft was transferred to Zhukovski in January 1960, and the prototype, SSSR-45000, made its maiden flight, with Aleksander Kalina in command, on 24 March 1960. Factory and state tests went smoothly, and the aircraft was put into production at factory 135 in Kharkov in the Ukraine.

Deliveries to Aeroflot directorates began in August 1962; once again, the Vnukovo unit of the Moscow general directorate was the first to receive it, and initial training was undertaken at the airport's training centre. Aviaremont N407 at Minsk was the maintenance centre. Other Aeroflot units to receive the -124 included Estonian and Lithuanian, Privolzhskoe, Georgian, Northern, North Caucasian, Belorussian and TsUMVS.

The first short- to medium-range Soviet jetliner, the Tu-124; the fourth and fifth aircraft, SSSR-45004 and -45005, are shown here over the town of Zhukovski about 1961
Maksimillian B. Saukke Collection

Passenger services began on the Sheremetyevo to Tallinn (Estonia) route on 2 October 1962. Soon it was serving a range of western Soviet cities from Moscow – Ulyanovsk, Gorki (now Nizhni Novgorod) and Vilnius in Lithuania were begun in 1962. Later services were begun in Mineralnie Vody, Volgograd, Murmansk, Kuibyshev (now Samara) and Sverdlovsk (now Ekaterinburg), Kazan, Krasnodar, Sochi and Minsk. On international routes, Helsinki and Stockholm were first served on 2 November 1965. Services to Warsaw began from Moscow–Sheremetyevo

in April 1964 and to Belgrade in February 1965. The -124 was not widely used on international routes.

Development continued throughout the early 1960s. The first new version was the -124V with first delivery in 1964. Passenger capacity was increased to fifty-six, range to 1,500km/932 miles, and maximum take-off weight by 3.5 tonnes to thirty-eight tonnes. This version began to gain a small number of export orders. Once again, the Czechoslovakian airline, CSA, was first. Its first two aircraft were delivered in November 1964, with the third arriving in Prague

Tu-124, Factory no. 1601, shown in VVS marks coded '50' at the ZLiDB at Sheremetyevo
Maksimillian B. Saukke Collection

in July 1965. They began service on routes to European destinations in November 1964, and served on short to medium routes until late 1973, when the two surviving aircraft were sold to Iraqi Airways, who operated them on mainly domestic routes until the early 1980s. They may have been transferred after that to the Iraqi Air Force.

Two more were delivered to the Iraqi Air Force in 1965, when they served in a transport role, possibly as executive transports until the end of the 1980s. One was reported to have been destroyed by US forces in Baghdad early in the 1991 Gulf War. Two went to East Germany in 1965, where they served mainly as VIP transports in Interflug colours, although occasionally, when needed, they supplemented the airline's fleet on passenger services. This practice was not unusual in the Soviet Union and other socialist countries. Another was delivered to the Air Force, also in 1965. All three were -124Vs. After ten years' service they were returned to the Soviet Union, probably to military service.

Three aircraft were delivered to the Indian Air Force in Delhi in September 1969; they were Tu-124Ks, the executive version, laid out with a deluxe twenty-two-seat interior, with two cabins which included facing seats, working/dining tables and a couch. These aircraft had wardrobes, a galley and a pantry. One was lost in a landing accident in 1977; the other two served at least until the early 1980s. In addition an unspecified number were delivered to the Chinese Air Force starting in 1966, where their role is thought to have been as VIP transports. As Tupolev are not aware of the Chinese deliveries, it is presumed that they were delivered from Soviet Air Force numbers. Other -124s were completed as flight trainers, and given the designation 124Sh-1, with the 'Sh' representing 'Shturmanski' (Navigators), indicating their training function. Later, some 124Sh-2s were delivered, but the reason for the different designation is not known. It may relate to equipment.

Altogether, a total of 163 aircraft were built, including the prototype; 111 of these were passenger models, thus implying that fifty-one may have been trainers. Production continued until 1966, and then switched to the -124A, which was by then already renumbered the -134.

The -124 stayed in service with Aeroflot until the end of 1979. In the 1990s, small numbers are known to exist, mainly in aviation museums. After severe damage in 1966, SSSR-45017 was superficially repaired and brought to the Civil Aviation Museum at Ulyanovsk, where it is preserved. SSSR-45025 is part of the Monino collection, and SSSR-45092 is preserved at Kharkov factory N135 where it was built.

Tu-126

With the development of long-range missiles and intercontinental ballistic missiles came a need for countries at risk to defend themselves. In 1954, the United States Air Force took delivery of its first EC-121D, a version of the Lockheed Constellation designed to use powerful radar systems to pinpoint ICBMs at an early stage of their flight towards the USA, and to warn defending aircraft of their approach, track and position. The Soviet Union needed a comparable system, and the arrival of the Tu-114 gave it an aircraft large enough, and reliable enough, to serve as a basis for a Soviet AEW (Airborne Early Warning) carrier. Its pressurised cabin was also an advantage, allowing equipment and operators to work effectively.

Nikolai Bazenkov headed the programme. The main external difference between the Tu-114 and what would become the Tu-126 (NATO codename 'Moss') was to be the saucer which carried the aircraft's AEW radar. The two metre/6.6 feet thick saucer was mounted some four metres/13.2 feet above the fuselage and the saucer itself was 12m/39.4 feet in diameter. The large fuselage also accommodated the intelligence data gathering and analysis equipment needed to make effective use of the 'Liana' radar. The AEW aircraft was intended to work closely with fighter interceptors and to direct them against incoming enemy aircraft. However, it soon showed that while it was effective over water, the different radar frequencies used over land did not give as good an image.

The prototype Tu-126 was completed in Kuibyshev in 1961, and it made its first flight from there on 23 January 1962, piloted by Ivan Sukhomlin. Despite the difficulties of achieving results with early AEW, it was put into production at Kuibyshev factory N18. A further eight aircraft were produced there.

Amazingly, the Tu-126 only came to Western attention in 1968, following the release of a Soviet documentary film which showed the aircraft. The Tu-126 entered VVS service in 1965, and the production aircraft were first based on the Kolar Peninsula, near the Finnish border. Later they were relocated to the Baltic area.

The Tu-126 had a crew of fifteen, and at a cruise speed of 650kph/404mph, it could stay airborne without refuelling for over nineteen hours. It was equipped with a refuelling probe, so the patrol duration could be extended if necessary. Its MTOW of 170 tonnes included 60.8 tonnes of fuel. Service ceiling was 13,000m/42,653 feet. It remained in service with the VVS until the late 1980s when the numbers of Il-78 'Mainstays' available to the VVS allowed the less effective 'Moss' to be withdrawn.

Tu-126

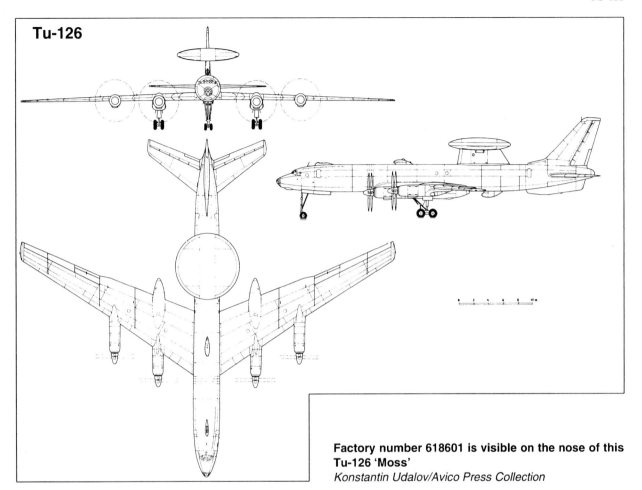

Factory number 618601 is visible on the nose of this Tu-126 'Moss'
Konstantin Udalov/Avico Press Collection

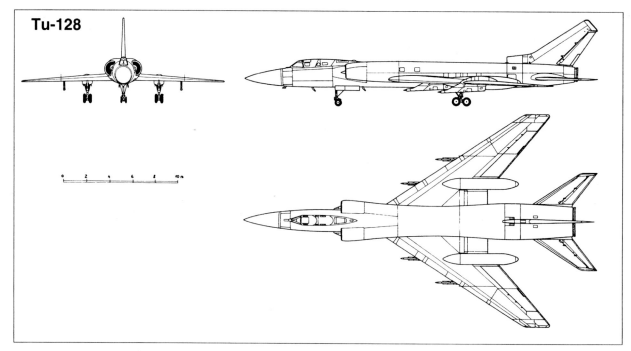

Tu-128

Tu-128

(NATO codename 'Fiddler')

In the late 1950s, controversy surrounded the question of strategic bombers – would they be manned, or would they be replaced by missiles? Most military and political leaders favoured missiles, but the B-52 continued in service, and the Soviet Union still regarded it as a major threat. The Soviet Union decided to develop a long-range interceptor, equipped with long-range radar to identify targets as far out as possible, and capable of carrying anti-aircraft missiles. It was not intended to be a fighter, in so far as it was not intended to engage in battles, and its weight would be substantially more than that of other fighters.

Because of its size and weight, the programme was given to Tupolev, who appointed Iosif Nezval as chief designer. Work began in 1958, and the project was given the number 128. Nezval took the Tu-98 design and adapted it for the new role; although intended as a bomber, the Tu-98 was similar in size to that required for the designated role of the new project. It had completed its state tests and gone on to serve as a research testbed (flying laboratory) gaining data on stability, durability and control at transonic and supersonic speeds, all of benefit to the new programme.

Nezval kept the -98's two AL-7F engines, this time choosing the -2 version with a static thrust of

10,000kg/22,046lb, and fitted with afterburners. He added radar-locating equipment designed by F. F. Volkov's OKB, the RP-S 'Smerch' (Waterspout), which could also serve as a long-range trajectory calculator when used with M. R. Bisnovat's K-8 long-range missile. The resulting weapons delivery system was given the VVS code Tu-28-80, although the aircraft itself was the Tu-28.

Construction of the first Tu-128 began at factory N156 in December 1959, although the -98 was regarded as the actual prototype. It was completed by summer 1960, but the RP-S and K-8 systems were not yet ready, so it was not until 18 March 1961 that Mikahil Kozlov took off from Zhukovski on the Tu-128's maiden flight; factory tests were combined with state tests, and they began immediately after the first flight.

One lesson learned from the Tu-98 was that its wheel track, at 2.5 metres/8.2 feet, was too narrow. On the new fighter, it was widened to 6.85 metres/22.5 feet to improve directional stability for take-off and landing.

The new fighter was unveiled to the public for the first time at the 1961 Aviation Day flypast at Tushino in August; many foreign observers were surprised by its size and its missile-carrying capacity, clearly visible under the fuselage.

As part of its test programme, the new interceptor was tasked in 1962 to locate and destroy an 'inbound enemy' – actually an Il-28 drone, radio-controlled and without crew. This it did with no operational difficulty. The Il-28 was destroyed at a range of some 30km/19 miles by an R-4RM air-to-air missile (NATO codename 'Ash' [AA-5]).

Unusually, the Soviet Ministry of Defence issued a decree as the test programme was being completed in July 1964 adopting the fighter's designation: not the VVS one, Tu-28, but the design bureau's Tu-128 with the suffix S-4 added. The aircraft was ordered into production in 1964, at factory N64 in Voronezh. It entered service with the VVS on 30 April 1965, with Tu-128S-4 being the first model to serve. It was an interceptor.

The design bureau and the VVS had both realised that it would be difficult to train pilots to fly the large and complex new fighter/interceptor, so the next version to enter service, in 1966, was a trainer, the Tu-128UT, adapted from production S-4s by replacing the radar-locating equipment, which was installed in the aircraft's nose section, with an instructor's cockpit. A small number of UTs were built from new, starting in 1966, but the instructor's restricted visibility limited the production run.

Iosif Nezval
Chief Designer of Tu-128 and Chief of serial production of Tu-4

The world's largest fighter was the Tu-128 'Fiddler' shown here with four R-4RM 'Ash' missiles mounted under its wing
Konstantin Udalov/Avico Press Collection

Navigators, who also served as weapons controllers, were trained on -128S-4s with only minor modifications needed. NATO gave the codename 'Fiddler' to the -128; the first two aircraft, seen at the 1961 Aviation Day flypast at Tushino with ventral fins mounted in the underbelly directly below the fin, both pre-production, were 'Fiddler As'; the -128S-4 was the 'Fiddler B'.

Production of the -128 came to an end in 1971, with just 198 aircraft built. By then, MiG had developed new MiG-25 variants in interceptor roles, and work had begun on the MiG-31. Despite this, Tupolev had developed a modernised model, the Tu-128S-4M, which made its first flight on 15 October 1970. This was equipped to intercept low-level incursions – the earlier aircraft were for high-level intercepts (tests were completed by 1974). As production had been discontinued by then, some VVS units arranged to have some aircraft converted at maintenance factories for the new role.

The -128 served with anti-aircraft/missile defence squadrons based near Arkhangelsk, Amderma, Omsk, Belaya and Semipalatinsk. Its service life was 2,300 flight hours/cycles and twenty years – low by Western standards, but good enough for a rapid response, high performance aircraft.

With a take-off weight of up to forty-three tonnes, it was the largest fighter/interceptor to enter service. Without missiles, its top speed was 1,920kph/1,193mph; with missiles mounted under the wings, it was 1,665kph/1,035mph. Service ceiling was 15,600m/51,184 feet, but on occasions, suitably lightened aircraft reached 20,000m/65,620 feet. The RP-S 'Smerch' radar could locate targets at up to 50km/31 miles, and the K-8 enabled missiles to be fired accurately at up to 35km/22 miles. Take-off run at MTOW without afterburners was 1,350m/4,430 feet and landing run was 1,050m/3,445 feet. The aircraft was stressed to withstand loads of 2.5G. Its normal armament was 2 × R-4RM plus 2 × R-4TM missiles (NATO codename 'Ash' [AA-5]); the RM had a 'semi-active head' with its own guidance system, while the shorter TM had a heat-seeking guidance system.

The -128 ended its VVS service in 1990, with most of the S-4M models being withdrawn in 1989.

A Tu-128 'Fiddler' taken from above by a helicopter-mounted camera
Konstantin Udalov/Avico Press Collection

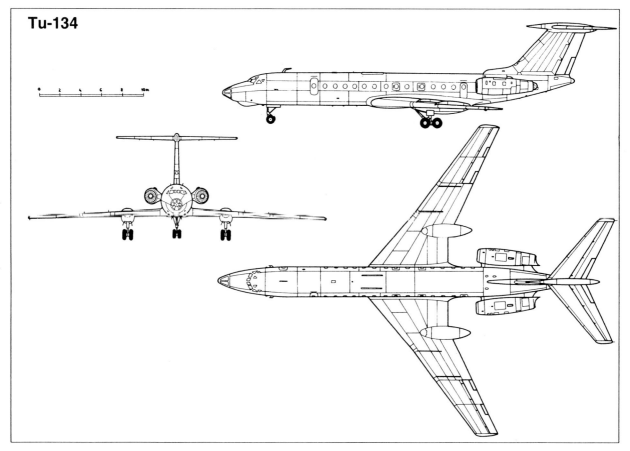

Tu-134

Tu-134

Early in 1960, Nikita Khrushchev, the Soviet leader, made a state visit to France, travelling there in a Tu-104. While there, he made several journeys in a Sud Caravelle, the French twin-engined medium-range jetliner which had entered service in 1959. While the Tu-104 had many excellent qualities, it was not a quiet aircraft, either for airports or for passengers, who sat almost alongside the engines mounted in the wing roots. The Caravelle, on the other hand, was the first jetliner to have tail-mounted engines, which reduced cabin noise considerably; Khrushchev was impressed.

On his return to Moscow, he summoned Tupolev and instructed him to design an airliner with a similar layout to the Caravelle. The Tu-124 had just made its first flight, and production at Kharkov was being set up. Dmitri Markov was again tasked for the project. He decided that the design should start from the Tu-124. Thus it was originally known as Tu-124A. He listed the advantages of the tail-mounted engines as being: better aerodynamics from a 'clean wing'; lower stress on the airframe from engine exhaust efflux; and

lower cabin noise levels. There were some difficulties: fuselage construction had to be stronger, and thus heavier; CG (centre of gravity) position was much further back, and to balance this, the wing position had to move back also; and the design and maintenance of the tailplane would be more complex.

By that time, Western designers were also working on tail-mounted engine layouts. It was almost a requirement for a jet airliner of the 1960s. Boeing's 727 entered service in 1963; the British Aircraft Corporation's VC-10 in 1964 and BAC 1-11 in 1965; and the Douglas DC-9, also in 1965. Later would come the Ilyushin Il-62, the Yakovlev Yak-40 and -42, and Tupolev's -154.

Markov started with the -124 fuselage. His original requirements were laid out as: forty passengers; four crew; five-tonne payload; 1,000kph/621mph maximum speed; 800 to 900kph/497 to 559mph cruising speed; and 1,500km/933 miles range with thirty minutes' fuel reserve. The design work was completed by early April 1961. Already some specifications had changed: to improve economical efficiency, passenger numbers had grown to forty-six in a mixed-class layout, and to fifty-six in an all-economy cabin.

Soloviev had developed a new version of the D-20P engine, the D-20P-125, with a thrust of 5,800kg/12,787lb. Markov selected these for the first trials. He had stretched the fuselage by 660mm/2.17 feet. The tailplane had been redesigned with the horizontal plane now at the top of the fin. The major new work was on the wings, which were a totally new design; the only similarity with that of the -124 was the sweep of 35°. The -134 had a span of 29m/95.1 feet compared to 25.55m/83.8 feet on the older aircraft. It featured a double-section aileron operated with geared tabs, and with a trim tab. Its flaps were operated through an electro-mechanical system, while the spoilers worked with a hydraulic system. The new wing had a different profile to that of the -124. There was a slight geometrical pivot designed into it to increase its strength. In the economics of the Soviet Union of the 1960s, it was of no importance that this increased fuel consumption by about 300kg/661lb per hour's cruise.

In December 1962, Markov began work on the Tu-145 project. The pressure of work made him resign from his airliner portfolios, so he was replaced by Leonid Seliakov, who, although in his late seventies by the mid-1990s, has stayed with the programme since then. Flight tests of some of the new aircraft's equipment began in 1963; the major equipment tested was the D-20P-125 engine, which was fitted on to three otherwise standard Tu-124s. Many Western sources state that the first -134s were converted -124s. Tupolev sources deny this, pointing out that moving the position of the wing roots would have been an impossible task.

Because of the similarities with the -124, and unusually for Tupolev, the parts of the first -124As were built

Leonid Seliakov
Chief Designer of Tu-134

at Kharkov and were brought to Moscow, assembled in N156, then wings and tail removed for transfer to Zhukovski. (The project was only redesignated to -134 in summer 1963.)

Aleksander Kalina was in command for the -124A/-134's first flight, which took place on 29 July 1963. State tests began soon afterwards and were carried out by the NII-VVS. It soon experienced the same problem encountered by Britain's BAC 1-11, the deep stall resulting from the new tailplane position. On 22 October 1963, while engaging in minimum speed tests and with flaps set in the take-off position, the first

The prototype Tu-134, SSSR-45075, at Kharkov in 1961
Tupolev

The first development Tu-134, SSSR-65600. The tail housing holds a parachute used in spin trials
Konstantin Udalov/Avico Press Collection

aircraft entered a deep stall and crashed. On the same day 2,000 miles away, the first BAC 1-11 also crashed for the same reason. Seliakov and his team studied the problem in detail, using the TsAGI wind tunnels. After a considerable amount of study, he increased the horizontal tailplane's area by thirty per cent. The problem was solved. The trials were completed on 6 November 1964.

Fortunately, Kharkov had built two prototypes (registered in the Tu-124 sequence), and the flight programme continued with the second aircraft. No more major problems came to light, and the results of the trials were incorporated into the next four aircraft, the first of which was completed in August 1964, and made its maiden flight on 9 September. In these aircraft, the fuselage was stretched a further 500mm/1.6 feet, increasing the number of passenger seats to sixty-four and extra fuel tanks were installed in the outer wing sections.

In 1965, Soloviev's new D-30 engine became available, with a power output of 6,800kg/14,991lb. This allowed the passenger load to increase to seventy-two, and was included into production models. The first D-30-powered aircraft, line number 00-04, SSSR-

After several incidents of engine failures when landing on wet runways, SSSR-65601, the second development Tu-134, was used in tests to find ways of avoiding water ingestion. It is shown here during these trials
Maksimillian B. Saukke Collection

Aeroflot Tu-134 SSSR-65656 at Sukhumi in an experimental colour scheme
Konstantin Udalov/Avico Press Collection

65602, made its first flight on 21 July 1966.

Meanwhile, another problem had been found in the flight test programme. On 14 January 1966, the second prototype -134, with D-20 engines, crashed with the loss of eight lives. Analysis of the Flight Data Recorder (FDR) showed that to speed up the test he was flying, the pilot had turned the rudder some twenty-five degrees without reducing speed. The aircraft turned sharply, entered a dive – it is not clear whether a spin resulted – and crashed. Seliakov put a limiter on the rudder control – at speed, the maximum rudder turn was now five degrees.

By then, Aeroflot was prepared for the introduction of the -134. Repair factory N400 was selected to provide maintenance. Later, as the numbers in service grew, factory N407 in Minsk was added. In the early 1990s, Minsk was the principal provider of -134 major overhaul and repair, and factory N412 in Rostov-on-Don was also added. Training was set up at Vnukovo – once again, this was to be the first Aeroflot unit to operate the aircraft. First, though, ground courses were established for aircrew and engineers. The first domestic passenger service was flown on 3 September 1967 between Vnukovo and Sochi. Before that, as was, and still is, usual with new aircraft, it had gained

some operational experience for crews, engineers and operators by flying cargo services for about a year.

Aircrew flying the new aircraft at first found its rate of climb to be very high; they, and the passengers, appreciated the lack of noise. And the new ventilation system gave a marked improvement in air quality, without the dryness that had been a feature of the old Tupolevs. Vnukovo pilots were also impressed with the aerodynamic qualities of the -134. Even thirty years later, it still feels exceptionally smooth in the air. And, once accustomed to the high tail, the aircraft could be quite forgiving. Vnukovo aircrew recall one occasion when the pilot of a -134, on take-off from Volgograd, noticed a cow standing on the runway. Normal unstick speed was 260kph/162mph. There was no possibility of stopping, so, at just 180kph/112mph, he pulled back the stick and the aircraft staggered into the air. They liked also the servo-operated rudder, the first time a Soviet airliner was so equipped, and the generator/APU introduced on the -134A, which made it independent of ground power. Engine reversers were liked too – although the first -134s were fitted with parachutes to slow them, the changes to the -134A added reverse thrust to the list of advantages.

Although the -134's glazed nose was due mainly to its Tu-16 and Tu-124 ancestry, it had the advantage of offering the navigator a clear view, subject to the weather, of conditions and the vista ahead. The -134

A Latavio Tu-134A, YL-LBA, at Sheremetyevo in 1994
Paul Duffy

Tu-134A SSSR-65098, at Kharkov after conversion to -134UBK
Maksimillian B. Saukke Collection

A line of eleven VVS Tu-134UBLs at Tambov Air Force Base, some 400km south-east of Moscow
Konstantin Udalov/Avico Press Collection

was equipped with some of the most up-to-date landing aids of the time – a 'semi-automatic' system which could guide the aircraft down to 30m/98 feet. As the technology improved, updated equipment was installed on production aircraft, and by the mid-1970s was compatible to and accepted as ICAO category II.

In the 1960s, systems of certification were being developed by the countries of eastern Europe, and on 9 November 1968 the Tu-134 received its first foreign certification. The Polish State Inspectorate certified that it met the standards of British Civil Airworthiness Requirements (BCAR) for aircraft, engines, systems and equipment. The -134 was sold to thirteen countries, with East Germany's Interflug receiving the first export aircraft in July 1968. All in all, Interflug took some thirty-nine aircraft, which it used to develop a wide network of routes from East Germany to Europe, the USSR, the Middle East and North Africa; Interflug also operated East Germany's government flights, and many of the -134s were dedicated to that service. When Interflug was closed down after Germany reunited, its remaining -134s were sold off, mainly back to Russia, with seventeen going to the Aeroflot division soon to become known as Komi Avia. Others went to Vietnam Airlines and Aeroflot–Russian International Airlines. Other countries and airlines to receive new -134s included:

Country	First Delivery	Operator	Quantity
Bulgaria	1968	Balkan	17
	1970	Air Force	2 (later to Balkan)
Poland	1968	LOT	11
		Air Force	6
Hungary	1968	Malev	10
	1975	Government	2 (later to Malev)
Yugoslavia	1969	Aviogenex	12
Iraq	1971	Iraqi Airlines	2
Czechoslovakia	1971	CSA	14
		Air Force	1
		Government	4
Angola	1978	Government/ Air Force	1
Vietnam	1980	Hang Khong	6
Mozambique	1980	Government	1
Syria	1982	Syrianair	6
North Korea	1982	CAAK	3
Cambodia	1984	Air Kampuchea	2

Meanwhile, delivery of the -134 to Aeroflot units was continuing. Thirteen aircraft were completed at

Tu-134A DDR-SDF of Interflug at Schönefeld in 1990
Paul Duffy

Aviogenex Tu-134A YU-AHX at Dublin in 1986
Paul Duffy

Kharkov in 1966; because of changes this slowed to six the following year. By the time the Tu-134A started to come off the production lines, in 1970, some seventy-eight of the standard model had been produced, with a maximum of twenty-eight rolled out in 1969.

The -134A added APUs and reverse thrust to the aircraft, along with a constant speed drive unit to allow alternating current electrical power. Other new features were an air conditioning system capable of being used while the aircraft was on the ground – this was very popular in hot summer conditions – and airstairs, installed for the first time on a Soviet airliner.

The -134A made its first flight on 22 April 1969, and entered service with Aeroflot seven months later. Kharkov speeded up production: twenty aircraft produced in 1970 grew to forty-nine in 1971; by 1974, fifty-nine were being produced annually.

By 1967, the Tu-134 was serving many of the medium-range inter-city routes in the Soviet Union, and with the newly named Central Department of International Air Services, the TsUMVS, also on routes to eastern Europe and near west Europe cities. First of these was Belgrade on 9 August, with Vienna

and Stockholm being added the next month. Warsaw, Helsinki and Zürich services began before the end of the year, and more followed in the next few years. The airlines of eastern Europe took more than 100 Tu-134s over the next fifteen years, and it was soon the standard medium-range jetliner of the region.

In 1980, the Tu-134B was introduced, allowing passenger numbers to rise to eighty. The first aircraft, -65720, is still in service, retained by Tupolev as a transport. Only twenty-eight were produced, serving with the Latvian and Azerbaijan Aeroflot divisions, while Syrianair, Hang Khong Vietnam and CAAK of North Korea each took this model.

By 1990, the Tu-134 and -154 were carrying seventy-five per cent of all Aeroflot passengers. In April 1991, Aeroflot carried its five hundred millionth -134 passenger. When the Soviet Union broke up at the end of 1991, Tu-134s were in service with Aeroflot units, soon to become new airlines, in the TsUMVS, Government Air Services, Central Regions, Mineralnie Vody, Arkhangelsk, St Petersburg, Astrakhan, Voronezh, Syktyvkar, Kaliningrad, Chelyabinsk, Perm, Nizhni Novgorod, Samara,

Orenburg, Rostov-on-Don, Volgograd, Grozni, Ivanovo, Tyumen, and in twelve of the other fourteen former Soviet Republics. By mid-1994, 608 -134s remained in service, including 410 in airline service. Another ten are the specialist agricultural version, the SKh (CX in Cyrillic letters), which was delivered to the Ministry of Agriculture and was equipped to make high-altitude passes over large areas of crops to survey their conditions, including water and fertiliser needs.

The SKh differed from the standard -134 by having two large removable nacelles mounted under the wings. These contained aerials for side surveillance radar. The lower fuselage contained three pressurised and one unpressurised glass compartments which could be sealed by sliding/folding doors. Nine work stations were located inside the aircraft, each with specialised equipment and a control panel. A processing laboratory was installed for the rapid analysis of data, which was capable of operating in six zones of the electromagnetic spectrum. It had a topographical camera, a multi-scanner filming system able to work in the six shifts simultaneously, four visual and infra-red opticals, and two for heat and infra-red. Eleven aircraft were delivered to the Agriculture Ministry, while Tupolev retained the development aircraft. In one hour, it could cover areas of up to 100km/62 miles square. Another 188 aircraft

Malev Tu-134A HA-LBP at Budapest–Ferihegy in 1989 in its first colour scheme
Paul Duffy

Malev Tu-134A HA-LBK at Budapest–Ferihegy in 1989 in its second colour scheme
Paul Duffy

A LOT Tu-134A, SP-LHD, at Warsaw–Okecie in 1990
Paul Duffy

served with the VVS as transports and also as crew trainers for long-range aviation (the long-nosed UBL version) and navigator trainers (the Sh version). These were the surviving aircraft from 199 converted -134s and -134As which were converted at Kharkov between 1971 and 1983. Most of the early -134s which served with Aeroflot and some foreign carriers, including some early ex-LOT, Aviogenex and CSA, were converted to Sh standards; the UBLs mainly came from conversions of new -134As.

In mid-1994, the high-time -134, RA-65683, had flown 35,659 hours, while the high-cycle aircraft RA-65840 had achieved 21,921 flights. Although the

original life was to be 30,000 hours and 20,000 cycles, strip down tests conducted by the GosNII GA and at the Minsk overhaul factory showed that these lives could be substantially extended. Technical staff at the factory are confident that the -134 can continue in service until between 2005 and 2010. By July 1994, 122 Tu-134s had exceeded their original hours of design life, including six which had exceeded 35,000 hours; and sixty-seven had exceeded 20,000 cycles, although, at the other end of the scale, one VIP aircraft had only flown 950 hours total time.

In military service, apart from training roles mentioned above, some -134s served as airborne command posts. Several -134s have served as flying laboratories; in Soviet/Russian terms, this can mean

Tu-134A, RA-65566, of Aeroflot–Russian International, started its service life with Interflug
Paul Duffy

anything from a vehicle to test new equipment to a fully equipped laboratory similar to that of the SKh version outlined above. The -134 has been used in a wide variety of aerial tests, including many radio, radar and electronics equipment flying testbeds. With the development of new business and industry in the countries of the former Soviet Union, some of the larger businesses have begun to buy airliners and convert them into business aircraft. In 1993, YL-LBB, an ex-Aeroflot Latvian -134A, was converted for a Latvian bank, and in 1994 RA-65099 was refurbished for the Stolichnii Bank of Savings.

The -134 has made a valuable contribution to the development of the Soviet Union's nations. Although by the mid-1990s, with airlines now having to pay for the fuel they use, its fuel burn of 2.3 tonnes per cruise hour at 10,000m/32,810 feet is high for a seventy-eight-seater, there is little replacement choice yet available. It will therefore have to stay in service for some time longer.

An impressive new executive interior for a Tu-134, as they become corporate jets in the new business world of the former Soviet Union. This is one for the Latvian Baltija Bank
Diamonite

Tu-134 Modifications

1. Prototype Tu-134: developed from Tu-124 design; first flight on 29 July 1963. Designation Tu-124A – Tu-134-1 (w/o in a crash on 22 October 1963).
2. Tu-134-2: second prototype, first flight 9 September 1964.
3. Tu-134 00-02: main aircraft of Kharkov aircraft factory. Maiden flight 14 August 1965.
4. Tu-134 00-04: first aircraft with D-30 engine. Maiden flight 21 July 1966. Entered into airline service on 9 September 1967.
5. Tu-134A (06-01): first Tu-134A. Maiden flight 4 April 1969. Entered service on 12 November 1970. D-30-2 engines.
6. Tu-134A with 'Groza' (Thunderstorm) radar. Modification for foreign airlines with a third cockpit crew member.
7. Tu-134A: eighty-six-passenger version for Aviogenex Jugoslavia.
8. Tu-134A: one only; 96 pax version, tail number SSSR-65966.
9. Tu-134 'Balkany' (Balkans): air command post for the Soviet Army.
10. Tu-134A-2: project only – planned to install D-30A engines (1977–1978).
11. Tu-134A-3: version with D-30-3 engines.
12. Tu-134B: version with 'Groza' (Thunderstorm) radar for Aeroflot; three crew members, 80 pax. Maiden flight in 1980.
13. Tu-134B-1: version with D-30-2 engines for 80 pax.
14. Tu-134B-1-3: version with D-30-3 engines for 80 pax.
15. Tu-134B-2: stretched project with D-30-2 engines; 100 pax.
16. Tu-134B-2-3: stretched project with D-30-3 engines; 100 pax.
17. Tu-134B-3: stretched project Tu-134B with D-30-3 engines.
18. Tu-134BV: version of Tu-134B for 'Buran' programme works. 1983 (space shuttle programme).
19. Tu-134V: update of Tu-134A with D-30A engines. Project only.
20. Tu-134G: update of Tu-134A, 1977. Project only.
21. Tu-134D: stretched Tu-134A for Yak-42 class with D-30A engines; 1975–1976. Cancelled at mock-up stage.
22. Tu-134I: advanced project on Tu-134SKh aerial laboratory.
23. Tu-134AK: VIP version made for United Air Detachment No. 235 – now Government Air Services, or Rossiya.
24. Tu-134L: project for aerial mapping at GDR's (East Germany's) request.
25. Tu-134LK: version for cosmonaut training. Two aircraft were built. First flight in 1980.
26. Tu-134M: project to modernise.
27. Tu-134OL: project for flying optomology laboratory for professor Viacheslav Federov.
28. Tu-134S: project with 'Groza' (Thunderstorm) radar convertible passenger/cargo, at the request of Aviogenex 1980/1981.
29. Tu-134SKh (CX): modification of Tu-134A for Agroprom (agricultural industry) system. First flight in April 1983.
30. Tu-134TS: project on the basis of Tu-134A; was developed, but did not find application.
31. Tu-134UB-K: one aircraft was built in 1982 (SSSR-65098).
32. Tu-134UB-L: modification of Tu-134B for training pilots of long-range aviation.
33. Tu-134Sh: modification for training Air Force navigators. Variants Sh-1 and Sh-2 Tu-134/As converted from 1971.
34. Tu-134Sh-SL: variant of Tu-134Sh for testing radar equipment. Modification of Tu-134Sh.
35. Tu-134LLShP (SSSR-65600): flying laboratory for testing an anti-diving parachute.

Tu-142

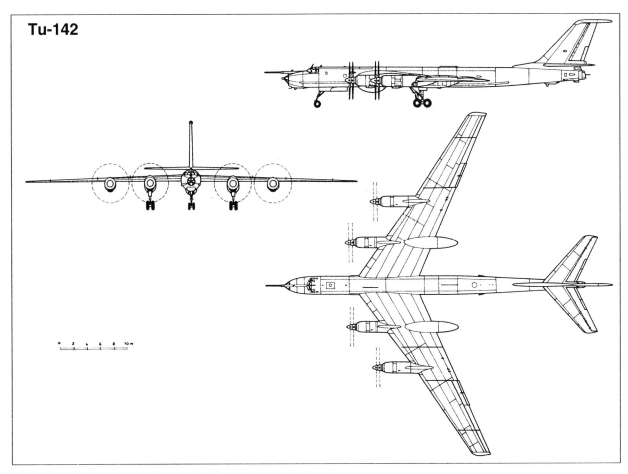

Tu-142

(NATO codename 'Bear F', 'H' and 'J')

In the mid-1960s, the Soviet Navy developed a require-ment for a long-range anti-submarine and maritime patrol aircraft to supplement the Il-38 medium-range aircraft. With the Tu-95 and Tu-114 in operation, Tupolev was asked to prepare proposals.

Nikolai Bazenkov was appointed chief designer for the project, which was given the number 142. He took the basic Tu-95 design but omitted all the strategic equipment. The wing was redesigned with increased span, up from 50.05 metres/164.2 feet to 51.10m/167.66 feet, which allowed more fuel to be carried, and with increased camber. Much of the defensive weaponry was also removed. Then he added the electronic equip-ment needed for its new role.

The prototype Tu-142 was built at the Oput factory (as N156 was by that time called) and it made its first flight from Zhukovski in July 1968, flown by Mikhail Nukhtikov. After flight tests by the designers and the

NII VVS, the aircraft was put into production at Kuibyshev and later at Taganrog factory N31. It entered service with Naval Long Distance Aviation in 1972; it was then, and still is, the world's largest anti-submarine aircraft. It served alongside the smaller Il-38, which was effectively the Soviet equivalent of the US Navy's P-3 Orion; but its long-range capability made it able to launch an attack on a submarine 5,000km/3,107 miles from the aircraft's base. With improvements in electronics, work began in 1973 on an improved version, the Tu-142M, and its first flight was made on 4 November 1975, flown by Ivan Vedernikov.

Nikolai Basenkov died in 1973; he was replaced by Nikolai Kirsanov, who stayed with the programme until the production line was closed in 1988. After that, Dmitri Antonov took charge of the continuous devel-opment and analysis of data for the -142.

The -142M was fitted with electronic equipment capable of early detection of low-noise submarines, a new and more accurate INS navigation system and

A Tu-142 'Bear F' at Zhukovski
Paul Duffy

automated radio communications. Its surveillance system worked on a 360º arc, and was more capable than that of the Il-38 at detecting magnetic abnormalities. Data was transferred immediately by satellite link back to base. With a capability to patrol for seventeen hours, the aircraft was provided with bunks for crew rest. Its internal fuel load was seventy tonnes, and it was equipped for in-flight refuelling which could extend the patrol duration beyond the seventeen hours when needed.

The VMS based its -142s, which were given the NATO codename 'Bear F', in the Northern and Pacific regions; some were also based in Cuba and Vietnam until 1990, when political developments prompted their return to Russia.

Nikolai Kirsanov
Deputy chief designer on special equipment (oxygen, ejection seats). Chief designer of Tu-95 and Tu-142 after Nikolai Bazenkov's death

Production continued at Taganrog until 1988, with one aircraft per month being completed. Total production run at both factories was 225 aircraft, including eight delivered to the Indian Navy starting in the mid-1980s and continuing until 1988. These figures have not been confirmed. With the political developments in the last few years, there have been some reports that a number of -142s have been converted to carry cargoes of twenty tonnes, but this has not been confirmed.

The standard armament of the -142 was two GSh-23 cannons mounted in the tail for defensive use. It could carry up to eight Kh-35/anti-shipping cruise missiles (NATO code AS-17) mounted on pylons under the wing, and internally, 450mm calibre anti-submarine torpedoes and/or 533mm calibre anti-shipping torpedoes. Depth charges could also be dropped. With a combat load of 11,340kg/25,000lb, its maximum range was 12,550km/7,779 miles. Normal take-off weight was 170 tonnes, but 188 was possible with little difficulty; its take-off speed was 300kph/186mph and landing speed was 270kph/168mph.

It was produced in four versions, with service entry dates:

Tu-142	'Bear F'	Long-range anti-submarine	(1972)
Tu-142M		Improved electronics	(1975)
Tu-142M2	'Bear H'	Improved radio and electronics	(1976)
Tu-142M3	'Bear J'	Improved radio and electronics	(1980)

The -142M2 was the first to carry cruise missiles, while the -142M3 carried VLF communications systems for instant data transmission to base and to friendly submarines.

Tu-144

World's First SST To Fly

The years following the end of the Second World War saw huge developments in civil aviation with aircraft becoming larger and faster, and also flying higher. The Soviet Union had kept pace with, and had sometimes been ahead of, many of these developments, and many research institutes, including TsAGI, had continued to work on the problems which needed to be solved before airliners could go any faster. Already high Mach numbers were being achieved; any higher, and the aircraft would be subject to the aerodynamic buffeting of transonic speeds. The alternative was to go through the sound barrier, to go supersonic.

In the early 1960s, research on the metals, alloys and plastics needed to build an aircraft capable of enduring the high temperatures resulting from sustained supersonic flight began to give results. Meanwhile, in

November 1962, France and Britain had signed an agreement for the development and production of an SST (supersonic transport), the Concorde.

Early in 1963, Tupolev set about the task of designing an SST. He appointed his son Aleksei as chief designer. Up till now, Aleksei had been working on the design of missiles and unmanned aircraft, aiming for the future as seen by military strategists of the 1950s. He received several awards for this work, and the experience gained on these high-speed projects added to his qualifications for the SST, which, as usual, had his father in overall command.

In the early 1960s, supersonic travel was seen as a means of saving valuable time and of easing the tiredness of jet lag that resulted from long flights. The arguments against SSTs were mostly economical, although that did not stop the Anglo-French project or Tupolev's one, and ecological, although at the time not very much was known about this aspect, except that the noise of sonic booms could be a problem for people living under the flight path.

An appropriately registered Tu-144, SSSR-77144, on climb-out; note the small aerofoils behind the cockpit which were used to improve performance at slow speeds and high angle of attack; these were retractable.
Konstantin Udalov/Avico Press Collection

Tupolev set to work and gathered his team. Despite the huge experience gained by the design bureau on the development of high-speed military aircraft, many problems remained to be solved. The aircraft's shape was one of the first. TsAGI, now situated at the Zhukovski test base, had some of the world's finest wind tunnels, and Tupolev's designs were formed into models and tested for aerodynamic quality here. This needed to be at least fifty per cent better than that of military aircraft of the period to assure passengers of a comfortable ride. For the same reason, it was necessary to study the effects of going through the sound barrier on the aircraft's stability and CG.

New heat-resistant materials needed to be in some cases developed, in others selected to meet the needs for cyclical heating – the aircraft's expansion when pressurised and heated by air friction followed by its contraction at low levels and speeds and on the ground. A 60m/197-foot fuselage would expand by 300mm/one foot in flight. Not much, perhaps, but its effects on a sealed, pressurised cabin had to be minimal. New lubricants were needed as were new sealants and even construction methods. New cabin environment systems had to be designed to allow passengers to experience normal living conditions at 20,000m/65,620 feet.

To carry out the work involved, which was regarded by the Soviet government as a matter of national prestige, over 1,000 staff were temporarily assigned to Tupolev from other aviation industry bodies. An early decision was taken to test the aerodynamic qualities of the wing design. This was done by modifying a MiG-21, by fitting a new -144-shaped wing to it. This was done by MiG at its design bureau workshop on Leningradskoe Shosse.

For the prototype, which was being constructed at the Opyt factory, many of the parts had to be chemically etched on to the material from which they were to be made, and then manually finished. The fuel tanks had to be sealed manually from the inside.

The visual similarity of Tupolev's aircraft and the Anglo-French Concorde has often led to charges of copying. These began in June 1965, when a model of the Tu-144 was shown at the Paris Air Salon. Although when compared in detail the differences are major, the aircraft certainly look alike. Tupolev's designers advise that the general shape of the aircraft was determined mostly by the laws of aerodynamics, combined with the needs (or market) for the aircraft and by materials available. They also point to the similarities of the DC-9 and the BAC1-11; the DC-8 and the Boeing 707; and the DC-10 and Lockheed TriStar. Computer-aided design was in the early stages of development in those days; today, the

air-raft might well be even more alike.

The prototype Tu-144 was completed in the summer of 1968. The Soviet government was anxious to see it fly before the Concorde, and at the 1965 Paris Air Salon, it had been announced that it would fly in 1968. As usual with Tupolev aircraft, it was disassembled for transfer to the test base at Zhukovski. Tupolev's works were (and still are) close to the centre of Moscow, with no available airfield nearby. Ilyushin, on the other hand, is based at Moscow's original city centre airport, Khodinka, and thus they don't need to take their aircraft apart before the first flight. It was reassembled at Zhukovski by October, and ground tests and engine runs were completed as a matter of priority. On 31 December 1968, hours before the deadline, Eduard Yelian pulled back the control column and SSSR-68001 lifted off Zhukovski's 5km/3.1-mile-long main runway with a MiG-21 escort, on the world's first SST flight. He had waited for sixteen days for reasonable weather conditions to make the flight.

Four aircraft were manufactured just for tests; two went to TsAGI for static tests. One went to Sib NII in Novosibirsk for heat tests, and the fourth was fatigue-tested at Zhukovski. The new airliner was powered by four newly developed NK-144 engines designed by the Kuznetsov engine design bureau which were fitted with afterburners used mainly on take-off. The airframe and wings were made from duraluminium, although the leading edge of the wings, where supersonic flight generated high temperatures, was manufactured of stainless steel and titanium.

The prototype Tu-144 was shown at the 1971 Paris Air Salon, already showing a number of design changes resulting from the experience gained during the flight test programme. It was an opportunity to compare the two SSTs, for further down the flight line was the French prototype Concorde. The -144 was larger and the wing roots began with a marked increase in sweep to help improve slow flying characteristics. On both aircraft, the engines were mounted in the underwing pods, but with very different arrangements. Later -144s would feature a small pair of wings just behind the cockpit, which pivoted outwards from the fuselage to assist low-speed performance, and was retracted at higher speeds.

With Aeroflot, enthusiastic at first, expressing the possibility of ordering large numbers of the Tu-144s, production was set up at Voronezh factory N64. Meanwhile, the flight test programme was proceeding.

On 5 June 1969, the Tu-144 went through the sound barrier for the first time, flying at an altitude of 11,000m/36,091 feet. A year later, on 26 May 1970, it exceeded Mach 2, flying at 2,150kph/1,336mph at an altitude of 16,300m/53,480 feet. It had been unveiled

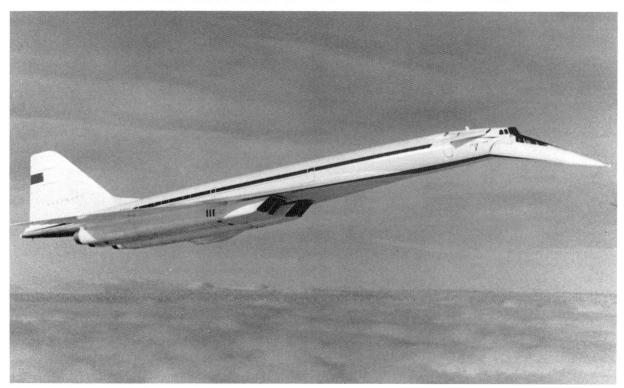

The second Tu-144, SSSR-77102, in flight
Konstantin Udalov/Avico Press Collection

to the public for the first time a few days earlier, on 21 May, when it was demonstrated at Sheremetyevo airport, and inspected by officials from the Ministry of Civil Aviation.

It was soon apparent that fuel consumption was much higher than calculated; while in Soviet economic terms this may not have been of great importance, it had a marked effect on the aircraft's range. Instead of the promised 6,500km/4,039 miles, it could only fly about 3,500km/2,175 miles, and could not reach many of the eastern and south-eastern cities of the Soviet Union without stopping for fuel and thus losing the time it was intended to save. To make matters worse, the second production aircraft crashed while giving a display at the 1973 Paris Air Show with 300,000 onlookers and the world's media present. No accident report was issued; this was not done in Soviet times, but there seems to have been no blame attributable to the aircraft. A major cause seems to have been the need to avoid an unidentified French Mirage filming the airshow. Nonetheless, the Soviet Union's determination to be first was widely interpreted as hurrying along the test programme, and drew much unfavourable comment.

By that time, five production aircraft had been completed, and five more were in the course of production. In 1973, Aleksei Tupolev, now appointed general designer of the OKB following his father's death, handed over the SST programme to Valentin Blizniuk, who would remain in charge until the programme ended in 1990.

The shortened range of the -144 had led the Soviet government to order the Kolesov Engine Design Bureau to develop a new, more efficient engine capable of delivering the same 20,000kg/44,092lb of thrust with afterburners on. The fifth production aircraft, SSSR-77105, was modified to take the new engine, designated the RD-36-51A, and flew as the Tu-144D with these engines for the first time in November 1974.

Valentin Blizniuk
Chief Designer of Tu-144 (after A. N. Tupolev's death), Tu-160, Tu-330

Captain Boris Kuznetsov of Aeroflot's Domodedovo division, who served as co-pilot for the flight, reporting to Marshal Boris Bugaev, the Minister of Civil Aviation immediately before the departure of the first Tu-144 service to Alma Ata on 1 November 1977.
Domodedovo CAPA

After the accident at Paris, Aeroflot's enthusiasm for the -144 diminished, although training of crews began in late 1974; with Tupolev test pilots as instructors, no Aeroflot pilot would ever command a Tu-144. Training flights were flown with the early Tu-144s over the Domodedovo (Moscow's new domestic airport)–Baku–Tashkent route. Later, from December 1975, cargo and mail were carried on regular services between Moscow and the Kazakhstan capital, Alma Ata. In February 1977, but with restricted payloads, cargo services began linking Moscow and Khabarovsk. On both these services, supersonic speeds were achieved over the sparsely populated regions below. Always, the pilot in command was from Tupolev.

At last, on 1 November 1977, the Tu-144 received its NLGS certificate of airworthiness, and on the same day passenger services began. But not Aeroflot services. Instead, the Ministry of Aviation Production operated the flights, providing pilots, engineers and technical support, although Aeroflot sold the tickets and retained the money. Aeroflot pilots served as co-pilots, but command was always with a Tupolev test pilot. The services were only on the Domodedovo–Alma Ata route. A total of fifty return flights were made; the ticket cost was eighty-two roubles (approximately $91) each way for an economy-class seat. The -144 held 122 economy- and eleven first-class passengers. Some 3,194 passengers were carried. Only two aircraft, SSSR-77108 and -77109, served. The service ended on 31 May 1978, a few days after the first production Tu-144D, flying on test from Zhukovski, experienced an in-flight fire, and was destroyed while making an emergency landing at Yegorievsk. The aircraft, SSSR-77111, had only recently been completed. The cause of the fire has never been revealed.

But the reason that the Tu-144 did not succeed had little to do with the aircraft or its teething problems. It was that political support for the SST had started to fade after the Paris accident. Aeroflot used the second accident as an excuse to stop services on an aircraft it had never actually operated. After the loss of SSSR-77111, four of the five aircraft still on the production line were completed. They were based at Zhukovski and flew occasionally as aerial laboratories with two continuing in service on ozone layer research until late 1990.

Altogether, the sixteen flying Tu-144s built made 2,556 flights, and totalled 4,110 flying hours. The high-time aircraft SSSR-77144 (sequentially, this should have been -77104) flew just 432 hours.

In the mid-1990s, ten Tu-144s remain, and four of

Tu-144 cockpit
Konstantin Udalov/Avico Press Collection

these are in museums: SSSR-77106 was flown to Monino on 29 February 1980 by Giorgi Voronchenko; SSSR-77107 was flown to Kazan on 29 March 1985 by Vladimir Matveev; SSSR-77108 was flown to Kuibyshev on 27 August 1987 by Boris Vasiliev; and SSSR-77110 was flown to Ulyanovsk on 1 June 1984 by Sergei Agapov. SSSR-77109 remains at Voronezh, at the factory where it was produced, and SSSR-77105 remains on the dump at Zhukovski. The four Tu-114Ds (excluding the fifth that crashed) SSSR-77112 to -77115 remain at Zhukovski.

In November 1993, an agreement was signed by Tupolev to make airworthy a Tu-144 (SSSR-77114 was chosen) to be used as a research vehicle for a future US supersonic transport. The other partners in the venture were Boeing, McDonnell Douglas, Rockwell Collins and NASA, with interests from England, France, Germany and Japan also involved. By then, the original engines, the RD-36-51As, were no longer available, so Aleksander Pukhov, the chief designer of the restoration project, chose to fit the NK-321 engine of the Tu-160 instead.

As the Tu-144 had not flown for some years, it was necessary to check and overhaul thoroughly all the aircraft's systems – hydraulics, electrical and mechanical. For the research programme, it was also necessary to fit a complex sensor system needed to gain the aerodynamic and engineering data required. A Damien computer was installed in the aircraft to record flight parameters. At the time of writing, the rebuilt Tu-144 is expected to make its second first flight in 1996. The agreement called for a thirty-five-flight programme to be undertaken from Zhukovski in order to gain an FAA experimental certificate of airworthiness, and then for the aircraft to be flown to the United States. A second aircraft is involved in the programme as a spares source to keep the primary aircraft airworthy.

Aeroflot pilots and engineers still regret the passing of the Tu-144; they regard it as a 'lost generation'. Tupolev pilots and engineers worked with Aeroflot staff at all times as the operational flying was regarded as developmental. Usually each aircraft would fly only once or twice per week. They recalled that you could not touch the aircraft for at least twenty minutes after a flight because of the high skin temperature (up to 120°C/230°F) of the metal.

On 16 March 1996, the fourth Tu-144D was rolled out at Zhukovski to begin a series of research flights for a second generation SST in a programme funded by an international group which included NASA, Boeing, McDonnell Douglas and PBN. Now called the Tu-144LL (for flying laboratory) it is shown there the next day
Paul Duffy

Project 145

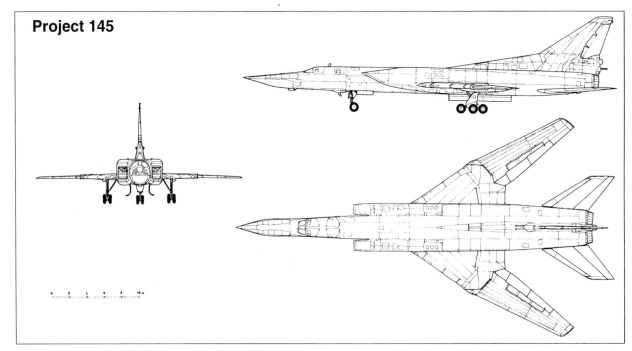

Project 145

The Tu-22 Again; NATO codename 'Backfire'

Late in 1962 work began on a major update programme for the Tu-22; some sources describe it as a totally new aircraft, and that the Tu-22M designation was kept in order to keep the development costs of a new strategic bomber hidden from outside observers.

The chief designer of the original Tu-22, Dmitri Markov, was at that time working on the Tu-134, but Tupolev decided that he was needed more on the Tu-22M programme, so Leonid Seliakov took over the airliner work, on transfer from the Myasishchev design bureau. The project number 145 was applied to the new work. At first, Tupolev decided that the Tu-22/Tu-105 layout would be retained but that variable geometry (VG) wings and new engines would be substituted. This concept was modelled and tested in the TsAGI wind tunnels at Zhukovski. Eventually, however, in 1967, the design was substantially modified: a new fuselage was conceived to allow higher speeds, the engine layout was changed, and an effect of this was an ability to carry a high bomb load.

The Tu-22M was equipped with an automatic control system, allowing the controls also to be manually operated. A hydraulic/mechanical system allowed the wings to change their sweep in flight, with a back-up electromechanical system. Sweep could vary from

a low-speed 20° angle to a maximum of 65°, with infinite choice between. The main undercarriage featured a six-wheel, three-axle layout on each bogey with a single-axle, two-wheel nose leg. The main legs retracted inwards to the lower fuselage. The aircraft's controls featured an all-moving horizontal tailplane for the first time on a Tupolev design. Leading edge slats ran the entire length of the wing and slotted trailing edge flaps were in three sections. Even with these, landing speed was 285kph/177mph and take-off speed 370kph/230mph. Take-off run at MTOW was 2,100m/6,890 feet and landing run '1,200 to 1,300 m'/3,938 to 4,265 feet.

Unusually for Tupolev, the prototype Tu-22M was built at Kazan factory N22. It was completed in July 1968, and after engine and ground tests the first flight took place on 30 August, with V. Borovoi in command. Nine M0s, as the prototype was designated, were built and all took part in the factory and state tests programme. Meanwhile, Markov was working on an M1 version, which he was fitting out for naval service. The noticeable differences between the M0 and the M1 were: the M0 had a smaller wing span and wing area; the M0 had a wider undercarriage track; the M0 had no tail-mounted cannon, whereas the M1 had a remotely operated GSh23M, with radio control and a closed-circuit television monitor operating system. The M1 made its first flight on 28 July 1971; nine M1s were built, and they served as development aircraft for naval aviation requirements. Seven were assigned to naval air regiments for service in a maritime patrol and reconnaissance role.

The West became aware of the Tu-22M and its variable geometry wings following intelligence reports in 1969; in 1970, it was photographed on the ground at Kazan by an overflying reconnaissance satellite. NATO then assigned it the codename 'Backfire'.

The Tu-22M was accepted into VVS service in 1976; production was now under way in Kazan, although the production aircraft had substantial modifications arising from the test programme and developing military requirements. The major changes resulted from improvements in equipment for flight, navigation and weapons systems. The production variant was designated Tu-22M2, and received the NATO codename 'Backfire B' to distinguish it from the earlier 'Backfire A'. External differences were a double horizontally mounted GSh-23 cannon in the tail and a Kh-22 rocket-propelled missile semi-slung into the bomb compartment. The -22M2 went into widespread VVS service starting from 1978. It was based in European Russia, the Northern units and in Siberia. With the VMF, it served from Murmansk, the Black Sea region and on the Pacific coast.

Another upgrade resulted in the Tu-22M3; a principal difference in the M3 resulted from the fitting of more powerful engines. The M2 and earlier versions had Kuznetsov NK-22 engines which gave a take-off power of 22,000kg/48,501lb with afterburners on; the new NK-25s on the M3 increased power to 25,000kg/55,111lb, again with afterburners. These resulted in newly designed air intakes, similar to those on the MiG-25, which sloped back from the shoulder to the lower fuselage; without reheat, the normal maximum thrust of the NK-25 was 14,500kg/31,967lb. Equipment changes included new onboard electronics, optical electronic bombsights, INS navigational, active and passive radio-jamming equipment, new ultra-short waveband radios and cyphercomms systems.

The M3 now had a single GSh-23M cannon in the tail, with a higher rate of fire – up to 4,000 rounds per minute, twice that of the early version on the M2. To carry the extra weights involved, the M3 had a strengthened wing construction, and Markov took this opportunity to improve aerodynamic qualities by minor design changes and by adding an automated flight control system. The M3's first flight took place on 20 June 1977. After exhaustive state tests, first

A Tu-22M1 in flight, with missile racks visible under the wings
Konstantin Udalov/Avico Press Collection

A Tu-22M3 in flight; a single missile, possibly an AS-15 'Kickback', is mounted underneath
Konstantin Udalov/Avico Press Collection

operational deliveries to the VVS and VMF began in 1981. Unusually, for several years both the M2 and M3 were in production together; in 1984, the last M2 of 211 built was delivered, although the M3 remained on the production line for another nine years. Some 286 M3s were produced before the political and economic changes in the Soviet Union and Russia brought an end to the line.

The normal combat range of the Tu-22M was 2,200km/1,367 miles. To augment this, the M2s and M3s were fitted with flight refuelling probes until the SALT treaties called for their removal. With the capability of refuelling in the air, the Tu-22M was a formidable strategic weapon; without it, its range did not bring it into a strategic category. The Tu-22M saw operational service at the time of the Afghan conflict

This TsAGI/LII Tu-22M3 was the first to be shown outside the former USSR when it appeared at the 1992 Farnborough Air Show
Paul Duffy

in December 1987 and January 1988; Tu-22Ms based at Hosta were used to bomb enemy/guerrilla positions with FAB500 bombs (500 = weight in kg, so 1,102lb). Later, in October 1988, as the Soviet Union was withdrawing from Afghanistan, it provided a protective screen for the manoeuvre with operational drops of FAB1500s (3,307lb) and FAB3000s (6,614lb).

A long-range reconnaissance version, the Tu-22MR, was introduced into naval service in 1985, but a proposed modernised M4 is unlikely to go ahead due to the defence budget costs of the 1990s.

All Tu-22Ms (which are sometimes referred to in the West, wrongly, as the Tu-26) carried a crew of four – pilot and co-pilot seated in the cockpit, and a navigator plus a weapons controller seated behind the cockpit. All four crew members were provided with zero/zero ejection seats (capable of use from ground level up); these could be fired either individually or collectively. The Tu-22M carried a formidable range of armaments – up to twenty-four tonnes of bombs and/or missiles constituted a load. As mentioned earlier, three Kh-22 (Kitchen AS-14) missiles could be carried, with one either semi-slung under the fuselage or in a drum installation in the bomb compartment, or ten Kh-15 (Kickback AS-16) missiles, six in the bomb bay drum and four underwing; sixty-nine FAB250 or eight FAB1500 bombs could also be fitted into the bomb bay, or a suitable combination of these. The Kh-22 missiles were for air-to-surface strikes, the Kh-15 were for close action attack. In the mid-1990s, the Tu-22M remains the backbone of Russia's medium-range bomber force, and seems likely to remain so for the foreseeable future.

The Tu-22M made its first public appearance outside the former Soviet Union at the 1992 Farnborough display, when a research Tu-22M3 operated by Tupolev made an appearance. At Farnborough, the Committee of Defence Industries announced that the Tu-22M3 was available for sale abroad; at the time of writing no orders have been announced.

Tu-154

In the early 1960s, Aeroflot was better equipped than it had ever been before. The Tu-114 was just beginning to serve long-range routes; the Tu-104 along with the Ilyushin Il-18 and the Antonov An-10 were serving medium-range flights, and the Tu-124 was being joined by large numbers of the new Antonov An-24s on short-range services.

By that time, the lead enjoyed by Aeroflot over Western carriers was beginning to be eroded as new jets and turboprops joined the Western fleets, and traffic in the Soviet Union continued its rapid growth fuelled by low fares and difficult surface travel conditions. The Ministry of Civil Aviation (MCA), the government department which was essentially the head office of Aeroflot, began to look for a replacement for its medium-range aircraft. It was felt that there should be no need for three different types to meet requirements that were close enough to be combined. The MCA defined its new requirements as: passenger capacity 150 to 160; range – 3,200 to 3,500km/1,988 to 2,175 miles; maximum runway required – 2,500m/8,202 feet. These combined most of the best features of the current types; it was also stated that the new aircraft should match the comfort of the Tu-104. Operating three very different aircraft in a similar category also had operational and financial penalties. This was just at the end of the golden years of the Soviet aviation industry; the resources available for new aircraft, particularly for civil aviation, would sharply reduce in the near future. It was the first time that economics had been a major factor in developing a new project since the 1930s. The MCA called for proposals from the MAP (Ministry of Aviation Production), and the MAP requested several design

Aleksander Shengardt
Chief designer of Tu-154 since 1975

Tu-154

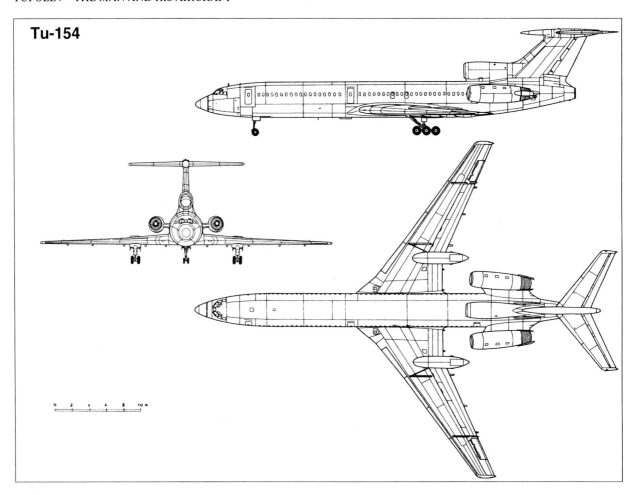

bureaux to submit projects. These included Tupolev, Ilyushin and Antonov. After examining the submissions, the MCA chose Tupolev's design proposals.

At that time the Soviet Union's priorities were changing to production of adequate food supplies and building new homes. The development of a totally new airliner, and not one evolved from military projects, was a major cost to the state; surprisingly, the funds were provided. Tupolev chose Sergei Yeger to lead the project. The first questions to be resolved were those of aerodynamics. A cruising speed of 950kph/590mph was needed with good stability and control response at all speeds and altitudes up to 12,000m/39,372 feet, so a suitable wing profile had to be selected and manufactured. Tupolev and Yeger decided to select a large wing area and to provide more engine power than was usual at that time – three Kuznetsov NK-8-2s each with a power of 9,500kg/20,943lb. Surprisingly, this helped to keep fuel consumption and engine wear down. As usual with Tupolev designs, the undercarriage retracted backwards into pods installed on the

back of the wing, but this was one of very few commonalities with other Tupolev aircraft.

Yeger had begun to work on the Tu-154 (as the project was designated) early in 1965. His work required many features new to Soviet aircraft including:

- Multiple systems redundancy. Each of the main systems on the aircraft – electrical, hydraulic, controls etc. – had three independent operational circuits, so that, in the event of any major failure, there would be two back-ups. Another system could fail without causing major control loss.
- Control boosters on all surfaces – ailerons, flaps, rudder and elevators – which reduced the force needed to be applied by the crew by between one and a half to five times. This also had multiple redundancy. Even if all three engines failed, the airflow passing through the autorotating engines would still provide enough power to operate the boosters.
- High-efficiency wing mechanisation, including slats,

Tu-154M, SSSR-85649, of Aeroflot's TsUMVS shown in flight in 1991
Paul Duffy

triple-slotted flaps, spoilers, all of which lowered the take-off and landing speeds, and augmented control on climb and descent.
• A six-wheel, three-axle mainwheel undercarriage bogey which reduced the stress force on runways to some sixty per cent of that of a Boeing 727-200A by spreading the load over a wider area.

The prototype Tu-154, SSSR-85000, was completed at the Opyt factory workshop beside Tupolev's design offices, in summer 1968; it was then disassembled and brought by road to Zhukovski, from where, after reassembly and ground tests, it made its first flight on 3 October 1968, piloted by Yuri Sukhov.

By then Yeger and his team were finalising the production drawings for hand-over to the factory where the -154 was to be built. Originally, production was to have been at Moscow factory N30 (MAPO), but the short runway available at the factory and the pressure of other programmes resulted in factory N18 at Kuibyshev being chosen, where Mitrofan Yevshin, the general director, was just completing production

A line of Aeroflot Tu-154s at Vnukovo in 1992
Paul Duffy

of the last Tu-114s. The -154 would keep factory N18 busy for the next quarter of a century.

As the flight test programme progressed, Aeroflot set about preparing for service entry. Again, the training centre at Vnukovo was used for ground courses for aircrew, technical and operations training; as -154s began to be delivered to the airline, some were assigned to the flight training unit at Ulyanovsk to provide aircrew for the new fleet.

The first aircraft delivered to Aeroflot (SSSR-85005 to -85009) were pre-production examples. They arrived at Vnukovo in October/November 1970 and were used at first to develop engineering and operating procedures for the -154 and for initial crew training. In May 1971, they began to operate cargo and mail flights; NLGS certification procedures up to the end of the Soviet Union required one year's operational experience on a new type before passenger services began. Routes served building up this experience were Vnukovo to Khabarovsk, with intermediate stops at Sverdlovsk, Novosibirsk, and Irkutsk; and Vnukovo to Sochi, Mineralnie Vody and Simferopol. As a matter of interest, -85007 continued in service with

Vnukovo until the end of 1993, when it was retired.

Passenger services began on the route Vnukovo–Mineralnie Vody on 9 February 1972; international services began from Moscow–Sheremetyevo to Prague in November that year, operated by the TsUMVS – the Central Department of International Air Services recently separated from the Moscow Transport Directorate of Aeroflot. Within a year, the TsUMVS was operating the -154 on twelve international routes, linking Moscow with major European cities.

But everything was not going so smoothly. In Novosibirsk, the Sib NII (Siberian Scientific Research Institute) had been conducting fatigue tests on a Tu-154 airframe and wing. The airframe gave little difficulty, but the wing was another matter. It turned out that the wing had no prospects of meeting the 30,000 flight hours or 20,000 flight cycles for which it was designed, or even to be developed to meet these needs. A new wing was needed. The reasons for this industrial catastrophe for Tupolev were:

• A design bureau belief that modification to meet any later needs could be built in (at that time, a motto in

COUNTRY	FIRST DELIVERY	OPERATOR	QUANTITY AND MODEL	REMARKS
Bulgaria	1972	Balkan	18 A/B/8M	
		VIA	4M	
Hungary	1973	Malev	10 A/B	
Egypt	1973	Egyptair	8A	One crashed, 7 returned 1975
	1992	Cairo Charter & Cargo	2M	
North Korea	1976	CAAK	4B	
Romania	1976	Tarom	12B	
Czechoslovakia	1980	Government	4B/2M	
	1988	CSA	7M	
Cuba	1980	Cubana	5B/4M	
Yemen	1981	Alyemda	1B/1M	Returned to Russia
Syria	1985	Syrianair	3M	
China	1985	China United	13M	
	1986	China Northwest	10M	
	1986	China Xinjiang	5M	
	1988	China Southwest	5M	
	1992	Sichuan	5M	
	1992	Air Great Wall	2M	
Poland	1986	LOT	14M	
	1990	Polish Air Force	1M	
Guyana	1986	Guyana Airways	1M	S. to Cuba
Afghanistan	1987	Ariana	2M	
East Germany	1989	Interflug	2M	(VIP) t/f Luftwaffe 90
Nicaragua	1989	Aeronica	1M	

Still showing evidence of its Aeroflot parentage, Tu-154M, 85700 (without country code), is shown at Shannon in 1992 with Air Ukraine titles
Paul Duffy

factory N156 stated 'Build it for static loads and we'll develop the service life!') This only became possible with the development of new methods following this major problem.

• The alloy chosen for the wing's lower panel, V95, which had excellent qualities under static test conditions, turned out to have problems in active service conditions, and to show major fatigue and cracks after a relatively short time.

• Normal experience in the industry at that time was to design a wing to meet eighty per cent of the maximum calculated loads, and that would meet all the operational needs expected. Sib NII tests showed that a change in the concept base was needed.

Tupolev sources today say that only a state-funded system could have borne the financial consequences of this failure; by that time, the 120th -154 was well advanced on the production line. After redesign of the wing, 120 aircraft had their wings replaced in a programme which would have bankrupted most Western manufacturers.

While the aircraft were in the repair factories having the new wings installed, the opportunity was taken to improve their control systems. Modifications were made which allowed the -154 to be certificated for ICAO Category II automatic landings.

Shortly after the 154's service entry, it began to attract orders from foreign airlines. The first customer was Balkan Bulgarian, and its first two aircraft were delivered to Sofia in May 1972. But these customers called for some changes, particularly in terms of service life. Thus the -154B came about. Although some -154Bs were involved in the rewinging programme, most of the earlier problems were

eliminated in the new model. Over the years, experience on the -154B and tests by bodies such as GosNII GA and Sib NII have permitted its service life to grow to 45,000 hours/18,000 cycles/twenty-three years.

The first non-aligned (i.e. not under Soviet influence) customer for the Tu-154 was Egyptair. The first four aircraft (of eight ordered) were delivered to Cairo in December 1973. Unfortunately, Egyptair did not like the Soviet interior, and Soviet industry at the time could not/would not provide any other; this, combined with the loss of one aircraft in a training accident, resulted in the fleet returning to the Soviet Union in March 1975.

Other countries, mostly under Soviet influence, bought substantial numbers of -154s. These aircraft were used to develop wide route networks for the larger operators. Balkan used the -154 to greatly expand the Bulgarian tourist market; the Bulgarian government, aware of the potential of the excellent beaches on the country's Black Sea coast, built new holiday towns there, and flew tourists from all over Europe with the -154s to fill these towns in the summer season. Balkan is also proud to have been the first to fly a -154 transatlantic.

As the Iron Curtain began to be lowered, Malev, the Hungarian national airline, anxious to improve its cabin standards, sent its fleet of -154s to Shannon in Ireland for new cabin interiors. With these fitted, most passengers did not realise that they were travelling in a Soviet airliner.

Guyana Airways took delivery of a single Tu-154M because the US authorities would no longer allow its ageing Boeing 707 to fly into US airports. Although the -154M was not noticeably quieter, its paperwork claimed to meet the noise requirements; but the difficulties of operating a single aircraft so far from its support lines caused Guyana to sell it to Cubana two years later. CSA and LOT were somewhat reluctant customers – the aircraft were accepted by their governments as a part payment of the Soviet Union's balance of payments deficit with the two countries. In turn, the Soviet Union was taking Polish-built An-2s and -28s, and Czech-built Let L-410s.

Meanwhile, back in the Soviet Union, the -154 was replacing older aircraft rapidly on Aeroflot's trunk routes. An accident to an Antonov An-10 at Kharkov in May 1972 led to the withdrawal of the entire An-10 fleet almost immediately, and put major pressure on the -154 programme to meet the resulting demand. It could not make up all the needs for 1972 or 1973 – Aeroflot's passenger numbers, even with virtually full flights, fell short of the eighty-seven million target by some four million. But by 1975, the numbers had grown to ninety-eight million. By the end of that year, more than 110 Tu-154s had joined the airline's fleet, and over ten million passengers were being carried on -154s every year.

Aeroflot's crews were growing used to the -154. Early in 1995, Vnukovo crews outlined some of their experiences:

'At first sight, it was a complex aircraft. There were many more systems and controls than on the -104 and -134 – mechanical and stabiliser systems, more redundancy and, of course, three engines – there was a lot of work on take-off. But we soon found that it was easier for the pilots. The extra power available gave us a latitude that we had never experienced before, and the additional slats and spoilers meant that landing speeds were lower.

The three engines increased our confidence – even if one failed, we could still depend on the other two to get us down safely. On the other hand, with the three engines mounted at the back, as soon as we had stopped, the engineer's first job was to fit a pole under the tail to prevent the aircraft from sitting down! We gradually learned how to get the best out of it, and as time went on, it became one of Aeroflot's best aircraft. The basic -154 needed some problems solved; on the -154A, there was better control of wing slats and flaps, and this gave improved stability. With the -154B, we had an automatic landing system certified to ICAO Category II conditions – that made schedules more reliable. The fuselage was one metre/3.28 feet longer, and passenger numbers grew from 158 to a maximum of 180. The CG position was better and we no

longer needed the pole to keep the tail up. And the automatic engine controls were greatly improved.

When flown by an experienced pilot, the -154 was very forgiving. On landing, we found that applying reverse thrust some two or three metres (six to ten feet) up usually resulted in a perfect landing, but could sometimes result in an element of drift. Different pilots varied the technique a little – some would wait until touchdown to apply reverse thrust, others would do it a few seconds earlier.

The -154M, which came in 1985, was fitted with Soloviev D30KU-154 engines. With this, fuel economy improved considerably. For example, whereas the 115-passenger -104 burned six tonnes per cruise hour at a lower speed, the -154B, with up to 180 passengers, burned just 6.4 tonnes at a higher speed, and the -154M burned a tonne less with the same load and speed. Thus the -154M could fly with a full load further than the B – it could make Irkutsk or Ulan Ude from Moscow with no problems.

Those of us who learned to fly jets on the -104 found it easy to switch to the -154. While at first we didn't want to leave our first love, we soon learnt to love the -154. We trusted it.'

The -154 was soon serving with almost all the major Aeroflot divisions. Of the thirty-four major operational divisions of Aeroflot at the end of 1990, only Domodedovo, Central Regions (mainly regional routes), Komi, Lithuanian, Estonian and the remote Kamchatka divisions were not -154 operators. There were other Soviet users too: Section 235, the Government Air Services of Aeroflot, now known as 'Rossiya' airline, operated Tu-154s. In 1995, along with long-range Ilyushin Il-62s, two Tu-154M-LK-1s are operated with long-range, and satellite, communications systems for presidential use plus nine others for governmental service. The Russian Air Force, the VVS, operate about twenty in mainly transport roles, with some -154Ts as flying hospitals; and a single LL-154 flying laboratory is in service, possibly as a cosmonaut trainer.

In 1982, work began on modernising the -154. Alexander Shengardt had taken over from Sergei Yeger as chief designer of the programme in 1975, and his task was to update the aircraft and to improve its operating economics. The major change was in the replacement of the old NK-8 engines with the Soloviev D30KU-154, a version of the engine used on the Il-62 and Il-76 for the previous ten years. A Tupolev-owned -154B was converted as the prototype -154M.

Tu-154, SSSR-85675, at Shannon in 1991 before painting.   Note its extra communications aerials marking it as a 154M-LK-1, for presidential use

Paul Duffy

A -154M airframe was also subjected to a full static and dynamic test programme at the Sib NII.

At first the new -154 version was called the 1-X-4, then the -164, before -154M was eventually decided upon. The first -154Ms were delivered to Vnukovo in 1985. They offered a reduction in fuel burn of one tonne per cruise hour, a saving of some fifteen per cent. The noise level was also improved. Again Balkan was the first export customer, quickly followed by several Chinese airlines, Guyana, Cubana and LOT. By the end of 1989, 130 -154Ms had been delivered.

In 1990, the last year of traffic growth for the Soviet Union, the still united Aeroflot carried 137.5 million passengers some 243.8 billion revenue passenger kilometres. Just over seventy-five per cent were carried on Tu-154s and Tu-134s, with some 580 -154s and 450 -134s in service with Aeroflot divisions by the end of 1990.

The Soviet Union officially ceased to exist on 31 December 1991. In the next few years, Aeroflot separated into several hundred airlines, and more new independent carriers began services. Although it was some time before many of these had painted their aircraft, soon -154s began to appear in a variety of new colour schemes.

Two Aviaremonts continue to provide Form 3 and Form 4 major overhauls, Plant N400 at Vnukovo, and N411 at Mineralnie Vody.

Late in 1994, the production factory at Samara became one of the first major industries to be declared bankrupt. The exact status of its bankruptcy is not clear at the time of writing, but it may mean the end of the production line.

By mid-1995, 606 Tu-154s, including the basic model, the A and the B, had been produced, some modified to Tu-154C/S standard for cargo operations, and 307 Tu-154Ms were completed although up to ten remained unsold. A proposed twin-engined -154M-2 is unlikely to go ahead, but the -154 is likely to serve for another twenty years.

Tu-154 Modifications

1. Tu-154: basic production model up to 158 passengers; NK-8-24 engines.
2. Tu-154A: improved production model up to 168 passengers.
3. Tu-154B: improved wing devices and comms equipment.
4. Tu-154B-1: equipment differences.
5. Tu-154B-2: equipment differences.
6. Tu-154B-2 Salon: VIP version of B-2 with improved interior and better communications equipment.
7. Tu-154C: conversion of basic model for cargo.
8. Tu-1X4 }re-engined version; became the -154M.
   Tu-164
9. LL-154: cosmonaut training laboratory.
10. Tu-154M: re-engined and improved production version with D-30KU-154 engines.
11. Tu-154M-LK-1: two aircraft equipped for Head of State flights.

Tu-155

Seeking an Alternative Fuel

The oil crisis at the end of the 1970s drew attention to the fact that the world's supply of hydrocarbon fuels would not last for ever. Because of this the Soviet government decided to request industry for proposals to find alternative fuels and new engines which could use these fuels.

The Soviet research institutes decided to concentrate on two potential fuels – liquid hydrogen (LH), and liquid natural gas (LNG). Hydrogen is perhaps the element in greatest abundance on this planet, but to serve as a fuel, it had to be kept at low temperature and under pressure. The Tupolev Design Bureau, under the leadership of Aleksei Tupolev, began working on cryogenic-fuelled aircraft at the beginning of the Soviet programme. It worked closely with the Kuznetsov Engine Design Bureau and a range of specialist subcontractors.

Kuznetsov developed an engine, the NK-88, from the NK-8 to be capable of running on either cryogenic or fossil fuel. Tupolev, who had appointed Vladimir Andreev to head the programme, then decided that

one engine should be installed on a modified Tu-154 which would act as a test vehicle. Thus SSSR-85035, an early Tu-154 'owned' by the design bureau, was taken out of service and extensively modified. Firstly, a second fuel system had to be installed; two of the aircraft's engines would continue to be fuelled by kerosene, and the third would serve as the testbed for LH and later LNG. So a second fuel system was installed in the fuselage cabin area, consisting of a large pressurised tank which had a high degree of thermo-isolation – in other words it maintained its own temperature, gaining or losing very little from outside influences. New centrifugal pumps were developed with higher than normal heat exchange efficiency, and new safety and alarm systems were installed. The engine also needed a re-regulation of its air intake to meet the revised requirements of airflow.

Another problem to be solved was the provision of airport refuelling facilities. For the test programme, a particular parking stand at Zhukovski was selected, some distance away from the normal line. A fuelling point was built beside it, and basic maintenance facilities were also located there, so that most of the aircraft's ground needs were provided from the same site. The fuel was brought to the site by trucks; up to

The converted Tu-155, SSSR-85035, at Zhukovski in 1993. Note the addition to the tail
Paul Duffy

four trucks could be simultaneously connected to the aircraft by pipelines equipped with safety locks, and fuelling was carried out semi-automatically from a remote control point.

The modified -154, now called the Tu-155, looked little different from the standard aircraft. Its most noticeable visual difference consisted of a small extra vertical fin mounted on top of the tailplane. Much internally modified, the Tu-155 with a single NK-88 mounted on the starboard side made its new 'first flight' on 18 April 1988 under the command of Andrei Talalakin. Only five flights were made using LH fuel. These tested the aircraft and engine's behaviour at altitudes of up to 7,000m/22,967 feet and at speeds of up to 900kph/556mph. The tests included air starts of the cryogenically fuelled engine, simulated failures and fire extinguishing systems. But two factors brought about the decision not to proceed with LH fuels – the high cost of the fuel, although it may be reasonable to presume that were it to be widely used the cost would come down, and the almost total lack of LH facilities at the world's major airports.

Natural gas, on the other hand, was already widely used and is piped from its sources to many cities and to airports. Much of the necessary infrastructure was already in place for industrial, domestic and motor use. In the late 1980s, Soviet researchers calculated that known LNG reserves came to 610 million tonnes, and that some fifty per cent was located on Soviet territory. While this is not an inexhaustible supply, it could serve as a stopgap while the technology and infrastructure needed to optimise the use of hydrogen was developed.

So the Tu-155 was modified to use LNG fuels. Some of the work was similar to that involved on the earlier LH programme. The engine itself needed only minor readjustment of the rate of air intake and fuel supply. But the fuel density was a problem: LNG is only one sixth of the density of LH. It was possible to increase the supply by a factor of three, so the flow of gas needed to be doubled. Again centrifugal pumps with improved heat exchange solved the problem. A more difficult problem was how to feed the fuel to the engine – as a liquid it would be best, but LNG turns from liquid to gas at minus 160°C/minus 256°F. Even this does not fully stop the fuel from boiling, which could mean a considerable loss in fuel volume. So the decision was taken to keep the fuel in a pressurised tank. Even so, it would have been difficult to ensure an even and continuous supply; instead it was heated to minus 70°C/minus 94°F before being fed to the fuel nozzles in gas form to avoid vapour generation in the fuel lines where it was more difficult to avoid boiling. This provided the necessary cavitation margin

upstream of the engine pump.

The first flight to use LNG fuel was made on 18 January 1989. In the next five years, more than eighty flights followed, testing the aircraft and engines in all aspects of flight at levels up to 13,000m/42,653 feet. The test programme resulted in considerable experience on both the design and operation of aircraft with cryogenic fuels, and this will assist in later manufacturing techniques. It has also resulted in new Soviet/Russian research and testing facilities for LNG fuels, and in better methods of preventing potential accidents, including fire or explosives-related accidents.

The Tu-155 was exhibited at three Western aerospace exhibitions – Nice in October 1989, Hannover (June 1990), and Berlin (July 1991), where it drew considerable attention. The work done on the Tu-155 was intended to lead to a production variant, the Tu-156, which was to be a modification of the Tu-154B capable of using cryogenic and kerosene fuel, and taking just five seconds to convert from one to the other. This has also been done in flight on the -155. The cryogenic fuel would be carried in an extra tank fitted above the passenger cabin. With the enormous political and financial problems being experienced by Russia in the 1990s, it is uncertain whether the programme will continue.

Tu-160

The Supersonic, Strategic 'Blackjack'

The development of the Rockwell B-1 for the US Air Force led to a Soviet government decision to launch a competition for the development of a supersonic strategic bomber intended to replace the Tu-95 'Bear', and replace/supplement the medium-range Tu-22M 'Backfire'.

Work began in the early 1970s and several design bureaux submitted proposals. It is understood that the best proposals were submitted by the Myasishchev design bureau, but the VVS considered that Myasishchev would be hard put to produce their design, so the competitive result went to the always capable Tupolev. The bureau's work on the Tu-144 was also a factor in this decision, as was the Opyt factory.

Aleksei Tupolev had succeeded his father as general designer of the bureau, which was officially given his father's name posthumously. This was unusual in Soviet industry – it is certainly the only time this has happened with an aircraft design bureau that a son succeeded his father. He appointed Valentin Blizniuk to act as chief designer for the programme, which was given the designation Tu-160.

Tu-160

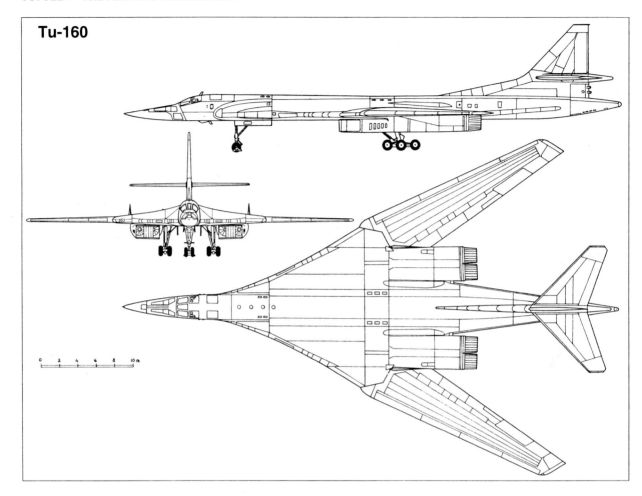

From the beginning, a variable geometry wing was proposed, even though the materials and technology needed for one of the necessary size were not then available. Different engine layouts were considered, including a vertical one, (with one engine mounted above a second on each side), but the complex airflow resulting would have needed a technically difficult air intake, so a side by side arrangement mounted in ducts under the inner wings was finally evolved. Many specialist staff in leading research institutes and even from other design bureaux worked on the programme, as did staff from other industries. For the first time in the Soviet Union, stealth technology was developed to reduce the possibility of the new bomber being detected by enemy radar.

The engine design bureau of Nikolai Kuznetsov developed a two-stage turbine engine, the NK-32, with reheat for the programme. When it was completed in 1980, it was installed on a Tu-95LL flying test aircraft for evaluation. Each NK-32 offered a thrust of 25,000kg/55,115lb with reheat. A number of systems

already in service on the Tu-22M3 were adapted for the Tu-160; electronic versions of artificial horizon, and turn and bank indicators were rejected as not yet meeting the standards needed. Titanium was used quite widely on the aircraft, accounting for some twenty per cent of the airframe. The high temperature leading edges were made from titanium alloys, as was the centreplane spar, a 12.4m/40.7-foot long by 2.1m/6.9-foot wide box with lateral ribs made from aluminium alloys. The centreplane spar was also used to carry fuel; some carbon fibre composites and fibre-glass materials were also used. The outer wings also served as fuel tanks. They were formed around a torsion box in which the fuel was carried, and the outer panels were manufactured from aluminium and titanium alloys. They were hinged to the centreplane and could vary the angle of sweep between 20° and 65°.

The crew of four was seated in a pressurised cabin and they were provided with K-36LM ejector seats, which could be operated from ground level. Entry to the aircraft was through an underbody hatch which held an extending ladder. The cabin was equipped for extended patrols with the provision of reclining seats for rest, together with cooking facilities and a toilet. Diving suits were also carried, presumably as a means of escape should the aircraft come down in the sea. The undercarriage had a steerable nose wheel, while the two main legs had telescopic extensions to lengthen them while being lowered, and to extend them outwards by 600mm/two feet in order to widen the wheel track.

The aircraft's equipment included an INS which served as back-up to an 'Astral' navigation system and long-range radar to locate ground and sea targets; an active/passive communications disruption system; optical/electronic bombsights; and a heat locator, capable of detecting approaching aircraft or missiles. Over 100 digital processors were fitted on the Tu-160 including eight digital navigation computers. The flying controls were rapid response, developed from fighter systems. The rear fuselage contained radar trapping and deflecting surfaces.

Two prototypes plus a static test airframe were built by the ANTK at the Opyt factory and at TsAGI at Zhukovski from parts made at the Kazan production factory. The centreplane was brought by river to Zhukovski and the wings were flown there, mounted under the belly of a Tu-95 piloted by Ivan Vedernikov, resulting in what was described as 'an interesting take-off'. As usual, when completed, the fuselages were disassembled and brought by road to Zhukovski, where they were reassembled, and joined to the wings in the Tupolev hangar at the test base.

When completed, one aircraft was rolled out on 26 November 1981. It was spotted parked beside two Tu-144s by an overflying satellite. When the KGB saw the resultant pictures, the quality was so good that they concluded that they had been taken from the roof of a building on the test base, and a major investigation was launched. A close examination revealed that the photographic angles could not be matched. Then a detailed analysis of records of possible overflights showed that none could match the sun positions. Finally, detailed scanning of the satellite overflights found the answer. Thereafter, no new aircraft were rolled out in daylight hours, although test flying was conducted both during the day and at night.

The photographs revealed to Western intelligence the largest combat bomber yet produced in the world, with the known size of the Tu-144 giving a clear measure against which to determine the bomber's dimensions.

The inaugural flight of the prototype Tu-160, codenamed 'Blackjack' by NATO, took place on 19 December 1981, the birthday of the then Soviet General Secretary, Leonid Brezhnev. It was made from Zhukovski, with Boris Veremei in command. As the factory and state tests progressed, the VVS decided that the requirement was for 100 aircraft, and production was established at Kazan. The first production aircraft joined the two built by factory N156 in the flight test programme. These tests were carried out at the Zhukovski flight test and development base of Tupolev. The second production aircraft was lost when it suffered an engine failure on take-off.

A Tu-160 'Blackjack' at Zhukovski in Soviet Air Force markings
Paul Duffy

Fortunately, there were no casualties.

The Tu-160 entered service with the VVS in May 1987, when the first aircraft were delivered to the Guards Bombing Air Force Regiment N184, based near the town of Priluki in the Ukraine. Nineteen aircraft, forming two squadrons, were delivered. A second base was set up near Engels, in the Saratov region of Russia, in 1991, with the first squadron expected to become active in 1992; the changing politics intervened and only four aircraft were delivered. They equipped Air Force Bombing Regiment N160.

In August 1988, US Secretary of Defense Carlucci became the first non-Soviet citizen to be allowed inside a Tu-160 which had been flown to the Kubinka air force base for the occasion. As he was climbing into the cockpit, he banged his head against an instrument panel. Since then, this has been nicknamed the 'Carlucci panel'.

The first occasion when Tu-160s flew beyond Soviet borders occurred in May 1991 when two aircraft flew to Cape Nordkyn in northern Norway, and then down the west coast as far as the town of Tromso. En route, they were intercepted by Royal Norwegian Air Force F-16s which accompanied them for some time.

But the changing political and economic climate of the Soviet Union brought its own difficulties to the Tu-160 programme. Early in 1992, the new Russian president, Boris Yeltsin, announced the end of the Tu-160 production line. Ministry of Defence sources quoted the production order as being cut from 100 to forty, but in fact only thirty aircraft were built, including those by the designers. In 1994, the officer commanding the VVS, Colonel-General Piotr Deinekin, stated that long-range military aviation was in a financial crisis, and that what was needed now was 'a cheaper bomber with better operational characteristics'.

At the time of writing, nineteen Tu-160s are grounded at Priluki, unused since 1992 as the Ukrainian Air Force has no resources to operate them. Russia and the Ukraine have held talks on a possible repatriation to Russia as a part offset of the Ukrainian debt for oil and gas, but no conclusion has, as yet, been reached. Tupolev sources indicate that, at this stage, it will be practically impossible to restore them to service condition.

A further four are based, and are operational, at Engels with the Russian Air Force; four production aircraft are at Tupolev's base in Zhukovski as are the two prototypes; the static test airframe is still at TsAGI; and one almost complete aircraft remains on the Kazan production line.

As a weapons system, the Tu-160 was formidable. All its weapons were mounted internally, and it could carry: twelve Kh-55 cruise missiles with a 3,000km/1,864-mile range, mounted in two drums in the bomb bay (NATO code 'Kent'/AS-15B); twenty-four Kh-15 missiles, similarly mounted (NATO code 'Kickback'/AS-16); and a range of freefall bombs and/or seamines, including nuclear bombs. Its combat load was up to forty-five tonnes. It could also be used as a first-stage satellite launch by using an underbody Burlak missile to take the satellite into a 300 to 500km/186 to 311-mile polar orbit at a fraction of the cost of a rocket launch. Maximum speed was 2,230kph/1,386mph at 13,000m/42,653 feet, practical ceiling was 15,000m/49,215 feet, and unrefuelled range was 12,300km/7,643 miles at MTOW. On patrol, its unrefuelled endurance was fifteen hours.

A Tu-160 'Blackjack' accompanied by four MiG-29s in Russian Air Force markings. It is being piloted by VVS Commander, Colonel-General Piotr Deinekin at the 1995 Victory Day parade.
Paul Duffy

This Tu-160 carries a Burlak satellite launcher under its fuselage (excuse the scratch)
Tupolev

Tu-204

In 1982, the Soviet government, through the Ministry of Civil Aviation, began to consider the question of replacing the Tu-154. At that time, experience showed that roughly seven years was the time taken from the beginning of plans for a new aircraft to the time of its first flight, and several more years would elapse before production aircraft started to be delivered. The Tu-154 was twelve years in production, and developments in engines and technology had advanced since the programme began in the mid-1960s. At the time, ecology was beginning to become a factor in aircraft design – aircraft needed to be quieter as ICAO began to promulgate the concept of Stage III noise rules, and fuel economy was gaining in importance. Also, Aeroflot's passenger numbers continued to grow. In 1981, 108.9 million travelled on Aeroflot services.

Tupolev was one of the bureaux asked to submit proposals, and in 1983 these were accepted. Aleksei Tupolev appointed Lev Lanovski to be chief designer.

Lanovski sought to bring the -204, as the project was named, as up to date as possible and aimed to match the latest Western standards. The Tu-204 title was chosen to reflect its second-generation replacement of the Tu-104.

The Soloviev Engine Design Bureau, based in Perm, had begun development of a new high bypass turbofan engine in the late 1970s intended to give a take-off power of 16,000kg/35,275lb, the PS-90A. It promised long life, technical reliability and a low fuel burn. It was chosen for the Tu-204.

Soviet industry was also aiming to match Western avionics, and Lanovski planned to feature two six-colour CRT screens with engine and systems data displays. He also installed full Category IIIA equipment allowing the aircraft to land at suitably equipped airports in weather conditions of zero vertical visibility and 200m/656 feet forward visibility. INS and satellite navigation systems were also fitted.

Tu-204

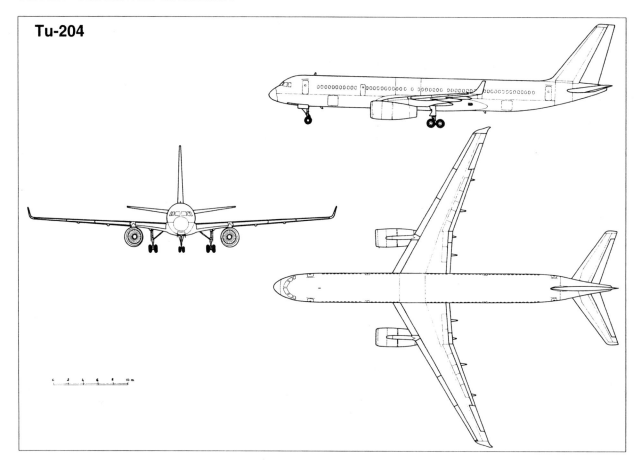

The Tu-204 was intended to have a two-crew cockpit, although Aeroflot required a flight engineer to supplement the pilot and co-pilot, so Lanovski left space for a fourth cockpit seat to be used by an instructor or for an observer. All major systems featured triple redundancy; the flying controls were a triple fly-by-wire system, with triple back-up systems, and design life was twice that of the -154 – 60,000 flight hours or 45,000 cycles. Lanovski considered installing a side stick in place of a conventional control column and tested one out on a Tu-154, but crew reaction to the side stick was not very good, so he stayed with the control column.

By the time the programme was hardened in 1985, Aeroflot had announced plans to take 350 Tu-204s. Production of the prototype began that year in the Opyt factory. It was completed in summer 1988, dissembled and brought by road to Zhukovski, from where, after reassembly at the test centre, it made its first flight on 2 January 1989, piloted by Andrei Talalakin.

Meanwhile, a number of events had occurred which would affect the -204 programme. First, the MAP had

assigned production of the new aircraft to the Ulyanovsk aviation production factory, which in 1991 would become Aviastar. This factory had been constructed in the 1970s originally to produce strategic bombers, but as the Cold War thawed out, it had instead been given the world's largest production aircraft, the Antonov An-124. But this left the huge facility under-used, so the -204 programme was added.

Secondly, Armand Hammar, the president of Occidental Oil and one of the very few Western businessmen to maintain contact with the Soviet Union throughout the previous seventy years, had established a programme with the Soviet government to modernise the civil aviation industry. His committee had selected two aircraft to begin work – the long-range Ilyushin Il-96-300 and the medium-range Tu-204. The primary objects of Hammar's work were to bring Soviet airliners up to Western standards in operational reliability and operating costs, and to begin the process of making them saleable in the West – in other words, to get them certificated by the Western airworthiness bodies. The committee's first tasks were to select Western engines and avionics for

Lev Lanovski
Chief designer of Tu-204

installation in the two programmes, and this led Tupolev to work with Pratt & Whitney, for the PW2240 engine, and with Allied Signals, Honeywell and Rockwell Collins for avionics.

The third change was only beginning to become evident at the time of the first flight – the impending collapse of the Soviet Union. While the leaders of the second superpower were well aware of the economic and consequent political crisis about to occur, to the average Soviet citizen things just seemed a bit more difficult. Money was becoming scarce, and the costs needed to get the Tu-204 up and running were only being met slowly and with severe restrictions. Still, the first -204 was shown at the 1989 Paris Air Salon, the long-time international display case of Soviet aviation.

1991 marked the end of the Soviet Union. It began a period of hyperinflation: in the next few years, prices in Russia went up some 12,000 times; what cost a rouble in 1990 cost at least 12,000 roubles in 1995. Any money provided by the government for projects like the -204 was paid six to twelve months in arrears, by which time its value had plummeted. Traditionally, the government had provided Aeroflot with its equipment; in the years after the Soviet collapse, the Russian government continued to do that for the state-owned airlines, but the resources available were much less in purchase power. In 1985, for example, it provided Aeroflot with seventy LET 410s, five An-28s, sixteen An-26s, the last two Tu-134As, five Yak-42s, eleven Tu-154s, three Il-62s, seventeen Il-76s and five Il-86s – and that was a low number; smaller aircraft and

SSSR-64001, the prototype Tu-204, at the Paris Air Salon in 1989
Paul Duffy

Tu-204, RA-64011, of Vnukovo Airlines, air to air in 1994
Paul Duffy

helicopters are omitted. In 1994, thirteen aircraft were provided to the airlines – two An-74s, two Yak-42s, four Tu-154s, two Tu-204s and three Il-96s, about one tenth of the 1985 numbers. 1991 also marked the end of the Hammar programme, for the American entrepreneur had died in 1990. But the venture had shown a way forward, and business connections built up by Aviastar and Tupolev led to a new joint venture with British partners. Called Bravia (an acronym for the British Russian Aviation Corp), the partnership equipped one of the development Tu-204s with Rolls-Royce RB211-535 engines.

The flight test programme progressed exceptionally slowly. Aeroflot had originally expected the -204 to enter service in 1990; late in 1990, it was expected by early 1992. It would take a further three years.

The Tu-204-220 (SSSR-64006), with RB211-535E4 engines, made its first flight on 14 August 1992, converted from a standard Tu-204-210 and with a new interior fitted by Huntings in East Midlands. Less than three weeks later, it was shown at the 1992 Farnborough Air Show.

The first -204s were -100s with an MTOW of 93.5 tonnes quickly increased to 99.5 tonnes. The series -200 (only development aircraft were in the series -100) raised the MTOW to 110.75 tonnes which significantly improved the maximum payload from twenty-one tonnes to twenty-five tonnes, and the range with full

payload from 2,500km/1,553 miles to 5,200km/3,231 miles. Amazingly, early flight tests showed that the PS-90A-powered Tu-204-210 had a two to five per cent lower fuel burn than the RB211-powered -220. But it was soon evident that the PS-90A needed a lot of development work to sort out its problems, and that finance for this work was not available. Both aircraft powered by the PS-90A in the early 1990s, the Il-96-300 and the Tu-204, experienced many problems with the engines; basically a good design, the snags seemed to originate from production line quality defects. And other difficulties were evident in the avionics.

A new Russian airline, Oriol Avia, bought the first Tu-204s in 1992, taking delivery before certification had been granted. Two aircraft it held for passenger services but the third (64010) it requested Tupolev and Aviastar to convert into a freighter. This was done at Zhukovski by a team led by chief designer Yuri Vorobiev. The aircraft was shown at the Paris Air Salon in 1993.

At the end of 1993, Vnukovo Airlines received its first -204. RA (Russia now had a new ICAO country code) -64011, and -64012 followed shortly afterwards. These aircraft, and -64013, the third for the airline, were bought by the State and given to Vnukovo who were requested to undertake the usual twelve months' operational trials before NLGS certification, and before passenger services could begin.

The Tu-204 went through its operational trials smoothly enough. -64011 was painted in Vnukovo's new colours by Expressair in Holland in June 1994 and shown at Farnborough in September. On 2 November, it flew its certification flight in the traditional Russian manner; a full load of VIPs and correspondents were brought on a trip to Sochi for a celebratory party. But near Rostov-on-Don, one of the PS-90 engines suffered an uncontained engine failure, and an emergency descent was followed by a landing at a military airfield. However, on 29 December the certification was approved; it was issued on 12 January 1995, subject to modification of the existing aircraft.

Certification of the Tu-204-210 allowed work to go ahead on the Rolls-Royce-powered -220, although the delays in the programme resulted in some strain in the partnership. But, even if finance was a problem for Russian and CIS airlines, the level of interest was high. In Soviet times, airline operators (Aeroflot divisions) did not have to pay for fuel; now they did. And the 5.5 tonnes per cruise hour of the Tu-154M carrying 168 to 180 passengers was a lot more expensive than the 3.4 tonnes of the -204, which can hold up to 214 economy-class passengers.

In autumn 1994, Aviastar claimed to have 268 'soft' orders for the -204. The 'soft' was explained by the manufacturer's reluctance to harden these orders until the certification conditions were known. But Tupolev only confirmed sixty-five. By then, Number 25 (64025) was in final assembly at Ulyanovsk. A second factory, N22 in Kazan, began to prepare for -204 production with the Rolls-Royce-powered version to be built here, and now designated the Tu-214, (according to Kazan officials); and the Minsk repair factory was appointed to undertake heavy maintenance on the Tu-204 when it became due.

Rossiya, the former Section 235, or Special Air Services Division of Aeroflot, and the operator of executive and presidential flights for the Russian government, took delivery of two -204-210s in autumn 1994.

By December 1995, the first two Vnukovo aircraft had completed their post-certification modifications, and passenger services began in February 1996 on the Moscow–Mineralnie–Vody route.

In April, ARIA (Aeroflot Russian International Airlines) took delivery of RA-64010, the Tu-204C modified for Oriol Avia. It had reached agreement

RA-64010, the first Tu-204C, showing its cargo hold at Zhukovski, March 1995
Paul Duffy

Tu-204, RA-64016, unpainted at Ulyanovsk, August 1994
Paul Duffy

with Oriol to operate its three -204s, plus the Tupolev-owned -64007, with 007, 008 and 009 to be converted to freighter standards 'before the end of 1995'.

That is the -204 story up to date. Hopefully it can now begin to work, even if five years late. It is a normal story for Russian industry in the traumatic times of the 1990s. Tupolev are also considering a cryogenically fuelled -204, although financial difficulties will constrain its development. It will be the Tu-214.

The chief designers of the 204 programmes beside the Tu-204C (L–R):
Yuri Alasheev, Chief Designer, Rolls-Royce-powered -220 version; Yuli Kashtanov, Deputy General Director of ANTK Tupolev; Yuri Vorobiev, Chief Designer Tu-204C; Lev Lanovski, Chief Designer of 204 programme
Paul Duffy

Tu-234

With Airbus Boeing and McDonnell Douglas, and others, developing families of aircraft by the simple method of stretching or shortening fuselage lengths to give larger or smaller cabins, Tupolev decided to do the same.

Tupolev's new general director, Valentin Klimov, had served as general director of Aviaexport, the Soviet/Russian state aviation marketing organization, before he rejoined Tupolev and was aware of the potential offered by having reduced spare holdings and crew flexibility on airline operating costs.

He appointed Lev Lanovski to develop a smaller version of the 204. Rather than start again, Lanovski took the Tu-204 prototype (RA-64001) in August 1993 and began the work of shortening it. As Ilyushin had done with the Il-96 prototype, he had the fuselage cut before and behind its wings. But instead of adding plugs as Ilyushin had done to stretch the 96-300 into the 96M, Lanovski instead removed 3 metres from the forward section and another 3 metres/9.84 feet from the rear fuselage. This reduced passenger numbers in a one-class arrangement from 214 to 160.

With no change in engines or engine power, the new member of the 204 was offered with either a MTOW of 84 tonnes or 103 tonnes.

The 84-tonne aircraft offered a range of 3000km/1864 miles from a 2000m/6561-foot runway. The 103-tonne model offered a range of 9000km/5593 miles. Both models could carry seven AK-07 containers for luggage and cargo in the lower fuselage.

As in the 204, flight data was displayed on six CRT tubes. With its close relationship to the Tu-204, Tupolev expects to achieve certification, with minimum work needed, relying on the 204's programme.

Tupolev expect a saving of 15% to 20% on operating costs compared to old generation aircraft with the Tu-234.

However the political and financial difficulties of Russian industry resulted in the rollout of the 234 taking place only on the 24 August 1995 at the Mosaeroshow, and the first flight had not taken place by the middle of 1996.

The first production Tu-234, RA-64026 was completed at Aviastar in early 1996.

Tu-334

If the Tu-154's replacement had taken a long time to arrive, then the Tu-134's took even longer. In 1985, Aeroflot, through the Ministry of Civil Aviation (MCA), sought proposals from the MAP.

Tupolev's provisional design for a low-winged 86- to 102-seat twin-engined airliner were accepted. Igor Kalygin was appointed chief designer, and he built up a team to work on the project. Aeroflot had wanted the new aircraft, which was given the title Tu-334 to indicate its relationship with its predecessor, to enter service in 1992, and a level of commonality with the Tu-204 was another requirement. This followed the Western trend whereby pilots rated on one aircraft could be licensed on another with little conversion costs, and thus be capable of flying both types resulting in worthwhile cost savings for both fleets.

In the mid-1980s, a lot of attention was being paid to the new propfan engines. These ultra-high bypass engines seemed to offer potential fuel savings of twenty-five per cent on advanced turbofan engines,

Igor Kalygin
Chief designer of Tu-334

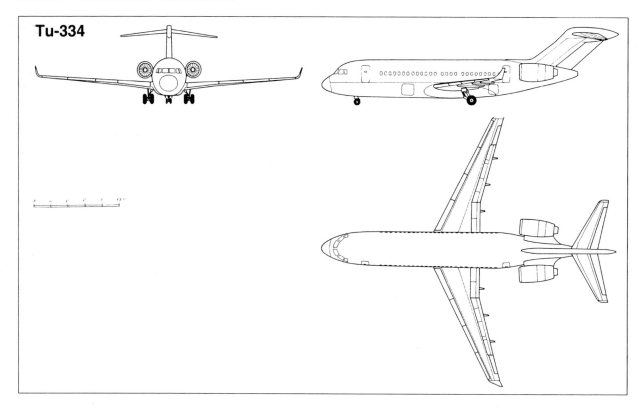

Tu-334

and up to fifty per cent on the then range of turboprops and jets. Tupolev decided that the proposed new Lotarev D-236 would be offered on the Tu-334, but that the propfan version, the D-436T would be the standard choice. Kalygin designed a wing similar to the -204 to incorporate similar handling characteristics; it included winglets to bleed off drag from the wingtips, as had the -204. The cockpit was also based on that of the -204, and controls were fly-by-wire. Surprisingly, in view of the concept of commonality, the new aircraft had its engines mounted at the tail, but this was necessary if propfans were to be fitted.

The fuselage of the initial standard aircraft (the -100) was 33m/108.3 feet in length, and the proposed propfan version was 3.9m/12.7 feet longer (the -200), which allowed maximum passenger numbers to increase to 137 at a tight 75 centimetre/29.5 inch pitch. The smaller aircraft relied on the standard doors only for evacuation in emergencies, but the stretched version had two extra overwing exits. Kalygin set the aims of design work to include a two-crew cockpit; operation from a 2,200m/7,218-foot runway; Category 3A operations – it could operate into suitably equipped airports with visibility down to zero feet in height and an RVR (Runway Visual Range) of just 200m/656 feet; annual utilisation of 2,600 hours (low by Western standards, but at least fifty per cent higher

than the Tu-134 and -154); and fuel burn (turbofan engines) of two tonnes per cruise hour. To achieve this, substantial use was made of composite materials: up to twenty per cent of the surface area of the aircraft used such materials, including much of the tailplane and the engine intakes.

For the first time in a Soviet/CIS airliner, the standard interior provided overhead lockers and oxygen masks. Kalygin paid a lot of attention to corrosion problems, with an improved heat insulation to minimise condensation, and underfloor enamelling and corrosion-resistant alloys were used in areas likely to gather water or hydraulic leaks. He also aimed for fast turnaround times, which are of particular value on short-haul routes; with multiple access points for service, a condition-monitoring data system and a flexible maintenance schedule, the aircraft should need no more than thirty-five minutes on stand by to be ready for its next sector. For operators wishing to use Western avionics and engines, Tupolev expected to offer a Rockwell Collins cockpit and BMW–Rolls-Royce BR715 engines.

The prototype -334 plus a second for static tests were constructed at Tupolev's Opyt factory; however, the delays which were now normal in the crisis-ridden former Soviet Union dragged out completion until late 1993. Already the aircraft was at least four years

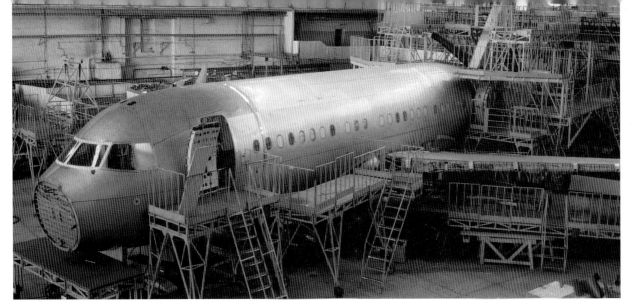

The prototype Tu-334 under reassembly at Tupolev's ZLiDB in Zhukovski in 1994
Paul Duffy

behind schedule. Once completed, the prototype was disassembled and brought by road to Zhukovski. There it suffered further delays, with inflation and shortage of funds combined with delays in payment of the promised governmental funding contributing to the programme's difficulties. In May 1993, Kalygin was confident that the first flight would take place by October or November of that year. In May 1995, with the prototype ninety-eight per cent complete, he was hoping, but with some doubts, to see it fly in the summer. In fact, the rollout took place on 25 August 1995, but funding shortages had not allowed the aircraft to fly by mid 1996.

The bureau sees the market for aircraft in the Tu-334's category as being in the region of 1,700 over the next twelve to fifteen years; with much competition, their major market is in the former Soviet Union and its traditional markets, including China and India. Here, it aims for 600 to 700 aircraft, principally as a replacement for the Tu-134.

Production lines were established in Kiev and Taganrog, and some 1,200 flights were expected to be made by the prototype and early production aircraft in the Russian certification programme. After this is achieved, it is likely that FAA and JAA certification will be sought.

Igor Kalygin, Chief Designer of the 334 (2nd from left) and Valentin Klimov, General Director of Tupolev (3rd from left) in front of the 334 after its rollout.
Paul Duffy

Future Designs

A design bureau is always considering a range of projects; some are in response to enquiries from potential customers, some originate in the bureau itself. Before an idea can become a reality, a likely customer/market base must be found, and project finance must be arranged.

In mid-1995, Tupolev are studying a range of potential projects ranging from a four-seat piston-engined light aircraft to a huge flying wing with a 100m/328-foot span which could carry up to 750 passengers in a three-class layout; and a Hotol category single-stage sub-orbital craft for long-distance travel. Some of these are outlined below.

Tu-24SKh(CX)   A single-engined agricultural sprayer.

Tu-34   A twin-engined business aircraft with a pusher layout. The project is being led by Aleksander Pukhov and is described as a 'light, multi-role passenger aircraft'. Unconfirmed reports suggest it may be manufactured in Tblisi, the Georgian capital, although Tupolev say this is not so.

Tu-130   A twin turboprop project using TV7-117S powerplants. This high-winged design should carry fifty-three passengers or a five-tonne payload. MTOW would be twenty-one tonnes, and range with a five-tonne cargo would be 2,000km/1,243 miles.

Tu-244   A second-generation SST. Aleksander Pukhov, who is also leading the Tu-144 restoration programme, is in charge of this project. In 1994 the project was studying the likely market up to 2025 for SSTs, and ways to achieve lower noise levels and high kinetic efficiency. It would carry up to 300 passengers for a maximum distance of 9,200km/5,717 miles. MTOW would be 350 tonnes, and empty weight 172 tonnes; speed would be Mach 2.05 and cruising altitude would be 18,000 to 20,000m/59,058 to 65,620 feet. It would be equipped for Category 3A operations.

Tu-330   Intended as an Antonov An-12 replacement, a role for which the prototype An-70T first flew in December 1994, the design of the high-winged Tu-330 makes considerable use of the Tu-204 programme, particularly for the wing and tailplane. It would be powered by two PS-90A engines. MTOW would be 103 tonnes and payload thirty-five tonnes. Its range with a thirty-tonne cargo would be 3,000km/1,864 miles, and a twenty-tonne cargo would increase this to 5,600km/3,480 miles.

Tu-404   Tupolev are considering an ultra-high-capacity flying wing, possibly to be powered by six propfan engines of twenty-two to twenty-five tonnes power. It could hold up to 750 passengers in a three-class layout. MTOW would be some 600 tonnes, and wingspan some 100m/328 feet. A disadvantage of this design would be a likely need to adapt airports to cater for parking, and for passenger through flows.

Tu-414   A proposed long-range biz jet for nine to twelve passengers, powered by two D-436T engines, the turbojet used on the Tu-334.

Tu-424   A fifty-seat regional version of the -414.

Tu-2000   Intended as a research aircraft for future sub-orbital programmes, Aleksander Pukhov is leading a team to develop an 'experimental spaceplane' in order to develop knowledge for airframe and engine layouts, aerodynamic characteristics, structured heating, new materials and air breathing engine operations in subspace at speeds of Mach 20 to 25. Liquid hydrogen would be the likely fuel for such a project, and MTOW would be fifty-five to sixty tonnes. The Tu-2000 would serve as a prototype single-stage reusable vehicle capable of delivering loads of up to ten tonnes to a low orbit – 200km/124 miles. It would take off and land from 'normal' runways, Hotol-style. The programme could be conducted in two stages: the first would be a hypersonic aircraft with a maximum speed of Mach 5 to Mach 6, with the second being the reusable delivery prototype.

Aleksander Pukhov
Chief designer of Tu-2000, Tu-34, Tu-144 (restoration)

The mock-up Tu-24SKh (CX) at the 1993 Mosaeroshow in Zhukovski
Paul Duffy

Tu-134 Production List – Aircraft in Service in 1995

Factory 135 in Kharkov produced 850 Tu-134s and two prototypes were assembled by Tupolev at their experimental works in factory 156.

Originally, the production aircraft had a seven-digit factory number – for example that of -65653 was 0351009 where 0 represented the year of manufacture (1970), 35 represented Kharkov factory 135, 10 was the batch number, and 09 was the number in the batch – usually there were ten in each batch.

Unfortunately in 1974 the system was changed; today, nobody seems to know why, although some have suggested that the KGB were alarmed to find how much seemed to be known about aviation production, particularly by Western enthusiasts. So a new system intended to confuse was conjured up and was regularly changed. Tupolev's production records are maintained still in batches and batch numbers, but it has not proved possible (as yet) to match the two. The few cases that did link up are given.

To make it worse, many of the early -134s were converted into the -134Sh and -134UBL for military training, and it seems that a new batch and number system was started from scratch for this. As Soviet/Russian Air Force aircraft have only a (usually) two-digit code as markings, and as this changes if the aircraft is posted to a different squadron, these aircraft are listed only by the new batch and number plus the appropriate model. And then, the original registrations on the -134s converted were reissued to aircraft arriving back into Russia after serving with Interflug and some other carriers.

So listed here are the -134s still in service as of 1 January 1995. Some may be questioned – for example, most of the Stigl fleet based at Grozni in Chechnia were destroyed in the battles in that unfortunate republic; those which survived are not known, so all are listed. And many of the aircraft are assigned still to their former Aeroflot unit – some may have been sold or leased onwards.

Tu-134

Factory No.	Registration	Model	Year Built	Operator
42230	RA- 65000	A	1975	Komi Avia
	RA- 65002	A	1976	Perm
44040	EY- 65003	A	1975	Todjikistan – Khujent Air Det.
44060	RA- 65004	A	1976	North West CAD
44065	RA- 65005	A	1976	Komi Avia
44080	RA- 65006	A	1976	Komi Avia
	RA- 65007	A	1976	Nizhegorodskie
46105	RA- 65008	A	1976	Volga
46120	RA- 65009	A	1976	Tyumen Avialinii
46130	RA- 65010	A	1976	Kaliningrad
46140	RA- 65011	A	1976	Kaliningrad
46175	RA- 65012	A	1976	Tyumen Avialinii
	65014	A	1976	Stigl (Chechnia)
48325	RA- 65015	A	1976	Cheboksari U.A.D.
48340	RA- 65016	A	1976	Donavia
48360	RA- 65017	A	1976	Tyumen Avialinii
48365	RA- 65018	A	1976	Ulyanovsk VAU-GA
48375	RA- 65019	A	1976	Kaliningrad
48380	RA- 65020	A	1976	North West CAD
48390	RA- 65021	A	1976	Nizhegorodskie
48420	RA- 65024	A	1976	Nizhegorodskie
48450	RA- 65025	A	1976	Tyumen Avialinii
48470	RA- 65026	A	1976	BAL-Bashkiri
48485	RA- 65027	A	1976	Kaliningrad
48490	RA- 65028	A	1976	BAL-Bashkiri
48500	RA- 65029	A	1976	Komi Avia
	65030	A	1976	Stigl (Chechnia)
48540	RA-65033	A	1976	Nizhegorodskie
	RA- 65035	A	1976	Perm
48700	ER- 65036	A	1976	Air Moldova (Lt Korov)
48850	UR- 65037	A		Air Ukraine – Kharkov Air Det.
48950	RA- 65038	A	1976	Tyumenaviatrans
	65039	A	1976	Stigl (Chechnia)

Factory No.	Registration	Model	Year Built	Operator
49100	RA- 65040	A	1976	BAL-Bashkiri
49350	RA- 65042	A	1976	North West CAD
	RA- 65043	A	1976	Nizhegorodskie
49450	EK- 65044	A	1976	Armenian Air Lines
49500	RA- 65045	A	1976	Nizhegorodskie
49700	RA- 65046	A	1976	Perm
49600	RA- 65047	A	1976	GosNII-GA/Poliot Chernobyl
49750	UR- 65048	A	1976	Air Ukraine
49755	EW- 65049	A	1976.	Belavia
49756	ER- 65050	A	1977	Air Moldova
49758	ER- 65051	A	1977	Air Moldova
49825	RA- 65052	A	1977	AVL-Arkhangelsk
49838	4L- 65053	A	1977	Taifun
49840	RA- 65054	A	1977	Kaliningrad
	RA- 65055	A	1977	Astrakhan
	RA- 65056	A	1977	Perm
	RA- 65057	A	1977	Voronezh
	RA- 65059	A	1977	Perm
	RA- 65060	A	1977	Kirov
49874	4L- 65061	A	1977	Taifun
49875	RA- 65062	A	1977	Voronezh
49880	RA- 65063	A	1977	Tyumen Avialinii
49886	RA- 65064	A	1977	Perm
49890	RA- 65065	A	1977	Nizhegorodskie ex XU-101
	RA- 65066	A	1977	AVL-Arkhangelsk
	RA- 65067	A	1977	Voronezh
49907	RA- 65068	A	1977	(ex ES-AAG)
49908	RA- 65069	A	1977	Komi Avia
49912	RA- 65070	A	1977	Komi Avia
	ER- 65071	A	1977	Air Moldova
49972	EK- 65072	A	1977	Armenian Air Lines
49980	UR- 65073	A	1977	Adjirian
49987	RA- 65074	A	1977	KMV-Mineralnie Vody
60001	UR- 65076	A	1977	Air Ukraine
60028	UR- 65077	A	1977	Air Ukraine

Factory No.	Registration	Model	Year Built	Operator
60043	RA- 65078	A	1977	Ulyanovsk VAU-GA
60065	RA- 65080	A	1977	Astrakhan
60081	EW- 65082	A	1977	Belavia
60090	RA- 65083	A	1977	AVL-Arkhangelsk
60115	RA- 65084	A	1977	AVL-Arkhangelsk (Occ. Lt Polis Air)
60123	EW- 65085	A	1977	Belavia
60130	RA- 65086	A	1977	Volga
60155	RA- 65087	A	1977	Kaliningrad
60180	UR- 65089	A	1977	Air Ukraine
65185	RA- 65090	A	1977	Kaliningrad
	UR- 65092	A	1978	Air Ukraine – Kharkov Air Det.
60215	UR- 65093	A	1978	Air Ukraine – Kharkov Air Det.
60255	ER- 65094	A	1978	Air Moldova
60257	RA- 65096	A	1978	AVL-Arkhangelsk
60540	RA- 65097	A	1978	Elf Air
	RA- 65099	A	1978	Stolichny Bank of Savings
60258	RA- 65100	A	1978	Donavia
60260	RA- 65101	A	1978	Orenburg
60267	RA- 65102	A	1978	Astrakhan
60297	RA- 65103	A	1978	AVL-Arkhangelsk
60301	R A- 65104	A	1978	Donavia
60315	EW- 65106	A	1978	Belavia
60328	UR- 65107	A	1978	Air Ukraine
60322	EW- 65108	A	1978	Belavia
60342	UR- 65109	A	1978	Air Ukraine – Kharkov Air Det.
60343	RA- 65110	A	1978	Orenburg
60346	EX- 65111	A	1978	Kirghizi
60395	UR- 65114	A	1978	Air Ukraine – Kharkov Air Det.
60380	RA- 65113	A	1978	(Industry operated)
	UN- 65115	A	1978	Kazair
60420	RA- 65116	A	1978	AVL-Arkhangelsk
60450	RA- 65117	A	1978	Orenburg
60462	RA- 65118	A	1978	Chelyabinsk
60475	EX- 65119	A	1978	Kirghizi
60505	UN- 65121	A	1978	Kazair
60518	RA- 65122	A	1978	Aerovolga
	UR- 65123	A	1978	Air Ukraine – Kharkov Air Det.
60575	EX- 65125	A	1978	Kirghizi
60588	RA- 65126	A	1978	KMV-Mineralnie Vody
60627	RA- 65127		1978	Tyumenaviatrans
60635	UN- 65130	A	1978	Kazair
60637	RA- 65131	A	1978	Chelyabinsk
60639	RA- 65132	A	1978	AVL-Arkhangelsk
60645	EW- 65133	A	1978	Belavia
60647	UR- 65134	A	1978	Air Ukraine
60648	UR- 65135	A	1978	Air Ukraine
60885	RA- 65136	A	1978	Orenburg
60890	RA- 65137	A	1978	Kirov
60907	UN- 65138	A	1978	Kazair
	RA- 65139		1978	KMV-Mineralnie Vody
60932	ER- 65140	A	1978	Air Moldova
	RA- 65141		1978	Perm
60967	RA- 65143	A	1979	AVL-Arkhangelsk
60985	EW- 65145	A	1979	Belavia
	UN- 65147	A	1979	Kazair
61025	RA- 65148	A	1979	Komi Avia
61033	EW- 65149	A	1979	Belavia
	RA- 65550	A	1984	Voronezh
	UN- 65551	A	1984	Kazair
66270	RA- 65552	A	1984	Rossiya (Occ. Lt ARIA)
66300	RA- 65553	A	1984	Rossiya
66320	RA- 65554	A	1984	Rossiya (Occ. Lt ARIA)
66350	RA- 65555	A	1984	Rossiya
66372	UR- 65556	A	1984	Air Ukraine
66380	RA- 65557	A	1984	Rossiya
	RA- 65558	A		ARIA
49909	RA- 65559	A	1977	ARIA (ex-Polish A/F 101)
60321	RA- 65560	A	1978	(Industry Operated) (ex-Avio Genex YU-AJW)
	RA- 65562		1984	LII – Gromov Flight Research Institute
	RA- 65563		1984	(Industry Operated)
63165	RA- 65564		1984	(Industry Operated)
63998	EW- 65565	A	1983	Belair
63952	RA- 65566	A	1982	ARIA (ex-Interflug DDR-SDS)
63967	RA- 65567	A	1982	ARIA (ex-Interflug DDR-SDR)
66135	RA- 65568	A	1983	ARIA (ex-Interflug DDR-SDU)
	RA- 65604	A		NPO Vzlet (Ministry of Radio Industry) – Used by Elf Air
09070	RA- 65605	A	1974	Chernomorskie (ex-Interflug DDR-SCU)
46300	RA- 65606	A	1976	Komiavia (ex-Interflug DDR-SDH)
48560	RA- 65607	A	1976	Komiavia (ex-Interflug DDR-SDI)
38040	RA- 65608	A	1975	Komiavia (ex-Interflug DDR-SDE)
46155	RA- 65609	A	1976	Komiavia (ex-Interflug DDR-SDG)
40150	RA- 65610	A	1975	Komiavia (ex-Interflug DDR-SDF)

Factory No.	Registration	Model	Year Built	Operator	
3351903	RA- 65611	A	1973	Komiavia	(ex-Interflug DDR-SCI)
3352102	RA- 65612	A	1973	Komiavia	(ex-Interflug DDR-SCN)
3352106	RA- 65613	A	1973	Komiavia	(ex-Interflug DDR-SCO)
4352205	RA- 65614	A	1974	Komiavia	(ex-Interflug DDR-SCP)
4352206	RA- 65615	A	1974	Komiavia	(ex-Interflug DDR-SCR)
4352207	RA- 65616	A	1974	Komiavia	(ex-Interflug DDR-SCS)
08068	RA- 65617	A	1974	Komiavia W/O Lagos 1995	(ex-Interflug DDR-SCT)
12095	RA- 65618	A	1974	Komiavia	(ex-Interflug DDR-SCV)
31218	RA- 65619	A	1975	Komiavia	(ex-Interflug DDR-SCW)
35180	RA- 65620	A	1975	Komiavia	(ex-Interflug DDR-SDC)
48320	RA- 65621	A	1976	Komiavia	(ex-Interflug DDR-SCX)
60495	RA- 65622	A	1978	Komiavia	(ex-Interflug DDR-SCY)
49985	RA- 65623	A	1977	ARIA (ex LOT SP-LHI)	
	RA- 65624	A		ANTK Tupoleva	
	RA- 65626	A		Air Transport School	
0351003	SSSR- 65648			Preserved Ulyanovsk Museum (WFU)	
	RA- 65649				
0351006	EK- 65650		1970	Armenian Airlines	
0351007	RA- 65651	A	1970	Tyumenaviatrans	
0351009	RA- 65653	A	1970	Sib NII Research Institute	
0351010	RA- 65654			RIGA (WFU)	
0351101	SSSR- 65655		1970	Preserved Kharkov	
1351109	EW- 65663			Minsk 1 Technical School	(WFU)
1351210	EW- 65664	A	1971	Belavia	
1351202	RA- 65666	A	1971	Donavia	
1351207	RA- 65667	A	1971	ANTK Tupoleva	
9350916	RA- 65669	A	1969	(Industry Operated)	
1351208	RA- 65671	A	1971	BAL-Bashkiri	
1351502	EW- 65676	A	1971	Belavia	
23249	RA- 65679	A	1972	VVS/223rd Flt Det	
62205	RA- 65684	A	1972	VVS/223rd Flt Det	
	RA- 65680	A	1972	VVS/223rd Flt Det	
49760	RA- 65681	A	1972	VVS/223rd Flt Det	
	RA- 65682	A	1972	VVS	
62199	RA- 65683	A	1972	VVS/223rd Flt Det UN-65683	leased to KAZA-R
	ER- 65686		1978	Air Moldova	
62575	RA- 65688	A	1972	VVS/223rd Flt Det	
	RA- 65689	A	1972	VVS/223rd Flt Det	
	RA- 65690	A	1971	VVS/223rd Flt Det	
63195	RA- 65691	A	1971	Volga	
63307	RA- 65697	A	1980	ARIA	
63375	4K- 65702	B	1980	AHY-Azerbaijan	
63383	4K- 65703	B	1980	AHY-Azerbaijan	w/o 1995
63415	4K- 65705	B	1980	AHY-Azerbaijan	
63435	ER- 65707	A	1980	Air Moldova	
63447	4K- 65708	B	1980	AHY-Azerbaijan	
63484	4K- 65709	B	1980	AHY-Azerbaijan	
63490	4K- 65710	B	1980	AHY-Azerbaijan	
63498	4K- 65711	B	1980	AHY-Azerbaijan	
63520	4K- 65713	B	1980	AHY-Azerbaijan	
63527	4K- 65714	B	1980	AHY-Azerbaijan	
63595	RA- 65716	A	1981	Komiavia	
63657	RA- 65717	A	1981	ARIA	
63668	UR- 65718	A	1981	Air Ukraine	
63637	RA- 65719	A	1981	Korsar	
62820	RA- 65720	B	1981	ANTK Tupoleva	Lt Arkhangelsk oro
	RA- 65721	(CX/SKh)		Ministry of Agriculture	
	RA- 65722	A		Ivanovo	
66440	RA- 65723	(CX/SKh)		Ministry of Agriculture	
66445	RA- 65724	(CX/SKh)		Ministry of Agriculture	
	RA- 65725	(CX/SKh)		Ministry of Agriculture	
63720	RA- 65726		1981	Korsar	
	EY- 65730	A		Todjikistan – Khujent Air Det.	
1351401	EK- 65731	A	1971	Armenian Air Lines	
	ER- 65736	A		Air Moldova	
	RA- 65738		1972	Sib NII Research Institute	
	RA- 65739			(Industry Operated)	
2351510	RA- 65740	A	1972	LII – Gromov Flight Research Inst.	
	ER- 65741	A	1972	Air Moldova	
2351608	UR- 65746	A	1972	Air Ukraine – Kharkov Air Det.	
61042	4L- 65750	A	1979	Orbi (Georgia)	
	RA- 65751	A	1979	Perm	
61079	UR- 65752	A	1979	Air Ukraine – Kharkov Air Det.	
61099	RA- 65753	A	1979	Aerovolga	
62154	EW- 65754	A	1979	Belavia	
62165	RA- 65755	A	1979	Komiavia	
62179	RA- 65756	A	1979	Voronezh	
62215	UR- 65757	A	1979	Air Ukraine	
62230	RA- 65758	A	1979	Samara	
62239	RA- 65759	A	1979	(Industry operated)	
62187	RA- 65760		1979	Volare	

Factory No.	Registration	Model	Year Built	Operator
62244	UR- 65761	A	1979	Air Ukraine – Kharkov Air Det.
62279	RA- 65762	A	1979	Voronezh
62299	EY- 65763	A	1979	Todjikistan – Khujent Air Det.
62305	UR- 65764	A	1979	Air Ukraine – Kharkov Air Det.
62315	UR- 65765	A	1979	Air Ukraine
	UN- 65767		1979	Kazair
62415	RA- 65769	A	1979	ARIA
62430	RA- 65770	A	1979	ARIA
62445	RA- 65771	A	1979	Donavia
62472	EW- 65772	A	1979	Belavia
62495	UR- 65773	A	1979	Air Ukraine – Kharkov Air Det.
62519	4L- 65774	A	1979	Orbi (Georgia)
62530	RA- 65775	A	1979	Perm
62545	UN- 65776		1979	Kazair
62552	RA- 65777	A	1979	Komiavia
	EX- 65778	A	1979	Kirghizi
62602	EX- 65779	A	1979	Kirghizi
62622	RA- 65780	A	1979	Komiavia
62645	RA- 65781	A	1979	ARIA
62672	UR- 65782	A	1979	Air Ukraine
62708	RA- 65783	A	1979	ARIA
62715	RA- 65784	A	1979	ARIA
62750	RA- 65785	A	1979	ARIA
62775	RA- 65786	A	1979	Chelyabinsk (Lt Aviaprima)
	UN- 65787	A	1979	Kazair
62835	EY- 65788	A	1980	Todjikistan – Khujent Air Det.
62850	EX- 65789	A	1980	Kirghizi
63100	UR- 65790	A	1980	Air Ukraine
	ER- 65791	A	1980	Air Moldova
	RA- 65792	A	1980	Aerovolga
63128	RA- 65793	A	1980	Komiavia
	RA- 65794	A	1980	Voronezh
63150	RA- 65796	A	1980	Donavia
63193	RA- 65797	A	1980	Aerovolga
63179	4L- 65798	A	1980	Orbi (Georgia)
	RA- 65800	A	1973	Samara
3352010	RA- 65801	A	1973	Ulyanovsk VAU-GA
3352101	RA- 65802	A	1973	Tyumen Avialinii
3552103	EW- 65803	A	1973	Belavia
3352105	RA- 65805	A	1973	Komiavia
332109	4L- 65808	A	1973	Taifun (Georgia – Sukhumi)
	4L- 65809	A		Orbi (Georgia)
3352201	4L- 65810	A	1973	Orbi (Georgia)
4352202	RA- 65811	A	1974	AVL-Arkhangelsk
4352204	RA- 65813	A	1974	Komiavia
4352208	EY- 65814	A	1974	Todjikistan – Khugent Air Det.
4352209	RA- 65815	A	1974	North West CAD
4352301	4L- 65817	A	1974	Taifun (Georgia – Sukhumi)
4352304	RA- 65819	A	1974	AVL-Arkhangelsk
08056	EY- 65820	A	1974	Todjikistan – Khujent Air Det.
08060	EW- 65821	A	1974	Belavia
09071	EK- 65822	A	1974	Armenian Air Lines
	RA- 65823	A	1974	Nizhegorodskie (Yukos Titles)
09074	RA- 65824	A	1974	Kaliningrad
09078	RA- 65825	A	1974	Astrakhan
12083	UR- 65826	A	1974	Air Ukraine – Kharkov Air Det.
12084	RA- 65827	A	1974	AVL-Arkhangelsk WFU
	RA- 65828	A	1974	Astrakhan
	RA- 65829	A	1974	Nizhegorodskie
12093	RA- 65830	A	1974	(Industry operated)
17102	EK- 65831	A	1974	Armenian Air Lines
17106	EW- 65832	A	1974	Belavia
17109	RA- 65834	A	1974	Donavia
17112	EY- 65835	A	1974	Todjikistan – Khujent Air Det.
17114	RA- 65837	A	1974	North West CAD
18116	RA- 65838	A	1974	Tyumen Avialinii
18118	RA- 65840	A	1974	Komiavia
18120	UR- 65841	A	1974	Air Ukraine
	RA- 65842	A	1974	Perm
18123	RA- 65843	A	1974	BAL-Bashkiri
	RA- 65844	A	1974	KMV-Mineralnie Vody
23231	RA- 65845	A	1974	Kaliningrad
	RA- 65846	A	1974	AVL-Arkhangelsk
23135	RA- 65847	A	1974	Orenburg
23136	EK- 65848	A	1974	Armenian Air Lines
	EK- 65850	A	1974	Armenian Air Lines
23241	RA- 65851	A	1974	North West CAD
23244	UR- 65852	A	1974	Air Ukraine
	RA- 65853	A	1974	BAL-Bashkiri
23248	RA- 65854	A	1974	North West CAD
23252	RA- 65855	A	1974	Air Transport School
23255	4L- 65857	A	1975	Orbi (Georgia)

Factory No.	Registration	Model	Year Built	Operator
	65858		1975	Stigl (Chechnia)
23264	RA- 65859	A	1975	Tyumen Avialinii
28265	RA- 65860	A	1975	Orenburg
28269	EW- 65861	A	1975	Belavia
28270	RA- 65862	A	1975	North West CAD
28283	RA- 65863	A	1975	Don avia
28284	UR- 65864		1975	Air Ukraine – Kharkov Air Det.
28286	4L- 65665	A	1975	Orbi (Georgia)
28292	RA- 65866	A	1975	Komiavia
	RA- 65867	A	1975	Nizhegorodskie
28305	65868		1975	Stigl (Chechnia) → AZZA
28306	RA- 65869	A	1975	Perm
28310	RA- 65870	A	1975	Kaliningrad
29312	RA- 65872	A	1975	North West CAD
29317	EY- 65875	A	1975	Todjikistan – Khujent Air Det.
31220	EY- 65876	A	1975	Todjikistan – Khujent Air Det.
31250	UR- 65877	A	1975	Adjiran
31265	4L- 65879	A	1975	Taifun
	RA- 65880	A	1975	Voronezh
35220	RA- 65881	A	1975	Voronezh
36150	EK- 65884	A	1975	Armenian Air Lines
36160	RA- 65885	A	1975	North West CAD
36165	4L- 65886		1975	Taifun (Georgia – Sukhumi)
36170	RA- 65887	A	1975	KMV-Mineralnie Vody
36175	UR- 65888	A	1975	Air Ukraine – Kharkov Air Det.
38010	RA- 65889	A	1975	Aerovolga
38030	RA- 65891	A	1975	Komiavia
38050	EW- 65892	A	1975	Belavia
40130	RA- 65894	A	1975	North West CAD
40140	EY- 65895	A	1975	Todjikistan – Khujent Air Det.
	65896		1975	Stigl (Chechnia)
42210	ER- 65897	A	1975	Air Moldova
	RA- 65898	A	1975	AVL-Arkhangelsk
42225	RA- 65899	A	1975	Tyumen Avialinii
63684	UN- 65900	A	1981	Kazair
63731	RA- 65901	A	1981	Komiavia
63742	RA- 65902	A	1981	Komiavia
63780	RA- 65903	A	1981	Volga
63953	RA- 65904	A	1982	Rossiya
63965	RA- 65905	A	1982	Rossiya
66175	RA- 65906	A	1983	(Research Instit.)
63996	RA- 65907	A	1983	(Step) Lt Alrosa Avia
63870	RA- 65908	A	1983	Elf Air operated for VAP Group
63972	RA- 65911	A	1983	Rossiya
63985	RA- 65912	A	1983	Rossiya
66109	RA- 65914	A	1983	Rossiya
66120	RA- 65915	A	1983	Rossiya
66152	RA- 65916	A	1983	Rossiya (Occ. Lt ARIA)
63991	RA- 65917	CX/SKh	1983	ANTK Tupoleva
63995	RA- 65918	CX/SKh	1983	Voronezh
66168	RA- 65919	A	1983	Rossiya (Occ. Lt ARIA)
63997	RA- 65921	A	1983	Rossiya
9350806	RA- 65924		1969	Industry Operated (ex LOT SP-LGE)
66101	RA- 65926	A	1983	LII – Gromov Flt. Research Inst. (Lt Volare)
66198	RA- 65927	A	1984	LII – Gromov Flt. Research Inst.
	RA- 65928	A	1983	Ivanovo
	RA- 65929	CX/SKh	1983	Ministry of Agriculture
66500	RA- 65930	CX/SKh	1983	Ministry of Agriculture
66405	RA- 65932	A	1983	Rossiya – Research Institute Lt KMV Mineralne Vodi
	RA- 65933		1983	Industry Operated (ex LOT) SP-L
66143	RA- 65934		1983	Industry Operated
66180	RA- 65935		1983	Rossiya – Research Institute
2351702	RA- 65950	A	1972	Tyumen Avialinii
2351707	RA- 65954	A	1972	Komiavia
2351708	RA- 65955	A	1972	AVL-Arkhangelsk
2351709	RA- 65956	A	1972	Korsar
2351802	EW- 65957	A	1972	Belavia
3351804	RA- 65958	A	1973	Komiavia
3351805	4L- 65959	A	1973	Taifun
3351806	RA- 65960	A	1973	Tyumen Avialinii
3351807	RA- 65961	A	1973	BAL-Bashkiri
	RA- 65962	A	1973	VVS
3351803	RA- 65965		1973	
3351902	RA- 65966	A	1973	ANTK Tupoleva
3351905	RA- 65967	A	1973	North West CAD
3351909	RA- 65969	A	1973	Komiavia
	RA- 65970	A	1973	Nizhegorodskie
3352001	RA- 65971	A	1973	Komiavia
3352002	RA- 65972	A	1973	Komiavia
3352004	EW- 65974	A	1973	Belavia
3352005	EK- 65975	A	1973	Armenian Air Lines
3352007	RA- 65976	A	1973	AVL-Arkhangelsk

Factory No.	Registration	Model	Year Built	Operator
63245	RA- 65977	A	1980	Komiavia
	RA- 65978	A	1980	Rossiya
	RA- 65979	A	1980	VVS/223 Flt. Det.
	RA- 65980		1981	VVS
	RA- 65981		1981	VVS
	RA- 65982	A	1981	VVS/223 Flt. Det.
	RA- 65983	A	1981	VVS/223 Flt. Det.
	RA- 65984	A	1981	VVS/223 Flt. Det.
63468	4K- 65985	A	1981	Azerbaijan Government
	RA- 65986	A	1981	VVS/223 Flt. Det.
63505	RA- 65987	A	1981	VVS/223 Flt. Det.
63550	RA- 65988	A	1981	VVS/223 Flt. Det.
	RA- 65989	A	1981	VVS/223 Flt. Det.
	RA- 65990	A	1981	VVS/223 Flt. Det.
	RA- 65991	A	1981	VVS/223 Flt. Det.
	RA- 65992	A	1981	VVS/223 Flt. Det.
	RA- 65993	A	1981	VVS/223 Flt. Det.
	RA- 65994	A	1985	Rossiya
	RA- 65995	A	1985	Rossiya
	RA- 65996	A	1981	VVS/223 Flt. Det.
1351204	RA- 93926		1971	(Progress Airline) (ex-Aviogenex YU-AHY)
2351508	RA- 93927		1972	(Industry operated) (ex-Aviogenex YU-AJD)
1351206*	RA- 93928		1971	(Industry operated) (ex-Aviogenex YU-AJA)
49890	RA- 64451		1977	(Industry operated) (ex XU-102)
	RA- 64454	A		LII – Gromov Flt Research Inst.
	RA- 64740	A		LII – Gromov Flt Research Inst.
49830	D2- EEC	A	1977	Government of Angola
48395	ES- AAE	A	1976	Estonian Air (ex-65022)
48565	ES- AAF	A	1976	Estonian Air (ex-65034) → OM-GAT
				sold to RA 65068
35270	ES- AAH	A	1975	Estonian Air (ex-65882)
60350	ES- AAI	A	1978	Estonian Air (to RA-65112)
60977	ES- AAK	A	1979	Estonian Air (to RA-65144) Orient
62350	ES- AAL	A	1979	Estonian Air (to RA-65768) Orient
62380	ES- AAM	A	1978	Estonian Air (ex-65113)
60560	ES- AAN	A	1978	Estonian Air (ex-65124)
62239	ES- AAO	A	1979	Estonian Air (ex-65759) sold to RA-65759
38020	ES- AAP	A	1975	Estonian Air (ex-65890)
1351301	HA- LBI	A	1971	Malev
1351302	HA- LBK	A	1971	Malev
12096	HA- LBN	A	1974	[2501] Malev (ex-Hungarian Gov. HA-YSA)
17103	HA- LBO	A	1974	[2503] Malev (ex-Hungarian Gov. HA-YSB)
63560	HA- LBP	A	1980	[6101] Malev
63580	HA- LBR	A	1980	[6102] Malev
3352003	LY- ABA	A	1973	Lietuva (ex-65973)
48415	LY- ABB	A	1976	Lithuanian Airlines (ex-65023)
60054	LY- ABD	A	1977	Lithuanian Airlines (ex-65079)
60076	LY- ABE	A	1977	Lithuanian Airlines (ex-65081)
60172	LY- ABF	A	1977	Lithuanian Airlines (ex-65088)
60195	LY- ABG	A	1977	Lithuanian Airlines (ex-65091)
60308	LY- ABH	A	1978	Lithuanian Airlines (ex-65105) to RA-65105
60628	LY- ABI	A	1978	Lithuanian Airlines (ex-65128)
49858	LZ- TUG	A	1977	Balkan (ex-Czech Gov OK-BYT)
1351209	LZ- TUK	A	1971	Balkan
3352303	LZ- TUL	A	1973	Hemus Air (ex-Balkan)
3351906	LZ- TUM	A	1973	Balkan
4352307	LZ- TUN	A	1974	Hemus Air (ex-Balkan) L. to Alberia
1351303	LZ- TUP	A	1971	Balkan (ex-Bulgarian Air Force 050)
60642	LZ- TUS	A	1978	Hemus Air
	LZ- TUT	A	1984	Balkan
1351409	LZ- TUU	A	1971	Balkan (ex-Czech Gov OK-BYQ)
1251408	LZ- TUV	A	1971	Balkan (ex-Czech Gov OK-BYR)
1351503	LZ- TUZ	A	1971	Balkan (ex-Czech Gov OK-BYS)
1351203	OB- R1489	A	1971	Imperial Air (Peru) (ex-Aviogenex YU-AHX)
60525	OB- R1490	A	1978	Imperial Air (Peru) (ex-65123)
60206	OB- R1553	A	1977	Imperial Air (Peru) (ex-65092)
1351407	1407	A	1971	Czechian Air Force (ex-CSA OK-AFD)
23128	OK- EFJ	A	1974	[2607] CSA
23130	OK- EFK	A	1974	[2608] CSA
49913	OK- HFL	A	1977	[4105] CSA
60142	OK- HFM	A	1977	[4305] CSA
60282	OK- IFN	A	1978	[4409] CSA

* Uncomfirmed

Factory No.	Registration	Model	Year Built	Operator
2351801	OK-CFH	A	1972	Pres as GAR/BRNO
66215	P- 813	B	1983	[6354] Air Koryo
66368	P- 814	B	1983	[6363] Air Koryo
	102	A		Polish Air Force
	103	A		Polish Air Force
	104	A		Polish Air Force
3351808	SP- LHA	A	1973	LOT
3351809	SP- LHB	A	1973	LOT
3351810	SP- LHC	A	1973	LOT
48400	SP- LHD	A	1976	[3506] LOT
48405	SP- LHE	A	1976	[3507] LOT
3352005	SP- LHF	A	1973	LOT
3352008	SP- LHG	A	1973	LOT
61055	VN- A104	A	1979	Vietnam Airlines (formerly Hang Khong)
49752	VN- A106	A	1977	Vietnam Airlines
62144	VN- A110	A	1979	Vietnam Airlines
62458	VN- A112	A	1979	Vietnam Airlines
66220	VN- A114	A	1984	Vietnam Airlines
66230	VN- A116	A	1984	Vietnam Airlines
66250	VN- A118	A	1984	Vietnam Airlines
66360	VN- A120	A	1984	Vietnam Airlines
49900	VN- A122	A	1977	Vietnam Airlines (ex-Interflug DDR-SDK)
60108	VN- A124	A	1977	Vietnam Airlines (ex-Interflug DDR-SDL)
60612	VN- A128	A	1978	Vietnam Airlines (ex-Interflug DDR-SDN)
62259	VN- A130	A	1979	Vietnam Airlines (ex-Interflug DDR-SDO)
63260	VN- A132	A	1980	Vietnam Airlines (ex-Interflug DDR-SDP)
49890	XU- 101	A	1977	[4007] Kampuchea Airlines S. to RA- 65065
66550	XU- 102	A	1985	[6375] Kampuchea Airlines S. to RA- 64491
63992	YK- AYA	B	1982	[6330] Syrianair
63994	YK- AYB	B	1982	[6331] Syrianair
63989	YK- AYC	B	1982	[6327] Syrianair
63990	YK- AYD	B	1982	[6328] Syrianair
66187	YK- AYE	B	1983	[6348] Syrianair
66190	YK- AYF	B	1983	[6349] Syrianair
61000	YL- LBA		1978	Latavio (ex-65146)
63215	YL- LBB		1980	Lat Charter/Baltija Bank (ex-65692)
63221	YL- LBC		1980	Latavio (ex-65693)
63235	YL- LBD		1980	Latavio (ex-65694)
63285	YL- LBE		1980	Lat Charter (ex-65695) to RA-65695
63295	YL- LBF		1980	Lat Charter (ex-65696)
63333	YL- LBG		1980	Latavio (ex-65699)
63340	YL- LBH		1980	Lat Charter (ex-65700)
63365	YL- LBI		1980	Latavio (ex-65701)
63410	YL- LBJ		1980	Latavio (ex-65704)
63425	YL- LBK		1980	Baltic International (ex-65706)
63515	YL- LBL		1981	Latavio (ex-65712)
63536	YL- LBM		1981	Baltic International (ex-65715)
63187	YL- LBN		1979	Latavio (ex-65799)

Tu-134As, Mostly Converted to UBL Standard, for the VVS

Batch No./Modification No.		Role
6401	134	UBL
6402	134	UBL
6403	134	UBL
6404	134	A
6405	134	A
6406	134	UBL
6407	134	UBL
6408	134	UBL
6409	134	UBL
6410	134	UBL
6501	134	UBL
6502	Not in Programme	
6503	134	A
6504	134	A
6505	134	UBL
6506	134	UBL
6507	134	UBL
6508	134	UBL
6509	134	UBL
6510	134	UBL
6601	134	A
6602	134	A
6603	134	A
6604	134	A
6605	134	UBL
6606	134	A
6607	134	A
6608	134	A
6609	134	UBL
6610	134	A
6701	134	UBL
6702	134	A
6703	134	UBL
6704	134	A
6705	134	A
6706	134	A
6707	134	UBL
6708	134	A
6709	134	A
6710	134	UBL
6801	134	A
6802	134	A
6803	134	A
6804	134	A
6805	134	A
6806	134	A
6807	134	UBL
6808	134	A
6809	134	A
6810	134	UBL
6901	134	A
6902	134	A
6903	134	A
6904	134	UBL
6905	134	A
6906	134	UBL
6907	134	A
6908	134	A
6909	134	A
6910	134	A
7001	134	A
7002	134	A
7003	134	UBL
7004	134	A
7005	134	UBL
7006	134	UBL
7007	134	UBL
7008	134	UBL
7009	134	UBL
7010	134	UBL
7101	134	UBL
7102	134	UBL
7103	134	UBL
7104	134	UBL
7105	134	UBL
7106	134	UBL
7107	134	UBL
7108	134	UBL

Total – 77 aircraft

The Tu-134As in this list are likely to be also included in the RA- section of this list.

Early Tu-134s Modified to Military Trainer Roles for the VVS

Batch No./Modification No.		Role
0001	134	Sh
0002	134	Sh
0101	134	Sh
0102	134	Sh
0103	134	Sh
0104	134	Sh
0105	134	Sh
0201	134	Sh
0202	134	Sh
0202	Not current	
0203	134	
0204	134	UBL
0205	134	Sh
0206	134	Sh
0207	134	Sh
0208	134	UBL
0301	134	Sh
0302	134	Sh
0303	134	UBL
0304	134	Sh
0305	134	Sh
0401	134	Sh
0402	134	Sh
0403	134	Sh
0404	134	Sh
0405	134	Sh
0501	134	Sh
0502	134	Sh
0503	134	Sh
0504	134	Sh
0505	134	Sh
0601	134	Sh
0602	134	Sh
0603	134	UBL
0604	134	UBL
0605	134	UBL
0701	134	UBL
0702	134	Sh
0703	134	Sh
0704	134	UBL
0705	134	Sh
0801	134	Sh
0802	134	Sh
0803	134	Sh
0804	134	Sh
0805	134	
0901	134	Sh
0902	134	
0903	134	Sh
0904	134	Sh
0905	134	Sh
1001	134	Sh
1002	134	Sh
1003	134	Sh
1004	134	Sh
1005	134	Sh
1101	134	Sh
1102	134	Sh
1103	134	Sh
1104	134	Sh
1105	134	UBL
1201	134	UBL
1202	134	Sh
1203	134	Sh
1204	134	Sh
1205	134	UBL
1301	134	Sh
1302	134	Sh
1303	134	Sh
1304	134	Sh
1305	134	Sh
1401	134	Sh
1402	134	UBL
1403	134	Sh
1404	134	Sh
1405	134	Sh
1501	134	Sh
1502	134	Sh
1503	134	Sh
1504	134	Sh
1505	134	Sh
1601	134	Sh
1602	134	Sh
1603	134	Sh
1604	134	Sh
1605	134	Sh
1701	134	UBL
1702	134	Sh
1703	134	Sh
1704	134	Sh
1705	134	UBL
1801	134	UBL
1802	134	UBL

Three aircraft role unconfirmed

Sh = Navigator trainer

UBL = ##

Tu-154

* = Enemy Action

Factory No.	Registration	Current Model	Operator	If W/O Year/Place
	85000		(Prototype)	(WFU)
001	85001			(WFU)
002	85002			(WFU)
003	85003			(WFU)
004	85004		Tech Test Aircraft	
005	85005		On Display – Moscow VDNK	(WFU)
006	85006		SVO Tech Training	
007	RA-85007		Vnukovo	(WFU)
008	85008			(WFU)
009	85009		Kiev Technical Training	(WFU)
010	85010		Egorevsk Tech Training	(WFU)
011	85011		Egorevsk Tech Training	(WFU)
012	85012			(WFU)
013	RA-85013	B	Ulyanovsk VAU-GA	
014	85014			(WFU)
015	85015			(WFU)
016	RA-85016	B	Ulyanovsk VAU-GA	
017	85017			(WFU)
018	RA-85018	B	Tatarstan Airways	
019	RA-85019	C	DAK – Far Eastern	
020	85020		Kiev Technical Training	(WFU)
021	EX-85021		Kirghizi	
022	85022			(WFU)
023	SSSR-85023			1973 Prague (W/O)
024	85024	B	LII-Gromov	
025	RA-85025	B	Ulyanovsk VAU-GA	
026	LZ-BTA		Balkan Bulgarian	
027	LZ-BTB		Balkan Bulgarian	1978 Damascus (W/O)
028	RA-85028	B	Vnukovo	
029	SSSR-85029			1981 Bratsk (W/O)
030	SSSR-85030			1973 Moscow (W/O)
031	RA-85031	B	DAK – Far Eastern	
032	85032		–	(WFU)
033	RA-85033	B	Vnukovo	
034	RA-85034	B	Samara – Aerovolga	
035	SSSR-85035	Tu-155	Converted to Tu-155 – ANTK Tupolev	
036	LZ-BTC	B	Balkan Bulgarian	
037	RA-85037	C	DAK – Far Eastern	
038	RA-85038	B	Baikalavia	
039	RA-85039	B	Vnukovo	
040	85040			(WFU)
041	RA-85041	B	Chita	
042	RA-85042	B	Samara – Aerovolga	
043	RA-85403	B	DAK – Far Eastern	
044	ER-85044		Air Moldova	
045	HA-LCA	B	Malev	
046	HA-LCB	B	Malev	(WFU)
047	HA-LCE	B	Malev	
048	SU-AXB		Egypt Air	1974 Cairo (W/O)
049	RA-85049		VVS – Air Force	(ex-SU-AXC Egypt Air)
050	RA-85050		VVS – Air Force	(ex-SU-AXD Egypt Air)
051	RA-85051		(WFU)	(ex-SU-AXE Egypt Air)

Factory No.	Registration	Current Model	Operator	If W/O Year/Place
052	RA- 85052		VVS – Air Force	(ex-SU-AXF Egypt Air)
053	SSSR- 85053/HA-LCI			(ex-SU-AXG Egypt Air) 1975 Beirut* (W/O)
054	LZ-BTN		Balkan Bulgarian	(ex-SU-AXH Egypt Air)
055	SSSR- 85055		LII-Gromov	(ex-SU-AXI Egypt Air)
056	RA- 85056		Bashkir	
057	RA- 85057		Vnukovo	
058	LZ-BTD	B	Balkan Bulgarian	
059	EW- 85059	B	Belavia	
060	RA- 85060	C	Far Eastern	
061	RA- 85061	B	Ulyanovsk VAU-GA	
062	RA- 85062	C	ARIA	
063	RA- 85063	C	ARIA	
064	RA- 85064	B	Omskavia	
065	85065	A		(WFU)
066	UN- 85066	B	Kazair	
067	SSSR- 85067	C		1989 Liberia (W/O)
068	UR- 85068	B	Air Ukraine	
069	RA- 85069	B	Far Eastern	
070	RA- 85070	B	Sibavia	
071	85071	A		(WFU)
072	85072	A		(WFU)
073	LZ-BTE	B	Balkan Bulgarian	
074	RA- 85074	B	Omskavia	
075	RA- 85075	B	Omskavia	
076	UN- 85076	B	Kazair	
077	LZ-BTF	B	Balkan Bulgarian	
078	RA- 85078	B	Ulyanovsk VAU-GA	
079	85079	A		(WFU)
080	RA- 85080	A	Nizhne Novgorod	
081	RA- 85081	C	ARIA	
082	85082	A		(WFU)
083	RA- 85083	A	LII-Gromov	
084	RA- 85084	C	Vnukovo	
085	85085	A		(WFU)
086	85086	A		(WFU)
087	85087	A		(WFU)
088	85088	A		(WFU)
089	RA- 85089	B	Samara – Aerovolga	
090	ER- 85090	A	Air Moldova	
091	RA- 85091	B	Ulyanovsk VAU-GA	
092	85092	B	Ulyanovsk VAU-GA	
093	UR- 85093	B	Air Ukraine	
094	RA- 85094	A	Barnaul	
095	LZ- 8TG	B	Balkan Bulgarian	
096	RA- 85096	B	North Western	
097	SSSR- 85097	B		1991 St Petersburg (W/O)
098	RA- 85098	B	Chelyabinsk	Lt Aviaprima
099	RA- 85099	B	Vnukovo	
100	85100	A		(WFU)
101	RA- 85101	B	North Western	
102	SSSR- 85102	A		1976 Eq. Guinea (W/O)
103	SSSR- 85103	A		1980 Orenburg (W/O)
104	RA- 85104	A	Uralskoe	
105	85105	A	Armenian Airlines	
106	RA- 85106	B	Sibavia	
107	RA- 85107	B	North Western	
108	RA- 85108	B	LII-Gromov	
109	85109	B		(WFU)
110	RA- 85110	B	Sibavia	
111	UN- 85111	B	Kazair	
112	RA- 85112	B	BAL-Bashkiri	
113	UN- 85113	B	Kazair	
114	RA- 85114	A	Chelyabinsk	Lt Aviaprima
115	RA- 85115	B	Tomsk	
116	UR- 85116	A	Air Ukraine	
117	RA- 85117	B	Barnaul	
118	UR- 85118	B	Air Ukraine	
119	RA- 85119	B	Volare	
120	85120	B		(WFU)
121	85121	B		(WFU)
122	SSSR- 85122	B	Chizovka Tech Instit.	
123	RA- 85123	B	Baikalavia	
124	RA- 85124	B	Krasnoyarskavia	
125	85125	B		(WFU)
126	HA- LCF	B	Malev	
127	HA- LCG	B	Malev	
128	HA- LCH	B	Malev	
129	P- 551	B	Air Koryo	
130	RA- 85130	B	Far Eastern	
131	4L- 85131	B	Orbi	
132	UR- 85132	B	Air Ukraine	
133	YL- LAA	B	Latavio	(ex-SSSR-85183)
134	SSSR- 85134	B	Krasnoyarskavia	(WFU)
135	RA- 85135	B	Kemerovo	
136	RA- 85136	B	Sibavia	
137	UR- 85137	B	Air Ukraine	
138	4K- 85138	B	AHY – Azerbaijan	
139	RA- 85139	B	North Western	
140	RA- 85140	B	Vnukovo	
141	RA- 85141	B	Uralskoe	
142	RA- 85142	B	Uralskoe	
143	P- 552	B	Air Koryo	
144	LZ- BTK	B	Balkan Bulgarian	
145	RA- 85145	B	Baikalavia	
146	RA- 85146	B	Baikalavia	
147	4K- 85147	B	AHY – Azerbaijan	
148	UR- 85148	B	Air Ukraine	
149	RA- 85149	B	Ulyanovsk Avia Predpriatie	
150	RA- 85150	B	Samara – Aerovolga	
151	UN- 85151	B	Kazair	
152	UR- 85152	B	Air Ukraine	
153	RA- 85153	B	North Western	
154	UR- 85154	B	Air Ukraine	
155	RA- 85155	B	Samara – Aerovolga	
156	RA- 85156	B	Vnukovo	
157	RA- 85157	B	DAK – Far Eastern	
158	4K- 85158	B	AHY – Azerbaijan	
159	YR- TPA	B	Tarom	
160	RA- 85160	B	Abakan Avia	
161	YR- TPB	B	Tarom	
162	EK- 85162	B	Armenian Airlines	
163	GA- 85163	B		1993 Sukhumi* (W/O)
164	RA- 85164	B	DAK – Far Eastern	near Khabarovsk 1995 (W/O)
165	RA- 85165	B	Krasnoyarskavia	
166	EK- 85166	B	Armenian Airlines	
167	RA- 85167	B	Chita	
168	4L -85168	B	Orbi	
169	SSSR- 85169	B		1978 Smolensk (W/O)
170	4L- 85170	B	Orbi	
171	RA- 85171	B	Chelyabinsk	
172	RA- 85172	B	Baikalavia	
173	UN- 85173	B	Kazair	
174	RA- 85174	B	Abakan Avia	
175	YR- TPC	B	Tarom	
176	RA- 85176	B	DAK – Far Eastern	
177	4K- 85177	B	AHY – Azerbaijan	
178	RA- 85178	B	DAK – Far Eastern	
179	UR- 85179	B	Air Ukraine	
180	RA- 85180	B	Chelyabinsk	Lt Aviaprima
181	RA- 85181	B	Krasnoyarskavia	
182	RA- 85182	B	Vnukovo	
183	RA- 85183	B	Chelyabinsk	Lt Aviaprima
184	RA- 85184	B	Krasnoyarskavia	
185	RA- 85185	B	DAK – Far Eastern	
186	4L- 85186	B	Orbi	
187	RA- 85187	B	DAK – Far Eastern	
188	4L- 85188	B	Orbi	
189	UK- 85189	B	Uzbekistan Airways	
190	RA- 85190	B	DAK – Far Eastern	
191	P- 553	B	Air Koryo	
192	4K- 85192	B	AHY – Azerbaijan	
193	RA- 85193	B	Uralskoe	
194	UN- 85194	B	Kazair	
195	RA- 85195	B	Abakan Avia	
196	EK- 85196	B	Armenian Airlines	
197	4L- 85197	B	Orbi	
198	4L- 85198	B	Orbi	
199	4L- 85199	B	AHY – Azerbaijan	
200	EK- 85200	B	Armenian Airlines	
201	RA- 85201	B	Krasnoyarskavia	
202	RA- 85202	B	Krasnoyarskavia	
203	4L- 85203	B	Orbi	
204	RA- 85204	B	Baikalavia	
205	RA- 85205	B	DAK – Far Eastern	
206	RA- 85206	B	DAK – Far Eastern	
207	RA- 85207	B	DAK – Far Eastern	
208	LZ- BTL	B	Balkan Bulgarian	
209	LZ- BTM	B	Balkan Bulgarian	
210	EK- 85210	B	Armenian Airlines	
211	4K- 85211	B	AHY – Azerbaijan	
212	RA- 85212	B	Uralskoe	

Factory No.	Registration	Current Model	Operator	If W/O Year/Place
213	RA- 85213	B	Krasnoyarskavia	
214	4K- 85214	B	AHY – Azerbaijan	
215	RA- 85215	B	Vnukovo	
216	RA- 85216	B	DAK – Far Eastern	
217	RA- 85217	B	Almazi Sakha	
218	UR- 85218	B	Air Ukraine	
219	RA- 85219	B	Uralskoe	
220	RA- 85220	B	DAK – Far Eastern	
221	UN- 85221	A	Kazair	
222	SSSR- 85222	B		1992 Tbilisi (W/O)
223	RA- 85223	B	Abakan Avia	
224	YR- TPD	B	Tarom	
225	YR- TPE	B	Tarom	
226	RA- 85226	B	KMV- Mineralnie Vody	
227	85227	B		(WFU)
228	RA- 85228	B	Nizhne Novgorod	
229	RA- 85229	B	North Western	
230	UN- 85230	B	Kazair	
231	UN- 85231	B	Kazair	
232	UR- 85232	B	Air Ukraine	
233	RA- 85233	B	Samara – Aerovolga	
234	RA- 85234	B	Aerovolga	
235	RA- 85235	B	Barnaul	
236	RA- 85236	B	North Western	
237	RA- 85237	B	Nizhne Novgorod	
238	RA- 85238	B	North Western	
239	YT- TPF	B	Tarom	
240	UN- 85240	B	Kazair	
241	EZ- 85241	B	Turkmenistan	
242	RA- 85242	B	North Western	
243	SSSR- 85243	B		1984 Omsk (W/O)
244	UR- 85244	B	Air Ukraine	
245	UK- 82545	B	Uzbekistan Airways	
246	EZ- 85246	B	Turkmenistan	
247	EY- 85247	B	Todjikistan	
248	UK- 85248	B	Uzbekistan Airways	
249	UK- 85249	B	Uzbekistan Airways	
250	EZ- 85250	B	Turkmenistan	
251	EY- 85251	B	Todjikistan	
252	EX- 85252	B	Kirghizi	
253	RA- 85253	B	Nizhne Novgorod	
254	SSSR- 85254	B		1988 Krasnovodsk (W/O)
255	RA- 85255	B	Tyumenaviatrans	
256	RA- 85256	B	Aerokuznetsk	
257	EX- 85247	B	Kirghizi	
258	LZ- BTO	B	Balkan Bulgarian	
259	EX- 85259	B	Kirghizi (Osh Air Detachment)	
260	EW- 85260	B	Belavia	
261	RA- 85261	B	Sibavia	
262	YR- TPG	B	Tarom	
263	RA- 85263	B	Nizhne Novgorod	
264	RA- 85264	B	Samara – Aerovolga	
265	RA- 85265	B	BAL-Bashkiri	
266	RA- 85266	B	DAK – Far Eastern	
267	RA- 85267	B	Orenburg	
268	SSSR- 85268	B		1990 Kutayissi (W/O)
269	UR- 85269	B	Air Ukraine	
270	LZ- BTK	B	Balkan Bulgarian	
271	UN- 85271	B	Kazair	
272	UK- 85272	B	Uzbekistan Airways	
273	RA- 85273	B	Omskavia	
274	4K- 85274	B	AHY – Azerbaijan	
275	RA- 85275	B	BAL- Bashkiri	
276	UN- 85276	B	Kazair	
277	YR- TPH	B	Tarom	
278	LZ- BTP	B	Balkan Bulgarian	
279	EK- 85279	B	Armenian Airlines	
280	RA- 85280	B	Chita	
281	EY- 85281	B	Todjikistan	
282	RA- 85282	B	Uralskoe	
283	RA- 85283	B	BAL-Bashkiri	
284	RA- 85284	B	Uralskoe	
285	ER- 85285	B	Air Moldova	
286	UK- 85286	B	Uzbekistan Airways	
287	RA- 85287	B	Nizhne Novgorod	
288	UR- 85288	B	Air Ukraine	
289	RA- 85289	B	Aerokuznetsk	
290	UN- 85290	B	Kazair – Karaganda Air Detach	
291	RA- 85291	B	Omskavia	
292	RA- 85292	B	Sibavia	
293	RA- 85293	B	North Western	
294	EX- 85294	B	Kirghizi	
295	RA- 85295	B	Donavia	
296	RA- 85296	B		(W/0) Chechnia 1993
297	RA- 85297	B	Vnukovo	
298	RA- 85298	B	North Western	
299	RA- 85299	B	Vnukovo	
300	RA- 85300	B	North Western	
301	RA- 85301	B	Vnukovo	
302	RA- 85302	B	AVL-Arkhangelski	
303	RA- 85303	B	KMV- Mineralnie Vody	
304	RA- 85304	B	Vnukovo	
305	RA- 85305	B	Donavia	
306	RA- 85306	B	Donavia	
307	RA- 85307	B	KMV- Mineralnie Vody	
308	RA- 85308	B	Donavia	
309	RA- 85309	B	KMV- Mineralnie Vody	
310	RA- 85310	B	Uralskoe	
311	SSSR- 85311	B		1985 Uch Kuduk (W/O)
312	RA- 85312	B	Tyumenaviatrans	
313	EX- 85313	B	Kirghizi	
314	RA- 85314	B	Tyumenaviatrans	
315	RA- 85315	B	Ulyanovsk VAU-GA	
316	UR- 85316	B	Lubansk Air Det	
317	RA- 85317	M	ANTK Tupolev	
318	RA- 85318	B	Nizhne Novgorod	
319	RA- 85319	B	Uralskoe	
320	RA- 85742	B	Amur Avia	(ex-SSSR-85320; LZ-BTR)
321	SSSR- 85321	B		1980 Chita (W/O)
322	UK- 85322	B	Uzbekistan Airways	
323	RA- 85323	B	Almazi Sakha	
324	ER- 85324	B	Air Moldova	
325	HA- LCM	B	Malev	
326	HA- LCN	B	Malev	
327	SSSR- 85327	B	SVO Tech Training	1986 DBR
328	RA-85328	B	Uralskoe	
329	4K- 85329	B	AHY – Azerbaijan	
330	RA- 85330	B	KMV- Mineralnie Vody	
331	EW- 85331	B	Belavia	
332	ER- 85332	B	Air Moldova	
333	RA- 85333	B	Poliot Chernobyl	
334	UR- 85334	B	Air Ukraine	
335	RA- 85335	B	Tyumenaviatrans	
336	RA- 85336	B	Uralskoe	
337	RA- 85337	B	Uralskoe	
338	SSSR- 85338	B		1984 Krasnoyarsk (W/O)
339	EW- 85339	B	Belavia	
340	RA- 85340	B	KMV- Mineralnie Vody	
341	RA- 85341	B	DAK – Far Eastern	
342	YR- TPI	B	Tarom	
343	RA- 85343	B	North Western	
344	UK- 85344	B	Uzbekistan Airways	
345	EZ- 85345	B	Turkmenistan	
346	RA- 85346	B	North Western	
347	RA- 85347	B	BAL- Bashkiri	
348	RA- 85348	B	Yakutaviatrans	
349	RA- 85349	B	BAL-Bashkiri	
350	UR- 85350	B	Air Ukraine	
351	RA- 85351	B	Aerokuznetsk	
352	EW- 85352	B	Belavia	
353	RA- 85353	B	VVS – Air Force	
354	RA- 85354	B	Yakutaviatrans	
355	SSSR- 85355	B		1980 Alma Ata (W/O)
356	UK- 85356	B	Uzbekistan Airways	
357	RA- 85357	B	Uralskoe	
358	RA- 85358	B	Omskavia	
359	4L- 85359	B	Orbi	
360	RA- 85360	B	VVS – Air Force	
361	RA- 85361	B	Tyumenaviatrans	
362	UR- 85362	B	Lubansk Air Det.	
363	RA- 85363	B	ARIA	
364	4K- 85364	B	AHY – Azerbaijan	
365	RA- 85365	B	AVL- Arkhangelsk	
366	RA- 85366	B	Tyumenaviatrans	
367	RA- 85367	B	Almazi Sakha	
368	UR- 85368	B	Air Ukraine	
369	EX- 85369	B	Kirghizi	
370	UK- 85370	B	Uzbekistan Airways	
371	RA- 85371	B	KMV- Mineralnie Vody	
372	FW- 85372	B	Belavia	
373	RA- 85373	B	KMV- Mineralnie Vody	

Factory No.	Registration	Current Model	Operator	If W/O Year/Place
374	RA- 85374	B	Uralskoe	
375	RA- 85375	B	Uralskoe	
376	RA- 85376	B	Yakutaviatrans	
377	RA- 85377	B	North Western	
378	RA- 85378	B	Tyumenaviatrans	
379	UR- 85379	B	Air Ukraine	
380	RA- 85380	B	VVS – Air Force	
381	RA- 85381	B	North Western	
382	RA- 85382	B	KMV- Mineralnie Vody	
383	EZ- 85383	B	Turkmenistan	
384	ER- 85384	B	Air Moldova	
385	EY- 85385	B	Todjikistan	
386	RA- 85386	B	AVL-Arkhangelsk	
387	UN- 85387	B	Kazair	
388	RA- 85388	B	Ulyanovsk VAU-GA	
389	RA- 85389	B	Kemerovo	
390	RA- 85390	B	North Western	
391	4K- 85391	B	AHY – Azerbaijan	
392	RA- 85392	B	Aerokutznetsk	
393	RA- 85393	B	KMV- Mineralnie Vody	
394	EZ- 85394	B	Turkmenistan	
395	UR- 85395	B	Lubansk Air Det.	
396	UN- 85396	B	Kazair	
397	UK- 85397	B	Uzbekistan Airways	
398	UK- 85398	B	Uzbekistan Airways	
399	UR- 85399	B	Air Ukraine	
400	RA- 85400	B	Donavia	
401	UK- 85401	B	Uzbekistan Airways	
402	RA- 85402	B	Barnaul	
403	EK- 85403	B	Armenian Airlines	
404	RA- 85404	B	Bashkir	
405	ER- 85405	B	Air Moldova	
406	EY- 85406	B	Todjikistan	
407	UR- 85407	B	Air Ukraine	
408	YR- TPJ	B	Tarom	1989 Romania (W/O)
409	RA- 85409	B	Donavia	
410	EZ- 85410	B	Turkmenistan	
411	EW- 85411	B	Belavia	
412	RA- 85412	B	Tatarstan Airways	
413	SSSR- 85413	B		1980 Pushkino* (W/O)
414	RA- 85414	B	Donavia	
415	YR- TPK	B	Tarom	
416	UK- 85416	B	Uzbekistan Airways	
417	RA- 85417	B	Krasnoyarskavia	
418	RA- 85418	B	Krasnoyarskavia	
419	EW- 85419	B	Belavia	
420	OK- BYA	B	Czechia Gov.	
421	RA- 85421	B	Tomsk	
422	LZ- BTS	B	Balkan Bulgarian	
423	UK- 85423	B	Uzbekistan Airways	
424	UR- 85424	B	Air Ukraine	
425	RA- 85425	B	Donavia	
426	RA- 85426	B	VVS – Air Force	
427	RA- 85427	B	Tyumenaviatrans	
428	YR- TPL	B	Tarom	
429	RA- 85429	B	Bratskoe	
430	4L- 85430	B	Orbi Georgia	
431	UN- 85431	B	Kazair	
432	RA- 85432	B	Uralskoe	
433	UK- 85433	B	Uzbekistan Airways	
434	RA- 85434	B	Tyumenaviatrans	
435	RA- 85435	B	Donavia	
436	RA- 85436	B	Donavia	
437	RA- 85437	B	Donavia	
438	UK- 85438	B	Uzbekistan Airways	
439	RA- 85439	B	Uralskoe	
440	EY- 85440	B	Todjikistan	
441	RA- 85441	B	North Western	
442	EK- 85442	B	Armenian Airlines	
443	RA- 85443	B	DAK – Far Eastern	
444	EX- 85444	B	Kirghizi	
445	RA- 85445	B	VVS – Air Force	
446	RA- 85446	B	VVS – Air Force	
447	CU- T1222	B	Cubana	
448	85448	B		(WFU)
449	UK- 85449	B	Uzbekistan Airways	
450	RA- 85450	B	Tyumenaviatrans	
451	RA- 85451	B	Tyumenaviatrans	
452	RA- 85452	B	Donavia	
453	RA- 85453	B	Baikalavia	
454	RA- 85454	B	Donavia	
455	UN- 85455	B	Kazair – Karaganda Air Detach.	
456	RA- 85456	B	Nizhne Novgorod	
457	RA- 85457	B	KMV- Mineralnie Vody	
458	RA- 85458	B	Nizhne Novgorod	
459	RA- 85459	B	Uralskoe	
460	UR- 85460	B	Air Ukraine	
461	RA- 85461	B	Sibavia	
462	RA- 85462	B	Baikalavia	
463	RA- 85463	B	VVS – Air Force	
464	UN- 85464	B	Kazair	
465	EW- 85465	B	Belavia	
466	EY- 85466	B	Todjikistan Air	
467	RA- 85467	B	Chelyabinsk	Lt Aviaprima
468	RA- 85468	B	AVL- Arkhangelsk	
469	EY- 85469	B	Todjikistan	
470	RA- 85470	B	Ulyanovsk VAU-GA	
471	RA- 85471	B	Aerokuznetsk	
472	RA- 85472	B	Samara – Aerovolga	
473	HA- LCO	B	Malev	
474	HA- LCP	B	Malev	
475	EY- 85475	B	Todjikistan	
476	UR- 85476	B	Air Ukraine	
477	RA- 85477	B	DAK – Far Eastern	
478	UN- 85478	B	Kazair – Karaganda Air Det.	
479	SSSR- 85479	B		1988 Syria (W/O)
480	SSSR- 85480	B		1981 Norilsk (W/O)
481	RA- 85481	B	Tyumenaviatrans	
482	UR- 85482	B	Air Ukraine	
483	LZ- BTT	B	Balkan Bulgarian	
484	LZ- BTU	B	Balkan Bulgarian	
485	RA- 85485	B	Tomsk	
486	RA- 85486	B	Almazi Sakha	
487	EY- 85487	B	Todjikistan	
488	RA- 85488	B	Tatarstan Airways	(ex-OK-LCP Czechia Gov)
489	RA- 85489	B	Krasnoyarskavia	
490	UR- 85490	B	Air Ukraine	
491	EX- 85491	B	Kirghizi	
492	EZ- 85492	B	Turkmenistan	
493	CU- T1224	B	Cubana	
494	RA- 85494	B	KMV- Mineralnie Vody	
495	RA- 85495	B	Donavia	
496	4L- 85496	B	Orbi	
497	EX- 85497	B	Kirghizi	
498	RA- 85498	B	Tyumenaviatrans	
499	UR- 85499	B	Air Ukraine	
500	RA- 85500	B	Samara – Aerovolga	
501	70- ACN	B	Alyemda	1986 Aden* (W/O)
502	RA- 85502	B	Tyumenaviatrans	
503	RA- 85503	B	Baikalavia	
504	RA- 85504	B	Kemerovo	
505	RA- 85505	B	Krasnoyarskavia	
506	RA- 85506	B	Chita	
507	EZ- 85507	B	Turkmenistan	
508	RA- 85508	B	Uralskoe	
509	EW- 85509	B	Belavia	
510	RA- 85510	B	VVS – Air Force	
511	EY- 85511	B	Todjikistan	
512	RA- 85512	B	Baikalavia	
513	UR- 85513	B	Air Ukraine	
514	RA- 85514	B	Chelyabinsk	
515	YL- LAB	B	Latavio	(ex-SSSR-85515)
516	YL- LAC	B	Latavio	(ex-SSSR-85516)
517	RA- 85804	B	Tatarstan Airways	(ex-OK-LCS Czechia Gov.)
518	4L- 85518	B	Orbi	
519	EX- 85519	B	Kirghizi	
520	RA- 85520	B	Yakutaviatrans	
521	UN- 85521	B	Kazair – Karaganda Air Det.	
522	RA- 85522	B	Tyumenaviatrans	
523	RA- 85523	B	ANTK Tupolev	
524	YL- LAG	B	Latavio	(ex-SSSR-85524)
525	RA- 85525	B	BAL- Bashkiri	
526	UR- 85526	B	Air Ukraine	
527	RA- 85527	B	Donavia	
528	EW- 85528	B		1992 Vladivostok DBR
529	RA- 85529	B	Krasnoyarskavia	
530	RA- 85530	B	North Western	
531	HA- LCU	B	Malev	(ex-SSSR-85531)
532	EZ- 85532	B	Turkmenistan	
533	UK- 85533	B		1993 Delhi (W/O)
534	RA- 85534	B	VVS – Air Force	
535	UR- 85535	B	Air Ukraine	

Factory No.	Registration	Current Model	Operator	If W/O Year/Place
536	EK- 85536	B	Armenian Airlines	
537	UN- 85537	B	Kazair – Karaganda Air Det.	
538	EW- 85538	B	Belavia	
539	YL- LAF	B	Latavio	(ex-SSSR-85539)
540	RA- 85540	B	MAK – Magadan	
541	CU- T1227	B		1991 Mexico (W/O)
542	RA- 85542	B	North Western	
543	HA- LCR	B	Malev	
544	HA- LCV	B	Malev	
545	EW- 85545	B	Belavia	
546	YL- LAE	B	Latavio	(ex-SSSR-85546)
547	4L- 85547	B	Orbi	
548	4K- 85548	B	AHY – Azerbaijan	
549	EZ- 85549	B	Turkmenistan	
550	RA- 85550	B	Tyumenaviatrans	
551	RA- 85551	B	AVL- Arkhangelsk	
552	RA- 85552	B	North Western	
553	RA- 85553	B	North Western	
554	RA- 85554	B	VVS – Air Force	
555	RA- 85555	B	VVS – Air Force	
556	YL- LAD	B	Latavio	(ex-SSSR-85556)
557	RA- 85557	B	MAK – Magadan	
558	YL- LAH	B	Latavio	(ex-SSSR-85558)
559	RA- 85559	B	VVS – Air Force	
560	EK- 85560	B	Turkmenistan	
561	RA- 85561	B	VVS – Air Force	
562	RA- 85562	B	MAK – Magadan	
563	RA- 85563	B	VVS – Air Force	
564	RA- 85564	B	ARIA	
565	ER- 85565	B	Air Moldova	
566	EK- 85566	B	Armenian Airlines	
567	RA- 85567	B	MAK – Magadan	
568	RA- 85568	B	Yakutaviatrans	
569	LZ- BTV	B	Balkan Bulgarian	
570	RA- 85570	B	ARIA	
571	RA- 85571	B	VVS – Air Force	
572	RA- 85572	B	VVS – Air Force	
573	P- 561	B	Air Koryo	
574	RA- 85574	B	VVS – Air Force	
575	UK- 85575	B	Uzbekistan Airways	
576	CU- T1253	B	Cubana	
577	RA- 85577	B	Yakutaviatrans	
578	UK- 85578	B	Uzbekistan Airways	
579	RA- 85579	B	North Western	
580	EW- 85580	B	Belavia	
581	EW- 85581	B	Belavia	
582	EW- 85582	B	Belavia	
583	EW- 85583	B	Belavia	
584	RA- 85584	B	MAK – Magadan	
585	RA- 85585	B	Samara – Aerovolga	
586	RA- 85586	B	VVS – Air Force	
587	RA- 85587	B	VVS – Air Force	
588	RA- 85588	B	Magadan	
589	UN- 85589	B	Kazair – Karaganda Air Det.	
590	EX- 85590	B	Kirghizi (OSH Air Detachment)	
591	EW- 85591	B	Belavia	
592	RA- 85592	B	ARIA	
593	EW- 85593	B	Belavia	
594	RA- 85594	B	VVS – Air Force	
595	RA- 85595	B	Samara – Aerovolga	
596	RA- 85596	B	MAK – Magadan	
597	RA- 85597	B	Yakutaviatrans	
598	SSSR- 85598	B		Stored Addis Ababa
599	CU- T1256	B	Cubana	
600	UK- 85600	B	Uzbekistan Gov.	
601	'0601'	B	Czech Air Force (ex-OK-BYD)	
602	RA- 85602	B	Orenburg	
603	RA- 85603	B	Orenburg	
604	RA- 85604	B	Orenburg	
605	RA- 85605	B	VVS – Air Force	
701	RA- 85606	M	LII – Gromov (converted Tu-154B)	
702	RA- 85607	M	LII – Gromov	
703	SSSR- 85608	M	'Industrial Test Airframe'	(WFU)
704	RA- 85609	M	Ulyanovsk VAU-GA	
705	RA- 85610	M	Vnukovo	
706	LZ- BTI	M	Balkan Bulgarian	
707	LZ- BTW	M	Balkan Bulgarian	
708	YK- AIA	M	Syrianair	
709	YK- AIB	M	Syrianair	
710	YK- AIC	M	Syrianair	
711	B- 4001	M	China United	
712	B- 4002	M	China United	
713	B- 4003	M	China United	
714	B- 4004	M	China United	
715	RA- 85611	M	Vnukovo	
716	B- 2601	M	China Northwest	
717	B- 2602	M	China Northwest	
718	B- 2603	M	China Xinjiang	
719	CU- T1276	M	Cubana	(ex-8R-GGA Guyana)
720	CU- T1264	M	Cubana	
721	RA- 85612	M	Vnukovo	
722	RA- 85613	M	Baikalavia	
723	RA- 85614	M	VVS – Air Force	
724	B- 2604	M	China Northwest	
725	B- 2605	M	China Northwest	
726	B- 2611	M	China Xinjiang	
727	4K- 727	M	LOT Turanair	(ex SP-LCA LOT)
728	B- 2606	M	China Xinjiang	
729	B- 2607	M	China Northwest	
730	B- 2612	M	China United	
731	RA- 85615	M	Vnukovo	
732	RA- 85616	M	VVS – Air Force	
733	4K- 733	M	LOT Turanair	(ex SP-LCB LOT)
734	B- 2608	M	China Northwest	
735	B- 2609	M	China Xinjiang	
736	RA- 85617	M	Ulyanovsk VAU-GA	
737	RA- 85618	M	Vnukovo	
738	RA- 85619	M	Vnukovo	
739	RA- 85620	M	Vnukovo	
740	B- 2610	M	China Northwest	1994 (W/O) China
741	B- 2614	M	China United	
742	RA- 85621	M	Vnukovo	
743	LZ- BTQ	M	Balkan Bulgarian	
744	LZ- BTX	M	Balkan Bulgarian	
745	SP- LCC	M	LOT	
746	RA- 85622	M	Vnukovo	
747	YA- TAP	M	Ariana	1992 Kabul* W/O
748	YA- TAR	M	Ariana	
749	RA- 85623	M	Vnukovo	
750	RA- 85624	M	Vnukovo	
751	CU- T1265	M	Cubana	
752	RA- 85625	M	ARIA	
753	RA- 85626	M	ARIA	
754	LZ- BTH	M	Balkan Bulgarian	
755	SP- LCD	M	LOT	
756	RA- 85627	M	LII – Gromov	
757	RA- 85628	M	Vnukovo	
758	RA- 85629	M	Rossiya	
759	RA- 85630	M	Rossiya	
760	RA- 85631	M	Rossiya	
761	RA- 85632	M	Vnukovo	
762	RA- 85633	M	Vnukovo	
763	RA- 85634	M	ARIA	
764	RA- 85635	M	Vnukovo	
765	B- 4022	M	China United	(ex-OK-SCA CSA)
766	RA- 85636	M	Ulyanovsk VAU-GA	
767	RA- 85637	M	ARIA	
768	RA- 85638	M	ARIA	
769	SP- LCE	M	LOT	
770	B-4023	M	China United	(ex-OK-TCB CSA)
771	RA- 85639	M	ARIA	
772	RA- 85640	M	ARIA	
773	RA- 85641	M	ARIA	
774	SP- LCF	M	LOT	
775	SP- LCG	M	LOT	
776	SP- LCH	M	LOT	
777	CU- T1275	M	Cubana	
778	RA- 85642	M	ARIA	
779	RA- 85643	M	ARIA	
780	RA- 85644	M	ARIA	
781	LZ- BTZ	M	Balkan Bulgarian	
782	RA- 85645	M	Rossiya	
783	B- 2615	M	China Southwest	
784	RA- 85646	M	ARIA	
785	RA- 85647	M	ARIA	
786	RA- 85648	M	ARIA	
787	RA- 85649	M	ARIA	
788	RA- 85650	M	ARIA	
789	B-4024	M	China United	(ex-OK-TCC CSA)
790	B- 2616	M	China Southwest	
791	B- 2617	M	China Southwest	
792	OK- TCD	M	CSA	
793	RA- 85651	M	Rossiya	
794	RA- 85652	M	Baikalavia	

Factory No.	Registration	Current Model	Operator	If W/O Year/Place
795	RA- 85653	M	Rossiya	
796	RA- 85654	M	Baikalavia	
797	B-2618	M	China Southwest	
798	RA- 85655	LL-154M	VVS – Air Force	(Cosmonaut Trainer)
799	11 + 01	M	Luftwaffe	(ex-DDR-SFA Interflug)
800	LZ-BTY	M	Balkan Bulgarian	
801	RA- 85656	M		1994 Novosibirsk (W/O)
802	RA- 85657	M	Baikalavia	
803	OM-BYO	M	Slovak Gov.	(ex-OK-BYO)
804	OK- UCE	M	CSA	
805	RA- 85821	M	LOT Samara	(ex-SP-LCI LOT)
806	RA- 85821	M	LOT Samara	(ex-SP-LCK LOT)
807	OK- UCF	M	CSA	
808	RA- 85658	M	Rossiya	Lt Korsar
809	RA- 85659	M	Rossiya	
810	RA- 85660	M	Baikalavia	Lt Iran Air Tours EP-ITL
811	RA- 85661	M	ARIA	
812	SP- LCL	M	LOT	
813	11 + 02	M	Luftwaffe	(ex-DDR-SFB Interflug)
814	B- 2619	M	China Northwest	
815	B- 2620	M	China Northwest	
816	RA- 85662	M	ARIA	
817	RA- 85663	M	ARIA	
818	SSSR- 85664	M		1990 Czechoslovakia (W/O)
819	RA- 85665	M	ARIA	
820	RA- 85666	M	Rossiya	
821	YN- CBT	M	Aeronica	(WFU)
822	RA- 85803	M	Krai Aero	(ex-70-ACT Alyemda)
823	B- 2621	M	China Xinjiang	
824	RA- 85810	M	ARIA	(ex-SP-LCM LOT)
825	RA- 85667	M	MAK – Magadan	
826	RA- 85668	M	ARIA	
827	RA- 85669	M	ARIA	
828	RA- 85670	M	ARIA	
829	RA- 85671	M	MAK – Magadan	
830	RA- 85672	M	Krasnoyarskavia	
831	RA- 85811	M	ARIA	(ex-SP-LCN LOT)
832	LZ- BTN	M	Balkan Bulgarian	
833	RA- 85673	M	Vnukovo	
834	RA- 85674	M	Vnukovo	
835	RA- 85675	M-LK-1	Rossiya	
836	RA- 85676	M	Abakan Avia	
837	'837 /01'	M	Polish Air Force	
838	OK- VCG	M	CSA	
839	RA- 85677	M	MAK – Magadan	
840	LZ- MIG	M	VIA	
841	RA- 85678	M	Krasnoyarskavia	Lt Kish Air EP-LAO
842	RA- 85679	M	Krasnoyarskavia	Lt Kish Air EP-LAP
843	RA- 85680	M	MAK – Magadan	
844	LZ- MIK	M	VIA	
845	LZ- MIL	M	VIA	
846	B- 2622	M	China Southwest	
847	B- 4014	M	China United	
848	RA- 85681	M	Abakan Avia	
849	RA- 85682	M	Krasnoyarskavia	
850	RA- 85683	M	Krasnoyarskavia	
851	RA- 85684	M	Chita Avia	
852	LZ- MIR	M	VIA	
853	RA- 85685	M	MAK – Magadan	
854	RA- 85686	M-LK-1	Rossiya	
855	B- 2623	M	China Northwest	
856	B- 4015	M	China United	
857	RA- 85687	M	Sibavia	
858	OK- VCP	M	Czechia Gov.	(ex-OK-BYP)
859	RA- 85688	M	Sibavia	
860	RA- 85689	M	Baikalavia	
861	RA- 85690	M	Baikalavia	
862	'862 /02'	M	Polish Air Force	(ex-SP-LCO LOT)
863	LZ- MIS	M	VIA	
864	EY- 85691	M	Todjikistan	
865	EY- 85692	M	Todjikistan	
866	RA- 85693	M	Sibavia	Lt Iran Air Tours EP-ITG
867	RA- 85694	M	Krasnoyarskavia	
868	RA- 85695	M	Baikalavia	
869	RA- 85696	M	MAK – Magadan	
870	RA- 85697	M	Sibavia	
871	4K- 85698	M	AHY – Azerbaijan	

Factory No.	Registration	Current Model	Operator	If W/O Year/Place
872	B- 4016	M	China United	
873	B- 4017	M	China United	
874	RA- 85699	M	Krasnoyarskavia	
875	UR- 85700	M	Air Ukraine	
876	UR- 85701	M	Air Ukraine	
877	RA- 85702	M	Krasnoyarskavia	Lt Iran Air Tours EP-ITK
878	EW- 85703	M	Belavia	
879	RA- 85704	M	Krasnoyarskavia	Lt AJT Air Int'l
880	RA- 85705	M	Sibavia	
881	EW- 85706	M	Belavia	
882	UR- 85707	M	Air Ukraine	
883	RA- 85708	M	Krasnoyarskavia	Lt Iran Air Tours EP-ITJ
884	RA- 85709	M	Sibavia	
885	RA- 85710	M	Vladivostok Avia	
886	B- 2624	M	Sichuan Airlines	
887	UK- 85711	M	Uzbekistan – Samarkand Det.	
888	RA- 85712	M	Alak	
889	RA- 85713	M	Alak	
890	RA- 85714	M	Alak	
891	RA- 85715	M	KMV- Mineralnie Vody	
892	RA- 85716	M	Aerovolga	
893	B- 2625	M	Sichuan Airlines	
894	B- 2626	M	Sichuan Airlines	
896	YL- LAI	M	Baltic Express	(ex-SSSR-85740)
896	ES- LTR	M	Estonian Air	(ex-SSSR-85741)
897	EY- 85717	M	Todjikistan	
898	EP- JAZ	M	Mahan Air	(ex-SU-AOC/Cairo Cargo Charter)
899	EP- ARG	M	Mahan Air	(ex-SU-AOD/Cairo Cargo Charter)
900	EX- 85718	M	Kirghizi	
901	UN- 85719	M	Kazair	
902	RA- 85720	M	Kasnoyarskavia	
903	RA- 85721	M	Aerovolga – Samara	1993 Tehran* (W/O)
904	RA- 85722	M	KMV- Mineralinie Vody	
905	RA- 85723	M	Aerovolga – Samara	
906	EW- 85724	M	Belavia	
907	RA- 85725	M	Rossiya	
908	RA- 85726	M	Mals	
909	ES- LTP	M	Estonian Air	(ex-SSSR-85727)
910	RA- 85728	M	Makhachkola Avia	
911	4K- 85729	M	AHY – Azerbaijan	
912	RA- 85730	M	Omskavaia	
913	RA- 85731	M	Aerovolga – Samara	
914	4K- 85732	M	AHY – Azerbaijan	
915	RA- 85733	M	Murmansk	
916	4K- 85734	M	AHY – Azerbaijan	
917	RA- 85735	M	Chita	Lt Sichuan B-2627
918	RA- 85736	M	Vnukovo	
919	B- 2629	M	Sichuan Airlines	
920	RA- 85737	M	LII – Gromov	
921	RA- 85738	M	Vitiaz	
922	RA- 85739	M	Aerovolga – Samara	
923	RA- 85766	M	Chita	
924	EW- 85748	M	Belavia	
925	RA- 85765	M	Chita	Lt Sichuan B-2628
926	RA- 85743	M	Vnukovo	
927	UN- 85744	M	Kazamat	
928	RA- 85745	M	Vnukovo	
929	RA- 85746	M	KMV- Mineralnie Vody	
930	RA- 85747	M	Aerokuznetsk	
931	RA- 85749	M	Aerokuznetsk	
932	RA- 85750	M	(Step) – Samara	
933	RA- 85751	M	Tyumenaviatrans	
934	RA- 85752	M	Amur Avia	
935	RA- 85753	M	Amur Avia	
936	EX- 85754	M	Star of Asia	Lt ARIA RA-85754
937	RA- 85755	M	Murmansk	
938	RA- 85756	M	Makhachkola Avia	
939	RA- 85757	M	Bratskoe	
940	RA- 85758	M	Aerokuznetsk	
941	RA- 85759	M	Murmansk	
942	RA- 85760	M	Bratskoe	
943	B- 4027	M	China United	
944	RA- 85761	M	Kogalim Avia	
945	EX- 85762	M	Star of Asia	
946	RA- 85763	M	Aerovolga – Samara	
947	UK- 85764	M	Uzbekistan Airways	
948	RA- 85767	M	North Western	
949	RA- 85768	M	Orenburg	
950	B- 4042	M	China United	

Factory No.	Registration	Current Model	Operator	If W/O Year/Place
951	RA-85769	M	North Western	
952	RA-85770	M	North Western	
953	RA-85771	M	Aerovolga – Samara	Lt C-Air
954	RA-85772	M	Aerovolga – Samara	Lt Sichuan B2630
955	RA-85773	M	BAL- Bashkiri	
956	RA-85774	M	BAL- Bashkiri	
957	RA-85775	M	Aerovolga – Samara	
958	RA-UK-85776	M	Uzbekistan Airways	
959	RA-85777	M	BAL- Bashkiri	
960	RA-85801	M	LII – Gromov	
961	RA-85802	M	Chita	
962	RA-85778	M	Rossiya	
963	RA-85779	M	North Western	
964	RA-85780	M	Aerovolga – Samara	
965	UN-85781	M	Kazair	Lt Iron Dragonfly RA-85781
966	RA-85782	M	Tatarstan	
967	RA-85783	M	LII – Gromov	to China United B-4028
968	RA-85784	M	Kogalimavia	
969	RA-85785	M	North Western	
970	RA-85786	M	Samara	
971	RA-85787	M	Kogalimavia	
972	RA-85788	M	Kaliningradsky	
973	RA-85789	M	Kaliningradsky	
974	RA-85790	M	Yakutskavia	
975	RA-85791	M	Yakutskavia	
976	RA-85792	M	Aerovolga – Samara	
977	RA-85793	M	Yakutskavia	
978	RA-85794	M	Yakutskavia	
979	RA-85795	M	Vak- Rosat	
980	RA-85796	M	Tyumenaviatrans	
981	RA-85797	M	Aviaenergo	
982	RA-85798	M	Aviaenergo	
983	RA-85799	M	Murmansk	
984	RA-85800	M	Baikalavia	
985	RA-85809	M	Aviaenergo	
986	RA-85805	M	Tyumenaviatrans	
987	RA-85806	M	Tyumenaviatrans	
988	RA-85807	M	Uralskoe	
989	RA-85808	M	Tyumenaviatrans	
990	RA-85813	M	Tyumenaviatrans	
991	EW85815	M	Belarus Gov'n	
992				Not yet sold
993				Not yet sold
994	RA-85814	M	Uralskoe	
995				Not yet sold
996				Not yet sold
997				Not yet sold
998				Not yet sold
999				Not yet sold
1000				Not yet sold
1001				Not yet sold
1002				Not yet sold
1003				Not yet sold
1004				Not yet sold
1005	RA-85812	M	Yakubskavia	
1006	RA-85816	M		

Tu-204

Factory No.	Registration	Model	Operator	Date
156001	RA-64001	23h	Tupolev	Converted to Tu-234
156002	64002		Static Tests	
164003	SSSR-64003		Tupolev	
164004	SSSR-64004		Tupolev	
164005	SSSR-64005			
164006	SSSR-64006		Converted to - 204M for Bravia	
164007	Rossiya 64007		Tupolev	#For conversion to Tu-204C
164008	Rossiya 64008		Oriol Avia	for Aeroflot – Russian
164009	RA-64009		Oriol Avia	International (ARIA)
164010	RA-64010	C	ARIA	04/95
164011	RA-64011		Vnukovo Airlines	1993
164012	RA-64012		Vnukovo Airlines	1993
164013	RA-64013		Vnukovo Airlines	1995
164014	RA-64014		Rossiya	1994
164015	RA-64015		Rossiya	1994
164016	RA-64016		Completed at Ulyanovsk 1994/95 but unsold pending certificate mods	
164017	RA-64017		Completed at Ulyanovsk 1994/95 but unsold pending certificate mods	
164018	RA-64018		Completed at Ulyanovsk 1994/95 but unsold pending certificate mods	
164019	RA-64019		Completed at Ulyanovsk 1994/95 but unsold pending certificate mods	
164020	RA-64020		Completed at Ulyanovsk 1994/95 but unsold pending certificate mods	
164021	RA-64021		Completed at Ulyanovsk 1994/95 but unsold pending certificate mods	
164022	RA-64022		Completed at Ulyanovsk 1994/95 but unsold pending certificate mods	
164023	RA-64023		Completed at Ulyanovsk 1994/95 but unsold pending certificate mods	
164024	RA-64024		Completed at Ulyanovsk 1994/95 but unsold pending certificate mods	
164025	RA-64025		Completed at Ulyanovsk 1994/95 but unsold pending certificate mods	
	64026		Completed as Tu-234	
	64027			
	64028			
	64029			
	64030			
	64031		in final assembly	
	64032		at Ulyanovsk	
	64033		1996	

Glossary of Terms

Abbreviations

AFB	= Air Force Base
AEW	= Airborne Early Warning.
AGOS	= (Otdel) Aviatsii Gidroaviatsii i Opytnykh Samoletov = Aviation Division of Hydro and Experimental Aircraft.
ANTK	= Aviatsionnii Nauchno Tekhnicheski Komplex = Aviation Scientific and Technical Complex.
APU	= Auxiliary Power Unit.
ATC	= Air Traffic Control.
AWACS	= Airborne Warning and Control System.
BB	= Bliznii Bombardirovshik = Short-Range Bomber.
BCAR	= British Civil Airworthiness Requirements.
bis	= Duplicate (or second example).
CG	= Centre of Gravity.
CRT	= Cathode Ray Tubes (Cockpit Instrumentation).
D	= Dalnii = Long-Range.
DB	= Dalnii Bombardirovshik = Long-Range Bomber.
DBR	= Damaged Beyond Repair.
DI	= Dvukhmestnii Istrebitel = Two-seat fighter.
DIP	= Dvukhmestnii Istrebitel Pushechnii = Two-Seat Fighter with Cannons.
FAA	= Federal Aviation Authority (later Administration).
FAB	= Fugasnaia Aviatsionnaya Bomba = High-Explosive Aviation Bomb.
FAI	= Fédération Aéronautique Internationale.
FDR	= Flight Data Recorder.
GAZ	= Gosudarstvenni Aviatsionnii Zavod = State Aviation Works (or Factory).
GosNII GA	= Gosudarstvennii Nauchno Issledovatelski Institut Grazhdanskoi Aviatsii = State Scientific and Research Institute of Civil Aviation.
GUAP	= Glavnoe Upravlenie Aviatsionnoi Promyshlennosti = Main Department of Aviation Industry.
GULAG	= Glavnoe Upravlenie Lagerei = Chief Main Department of Labour Camps.
HOTOL	= Horizontal Take-Off and Landing (sub-orbital travel).
HQ	= Headquarters.
I	= Istrebitel = Fighter.
ICAO	= International Civil Aviation Organisation.
IFF	= Identity: Friend or Foe (Instrument to avoid attack by friendly forces)
IMTU	= Imperatorskoe Moskovskoe Tekhnicheskoe Uchilishe = Moscow Imperial Technical High School.
INS	= Inertial Navigation System.
JAA	= Joint Airworthiness Authorities (the combined body of European authorities).
JATO	= Jet Assisted Take-Off (usually small booster jets fitted for take-off, then dropped off).
KGB	= Kommitet Gosudarstvennoi Bezopastnosti = Committee on State Security.
KOSOS	= Konstruktorski Otdel Stroitelstva Opytnykh Samoletov = Design Division for the Construction of Experimental Aircraft.
LH	= Liquid Hydrogen.
LII	= Letno Issledovatelsky Institut = Flight Research Institute.
LNG	= Liquid Natural Gas.
Lt	= Leased to.
MAP	= Ministerstvo Aviatsionnoi Promyshlennosti = Ministry of Aviation Industry/Ministry of Aviation Production.

MCA = Ministerstvo Grazhdanskoi Aviatsii = Ministry of Civil Aviation.
MDR = Morskoi Dalnii Razvedchik = Naval Long-Range Reconnaissance.
MI = Mnogomestnii Istrebitel = Multi-Seat Fighter.
MK = Morskoi Kreiser = Naval Cruiser.
MMZ = Moskovski Mashinostroitelnii Zavod = Moscow Engineering Factory.
MP = Morskoi Passazhirski = Passenger Seaplane.
MTB = Morskoi Torpedonosets Bombardirovshik = Naval Torpedo Bomber.
MTK = Million Tonne Kilometres.
MTOW = Maximum Take-Off Weight.
MVTU = Moskovskoe Visshee Tekhnicheskoe Uchilishe = Moscow Higher Technical College.
NASA = National Aeronautics and Space Administration (USA).
NATO = North Atlantic Treaty Organisation.
NII = Nauchno Issledovatelski Institut = Scientific Research Institute.
NII VVS = Nauchno Issledovatelski Institut Voenno Vozdushnykh Sil = Scientific Research Institute of the Air Force.
NKTP = Narodnii Komissariat Tiazheloi Promyshlennosti = People's Commissariat (Ministry) of Heavy Industry.
NKVD = Narodnii Komissariat Vnutrennikh Del = People's Commissariat (Ministry) of Interior Affairs.
OKB = Opytno Konstruktorskoe Buro = Experimental Construction (or Design) Bureau.
PS = Passazhirski Samolet = Passenger Aircraft.
R = Razvedchik = Reconnaissance.
RK = Razreznoe Krylo = Slotted Wing.
RPK = Revenue Passenger Kilometres.
RVR = Runway Visual Range.
SALT = Strategic Arms Limitations Talks.
SB = Skorostnoi Bombardirovshik = High-Speed Bomber.
SOS = Sektsiia Opytnogo Samoletostroeniia = Section for Experimental Aircraft Construction.
SST = Supersonic Transport.
START = Strategic Arms Limitations Talks/Treaties.
T (suffix) = Torpedonosets = Torpedo Carrier.
TB = Tiazheli Bombardirovshik = Heavy Bomber.
TKM = Tonne Kilometres.
TsAGI = Tsentralnii Aerogydrodinamicheski Institut = Central Aero and Hydrodynamics Institute.
TShB = Tiazheli Shturmovik Bronirovanni = Heavy Armoured Ground Attack.
TsIAM = Tsentralnii Institut Aviatsionnogo Motorostroeniia = Central Institute of Aviation Motors.
TsKB = Tsentralnoe Konstruktorskoe Buro = Central Construction (or Design) Bureau.
USB = Uchebnii Skorostnoi Bombardirovshik = High-Speed Training Bomber.
UTB = Uchebno-Trenirovochnii Bombardirovshik = Learning Trainer Bomber.
VG = Variable Geometry – wings that can have an angle of sweep adjusted in flight to meet the aerodynamic needs of the flight speed.
VI = Vysotnii Istrebitel = High-Altitude Fighter.
VLF = Very Low Frequency (radio transmissions).
VMF = Voenno Morskoi Flot = Military Sea Fleet = Navy.
VMS = Voenno Morskie Sili = Military Sea Force = Navy.
VVS = Voenno Vozdushnie Sili = Military Air Force = Air Force.
W/O = Written off.
WFU = Withdrawn from use.
ZLiDB = Zhukovskaya Letnaya i Dovodochnaya Baza = Zhukovski Flight Test and Development Base.
ZOK = Zavod Opytnykh Konstruktsii = Factory of Experimental Constructions.

Bibliography

1. Gallai, M., *Izbrannoe* (Selected Works), 2 vols., Voenizdat (Military Publishers), Moscow, 1990.
2. Danilin, A. S., *Cherez Severnii Polius* (Through the North Pole), DOSAAF, 1981.
3. Duz, P. D., *Istoria Vozdukhoplavania i Aviatsii v Rossii* (The History of Aeronautics and Aviation in Russia), Mashinostroenie (Engineering Publishers), Moscow, 1981.
4. Tsikin, A. D., *Ot Ilii Muromtsa do Raketonostsa* (From Ilia Muromets to Missile Carrier), Voenizdat (Military Publishers), Moscow, 1975.
5. Beliakov, A. V., *v Polet Skvoz Gody* (To Flight through Years), Voenizdat (Military Publishers), Moscow, 1988.
6. Baidukov, G. F., *Pervye Pereleti Cherez Ledovitii Okean* (First Overflights over the Arctic Ocean), Detskaia Literatura (Children's Literature Publishers), Moscow, 1977.
7. Beliakov, A. V., *Valery Chkalov*, DOSAAF Publishers, Moscow, 1977.
8. Ponomarev, A. N., *Sovetskie Aviatsionnye Konstruktori* (Soviet Aviation Designers), Voenizdat (Military Publishers), Moscow, 1986.
9. Gromov Cherez, M. M., *Vsiu Zhizn* (Through the Whole Life), Molodaia Gvardiia (The Young Guard Publishers), Moscow, 1986.
10. Shavrov, V. B., *Istoria Konstruktsii Samoletov v SSSR* (The History of Aircraft Designs in the USSR), 2 vols., Mashinostroenie (Engineering Publishers), Moscow, 1978.
11. Tupolev, A. N., *Grani Derznovennogo Tvorchestva* (Aspects of Technical Frontiers of Tupolev) Selected Works, Nauka (Science Publishers), Moscow, 1988.
12. *60 Let OKB A. N. Tupoleva* (60 Years of the A. N. Tupolev Design Bureau), TsAGI Publishers, Moscow, 1982.
13. Tupolev, A. N., *Zhizn i Deiatelnost* (Life and Creative Activities), TsAGI Publishers, Moscow, 1989.
14. Shakhurin, A. I., *Krylia Pobedy* (The Wings of Victory), Politicheskaia Literatura (Political Literature Publishers), Moscow, 1985.
15. Riabchikov, E., Magid, A., *Stanovlenie* (Establishing), Znanie (Knowledge Publishers), Moscow, 1978.
16. Arlazorov, M., *Grazhdanskaia Reaktivnaia Sozdavalas Tak . . .* (Civil jet aviation was created like this . . .), Politicheskaia Literatura (Political Literature Publishers), Moscow, 1976.
17. Lazarev, P., *Vzlet* (Take-Off), Profizdat (Professional Publishers), Moscow, 1978.
18. Arlazorov, M., *Konstruktori* (Designers), Sovetskaia Rossiia (Soviet Russia Publishers), Moscow, 1975.
19. Magid, A., *Bolshaia Zhizn* (Long Life), DOSAAF Publishers, Moscow, 1968.
20. Gai, D., *Profil Kryla* (Profile of a Wing), Moskovsky Rabochii (Moscow Worker Publishers), Moscow, 1981.
21. Yakovlev, A. S., *Sovetskie Samolety* (Soviet Aircraft), Nauka (Science Publishers), Moscow, 1979.
22. Tabachnikov, S., *Krylia* (Wings), Kiubyshevskoe Knizhnoe Izdatelstvo (Kuibyshev Books Publishers), 1987.
23. Kerber, L. L., *Tu – Chelovek i Samolet* (Tu – A Man and an Airplane), Sovetskaia Rossia (Soviet Russia Publishers), Moscow, 1973.
24. Papanin, I. D., *Zhizn Na Ldine* (Life on an Ice Flow), Mysl (Conception Publishers), Moscow, 1966.
25. Lebedev, A. A., and Mazuruk, I. P., *Nad Arktikoi i Antarktikoi* (Over Arctic and Antarctic), Mysl (Conception Publishers), Moscow, 1991.
26. Saukke, M. B., *Neizvestnii Tupolev* (Unknown Tupolev), Manuscript, Moscow, 1993.
27. Saukke, M. B., *Samolety Tu v Velikoi Otechestvennoi Voine 1941–1945* (Tu Airplanes in the Great Patriotic War of 1941–1945), Manuscript, 1981.
28. Petliakov, Unger Ulrich, *Pe-8 der Sovietishe Fernbomber*, Brendenburgishes Verlagshaus, Berlin, 1993.
29. *Aviatsiia (Entsiklopediia)* (Aviation Encyclopedia), Bolshaia Rossiiskaia Entsiklopedia, TsAGI Publishers, Moscow, 1994.

30. Zuzenko, Yu., Korostelev, S., *Boevye Samoleti Rossii, Spravochnik* (Combat Aircraft of Russia, Reference Book), Elakos Publishers, Moscow, 1994.
31. Bugaev, B. P. (ed.), *Istoriya Grazhdansoi Aviatsii SSSR* (History of Civil Aviation of the USSR), Vozdushni Transport Publishers, 1983.
32. Nemecek, V., *The History of the Soviet Aircraft from 1918*, Willow Books/Collins, London, 1986.
33. Taylor, John W. R. (ed.), *Jane's All The World's Aircraft* (different editions), Jane's Publishers, London.
34. MacDonald, Hugh, *Aeroflot: Soviet Air Transport since 1923*, Putnam.
35. Stroud, John, *Soviet Transport Aircraft since 1945*, Putnam, London, 1968.
36. *Chudesa i Priklucheniia* (Miracles and Adventures), No. 5, 1993. *(Magazine)*
37. *Aviatsiia i Kosmonautika* (Aviation and Space), No. 5–6, 1992. *(Magazine)*
38. *Nauka i Zhizn* (Science and Life), No. 11, 1988. *(Magazine)*
39. *Krylia Rodiny* (Wings of the Motherland), No. 1, 1988, No. 1–2, 10, 1989. *(Magazine)*
40. *Izobretatel i Ratsionalizator* (Inventor and Rationaliser), No. 3–9, 1988. *(Magazine)*
41. *Grazhdanskaia Aviatsiia* (Civil Aviation), No. 11, 1988. *(Magazine)*
42. *Vozdushnie Transport Newspaper* – various editions. *(Magazine)*
43. Duan Zizun China Today = Aviation Industry, Chinese Social Science Press (1989)
44. Paul Duffy *Commercial Aviation in the Soviet Union*, CAR 1991

Designs of A. N. Tupolev OKB
1923–1993

Official Designation/ Official Variants	Date of First Flight/Pilot	Stage of Development Achieved	Short Characteristic of Aircraft	OKB Designation
ANT-1	21 October 1923 E. I. Pogosski	Experimental	Light sports single-seat monoplane of mixed construction. One Anzani engine	ANT-1
ANT-2	20 May 1924 N. I. Petrov	Experimental Two aircraft by TsAGI Serial 5 aircraft	First Soviet all-metal, passenger aircraft (for 2). Monoplane. One Bristol Lucifer engine	ANT-2
R-3 R-3LD R-3 (M-5)	August 1925 V. N. Filippov	Serial 101 aircraft	Reconnaissance, sesquiplane. One M-5 engine. First aircraft in serial production. Two overflights: 1926 – *Proletarii* – Western; 1927 – *Our Reply* – Eastern.	ANT-3
TB-1 TB-1-P	26 November 1925 A. I. Tomashevski	Serial	First all-metal monoplane bomber in the world. Heavy-bomber, two-seat cantilever monoplane (first in its class) two M-17 engines. First aircraft carrier for Zveno project.	ANT-4
I-4	August 1927	Serial aircraft	Single-seat fighter, sesquiplane, M-22 engine.	ANT-5
TB-3 TB-3 (4 x M17) TB-3 (4 x M-34R) TB-3 (4 x M-34RN) TB-3 (4 x M-34FRN)	22 December 1930 M. M. Gromov	Serial	Four-engined heavy bomber. Development from TB-1. Four M-17 engines. World's first four-engined monoplane bomber with cantilever wing. Was the basis of the USSR Strategic Aviation in 1932–1938. Paratroop forces and transport aviation were set up with it.	ANT-6
R-6 KR-6 MR-6 KR-6A PS-7 MP-6	11 September 1929 M. M. Gromov	Serial	Multi-purpose reconnaissance, bomber, fighter development from TB-1, two M-17 engines. The first Soviet aircraft to fly over the North Pole.	ANT-7
MDR-2	30 January 1931 S. Riballschuk	Experimental	Naval, long-range, reconnaissance, flying boat, two BMW-IV engines. First all-metal seaplane.	ANT-8
PS-9 PS-9 (3 Wright-Whirlwind) PS-9 (2 x M-17F)	May 1929 M. M. Gromov	Serial – sixty-six built	Passenger aircraft, nine seats, two M-17 engines. First production all-metal aircraft with three engines	ANT-9
R-7		Experimental	Reconnaissance, development of R-3. One BMW-VI engine.	ANT-10
ANT-11		Project was not implemented	Multi-purpose seaplane, flying boat.	ANT-11
I-5	29 April 1930 B.L. Bukholts	Project transferred to Polikarpov; was in serial production in service for about nine years.	Single-seat fighter biplane. One Bristol Jupiter engine.	ANT-12
I-8 *Zhokei; Public Aircraft*	12 December 1930 M. M. Gromov	Experimental	Single-seat fighter-interceptor. One Curtiss Conqueror engine. First USSR aircraft to exceed 300kph. Was not in serial production due to a lack of Soviet-made engines for it.	ANT-13
ANT-14	14 August 1931 M. M. Gromov	Experimental	Passenger aircraft, thirty-six seats. Five Bristol Jupiter VI engines. One of the largest passenger aircraft of its time. Was built for expected transcontinental route MOW–Vladivostok, but because of not enough passengers was not in serial production.	ANT-14
ANT-15		Project		ANT-15
TB-4	3 July 1933 M. M. Gromov	Experimental	Heavy bomber, development of TB-3, six M-34 engines. Had largest bomb compartments in the world. Design was later used in ANT-20 construction.	ANT-16
TS1-B		Project	Armoured assault aircraft – twin-engined biplane.	ANT-17
R-6SL		Project	Armoured assault aircraft. Development of R-6; two M-34 engines.	ANT-18
ANT-19		Project		ANT-19

Official Designation/ Official Variants	Date of First Flight/Pilot	Stage of Development Achieved	Short Characteristic of Aircraft	OKB Designation
MG (*Maksim Gorki*) PS-124 (SSSR-L760) PS-124 (ANT-20bis)	17 June 1934 M. M. Gromov 15 May 1939 E. I. Shwarts	Experimental	Propaganda aircraft. Eight M-34FRN engines. Six M-37FRNV engines, sixty to sixty-four passengers on second aircraft, served with Aeroflot on Moscow–Mineralnie Vody route. From the beginning of the war till the end of 1942 was used as a cargo/passenger aircraft on short routes.	ANT-20
MI-3 MI-3D (ANT-21bis)	23 May 1933 I. F. Kozlov	Experimental	Multi-seat fighter, retractable undercarriage, two M-34 engines.	ANT-21
MK-1	8 August 1934 T.V. Riabenko	Experimental	Sea cruiser, long-range reconnaissance flying boat, six M-34R engines. World's largest built with twin hull.	ANT-22
I-12 (*Baumanski Komsomolets*)	29 August 1931 I. F. Kozlov	Experimental	Single-seat fighter of twin-boom scheme, two M-22 eingines.	ANT-23
ANT-24		Project		ANT-24
RD Range Record	22 June 1933 M. M. Gromov	Experimental Built in small series as ANT-36	Record-beating long-range aircraft, one M-34R engine.	ANT-25
TB-6		Project	Heavy bomber, development of TB-4 twelve M-34FRN engines. Construction started but was stopped in 1936; it lacked speed, altitude, defensive armaments.	ANT-26
MDR-4	March 1934 T.V. Riabenko	Experimental	Naval, long-range, reconnaissance, heavy bomber, flying boat with three M-34RN engines. 15 April 1934 crashed at take-off during factory tests.	ANT-27
MTB-1 (ANT-27bis)	29 October 1934 T. V. Riabenko	Serial	Naval torpedo carrier, bomber/flying boat, was in small serial production (ANT-27bis).	ANT-27bis
ANT-28		Project	Passenger variant of TB-6/ANT-26.	ANT-28
DIP 'To Catch Up and Overtake'	14 February 1935 S. A. Korzinshikov	Experimental	Two-seat cannon fighter, two M-100 engines.	ANT-29
SK-1		Project beginning of 30s	'High-Speed' fighter of convoy, two M-38 engines.	ANT-30
I-14	27 May 1933 K. K. Popov	Serial	Single-seat fighter, one M-25 engine. First monoplane fighter in the USSR to go into production. Retractable undercarriage was used for the first time. ANT-31bis was in small serial production.	ANT-31
ANT-32		Project	Single-seat fighter. Work was stopped at the stage of drawing project (1934).	ANT-32
ANT-33		Project		ANT-33
ANT-34		Project		ANT-34
PS-35 PS-35 (2 x M-62iR)	20 August 1936 M. M. Gromov	Serial	Passenger aircraft, ten seats; two M-621R engines. Served with Aeroflot till 1941, participated in WWII.	ANT-35
DB-1 (RD-VV)	22 July 1936 G. F. Baidukov	Serial	Long-range bomber, variant of RD, one M-34 engine.	ANT-36
DB-2	15 June 1935 K. K. Popov	Experimental	Long-range bomber. Broke up in air due to vibration of horizontal empennage.	ANT-37
ANT-37bis *Rodina*	25 February 1936 M. Yu. Alekseev	Experimental	Record-beating aircraft. Two M-85 engines. Staged women's world record in non-stop direct flight range on 24 to 25 September 1938.	ANT-37bis
ANT-38		Project		ANT-38
ANT-39		Project		ANT-39
SB (2 x M-100) SB (2 x M-100A) SB (2 x M-103) SB (2 x M-105) AR-2 PS-40 V-71 (Czechoslovakia)	7 October 1934 K. K. Popov	Serial	High-speed front-line bomber. Two M-100A engines. By the beginning of the Great Patriotic War (22 June 1941) SBs made up 94% of the front/combat bombers' aviation.	ANT-40
T-I	2 June 1936 A. P. Chernavski	Experimental	Torpedo carrier. Two M-34FRN engines.	ANT-41
TB-7 (PE-8)	27 December 1936 M. M. Gromov	Serial	Heavy bomber of 'Flying Fortress' class. Four AM-35A engines.	ANT-42

Official Designation/ Official Variants	Date of First Flight/Pilot	Stage of Development Achieved	Short Characteristic of Aircraft	OKB Designation
ANT-43		Project		ANT-43
MTB-2 *Chaika* (Seagull)	19 April 1937 T. V. Riabenko	Experimental	Naval heavy bomber. Flying boat; four M-85, M-87A (ANT-44bis).	ANT-44
ANT-45		Project	Two-seat fighter. Work stopped at the project drawings stage.	ANT-45
DI-8	1 August 1935 M. Yu. Alekseev	Experimental	Long-range fighter. Two Gnôme-Rhône 14K engines. Was not handed over for state tests.	ANT-46
ANT-47		Project		ANT-47
ANT-48		Project – 1935	High-speed sports aircraft.	ANT-38
ANT-49		Project		ANT-49
ANT-50		Project	Passenger aircraft. Two AM-34 engines. Work was stopped at the project drawings stage.	ANT-50
SZ *Stalin's Task*	25 August 1937 M. M. Gromov	Experimental	Reconnaissance, light bomber. Prototype of Su-2 serial aircraft; one M-62 or M-87 engine.	ANT 51
ANT-52		Project		ANT-52
ANT-53		Project	Four-engined passenger aircraft; four AM-34FRN engines. Work was stopped at project drawings stage.	ANT-53
ANT-54		Project		ANT-54
ANT-55		Project		ANT-55
SRB		Project 1940	High-speed reconnaissance bomber aircraft.	ANT-56
PB-4		Project 1939	Dive bomber. Four M-105 engines. Beria's programme.	ANT-57
103	29 January 1941 M. A. Nukhtikov	Experimental	Front-line dive bomber. Two AM-37 engines.	ANT-58
103U	18 May 1941 M. A. Nukhtikov	Experimental	'103' Development. Two AM-37 engines.	ANT-59
103V	15 December 1941	Experimental	'103' Development. Two M-82 engines.	ANT-60
Tu-2 Tu-2VS Tu-2S Tu-2T Tu-6	February 1942	Serial	Production variant of '103V'. Two ASh-82A engines. ASh-82FN engine (Tu-2S). 2,527 aircraft built. (Tu-2 variants total)	ANT-61
Tu-2D '62T'	October 1944	Serial	Long-range bomber, development of Tu-25. Two ASh-82FN engines.	ANT-62
SDB Tu-1	21 May 1945 A. D. Pereliot	Experimental	High-speed day bomber version of the '103' and Tu-2S fighter-interceptor. Two AM-39, AM-39F, AM-43V (Tu-1) engines.	ANT-63
ANT-64		Project	Long-range bomber. Four AM-43TK; AM-46TK; ACh-30BF engines.	ANT-64
Tu-2D	1 July 1946	Experimental	Development of '62'. Two AM-44TK engines.	ANT-65
ANT-66		Project	Passenger aircraft for fifty-two seats; variant of '64'.	ANT-66
Tu-2D	12 February 1946	Experimental	Development of '62'. Two ACh-30BF engines.	ANT-67
Tu-10 (Tu-4)	19 May 1945	Serial	Variant of Tu-2S. Two AM-39FNV engines.	ANT-68
Tu-8	19 July 1947	Experimental	Development of '62'. Two ASh-82FNV engines	ANT-69
Tu-4 Tu-4A Tu-4R Tu-4KS Tu-4T Tu-4 (aircraft of radioelectronic patrol)	19 May 1947 N. S. Rybko	Serial	Long-range bomber; copy of B-29. Four ASh-73TK engines; 847 aircraft were built. Last production heavy bomber with piston engines.	B-4
Tu-12 (1)	27 November 1946 F. F. Opadchi	Experimental	First USSR aircraft built with pressurised passenger cabin. B-29/Tu-4 development. Four ASh-73TK engines. Seventy-two seats.	Tu-70
Tu-71		Project 1946	Variant of Tu-2S with new nose. Two M-82M or M-93 engines.	Tu-71
Tu-72		Project 1946	Medium bomber. Two ASh-2TK engines.	Tu-72
Tu-72		Project 1947	Variant of '69' with two 'Nene-1' engines.	Tu-72

Official Designation/ Official Variants	Date of First Flight/Pilot	Stage of Development Achieved	Short Characteristic of Aircraft	OKB Designation
Tu-20 (1)		Project 1947	Front-line jet bomber; two 'Nene-1' engines.	Tu-73
Tu-14 (1)	29 December 1947	Experimental	Front-line jet bomber. Two 'Nene-1' and one 'Derwent' engine.	Tu-73
Tu-22 (1)		Project 1947–1948	High-altitude reconnaissance; two M-93 or ASh-84TK engines. High-altitude reconnaissance aircraft, two ASh-84TK and one 'Nene-1' engine.	Tu-74
Tu-75	22 January 1950 V. Marunov	Experimental	Military transport variant of '70'.	Tu-75
Tu-76		Project 1947–1948	Bomber variant of '74'. Two ASh-73TK and one 'Nene-1' engines.	Tu-76
Tu-12 (2)	27 July 1947 A. D. Pereliot	Serial	Bomber with jet engines developed from the Tu-2S. First Soviet jet bomber.	Tu-77
Tu-16 (1) Tu-73R	7 May 1948	Experimental	Reconnaissance aircraft, variant of '73', two RD-45 and one RD-500 engines.	Tu-78
Tu-79 Tu-20 (2)		Project 1949	Reconnaissance aircraft version of '73' with two VK-1 and one RD-500 engines.	Tu-79
Tu-80	1 December 1949 A. D. Pereliot	Experimental	Variant of Tu-4. Four ASh-73TKFN engines.	Tu-80
Tu-18		Project	Front bomber, development of '73'. Two VK-1 engines.	Tu-81
Tu-14 Tu-14T	13 October 1949	Serial	Front-line bomber, development of Tu-18, torpedo carrier. Two VK-1 engines.	Tu-81T
Tu-22 (2)	24 March 1949 A. D. Pereliot	Experimental	First Soviet bomber with swept wing (sweep of 35°), front-line bomber on the basis of '73'. Two RD-45 engines.	Tu-82
Tu-83		Project 1949	Development of '82'.	Tu-83
Tu-84		Project 1949	Development, variant of '74'. Two VK-2 and one VK-1 engine.	Tu-84
Tu-85	9 January 1951 A. D. Pereliot	Experimental	Intercontinental strategic bomber. Four VD-4K engines.	Tu-85
Tu-86		Project 1951	Long-range bomber. Development of '82'. Two AM-2 or Tr-3 engines.	Tu-86
Tu-87		Project 1951	Development of '86'.	Tu-87
Tu-16 Samolet N	27 April 1952	Serial	Long-range bomber, reconnaissance aircraft, missile carrier. Two AM-3 or RD-3M engines.	Tu-88
Tu-16A Tu-16KS Tu-16R Tu-16P Tu-16T Tu-16E Tu-16 'Refueller' Tu-16K-10 Tu-16KSR-2 Tu-16KSR-5 Tu-16K-11-16 Tu-16K-26 Tu-16M Tu-16S Tu-16N	N.S. Rybko			
Tu-16 (2)	February 1951	Experimental	Reconnaissance aircraft. Variant of '81'. Two VK-1 engines.	Tu-89
Tu-90		Project 1951	Variant of '88'. Four Tr-3F engines.	Tu-90
Tu-91	Autumn 1954	Experimental	Assault aircraft dive bomber. One TV-2M engine.	Tu-91
Tu-16R	1955	Serial	Reconnaissance variant of Tu-16 (see '88')	Tu-92
Tu-93		Project 1952	Torpedo carrier bomber, minelayer, development of Tu-14T; two VK-5 or VK-7 engines.	Tu-93
Tu-94		Project Beginning of the 1950s	Modernisation of Tu-4 for turboprop engines, four TV-2 or NK-4 engines.	Tu-94

Official Designation/ Official Variants	Date of First Flight/Pilot	Stage of Development Achieved	Short Characteristic of Aircraft	OKB Designation
Tu-95A Tu-95M Tu-95K Tu-95KM Tu-95MR Tu-95RTs Tu-95K-22 Tu-95MS	12 November 1952 A. D. Pereliot	Serial	Intercontinental strategic bomber, missile carrier; reconnaissance aircraft. Four NK-12MV engines.	Tu-95
Tu-96	1956	Experimental	High-altitude intercontinental strategic bomber, development of '95'. Four NK-16 engines.	Tu-96
Tu-97		Project Beginning of the 1950s	Long-range bomber; development of '88'; two VD-5 engines.	Tu-97
Tu-24	Spring 1956	Experimental	Supersonic bomber became prototype of fighter Tu-128. Two AL-7F engines.	Tu-98
Tu-99		Project Mid 1950s	High-altitude intercontinental strategic bomber on the basis of '96'. Four VD-7 engines.	Tu-99
T-100		Project Mid-1950s	Piloted or unmanned aircraft intended to be suspended under Tu-96, -108 or -109 for airborne launching. Two AM-11 engines.	Tu-100
T-101		Project Beginning of the 1950s	Military transport aircraft. Two TV-2F engines.	Tu-101
Tu-102		Project Beginning of the 1950s	Passenger variant of '101'.	Tu-102
Tu-103		Project Beginning of the 1950s	Long-range transonic bomber, development of '88'. Four VD-7 or AM-13 engines.	Tu-103
Tu-104A (70 pax) Tu-104V (100–115 pax) Tu-104B (100 pax) Tu-104D (85 pax)	17 July 1955 Yu. T. Alasheev	Serial	First Soviet jet passenger aircraft developed from the Tu-16. 50–115 seats. RD-3M engines. Twenty-six world records set with the aircraft.	Tu-104
Tu-22 Tu-22B(A) Tu-22R Tu-22P Tu-22K Tu-22U	21 July 1958 Yu. T. Alasheev	Serial	Long-range supersonic bomber, reconnaissance missile carrier. Two VD-TM or RD-TM-2 engines.	Tu-105
Tu-106		Project Second half of the 1950s	Development of the '105'. Two NK-6 engines.	Tu-106
Tu-107	1958	Experimental	Military transport aircraft, variant of -104A	Tu-107
Tu-108		Project Mid-second half of the 1950s	Intercontinental supersonic bomber. Carrier of of '100' aircraft; six VD-7M engines.	Tu-108
Tu-109		Project. Second half of the 1950s	Development of '108'. Six P-4 or NK-6 engines.	Tu-109
Tu-110	11 March 1957 D. V. Zuzin	Experimental	Passenger aircraft; four-engined variant of Tu-104. Four AL-7P or D-20P engines.	Tu-110
Tu-111		Project Mid-1950s	Passenger aircraft, twenty-four seats; two TV-2F or TV-2M engines.	Tu-111
Tu-112		Project Mid-1950s	Front-line bomber	Tu-112
Tu-113		Project 1956	Rocket-aircraft of 'Air-to-Ground' class.	Tu-113
Tu-114 (up to 220 pax) Tu-114D (long-range for flights to Cuba)	15 November 1957 A. P. Yakimov	Serial	Intercontinental passenger aircraft, 170–220 seats, developed from the Tu-95; four NK-12MV engines.	Tu-114
Tu-115		Project 1955	Military transport variant of Tu-114.	Tu-115
Tu-114D (Diplomatic)	1958	Serial	Two Tu-95s converted for governmental passenger delegations; twenty to twenty-four seats.	Tu-116
Tu-117		Project Second half of the 1950s	Military transport variant of Tu-110.	Tu-117
Tu-118		Project Second half of the 1950s	Passenger aircraft, variant of Tu-104 with four turbofan engines.	Tu-118
Tu-119		Project Second half of the 1950s	Intercontinental strategic bomber with nuclear power installation. Flying laboratory – Tu-95LAL – was built for '119' programme. It had nuclear reactor. Two NK-14A and two NK-12MV engines.	Tu-119

Official Designation/ Official Variants	Date of First Flight/Pilot	Stage of Development Achieved	Short Characteristic of Aircraft	OKB Designation
Tu-120		Project Second half of the 1950s	Long-range supersonic bomber with nuclear power installation; four RD-A engines.	Tu-120
'S'	1959	Experimental	Operational strategic strike missile.	Tu-121
Tu-122		Project Second half of the 1950s	Bomber development of '98'.	Tu-122
DBR-1	1960	Serial	Long-range operational strategic reconnaissance missile in the 'Yastrebi' (Hawk) system of reconnaissance missiles.	Tu-123
Tu-124 (44 pax) Tu-124V (56 pax) Tu-124Sh	24 March 1960 A. D. Kalina	Serial	Short-range passenger aircraft; 44–56 seats. Two D-20P engines.	Tu-124
Tu-125		Project Second half of the 1950s	Long-range, single-engined, supersonic, strike/attack aircraft 'Ukta' (Duck) scheme. Two NK-6 or NK-10 engines.	Tu-125
Tu-126	23 January 1962 Ivan Sukhomlin	Serial	Aircraft of long-range radar surveillance with 'Liana' complex, on the basis of Tu-114. Four NK-12MV engines/AWACS equivalent.	Tu-126
Tu-127		Project End of the 1950s	Military transport aircraft, variant of Tu-124.	Tu-127
Tu-128/UT	18 March 1961 M. Kozlov	Serial	Long-range supersonic fighter-interceptor armed with missile installation R-4T and R-4R of air-to-air class; two AL-7F-2 engines.	Tu-128
Tu-129		Project End of the 1950s	Front attack aircraft. One VD-7M engine.	Tu-129
Tu-130	Beginning of the 1960s	Experimental	Space missile.	Tu-130
Tu-131		Project End of the 1950s	Ground-to-air guided missile.	Tu-131
Tu-132		Project End of the 1950s	Low-altitude transonic attack aircraft.	Tu-132
Tu-133		Project Beginning of the 1960s	Strategic attack missile–rocket development of '121'.	Tu-133
Tu-134 (72 pax) Tu-134A (76 pax) Tu-134B (80 pax) Tu-134Sh Tu-134UBL Tu-134SKh	29 July 1963 A. D. Kalina	Serial	Short-range passenger aircraft. Modernisation of Tu-124V; 72–90 seats. Two D-30 engines. First Tupolev aircraft with new engine layout, on pylons in the rear fuselage.	Tu-134
Tu-135		Project Beginning of the 1960s	Long-range single-role strategic supersonic aircraft. 'Ukta' (Duck) scheme; passenger version – '135P'. Four NK-6 or NK-10 engines.	Tu-135
'Zvezda' (Star)		Project End of the 1950s	Piloted air space aircraft. Equivalent American X-20 'Dinosaur' project.	Tu-136
Tu-136		Project 1976	Medium-range passenger aircraft; 165 seats. Two D-30KU engines.	Tu-136
Tu-137		Project Beginning of the 1960s	Development of '135'.	Tu-137
Tu-138		Project Mid-1960s	Development of '128'. Two VD-19 engines.	Tu-138
DBR-2	July 1968	Experimental	Long-range operational, strategic reconnaissance missile of multiple use, development of '123', part of 'Yastreb-2' (Hawk) air reconnaissance system.	Tu-139
Tu-140		Project Beginning of the 1960s	Guided missile of 'air-to-ground' class.	Tu-140
Tu-141	December 1974	Serial	Operational-tactical reconnaissance missile; part of 'Strizh' (Swift) air reconnaissance system.	Tu-141
Tu-142 Tu-142M Tu-142M-3	July 1968 M. Nukhtikov	Serial	Anti-submarine aircraft; modernised variant of Tu-95. Tu-95MS strategic missile carrier was built at the end of the 1970s on the basis of the Tu-142M; carrier of cruise missiles of Kh-5 type, 4 x NK-12MV or NK12MP engines.	Tu-142
Tu-143	December 1970	Serial	Tactical reconnaissance missile; part of the 'Reis' (Flight) air reconnaissance system.	Tu-143

Official Designation/ Official Variants	Date of First Flight/Pilot	Stage of Development Achieved	Short Characteristic of Aircraft	OKB Designation
Tu-144 (NK-144A) Tu-144 (RD-36-51A)	31 December 1968 E. V. Yelian	Serial	The world's first supersonic passenger aircraft; 100–120 seats; four NK-144A or RD-36-51A engines.	Tu-144
Tu-22M Tu-22M-0 Tu-22M-1 Tu-22M-2 Tu-22M-3 Tu-22MR	30 August 1969	Serial	Twin-engined supersonic bomber, missile carrier with variable sweep wing. Two NK-22, NK-25 engines.	Tu-145
Tu-148		Project Second half of the 1960s	Development of '128'; with variable geometry wing.	Tu-148
Tu-154 (152 pax) Tu-154A (158 pax) Tu-154B (160–180 pax) Tu-154C (cargo) Tu-154M (180 pax)	3 October 1968 Yu. V. Sukhov	Serial	Medium-range passenger aircraft, 152–180 seats. Three NK-8-29, D-30KU-154 engines.	Tu-154
Tu-155	15 April 1988 A. I. Talalakin	Experimental	Flying laboratory for testing engines fuelled by liquid hydrogen or natural gas on the basis of Tu-154; two NK-8-29 engines and one NK-88.	Tu-155
Tu-156		In the process of design	Medium-range passenger aircraft, variant of Tu-154B, and Tu-154M for engines on liquid natural gas. Three NK-89 engines.	Tu-156
Tu-154M-2		In the process of design	Medium-range passenger aircraft, modernisation of Tu-154M for two PS-90A engines.	Tu-154M-2
Tu-156		Design is just starting	Aircraft of long-distance radar surveillance and aiming; four D-30KP engines.	Tu-156
Tu-160	18 December 1981 B. Veremel	Serial	Multi-regime supersonic strategic bomber missile carrier with variable sweep wing. Four NK-32 engines.	Tu-160
Tu-164		Project Beginning of the 1970s	Development of Tu-134. First/initial definition of Tu-154G, then Tu-154M.	Tu-164
Tu-202		Project End of the 1970s	Basic anti-submarine 'Argon' aircraft.	Tu-202
Tu-184		Project Beginning of the 1970s	Short-range widebody passenger aircraft 'Airbus' class for 140–160 seats; two D-30KP engines.	Tu-184
Tu-204 Tu-204-100 Tu-204-120 Tu-204C Tu-204-200 Tu-204-220	2 January 1989 A. I. Talalakin	Serial	Medium-range passenger aircraft for 214 seats. Two PS-90A engines. -204 version with RB211 engines.	Tu-204
Tu-214		In the process of design	Variant of Tu-204 for engines on liquid natural gas.	Tu-214
Tu-234		Project	-204 version with PW2240 engines.	
Tu-23u (2)		Experimental	-20u shortened with 160 seats	Tu-234
Tu-334		Experimental aircraft is being built – first flight likely 1996	Short-range passenger aircraft with 102 seats. Two D-436T engines.	Tu-334
Tu-304		In the process of design	Long-range passenger aircraft.	Tu-304
Tu-244		In the process of design	Supersonic passenger aircraft of the second generation (SPS-2) – abbreviation for Sverkhzvukovoi Passazhirsky Samolet = supersonic passenger aircraft.	Tu-244
Tu-2000		In the process of design	Air space aircraft in HOTOL category.	Tu-2000
Tu-404		In the process of design	Passenger aircraft for 600–800 seats.	Tu-404
Tu-24Skh		In the process of design	Multi-purpose agricultural aircraft.	Tu-24Skh
Tu-34		In the process of design	Light multi-purpose passenger aircraft.	Tu-34
Tu-414/424		In the process of design	Long-range business aircraft for nine to twelve passenger seats (Tu-414). Tu-424 – medium-range airliner for fifty passengers. Two D-436T engines.	Tu-414/424
Tu-330		In the process of design	Medium transport, high-wing aircraft on the basis of Tu-204 elements, to replace An-12. Two PS-90A engines.	Tu-330
Tu-130		In the process of design	Light transport aircraft of cargo class (twelve tonnes).	Tu-130

**CORPORATE STRUCTURE OF
A. N. TUPOLEV ANTK**

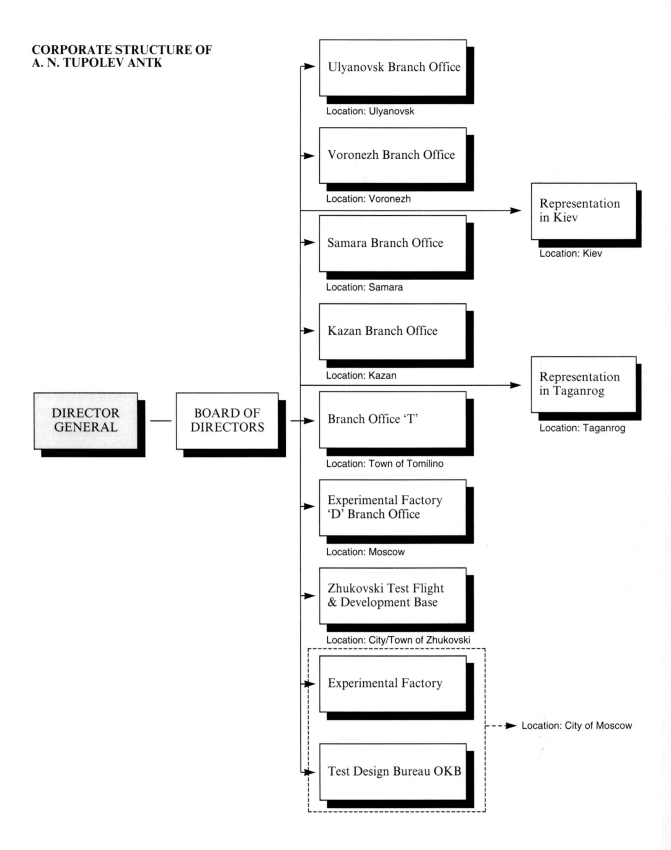

SPECIFICATIONS OF ANT AEROSLEIGHS

NAME	YEAR OF PRODUCTION	NUMBER OF SEATS	TRACK (METRES)	MAX WIDTH (M)	LENGTH OF BASE (M)	MAX LENGTH ON SKIS (M)	MAX HEIGHT (WITH PROPELLERS) (M)	WEIGHT WITHOUT/ WITH LOAD (KG)	ENGINE AND HORSE-POWER
ANT-1	1921	2	1.70	–	2.70	5.13	–	290/450	Anzani/38
ANT-1bis	1925	2	1.70	2.35	2.70	5.13	–	282/442	Anzani/38
ANT-II	1922	5	–	–	–	7.00	–	680/1160	Clerget/115
ANT-III	1923	3	–	–	–	6.00	2.68	410/716	Gnôme-Rhône/80
ANT-IIIbis	1926	3	1.80	2.40	3.23	6.00	2.68	406/646	Khakke/50
ANT-IV	1924	5	2.00	2.50	3.74	6.62	2.75	620/1060	Mikulin M-11 /100
AN1-V	1924	3	1.98	2.30	3.70	6.56	2.50	460/785	Bristol Lucifer/ 100
ANT-Vs	1925	3	2.00	2.50	3.74	6.62	2.75	542/862	Bristol Lucifer/ 100
ANT-VI	1926	3	1.80	2.40	3.23	6.00	2.68	–	Khakke/50
ANT-VII	1934	5	–	2.50	–	6.62	2.75	–	M-11/100
A-3	1961	2–6	–	2.16	–	6.11	2.21	–	Mikulin M-14B /350

AIRCRAFT SPECIFICATIONS

	ANT-1	ANT-2	ANT-3 (R-3)	ANT-4 (TB-1)	ANT-5 (I-4)	ANT-6 (TB-3)	ANT-6 *Aviaarktika*
First Flight/Year	1923	1924	1925	1925	1927	1930	1936
Beginning of Serial Production/Year		1926	1927	1929	1928	1932	1936
Number and Type of Engines	1 Piston 'Anzani'	1 Piston Bristol Lucifer	1 Piston M-5	2 Piston M-17	1 Piston M-22	4 Piston M-17F	4 Piston M-34R
Engine Power hp Engine Thrust kgp	25.7	73.5	449.7	500–679.3	479.6	500–729.6	610
Length, m	5.4	7.6	9.5	18.0	7.28	24.4	25.18
Height, m	1.7	2.12	3.1	5.1	2.8	6.5	6.5
Wing Span, m	7.2	10.45	13.0	28.7	11.4	39.5	41.85
Wing Area, m²	10	17.5	24.5 & 12.5 (biplane)	120.0	23.8	230.0	234.5
Wheel Track, m		1.75	1.89	5.8	1.6	7.0	7
Take-Off Weight: Normal (tonnes)	0.36		2.13	6.81	1.43	16.38	24.05
Maximum (tonnes)		0.836		8.79		18.01	24.50
Empty Weight, tonnes	0.229	0.523	1.34	4.52	0.98	11.21	12.5
Maximum Payload, tonnes	0.13	0.31		0.73		4.0	
Maximum range, km	540	750	950	1,350	840	2,700	2,500
Maximum speed, kph	135		194.0	198	231	177	275
Cruising Speed, kph		155					
Service Ceiling, km	0.4		5.0	4.8	7.0	3.8	4.5
Number of Crew	1	1	2	6	1	8	8
Number of Passengers		2–3					

* Payload is commercial load or, for military aircraft, weapons load

	ANT-7 (R-6, KR-6)	ANT-8 (MDR)	ANT-9 (PS-9)	ANT-10 (R-7)	ANT-13	ANT-14 *Pravda*	ANT-16 (TB-4)
First Flight/Year	1929	1931	1929	1930	1930	1931	1933
Beginning of Serial Production/Year	1931		1933				
Number and Type of Engines	2 Piston M-17F	2 Piston BMW-VI	2 Piston M-17	1 Piston BMW VI	1 Piston Curtiss Conqueror	5 Piston Gnôme-Rhône Jupiter-VI	6 Piston M34
Engine Power hp	500–679.3	500	500	500	515	353	610
Engine Thrust kgp							
Length, m	15.1	17.03	17.01	10.9		26.49	32
Height, m	5.45	5.67	5	3.6		8.29	11.73
Wing Span, m	23.2	23.7	23.85	15.2	9.03	40.4	54
Wing Area, m²	80.0	84	84	49	20.09	240	422
Wheel Track, m	4.61		5.07			8.05	10.64
Take-Off Weight: Normal (tonnes)	6.13	6.92		2.92	1.235		33.28
Maximum (tonnes)	7.25	8.16	6.2		1.454	17.53	37
Empty Weight, tonnes	3.9	4.56	4.4	1.72	1	10.828	21.4
Maximum Payload, tonnes	0.74		0.81			3.78	
Maximum range, km	1,680	1,062	1,800	1,100	545	2,400	2,000
Maximum speed, kph	212	166		235	303		200
Cruising Speed, kph			180			195	
Service Ceiling, km	5.6	3.35		5.5	5		2.75
Number of Crew	3–4	5	2	2	1	5	12
Number of Passengers			9			36	

	ANT-20 *Maksim Gorki*	ANT-21 (MI-3)	ANT-22 (MK-1)	ANT-23 (I-12)	ANT-25 (RD)	ANT-27bis (MTB-1)	ANT-29 (DIP)
First Flight/Year	1934	1933	1934	1931	1933	1934	1935
Beginning of Serial Production/Year						1935	
Number and Type of Engines	8 Piston M-34FRN	2 Piston M-17	2 Piston AM-34R	2 Piston 'Jupiter VI'	1 Piston M-34RF	3 Piston AM-34R	2 Piston M-100
Engine Power hp	662	500	610	353	699	610	633
Engine Thrust kgp							
Length, m	32.476	12.3	24.1	9.5	13.4	21.9	13.2
Height, m	11.253	5.95	8.96		5.5	8.6	5.3
Wing Span, m	63	20.76	51	15.6	34	39.4	19.19
Wing Area, m²	486	55.1	304.5	30	87.1	177.5	55.1
Wheel Track, m	10.645	4.94	12		7.3		4.85
Take-Off Weight: Normal (tonnes)	42	5.26	29.45	2.4		˙16.25	5.3
Maximum (tonnes)	53		43		11.5		
Empty Weight, tonnes	28.5	3.8	21.663	1.75	3.78	10.521	3.9
Maximum Payload, tonnes	6.72 (ANT-20bis)						
Maximum range, km	2,000	2,100	1,330		13,000	2,000	
Maximum speed, kph	220	351	205		246	225	3.52
Cruising Speed, kph				259			
Service Ceiling, km	4.5	7.89	3.5	8.5	7.85	4.47	
Number of Crew	8	4	8	1	3	5	2
Number of Passengers	72						

	ANT-31bis (I-14)	ANT-35 (PS-35)	ANT-37 (DB-2)	ANT-40 (SB)	ANT-41 (T-1)	ANT-42 (TB-7, Pe-8)	ANT-44bis (ANT-=44D)
First Flight/Year	1934	1936	1935	1934	1936	1936	1938
Beginning of Serial Production/Year	1934	1937		1936			
Number and Type of Engines	1 Piston M-25	2 Piston M-621R	2 Piston M-85	2 Piston M-100A	2 Piston M-34FRNV	4 Piston ASh-82FN	4 Piston M-87
Engine Power hp Engine Thrust kgp	699.7	735	625	859.4	883	1,849.2	669
Length, m	6.11	15.4	15	12.7	15.54	23.59	22.42
Height, m	3.14	5.66	3.825	4.24	3.86	6.4	7.88
Wing Span, m	11.25	20.8	31	20.33	25.73	39.01	36.45
Wing Area, m²	16.8	57.8	85	56.7	88.94	188.4	144.7
Wheel Track, m	2.9	5.55	5.72	5.10	5.88	6.54	20.46
Take-Off Weight: Normal (tonnes) Maximum (tonnes)	1.54	7	9.456 11.5	5.71 8.05	8.925	25.0 32.0	19 21
Empty Weight, tonnes	1.17	5.01	5.8	4 14	5.846	18.4	13.0
Maximum Payload, tonnes		1.1		1.5		4–5	3.0
Maximum range, km	1,050	1,200	5,000	2,150	4,200	4,700	4,500
Maximum speed, kph	449		342	423	435	345	355
Cruising Speed, kph		372					
Service Ceiling, km	9.43		8	9.56	9.5	10.3	7.1
Number of Crew	1	2	4	3	4	11	6–7
Number of Passengers		10					

	Tu-2 (ANT-58)	Tu-4	Tu-70	Tu-12 (Tu-77)	Tu-14T (Tu-81)	Tu-80	Tu-82
First Flight/Year	1941	1947	1946	1947	1950	1949	1949
Beginning of Serial Production/Year	1942	1947			1950		
Number and Type of Engines	2 Piston ASh-82FN	4 Piston ASh-73TK	4 Piston ASh-73TK	2 Turbojet 'Nene-1'	2 Turbojet VK-1	4 Piston ASh-73FN	2 Turbojet VK-1
Engine Power hp Engine Thrust kgp	1,360	1,770	1,770	22.3	26.5	1,770	26.5
Length, m	13.8	30.18	35.61	15.75	21.95	36.6	17.57
Height, m	4.5	8.95	9.75	4.19	5.95	8.91	6.2
Wing Span, m	18.86	43.05	43.05	18.86	21.69	44.3	17.81
Wing Area, m²	48.8	161.7	161.7	48.8	67.36	173.1	45
Wheel Track, m	5.4	8.67	9.48	6.06	6.60	8.67	6.93
Take-Off Weight: Normal (tonnes) Maximum (tonnes)	10.86 11.36	47.60 54.50	51.4	14.7 15.72	21.0 25.35	51.5 67.2	13.5 18.34
Empty Weight, tonnes	7.47	35.27	38.29	8.993	14.49	41.03	9.526
Maximum Payload, tonnes	3–4	6–8					
Maximum range, km	2,100	6,580	4,900	2,200	3,010	7000–8,000	2,395
Maximum speed, kph	547	558		783	845	650	934
Cruising Speed, kph			56.3				
Service Ceiling, km	9.5	11.2		11.36	11.2	11.18	11.4
Number of Crew	3–5	11	6	4	3	11	3
Number of Passengers			48				

	Tu-85	Tu-16 (Tu-88)	Tu-91	Tu-95	Tu-98	Tu-104B	Tu-22 (Tu-105)
First Flight/Year	1951	1952	1954	1952	1956	1955	1958
Beginning of Serial Production/Year		1953		1955		1956	1959
Number and Type of Engines	4 Piston VD-4K	2 Turbojet AM-3M	1 Turboprop TV-2M	4 Turboprop NK-12	2 Turbofan AL-7F	2 Turbojet AM-3M	2 Turbojet RD-TN-2
Engine Power hp Engine Thrust kgp	3,160	9,500	7,650	12,000	6,850–8,000	9,500	16,500

	Tu-85	Tu-16 (Tu-88)	Tu-91	Tu-95	Tu-98	Tu-104B	Tu-22 (Tu-105)
Length, m	39.31	34.80	17.7	46.17	32.06	38.85	41.6
Height, m	11.36	10.36	5.06	12.5	8.63	11.9	10.0
Wing Span, m	55.94	34.54	16.4	50.1	17.27	34.54	23.60
Wing Area, m²	273.6	164.65	47.48	284.9	87.5	169.7	162
Wheel Track, m	9.1	9.78	3.37	12.55	2.5	11.325	
Take-Off Weight: Normal (tonnes)	75	75.8	12.85	171	39.0		85
Maximum (tonnes)	107		14.4	190		78	94.0
Empty Weight, tonnes	55.4	37.20		120.0		44.2	
Maximum Payload, tonnes	13.0	9.0	1.5	25		12	9.0
Maximum range, km	13,000	7,800	2,350	12,500+	2,440	4,200	5,650
Maximum speed, kph	665	1,050	800	910+	1,238	1,000	1,640
Cruising Speed, kph	563			711		800	
Service Ceiling, km	13.0	15.0	11.0	17	12.75	11.9	13.5
Number of Crew	11–16	6	2	10	3	5	3
Number of Passengers						100	

+ *with combat load*

	Tu-114	Tu-116	Tu-124	Tu-126	Tu-28 (Tu-128)	Tu-134A	Tu-142*
First Flight/Year	1957	1958	1960	1960	1961	1963	1968
Beginning of Serial Production/Year	1958		1961	1961		1964	1972
Number and Type of Engines	4 Turboprop NK-12MV	4 Turboprop NK-12MV	2 Turboprop D-20P	4 Turboprop NK-12MV	2 Turbofan AL-7F-2	2 Turbofan D-30	4 Turboprop NK-12MP
Engine Power hp	12,000	15,000		15,000			15,000
Engine Thrust kgp			5,800		6,900–10,100	6,800	
Length, m	54.1	47.5	30.58	55.20	39.1	37.1	49.50
Height, m	15.5		8.08	16.05		9.02	12.12
Wing Span, m	51.1	51.1	25.55	51.20	17.53	29	51.10
Wing Area, m²	311.1	311.1	105.35	311.10	96.94	115	295
Wheel Track, m	13.7		9.05			9.45	
Take-Off Weight: Normal (tonnes)							170
Maximum (tonnes)	179	121.920	37.6	170	43.0	47	188
Empty Weight, tonnes	95		23.16		25.96	29	80
Maximum Payload, tonnes	22.5		6		1.9	8.2	20
Maximum range, km	8,400	10,500	2,040	12,550	2,565	3,060	12,550
Maximum speed, kph			1,000	850	1,910		925
Cruising Speed, kph	750	770	750–850	650	1,665	750–850	
Service Ceiling, km		12.0		13	15.6		13.5
Number of Crew	5		3	15	2	3	10
Number of Passengers	170–224		44–56			80–86	

* For Tu-142M3

	Tu-144	Tu-22M (Tu-145)	Tu-154	Tu-160	Tu-204	Tu-334	Tu-234
First Flight/Year	1968	1977	1968	1981	1989	Expected	Expected
Beginning of Serial Production/Year	1969		1969		1990	1996	1996
Number and Type of Engines	4 Turbofan with afterburn NK-144	4 Turbofan with afterburn NK-25	3 Turbofan NK-8-2	4 Turbofan with afterburn NK-32	2 Turbofan PS-90A	2 Turbofan D-436	2 Turbofan PS-90A
Engine Power hp							
Engine Thrust kgp	20,000	25,000	93kn	25,000	157kn		157kn
Length, m	65.7	42.16	47.9	54.1	46	33.0	40.0
Height, m	12.5	11.05	11.4	13.2	13.9	8.8	13.9

	Tu-144	Tu-22M (Tu-145)	Tu-154	Tu-160	Tu-204	Tu-334	Tu-234
Wing Span, m	28	34.28/23.3	37.55	55.7/35.6	42	29.8	42.8
Wing Area, m²	507	183.58	180	232	168		168
Wheel Track, m	6		11.5	5.4	7.8		7.8
Take-Off Weight: Normal (tonnes) Maximum (tonnes)	207 (Tu-144D)	124	98	275.0	93.5		
Empty Weight, tonnes	97 (Tu-144D)		52	110	56.5		
Maximum Payload, tonnes	15	24	18	45.0	21	11	
Maximum range, km	6,500	2,500	4,500	12,300	4,600	3,000	9,000
Maximum speed, kph		2,450		2,200			
Cruising Speed, kph	2,200 (Tu-144D)		850		810–850*	800–820*	810–850*
Service Ceiling, km	18*	15,000	11.9*	18.0			
Number of Crew	4	4	3–4	4	2–3	3	2–3
Number of Passengers	150 (Tu-144D)		164–180		214	86–102	160
		* Maximum cruising level					

WORLD RECORDS STAGED ON ANT-6

No.	Date	Crew	Aeroplane Number Type of Engines, Their Power (hp)	Type of Record	Showing
1	11 September 1936	A. B. Yumashev – *1st Pilot* A. Kalshnikov – *Mechanic*	ANT-6, Four AM-34FRN, (Russian), 900hp	Altitude with the load of 5,000kg	8,102m
2	16 September 1936	A. B. Yumashev – *1st Pilot*	ANT-6 Four AM-34FRN, 900hp	Altitude with the load of 10,000kg	6,605m
3	20 September 1936	A. B. Yumashev – *1st Pilot* L. I. Sheverdinsky *Mechanic*	ANT-6, Four AM-34FRN, 900hp	Lifting the load to the altitude of 2,000m	12,000kg
4	28 October 1936	A. B. Yumashev – *1st Pilot*	ANT-6, Four AM-34FRN, 900hp	Altitude with the load of 5,000kg	8,980m

Source Used: '1. World aircraft records of the USSR'
(A. S. Yakovlev *Soviet Aeroplanes*, Moscow 1982, pages 326–327).

WORLD RECORD STAGED ON ANT-20 (*MAKSIM GORKI*)

No.	Date	Crew	Aeroplane Number Type of Engines, Their Power (hp)	Type of Record	Showing	Source
1	1934	M. M. Gromov – *1st Pilot* I. S. Zhurov *2nd Pilot*	ANT-20, Eight M-34FRN (M-3490PH), 900hp	Altitude with the load (kg): 1. 10,000 2. 15,000	5,000m	*Samolet* (aeroplane) No. 1, 1936 page 46

WORLD RECORD STAGED ON ANT-22

No.	Date	Crew	Aeroplane Number Type of Engines, Their Power (hp)	Type of Record	Showing
1	8 December 1936	T.V. Riabenko – *1st Pilot* D. Iliynsky – *2nd Pilot* V. Kochetov – *Mechanic*	ANT-22, Six AM-3YP (Russian), 800hp	Altitude with the load of 10,000kg/seaplanes	1,942m

WORLD RECORDS STAGED ON ANT-25

No.	Date	Crew	Aeroplane Number Type of Engines, Their Power (hp)	Type of Record	Showing	Source
1	12 to 15 September 1934	M. M. Gromov – *1st Pilot* A. I. Filin – *2nd Pilot* I. T. Spirin – *Navigator*	ANT-25, AM-34P (Russian) (Duplicate RD-2) 950hp	Range on straight line distance (length of flight – 75 hours)	12,411km	Not registered by FAI (USSR not a member)
2	20 to 22 July 1936	V. P. Chkalov – *1st Pilot* G. F. Baidukov – *2nd Pilot* A. V. Beliakov – *Navigator*	ANT-25 AM-34P (Russian) (Duplicate, RD-2) 950hp	Range on broken line (length of flight – 56 hours 20 min)	9,374km	
3	12 to 14 July 1937	M. M. Gromov – *1st Pilot* A. B. Yumashev – *2nd Pilot* S. A. Danilin – *Navigator*	ANT-25; AM-34R (Experimental, RD-1) 950hp	Range: (1) On broken line. (2) Straight line (length of flight – 62h. 17 min.)	two records	10,148km

WORLD RECORD STAGED ON ANT-37 (*RODINA* = MOTHERLAND)

No.	Date	Crew	Aeroplane Number Type of Engines, Their Power (hp)	Type of Record	Showing	Source
1	24 to 25 September 1938	V. S. Grizodubova – *1st Pilot* P. D. Osipenko – *2nd Pilot* M. M. Raskova – *Navigator*	ANT-37, Two M-86, 800hp	Range in straight line, by women's crew (length of flight – 26 hours, 29 minutes)	5,908km	B.V. Shavrov *The History of Aeroplane Design in the USSR before 1938* Moscow, 1969

WORLD RECORD STAGED ON ANT-40 (SB) AIRCRAFT

No.	Date	Crew	Aeroplane Number Type of Engines, Their Power (hp)	Type of Record	Showing	Source
1	2 September 1937	M. Y. Alekseev – *1st Pilot*	ANT-40 Two M-103, 860hp	Altitude with load (kg) 1,000	12,246m	*Tekhnika Vozdushno Go Flota* (Equipment of the Air Fleet) No. 10 1937 pages 113–114

WORLD RECORDS STAGED ON ANT-44

No.	Date	Crew	Aeroplane Number Type of Engines, Their Power (hp)	Type of Record	Showing
1	17 June 1940	I. M. Sukhomlin – *1st Pilot*	ANT-44D Four M-87, 840hp	Altitude with load (kg) 1. 1,000/seaplane	7,134m
2	19 June 1940	I. M. Sukhomlin – *1st Pilot*	ANT-44D, Four M-87,840hp	Altitude with load (kg) 1. 2,000/seaplane 2. 5,000/seaplane	6,284m 5,219m
3	19 June 1940	I. M. Sukhomlin *1st Pilot*	ANT-44D, Four M-87, 840hp	Lifting a load to the altitude of 2,000m/seaplane	5,000kg
4	28 September 1940	I. M. Sukhomlin – *1st Pilot*	ANT-44D, Four M-85, 750hp	Speed at 1,000km of closed circuit with the load of 1,000kg/seaplane	277.466kph
5	7 October 1940	I. M. Sukhomlin – *1st Pilot*	ANT-44D, Four M-85, 750hp	Speed at 1,000km of closed circuit with 2,000kg of load/seaplane	241.909kph

WORLD RECORDS STAGED ON Tu-104

Materials Used:
1. Reference book – photo album of the museum of A.N. Tupolev
2. Copies of the FAI Diplomas on the records (from the friends of A.N. Tupolev museum).
3. 'Materials to the TsAGI History. International and Soviet records staged on the USSR aeroplanes. 1934–1967'
(Museum of N.E. Zhukovsky. Ref. No. 6899 dated 18.09.1967).

No.	Date	Crew	Type of Aeroplane	Type of Record Flight From	Showing
1	9 September 1957	Y. T. Alasheev – *1st Pilot* V. F. Kovalev – *2nd Pilot* K. I. Malkhasian – *Navigator* V. N.Benderov – *Engineer* N. F. Maiorov *Radio Operator* I. D. Ivanov – *Mechanic*	Tu-104A (SSSR-L5421) Two RD-3 - 8,700kg	Altitude with payload (kg) 1. 20,000 2. 40,053 Vnukovo, Moscow airport	11,221m 2,000m two records
2	11 September 1957	Y. T. Alasheev – *1st Pilot* V. F. Kovalev – *2nd Pilot* R. I. Malkhasian – *Navigator* V. N. Benderov – *Engineer* N. F. Maiorov – *Radio Operator* I. D. Ivanov – *Mechanic*	Tu-104A (SSSR-L5421) 2 RD-3 - 8,700kg	Speed at 2,000km closed circuit with load (kg): 1. 2,000 2. 1,000 3. Without load Institute named after Shternberg, South Bazisnaya	897.798 (km/h) three records
3	24 September 1957	V. F. Kovalev – *1st Pilot* I. M. Sukhomlin – *2nd Pilot* R. I. Malkhasian – *Navigator* B. N. Grozdov – *Engineer* N. F. Maiorov – *Radio Operator* V. A. Golubkov – *Mechanic*	Tu-104A (SSSR-L5421) 2 RD-3 - 8,700kg	Speed on 1,000km closed circuit with payload of (kg) 1. 10,000 2. 5,000 3. 2,000 4. 1,000 5. Without load Institute named after Shternberg 'Zorino'	970.821 (km/h) five records

No.	Date	Crew	Type of Aeroplane	Type of Record	Showing	Source
4	1 August 1959	V. F. Kovalev – *1st Pilot*	Tu-104B	Speed at 1,000km of closed circuit with payload (kg): 1. 15,000 2. 10,000 3. 5,000 4. 2,000 5. 1,000 6. No load	1,015.866 kph six records	Reference – Book 1 Photo Album page 118, point 3
5	August 1959	Y. T. Alasheev – *1st Pilot*		Max load lifted over an airfield	12,799kg three records	Reference – Book 1 Photo Album page 118, point 4
6	4 August 1959	Y. T. Alasheev – *1st Pilot*	Tu-104B	Altitude with payload 25,000kg	12,896m one record	Diploma of the USSR Record Holder awarded to Y.T. Alasheev by the Central Council of the Union of Sports, Societies and Organisations, April 1960
7	2 April 1960	V. F. Kovalev – *1st Pilot* Y. Minin	Tu-104E 2 TRD-3M 9,500kg	Speed at 2,000km closed circuit with payload 1. 15,000 2. 10,000 3. 5,000 4. 2,000 5. 1,000 6. No load	959.940 kph six records	FAI Record 1961, 1962 Reference – Book 1 Photo Album page 118, point 5

In total on different modifications of Tu-104, twenty-six world records were staged during the period from 6 September 1957 until 2 April 1960.

RECORDS REGISTERED WITH THE FÉDÉRATION AÉRONAUTIQUE INTERNATIONALE SET BY TUPOLEV AIRCRAFT
AND CURRENT AT 1 JUNE 1995.
SOURCE: FÉDÉRATION AÉRONAUTIQUE INTERNATIONALE/THIERRY MONTIGNEAUX.

GROUP 2: TURBOPROP ENGINES
Sub-Class C-1 (Unlimited Weight)
(35 Records)

Crew	Aircraft	Record	Performance	Date	Comment
	Tu-142	altitude with 1,000kg payload	12,265m	05/10/89	superseded
	Tu-142	altitude with 2,000kg/5,000kg payload	12,265m	05/10/89	
Sukhomlin – *First Pilot* Timoshok – *Second Pilot* Zhila, Malkhasian – *Navigators* Kutakov – *Radio Operator* Seliverstov, Korolev – *Engineers* Aristov, Komissarov – *Mechanics*	Tu-114	altitude with 25,000kg/30,000kg payload	12,073m	12/06/61	
Sukhomlin – *First Pilot* Timoshok – *Second Pilot* Zhila, Malkhasian – *Navigators* Kutakov – *Radio Operator* Seliverstov, Korolev – *Engineers* Aristov, Komissarov – *Mechanics*	Tu-114	speed over a 1,000km closed circuit without payload speed over a 1,000km closed circuit with a 1,000kg/2,000kg/5,000kg/10,000kg/ 15,000kg/20,000kg/25,000kg payload	871.38kph	24/03/60	
Sukhomlin – *First Pilot* Timoshok – *Second Pilot* Zhila, Malkhasian – *Navigators* Kutakov – *Radio Operator* Seliverstov, Korolev – *Engineers* Aristov, Komissarov – *Mechanics*	Tu-114	speed over a 2,000km closed circuit without payload speed over a 2,000km closed circuit with 1,000kg/2,000kg/5,000kg/10,000kg 15,000kg/20,000kg/25,000kg payload	857.28kph	01/04/60	

Crew	Aircraft	Record	Performance	Date	Comment
	Tu-142	speed over a 2,000km closed circuit with 30,000kg payload	834.82kph	28/09/89	
Sukhomlin – *First Pilot* Timoshok *Second Pilot* Zhila, Malkhasian – *Navigators* Kutakov – *Radio Operator* Seliverstov, Korolev – *Engineers* Aristov, Komissarov – *Mechanics*	Tu-114	speed over a 5,000km closed circuit without payload speed over a 5,000km closed circuit with a 1,000kg/2,000/5,000kg/10,000kg/15,000kg/20,000kg/25,000kg payload	877.21kph	09/04/60	
Sukhomlin – *First Pilot* Timoshok – *Second Pilot* Zhila, Malkhasian – *Navigators* Kutakov – *Radio Operator* Seliverstov, Korolev – *Engineers* Aristov, Komissarov – *Mechanics*	Tu-114	speed over a 10,000km closed circuit without payload speed over a 10,00km closed circuit with 1,000kg/2,000kg/5,000kg/10,000kg payload	737.35kph	21/04/62	

GROUP 2: TURBOPROP ENGINES
Sub Class C-1-P (Landplanes – Take-Off Weight 100,000 to 150,000kg)
(27 Records)

Crew	Aircraft	Record	Performance	Date	Comment
Malyshev Bashkirov Egorov	Tu-142	altitude without payload altitude with 1,000kg/2,000kg/5,000kg payload	12,265m	05/10/89	
Alferov Nikolaev Vydrin	Tu-142	altitude with 10,000kg/15,000kg/20,000kg payload	12,240m	28/11/90	
Bashkirov Samorodov Lushnikov	Tu-142M	altitude with 25,000kg/30,000kg payload	11,410m	22/11/90	
Mosolov Chalov Kashitski Bezhenari	Tu-95	speed over a 1,000km closed circuit without payload speed over a 1,000km closed circuit with 1,000kg/2,000kg/5,000kg/10,000kg/15,000kg/20,000kg/25,000kg/30,000kg payload	807.37kph	26/09/89	
Naimushin Osipov Ivlev Zolotarev	Tu-142	speed over a 2,000km closed circuit without payload speed over a 2,000km closed circuit with 1,000kg/2,000kg/5,000kg/10,000kg/15,000kg/20,000kg/25,000kg/30,000kg payload	834.82kph	28/09/89	

GROUP 2: TURBOPROP ENGINES
Sub-Class C-1-Q (Landplanes – Take-Off Weight 150,000 to 200,000 kg)
(28 Records)

Crew	Aircraft	Record	Performance	Date	Comment
Kabanov Alferov	Tu-142	altitude without payload altitude with 1,000kg/2,000kg/5,000kg payload	10,823m	05/10/89	
Bobylev Makarov Shishko	Tu-142	altitude with 10,000kg/15,000kg/20,000kg payload	11,100m	28/11/90	
Nikolaev Kobiakov Tsiberkin	Tu-142	altitude with 25,000kg/30,000kg payload	10,110m	16/11/90	
Kozlov Popov Maltsev Merzliakov	Tu-142	speed over a 1,000km closed circuit without payload speed over a 1,000km closed circuit with 1,000kg/2,000kg/5,000kg/10,000kg/15,000kg/20,000kg/25,000kg/30,000kg payload	816.25kph	26/09/89	

Crew	Aircraft	Record	Performance	Date	Comment
Pripuskov Baskakov	Tu-142	speed over a 5,000km closed circuit without payload speed over a 5,000km closed circuit with a 1,000kg/2,000kg/5,000kg/10,000kg/15,000kg/20,000kg payload	785.30kph	10/10/89	
Pavlov Sattarov Tsarakhov Oshepkov	Tu-142	speed over a 10,000km closed circuit without payload speed over a 10,000km closed circuit with a 1,000kg/2,000kg payload	647.89kph	31/10/89 to 01/11/89	

GROUP 3: TURBOJET ENGINES
Sub-Class C-1 (Unlimited Weight)
(4 Records)

Aircraft	Record	Performance	Date	Comment
"Tu-160"*	speed over a 1,000km closed circuit with 15,000kg/25,000kg payload	1,731.40kph	31/10/89	
"Tu-160"*	speed over a 2,000km closed circuit with 15,000kg/25,000kg payload	1,678.00kph	03/11/89	

Here it is worth mentioning that there are a number of records which have been set by aircraft referred to as 'Aircraft 101'. The exact type was not indicated, but it may be that it was a 'Blackjack' bomber. Also note the Tu-160 is sometimes referred to as 'Aircraft 70' in some record lists, as they did not give its name at first. We identified it from the photographs included with the record documents. This comment is by FAI. They are not correct. Aircraft 101 is in fact a Tu-144D, SSSR-77114.

GROUP 3: TURBOJET ENGINES
Sub-Class C-1-M (Landplanes – Take-Off Weight 45,000 to 60,000kg)
(7 Records)

Aircraft	Record	Performance	Date	Comment
Tu-16	altitude without payload	14,120m	27/09/91	
Tu-16	altitude with 1,000kg/2,000kg/5,000kg payload	14,180m	24/09/91	
Tu-16	altitude in horizontal flight without payload	14,590m	26/02/91	
Tu-16	speed over a 1,000km closed circuit with 2,000kg payload	913.00kph	22/07/91	
Tu-16	speed over a 1,000km closed circuit with 5,000kg payload	881.45kph	01/10/91	

GROUP 3: TURBOJET ENGINES
Sub-Class C-1-N (Landplanes – Take-Off Weight 60,000 to 80,000kg)
(14 Records)

Aircraft	Record	Performance	Date	Comment
Tu-155*	altitude without payload	9,546m	04/08/89	superseded
Tu-155*	altitude with 1,000kg payload	9,546m	04/08/89	
Tu-155*	altitude with 2,000kg payload	9,546m	04/08/89	superseded
Tu-16	altitude with 5,000kg payload	14,010m	28/02/91	
Tu-155*	altitude in horizontal flight	9,475m	07/08/89	superseded
Tu-16	greatest payload carried to 2,000 metres	8,406kg	22/03/91	

Aircraft	Record	Performance	Date	Comment
Tu-16	speed over a 1,000km circuit without payload speed over a 1,000km closed circuit with 1,000kg/2,000kg/5,000kg payload	897.16kph	05/03/91	
Tu-16	speed over a 2,000km closed circuit without payload speed over a 2,000km closed circuit with 1,000kg/2,000kg/5,000kg payload	889.42kph	20/03/91	

* Cryogenic Fuel

GROUP 3: TURBOJET ENGINES
Sub-Class: C-1-0 (Landplanes – Take-Off Weight 80,000kg to 100,000kg – Cryogenic Fuel)
(5 Records)

Aircraft	Record	Performance	Date	Comment
Tu-155	altitude without payload altitude with 1,000kg/2,000kg payload	12,170m	04/12/90	
Tu-155	altitude in horizontal flight	12,130m	04/12/90	
Tu-155	greatest payload carried to 2,000 metres	2,308.2kg	22/03/91	

GROUP 3: TURBOJET ENGINES
Sub-Class: C-1-R (Landplanes – Take-Off Weight 200,000 to 250,000kg)
(37 Records)

Aircraft	Record	Performance	Date	Comment
Tu-160	altitude without payload altitude with 1,000kg/2,000kg/5,000kg/10,000kg/ 15,000kg/20,000kg/25,000kg/30,000kg payload	13,894m	31/10/90	
Tu-160	altitude in horizontal flight	12,150m	31/10/90	
Tu-160	speed over a 1,000km closed circuit without payload speed over a 1,000km closed circuit with 1,000kg/2,000kg/5,000kg/10,000kg/15,000kg/ 20,000kg/25,000kg/30,000kg payload	1,731.40kph	31/10/90	
Tu-160	speed over a 2,000km closed circuit without payload speed over a 2,000km closed circuit with 1,000kg/2,000kg/5,000kg/10,000kg/15,000kg/ 20,000kg/25,000kg/30,000kg payload	1,195.70kph	22/05/90	
Tu-160	speed over a 5,000km closed circuit without payload speed over a 5,000km closed circuit with 1,000kg/2,000kg/5,000kg/10,000kg/15,000kg/ 20,000kg/25,000kg/30,000kg payload	920.95kph	24/05/90	

GROUP 3: TURBOJET ENGINES
Sub-Class C-1-S (Landplanes – Take-Off Weight 250,000 to 300,000kg)
(18 Records)

Aircraft	Record	Performance	Date	Comment
Tu-160	altitude without payload altitude with 1,000kg/2,000kg/5,000kg/10,000kg/ 15,000kg/20,000kg/30,000kg payload	14,000m	03/11/89	
Tu-160	speed over a 2,000km closed circuit without payload speed over a 2,000km closed circuit with 1,000kg/2,000kg/5,000kg/10,000kg/15,000kg/ 20,000kg/25,000kg/30,000kg payload	1,678kph	03/11/89	

WORLD RECORDS STAGED ON Tu-144

Crew	Class	Aircraft	Record	Performance	Date	Comment
		Tu-144 (Avion 101) SSSR-77114	Speed over 1,000km closed circuit with payload 5,000kg/10,000kg/ 20,000kg/30,000kg	2,031.546kph	13/7/83	Superseded
		Tu-144 SSSR-77114	Speed over 2,000km closed circuit with payload 5,000kg/10,000kg/ 20,000kg/30,000kg	2,012.257kph	20/07/83	
		Tu-144 SSSR-77114	Altitude with payload 5,000kg/ 10,000kg/20,000kg/30,000kg	18,200m	20/07/83	

WORLD RECORDS TIME TO ALTITUDE/PROPELLER AIRCRAFT

Crew	Class	Aircraft	Record	Performance	Date	Comment
Artukhin Vanshin Sadov Donskov	C-1-P	Tu-142L	Time of climb to altitude 6,000m/9,000m	4 min 23 sec/ 6 min 35 sec	30/5/90	
	C-1-P	Tu-142	Altitude without payload	12,265m		

SPECIFICATIONS OF TORPEDO BOATS

TKA	Displacement	Length & Width = Draught	Number/Type of Engines hp	Engine Power	Max Speed	Range Miles	Armaments Number & Type	Crew
GANT-3 First Born	8.9 tonnes	17.3 x 3.3 x 0.9	2 Wright Cyclone	600	54.0	340	1 x 450mm Torpedo 2 x 7.62mm machine-guns 2 mines	3 – 4
GANT-4 *Tupolev*	10.0 tonnes	16.8 x 3.3 x 0.8	2 Wright Cyclone	600	50.5	300	2 x 450mm Torpedos 1 x 7.62mm machine-gun 2 mines	5
SL-4 Serial GANT-4	10.0 tonnes	16.8 x 3.3 x 0.8	2 Wright Cyclone	600	50.5	300	2 x 450mm Torpedos 1 x 7.62mm machine-gun 2 mines	5
GANT-5	14.5 tonnes	19.1 x 3.4 x 1.2	2 ASSO	1,000	58.0	232	2 x 533mm Torpedos 2 x 7.62mm machine-guns 4 mines	6
Serial GANT-5	17.8 tonnes	19.1 x 3.3 x 1.2	2 GM-34	800	52.0	200	2 x 533mm Torpedos 1 x 7.62mm machine-gun 1 x 12.7mm mines	6
G-6	86.0 tonnes	36.4 x 6.6 x 1.9	8 GM-34	800	49.8	435	6 x 533mm Torpedos 1 x 45mm cannon 1 x 12.7mm machine-gun 4 x 7.62 machine-guns 3 mines	20
G-8	31.3 tonnes	24.2 x 3.8 x 1.5	4 GM-34APF	1,000	48.0	350	2 x 533mm Torpedos 2 x 12.7mm machine-guns 1 x 7.62mm machine-gun 6 Depth Charges	8 – 10
SM-4 (Serial G-8)	42.0 tonnes	22.0 x 4.1 x 1.8	4 GM-34APF	1,000	30.0	–	2 x 533mm Torpedos 3 x 12.7mm machine-guns 10 Depth Charges	8 – 10

PRODUCTION FIGURES

Design Bureau Designation	Military Aeroflot Designation	Produced By Designer	Serial Production		Remarks
ANT-1		1	–		
ANT-2		2	5		
ANT-3		2	101	79	Lorraine-Dietrich engines
				1	BMW VI
				21	Mikulin M-5
ANT-4	TB-1	2	216		
ANT-5	I-4	2	369		
ANT-6	TB-3	1	819		
ANT-7	R-6	1	410	404	Standard
				5	KR-6P Floatplanes
				1	'Limo'
ANT-8	MDR-2	1	–		
ANT-9	PS-9	1	66	60	3 Wright Whirlwind engines
				6	2 Mikulin M-17
ANT-10	R-7	1	–		
ANT-12	I-5	–	–		Transferred to Polikarpov
ANT-13	I-8	1	–		
ANT-14		1	–		
ANT-16	TB-3	1	–		
ANT-17		(1)	–		Not completed
ANT-20	*Maksim Gorki*	1	–		
ANT-20bis	PS-124		1		
ANT-21	MI-3	2	–		
ANT-22	MK-1	1	–		
ANT-23	I-12	1	–		
ANT-25	RD	2			Plus one replica
ANT-27	MDR-4/MTB-1	2	15		
ANT-29	DIP	1	–		
ANT-31	I-14	2	18		
ANT-35	PS-35	1	11		
ANT-36	DB-1	–	20		

Design Bureau Designation	Military Aeroflot Designation	Produced By Designer	Serial Production	Remarks
ANT-37	DB-2	2	–	
ANT-40	SB/PS-40/AR-2 SB-1, SB-2, SB-3	3	6,992	Including Czechoslovakian production
ANT-41	T-1	1	–	
ANT-42	TB-7, Pe-8	2	93	
ANT-44	MTB-2A	2	–	
ANT-46	DI-8	1		
ANT-51		1		Design transferred to Sukhoi
ANT-58	Samolet 103	1		
ANT-59	Samolet 103U	1		
ANT-60	Samolet 103V			
ANT-61	Tu-2/VS/S/T/Tu-6	–		Total Tu-2 production
ANT-62	Tu-2D/Samolet 62T	–		including related versions
ANT-63	SDB/Tu-1	–	2,527	excludes Chinese production
ANT-65	Tu-2D	–		numbers
ANT-67	Tu-2D	–		
ANT-68	Tu-10	–		
ANT-69	Tu-8			
B-4	Tu-4	–	847	Copy of B-29
Tu-70		1		Using B-29 parts
Tu-73	(Tu-14)	1	–	
Tu-75		1	–	
Tu-77	Tu-12	1	3	
Tu-78	(Tu-20) Tu-73R	1	–	
Tu-80		1	–	
Tu-81	Tu-14T	1	87	
-82	(Tu-22)	1		
Tu-85		1		
Tu-88	Tu-16 'Badger'	1	1,507	
	H-6		+120 (estimate)	Built in China
Tu-89	(Tu-16)	1		
Tu-91	'Bychek'	1	–	

Design Bureau Designation	Military Aeroflot Designation	Produced By Designer	Serial Production	Remarks
Tu-92				Included in Tu-88 figures
Tu-95	Tu-20, 'Bear' A-E, G	2	172	
Tu-96		(Nil)	1	
Tu-98	(Tu-24) 'Backfin'	2	–	
Tu-104		2	201	Includes tests airframe
Tu-105	Tu-22 'Blinder'	2	311	
Tu-110		1	2	Prototype assembled from production factory parts
Tu-114		1	32	
Tu-116		–	2	
Project 121	'S'	1	–	Missile – ICBM
Project 123		1	52	Missile – strategic reconnaissance
Tu-124	DBR-1	1	162	
Tu-126	'Moss'	(Nil)	9	
Tu-128	'Fiddler'	1	198	
Project 130		1	–	Missile – space
Tu-134		2	850	
Project 139		1	–	Missile – strategic reconnaissance
Project 141		1	152	Missile – tactical reconnaissance
Tu-142	'Bear' F, H and J	1	225	Number unconfirmed
Project 143		1	950	Missile – tactical reconnaissance
Tu-144		1	15	Flyable, and one not completed
			4	Test airframes
Project 145	Tu-22M 'Backfire'	–	497	
Tu-154		1	911	*Still in production
Tu-160		2	27	Last one incomplete as yet (would leave total 30)
			1	Static test airframe
Tu-204		1	32	*Continuing
		1		Static test airframe
Tu-334		1		Not yet in production
		1		Static test

PRODUCTION OF TUPOLEV DESIGNS

Total	Type	Factory Number	Location	1925	1926	1929	1930	1931	1932
	ANT-4/TB-1								
2	Prototypes	TsAGI/ZOK	Moscow	1	1				
216		22	Kazan			2	66	146	2
218				*1*	*1*	*2*	*66*	*146*	*2*

Total	Type	Factory Number	Location	1930	1932	1933	1934	1935	1936	1937	1938
	ANT-6/TB/3										
1	Prototypes	TsAGI/ZOK	Moscow	1							
763		22	Kazan		155	270	126	74	115	22	1
6		18	Voronezh				5		1		
50		31	Taganrog		5	37	8				
820				*1*	*160*	*307*	*139*	*74*	*115*	*23*	*1*

Total	Type	Factory Number	Location	1934	1935	1936	1937	1938	1939	1940	1941
	ANT-40/SB										
3	Prototypes	TsAGI/ZOK	Moscow	2	1						
5,695		22	Kazan			268	853	1,250	1,435	1,820	69
1,136		125	Irkutsk				73	177	343	375	168
161			Czechoslovakia	Years not confirmed				161			
6,995				*2*	*1*	*268*	*926*	*1,427*	*1,778*	*2,195*	*237*	*161*

Total	Type	Factory Number	Location	1952	1953	1954	1955	1956	1957	1958	1959	1960	1961	1962	1963	
	Tu-16 'Badger' (Tu-88)															
2	Prototypes	156	Moscow	1	1											
800		22	Kazan		2	70	200	133	170	75	–	–	30	70	50	
543		18	Kuibyshev			10	130	131	150	50	30	42	–	–	–	
166		64	Voronezh				25	86	55							
120 (approx)			China	Exact Numbers and Years Not Confirmed												±120
1,631				*1*	*3*	*80*	*330*	*289*	*406*	*180*	*30*	*42*	*30*	*70*	*50*	*±120*

Total	Type	Factory Number	Location	1952	1953	1954	1955	1956	1957	1958	1959	1960	1961
	Tu-95												
2	95/95M Prototypes	156	Moscow	1	–	1							
49	95/95M	18	Kuibyshev					4	23	8	14		
70	95/K/95M/95KD									3	17	17	10
53	95RTS												
174													
1	Tu-96	18	Kuibyshev						1				
175				*1*	*–*	*1*	*4*	*24*	*8*	*17*	*17*	*17*	*10*

	Type	Factory Number	Location	1962	1963	1964	1965	1966	1967	1968	1969
	Tu-95										
	95/95M Prototypes	156	Moscow								
	95K/95KM/95KD		Kuibyshev	10	8	4	1				
	95RTS			1	2	5	10	10	10	10	5
	Tu-96	18	Kuibyshev								
				11	*10*	*9*	*11*	*10*	*10*	*10*	*5*

Total	Type	Factory Number	Location	1955	1956	1957	1958	1959	1960
	Tu-104								
1	Prototype	156	Moscow	1					
96		22	Kazan			17	35	44	
45		135	Kharkov		7	12	16	10	
60		166	Omsk		5	13	21	15	6
202				*1*	*12*	*25*	*54*	*60*	*50*

Total	Type	Factory Number	Location	1957	1958	1959	1960	1961	1962	1963	1964	1965	1966
	Tu-105/Tu-22												
2	Prototype	156	Moscow	1	1								
311		22	Kazan			5	20		33	36	49	35	40
313				*1*	*1*	*5*	*20*		*33*	*36*	*49*	*35*	*40*

	Type	Factory Number	Location	1967	1968	1969					
	Tu-105/Tu-22										
	Prototype	156	Moscow								
		22	Kazan	50	27	16					
				50	*27*	*16*					

Total	Type	Factory Number	Location	1957	1958	1959	1960	1961	1962	1963	1964
	Tu-114										
1	Prototype	156	Moscow	1							
31		18	Kuibyshev		2	6	3	6	6	4	4
32				*1*	*2*	*6*	*3*	*6*	*6*	*4*	*4*

Total	Type	Factory Number	Location	1962	1963	1964	1965	1966	1967	
	Tu-126									
1	Prototype	156	Moscow	1						
8		18	Kuibyshev				2	3	3	
9				*1*			*2*	*3*	*3*	

Total	Type	Factory Number	Location	1959	1960	1961	1962	1963	1964	1965	1966	1967	1968
	Tu-124												
1	Prototype	156	Moscow	1									
163		135	Kharkov		5	12	20	27	32	33	13	15	6
164				*1*	*5*	*12*	*20*	*27*	*32*	*33*	*13*	*15*	*6*

Total	Type	Factory Number	Location	1960	1961	1962	1963	1964	1965	1966	1967	1968	1969	1970	1971
	Tu-128															
1	Prototype	156	Moscow	1											
198		64	Voronezh		2	2	2	3	4	42	37	31	38	27	10
199				*1*	*2*	*2*	*2*	*3*	*4*	*42*	*37*	*31*	*38*	*27*	*10*

Total	Type	Factory Number	Location	1963	1966	1967	1968	1969	1970	1971	1972	1973	1974
	Tu-134												
80	Tu-134	135	Kharkov	2	13	6	20	28	11				
683	134A & 134B	135	Kharkov						9	45	39	41	59
77	134A/UBL (Conversion into UBLs)	135	Kharkov										
12	134SKh	135	Kharkov										
852				*2*	*13*	*6*	*20*	*28*	*20*	*45*	*39*	*41*	*59*
122	Conversion of Tu-134/Tu-134As to 134ShNavigation Trainers	135	Kharkov							2	12	9	8

Type	Factory Number	Location	1975	1976	1977	1978	1979	1980	1981	1982	1983	1984
Tu-134												
Tu-134	135	Kharkov										
134A & 134B	135	Kharkov	56	53	56	59	56	58	48	57	23	24
134A/UBL (Conversion into UBLs)	135	Kharkov							31	32	14	
134SKh	135	Kharkov								2	4	6
			56	*53*	*56*	*59*	*56*	*58*	*79*	*91*	*41*	*30*
Conversion of Tu-134/ Tu-134As to 134Sh Navigation Trainers	135	Kharkov	10	10	12	14	15	15	15			

Total	Type	Factory Number	Location	1968	1971	1972	1973	1974	1975	1976	1977	1978	1979	1980	1981
	Tu-144														
1	Prototype	156	Moscow	1											
15		64	Voronezh		1	1	1	1	3	1	2	1	1	–	3
16				*1*	*1*	*1*	*1*	*1*	*3*	*1*	*2*	*1*	*1*	*–*	*3*

+ 3 test airframes. One incomplete.

Total	Type	Factory Number	Location	1968	1969	1970	1971	1972	1973	1974	1975	1976	1977
	Tu-142 – incomplete; Later details classified												
1	Prototype	156	Moscow	1									

Total	Type	Factory Number	Location	1968	1969	1970	1971	1972	1973	1974	1975	1976	1977
18		18	Kuibyshev	2	5	5	5	1					
	Incomplete details	31	Taganrog							2	6	6	6
				3	*5*	*5*	*5*	*1*		*2*	*6*	*6*	*6*

Total	Type	Factory Number	Location	1969	1970	1971	1972	1973	1974	1975	1976	1977	1978	1979	1980	1981
	Tu-145/Tu-22M															
9	22M0	22	Kazan	5	2	2										
9	22M1	22	Kazan		1	8										
211	22M2	22	Kazan			3	14	15	17	17	21	22	26	23	23	
268	22M3	22	Kazan							1	1	3	5	7	7	
497				*5*	*2*	*3*	*11*	*14*	*15*	*17*	*18*	*22*	*25*	*31*	*30*	*30*

Type	Factory Number	Location	1979	1980	1981	1982	1983	1984	1985	1986	1987	1988	1989	1990	1991	1992	1993
Tu-145/ Tu-22M																	
22M0	22	Kazan															
22M1	22	Kazan															
22M2	22	Kazan	26	23	23	20	10										
22M3	22	Kazan	5	7	7	10	20	30	28	30	28	27	25	20	17	6	3
			31	*30*	*30*	*30*	*30*	*30*	*28*	*30*	*38*	*27*	*25*	*20*	*17*	*6*	*3*

Total	Type	Factory Number	Location	1968	1969	1970	1971	1972	1973	1974	1975	1976	1977	1978	1979	1980	1981
	Tu-154																
1	Prototype	156	Moscow	1													
3	Pre-Production	18	Kuibyshev		2	1											
602	154/A/B	18	Kuibyshev			7	12	13	18	36	46	56	61	67	70	77	57
288	154M – Continuing	18	Kuibyshev														
*894**				*1*	*2*	*8*	*12*	*13*	*18*	*36*	*46*	*56*	*61*	*67*	*70*	*77*	*57*

* Continuing

	Type	Factory Number	Location	1982	1983	1984	1985	1986	1987	1988	1989	1990	1991	1992	1993
	Tu-154														
	Prototype	156	Moscow												
	Pre-Production	18	Kuibyshev												
	154/A/B	18	Kuibyshev	43	29	10									
	154M –	18	Kuibyshev			8	14	21	23	31	32	35	41	41	42
				43	*29*	*18*	*14*	*21*	*23*	*31*	*32*	*35*	*41*	*41*	*42*

1994 figures not available

Total	Type	Factory Number	Location	1981	1982	1984	1985	1986	1987	1988	1989	1990	1991	1992
	Tu-160													
2	Prototypes	156	Moscow	1	1									
1	Static Test	156	Moscow		1									
27	Production	22	Kazan			2	1	1	4	5	3	5	3	3
30				*1*	*2*	*2*	*1*	*1*	*4*	*5*	*3*	*5*	*3*	*3*

General Index

Aeroflot – Russian International Airlines 27
Agapov, Sergei 157
Alasheev, Oleg *26*
Alasheev, Yuri 119, 121, 124, *178*
Aleksandro, V.L. 23
Alekseev, Anatoli 46
Alekseev, Lt-Col 112
Alekseev, Mikhail 78, 82, 87
Allen, Eddie 95
Andreev, Vladimir *27*, 168
Anikeev 76
Anisimov, A.F. 38, 40
ANT throughout book; *10, 15, 18, 25, 31*
Antonov, Dmitri 151
Arkhalinin 131
Arkhangelski, Aleksander *23*, 23, 64, 74, 76, 77, 80, 82, 83, 86
Arroshar, Michel 34
Aviadvigatel (Perm) 27
Aviastar (Ulyanovsk) 27, 174, 176, 177
Aziamov 86

Baidukov, Georgi 45, 71
Balbo, Marshal 65
Bashilov, Trifon 131
Bauman 67
Bazenkov, Nikolai 113, *114*, 114, 126, 131, 136, 151
Belyakov, Aleksander 71
Beria, Lavrentia 13, 23, 89
Bisnovat, M.R. 138
Blagin, N.P. 62, 63
Blizniuk, Valentin 155, *155*, 169
Bolotov 38
Bondaruk 103
Bonin, Aleksander *26*
Borovoi, V, 158
Brezhnev, Leonid 171
Bugaev, Boris 122, *156*

Carlucci 172
Chamberlain, Austin 35

Charomski, Aleksei 92
Cheremukhin, Aleksei *22*
Chernyshov, Vladimir 67
Chetvertikov, Igor 73
Chizhevski, Vladimir 77, 78, 112
Chkalov, Valeri P. 13, 38, 71, 78
Churchill, Winston 86
Codos, Paul 70

Danilin, Sergei 72, 76
Deinekin, Col.-Gen Piotr 172
de Lavo, Henri 72
Dobrynin, Vladimir 106

Fainshtein, Abram *26*
Federov, Viacheslav 150
Filin, Aleksander 70, 78
Filippov V.N. 34
Franco, General 81
Frenkel, Georgi 13, 14

Gallai, Mark 97, 98
Golovachev 45
Golovin, Pavel 46, 48
Golubkov, Aleksander, P. 21, 23, 73, 86
Gorki, Maksim 57, 60, 61, 62
Grizodubova, Valentina 79, *79*
Grokhovski, P.I. 45
Gromov, Mikhail M. 13, 34, 35, 40, 42, 47, 51, 52, 53, 55, 56, 57, 60, 62, 69, 70, 71, 72, 76, *76*, 78, 84, 88

Hammar, Armand 174, 176

Ilynski, 66
Ilyushin, Sergei, V. 12, 23, 37

Junkers 11, 12, 32

Kalina, Aleksander 134, 142
Kalygin, Igor *27*, 179, 180
Kandalov, Andrei I. *7*, 13
Kashtanov, Yuli *26*, *178*

Kellet, Squadron Leader 72
Kerber, Leonid *26*
Khrushchev, Nikita 14, 18, 63, 112, 113, 116, 128, 131, 132, 141
Khrushcheva 18
Kirsanov, Nikolai 151, *152*
Klimov, Valentin, T. 20, *20*, 25, *26*, 27, 179
Klimov, Vladimir 16, 105
Kolesov, Piotr 123
Koltsov, Mikhail 61
Konoplev, Evgeni 84
Kondorski, Boris M. 21, 112
Korolev 13
Korzinshikov, Sergei 75, 76
Kovaliov, Valentin 116, 121
Kozlov (Deputy Premier) 18, 120
Kozlov, A. 40
Kozlov, Ivan 64, 67
Kozlov, Mikhail 138
Kulokov, Leonid *26*
Kurchevski 41
Kurchevski, Leonid 67
Kuznetsov, Capt. Boris *156*

Lanovski, Lev *27*, 173, *174, 178*, 179
Leonov 45
Levanevski, Sigismund 12, 70, 71
Levanovich, Boris *27*
Lillenthal (Otto) 9
Lisitsyna, Anna V. 9
Li Yuanyi 111
Lyapidevski, Anatoli 39
Lyulka, Arkhip 104, 116

Makhotin, G. 28
Malkhasian, Konstantin 112
Markov, Dmitri 95, 96, 101, 103, 104, 106, 108, 116, 118, 119, 123, 126, 134, 141, 158
Marshall, General 72
Marunov, Viacheslav 103
Matveev, Vladimir 157

Mazuruk, Ilya 46
Mesheriakov, Aleksei *26*
Mikhailov, Capt. L.V. 81
Mikheev 51
Mikoyan 18
Mikulin, Aleksander 38, 90, 108
Molonov, Vassili 46
Molotov, Viacheslav 86
Mussolini, Benito 53
Myasishchev, Vladimir M. 13, 23, 84, 95

Nadashkevich, Aleksander *26*
Nekrasov, N.S. 13, 21 *22*, 23
Nezval, Iosif F. 21, 85, 138
Nizhevski, R.N. 29
Nukhtikov, Mikhail 14, 90, 91, 92, 114, 151

Opadchi, Fiodor 91, 92, 101, 102
Osipenko, Polina 79, *79*
Osipov, D.N. 21
Ozerov, Georgi A. 21, *22*

Papanin, Ivan 46
Pavlov 86
Pereliot, Aleksander 17, 92, 104, 105, 106, 114
Petrov, M.N. 23
Petrov, Nikolai 1, 11, 21, 33
Petliakov, Vladimir M. 13, 21, 23, 37, 42, 43, 44, 47, 57, 59, 63, 73, 84, 85
Pinedo, 65
Piskok, Col. I. 92
Podluchnikov, N. I. 21
Pogosski, Yevgini 11, 21, 23, 31
Pogosski, Ivan 21, 23, 47, 50, 51, 52, 65, 73, 86
Polikarpov, Nikolai 55
Polishuk, Konstantin *22*
Popov, Konstantin 75, 78, 80
Portasov, Capt. A.S. 81
Pukhov, Aleksander *26* 157, 182
Pusep, Endel 86

Putilov, A. I. 21

Radzevich, Yevgeni 34
Razkova, Marina 79, *79*
Riballschuk, S. 50
Riabchenko 45
Riabenko, Timofei 66, 73, 86
Riabinin, Nikolai 131
Rodionov, Vladimir 56
Roosevelt, President Franklin D. 86
Roosevelt, President Theodore 72
Rossi, Maurise 70
Rumer 13
Rusakov 52, 53
Rybko, Nikolai 84, 97, 98, 108

Sapelkin, K.P. 120
Saprykin, T.P. 21, *22*
Schmidt, Otto 46
Scillard 13
Seliakov, Leonid 134, 142, *142*, 143, 144, 158
Shavrov, Vadim 54
Shengardt, Aleksander *161*, 166
Shestakov, Semion 35, 38
Shishmarev, M.M. 71
Shukov, Yuri 163
Shvetsov, Arkadi 12, 98, 99, 103, 104
Sidorin, I.I. 21
Sikorski, Igor 36
Sizov, Major 112
Sokolov 45
Soloviev, Pavel 134
Spirin, Ivan 51, 70
Stalin, Josef (Iosif) 13, 14, 16, 23, 38, 57, 61, 62, 63, 71, 76, 86, 88, 89, 94, 95, 96, 97, 99, 101, 112
Stalin, Vasili 101
Stefanovski, Piotr, M. 44, 77
Stepanchenok, Vasily 44
Stoman, Evgeni *22*
Sukhoi, Pavel O. 23, 40, 67, 68, 69, 75, 77, 78, 80, 88, 92, 112
Sukholim, Ivan 86, 87, 128, 136

Talalakin, Andrei 169, 174
Temple, Shirley 72
Tomashevski, Apolinari 13, 37
Troianovski, Ambassador 72
Tupolev, Aleksei A. 13, 18, 19, *19*, 24, *26*, 132, 153, 155, 168, 169, 173
Tupolev, Nikolai I. 9
Tupoleva, Julia A. 13, 18
Tupoleva, Julia N. 8, 10, 13, 18
Twining, Gen. Nathan 116

Universal Scientific Production Centre 27

Vakhmistrov V.S. 38, 39, 40, 44
Vasilchenko, Aleksander 97
Vasiliev, Boris 157
Vedernikov, Ivan 151, 171
Veremei, Boris 171
Vodopianov, Mikhail 46, 48
Volkov, F.F. 138
Vorobiev, Yuri *26*, 176, *178*
Voronchenko, Giorgi 157

Whitcomb, R.T. 16

Yakimov, Aleksei 127
Yefimov 45
Yeger, Sergei 102, 104, 105, 162, 163, 166
Yelian, Eduard 154
Yeltsin, Boris N. 27, 172
Yevshin, Mikrofan 114, 128, 163
Yumashev, Andrei B. 40, 43, 45, 72

Zalevski A.I. 38
Zhadanov, Konstantin 114
Zheltiakova, Julia N. 10
Zhukovski, Nikolai E. 9, 10, 20, *28*, 29
Zhurov, K. 80
Ziuzin, Dmitri 112, 126

Operators and Aircraft Index

Aeroflot 35, 39, 45, 48, 54, 57, 63, 77, 82, 99, 101, 154, 156, 157, 161, 163, 164, 166, 167, 173, 174, 175, 176, 177, 179
Aeronica 164
Aerosleighs 11, 28, *28*, 32
Air Great Wall 164
Air Kampuchea 145
Airships 29
An-2 119, 166
An-12 118, 182
An-14 118
An-24 118, 161
An-26 175
An-28 166, 175
An-70T 182
An-124 174
Alyemda 164
Angolan Airforce 145
ANT-1 11, 21, *30, 31*, 31
ANT-2 11, 21, 32–3, *32, 33*, 40
ANT-3 11, 34–35, *34, 35*, 40
ANT-4 12, 21, 36, 39, *37, 39*, 40, 42, 47
ANT-5 12, *37*, 38, 40–1, *40–1*
ANT-6 12, 38, 42–6, *43, 44, 45*, 57, 59
ANT-7 12, 46, 46–9, *48, 49*, 51, 60
ANT-8 50, *50*
ANT-9 12, 50, 51–4, *52, 53, 54*, 57
ANT-10 55, *55*
ANT-11 55, 65
ANT-12 55
ANT-13 56
ANT-14 12, 50, 57–8, *58, 59*
ANT-15 59
ANT-16 23, 59–60, *60*, 61, 62, 73
ANT-17 60
ANT-18 60
ANT-19 60

ANT-20 12, 18, 61–3, *62, 63*
ANT-21 64, *64*
ANT-22 65–6, *65, 66*, 73
ANT-23 67, *67*, 74
ANT-25 12, 13, 68–72, *69, 71, 72*, 76, 78
ANT-26 73, 74
ANT-27 47, 73–4, *74*
ANT-28 74
ANT-29 74–5, *74*
ANT-31 75, *75*
ANT-32 76
ANT-34 76
ANT-35 12, 76–7, *76*
ANT-36 77–8, *77*
ANT-37 78, *78*, 79, *79*, 80
ANT-38 79
ANT-39 79
ANT-40 12, 76, 80–4, *81, 82, 83*, 86
ANT-41 84
ANT-42 12, 84–6, *85*
ANT-43 86
ANT-44 86–7, *87*
ANT-45 87
ANT-46 87, *87*
ANT-47 88
ANT-48 88
ANT-49 88
ANT-50 77, 88
ANT-51 88, *88*
ANT-58 13, 14, 15, 24, 91
ANT-59 91
ANT-60 91
ANT-61 91, *91*
ANT-62 91
ANT-63 92, 99
ANT-63P 94, *94*
ANT-64 94
ANT-65 92
ANT-67 92
ANT-68 99
ANT-69 99
Antoinette biplane 9

Antonov:
An-2 119, 166
An-10 118, 126, 161, 166
An-12 118, 182
An-14 118
An-24 118, 182
An-26 175
An-28 166, 175
An-124 174
An-70T 182
Ansaldo A-1 40
ARIA – Aeroflot Russian International Airlines 145, 177
Ariana 164
Arkhangelsk AR-2 (ANT-40) 83
Avia Arktika 39, 45, 48, 98, 99
Aviaexport 179
Aviogenex 145, 148

BAC 1-11 141, 142, 143, 154
Balkan Bulgarian (Airlines) 145, 164, 165, 167
BB-1 (ANT-51/Su-2) 88
Beriev MBR-2 50
    MP-1 79
Blériot 110 70
Boeing:
B-29 15, (16), 94, 95, 96, 97, 98, 99, 101, 103, 104
B-52 (Stratofortress) 138
B-377 Stratocruiser 101
B-707 154, 165
B-727 141, 163
B-747 127
BOK (ANT-36) 77
Brabazon Committee 17
Bravia 176
Bristol Brabazon 61
        Britannia 113
British Aircraft Corp/Vickers VC-10 141
Bulgarian Air Force 145
Bychek 112

CAAK (North Korea) 145, 146, 164
Cairo Charter and Cargo 164
Cheluskin (Ship) 39
China Northwest 164
China Southwest 164
China United 164
China Xinjiang 164
Chinese Air Force 137
Concorde 153, 154
CSA – Czechoslovakian Airlines 121, 135, 136, 145, 148, 164, 166
Cubana 164, 166, 167

DB-A (Shishmarev) 71
DB-1 (ANT-25) 68, 77
DB-2 (ANT-37) 78–9, *78*, *79*, 80
de Havilland :
  Comet 17, 108, 117, 118
  DH-4 33
  DH-9 33
  DH-95 Flamingo 86
Deruluft (Deutsch-Russisch Luftverkehrs) 54
DIP (ANT-29) 74–5
DI-8 (ANT-46) 87, *87*
Dobrolet 54, 57
Dornier WAL 73
Douglas DC-3 12, 101, 118
      DC-8 154
      DC-9 141, 154
      DC-10 154
      Skyshark 112
Duraluminium 11
Dux R-1 33

East German Air Force 136
EC-121D 136
Egyptair 164, 165

Fairey Gannet 112, 113
Fokker DX1 40

G-1 (ANT-4) 39
G-2 (ANT-6) 45
Gliders 9, *9*, 29, 32
Gloster Javelin 110

Goodrich, B.F. (tyre manufacturer) 86, 97
GOS NII GA 122, 148, 165
Grigorovich I-2 40
Grigorovich I-Z 44
Grigorovich MT-1 12
Guyana Airways 164, 165

H-5 (Il-28) 111
H-6 (Tu-16/88) 111
Handley Page Harrow 38
Hang Khong 145, 146
Hughes Hercules 61, 127
Hispano Suiza (engine) 12

I-3 (Grigorovich) 40
I-3 (Polikarpov) 40
I-4 (ANT-5) 38, 40–1
I-5 (ANT-12) 55
I-5 (Polikarpov) 44, 55, 62
I-8 (ANT-13) 56
I-12 (ANT-23) 67, 74
I-14 (ANT-31) 75
I-15 (Polikarpov) 39
I-16 (Polikarpov) 39, 44, 75
I-142 (ANT-31bis) 75
I-153 (Polikarpov) 81
I-Z (Grigorovich) 44
Ilya Muromets (Sikorsky) 36
Ilyushin Il-2 14
Ilyushin Il-4T 91
Il-12 101, 118, 129
Il-14 118, 120, 129
Il-18 (piston) 101
Il-18 (turbine) 118, 126, 129, 161
Il-28 111, 138, 139
Il-38 151, 152
Il-62 118, 131, 141, 166, 175
Il-76 166, 175
Il-78 'Mainstay' 136
Il-86 175
Il-96 174, 176, 179
Indian Air Force 136
Indian Navy 152
Interflug 136, 145, 164
Iraqi Air Force 136
Iraqi Airlines 136, 145

Kalinin K-5 57

Kharkov KhAI-5 88
Kolchuginsk metallurgical factory 11, 32
Komi Avia 145
KR-6P (ANT-7) 47–8

Lavochkin La-15 93
LET L-410 166, 175
LII Flight Research Institute 15, 96, 97, 104
Lishunov Li-2 12, 101, 118, 120
Lockheed Constellation 136
Lockheed Electra 110
Lockheed Hercules 113
Lockheed TriStar 154
LOT-Polish Airlines 145, 148, 164, 166, 167
Luftwaffe 164

Maksim Gorki Agitation Squadron 54, 57, 58, 62
Maksim Gorki (ANT-20) 61, 62, 63
Malev (Hungarian Airlines) 145
Martinsyde F-4 Buzzard 40
MBR-2 (Beriev) 50
MDR-2 (ANT-8) 50
MDR-3 (TsKB-11) 73
MDR-4 (ANT-27) 73–4
Messerschmitt Bf 109 81
MI-3 (ANT-21) 64
MiG-3 81, 85
MiG-15 (bis) 93, 104
MiG-21 154
MiG-25 140, 159
MiG-31 140
Missiles 132–3, *132*
MK-1 (ANT-22) 65, 66, 73
Monino Museum 33, 72, 84, 97
MP-1 (Beriev) 79
MP-6 (ANT-7) 48
MR-2 (ANT-7) 48
MTB-1 (ANT-27) 73
MTB-2A (ANT-44) 86–7

NII-VVS 14, 38, 40, 42, 47, 51, 90, 112, 142, 150
Normandie (Liner) 72

Oriol Avia 176, 177, 178

P-3 (Lockheed) Orion 151
Petliakov Pe-2 8, 14, 81, 89
Petliakov Pe-8 12, 84, 86, *85*, 92
Polikarpov I-3 40
    I-5 44, 62
    I-15 39
    I-16 39, 44, 75
    I-153 81
    R-5 38, 55
    U-2 69
Polish Air Force 164
Project 101 13
    102 13
    103 13, 14, 24
    103U 14
    110 13
    507 112
    509 112
    N6Y 13
PS-3 (ANT-3) 35
PS-7 (ANT-7) 48
PS-9 (ANT-9) 54
PS-35 77
PS-124 (ANT-20bis) 63

R-3 (ANT-3) 34, 35, *35*
R-4 35
R-5 (Polikarpov) 38, 55
R-6 (ANT-7) 47–49, *48, 49*, 60
R-7 (ANT-10) 55
Rodina (ANT-37bis) 79
Rossiya (Airline) 177

Samolet 103 89, 91
    103S 91
    103U 91
    103V 91
Savoia Marchetti SM-55 45, 65
SB (ANT-40) 80, *81, 82, 83*
SB-1 (ANT-40) 80
SB-2 (ANT-40) 76, 80
SB-3 (ANT-40) 82
Sib NII 154, 164, 165, 167
Sichuan Airlines 164
Speedboats 11, 21, 29, 32
Sud Caravelle 141
Sukhoi Su-2 (ANT-51) 88

Sukhoi UTB (Tu-2) 92
Syrian Air 145, 146, 164

TsAGI 10, 11, 12, 13, 17, 20, 29,
    31, 32, 33, 34, 36, 40, 43, 47,
    50, 51, 55, 57, 59, 60, 61, 62,
    63, 64, 65, 66, 67, 69, 73, 74,
    75, 76, 77, 78, 80, 81, 84, 86,
    87, 88, 104, 108, 112, 142,
    153, 154, 158, 171
Torpedo Boats *29,* 29
T-1 (ANT-41) 84
TB-1 (ANT-4) 36–39, 40, 42, 59
TB-3 (ANT-6) 38, 42–46, *43*, 44,
    45, 57, 59, 60
TB-4 (ANT-16) 59, 60, 61, 73
TB-6 (ANT-26) 73
TShB (ANT-17) 60
TsKB-11 (MDR-3) 73
TB-7 (ANT-42/Pe-8) 84–86, 85
Tarom (Romanian Airlines) 164
Tu-1 94, *94*
Tu-2 13, 14, 15, 16, 24, 89–94,
    91, 92, 93, 94, 108
Tu-4 15, 16, 24, 94–9, *96, 97, 98,*
    99, 103, 104, 108, 112, 113
Tu-6 92, 99
Tu-8 92, 99
Tu-10 92, 99, *100*
Tu-12 16, 92, 103, 104
Tu-14 16, 105, *105*, 112
Tu-16 17, 19, 24, 108–111, *109,*
    110, 111, 112, 116, 117, 118,
    119, 120, 122, 123, 125, 144
Tu-20 19, (i)102, 114
Tu-22 18, 19, 24, (i)102, 105,
    123–25, *124–25,* 158
Tu-22M 18, 19, 20, 24, 134,
    158–61, *159, 160,* 170
Tu-24 SKh (CX) 182
Tu-28 19, 138, 140, *139, 140*
Tu-34 182
Tu-70 16, 17, 97, 99–101, *101,*
    103, 104, 108, 118
Tu-72 102, 105, 108
Tu-73 16, 102, *102,* 105, 108
Tu-74 102, 105, 108
Tu-75 16, 103, *103,* 104, 108,
    118

Tu-77 16, 103, *103*, 104, *104*
Tu-78 102, 105, 108
Tu-79 102, 105, 108, 125
Tu-80 104–5, *104,* 108, 118
Tu-81 16, 105, *105,* 108, 112
Tu-82 16, 105–106, *106,* 125
Tu-85 16, 17, 106, *107,* 108, 113,
    114, 118
Tu-86 106
Tu-88 16, 17, 108–111, *109, 110,*
    111, 112, 116
Tu-89 112
Tu-91 112–13, *112*
Tu-92 113
Tu-95 17, 18, 24, 113–15, *115,*
    116, 118, 126, 151, 169, 170,
    171
Tu-96 116, *117*
Tu-98 116, *116,* 138
Tu-104 17, 18, 24, 117–22, *118,*
    119, 121, 131, 134, 141, 161,
    166, 173
Tu-104G 110, 119, 120, 122, *122,*
    126
Tu-105 123–5, *124, 125,* 158
Tu-107 122
Tu-110 24, 118, 126, *126*
Tu-114 18, 24, 118, 126–31, *128,*
    129, 130, 131, 136, 151, 161
Tu-116 131–2, *132*
Tu-119 132
Tu-121 132
Tu-123 19, 132, *133,* 133
Tu-124 18, 24, 118, 134–6,
    134–5, 144
Tu-126 136, *137*
Tu-128 18, 24, 138–40, *139–40*
Tu-130 132–3, 182
Tu-134 18, 19, 24, 141–50,
    142–9, 158, 166, 167, 175,
    179, 180, 181
Tu-139 133
Tu-141 133
Tu-142 24, 151–2, *152*
Tu-143 133
Tu-144 18, 19, 24, 153–7, *153,*
    155, 156, 157
Tu-145 24, 142, 158–61, *159–60*
Tu-154 18, 19, 20, 24, 141, 146,

161–7, *163*, *165*, *167*, 168, 169, 173, 174, 175, 176, 177, 179, 180
Tu-155 19, 20, 25, 168–9, *168*
Tu-156 169
Tu-160 19, 20, 24, 25, 157, 169–72, *171*, *172*
Tu-164 167
Tu-204 19, 20, 24, 25, 27, 173–8, *175*, *176*, *177*, *178*, 179, 180, 182
Tu-214 178
Tu-224 177
Tu-234 179
Tu-244 182

Tu-1X4 167
Tu-334 24, 25, 27, 179–81, 182
Tu-330 182
Tu-404 182
Tu-414 182
Tu-424 182
Tu-2000 182–3

U-2 (Polikarpov) 69
USB (ANT-40) 82
UTB (Sukhoi/Tu-2) 92

VI-1000 (Pe-2) 88
VIA (Bulgarian Airline) 164

Vickers Viscount 113
Wellesley 72
Vietnam Airlines 145
Vnukovo Airlines 176
Vozdushni Transport (Journal) 83

Westland Wyvern 112
Wright Cyclone (engine) 12

Yakovlev Yak-1 91
Yak-9 15
Yak-40 141
Yak-42 141, 175, 170

Zveno *37*, 38, 39, 41, 44